NANSEN

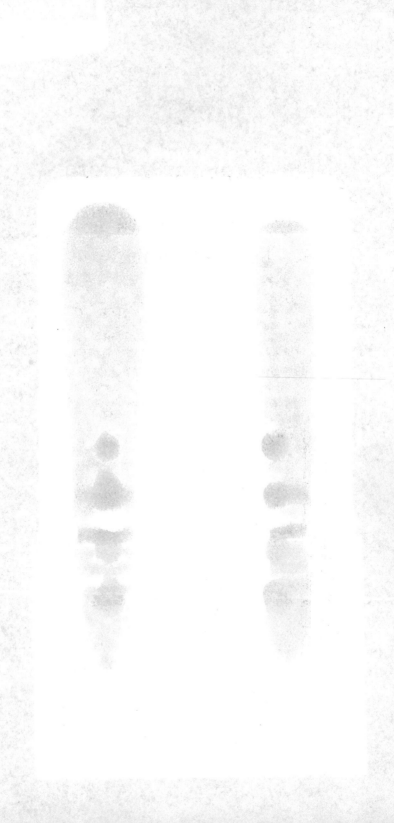

NANSEN

The Explorer as Hero

Roland Huntford

BARNES
&NOBLE
B O O K S
NEW YORK

First published in 1997 by
Gerald Duckworth & Co. Ltd.

This edition published by Barnes & Noble, Inc.,
by arrangement with Gerald Duckworth & Co. Ltd.

1998 Barnes & Noble Books

ISBN 0-7607-1262-X

Printed and bound in Great Britain

98 99 00 01 M 9 8 7 6 5 4 3 2 1

Contents

Contents

Contents

To my ever-patient wife, Anita

Introduction and Acknowledgements

This biography completes a cycle of modern polar exploration, the other parts of which are *Scott and Amundsen* and *Shackleton*. Nansen belonged to the Scandinavian ascendancy in high latitudes. He launched the process which culminated in the race for the South Pole, and founded the technique of modern polar travel. Behind the polar explorers of our time, his figure looms. He was the mentor of them all. He came close to that semi-mythical figure, the archetype.

This is the first biography of Nansen in the English language for some years, and the first to be based on original sources. Much of the material has not been tapped for the subject in any language.

Because Nansen was more than just a polar explorer, the sources are many and scattered. The book has had a long gestation, in the couse of which I have contracted many debts of gratitude.

First of all, I thank Dr P.G.F. Nixon and his wife, Susie, to both of whom I owe more than can ever be adequately repaid. They will know why.

Next I wish to thank the Warden and Fellows of St Antony's College, Oxford, for great hospitality in the best traditions of the republic of letters, especially in piloting me through the morass of modern Russian history. Also, I thank them for a humane and timely grant. In particular, I should like to thank Sir Raymond Carr, Alistair Horne, Lord Dahrendorff, Dr J.D. Bailey, Dr Michael Kaser, Dr R. Kindersley and Dr Harry Shukman.

I also thank the President and Fellows of Wolfson College, Cambridge for their help; Sir David Williams and Dr Gordon Johnson in particular. I owe a special debt of gratitude to the late Mr Plantagenet Somerset Fry.

I wish especially to thank my Norwegian publishers, Aschehoug, for unbelievable loyalty, generosity, kindness and patience. For special thanks, I single out Marit Notaker and William Nygaard – the latter surely one of the bravest men in publishing, anywhere.

I much appreciate the help given me by the Nansen family, and thank them warmly for opening all material, and giving permission to quote.

I pay tribute to the memory of Colin Haycraft, of Duckworth, a gentleman and scholar, who supported me through difficult times. I only regret that he did not live to see his faith in this book vindicated. I also take the opportunity of thanking Deborah Blake and Ray Davies and their staff at Duckworth for seeing the work through the press.

To my editor, Rivers Scott, I am exceedingly grateful in more ways than one.

To the Earhart Foundation of Ann Arbor, Michigan, I give unbounded thanks for a more than generous grant which largely enabled me to finish this book.

I am also deeply grateful to the Royal Literary Fund in London for coming to the rescue in an hour of need. In particular, I must thank the Secretary, Mrs Fiona Clarke, for her rare ability to be both businesslike and kind.

At an early stage, the Hélène Heroys Literary Foundation in Geneva gave me a grant, for which I am very grateful.

My thanks are also due to the Society of Authors in London for a grant.

I must also thank *Nansenfondet* – the Nansen Fund in Oslo – for a timely grant.

To Professor Robert Cluett of Toronto, I owe more than I can repay in help, encouragement and advice. For vital help, I also wish to thank Stephen Durbridge and Arne Naess.

To the University Library in Oslo, I cannot adequately express my thanks. The Department of Manuscripts has shown the patience of Job, and never failed to help, even in matters outside their remit. I especially thank Mr Oddvar Vasstveit for taking a personal interest in my problems, and for willing help far beyond the call of duty. To his subordinates, especially Sigbjørn Grindheim, Tone Modalsli, Kari Karlsson and Odd Røstvig, thanks are also due.

For much patient and friendly help, I thank the librarians at the Bodleian Library, Oxford, and the Cambridge University Library.

Also, I must thank the Archives Centre of Churchill College Cambridge, especially the former Keeper of the Archives, Mr Correlli Barnet, for generous help. Special thanks are also due to the Library of the Department of Modern and Medieval Languages of the University of Cambridge.

I am most grateful for the help and patience of the League of Nations Archives in Geneva, especially Mr Guindi, and the former archivist, Mr Sven Welander. Likewise, I thank the International Committee of the Red Cross in Geneva for opening their archives to me.

I acknowledge the gracious permission of Her Majesty the Queen to use the material in the Royal Archives, Windsor.

Also I express my thanks to His Majesty King Carl XVI Gustav of Sweden for opening the Bernadotte Family Archives to me.

I particularly wish to thank the Countess of Sutherland for helping with the papers of her grandmother, Millicent, fourth Duchess of Sutherland.

For help in evaluating Nansen's contribution to neuroscience, I am greatly indebted to Professor John Edwards, of Washington State University, Seattle, the Departments of Anatomy and Zoology, University of

Introduction and Acknowledgements

Cambridge, Professor Karen Helle of the University of Bergen, Dr Jan K.S. Jansen of Oslo.

For guiding me through polar history, I am particularly indebted to Clive Holland, Librarian of Wolfson College, and Mr A.G.E. Jones.

For much generous and unstinted help in research, I must thank Torkel Fagerli, of Oslo. Thanks are also due to Major Bertil Flodin, of Stockholm, for help with the military aspects of the Norwegian-Swedish crisis of 1905. For an analysis of nationalism in music, I am indebted to Professor Michael Beckerman of Santa Barbara, California.

I am extremely grateful to Professor Geir Kjetsaa of the University of Oslo, for sharing his knowledge of Maxim Gorky. I also wish to thank Professor Vigdis Ystad, also of the University of Oslo, for enormous help in the interpretation of Norwegian history and literature.

I wish to express my gratitude for willing help from the Danish State Archives in Copenhagen, the Norwegian Polar Institute and the Norwegian State Archives in Oslo; the Swedish State Archives, the Library of the Royal Academy of Science, and the Bernadotte Family Archives – particularly the Archivist, Dr Ingemar Carlsson – in Stockholm, the Stefansson Collection at Dartmouth College Library, the Hoover Institute at Stanford, California, the National Archives in Washington, DC, Yale University Library, Harvard Law School Library, the University Library in Bergen; the Public Record Office, the Royal Geographical Society and the Zoological Society in London; the Library of the University of Reading, the National Library of Scotland, and the University Library of St Andrews. For the history of the Primus stove, I am much indebted to Tekniska Muséet, Stockholm. Thanks are due to Professor Brian Simon for the papers of Henry Simon.

Many others have unstintingly given help and encouragement, and I thank them all. In particular, I want to thank Steen P. Aasheim, Don Aldridge, Sten Andersen, Thomas and Kyra Andreasson, Professor Robert Baldwin of Stanford University, Karl H. Brox, Professor Evan Bukey of the University of Arkansas, David Burnett, Jan Christensen, Professor Martin Dubin of Dekalb University, Illinois, Lennart and Gunilla Forsling in Stockholm, Professor H.E. Huppert, of King's College, Cambridge, Morten Chr. Jakhelln, Julie Jones, Erik Klavenesss, William McCoy, Dr A.D. Martinez-Arias of the Department of Zoology University of Cambridge, Herman Mehren, Olav and Kajsa Momyr, O.R. Norland, Liz and Beau Riffenburgh, Bertil Roos, Bo and Anne Sahlin, Dr Charles Swithinbank, Alison and Per Thuesen, Dr Michael Stevens of Stockholm University, Professor Ian Whitaker of Simon Fraser University, Vancouver.

Lord Noel-Baker very kindly allowed himself to be interviewed, but has since passed away.

Mr R.F. Perachie, who helped enormously with research, and made some essential discoveries, has sadly passed away. Venetia Pollock, to

xi

whom as friend and editor I owe a great deal, died before she could help with this book. To their memory, I pay tribute.

Gratitude for help does not imply endorsement of the views expressed in this book. These, together with any errors, are my responsibility alone.

If I have overlooked anybody, or failed to trace copyright holders, I hope they will forgive me.

Finally, I want to thank my wife, to whom this book is dedicated, for unexampled help, patience and understanding through some difficult times. My sons, Nicholas and Anthony, deserve credit for some patience too.

Cambridge   R.H.
August 1997

Note

In the interests of historical authenticity, place names have been used in their contemporary form. Thus Oslo will be found as Christiania, sometimes Kristiania, until the change was made in 1925. Istanbul is called Constantinople. St Petersburg appears as Petrograd when required. Since the demise of the Soviet Union, most place-names have reverted to their original pre-revolutionary names, and those are the forms I have used.

So too with personal names. The Swedish Crown Prince and later King is called Gustaf, as he was until a later spelling reform changed it to Gustav.

Similar reasoning has been applied to units. Altitude and distances on land are given in the metric system. At sea and on the pack ice, however, traditional measures are used. Soundings are given in fathoms – 6ft or about 180 cm. Distance is measured by the nautical mile. This is one sixtieth of a degree, or one minute of latitude. It is fixed at 6,080 feet, equivalent of 1 1/7 statute miles, or 1.85 kilometres. The unit of speed is the knot, one nautical mile per hour. All temperatures are in Centigrade.

Sastrugi are irregularities formed by the action of the wind on the surface of the snow. They vary in height from a few centimetres to a metre or more, and in shape from gentle ripples to harsh, gouged, sweeping forms.

The Norwegian letter a is pronounced like u in run; aa or å like aw in law; j like y in yell; ø like i in first, and u like oo in loose.

Until 1914, the rate of exchange of the Norwegian krone remained at about 18.5 to the £ sterling, and 3.8 to the US $.

Conversion of money into present terms refers to the first quarter of 1997.

Translations from foreign languages are the author's own.

Illustrations

Illustrations

Nansen's new home at Lysaker, *Polhøiden* (later *Polhøgda*).
Nansen with visitors at Sørkje in 1901.
Caricature of Nansen replacing King Karl Johan on the equestrian statue in front of the Royal Palace in Christiania.
Nansen on horseback in London.
The Norwegian Royal couple and Roald Amundsen with Nansen and his children at *Polhøgda*.
The Duchess of Sutherland.
Marie Lewis.
Kathleen Scott
Sigrun Munthe, Anna Schøtt and Eva, *c*. 1900.
Philip Noel-Baker with Nansen at Polhøgda in the 1920s.
Nansen and Amundsen at an open air meeting in Oslo on 16 July.
Nansen delivers a speech at an open air meeting in 1928.

Maps

Prologue

One day in November 1892, as a train was starting from Victoria Station, a hotel messenger jumped up, seized the hand of someone standing at the entrance to one of the carriages, and dropped back onto the platform, shouting: 'I'm the last man in London to shake hands with him!'

The man on the train was Fridtjof Nansen. 'Of all the Arctic explorers of our day,' *The Times* declared in an expansive leader devoted to Nansen, 'none has shown greater daring and originality than this young Norwegian.' Nansen was thirty-one years old. He had just visited London to lecture on his next expedition, and was now going home to resume his preparations.

Nansen was one of the surprising figures who emerged from northern mists and helped to mould the age. He was the father of modern polar exploration – in its turn, the prelude to the leap into space. His life was intertwined with those of the discoverers who came after him.

In the spirit of the age, Nansen had an urge to demolish reigning concepts. He was, among other things, a skiing pioneer, and revolutionised polar travel by the use of skis. He had turned to polar exploration, or so he said, as a holiday from the mental fatigue of scientific research – into the structure of the central nervous system. There too he was a pioneer – as also in exploiting his fame for political purposes to benefit his country.

In the polar regions he broke a muddied mould. He became the incarnation of the explorer as hero. He had the power of inspiring men to act. He opened what is called the heroic age of polar exploration. His successors tried to build themselves in his image. The combatants in the race for the South Pole, Amundsen, Shackleton and Scott, were all his acolytes.

Parallel with Nansen's heroic aura there ran a streak of vanity, a fragmented personality, and a startling selection of paradoxes. Severely anti-clerical, he yet had the religious temperament, albeit of a pagan kind. He could only make friends with women, and never with a man. Yet although he fell deeply in love, he was incapable of living with a woman. But through all his contradictions he was genuine, incapable of dissimulation. Partly on that account he was, when it came to it, a political innocent.

Restless, ever seeking satisfaction, whether in science, exploration or politics, he was trapped by the illusory search for happiness. Nansen was

1

like Faust, the personification of modern man. Faust's compact with the devil was that he would barter his soul for the apparent certainty of being fulfilled.

For Nansen in his prime there was fulfilment in geographical discovery. It had seized the public imagination. Ever since Columbus landed in America, four hundred years before, any part of the earth still undiscovered had been abhorrent to the European mind. By now, in the last decade of the nineteenth century, Western Europe had colonised most of Africa, removing yet another patch of the unknown from the globe. The empty spaces were shrinking. The ambit of attainment was becoming circumscribed. The polar regions were the last great blanks on the map.

This was the stage onto which Nansen came hurrying, before it was too late. He craved the grand passion which, for the moment, he believed he would find in exploration. He really felt lurking within himself a sense of tortured kinship with Faust, as the figure is protrayed by Goethe.

In Nansen's own words during an outburst of despair: 'Goethe's Faust never reached a place where he wanted to "remain". I cannot even glimpse anywhere worth the attempt.' That echoed the haunting words of Goethe in which Faust makes his compact with the devil. Faust, in his portrayal, would be granted what he wished in return for giving up his soul – *at some time that depended on himself*. As long as he was dissatisfied, he was safe, but:

> *Werd ich zum Augenblicke sagen:*
> *Verweile doch! Du bist so schön!*
> *Dann magst du mich in Fesseln schlagen,*
> *Dann will ich gern zu grunde gehn!*
> *Dann mag die Totenglocke schallen.*

> 'If to the passing hour I say
> "Remain, thou art so sweet, remain!"
> Then bind me with fetters on that day,
> For I will gladly perish then.
> Let the death-bell start to toll.'

Part I

Beginnings

1

A Boy and his Skis

Fridtjof Nansen was born in Christiania, as Oslo, the capital of Norway was then called, on 10 October 1861. His father, Baldur Nansen, was a lawyer; a short, thin man, with a reddish complexion, tiny pinpoint blue eyes, and an air of perpetual worry. His mother, Adelaide Johanne Thekla Isidore, was the opposite of her husband in both background and appearance. She belonged to the Wedel-Jarlsbergs, one of the few Norwegian aristocratic families. Taller than Baldur by a good half a head, she was dark-haired, big-boned; a Valkyrie-like figure with a long nose, broad nostrils, high cheekbones, eyes which, though blue like her husband's, were slanting and large, and a mouth turned down at the corners. She had views of her own and was free-spoken to a fault.

For both parties, this was their second marriage. In 1844, at the age of twenty-three, Adelaide had married an army lieutenant called Jacob Bølling, a union that scandalised her well-born family, for Bølling was the son of a baker. Bølling died in 1853, during a cholera epidemic in Christiania. A year later, Baldur Nansen's first wife also died, of puerperal fever, a week after giving birth to their only child, a son called Moltke. The future couple were already on terms, Baldur happening to be Adelaide's lawyer, and in March 1858 they became husband and wife. Baldur was forty-one, four years older than Adelaide.

Again, Adelaide's family protested that she had married beneath her. But, left a widow with five children to care for, she was looking for security. For his part, Baldur wanted someone to give Moltke a mother's attention. Together with all their children, the couple moved into a house which Baldur had bought on behalf of his new wife when they were still only lawyer and client.

This house was Nansen's childhood home. Built of wood, it was large and comfortable, surrounded by outbuildings, and stood in its own grounds, on the outskirts of Christiania. It was called *Lille Frøen*; by derivation, probably 'The little fertile meadow'. Not long since, it had been a working farm. To the south, glinted the quiet waters of the fjord. Close by, the forest began; the 'deep, sombre pine forest', as Nansen once called it in a moment of harkback: 'you were the only confidante of my lonely childhood ... From you I learned all [the] wildness and ... heavy melancholy of Nature ... You gave my spirit its colour for life.'

5

The city meanwhile was stealthily encroaching. It still numbered fewer than 60,000 souls. Paris then had 1,700,000 inhabitants; roughly the same as that of all Norway at the time.

A second son, Alexander, was born to the Nansens in 1862. He was in fact their third child. In 1859, Adelaide had given birth to another son, also baptised Fridtjof, but he died after little more than a year.

At about the age of two, Fridtjof Nansen was taught to ski by a spirited seven-year-old girl called Inga Schjøtt, who lived nearby. A few years later a kindly but reputedly acerbic neighbour gave him his first 'proper' pair of skis. The memory of this gift remained vivid throughout his life. His very first pair, as he later recalled, were 'dismal and decrepit, made out of old skis ... not even the same length'. But as for the new ones:

> I can still see [the] long long parcel ... It [contained] a pair of red enamelled ash skis with black stripes. And then there was a long stick, with shiny, blue enamelled shaft and basket.

Nansen used those skis for years. He was wearing them still when, at the age of ten or eleven, he made his first big jump. That was on the Huseby jumping hill, very much an adult installation, although freely used by daring boys. Nansen's parents, however, declared it out of bounds to him. From his home, Nansen could see the forbidden slope. In his own words, it 'tempted me for so long, until [one day I] couldn't resist any more'.

> I started down, took off at a tremendous speed, swooped through the air for an eternity, and then my skis dug into a snowdrift. [They] remained standing in the drift, and I described a long curve in the air, head first ... When I landed, I bored my way into the snow right up to my waist ... The other boys [broke into] an endless peal of mocking laughter.

In the late summer of 1868, just before his seventh birthday, Nansen started school. From the outset, with his blotted and irregular attempts at copperplate handwriting, he mildly exasperated his teachers. He had an irritating capacity to manage without much apparent effort. He followed the curriculum, from mathematics through to drawing, and taking in English, French and German. He acquitted himself adequately, without any particular leaning. He seemed to care for sport alone.

To Nansen, as he grew up, the seasons were delimited by sport. Summer was the time for fishing and swimming in the sharp, cold waters of the fjord on which Christiania lay. (Nansen was unusual in his enthusiasm for this.) Autumn, with the conifers interlaced by yellowing birches, meant hunting. As a child (so the story runs) Nansen made bows and arrows, hopefully dipping the arrowheads in fly agaric, supposedly the most poisonous of fungi, with squirrels as his quarry. In time, he graduated to guns, game pouches, and the real thing.

But winter was the climax of the year, bringing snow, and skiing in its wake. During Nansen's childhood occurred the technical revolution which gave rise to skiing as we know it.

In Norway, skiing was historically a part of life, and an instrument of national consciousness, although to the outside world it still remained a curiosity of travellers' tales. Not that the ski was exactly a Norwegian invention. Its origins are prehistoric, with traces along a crescent running from Central Asia across Siberia to Scandinavia. Norway, however, was the home of modern skiing. There it evolved from what was a means of winter travel into a universal sport. It was in Norway too that the ancient form of skiing, cross-country, or Nordic, had evolved into the downhill kind as well.

By a complex interplay of men and mountains, the province of Telemark, to the west of Christiania, was pre-eminent in the development of downhill skiing. In Telemark, according to one contemporary writer,

> It was a terrible disgrace to take a tumble ... Anyone who had too many falls couldn't dance with the girls on Sunday evening, and if he asked them, they just laughed.

Out of Telemark came Sondre Nordheim, a poor farmer's son, arguably one of the greatest of the skiing pioneers. He is credited with introducing the two fundamental turns: one elegant, balanced and adapted to deep snow, soon appropriately called the Telemark, the other based on side-slipping, eventually dubbed the Christiania or 'Christie', after the city, and the foundation of all downhill technique. Nordheim also devised a new form of binding, the vital link between the skier and his skis. It was a rigid model made of thin birch root threaded over the toe and round the heel of the boot. It was the first device to give proper lateral control of the skis, and hence the first modern binding.

Although Nordheim may not exactly have invented all this, he perfected it. He was one of those historic individuals who appear opportunely to encapsulate a trend. A turbulent character, he may decently be called the father of skiing as we know it, and his native valley of Morgedal the crucible of the sport.

By contrast, when Nansen was a child, Christiania was a backwater, where skiers still practised stick riding – a clumsy method using a single stick both for balancing and as a brake. Nordheim, with his beautiful sense of balance, disdained this. On Sunday 9 February 1868, invited by those concerned by the state of the sport, he demonstrated in a ski race his technique to the inhabitants of Christiania. He was a sensation; the stuff of encomiastic journalism. The event may be called the birth of modern skiing. It took place within sight of Nansen's home.

Adelaide Nansen was herself an impassioned skier. She defied convention which at that time decreed, in the cities at least, that females, once past childhood, should leave this sport to the men. Baldur took no interest in any sport at all. But finally he grasped what sport and the open air meant to his sons, and helped them to the extent of paying for their equipment.

One of Nansen's playmates observed in later years that Nansen did not feel close to his father, who was 'an old maid', and that 'Old Madame Nansen was ugly to look at, strict, but kind. Fridtjof loved her.' This is borne out by a letter he wrote to his parents in March 1870, when he was eight and a half years old and they were away on a foreign trip. 'I think it's sad to be alone at home,' he told them. 'I and Alexander miss you a lot.'

Whether Adelaide returned his affection, was another matter altogether. She was preoccupied with running the household which, in the early years, with all the children at home, numbered ten, not counting servants. Nansen in later years seldom referred to her. She remains a distant, shadowy figure; a prisoner of circumstance perhaps, trapped in a marriage of convenience, with enigmatic feelings towards her second family.

'I did not get on with my father, and I had no mother,' was her son's own bleak summing up. For mother love, he turned in the first place to the housekeeper, Marthe Larsen; then to his half-sister Ida Bølling, twelve years his senior. It was the beginning of a lifelong quest.

There was in Nansen a persistent strain of melancholy. On his own admission, he was 'a bit of a lone wolf'. 'I had ... companions with whom I played – but no friends.' Alexander remembered his brother as 'the boss', adding: 'I used to tease him, and we kept on quarrelling and fighting.' Both boys were moody, a trait they are said to have inherited from their mother.

In 1867 Moltke died, at the age of thirteen, having been sickly all his life. By the time Nansen was ten or so Adelaide's three oldest sons had all left home, so that from her first marriage there remained behind only her two daughters. But even with four fewer mouths to feed, money was tight. Baldur was plagued by financial difficulties. Besides, whatever his circumstances, he believed in Spartan principles. Food stayed simple; pocket money, low. Adelaide was forced to continue economising. Amongst other things, she made clothes for Fridtjof and Alexander by altering Baldur's cast-off suits.

All this did not bode well for Nansen when he began the usual adolescent pursuit of girls. He was tall for his age and flaxen-haired, with a fierce glint behind frank, childlike eyes. Unfortunately, he was also fat and gauche. To the knowing young female, it was not a figure that appealed.

He himself seemed to alternate between fits of brooding and spasms of exuberance. He could appear hard and unfeeling. But underneath the shell were glimpses of something softer and more emotional.

Poetry of a certain kind gripped him, notably the work which had inspired his own christian name. This was an epic called *Frithiof's Saga*; an early nineteenth-century Swedish work romanticising the Norwegian Vikings. Translated into various languages, it was much admired at the time. As a schoolboy, Nansen knew long passages by heart, which he insisted on reciting. One stirring stanza runs:

> But Frithiof laugh'd: 'I count my race
> From foes I conquered in the chase:
> I slew the forest monarch grim;
> My glories all descend from him.'

2

'That Strange City'

Nansen grew up in 'that strange city' – to quote a classic characterisation of nineteenth-century Christiania – 'which nobody leaves before he has been marked by it.' The words are those of Nansen's exact contemporary Knut Hamsun, the greatest of the Norwegian nineteenth-century novelists, and a pioneer of the stream of consciousness, influencing James Joyce.

Christiania was a small town trying to be a capital. Its one metropolitan touch was the short, newly completed boulevard that formed its main thoroughfare and, since the middle of the century, had been called Karl Johansgate, 'Karl Johan Street' – in honour of a Swedish king.

Norway was one of the subject nations of Europe. After the distant glories of the Viking age, she had steadily declined. For over four hundred years she belonged to Denmark and was ruled from Copenhagen. In consequence, many Norwegians, including both Nansen's parents, had Danish blood in their veins. Indeed the founder of the Nansen family, Hans Nansen, was a celebrated Dane of the seventeenth century. As a young man he made some audacious journeys through Arctic Russia, eventually becoming Mayor of Copenhagen and stalwart defender of the burgesses against the King.

During the Napoleonic Wars, Norway was caught up in the whirlwind. In 1814, the year before Waterloo, she found herself summarily transferred to Sweden. 'Your fate is sealed,' the Swedish regent bluffly told the Norwegians. 'Small countries,' he cheerfully proclaimed, 'are always the pawns of stronger ones.'

The Norwegians begged to disagree. They immediately asserted their independence. The Swedish regent, however, was not to be trifled with. He was in fact a Frenchman: the celebrated Jean-Baptiste Bernadotte, one of Napoleon's wiliest marshals. Bizarre political convolutions had brought him to Sweden, technically as Crown Prince to an ineffectual sovereign, in reality to rule. He founded the present Swedish reigning house.

By declaring independence, the Norwegians had set a sinister example for nationalist ambitions elsewhere. They threatened to torpedo the looming post-Napoleonic settlement. In July 1814 Bernadotte marched on Norway. After a war lasting eleven days the Norwegians sued for peace. As wars go, it was not much, but for Bernadotte it was enough. He was faced with pressing foreign military and diplomatic complications. So, in August, he galloped through negotiations for peace. As part of the price for speed he accepted the Constitution adopted by a Norwegian national convention on 17 May that year – the anniversary of which became the Norwegian national day and which, much revered, with few amendments, still remains in force.

Instead of a conquered province, Norway became an autonomous, constitutional monarchy joined to Sweden in a personal union under one king. She had her own national Parliament and Cabinet, with sovereign power to raise taxes. Only in foreign affairs was she really subject to the Swedes.

Thus by an ironic twist of history, union with Sweden had brought self-determination to Norway. She was pitchforked from absolutism to representative democracy, with a unicameral parliament on the best modern lines. Because of the profound centralisation of the Danish state, Norway had long had no separate existence; no capital city even. *Faute de mieux*, Christiania now became the capital.

In 1818, Bernadotte formally ascended the throne of Sweden-Norway with the dynastic name of Karl XIV Johan, always shortened to Karl Johan, hence the Christiania street name. He was everybody's favourite fairy tale come to life. The son of a lawyer, he had started as a humble private soldier, became one of the military leaders of the French revolution, and ended as a king.

This resembled the national Askeladden myth, in which Norwegians see themselves. Askeladden is an Aladdin-like figure; the archetypal hero, or rather anti-hero, of many a Norwegian folk tale. He is a happy-go-lucky scapegrace of a boy, often a younger brother, who, by the exercise of cunning and a quick tongue but, above all, by good luck, overtakes his worthy betters to rise from rags to riches and get the girl as well. As a result Karl Johan, although he had defeated them in war, was hugely popular among the Norwegians.

Nonetheless, they chafed under Swedish overlordship. Yet from a certain point of view, Norway got the best of the bargain. She was given peace and stability while she underwent the disturbing change from a backward, isolated country of farmers and fishermen to a modern state.

It was an abiding irony that Karl Johan, who subjugated the Norwegians, presided over the gestation of their extraordinary renaissance of the nineteenth century which produced, among its geniuses, Nils Henrik Abel, one of the founders of modern mathematics, Ibsen, Grieg, and Nansen too. Like the Italian original, from which it was lineally descended, this latter-day version was devoted to the cultivation of individuality and the universal man. It was overlaid by a Romantic veneration for the man of action and conspicuous achievement.

When Karl Johan died, in 1844, at the age of 81, the Norwegians were grappling with the transition from an inchoate national feeling to romantic, self-conscious and militant nationalism. It was a metamorphosis of the times. Nonetheless, in 1848, the year of nationalist insurrections, an English visitor to Norway observed that, 'of all the states of Christendom', it appeared to be 'almost the only one exempt from the desire or the apprehension of change'. From another point of view, a Norwegian writer observed darkly that 'the great European wave is not yet running up here, but we can hear the murmur of the swell'.

Intellectual ferment and the power of nationalism had, after all, been at work. 'The rebirth of springtime' was, tellingly enough, an image used by Norwegians themselves to evoke their exhilarating sense of a country waking up.

The same forces of unrest produced in a small nation like Norway a suffocating sense of claustrophobia that drove original spirits to escape. Ibsen was a notable example. He lived abroad for most of his productive life, and in all seriousness considered one of his tasks 'to awaken the people and make them think big'. Yet because the population was thinly spread in an untamed landscape there was an internal path to freedom. Nansen had his within view of his very own doorstep in the form of the wild, undulating upland called Nordmarka.

Swathed in pine forest, in winter mantled with snow, Nordmarka was threaded with lake, moor, marsh, and stream. Here and there were lonely mountain farms. So far, it had been left to the few foresters, hunters, and others whose business took them there. Now, it was beginning to be explored for pleasure by city dwellers driven to flee brickbound streets, especially grim when the fog rolled in from the fjord. Nor did they have to flee far. This tract of country began only a few miles to the north of the capital.

Nansen was introduced to Nordmarka by Einar Bølling, one of his half-brothers; fifteen years older than himself, and an army officer. Einar taught him how to hunt, how to fish, and how to survive in the wilderness.

In their teens, when winter came, Nansen and his brother took to Nordmarka on their skis, year by year penetrating deeper into the hinterland. In this they were pioneers. There were no prepared tracks. They had to find their own way alone through the forest, usually on virgin snow; on memorable occasions, light and powdery, hissing beneath the skis, like the spume of a yacht driving before the wind. When they set out, they never knew exactly where they would finish. It was exploration on their doorstep.

Year in and year out, in all weather, Nansen walked to school and home again; into Christiania and back to where the rough country roads began; three kilometres each way. Perhaps this helped him, early in 1877, at the age of 15, to win a boys' speed skating race over five kilometres. It was held before a large crowd on a frozen inlet of the Christiania Fjord. In the same season he came 14th in the boys' class of a combined ski jumping and cross-country competition – a classic Nordic event – just outside Christiania.

That summer, Nansen's mother died. She had been ailing for some time. For what remained of the once large family the Nansen property was now

2. 'That Strange City'

patently too big. Baldur quickly sold up and moved to a flat in Christiania itself. Sadly, clumsily, without complaint, this conscientious provider tried to be both father and mother to the two sons still in his care. He had, in his quiet way, come to expect great things from Fridtjof, though sensitively trying to hide these feelings from Alexander.

During the summer of 1878, when Nansen was almost seventeen, Baldur sent both him and Alexander on their first walking tour to Jotunheimen, in the charge of another half-brother, Harald Bølling.

Jotunheimen is the mountain range of western Norway; the highest in the country, and the summit of Scandinavia. It was another paradigm of escape. In Norway, because the sun is so low for much of the year, the valleys, although the seats of habitation, have always been associated with darkness and a sense of being trapped. By contrast, the mountains have come to mean light and liberty. It is an antithesis that happens to mirror, and perhaps help explain, the moody streak and violent contrasts in the Norwegian psyche. It lay behind a poem by Ibsen that in time greatly influenced Nansen. This was *På Viddene*; roughly, 'On the Heights'. An eerie evocation of the Norwegian mountain atmosphere, the poem ends with the telling lines:

> Up here on the heights, God and freedom reign,
> Down below the others flounder on.

Up in Jotunheimen Nansen, in his adolescent way, responded to this sentiment. 'One day we saw a big reindeer stag crossing a glacier ... The loveliest experience we have yet had,' he reported back to Baldur. Whatever his true opinion of his father, he was a dutiful correspondent, and absence brought pity to the surface: 'But we are enjoying ourselves, and poor you, who pay for our pleasure, are sitting at home and slaving away.'

Still, summer was only the interval between two winters, and skiing was the Nansen brothers' passion. They joined the Christiania Ski Club, the first of its kind in the capital, soon after its foundation in 1877. To Alexander, skiing was a pastime, and in other respects he showed all the signs of following a conventional career. Fridtjof, on the other hand, caused Baldur considerable misgivings. Approaching adulthood, the youth still seemed obsessed by sport. Like most of his fellow-countrymen, he was too much of an untamed individualist to take kindly to team games; but he was devoted to skiing, swimming and gymnastics.

Meanwhile, there was the looming prospect of the *Examen Artium*; Artium for short, the university entrance examination still exclusively reserved for males, which marked the culmination of every young man's school career and his entrée into adulthood.

Nansen took it in 1880 (two years before the first woman was admitted) and found that he had passed within 1 mark of distinction. Most students celebrated the end of this ordeal with a hefty bout of organised drinking.

13

Nansen chose instead to recuperate from his exertions with an extended visit to the country estates of two wealthy familes. The gossip drifting down to Christiania did not reassure Baldur, who admonished his son in a letter:

> That extravagant life is not healthy for you ... To live *only* for pleasure will do for a little while, but not for long. You will acquire a taste for a way of life very far from that you are accustomed to ... and from what I wish you to lead ... To amuse yourself with the ladies can be pleasant for you, so long as the ladies agree ... But beware, and watch your behaviour, so that you do not give any cause for comment ... I find it *unworthy* of a young person to let himself be used as a plaything by the ladies, because they lack other playthings ... But – the game goes on just so long as they have nobody better.

It was his wish, he concluded, that Nansen should come home soon. 'See that you are back by the 16th or 17th of this month.'

Nansen was by now within a few days of his nineteenth birthday. He had lost his puppy fat. He had grown up tall, slim, well-proportioned and undeniably attractive to women, especially those older than himself. But he was not yet free of his father's legal tutelage and had still to decide on a career.

It was not Baldur's wish to influence his son's choice; he only wanted him to make up his mind – an attitude astonishingly tolerant for the times. Nansen himself first thought of engineering: Baldur concurred. Then he felt that the prospects were poor and decided instead to be an army officer. Baldur entered him in the cadet school. Then he switched to forestry and then, finally and somewhat surprisingly, settled on zoology, with the aim of specialising in the lower marine creatures. He was, he wrote later,

> a passionate hunter and angler and man of the forest, and in my youthful inexperience believed that such a subject meant a life constantly in the open air.

Baldur was pleased, but for different reasons. In his own words:

> As by this choice he will have work of consuming interest for his whole life, I raised no objections, but spoke to scientists at the University ... They very much wanted someone to devote himself completely to that subject, but also explained that it would not bring in much money. However, I do not think that so important, as long as Fridtjof is interested in his career.

Nansen began university early in 1881. Meanwhile there was more skiing. On 7 February 1881, in the course of a winter marked by phenomenally abundant snowfalls, Nansen entered a competition arranged by the Christiania Ski Club at Huseby, where he had once so notably come to grief.

The event was conceived as the microcosm of a ski tour. The course opened with a jump, followed immediately by a cross country sprint of about three kilometres over violently undulating terrain. Starting was consecutive, at intervals of one minute. The intention was to reward the complete skier; he who could jump, climb, run downhill, and ski well on level ground. It was a fusion of what later separated into Nordic and alpine skiing. To ensure a proper standard for the Huseby race of 1881, competitors had been invited from Telemark.

To modern eyes, it would all have seemed inexpressibly quaint. The jumping hill was not an artificial structure, but a natural slope, the lip built up with blocks of snow. Jumps were only about 18 metres, against the 80-90 metres that is usual today at the top. The style was with body bolt upright, not lunged aerodynamically forward. 'Of falls there were plenty,' so one journalist reported,

> and not only minor prophets bit the dust ... only 12 or 13 [of 47] managed the big jump, and of these 2 were stick-riders, but of the remainder of those who did not fall, only [a handful] set off with full speed in the approach run without braking, including ... F. Nansen.

Nansen finished seventh, winning a pair of skis, beating ten of the fifteen Telemark skiers and also winning a cup for the best skier from Christiania. Since this cup had been donated by his father, he felt he could hardly accept it. He returned it to the organisers, for use on another occasion.

By his performance, Nansen had proved himself one of the best skiers in the country, and incidentally secured a place among the skiing pioneers. But in the public debate that ensued, he was far from content. The question was: should competitive skiing become specialised and artificial, or should it keep its roots as a way of travelling over natural terrain? Nansen unequivocally took the view that skiing was 'a means of travel' and should not run the risk of being 'turned into a performing art'.

> It is not the jump that plays the leading rôle [he went on to say], but the unexpected obstacles that arise in moving through unknown country; and there generally it is a question of instantly *avoiding* a jump, instead of carrying it out.

An unexpected obstacle of a different sort was provoked by his passion for hunting, when, in the autumn of 1881, his kinsman, Harald Wedel Jarlsberg, accused him of illicitly shooting on his estate. Jarlsberg threatened to take him to law, and only after strenuous efforts on the part of Nansen's father did he agree to drop proceedings.

Meanwhile there was his first year at university to be got through. In December 1881, he sat and passed with distinction the so-called 'second examination' required of all students before they were allowed to specialise, then answered a call from the department of zoology (the only person to do so) which wanted someone to visit the Arctic to collect specimens of marine life. Once more Baldur agreed. 'It is a little hard', he wrote to a relative, 'to have him away for so long without news ... and people are surprised that I immediately gave permission. But I decided it was a sensible first step on his chosen career.'

Nansen had to arrange his own passage. Through his father's contacts, he found a comfortable berth on the sealer *Viking*, of Arendal, a port on the south coast of Norway, and sailed on 11 March 1882.

> We steamed out [he wrote in his newly begun diary] exactly as the sun rose majestically over the islands ... It was with a strange feeling I departed from islands and ... forests and hills, to be consigned to the sea and its waves ... it was the first Spring I would not be able to wander about in the conifer forests of my birthplace, and absorb the air of springtime; and with it the wonderful, invincible sense of life returning.

3

Viking

Out in the Atlantic, off the Faeroes, the sea birds, which had been companionably following the ship, all vanished, except for a few petrels and kittiwakes, creatures of the storm. After days of gently dipping on an easy swell *Viking*, with close-reefed tops'l, heeled over to a gale that swept out of the south-west. She heaved and lurched violently to the rhythm of a capricious, remorseless sea. The wind screamed through the rigging and tore at the masts; the backstays thrummed; the mainyard was wrenched from its mountings and swung tangled in the halliards. The deck was raked by hissing green seas whipped to spume which, when darkness fell, glittered with phosphorescence like a ghostly firework display. All this Nansen tersely recorded in his diary while seasickness took its course.

So far, it was little different from any first voyage. Nansen had grown up by the fjord, familiar with the sight of ships, but he knew little of seamen or the sea, and aboard *Viking* he faced a profound initiation. On 17 March he crossed the Arctic Circle for the first time in his life. Next day, he came on deck to see small white isolated fragments of ice drifting past on the sombre swell. Over the northern horizon hung an eerie glow; the loom of the pack ice ahead. *Viking* closed, and began cruising along the edge. During the night there was, appropriately, a display of the aurora borealis.

The auroras are the emblem of high latitudes; mirages of both desert and ice. This was how Nansen recorded his first mirage:

> Pieces of ice, at or under the horizon, were lifted up, hovering above it ... naturally I tried to sketch this, but ability is not always as great as intention.

Nansen's position on board *Viking* was anomalous. When the sealing started, he would be expected to take part. Until then he was a passenger, living aft under the half deck among the officers with a cabin of his own. He had the leisure to assimilate the new sensations with which he was being bombarded. The end of seasickness he celebrated by lying in his bunk and reading a pirate story. In the saloon, he lapped up every yarn that was spun, including some about ships deliberately wrecked to cover the losses of a bad season by cashing in on the insurance money. Finally, at the end of April, around 75°N and five hundred miles beyond the Arctic

17

Circle, he had his first glimpse of the Midnight Sun, flaming crimson through a gap in leaden clouds. His rites of passage to the polar world were now complete.

Seals are marine mammals, who partly live out of the water, especially to have their young. Sealers of those days were likewise a breed of their own: tough, highly specialised, independent, and by ordinary mariners treated warily; outcasts among outcasts. Even a sealing vessel was not as other ships. For one thing, at the masthead was the tell-tale crow's nest, the barrel-like perch for the lookout to spy out over the ice.

Of 650 tons burden, *Viking* was big for a sealer. She was a sailing ship, barque rigged, with auxiliary steam engines, coal fired. Like any sealing vessel she was built of wood which, even in the age of the iron ship, was still the only construction yet known to ensure an elastic hull and with-stand the pressure of the polar ice. Vulnerable parts were reinforced. The bows, for example, were cross-braced and built up with solid timber four or five feet thick. *Viking* had just come off the stocks, and this was her maiden voyage.

To rule such a ship and such a crew required a particular kind of man. *Viking*'s captain, Axel Krefting, a sturdy, bearded figure, about thirty years of age, was no ordinary mariner. He was part seaman, part trader, part farmer, with a great fund of shrewdness: rather like an old Viking chieftain, in other words. His roots indeed lay in an old aristocratic hunting society in which the best hunters ruled.

He was also a kind of explorer, for the Arctic was still mostly a blank upon the charts. Waning catches had driven Norwegian sealing skippers further out in search of better luck. Northwards, they skirted the still mysterious ice calotte around the pole. To the east, they probed the imperfectly charted waters off Siberia and opened the Kara Sea. One of them, Edvard Holm Johannesen, was the first known to have circumnavigated Novaya Zemlya. Those sealers did duty for Norwegian polar explorers, for in Norway polar exploration, as such, did not then exist. To avert the tedium of being cooped up on board for months on end, Krefting drove men and ship hard. But he tried never to cross the thin line that divides daring from foolhardiness.

Nansen got on well with Krefting, and they were glad of each other's company. With the crew, his relations were more complex. Living their communal life in the foc'sle, they found him an enigma. On the one hand, his impressive stature made him one of the chieftain figures they respected and understood. On the other, his habit of dissecting the sea birds he had shot, taking water temperatures, and doing other mystifying things, seemed to them inexplicable. Yet these men of rough appearance and brutish calling had great respect for learning. Some of them, indeed, were surprisingly well-read. For his part Nansen found them 'childlike souls ... content with little. They are happy as long as they have something to eat and drink.' But neither was he blind to their other side. In the toils of life ashore they could be wild, drunk and improvident.

As *Viking* sailed on, the hunter in Nansen stirred, and incessantly he clambered up to the crow's nest to scan the ice with its jagged network of dark open water leads for his first sight of seal.

But it was not only a question of finding the seal. There was also a cat-and-mouse game with other sealing vessels. Nobody willingly shared his luck. *Viking* had found the ice at 70°N, about 150 miles east of Jan Mayen and, as it happened, 80 miles to the west of where the pups had been found the previous season. Other sealers soon appeared. After a few days searching in company, Captain Krefting used his superior engine power to break out into open water and scuttle off on his own. The weeks passed; *Viking* threaded her way through the pack, but in vain. Nansen filled the hiatus by sketching and painting and with telling diary observations of the natural scene. 'Most people,' he wrote in what was almost a profession of faith,

> might be oppressed by such surroundings, with its silence and inhuman expanses ... But he who seeks peace and quiet in Nature, undisturbed by human activity ... will find here what he seeks ... even although, beset in the ice, one is a plaything of the forces of Nature.

This was, by common consent, the strangest season in living memory. It was only on 10 April, at around 73°N, that Nansen finally saw his first seal. At last, a fortnight later, more than a month after *Viking* entered the pack, the lookout in the crow's nest sighted the first proper herd.

The boats were ordered away. Now Nansen's strange shipmates came into their own. In their fur caps, with flaps hanging down loose over their ears, they looked like primitive tribesmen. With short, powerful strokes they rowed their whaler down a channel to the chosen floe. Nansen himself was not at an oar. He sat in the bow with his rifle, an apprentice marksman, one of the elite, together with an experienced shot who had been detailed to teach him the trade.

Nansen's boat approached the herd – all adults, no pups. The only movement on the ice was a periodic bobbing of wary seal heads keeping a lookout. With equal wariness, the boat's crew rowed within rifle range, and shipped their oars. The skill was to place a bullet exactly in a certain part of the skull. Anywhere else, and the seal would survive at least long enough to escape into the water. Once a marksman had scored, men landed on the ice and, with surgical exactitude, flensed the fallen seal, for they wanted only the pelts, leaving the carcasses behind on the blood-stained ice for the gulls to scavenge. Back and forth went the boats. In the midst of all the excitement, Nansen remembered material for his zoological collection. What thrilled him most was when his boat turned out to have the largest bag that day: 44 pelts in all. But one day, in thick weather, a squadron of sealers loomed out of the Arctic mist, all sail set, weighed down with their catch. While *Viking* had dodged about in vain, the others had found the pups. 'Disappointed hope,' so Nansen jotted in his diary, 'was to be seen on every face' – for *Viking*'s crew understood they would not become rich from this voyage.

For two months longer, *Viking* ranged about, northwards at first until the shattered peaks of Spitsbergen were briefly raised and Nansen had to contain 'an unbearable longing' for its 'reindeer herds and eider rookeries'; south again to reach the pack ice in the Denmark Strait between Greenland and Iceland.

But the slowly pulsating ice soon closed up; sealing again had to stop. Nansen, however, noticed Greenland sharks in some narrow, open leads. The oil from the liver, he knew, was valuable; but on a sealer, shark fishing was unheard of. Nansen nonetheless had by now imposed his personality to the point where he was able to overcome the terrible conservatism of the sea and cajole Captain Krefting into letting him try. With a few seamen, he went out onto the ice, and led an assault on the sharks, using seal picks as improvised harpoons. Large beasts, some of them five metres long, the sharks were sluggish and easy prey.

By now, Nansen had acquired the knack of stalking seal and shooting them. On 4 June, with no little pride, he recorded that his boat killed 200 seal, the biggest catch that day.

Then, towards the end of the month, fog rolled in; the ice closed up. An unrelieved plain of compacted floes stretched, greenish white, all round to the horizon. *Viking* was beset. The seal, needing open water, had disappeared once more. Nansen now tried his hand at shooting polar bears. Aided by the crew, who warmed to his schoolboy eagerness, he soon made his first kill. But dissatisfaction marred the hour, for he had taken four shots where one should have done. He was reassured when the ammunition, not his marksmanship, turned out to be at fault. He had used hollow shells, which disintegrated on impact; thenceforth he would use solid bullets instead.

But as much as the hunt itself, Nansen enjoyed Krefting's companionship. These 'pleasurable hours' would remain, as he put it,

> shining pearls in the treasure chest of memory. Memories, the wonderful memories, are the most precious possession of the hunter; a ... fortune ... that is never lost.

Early in July, Nansen felled a young bear. Some of the meat was cooked and served. Nansen appropriated the heart, sharing it with Captain Krefting,

> who now was persuaded that it was especially delicate, although he laughed when I first said I wanted to eat the heart of a bear – 'that hard, stringy muscle'.

20

3. Viking

There was an ancient Nordic superstition that to eat the heart of a bear was to acquire its courage and strength. Nansen half believed this, wantonly interrupting a spate of scientific work – notably trawling for marine life through a hole in the ice – with this arguably atavistic rite. At the same time he could reflect:

> How beautiful is this proud animal, that now lies in the snow in its yellow-white fur, while the fresh red blood drips from its chest [he wrote]. One becomes half melancholy with the thought that even such a creature must succumb to human ingenuity ... One almost falls into a tragic mood with the thought that, with [a rifle] in his hand, even the most miserable and cowardly human creature can ... murder ... at long range, in cold blood ... the bravest and strongest animal on the face of the earth.

The crew became dispirited or worse when, at the beginning of July, Greenland hove into sight. They feared that *Viking*, still hopelessly gripped in the pack, was about to re-enact one of the dismal sagas of shipwreck by which their folklore was darkened. But Nansen, in the crow's nest, had spotted what is now called Christian IX Land, but was then one of the last unexplored parts of the east coast of Greenland. Nobody was known yet to have landed there. Nansen instantly wanted to go ashore, but was stopped by one 'decisive objection':

> The Captain naturally could not himself leave the ship, nor could he permit others to do so. If the pack ice slackened, and that could not be predicted, he had to be prepared instantly to sail free ... Thus ... my splendid dream of setting foot on the shore so often sought by explorers in vain, went up in smoke.

Viking had been beset just under the 66th parallel. She was swept north about 20 miles above the Arctic Circle until, on 12 July, she began to drift south again. For much of the time, she was off *Schreckensbucht*, 'The Bay of Horrors'. The only feature on that coast with a name, it commemorated the failed attempt by a German expedition to reach the North Pole in 1870 and thereby place another feather in the cap of a triumphant Bismarck. The bay was named in 'eternal memory', to quote one expedition member, 'of the deadly dangers we had survived'.

On 17 July *Viking* at last broke out of the pack and, next day, was homeward bound, with a mediocre cargo of sealskins to show for her maiden voyage.

Except for a brief landing in Iceland on the way down to the Denmark Strait, Nansen had now been at sea continuously for over four months. He was returning with a full collection of zoological specimens and so had succeeded in what he had been sent out to do. Nonetheless it was 'with melancholy', as he put it, that he watched the coast of Greenland 'sink gradually towards the horizon'.

21

4

Dr Jaeger Ordains

'It is very odd; if anyone was tempted to believe in a genie specially appointed for him by Fate, it must be me,' Nansen once wrote. 'So often, at a crisis in my life, it has happened that some strange chance has shown the way ahead.'

On 11 August 1882, he came home from *Viking*, prepared to return to university. On that very same day a lecturer in the zoology department, Robert Collett, who had sent him out to the Arctic in the first place, came round to urge him to apply instead for a position at the museum in Bergen, on the west coast of Norway.

A post as curator in the zoological department was about to fall vacant, and no qualified applicants had so far appeared. Nansen himself was scarcely qualified either, but such was the state of the sciences in Norway at that time that he was the only candidate whom Collett, when approached, could suggest.

After barely a year at university, and a few weeks before his twenty-first birthday, Nansen was thus presented with financial independence. He wished to seize the moment. In all decency, however, he felt obliged to consult his father, then staying in the country, and hastened to put his case. In Baldur's own words:

> When I heard that Collett unreservedly believed that the [move] would greatly help him in getting ahead ... in his profession ... it was obvious that I had to give my consent ... even although [I had] looked forward ... to keeping him here with me for the years I might still have to live.

Nansen applied for the post, was appointed by telegram, and left for Bergen without delay.

The move was an escape, from his father first of all, but also from an educational straitjacket. The University in Christiania imposed rigid, lacklustre, formalised instruction in the lecture room. By contrast, the Bergen Museum, founded some sixty years before by public-spirited citizens, was an easygoing combination of a centre for popular improvement and a scientific research institute.

It was an age when individuals, working on their own, were still making fundamental discoveries. Of that, Nansen now had living proof. On the staff of the museum was Dr Gerhard Armauer Hansen who, in 1873, had discovered the leprosy bacillus.

This was a milestone in the history of medicine. Pasteur and others were then developing the germ theory of infection. By his discovery, Armauer Hansen provided early confirmation, for he was one of the first to associate a specific agent with a particular disease. Here was an example to inspire. Nansen was stirred by the vision of the scientist in his laboratory.

In other respects, he found it difficult to settle down. Bergen was somehow a place apart. With a population of only 40,000, this ancient Hanseatic port was still the second city in Norway. But while Christiania was linked by valleys to the interior, Bergen was cut off, isolated by mountains from the hinterland and with only the sea to link it to other places along the coast.

The inhabitants too were of an unfamiliar temperament – livelier than those of Christiania, less prone to brood, more given to sudden outbursts of emotion which then passed away. They were men of a frontier world between mountain and sea. They spoke a distinctive dialect which, with a flat cadence and rolled r's, was quite unlike the sing-song of eastern Norway with which Nansen had grown up.

Most different of all was the weather. Christiania, on a landlocked sound, had a more or less stable, continental climate. Bergen, on the edge of the Atlantic, was exposed to the volatile force of the sea. One day the mountains might be glistening with snow; the next, black and brown in the drizzle. Against this, the exotic charms of the old Hanseatic quarter, and the drama of its setting under gnarled and weatherbeaten peaks, were not enough to console Nansen for the sights and sounds he had lost. He was a man of the forest, as he himself once said, 'and nobody escapes from his origins'. He was one of those who are prisoners of landscape. A letter from Krefting saying he was back on *Viking*, and adding, 'It is almost laughable how I miss you,' did not help. As winter approached Nansen felt a restlessness for snow, the skier's intolerable yearning for the ski track. At Christmas, he decided to take leave from the museum and go home.

This was easier said than done. There was no railway yet. To sail round the coast would take too long. Nansen's solution was to use his skis. This was unheard of. Mountain skiing as a pastime hardly existed; few winter crossings were recorded.

Nansen first took a boat from Bergen up the Sogne Fjord, the longest of the west Norwegian fjords, disembarking at Lærdal, near its head. He then skied over the mountains along the postal road via the valley of Hemsedal which, when conditions allowed, connected eastern and western Norway. The crossing was uneventful except for a blizzard. 'One is merely egged on to ... overcome the forces of Nature,' was how he recorded the event. 'One feels it refreshing to bathe in the storm, it is the wildness, the rebelliousness in one that is spurred.'

On the other side there was plenty of good snow, and all the skiing gave Nansen 'wonderful exercise, and refreshing enjoyment, which [as Baldur put it in a letter] would be so good for him, as he sits still at his work nearly all day'. Helpfully the old man added: 'So that he could meet some of his ... girl friends, I arranged a little dance.'

Nansen's method of travel had been characteristically pioneering but, back in Bergen at the beginning of the New Year, he ruefully told his father:

> no snow to be seen except a spot here and there up on the highest mountain ridges ... there is no skiing here ... but one cannot have all good things.

What Nansen did have by now was a new microscope. He had soon become dissatisfied with the instruments provided by the museum, and a month or two after starting work had asked his father to lend him the money to buy one of his own. Within a week Baldur obliged and in the New Year the microscope arrived.

As Nansen proudly told his father, it was better than anything else in the museum. What he had obtained was a Zeiss microscope with one of the first oil immersion lenses. In the vanguard of technology, it had just come onto the market. It was an enormous advance: great magnification, combined with high resolution and lack of distortion.

All this power Nansen was burning to exploit. Baldur sympathised. But when he sent the money for the microscope it was with the rider that 'I would also like you to be together with people of your own age'. There was cause for this concern.

Nansen had found lodgings with a parson called Vilhelm Holdt and his wife, Maria. They were childless, and soon after Nansen moved in, Holdt was calling him 'Esau', the former lodger having been 'Jacob'. Holdt, of course, was Isaac, and his wife, Rebecca. Nansen played up to this biblical whimsy, protesting however that his own nickname was essentially unjust. Esau, Isaac's favourite son, was a distinctly turbulent character; 'a cunning hunter, a man of the field', in the words of Genesis. Nansen, as he told his father, had 'become a slippered stay-at-home of the purest vintage'. The Holdts were giving Nansen the home that Baldur had never managed to provide.

By comparison with Nansen's Viking-like aspect, the Holdts were physically unimposing. He was dark-haired, conventionally bearded, of medium height; she plain and dumpy. Nansen remarked to Baldur that Holdt did not 'exactly give an impression of manliness, but his is the strangest yet one of the pleasantest characters I have come across; a mixture of greybeard and child'. Mrs Holdt was, revealingly, 'a wife who is that half of him that is completely lacking'. Both were thirty-eight; only sixteen years older than Nansen – with Maria one more substitute for the mother he claimed that he had never had. The Holdts on their side were plainly clinging to a make-believe son.

Dr Daniel Cornelius Danielssen, Director of the museum, was an altogether more dramatic character. He walked with a limp, the result of a tubercular hip in youth. He had lost three of his four children at an early age from lung disease. This left him with a profound regard for physical perfection and now, in his late sixties, a wistful longing for a young son. He was said to have confirmed Nansen in his post on account of his good looks. A patriarchal figure with a flowing beard, affecting always a skull cap, Danielssen was a master of the quick, barbed wit peculiar to Bergen. He was a genuine eccentric, given to the impulsive outburst and sweeping generalisation. (By contrast Armauer Hansen, like many medical pioneers, was surprisingly ordinary.)

For that matter, Nansen seemed something of an eccentric himself. He was a disciple of Dr Gustav Jaeger, the celebrated physician and clothing reformer from Stuttgart, whose name survives as a trade mark in the fashion business still. Jaeger advocated pure woollen garments to allow 'evaporation of the "noxious" emanations'. Nansen had for some years dressed exclusively in what the great clothing reformer had patented as his Sanitary Woollen Clothing. He revelled in the light, simple garments Dr Jaeger ordained, along with tight trousers and short jacket. 'I admire you, Herr Nansen,' someone once sardonically remarked, 'because you flaunt that member we others prefer to hide.' Nansen also went clean-shaven when to be bearded was still the norm. In all weathers he was to be seen striding about the streets of Bergen, a defiantly conspicuous figure, without an overcoat and, worst of solecisms, bareheaded. In Christiania, Nansen reminded his father, 'people laughed at me, and called it showing off, when I first began to dress in this way'. Now, in Bergen, he was accepted as just one more in the rich historical gallery of characters, almost lampoons of themselves, that was part of local pride.

Secure in his surrogate family, Nansen plunged into his work, labelling and classifying specimens dredged by others from the sea, while frenziedly teaching himself zoology to overcome the defects in his theoretical education. The Bergen Museum was far from the great centres of learning but nonetheless had a well-stocked scientific library. The company also was surprisingly stimulating. To begin with, there was Armauer Hansen himself, a pioneer in Norway of Darwinism, to which he quickly converted Nansen. Like Armauer Hansen, Dr Danielssen too was known abroad, as another expert on leprosy, by which Norway was, mysteriously, one of the last European countries to be seriously afflicted.

'I live quietly in our little circle,' Nansen told his father in the spring of 1883, 'caring little about the world outside … which could almost collapse without my noticing … I busy myself alternately with science and literature.'

Bergen possessed a theatre with its own professional company. There, on 24 January 1883, Ibsen's *An Enemy of the People* was produced, the first performance having taken place in Christiania a mere ten days before. In a letter to his father, reviling the dead weight of accepted beliefs, Nansen railed against 'the compact majority', which happened to be a direct quotation from the play. His creed was that of its hero, Dr Stockman: 'The minority is always right.' Another line from Ibsen, 'Compromise is Satan's work!' also appealed powerfully to Nansen.

Surprisingly enough, his mild-mannered landlord, Vilhelm Holdt, probably agreed with him in this. Unusually for a clergyman, Holdt was a devotee of Ibsen, and though in no way academic was a man of wide learning who encouraged Nansen's interest in literature in many ways.

Soon Nansen, like many other educated Norwegians, was turning to foreign literature, first to Byron's poetry, then more significantly to Goethe's *Faust*. 'The questing human spirit is not satisfied,' Nansen wrote to his father in the first flush of enthusiasm:

> It sometimes dares to penetrate where its power ends, like Prometheus of old who was bound to the rock, and Faust who entered into an alliance with the Devil, and that is the spirit that has emerged nowadays more powerfully than ever.

Indeed, there was about Nansen himself, bending over his microscope in the dark recesses of the museum, turbulent with an inchoate sense of power looking for direction, the hint of a Faustian figure.

Nansen was briefly torn in two directions. Microphotography did not yet exist, and to depict what he saw in the microscope Nansen took drawing lessons. His teacher is supposed to have told him to abandon science for art, because that was where his talent lay. After some wavering Nansen regretfully (perhaps) decided that, after all, he had better stick to biology.

All winter, Bergen seemed in a doze, turned inwards on itself. Then suddenly, one day in early summer, the city was jolted into life again by throngs of foreign tourists, English in the main. They had arrived with the first ships of the holiday season to appear out of the North Sea, for this was the port of entry for the spectacular landscape of the fjords.

Another kind of visitor used to arrive with the advent of spring. Marine biology was now veering away from the classification of dead specimens that was an essential stage in the evolution of the science, but which so irked Nansen, to the study of living creatures from the sea. There, the Bergen Museum was actually in the vanguard. The waters round about teemed with oceanic life. A coastal archipelago gave protected channels. That in turn offered unrivalled opportunity for dredging from the depths. A notable consequence was that the museum attracted scientists from abroad, and Nansen was brought into contact with people he might not otherwise have met.

In the spring of 1883, perhaps six months after Nansen took up his post, there arrived on an extended visit Dr Willy Kükenthal, a German zoologist from Jena.

It was a timely encounter. Kükenthal was exactly the same age as Nansen. He had an engaging personality, and quickly acquired great influence on Nansen at this crossroads of his life. Amongst other things, Kükenthal was interested in marine invertebrates – their nervous systems in particular. Nansen followed his lead, and decided to specialise in the neuroanatomy – that is, the structure of the nervous system – of lower marine creatures.

The whole subject of the nerves was in the air – a direct consequence of the development of the microscope. The nervous system of any creature was little understood and now, for the first time, as part of the advance in microscopical anatomy, its structure could be properly observed. There was a concerted desire to penetrate its mysteries. Within Western Europe there arose a spontaneous wave of research.

This followed in the wake of the cell theory, launched during the early part of the nineteenth century. It proposed that all living matter was made up of individual cells. This is now axiomatic but it took time to be generally accepted. (Darwin was able to propound the theory of evolution without once mentioning cellular structure.) In the late nineteenth century there was burgeoning interest in the study of cells, of which nerves are merely a specialised case.

One consequence of Darwin's theory of evolution was a sense that all forms of life are kin. If man really originated from protozoa, then any simpler creature was a model of himself. Invertebrate anatomy, therefore, was not an end in itself. It would help to understand the human nervous system and the working of the brain; ultimately perhaps the secret of thought itself. This was the quest on which Nansen was now preparing to embark.

5

Winterreise

Nansen's attention was divided nonetheless. The Arctic was once more haunting his desires. To begin with, Captain Louis Alphonse Mourier, the editor of the *Geografisk Tidskrift*, the Danish Geographical Journal, asked him for an article about his voyage in the *Viking*. He had already written a series on the subject for a Norwegian sporting journal. Mourier's invitation, however, first made personally at Christmas when he was staying in Norway with some relations who happened to know Baldur, and followed by a gentle reminder in the spring, came at a particular juncture. Nansen had been put in mind of a ship called *Vega*, probably for a short season the most famous vessel afloat. She had been sighted the previous year from the decks of *Viking*. 'With a certain awe,' Nansen's journal of that time records, 'I looked upon her celebrated form.'

As well he might. *Vega* was the expedition ship of one of the heroes of the age, the Swedish explorer Baron Nils Adolf Erik Nordenskiöld. In her, between 1878 and 1880, he had circumnavigated Europe and Asia, on the way completing the North-East Passage, the legendary route between the Atlantic and the Pacific along the coast of Siberia, and through the Bering Strait – the first time either had been accomplished. Thereafter, *Vega* returned to the seal fishery for which she had originally been built. When Nansen received Mourier's reminder, he had just heard that Nordenskiöld was preparing to explore the interior of Greenland.

Memories of the meeting with *Vega* in the ice welled up. 'My wanderlust,' he told Mourier in his reply, 'was roused again!' Some months later, in September 1883, while listening to Holdt reading out items from the newspaper, he heard that Nordenskiöld had just come back, having reached the ice cap that covers the interior of Greenland, and penetrated further inland than anyone yet. What is more, Nordenskiöld had succeeded in landing on the east coast, which Nansen himself, on *Viking*, had signally failed to do. In fact, nobody had done so in that region since the Vikings. As Nansen wrote to Mourier: 'I was all afire.' In the meanwhile, he had obliged with the article, which substantially turned out to be a plan of his own for finally landing on the east coast of Greenland.

Thus unsettled by the turbulence within, Nansen had also to console his father, who was now becoming chronically depressed and whose letters were often budgets of complaint. Baldur aspired only to win the love of his children which he sadly and all too justifiably grieved that he was incapable of doing. In May 1883, he suffered a minor stroke, but was well on the way to recovery by the time the news reached his son. In any case, Nansen wanted to spend his first summer in Bergen with the Holdts. He had been building up a variegated circle of acquaintances in Bergen, but Vilhelm and Maria Holdt, so he said, were 'the only people to whom I really became attached'. He went with them to Askøy, an island not too distant, in the coastal archipelago, on the edge of the open sea.

They could only find a single room to rent. Nansen slept in a neighbouring shed, with an earthen floor, in a hammock which he bought for the occasion. And there he stayed contentedly, dredging for specimens with local fishermen out among the islands, until the all too short Scandinavian summer waned and it was time to move back to town.

Towards the end of the year, Nansen received a more than usually agitated letter from his father. Baldur had heard that he might be going to America. Nansen had to explain that the scheme had been proposed during a visit to the Bergen Museum that summer by an unnamed English amateur zoologist who knew Professor Othniel Charles Marsh, head of the US Paleontological Survey. Overwhelmed by Nansen's personality, the Englishman recommended him to Marsh, then visiting Europe. The outcome was a flattering offer to Nansen of a post with the Survey.

Baldur was appalled. Not only would his son be going even further away from home than he was now; he would also be joining the landless farmers and others then emigrating in a flood to the United States. To join this flow would be a disgrace to his class and family.

Nansen reassured him:

> Mrs Holdt said that *I was not allowed to leave* ... and so I had to submit. As you know, my stiff-necked self finds it all too easy to submit.

Clearly he felt unready to move out into the wider world just yet.

Meanwhile, another winter was closing in, and once more, oppressed by rain beating on the windows, Nansen pined for the Christiania snows. He was also pining for a dark-eyed Christiania beauty called Emmy Caspersen. Her father disapproved and it was hard to get messages through to her except with the help of his half-sister Ida. At the end of January, he decided to solve all by returning home to run in the Huseby ski races. Once more, he decided to ski across. Dr Danielssen granted him leave. Early on Monday morning, 28 January 1884, skis over his shoulder, Nansen started off through the cobbled streets of Bergen. Trotting at his heels was a little dog called Flink ('Clever'), a mongrel whom he used for hunting.

*

The year before Nansen had started off by boat. In between, a railway had been completed, so now he took the train instead. On a narrow gauge line, round cramped curves, through tunnels, along ledges blasted out of the living rock, it puffed and rattled into the hinterland. The line stopped at Voss, some 100 kilometres to the east of Bergen.

Instead of following the postal road, Nansen proposed making a beeline to the east. This meant traversing a wild mountain range, uninhabited in winter. Mist, rain and thaw pursued him all the way. Carrying his skis, and followed by the trusting Flink, he started trudging hopefully up a valley to the heights. After a few miles on unskiable ice he decided to turn and, reluctantly, take the postal road after all. That meant first making for an arm of the Sogne Fjord to catch a boat. Shortly after turning he met a man with a horse and sledge, going the same way. The man offered to carry Nansen's skis, which were made of solid ash, each one weighing more than a whole modern pair including sticks. Gratefully he accepted the offer.

Late in the evening, after something like twenty kilometres, they reached their destination for the night, a place called Vinje. Next morning, Nansen woke to frost crystals on the windowpane, fresh snow that had fallen in the night – and no sign of his friend the sledge-driver. He had left half an hour earlier, taking the skis with him. Nansen hastened off in pursuit. He made short work of the chase. Glimpsing his quarry in the weak winter sun at a bend in the road, he sprinted down a slope and finally caught up.

I was inexpressibly glad to be on skis again [he recorded]. How I gathered speed; the sledge … was soon out of sight. What sense of elation I felt within me each time I swooped down a slope at breakneck speed.

Then he observed

the possibility of a good jump over the road. A desire to try my old skill awakened instantly; once more I would feel that wonderful lifting sensation of a proper flight through the air … I fly down like a gull. One feels that there is still a little sap in one's unpractised limbs.

The result was unexpected. Like 'ants swarming out of an ant heap', as he put it, people emerged from

all the farmhouses round about … Young and old … wanted to see 'what sort of man it was, who flew up there … he must be tired of life, or was it perhaps the Evil One himself?'

And worse was to follow. By now Nansen was thirsty and skied straight down the mountainside to the nearest farmhouse in search of a glass of milk.

But if there had been haste to come out, now there was even more desire to get inside again. People were scrambling through the door, with terror in their faces.

Nansen followed them in, and after a surrealistic conversation managed to prove that he was not the devil incarnate. He obtained his milk and slaked his thirst, undeterred by doubtful hygiene. Outside once more he found that

> naturally ... my extraordinary skis had attracted ... delegates from the neighbouring farms ... And when the man himself appeared, he was naturally surveyed from top to toe.

Skiing lay fallow in Western Norway. 'Not a ski track anywhere,' Nansen observed. The inhabitants 'simply hibernate ... Teach them to ski, and they would once more be the men they used to be.' Performing one or two jumps to satisfy his audience, he put on his rucksack and, followed by a string of comments, which encompassed Flink as well, regained the road. There once more he met someone with a horse and sledge, with whom he kept company to a place called Stalheim. Here the valley plunged down in a cleft to the level of the fjord. In Nansen's own words, he 'could not see the bottom; everything dropped away ... I stared into this chasm.' Involuntarily, his thoughts turned to a passage in Ibsen's *Brand* about the Ice Church, where

> '... A gust of wind
> has sometimes made the ice-fall crack;
> A cry, a rifle-shot as well – '

It was the climax of the route, and a terrifying scene at that:

> Nothing could possibly be worse than what I saw, and I could not wrench my eyes away. Undeniably, it is the wild and torn side of Nature that exerts the greatest power over the senses; irrespective of whether that power is good or evil.
>   Suddenly I stopped; the road dropped away at my feet. [I] looked straight into the abyss.

The man with the sledge offered to carry Nansen's skis down the road. 'Something snapped in me,' as he put it. It was like a cold douche:

> I had forgotten human beings, but one is not allowed to do that for long ... And saying 'No thanks, I'll look after them myself,' to the man's horror I started off downhill.

The snow was good. With 'lightning speed', as he said, Nansen

> raced down into the gorge, sometimes at the edge of one chasm; sometimes

31

of the other. The bends are many and sharp; I braked a little before each, kept well into the turn, and then was able to come out into the straight with even greater speed. It was no use trying to stick-ride here; I had to depend on my legs alone.

Even with modern equipment, it would have been a test of skill. Nansen's skis had no steel edges, they could not bite into the snow. He had to rely on sheer strength. Neither boots nor bindings gave precise control over the ski.

Half way down, the image of a farmer's face, distorted by dismay, flashed past. In sheer terror, he was pressed up against the mountain wall. Before I had time for second thoughts I was at the bottom of the valley. Up in the bends of the road the dog was tumbling down like a brown skein of wool.

Now it was a gentle descent all the way to Gudvangen, the village on the Sogne Fjord where Nansen was to catch the boat. He had no desire to linger on the way. The road, following a river, ran at the bottom of an eerie gorge called Nærødalen. At Gudvangen, where the fjord lies in a prolongation of the gorge, Nansen saw the débris of an avalanche which had fallen just before he arrived.

Waiting for the boat, he was regaled by local inhabitants with tales of disaster. One concerned the selfsame vessel, which

escaped an avalanche by the skin of its teeth ... full speed ahead was ordered [and] only the after part [was caught]. If the steamship had been a few lengths astern, it would [have been] buried, never to rise to the surface again.

After an overnight voyage Nansen landed at Lærdal, his starting point of the year before. But compared with the downhill run from Stalheim, and the ski jumping of the previous day, what followed was now prosaic. Nansen started up the postal road over the Filefjell pass, at first bare of snow. Once more he had to put his heavy skis over his shoulder, and trudge interminably along a twisting valley. Above him glittered snow, plentiful and promising.

Eventually he was able to put on his skis again and once more swing rhythmically along the contours of the landscape, hauling himself hand over hand with his single stick like someone propelling a punt. By now it was Wednesday. The race was on the following Monday, and there were still over 200 kilometres to go. When darkness fell, Nansen had only reached Breistølen, the first post house up the pass. There he had to sleep.

Next morning, when Nansen left, in his own words, 'the sun had begun to rise, and spread its shining glow on the sea of mist below, and on the mountain summits that broke the surface like red and white tents'. The temptation was too great; he left the road and struck out into the terrain in search of

> those wonderful, long, steep mountainsides, where the snow lies soft as eiderdown, where one can ski as fast as one desires ... From the tips of the skis ... the snow sprays knee-high, to swirl up in white clouds behind; but ahead all is clear. You cleave the snow like an arrow ... you just have to tense your muscles, keep your body under control, and let yourself wing downwards like an avalanche.

This is one of the earliest pæans of praise to skiing in powder snow. But of course there was a price to pay. It was late in the day when Nansen reached the next post house, Bjøberg, scarcely twenty kilometres up the road. There he found two exuberant hunters who had been out shooting ptarmigan and who invited him to dinner. Nansen compared them with people whom

> one could meet for years and never get to know; they are wrapped in a thick cocoon of stiffness and formality, strangers to each other away in the teeming towns, those greenhouses of everything unnatural and unhealthy. No; it is here in the mountains that people become themselves. One becomes a child of nature once more; all the corruptive frills of society, etiquette and fashion are stripped away. One has to have a very tough hide to drag all that up here.

Thus he enunciated the romantic philosophy of the emergent mountain skier.

It was dark, and late in the evening, when he reached the next post house, Tuft in Hemsedal. Still he insisted on going on. After some acrimony he managed to obtain a horse and sledge, and reached the next stage, Kleven, around midnight.

Next morning at nine o'clock, he was on his skis again, Flink trotting as usual imperturbably behind. They stuck to the road but by now it was Friday, and after another 40 kilometres Nansen once more had to put up for the night. The following day, with the help of a horse and sledge over the last ten kilometres, he reached the railhead, caught the train at three o'clock in the afternoon, and arrived at his father's flat in Christiania the same evening.

Nansen had been travelling hard for six days, and had covered at least 300 kilometres. He was reasonably content, for he had 'the whole of Sunday to rest and practise a little'. But where was the snow? He had come all the way in search of winter, to be greeted by a thaw that, over the past decade, had been growing all too familiar.

On the Monday morning, when he arrived at the jumping hill, the thermometer showed 6°C above zero. He also found there a large block of fat cheese provided by the organisers as a communal ski wax. Some competitors are said to have preferred to eat their ration. Be that as it may, this was the first time that waxing was officially accepted in a competition as a means of overcoming the natural limitations of snow.

This year, the cross-country event had been dropped, and only the jumping took place. Nansen started No. 9. In the words of one reporter, he 'had the same elegant style as before, although he was noticeably off colour'. Given his experiences, this was hardly surprising. Moreover, he had not raced since 1881, and for almost a year he had not skied at all. Nonetheless, he came ninth overall, out of 53 entered, only two down from his previous appearance.

After the serious jumping, there was, as one newspaper put it, 'a bit of fun'. Some competitors

> went over in pairs. Some actually managed to hold each other's hands in the air, and land on their feet. That showed control of their skis. One man tried to jump on one ski – but did not succeed ... The mass of spectators returned to town in a huge black stream. I believe most of them took pleasant memories home.

But the newspaper ended with a stern admonition:

> Why all these barbaric outfits? One does not need to be dandified, but one can dress in a reasonably tasteful and practical way, instead of partly disrobing, when one does not have a respectable woollen shirt underneath.

The response of the competitors to this rebuke is not recorded.

6

A Foolhardy Trip

Nansen stayed on ten days after the races, mainly to see Emmy. He started back on 13 February, still supposedly mid-winter. The thaw, however, had wrought havoc with the seasons. The trees were dark and bare; the rooftops of the scattered farms had lost their white canopies of snow. The air was gloomy with mist and hint of rain. It was in these conditions that he embarked on a pioneering ski tour, by timorous friends considered foolhardy, and later described by him in vigorous and dramatic detail in a series of articles in a Christiania newspaper.

On Thursday 14 February, having travelled variously by train, horse and sleigh and on skis, Nansen reached Gol, at the bottom of the pass through Hemsedal, whence he had come on the outward journey. He could have returned the same way, but although Hemsedal was undoubtedly the safest route, there was also 'something undeniably tame' about it. The weather too 'was now enticing; there was certainly good snow up in the mountains'. He therefore chose another crossing, more direct and much wilder.

This meant following the road along Hallingdal, the long valley cleaving the massif to the west. Already it was being considered as the path of the future railway, but at present all that Nansen had at his disposal was a Norwegian road typical of the time. It was rough, unsurfaced, uncambered, and switchbacked violently.

Normally, winter meant improvement with a neat layer of compressed snow. Now, the long thaw had turned that into a greenish ribbon of grainy ice. Nansen tried to ski but ended up carrying his skis for almost twenty kilometres to the next posting station, at the village of Ål. There, he hired a horse and sleigh and, after going some distance and changing horses once, struck off north-west up the start of the mountain pass.

'If the road had been bad before,' said Nansen, 'it hardly improved now.'

In many parts, it ran through narrow gorges, with a rock face on one side, and a precipice on the other, while below a river frothed and roared its way down. The road became more domed and slippery than ever; I almost had to carry the sledge more than it carried me ... I had to depend on the horse. With his spiked shoes, he found a foothold on the ice – as long as it held.

35

At one point,

> the sledge started sliding into the abyss. It was halted momentarily by a
> stone, but the post-boy behind was on his way down into the waterfall.

The post boy was a feature of Norwegian travel at the time. He was there
to take the sledge – or, in summer, a two-wheeled cariole – back to the
previous stage.

> With one hand [said Nansen], I grabbed the boy by the collar, and with the
> other, I held the sledge, and got both on an even keel again. One had to be
> constantly on one's guard.

Late at night, in the dark, Nansen, Flink, and the post boy reached an
isolated mountain farm, and the end of the post road. After a few hours'
sleep, they were woken at half past two in the morning, and breakfasted
on a special kind of porridge made with cream. Nansen was touched to
consider that the womenfolk, now bustling about, must have stayed up all
night to prepare that particular dish for him. His thanks were brushed
aside, with the explanation that this was the right food for mountain
travel: it nourished without causing thirst.

Nansen set off under clear skies, in moonlight. After a long climb, he
found a downhill run, but:

> The route ahead was obscured by shadows; thick birch scrub lay on each side.
> It was difficult to see – I knocked up against something, and I lay on my nose
> on the grainy crust. It was not the only occasion on which I made the
> acquaintance of the hardness of the snow.

At daybreak, Nansen arrived at Myrstølen, another lonely mountain
farm, on the shore of a frozen lake. There, he found only the womenfolk at
home. The man of the house was away somewhere tending a reindeer
herd. Nansen had hoped, or rather been half persuaded along the way, to
take him as a guide over the mountain crossing proper. He decided not to
lose time but go on alone, with his dog. So appalled were the women when
he told them what route he had in mind that at first they refused to provide
him with food for his journey. Eventually, after approaching 'a bright
young girl', he got what he desired – a piece of cheese and some pieces of
home-made crispbread, along with a box of matches – and continued on
his way. Now he was truly on his own, except for Flink. The terrain ahead
was wild and uninhabited. When he left Myrstølen, he had vanished from
the sight of man as effectively as if he had been swallowed by the
unexplored polar regions.

After another climb, Nansen found another downhill run. But now he
was in open terrain, above the treeline and in full daylight. In his own
words, he

swooshed for miles down long slopes. The skiing was as good as it is possible to be. Storms had raged for weeks, and compacted the snow; the thaw generated a thin crust on top, and over that a thin layer of loose snow had fallen. That produced the finest conditions a skier can imagine. My skis just about left tracks in the snow, and on the flat, they almost moved of their own accord, with a light wind behind.

Nansen was passing over the watershed, headed for a ridge called Vosseskavlen, but in his orgy of sensual enjoyment he had all but forgotten about time and place. The only signs of life were animal tracks in the snow, including those of at least three wolves. That intrigued Nansen for, hounded by the reindeer owners, the wolf was supposed to be extinct in that region.

Nansen forgot the landscape, followed the spoors, and found himself in a narrow valley dropping sharply down in a succession of steps, with a river, defying winter, in full spate. At one point, he had to take off his skis and descend a precipice, driving his stick into a precarious smooth, hard snow cladding to obtain some kind of hold, and then negotiate an overhanging cornice.

Nansen had neither map nor compass. He depended on the recollection of a mountain walk the previous summer. Nothing seemed familiar, but still he persisted in climbing upwards. Eventually he got his bearings: he had blundered into the Flaam valley which ran down to the Sogne Fjord, and an easy way home.

That, however, was not the way he had decided to go. He was determined to go via Vosseskavlen.

Therefore, I simply had to turn back … The worst thing was I had once more to pass the gorges I had just negotiated, glad to have got through safe and sound. Anyway, where I had gone once, I could return.

Night had long since fallen. After some awkward moments carrying Flink across a sheer drop, Nansen reached the head of the valley again. But still he could not get his bearings. In the starlight, he could just make out the hands of his watch, and saw it was half past nine. He had been on the way continually for eighteen hours. He had neither tent nor sleeping bag, and rest was now imperative. He found shelter between a boulder and a snow hummock carved by the wind. There, he lay down having put on a woollen sweater, his only extra clothing. In his own words,

With my rucksack as a pillow, and the dog rolled up in a ball next to me with his head under my arm, we both placidly fell asleep.

Nansen woke after a few hours to find the moon had risen. By his own account, only his legs were cold. He stood up and looked around, but the dog clearly had not the slightest wish to rise so early. He gave his master a long, quizzical look, curled up again, and went on sleeping.

It was, after all, only 3 a.m. Nonetheless it was time to go. Nansen put on his skis and, followed somewhat reluctantly by Flink, continued on his way. Surrounded by indistinguishable shadowy silhouettes towering on all sides, he was still lost. He climbed a convenient ridge to see where he was, but found the moonlight confusing, so he dug himself down into the snow again, and slept until first light. When he woke, he finally got his bearings. But, as he put it, 'the view was too grand to rush off.' He settled down to wait for sunrise, and eat what food he had.

> At last the sun appeared, a clear ray of light rolled through space, played over the mountain range, and touched the summits. Then a veritable sea of sunrays broke through, and enveloped everything in its glow of colour, the peaks reddened, cornices sparkled with colour and blinked, the valleys rested in their cold shadows. Truly this is a breathtaking sight; one seems to lose one's identity, and melt into the surroundings, to sense other Powers, to be lifted towards unknown worlds, as it were to have a glimpse of eternity. And if one has ever felt a moment such as this, one never forgets it. One is as if bewitched ... the spirit of the mountains has put its stamp on one's mind, and afterwards one often longs to go back again.

Eventually, Nansen tore himself away, skied down from the ridge, along a valley and, at long last, started climbing Vosseskavlen. That involved, once more, taking skis off and carrying them over steep snow cornices.

> The dog, poor devil, had a bad time. As long as it was merely steep, he was infinitely superior to me with his four legs. But on an overhang, where his claws could not get purchase, he stood confused, and began to shiver and whine. But he generally found a place where he could get up. Often, I had to admire his courage; how on the edge of an abyss, he would make daring jumps up the mountain wall. One false step, and we would never have seen each other again.

Meanwhile, for more than twenty-four hours, Nansen had not had a proper meal. He was gripped by a raging thirst, as if in the Sahara. He ate his last orange; now frozen as hard as a coconut. He even ate the skins, mixed with snow, to try to slake his parched throat.

At last Nansen and his dog reached the top and, in a sense, the purpose of the whole journey. Beneath them, there opened a long, steep slope, down which nobody, at least in recent times, was known with certainty to have skied before. It had a vertical drop of nearly a thousand feet; the wind had packed the snow to a hard, crystalline crust. It would hardly require circumspection on modern skis with steel edges. Nansen had no such luxury. By now, his skis were rounded at the edge, they could not grip the snow and, in his own words, 'it will be hard to steer'.

> But never mind: I threw myself over the edge, and down I went like an arrow, faster and faster, the air rushed by louder and louder; sometimes I sailed through the air; sometimes over the tops of frozen waves, sometimes back on the ground. In the end, I hardly felt the difference ... It was like aerial gymnastics *à la Daedalus* ...
>
> I tried to reduce speed with some turns; but nothing helped. The snow was too hard, and the skis simply slipped sideways. There was nothing for it but to go straight down. Before I knew exactly what had happened, I was at the bottom, on the far side of a small frozen lake. I stood still; I trembled in every limb after the run. I looked up, and far away, near the top, a dark point was working its way down. It was the dog ... it reached me, and great was his joy at our reunion.

Now the going became worse. Nansen

> began to notice the warming effect of the nearby ocean for, over the snow, there now appeared patches of thin, smooth, glass-like ice, fatal for skis and hands if one came too close, but I flew down the narrow gulley.

At the edge of an overhanging cornice, he managed to stop, just in time, turn the obstacle, and clamber down to a skiable slope again. By now, he was within sight of the first habitation since Myrstølen, two days before. A long, reasonable slope was all that remained. Nansen set off straight down the fall line:

> At full speed, I swooped down, sometimes over wind crust, sometimes in loose snow. But then I came to a long patch of ice; the skis slid sideways, I lost control, fell head over heels, and slithered down. I broke through the crust, and the ice gripped my wrist. I wrenched it free, and luckily escaped with nothing worse than a few grazes. The blood trickled red and beautifully on the snow.

*

All this, and more, Baldur was able to read in a series of newspaper articles written by his son once he was safely back in Bergen. 'I am distressed to see the danger you have courted because of sheer obstinacy, and an insistence on carrying out the journey in the way you had decided,' Baldur wrote to him at the end of April.

Nansen protested that he was the best judge of danger. But he had taken unjustifiable risks – notably starting off without enough food or extra clothing. As for the newspaper articles, on which Baldur was pleased to receive congratulations, they were dismissed by his son as having been 'far from as thoroughly prepared as they might have been'. In fact, however, they played a leading rôle in the history of skiing. They stimulated the popularisation of mountain touring. It was not so much that Nansen had blazed a trail. Farmers and hunters must certainly have made unrecorded winter crossings down the centuries, and the articles themselves had had one or two precedents. But Nansen was the first of the skiing pioneers with the power and the literary craft to inspire. He had appeared at the right time. He had caught the spirit of the age. He had proved, what till then was still not certain, that skis could be used in most kinds of snow and terrain.

Soon he was writing to Captain Mourier in Copenhagen:

> I have been constantly hatching a plan ... to cross the interior of Greenland with skiers. Given ... what I might be permitted to call my not insignificant knowledge of skis as a means of transport when attached to the legs of good skiers, I cannot get it out of my head that this must be one of the more easily accomplished of the many interesting challenges offered by polar exploration at the present time.

In one way this was factitious, but there was a mystique about Greenland, if only because of the forbidding enigma of the ice cap covering the interior, the largest of its kind by far in the Northern Hemisphere – about 1,700,000 square kilometres, as we know today, 2,000 metres thick on average. There was also a sense of urgency. Already, twelve years earlier, the Yellowstone National Park had been founded in Wyoming, the first of its kind anywhere. Even before the surface of the planet was completely known, there was a feeling that something in a state of nature had to be preserved while there was still time. In a world being so rapidly opened up, the crossing of Greenland, together with the attainment of the Poles, had become one of the last great symbolical geographical prizes.

7

A Question of Nerves

The threshold of 1885 was even unhappier for Nansen than an ordinary New Year, that gloomy festival of retrospection and regret. His dog Flink, his companion on the ski track and many a hunt, had bitten people and had to be put down. Nordenskiöld's penetration of the Greenland Ice Cap was plaguing him with restlessness and – another added goad – in July the American explorer, Adolphus W. Greely, had returned from Lady Franklin Bay on Ellesmere Island in the Canadian Arctic after an admittedly lurid bungle of an expedition but with a new Furthest North of 83° 23.8′. 'If one looks back and surveys what one has done,' Nansen wrote to Emmy at the end of 1884, 'it is anything but a satisfactory sight.'

By then, their love affair had also reached its height. During the summer, he was in Christiania to do his military service and, going back to Bergen by walking across Jotunheimen, had found Emmy at a health resort in the foothills, without her father, keeping her mother company.

In the narrow circles of Norwegian society, news travelled fast. Nansen's father soon wrote to say that he had heard 'many people remark on the conspicuous interest Miss Caspersen was showing in you'. Baldur found her 'loud and unwomanly'. She cheerfully admitted to being 'a madcap ... never mind dignity, you must be allowed to be natural'. She was, in fact, like many other young women, infected by the spirit of Ibsen's *A Doll's House*, which had first been performed four years earlier, with devastating effect. Nora, the drama's disturbing heroine, personified sexual liberation and revolt. They were a message for the times, to the distaste of such as Baldur.

Nansen and Emmy had a glorious five days together, after which he wrote her a letter twenty pages long. It started off ostensibly as an account of his journey back to Bergen. In fact it belonged to a characteristic Norwegian half-world, between imagination and reality.

Most of it was devoted to what Nansen declared to be an anonymous essay he had just discovered, which exactly reflected his feelings, and which, for Emmy's benefit, he copied *in extenso*. It was, he said, called *Twilight and Mountain Solitude*. 'There is no life here,' began an all too typical passage,

and yet, on a stone there in the scree underneath the glacier there is something; yes, it is a lonely wanderer, resting here in the heart of the wilds after the efforts of the day ... his eyes rest deamily on the mountain tops and the glowing land of colour in the west ...

Then:

> A smile played over the lips, and a warmer look appeared in the eye of ... the lonely wanderer, and ... revealed clearly what was happening inside him ... Yes, it was ... the ... most wonderful mystery that has borne history onwards ... It was humanity's richest blessing – love – which ... so few know completely, and none in the same way.

And so on and so forth. Of the whole epistle, Nansen kept a carbon copy.

Emmy soon replied; to break off what had become a tacit engagement. Admittedly, her father remained opposed to the match but the decision, all the same, was probably Emmy's own. After an interval, Nansen replied:

> You ask me, dear Emmy, not to be sad about what has happened ... You can console yourself with the thought that, on the contrary, I am glad; because I had begun to doubt myself, whether my love for you ... was not partly self delusion.

Therefore, he went on,

> I am glad that things have turned out as they have. We pledge our genuine friendship to each other, we will take pleasure in each other's future happiness.

In March 1885, Nansen resigned from the museum. In his own words, he had had to 'stumble forwards, alone, and entirely by my own efforts'. He felt a craving for wider horizons, and wanted now to study abroad.

As usual, Baldur was distressed by the prospect of his son travelling far away and out of reach. He put his objections in financial terms. 'When I last made up my accounts, I had spent [far] more than my income,' he wrote. 'Where is the money to come from?'

'It had never occurred to me to be a burden to you, to whom I owe everything so far,' Nansen protested. 'Quite frankly, I imagined that you thought better of me ... I have ... all too many faults ... but if you could turn me inside out, I do not think you would find ingratitude amongst them.'

Dr Danielssen declined to accept Nansen's resignation. Cheerful and understanding as ever, he suggested a year's leave instead, with the salary available for travel. Nansen commented in a letter to his father: 'I had expected friendliness, but not consideration to this degree.' Baldur probably never read this. He died on 2 April, three days after it was written. For Nansen, distance and the presence of the Holdts softened the blow. He threw himself into his work, and finished his first scientific paper – rewarded by the museum, incidentally, with a gold medal.

The paper presented his research on an obscure marine creature called a myzostome, concentrating on its nervous system. The myzostome is a small parasite, about the size of a flea, found in starfish. A primitive creature, it was the simplest to hand with a nervous system, and hence an appropriate point at which to begin the study of the nerves. What clinched the matter for Nansen was that, at the museum, a supply of preserved specimens was available.

Nansen was struck by the fact that some of his work on the myzostomes agreed with that being done elsewhere on the central nervous system of man. So, before going abroad, he decided to pursue this lead in 'animals lying between these widely separated forms', as he drily put it. He settled on the ascidians, pulpy marine creatures, primitive forerunners of the vertebrates. He also chose *Myxine glutinosa*, the hag fish, a very primitive kind of fish.

Nansen now wanted to work on fresh, as distinct from preserved, specimens. To collect material, he spent the summer of 1885 on an island in the coastal archipelago north of Bergen, dredging the surrounding waters. The museum made a grant to cover the expenses. Less happily, for part of the time, Armauer Hansen imposed his company. He had long since extended his interests from leprosy to Nansen's field of marine biology, concentrating on invertebrates. 'He feels that he will gain by working *together with someone else*,' Nansen had written to his father, 'but I do not feel that I will gain by collaborating with him.' For one thing, Nansen had no desire for an elder on his back. For another, Armauer Hansen had a peculiar and irritating personality. It was a strange blend of brusqueness and naïveté, combined with an unimaginative devotion to observable facts alone. For all that, Nansen knew that he meant well and did not want to hurt his feelings. Without exactly quarrelling, he managed to keep his distance.

The ships steaming past along the coast brought two celebrated visitors among the crowd of tourists to Bergen that summer. One was Ibsen, on a rare visit home; another Gladstone, lately out of office, in *Sunbeam*, Lord Brassey's yacht, come to study the Swedish-Norwegian Union which he egregiously insisted on believing to be untroubled and a model for his scheme of Home Rule for Ireland.

On the island itself, as Nansen wrote to his half-sister, Ida, he found among the summer visitors 'two fine (indeed some say very fine) young ladies', both Norwegian, and both 'attractive and easygoing ... which could have made the whole thing perilous: I mean two months ... under the same roof.' There was also a Russian woman 'who was not less pleasant'.

In spite – or because – of this distraction, Nansen returned to Bergen with a good haul of specimens. When he got them under the microscope, he found himself preoccupied with the question of how the nerves communicated with each other. Although it was still below the horizon, he recognised this to be the central issue of the whole nervous mechanism, including that of mankind.

Nerve fibres were supposedly fused to form a continuous network, like electrical conductors. This network or, as it is usually called, the reticular theory, then held almost undisputed sway. Nansen, seeing only free nerve endings where others saw coalescing junctions, took leave to doubt.

Armauer Hansen probably pointed him in that direction. Some time before Nansen joined the Bergen Museum, Armauer Hansen had published some research he had carried out in Paris under Professor Louis Antoine Ranvier, a specialist in the nervous system, and one of the founders of neurology. Ranvier was then interested in the way motor nerves were connected to muscles. When Armauer Hansen, already famous for his work on leprosy, turned up on a visit, Ranvier invited him, with his added experience of invertebrate zoology, into his own laboratory to investigate the motor nerves of the leech. Armauer Hansen demonstrated that these nerves 'divide ... without anastomising [fusing into] the muscles', as he put it. 'They terminate ... in a triangular thickening.' This was in fact one of the earliest recorded observations of discontinuity in the peripheral nervous system.

Armauer Hansen did not see the implications of what he had observed. As far as Nansen knew, he himself was alone among his contemporaries in applying that same view of discontinuity to the central nervous system and the connection between nerve and nerve. He was, however, labouring under mounting frustration. For one thing, he was working at the limits of even his then advanced microscope. For another, the modern technique of cutting thin sections, the very basis of advanced microscopy, was quite new. Nansen had to teach himself. He was among the first to apply it to the invertebrate nervous system.

In studying nervous tissue, however, the great difficulty lay in staining sections, to bring out the details by the use of colour, and thus make the structure visible in the microscope. The best available method was one developed by an Italian, Camillo Golgi, using silver nitrate. Nansen could not make it work properly, which meant that his observations were bedevilled by uncertainty. The obvious solution was to learn from Golgi in person. So Nansen added to his maturing travel plans a visit to Golgi in his laboratory at Pavia.

Such a change was sorely needed, for in the autumn of 1885, as the dark season approached, and with no skiing again in prospect, Nansen fell into another fit of gloom. He sought relief in yet another of his periodical outbursts – to his half-sister Ida on this occasion. 'I know you find me strange,' Nansen wrote.

I am always brooding, except about those things that can keep my emotions

44

balanced. I know I have always been a demanding creature, that has not understood the art of being content with what one has ... or what one can obtain; for whom the ordinary was too little and who, when the extraordinary was unattainable, simply lost interest. That is precisely the fatal flaw ... the key to your spiritual life, my great Herr Fridtjof. But once it has emerged, no earthly power can eradicate it; it stays where it is, and can be the cause of a whole lifetime's discontent, a life of scattered powers, scattered possibilities, scattered longings, and without unity.

On 17 February 1886, Nansen finally sailed off. At the age of twenty-four, he was emerging at last onto continental Europe for the first time in his life.

8

Innocents Abroad

Nansen's journey began with Germany – now, under Bismarck, bursting with vitality and pre-eminent in scholarship and the sciences. For three weeks, he hurried across the country, visiting the leading biologists of the day. They included Professor Ernst Haeckel in Jena. The leading German apostle of Darwin, Haeckel, besides his scientific achievements, was a pioneer of social Darwinism. He believed strongly that the survival of the fittest applied especially to human beings. He exercised a formative influence on Nansen.

In the middle of March, Nansen crossed the Alps into Italy, via Switzerland, on a train steaming through the St Gotthard tunnel. It had been opened for barely four years and was one of the wonders of the age.

In Italy, he went straight to Pavia and presented himself to Camillo Golgi, unannounced. Bearded, solid, dignified, Professor Golgi was amused by this youthful looking stranger who had dropped in, without credentials, but radiating an extraordinary personality. In contrast to many university professors, Golgi actually liked students. He allowed Nansen into his laboratory, to learn his method of staining nerve tissue.

In a few days, Nansen had learned Golgi's method of staining – the 'reazione nera' and, in his own words, 'never in my life had I imagined it was possible to prepare such elegant and distinct nerve sections'.

After a week or so, he was on his way to Naples, where he proposed to work at a unique marine biological station. Independent and academically unfettered, its purpose was to attract scientists from all over the world and let them pursue their own work in their own way. It was the forerunner of international research institutions as we know them now and was the brain-child of Anton Dohrn, a German professor of zoology from Jena.

By his own admission, the rigours of research itself did not appeal to Dohrn. His 'inner need', as he put it, was to 'be of service to others'. He was a fervent early Darwinist, and he wanted to change zoology, prophetically, from a sterile exercise in classification to a living science set within its proper environment. With these aims, Dohrn opened the Naples station in 1873, paying for it out of his own pocket, and with loans from friends.

Nansen had been attracted by the promise of a proper scientific milieu. Not only were there laboratories and an aquarium, but steam launches, with crews to dredge for specimens on demand. There was even diving equipment, which had enabled a German lithographer called Werner to make what were probably the very first illustrations of marine organisms, from life, on the sea bottom.

Unannounced here too, Nansen was rather less cordially received than in Pavia. 'It took some time before the great man, Prof. Dohrn, deigned to make a decision,' he crossly wrote. By now, Dohrn had secured international support. Various countries paid for their scientists to work at the station, but Sweden-Norway was not among them and Nansen, as Dorhn put it, was 'only a hopeful young man'. But he did finally admit him.

Dohrn had chosen Naples for his station because of protected waters, abundant marine life – and persuasible city fathers who gave him land on which to build. But he also had an eye to the setting – a park on the waterfront with a view of the bay. 'If only I could send it to you as it lies before me now, as I look out of the window,' Nansen wrote, touchingly, to Dr Danielssen, 'with Castellamare, Sorrento and Capri in the distance, all dreaming in the misty morning light; ah then I could repay all your warmheartedness.' This was the milieu, incidentally, in which Ibsen had written both *Peer Gynt* and *A Doll's House*.

Nansen proceeded now to apply on his own what he had learned at Pavia of Golgi's staining method. It was distinguished by picking out nerve cells selectively, but completely, to their finest ramifications. On a translucent yellow background there appeared an intricate tracery of black filaments. This was the vivid spectacle that burst upon Nansen in his microscope, to match the view from the laboratory window. Nerve cells were frozen in mysterious forms; some, like cyclopean creatures from another world, staring enigmatically from a single eye; others bursting with elaborate eruptions of branches as if they were trees in a lush and fertile forest.

Nansen was working with ascidians, and a primitive fish-like animal called the lancelet (*Amphioxus*). This was a piece of pioneering. Golgi was a doctor, working on mammals and, especially, Man. Nansen was probably making the first attempts to use Golgi's technique on the lower vertebrates. Almost certainly he became the first to apply it to invertebrates.

Nansen was now among others like himself, devoted to the central nervous system. He was stimulated by the select company of first-class minds. He stood out by an impression of overflowing vitality that no laboratory could contain. But he had been driven to Naples not only by a thirst for knowledge but also by the historic Scandinavian longing for the south. He sought in the sun, in the sensuous colours of the Mediterranean littoral and the spirit of the Latin world a cure for a mysterious sickness of the soul. 'Look and learn from the children of the South' was his somewhat naïvely expressed feeling.

Do you think they are better inside themselves than us? Oh no; the difference is simply that they are ... carefree and natural without the dull toil of the North, with its reminders of times past and worries for the morrow.

Nansen lived up to this precept. Away from the laboratory, he was to be found in a convivial coterie of neuroscientists, mainly German, Swiss and Hungarian, who frequented the cafés of the region. German was their common language, and Nansen spoke it tolerably. Adolf Ónodi, one of the Hungarians, said that he was 'largely responsible for our happy mood'.

But his own moods remained complex. Ónodi, who particularly attached himself to Nansen, was struck by his arbitrary and sudden descents into fits of brooding. One evening, on an excursion to Vesuvius, Nansen abruptly broke off from the hilarity, and disappeared. He was found sitting alone on a block of lava in the moonlight, gazing over the ruins of St Sebastian, a village destroyed by an eruption twelve years before. He did not answer when spoken to and seemed almost in a trance. Only with great difficulty was he roused and persuaded to start walking back to Naples. In Ónodi's own words, Nansen

> moved slowly, with heavy steps. I took his arm, and the whole way I tried to get something out of him, but he remained absolutely silent, and said not a word until we parted.

Next day, or soon after, Nansen returned to his irrepressible wildness; dancing a tarentella here, running alongside a horse and carriage there, pretending to be a ghost in the Blue Grotto on Capri. Tall, blond and unmistakable, self-consciously playing the Dionysus with vine leaves in his hair, as if he were acting out a part in one of the frescoes of Pompeii, he acquired a certain notoriety. The Neapolitans had his measure; to his amused satisfaction, he was nicknamed *il gran' giovane*, 'the overgrown boy'. From another point of view, an artist once said that Nansen was difficult to draw, because 'his face was always changing'.

Early in May Nansen was visited by Johanne Sylow, a Christiania schoolteacher who had known him when he was a child. In her forties, and unmarried, Miss Sylow was making the then customary tour of Italy. She found Nansen somewhat mixed-up. She lectured him on his behaviour and, on leaving for Rome late in May, half-seriously demanded from him a written self-analysis. Somewhat to her surprise, she actually received one. Dance music, he declared, in exculpation of his wilder flights,

> has a special influence on me ... I don't know what it is, ... the body is swept away without conscious effort by the rhythm of the music.

But: 'The more my thoughts concentrate on this vital subject, my own dear self, the more that same self becomes an enigma.'

> Much of it is mood; much sentimentality coupled with the coldest realism ... desire for knowledge coupled with contempt for civilisation and thirst for the primitive and nature in the raw; in a word, it is ... a chaos of discord.

It was, he went on, 'just these crying inconsistencies [coupled with] undiluted egoism, that drives one forwards; it is the spring driving the whole mechanism.'

'There is one characteristic you have omitted from your self-portrait,' Miss Sylow hastened to reply. 'It is great kindness and consideration for elder ladies; even for old maids, and that is the height of consideration.'

Nansen's outpouring was an extension of what he had written to his half-sister Ida, at the end of the previous year. In both, he showed a characteristic gusto for turning himself inside out; at least before women. In a cryptic passage to Miss Sylow he said that in Naples she was an 'as yet not unthroned, fugitive Madonna'. If he gave the impression – sometimes – of a would be Don Juan, he also seemed still to be a little boy searching for a mother. Perhaps the difference, after all, is not that great.

In any case, Miss Sylow told Nansen that in Rome she had heard rumours of how he 'had moved heaven and earth to arrange a dance, where he had made tempestuous advances to a young Englishwoman'.

It was substantially true. Marion Sharp was the 'young Englishwoman's' name – although in fact she was an Edinburgh Scot. Nansen had had other contacts with late Victorian middle-class ladies from the British Isles; notably a mysterious encounter in Venice on the way from Pavia. He spoke English well enough to talk convincingly about himself. Marion called him variously her 'Viking' and 'fair haired barbarian'.

Marion was on a continental tour with her mother. They were living in Hong Kong, where her father was a teacher. As a duenna, the mother left something to be desired. Her daughter could slip away to explore the Bay of Naples alone with Nansen. For the first time since the affair with Emmy Caspersen, he found himself in love again. When Marion and her mother left Naples, in the middle of June, Nansen cut short his work at the zoological station and went with them.

By way of Rome, they reached Florence. Nansen, having already seen both on his way to Naples, now earnestly played the cicerone. He found it hard going. Though physically attractive Marion was, as she cheerfully admitted in retrospect, 'impatient and frivolous'. In Florence, she was lukewarm about the splendours of the Renaissance, which were generally the reason for a visit, but was charmed to see the house where Robert Browning and his wife, Elizabeth Barrett Browning, once lived. Like a conventional Victorian, she was devoted to Browning's poetry, but perhaps admired Elizabeth Barrett's verses just that bit more. She herself was trying hopefully to write. But, she told Nansen, with a dramatic flourish, she was not meant 'only to be a novel-writer ... I want to be *in* the battle of life, not merely a spectator.'

From Florence Nansen, Marion and her mother took the train to Brunnen in Switzerland. There, among the Alps, in the romantic surroundings of Lake Lucerne, Nansen found once more that the woman of his desires had thought better of it, and the affair ended. 'I cannot tell you

... how more than glad I was to have your assurance that you were happy & not the worse for knowing me,' she wrote to him from Brunnen, after he had left.

Her mother was less contented. 'My dear young Friend, Why don't you write,' she plaintively enquired. 'I gave you a week patiently but hopefully in which to send me a line ... and now it is four! Has the warmth of Italy become stiffened by the cold of the North?' Eventually a letter arrived and Marion's mother wrote in reply:

> If you knew how many times I have read it ... in that most perhaps earnest hour of all the twenty four, before putting out my candle, when one seeks a bright influence to color our dreams or the sense of a love to warm our heart.

Designedly or not, Nansen had added Mrs Sharp to Miss Sylow and his other elderly conquests. Perhaps he had succumbed to mother and daughter as separate manifestations of a single image.

Nansen meanwhile had returned to Norway for military service, and Marion, more crisply perceptive than her mother, wrote to him: 'What a change it will be for you to be thrown entirely with men ... a healthy change.'

Nansen undoubtedly clung to the company of women and was soon anxious for a new meeting with Miss Sylow, also back from her travels, so that 'we could once more be in Italy for a little while', and

> relive those unforgettable days that have been, and will never come back; days that have brought fresh young shoots in the soul of the *gran' giovane*, shoots which in the future, let us hope, will bear fruit.

He returned to Bergen in August, thoroughly unsettled. Nor did the arrival of a letter from Ónodi, now also back home in Budapest, resign him better to his lot. 'My dear Herr Nansen!,' Ónodi wrote, 'Most valued friend!'

> Time passes quickly, but it cannot erase those wonderful, congenial hours that we spent in Naples and the environs ... wonderful days I will never forget, we enjoyed ourselves in a way one cannot plan. Those repasts in the Syrene, the Batafina, the Toledo; Sorrento, Capri, Ischia, etc. etc!!! It was wonderful!

Nansen had been obsessed by the figures on the Medici tombs in Florence. Now, after months of rumination, he was driven to express his feelings in the kind of private essay which was becoming a habit with him. He began with his old theme of having the courage to say what one thinks. So, if one was independent enough 'not to crow in chorus' with the others gazing on the statuary, 'you would laugh at the disgusting flock of sheep and call Michelangelo Buonarroti a deluded crank'.

> Undoubtedly you have to acknowledge an overpowering technical brilliance, but you can also find that in a madman. If it is the only aim of art to seek

beauty in Nature's forms ... then, in that case, Michelangelo, the giant, topples from his pedestal.

That, said Nansen, was undoubtedly his 'first impression of this extraordinary spirit'. He was forced to consider 'the old question of what was the aim of art. Was it to imitate Nature as closely as possible, or was it to seek perfection? ... Between these two poles, art had swung like a pendulum that never comes to rest.' Michelangelo had 'not even attempted to do either'. He had 'truly blazed new trails'.

Ruthlessly, like a Titan, he had heaved the globe of the pendulum out towards a new goal ... One unmistakably notices that here all barriers are broken; ordinary standards do not hold ... This spirit has followed its own course with a rush; not like the most violent of violent Titans, but rather like an eagle with mighty beats of its wings, soaring through the Cosmos: but where was it heading, and what was the goal ... ?

9

Back to Bergen

In Bergen – to which, incidentally, he had returned by crossing the mountains once more on foot – Nansen resumed the work interrupted by his travels. In December, however, he was off again; this time to England.

Ostensibly, it was to further his research. Nansen did indeed visit zoologists at Cambridge. He also appeared at a new marine biological laboratory at St Andrews in Scotland. But the underlying reason for his journey was something else. 'He had loved,' to quote another private monologue of his, written in the autumn, after hunting, as it happened.

> Did he love now? His thoughts turned to her; could she now make life happy, or would she ... like the others, be played out after a time, and would he not be bored with her, as with anything else when it became familiar ... Did life have no deeper meaning [than] this unhappy yearning for the unattainable?

This was directed towards Marion. She it was who had really drawn him over the North Sea. She had wished to remain friends – or a little more? Clutching at straws, Nansen kept up a correspondence. Now he wanted to know whether her rejection was as final as it seemed.

They were united in Edinburgh. Marion was without her mother, who had rejoined her father in Japan, where he had now moved, and was staying with her married sister. She was now, she insisted, thoroughly independent. They went on long walks together. Endlessly, they talked. They went to the theatre. They saw *Hamlet* at the Royal Lyceum and, between the acts, Nansen revealed his intention of crossing Greenland one day.

When Nansen left Edinburgh for London on his way home it was Marion's turn to pursue him with letters, which she then immediately asked him to destroy. Nansen had found the answer he was seeking – after a fashion. He himself was reverting to form. When he returned a silver watch that Emmy Caspersen had lent him, he had had '7th August 1884', the date of their parting, engraved on the back. To Marion, he gave a brooch to mark the end of their encounter. With a confusing blend of regret interwoven with relief he returned to the motherly comfort of Maria Holdt in Bergen.

9. Back to Bergen

There, soon afterwards, on 17 January 1887, in the austere precincts of the National Theatre, another first performance of an Ibsen play took place. This time it was *Rosmersholm*. In a letter at the time Nansen complained of 'this ceaseless buzzing around one, where everything is discussed and mulled over ... everything is topsy-turvy, people even question the difference between black and white'. Once more, he was echoing the play. Like most of Ibsen's later dramas, *Rosmersholm* revolved round the confrontation of the old order with the new. 'Almost every single concept,' one of the characters is made to say, 'has been turned upside down.'

This neatly encapsulated the spirit of the age. As Nansen drove himself back to his microscope, Heinrich Hertz in Karlsruhe was producing the first radio waves. And in Prague, a physicist called Ernst Mach had just published a book rejecting as 'an idle metaphysical conception' the classical view of time as fixed and absolute. That begot Einstein's theory of relativity, and the scientific revolution which, amongst other things, unleashed the power of the atom. It was in this decade of the 1880s that the seeds of the modern world were being sown.

Nansen's Italian journey had given him new vigour. 'I have never learned so much in so short a time,' he wrote to Golgi, whose staining method had 'opened a new epoch in my scientific training'.

Nansen was also helped by another technical advance. The Zeiss apochromatic microscope had recently appeared. This was the first fully colour-corrected instrument. By eliminating chromatic aberration – the rainbow-like fuzziness at the edges – it enhanced resolution and clarity. It was the culmination of a decade of systematic development. With this design the optical microscope, an invention of the sixteenth and seventeenth centuries, had achieved its modern form.

While in Naples, Nansen had finally written up his research into the nervous system of the ascidians and the hag fish that he had finished before leaving home. It was published by the Bergen Museum, in Norwegian, during the summer of 1886, and given wider circulation by a translation in a well-known English scientific journal. 'Anastomoses or unions between the different ganglion [nerve] cells,' Nansen announced, 'I have been unable to demonstrate with certainty.'

This was a historic declaration. Unknown to Nansen at the time, a Swiss embryologist, Wilhelm His, had discovered that in human embryos during early stages of development nerve cells definitely were *not* in contact, which led His to similar views. Nor did Nansen know about the work of August Forel, a Swiss psychiatrist, who observed that degeneration in the nervous system did not spread, but was bounded by the limits of the cell, which led him also to deny continuity. These three, Forel, His and Nansen, from different points of view, had launched the first onslaught on the orthodox reticular theory. They thus became the co-founders of the modern view of the nervous system. Nansen's English translation appeared in September 1886, followed by His's paper on the subject in October, and Forel's in January 1887. Thus, by a quirk of publication, Nansen had secured technical priority.

Meanwhile Nansen had been offered another chance of going to America, this time as Associate Professor of biology at the University of Indiana in Bloomington. Once more, as at Bergen, Robert Collett was the intermediary. Nansen's formal application arrived in Bloomington too late, and the post went to someone else. But the President of the University, David Starr Jordan (later of Stanford), invited him to try again.

Nansen's own views on this episode were mixed. On the one hand, at the age of 25, it was a flattering proposal. He saw an escape from the routine work of the museum, which was becoming ever more irksome with the years. But also he feared that, tied to landscape as he was, in an alien environment he might wither on the vine. In any case, Bloomington was too far from the sea, and hence unsuited to marine biology.

He also wanted to finish his work and publish without delay. He had the warning example of Armauer Hansen to remind him that in scientific research, as in other things, priority was nine points of the game. Because Armauer Hansen had delayed publication of his final results he had had to fight for recognition as the true discoverer of the leprosy bacillus against a German doctor, Albert Neisser, who had already discovered the gonorrhoea bacillus, and who had actually visited him and seen his work. Personal ambition aside, the same force of nationalism that was giving men their creative vitality also meant using scientific advances to promote patriotic glory.

During August 1887, Nansen published a German translation of that part of his paper on the myzostomes that concerned the nervous system. It appeared in the *Jenaische Zeitschrift für Naturwissenschaft*, a well-known German scientific journal in Jena where, incidentally, his old friend Willy Kükenthal was becoming established and doubtless lent his support. Nansen took the opportunity to add a coda embodying his latest work which, as it turned out, was also ground-breaking.

The cardinal theory of the structure of the nervous system had been constructed over the decades since the middle of the century. In succession it had been shown that what conducted nervous impulses were the nerve fibres, and not the jelly-like substance in which they were packed; that the fibres and the nerve cells were part of the same unit, and that the fibres were outgrowths of the cell body. When Nansen arrived on the scene, essentially what remained was the question of how these cellular units combined to form the central nervous system. He had the good fortune to have the right ideas at the right time.

In the German version of his paper on the myzostomes – 'Anatomie und Histologie des Nervensystemes der Myzostomen' – Nansen repeated with greater vehemence his original statement that the cellular nerve units were not fused, but only touched each other. However, he went further now. To begin with, he declared that the nerve units all had membranes. That cells are enclosed by membranes is now axiomatic, but was then still a matter of debate. It did however provide a logical explanation for discontinuity in the nervous system, and in that Nansen was alone. In other words, he had declared the independence of the nervous cellular unit. This is the basis of modern neurology.

He went further still in formulating modern concepts. There was a well-known feature in microscopical observations of the nervous system then called the 'dotted substance'. It was conventionally seen as a spongy material fusing the nerve endings together. Nansen was the first correctly to interpret the phenomenon as the result of cutting sections through nerve bundles; the dots which gave the substance its name being minute stained nerve fibres sliced across. Moreover, Nansen declared that it was in this 'dotted substance' that the nerve fibres communicated with each other. And in a few prophetic words: 'This tangle of [nerve] fibres ... is the true seat of the psyche.'

Indeed, the 'dotted substance', in vertebrates later called the grey matter, in invertebrates the neuropil, was subsequently shown to be where nerves communicate – across points of contact now called the synapses – and hence where mental processes occur. Since Nansen's day, much has been discovered about the staggering complexity of the central nervous system, especially the transmission of signals. But even now, for a lapidary definition of the mechanism of nerve and brain, he could hardly be bettered.

To round off his paper, Nansen broke yet more new ground with an explanation of the reflex arc. This is the mechanism by which sensory impulses are conducted via motor nerves to become physical actions. The reigning view was that the conduction path ran through fusions of the cell bodies in the peripheral nervous system. Nansen drew other conclusions from his model of the independent cellular unit. He proposed instead that sensory nerves conducted information from the periphery, central nerve cells then relaying the impulses to motor nerves, which in turn activated the muscles. Nansen had become the first to give the correct theoretical explanation, long before the reflex arc in any species had been adequately described.

The German paper on the myzostomes was a compressed summary rushed out to bring the ideas to market and avoid being forestalled. Nansen was meanwhile writing up his research comprehensively; not in Norwegian, because of its limited currency, but in English. This was odd in a way. Mainly due to intellectual isolation, neurology was languishing in England, so that Nansen would have done better to continue publishing in German, then the scientific language par excellence. But Nansen was by now well on the way to becoming an Anglophile.

In part at least, this was thanks to the attractions of Marion, with whom, in spite of all, he was still corresponding. He wrote her long letters unburdening himself, as before. She sent him gossipy budgets, and lectured him on English literature. Above all, at a distance, she helped him to write his paper.

It was finished during the early summer of 1887, and published in December, in the original English, by the Bergen Museum under the title *The Structure and Combination of the Histological Elements of the Central Nervous System*. It was something of a *tour de force* – a revolutionary theory presented in a foreign language, with clarity and vigour. Moreover, Nansen had prepared all the illustrations himself, drawing directly from the microscope onto the stone for lithographic reproduction.

In his central thesis, he was showing greater insight than Dr Sigmund Freud, who at that point was only starting his work on psychology but – a little known fact even today – had been working in Vienna on the anatomy of the nerves and publishing papers in which, following the crowd, he subscribed to the nerve-net theory. Years later, finding that he had backed the wrong horse, Freud covered his tracks by destroying his laboratory notes and suppressing knowledge of the incriminating published papers.

Nansen, by contrast, was well ahead of his time, and stuck to his guns. 'Direct anastomosis [fusion] between the processes [nerve fibres] ... does not exist,' was his categorical summing up. Therefore: 'We are obliged to abandon the theory of the direct combination of the [nerve] cells.' This is the original definition of the modern view of the independence of the nervous cellular unit. It was also the first explicit concomitant rejection of the reigning orthodoxy.

Nansen's concept of the nervous cellular unit as independent, in his own words, gave 'a new view' of the functioning of the nerves and the brain. 'According to this view,' as he pregnantly put it, there could be 'a *localisation* in the central nerve-system but *no isolation*. This view will also I think possibly be able to explain the fact that other parts of the brain can take up the function of lost parts.' Even today, after more than a century, it could hardly be put better.

Nansen's paper was ahead of its time not only in content, but in style too. Instead of the usual academic obfuscation, it was written in simple, clear and unambiguous language. This might well have merely been a by-product of the Norwegian love of argument. At least it left no doubt as to what Nansen really meant, and thus removed one source of dispute.

His rôle was that of the often underrated historical figure; the enunciator of principles. He was one of the great simplifiers. He had done what he could to achieve priority of publication. He had secured his place among the founders of neurology.

What remained was to ensure that his research brought him full academic recognition. He decided to present *The Structure and Combination of the Histological Elements of the Central Nervous System* for a Ph.D. in Christiania. All academic dissertations, however, then had to be in Norwegian. So Nansen produced a translation into his mother tongue; not, however, all 214 pages and 113 illustrations, but a précis one tenth as long. By the autumn of 1887 the work was all finally done.

In his tussle with the nerve cells Nansen had, perforce, to keep the thought of skiing across Greenland in quiescence. He was now free, at last, to go. It was just as well. Time was running out.

Part II

Greenland

10

Plans and Preparations

In the summer of 1886, Robert Edwin Peary, an engineer in the United States Navy, had penetrated the ice cap about 100 miles in from Disko Bay. Peary intended to return the following year and make the first crossing of Greenland from coast to coast. Circumstances sent him instead to Nicaragua to survey the route for an abortive precursor of the Panama Canal. This gave Nansen an uncovenanted breathing space. He decided to make his own attempt the next year, and wrote to Marion to tell her so. She wrote back reminding him of his announcement between the acts of *Hamlet* that now seemed so long ago. 'The idea has remained in my mind ever since,' she told him. 'There is something essentially suited to your nature ... in following your own will. I hope you are also led by a wise Fate.'

Nansen had barely six months to prepare. Characteristically, he started at the top. In 1886, he had gone all the way to Golgi in Pavia as the fountainhead of laboratory technique. Now, in November 1887, having handed in his thesis, he abruptly left for Stockholm in order to consult Nordenskiöld who, after a quarter of a century exploring high latitudes, was the acknowledged master of polar travel.

The arrival of the young man in the everlasting Jaeger suit caused something of a stir. Sven Hedin, the Swede who subsequently became famous as an explorer in Central Asia, found him 'really a thoroughly unusual apparition'. The Professor of Mineralogy at the Stockholm Technical University, a Norwegian called Waldemar Brøgger, to whom Nansen, as a compatriot, first introduced himself unannounced, began by being taken somewhat aback. But soon he too had succumbed to Nansen's overwhelming personality. Nansen had approached him as a means of effecting an introduction to Nordenskiöld, who was a Professor of Mineralogy too, and therefore an academic colleague. At what was the beginning of a lifelong friendship, Brøgger hurried over to present Nansen to Nordenskiöld in his laboratory at the Academy of Sciences.

Tall and forbidding, Nordenskiöld, the illustrious conqueror of the North-East Passage, was every inch the professorial autocrat. A Finn by birth, he spoke with the characteristic harsh accent and melancholy cadence of the Swedish-speaking elite which had governed his native land since the Middle Ages, first when it was part of Sweden, and then, after the Napoleonic Wars, when the Russians had supplanted the Swedes as its overlords.

Among polar explorers, Nordenskiöld was distinguished by a technical approach. He had long since decided that skis were the best means of snow travel. The uncertainty was whether the snow on the Greenland Ice Cap was the same as that in lower latitudes and, therefore, whether skis would be equally effective there. It was partly to settle the question that Nordenskiöld's expedition to Greenland in 1883 – which so inspired Nansen – had been conceived.

Unfortunately, since skiing was much rarer among Swedes than Norwegians, neither Nordenskiöld nor his companions could ski. In so far as skiing had been preserved in Sweden, this was mainly thanks to the Lapps. They are a distinct people, with their own language, inhabiting the north of Scandinavia, arguably having migrated from Central Asia. For centuries skiing had been part of their culture. So Nordenskiöld took with him two Lapps, Pavva Lars Tuorda and Andars Rassa, from Jokkmokk, in Northern Sweden.

Nordenskiöld was living proof of the power of illusion in the process of discovery. He was driven by an urge to substantiate his belief that the interior of Greenland was ice-free and fertile. Starting at Disko Bay, he travelled about 120 kilometres over the ice cap, without a sign of bare land. On 22 July, he stopped, and sent Tuorda and Rassa on ahead alone. They returned after 57 hours. They found no oasis. What they saw was the ice cap sweeping on unbroken to the horizon. They claimed to have skied 230 kilometres each way, only resting for four hours. Tuorda, said Nordenskiöld, 'had never seen such even skiing terrain before; the skis slid with the utmost ease.'

The only doubt was whether Tuorda and Rassa, as they claimed, had really skied 460 kilometres in 57 hours. To settle the point, a ski race was organised, on 4 April 1884, betweeen Jokkmokk and Kvikkjokk in Swedish Lappland. The distance was 200 kilometres. The winner was Tuorda, in 21 hours, 22 minutes, including rests, in snow that was wet and foul. To Nansen, all this had merely confirmed what he already believed. The snow on the Greenland Ice Cap was not significantly different from that in his own familiar mountains, and skis were thus equally effective in both. What Nansen wanted to learn from Nordenskiöld was the technique of polar travel.

Once he had grasped this, Nordenskiöld very soon unbent. For one thing, Nansen was almost thirty years younger, and Nordenskiöld enjoyed playing the mentor. While Nansen was in Stockholm Nordenskiöld, it seemed, never stopped talking.

In Stockholm, Nansen also met another seminal figure in the person of Sven Lovén. An invertebrate zoologist, Lovén had first shown the existence of a nervous system in the myzostome, which had been so important to Nansen in his own research. In 1837 Lovén had briefly visited Spitsbergen, and become the precursor of scientific research as an aim of polar exploration. From him descended a whole school of Swedish polar explorers who began the Scandinavian ascendancy in high latitudes.

A gentlemanly, versatile, and genial septuagenarian, Lovén was unenthusiastic about the crossing of Greenland. He suggested that Nansen was 'too valuable [a scientist] to go on such an adventure'. Nonetheless, on returning home, Nansen sent Lovén a photograph of himself as a souvenir – his habit when meeting people for whom he formed a high regard.

To Nordenskiöld, Nansen wrote: 'I hope that the help you have given me … will bear fruit, and help me attain the goal I have set myself. Thus, Herr Baron, you will not be ashamed of your Scandinavian successors on the Greenland Ice Cap.'

For Nordenskiöld, it could scarcely have been more aptly put. Although born a Russian subject, he was a passionate Scandinavian. It pleased him greatly that, in navigating the North-East Passage, he had finally accomplished under the Swedish flag what English explorers had first attempted three centuries before.

Since the first expedition – by Danes, in 1751 – there had been eight known attempts to penetrate the Greenland Ice Cap. All, including Nordenskiöld's, had started on the west coast and headed east. The west coast of Greenland was inhabited; the east coast, except for a few little-known Eskimo settlements, was not. 'In polar expeditions, as in war,' was Nordenskiöld's decided view, 'to maintain the confidence of the men, a line of retreat is necessary. Without it, discipline is soon at an end.'

Nansen quietly but diametrically disagreed. Cutting off all lines of retreat was the philosophical kernel of his plan. As he put it, 'there would be a correspondingly greater incentive to try one's uttermost to reach the west coast' if he started from the east, which is what he had decided to do. Later, and even more dramatically, he proclaimed: 'Death or the west coast of Greenland.' Nansen, in other words, was harnessing the instinct for self-preservation. It had worked against his predecessors, for safety tugged them from behind and danger drove them back. It was turning conventional wisdom upside down. But that, as he had already discovered in the laboratory, was the way ahead.

So far, Arctic expeditions had been mostly large and cumbrous affairs. Down the centuries, they had been attended by disaster. Nansen, once more, spurned orthodoxy. He espoused the small expedition, and put his faith in mobility. He was not exactly the first to think in this way. In the Canadian Arctic, servants of the Hudson's Bay Company had pioneered the small expedition. They included Dr John Rae, an Orkneyman, among the greatest polar explorers and, as it happened, one of Nansen's models. Nansen's originality lay in the application of skis, and seeing safety not only in compactness but in sheer speed.

His proposed route across Greenland was 700 kilometres long; he assumed a daily run of about 30 kilometres. This was at least double the speed of most polar expeditions but, in his own words, 'for skiers it is a very conservative estimate'. He estimated that the crossing of the ice cap would take a month, but planned to carry supplies for twice that time. The concept of a margin of safety rounded off his radical approach.

His skiing exploits had so far been solitary affairs. Now, for the first time, he would need companions. Their choice required circumspection. History amply proved that the wrong men could bring disaster.

To Nordenskiöld Nansen wrote asking cautiously whether the Lapps he took to Greenland had other virtues, or 'were they merely superior in skiing?' Nordenskiöld replied that 'On expeditions in snow deserts, a couple of Lapps are invaluable, if only because they can always find their way.' But he warned that 'Lapps are difficult to handle – they are mistrustful and very easily offended.' This was not racial prejudice; Nordenskiöld was in fact a sympathetic observer of alien cultures.

In any case Swedish and Norwegian attitudes towards their Lapp subjects were profoundly different, reflecting different circumstances. In Sweden, the Lapps occupied land desirable for farming and mining; so they found themselves in conflict with the Swedes colonising the north of their country. In Norway, on the other hand, the Lapps lived on poor sub-Arctic heathland, useless for anything else. As a result, they were left more or less to their own devices. As an English traveller who visited the Lapps was moved to write:

> I am not aware of any other instance ... of a people so weak ... remaining for centuries in contact with an ... altogether stronger people, and never attacked, pillaged, enslaved.

Nansen, at all events, decided to take Lapps. But Finnmark, the northernmost province of Norway, and the home of the Norwegian Lapps, was so remote that he now had no time to travel there personally to make his own selection. He asked Norwegians living in Finnmark to find him two suitable Lapps, and turned to other matters.

Meanwhile, on 24 November, about a fortnight after Nansen's return from Stockholm, a Christiania newspaper printed an article on his plans. It was the first time they had been revealed in print. The very same day, as a result, the first candidate applied to join the expedition. It was in the shape of a Norwegian army lieutenant called Henrik Angell, another skiing pioneer. In January 1884, the same season that Nansen skied to Christiania for the Huseby races, Angell had made what appears to have been the first recorded crossing on skis of Hardangervidda, the plateau between Western and Eastern Norway, and like Nansen had written up his exploit in a Christiania newspaper.

A few days after Angell, another army lieutenant, Oluf Christian Dietrichson, also asked to be considered. As a 'possible indication that I possess the necessary qualifications', he modestly wrote,

10. Plans and Preparations

I take the liberty of pointing out that, besides being used to hardships from the hunting trips that I carry out for a few months every year, in the winter of 85-86, without a guide, I did a ski tour.

And he mentioned a route from Tynset, in central Norway, through assorted mountain ranges to Lake Hittedal, in Telemark; more than 500 kilometres, end to end. It was about twice the length of Nansen's longest ski tour so far.

Both Angell and Dietrichson featured as their prime accomplishments skiing and inurement to exertion in deep cold. In other words, they presented themselves as already qualified for the Arctic. To them, crossing Greenland would be merely another ski tour. This unadorned approach, free of heroic yearning, was the hallmark of the skier. It was also something new in polar exploration, an ideal to which not even Nordenskiöld had aspired, and absolutely what Nansen demanded.

The only drawback was that these applicants, and several others, were what Nansen called 'educated'. For reasons of general toughness and adaptation to the wilds, he sought countryfolk with simpler backgrounds. For example, he wanted the man who had won the Huseby ski jumping of 1884, when he himself was seventh. This was Mikkel Hemmestveit, one of the Telemark skiing pioneers. Hemmestveit declined, as did others whom Nansen approached. The closer to the soil, as he now began to learn, the more earth-bound.

It was the 'educated' Norwegians whose imagination was fired by the thought of crossing Greenland. They were not many in number, ten or twenty at most; to whom were added, now that the news had filtered out, a sprinkling of hopefuls from abroad. Someone, for instance, wrote from a suburb of Paris that he had 'an idea for rapid travel over the ice ... I know a little about mechanics and also chemistry, but I do not know fear.' Those who refused Nansen's invitation believed that the crossing of Greenland was foolhardy, and against all common sense. This turned out to reflect the views of the great majority. Returning to Bergen, Nansen found himself up against a solid wall of disapproval. But through the chorus of condescending censure the voice of reasoned criticism was heard, for he was systematically consulting explorers who knew Greenland. Since Greenland was a Danish colony, most of these were Danes; amongst them one called Gustav Holm. To him, in January 1888, Nansen sent his plans.

'With 3 or 4 of the best skiers to be found,' Nansen wrote, 'I propose to sail on a Norwegian sealing ship at the beginning of June and ... around 66° North latitude, attempt to approach the coast as closely as possible.' Immediately thereafter, he intended to cross the ice cap. Like Nordenskiöld and Peary before him, he wanted to complete the whole expedition in one season, and be home before the year was out.

'I see you have the qualities required for success,' Holm replied. But, he mildly suggested, Nansen ought first to 'spend the winter in East Greenland [to] become familiar with the difficulties you will have to face'. Because of ice,

> you cannot count on reaching the East Coast by ship before the end of the summer [and] you naturally want to use the best part of the summer, when the nights are light, and the weather is good.

Holm was further concerned that Nansen wanted to start north of Cape Dan, which was still unexplored.

Holm knew what he was talking about. In 1884 and 1885, he had led a celebrated Danish expedition to East Greenland, travelling with Eskimos in an umiak, a flat-bottomed skin boat rowed by women. Nansen took his advice to the extent of agreeing to land, not in unexplored and uninhabited terrain, but near the Eskimo settlement of Angmagsalik, which was at the limit of what was known, and which Holm had discovered.

Meanwhile Nansen was faced with the task of fitting out and here, once again, he departed from convention. Tradition, based on many hands to haul, squandered weight and generated complexity. Nansen would depend on speed, simplicity and mobility. As a result, however, little could be bought ready made. Almost everything had to be specially designed. That included skis, for even they were not yet standardised. Nansen brought to polar exploration the skier's happy preoccupation with equipment. Advice descended on him, generously and unsolicited, from the small elite of mountain skiing pioneers. Someone, for example, wrote to explain that skiers from one of the wilder fjords, 'had invented a means of preserving the edges of their skis ... which they do by attaching a strip of galvanised iron 3/4" wide to both sides of their skis, so that they will grip on the snow crust'. This is the first record of steel edges on skis, half a century before they were officially 'invented'.

In the ski Nansen at least had a device which basically worked. The same could hardly be said of anything else. There was certainly no satisfactory sleeping bag; he had to design his own from scratch. Even the material was a matter of debate. Down-filled bags did not exist. Nordenskiöld had used woollen blankets; some Americans used buffalo fur. Nansen decided on reindeer fur. The Lapps used it for their winter clothing; it offered the best combination of warmth and light weight. Nansen got a Bergen furrier to make up a sleeping bag with a hood that could be completely closed, to prevent all escape of heat.

Transport was also a problem. To cross Greenland, the expedition would have to carry all supplies required by about half a dozen men for six weeks. That naturally meant hauling sledges. In his extensive reading, Nansen was struck by the example of Elisha Kent Kane and Charles Francis Hall, American explorers, who had pioneered the practice of learning from the polar Eskimos how to adapt to the surroundings. Both advocated sledge dogs as the best means of transport.

10. Plans and Preparations

Nansen, however, had never driven dogs in his life. Dogs as draught animals were virtually unknown in Scandinavia. Following Nordenskiöld's example, he toyed with the idea of reindeer instead, because they were the draught animals of the Lapps and could be obtained in Northern Norway. It was soon clear, however, that transporting them would be difficult. Besides, reindeer were herbivorous, existing on lichen, which did not grow in the part of Greenland for which they were intended. Every scrap of fodder would have to be shipped with them. Nansen was reduced to man-hauling.

Doing so on skis was an apparent contradiction. The ski is meant to slide, not grip. Nansen certainly had no experience in the matter, and someone who wanted to join the expedition told him: 'I have often tried to pull a sledge on skis, and I discovered it was so incredibly hard.' The type used so far by European explorers was heavy, clumsy and, with narrow runners, sank into soft snow. Since the first British expeditions had gone out, seventy years before, the design had not been changed. So Nansen obviously had to design a sledge that was light in weight and easy to pull.

Nansen had no desire to repeat the mistakes of his predecessors. He considered the boat-like pulka of the Lapps, but that was designed for soft snow and unsuited to hard crust and steep slopes. The same held for the flat-bottomed North American toboggan.

These drawbacks were avoided by the sledge traditionally used by Norwegian farmers. It ran on broad runners like skis. It therefore possessed the versatility of the ski in coping with all kinds of snow, and being able to traverse a slope. Nansen decided to adopt this form. This was one of his great innovations. (The irony is that today, with modern plastics, and the ability to mould thin strong shells of any shape, and any chosen elasticity, it is the pulka form that dominates, because that is the lightest, least cumbersome pattern, most easily hauled.)

He got a carpenter to make up an experimental model. It was considerably lighter in weight and more sophisticated in concept than the original. No iron was used in its construction. All joints were lashed with leather thongs. This was for elasticity, so as to ensure efficient running, and avoid damage in moving over rough terrain.

At the end of January 1888, Nansen once more skied from Bergen to Christiania to test his newly designed equipment. Hauling the prototype of his sledge, he followed Angell's route over Hardangervidda. In his reindeer sleeping bag he slept out in the snow, seeing among other things an eclipse of the moon. 'I slept out,' he told Nordenskiöld, 'in more than 20° of frost, and I was *too* warm.'

11

Danish Gold

Meanwhile there was the matter of money. The previous November, Nansen had asked the university in Christiania for a grant. 'Not a single Arctic expedition has yet been organised by Norway,' he argued.

> This seems all the more peculiar since ... Norwegians are undoubtedly the nation best suited to polar exploration. We have the ability to stand the climate better than most, and in our skiers we have a considerable superiority.

He also suggested that his expedition held 'scientific interest', if only because Greenland was now in an ice age, as other parts of the globe had been before. The university was impressed. But money it unfortunately had none to spare. So the university went to the government, and was summarily rebuffed.

Nansen had asked for 5,000 kroner, which he estimated the expedition would cost. This is equivalent to about £12,000 or $20,000 today. He was prepared to pay it all himself; spending his patrimony if need be. He afterwards maintained that he had only been persuaded to ask for public money in order to give the expedition the stamp of a national undertaking. In other words, he was voicing the ever-present nationalistic urge, but basing it firmly on the Nietzschean principle that what was good for the individual was good for the country, and not the other way about. The appeal to science was humbug. Nansen was more convincing when he told Dr Danielssen that after all his work on the central nervous system, he simply wanted to 'get some rest for my brain'.

The government announced its rejection of the pleas for funds on 4 January 1888. A few days later Professor Amund Helland, one of Nansen's supporters at the university, received a letter from – of all places – Copenhagen, hinting at private patronage. The writer was a wealthy Danish businessman called Augustin Cyrille Victor Vilhelm Gamél.

Helland had written the newspaper article that first publicised Nansen's plans. Geologist by profession, a humorist and an eccentric, he had himself been to Greenland. He was the man who discovered that glaciers flowed. Nansen, he told his readers, 'is one of the best skiers in the country, ... and a scientist who is also a first class skier is among the greatest rarities.' He ended by saying that Nansen needed money soon, so that he could set off the following season.

On New Year's Day a Copenhagen newspaper reprinted Helland's article, which was how Gamél heard of Nansen, and why he wrote to Helland in the first place. Gamél was quickly sent Nansen's own résumé of his plans, published early in January. The Norwegian government having refused Nansen his grant, Gamél decided to give the money, and by the end of the month had already paid it over. Nansen was regrettably late in expressing his thanks. However, he explained, when 'one leads a nomadic life, as I do at the moment, it is not easy to do everything at the right time'.

By then, having finished his trial ski tour with sledge and sleeping bag, Nansen was in Christiania. He now had to find a ship. After some difficulty, he picked on the sealer *Jason* of Sandefjord, 'well suited to the ice', as he told Gamél, 'and with a captain who is not timid, which is most important'. *Jason* was to land the expedition in Greenland in the course of her normal sealing operations. Nansen signed the contract on 23 February.

With a bare two months to go, the ship was all that had yet been settled. Nansen had still not found his men. His equipment remained far from complete. His latest trip had shown his ski boots to be too stiff and cold. Moreover, he still had to design a satisfactory cooker.

In polar travel, where every scrap of food and fuel had to be carried, probably the greatest single impediment at that period was the lack of an efficient portable stove. Especially was this true of Nansen's new style with skis, where speed and mobility were all. The spirit stove was the only kind available. It was primitive, burned with a wick, and seemed oddly out of step with the technical advances of the age. The only obvious improvement lay in the cooking vessels to make better use of the heat.

Towards the end of February, still in Christiania, Nansen was reading *Three Years of Arctic Service*. This was the book by Adolphus W. Greely about his Arctic expedition which had attained a new Furthest North: a record, by the way, which still stood. For all his faults, Greely was a technical pioneer, and one of his innovations was a more efficient cooking vessel. It had a central flue to absorb heat from the hot gas of the burner. On top was a conventional saucepan to act as a lid and utilise residual heat to melt snow. Nansen seized on the basic idea but reduced the number of parts, added insulation, and generally improved the design.

He ordered a prototype from a Christiania workshop. At the beginning of March, before the work was done, he returned to Bergen. There he pursued his other preparations. He took nothing for granted.

Hitherto, expedition members had been dressed in tight and heavy garments, like armour plating. Skiing required something looser, lighter, and capable of variation. Nansen introduced what has come to be known as the layer principle. Still faithful to Dr Jaeger's precepts, he stuck to pure wool. There were to be four layers: underwear, shirt, sweater and, finally, jacket, knee breeches and leggings made of a tough, thick Norwegian woollen material called vadmel. These could be combined according to temperature: in skiing, the problem is very rarely that of cold, but of overheating. Nansen also designed an outer wind jacket, with hood attached, like the Eskimo anorak. That had been used before, notably by the Austro-Hungarian expedition under Carl Weyprecht and Julius Payer, which discovered Franz Josef Land in 1872. But it had then been made of fur. Nansen's innovation had been to make his anorak of light, proofed cotton, separating protection against the wind from the warming function altogether.

Nansen was working against time. Even his skis were not ready yet. To every detail, he brought the same experimental zeal. He even found time to write an article on his expedition for a children's magazine. It was clear that he would win through not by heroic endeavour but by ingenuity. Tellingly, he implied that if a thing was not fun it was not worth doing.

Preparation was complicated by the fact that much was unobtainable in Norway and had to be ordered from abroad. A tent, for example, had to come from Copenhagen. There Carl Ryder, a Dane with great experience of Greenland, was having a tent specially sewn up. Towards Ryder and other polar authorities Nansen was humble, almost self-abasing; a noticeable contrast to his behaviour when dealing with scientists and academics. That did not prevent him from injecting his own ideas. He told Ryder, for example, to have the tent made of several pieces that could easily be separated. They were to double as sails on the sledges and make use of the wind.

Food was Nansen's intractable concern. Polar history was of little help, except repeatedly to prove that the destiny of a traveller was decided not by storm and frost but by what he ate.

Deficiency diseases, as they are now known, were the overhanging threat. Scurvy was the most common and most serious of them all. Its cause was not yet understood, but since it took long to develop, and Nansen's aim was speed, all being well it could be discounted. Other problems of nutrition had to be faced. Nansen's task was to feed men working long and hard in deep cold. What we would call a high calorie diet was the solution, as he knew from his own mountain tours.

Because everything had to be carried along, Nansen needed food that was both light and highly concentrated. To save weight, dehydrated food was required, but production techniques were still rudimentary. Diet would be based on pemmican, the customary ration of the polar traveller. It was one of the techniques borrowed by European explorers from native polar tribes. Originating among the Chree Indians of North America, pemmican consists of dried meat, ground up, mixed with melted fat, and cast into solid cakes. It is nourishing, concentrated – 6000 calories per kilogram – and highly indigestible.

The only European manufacturer was the firm of Beauvais in Copenhagen. Gustav Holm, who had used these supplies himself, was Nansen's local intermediary. 'From my few remarks,' Holm, with gentle irony, had written, 'you will have gathered that I do not consider your plan to be prepared well enough.' Nonetheless, he gracefully added, 'it would give me great pleasure to be of any help'. Holm had taken a year or more to organise his own expedition. Nansen was cramming his preparations into a few months.

Beauvais only made pemmican on request. Nansen sent his order in March; he required everything by the first week in April. Like other suppliers, Beauvais found this too rushed; Nansen would have to wait a little longer. But Beauvais did proudly explain that his pemmican would be packed in 'tins with a new, convenient method of opening, patented by myself, which makes knife or scissors superfluous'.

All this and more required detailed correspondence. In Bergen, meanwhile, Nansen had to suffer the solicitous, paternal reproaches of Dr Danielssen, who feared that he would be lost to the museum. Desperate to keep some kind of hold over his protégé, he gave him, as before, a year's leave.

Finally, there was the harrowing process, after five and a half years, of parting from Vilhelm, and especially Marie, Holdt. On Friday 29 March, as Marie reminded him afterwards, 'I accompanied my dear Fridtjof to the railway station and bade you the last farewell.'

So, after yet another mountain crossing on skis, Nansen returned to Christiania, but not immediately to conclude his preparations. Before leaving for Greenland, he was determined on taking his Ph.D., which first involved three solid days of irksome preliminary examinations.

For almost four months, the university had been vacillating over whether to accept as Nansen's thesis his paper on the central nervous system. To make sure that it did not languish unnoticed, he had presented it to leading scientists abroad, well aware, as he said, that his conclusions were 'in several respects very radical'. The university in Christiania evidently agreed with this view. It was less than a month before his departure for Greenland that his thesis was finally accepted.

The question of companions for his expedition was still hanging fire too. Crossing Greenland was not merely a matter of skiing. It also involved climbing up to the ice cap and descending through the coastal mountains. The enterprise lay in the frontier zone between skiing, climbing and glacier travel.

Of the last-mentioned, Nansen knew little. He needed a mountaineer, and the acceptable candidates were skiers alone. In his perplexity, he wrote for help to a Danish climber, Carl Christian Hall in Copenhagen, a distinguished pioneer of mountaineering in Norway with several first ascents to his credit, and the only Scandinavian member of the Alpine Club in London. Hall recommended some Norwegian mountain guides and porters he had employed; they all declined Nansen's invitation. There was going to be no mountaineer. Hall was, however, able to help with equipment, notably crampons and alpine rope.

Meanwhile, early in February, a certain Otto Sverdrup had applied to join the expedition. Sverdrup, although no mountaineer, was 'a man of the open air, tough, spartan, with great endurance', to quote the testimonial he enclosed from a past chairman of the local ski association.

> For years he has done forestry work on ski in impassable [terrain] and I can testify that he shows great stamina ... He is well mannered, and easy to get on with.

Sverdrup was in Steinkjær, three hundred miles to the north. Nansen's brother Alexander, however, who had taken up law, was then, as part of his training, a court official in a nearby town. He happened to know Sverdrup; which was probably why Sverdrup applied to Nansen in the first place. In any case, Nansen asked for Alexander's opinion. 'Small very well built indomitable self-controlled pleasant fellow,' Alexander telegraphed, 'can only recommend.' Without more ado, Nansen accepted Sverdrup. That was the first definite appointment to the expedition. It was by now late March.

Nansen and Sverdrup met for the first time early in April in Christiania. Sverdrup was not just another skier. In his own words, he had 'undergone many hardships both at sea and ashore'. He was that authentic Norwegian type, part seaman, part farmer.

Born in Northern Norway, although he spent most of his life in the central province of Trøndelag, he grew up on a farm between mountain and fjord. Like many of his kind, he never went to school but was taught at home by a tutor. At the age of 17 he went to sea before the mast and after six years had his master's certificate. He had led a roaming life, much of the time in sail, but at the time he joined Nansen he had not been to sea for several years and was working on his father's farm mainly because the Norwegian merchant fleet was then in a period of depression and it was hard to get a decent berth. Like a soft-spoken Viking, Sverdrup was only resting between forays. Without exactly having that intention, he seemed to slip naturally into the position of second-in-command.

Before actually meeting Sverdrup, Nansen had settled on Dietrichson as his other companion. At the eleventh hour, Nansen – or Sverdrup – felt that one more was needed. It was Sverdrup who arranged it. Near his father's farm, he was able to call at short notice on a woodcutter, seaman and skier called Kristian Kristiansen. It was Sverdrup, too, who went down to the railway station in Christiania to meet the expedition's Lapps.

Since two Lapps had been 'ordered' by Nansen during the previous autumn, he had heard very little more of them. In the end, there was a flurry of telegrams and during the first week of April, they were reported to be on their way. On 16 April, when they finally arrived in Christiania, Nansen was in the throes of delivering three trial lectures, another part of the preliminaries for his Ph.D. As soon as he could, he hurried round to inspect the newcomers in their hotel. This was his first encounter with Lapps of any kind, and it came as quite a surprise. 'In the middle of the floor,' as he described the scene,

> stood a handsome young man ... away in a corner sat an old man with long, black hair hanging down to his shoulders; he was very small [and] looked more like a Lapp than the young one.

The man to whom this applied was called Ole Nielsen Ravna; his younger (and taller) companion was Samuel Johannesen Balto. Both were dressed in the Lapp national costume of blue serge jerkins, decorated with red and yellow stripes. They spoke broken Norwegian. They came from the vicinity of Karasjok, a settlement in Northern Norway, almost a thousand miles away, and had never before been south of the Arctic Circle. They were wholly exotic.

Finding them had not been easy. Candidates were interested chiefly in the money to be earned. Norwegian Lapps were only partly Europeanised. They had learned to read and write. They had been converted, more or less, from their old pagan, shamanistic beliefs to a local variant of protestant fundamentalism. More willingly, they had embraced tobacco, alcohol, firearms and coffee, especially coffee; hot, strong, and in huge quantities.

Living in the polar regions, on the very edge of the habitable world, they saw life as a struggle for survival against the forces of Nature. Exploration was an alien concept; they did not need to seek adventure. Balto and Ravna had to be enticed with 800 kroner (£2,000 or $3,200 in present terms), plus travel expenses, for what was estimated as an absence of six months. It was what they might have earned in a good season from reindeer keeping and fishing. Nansen's own annual salary at the Bergen museum was still only 1,600 kroner.

Balto – who could write Lappish, but not Norwegian – has recorded that it was through Nansen's approach that he 'heard about the foreign country Greenland for the first time'. He was comforted to learn that 'it was not colder in Greenland during the summer than during the winter in ... Karasjok'. On 4 April, he and Ravna started over the spring snow from Karasjok. Balto described how 'many people followed us for several miles ... and they all had a farewell drink from me'.

They travelled for twelve days; first by reindeer-drawn *pulka* to the coast; then by boat, and finally by train; the first time they had ever seen one. On the way Balto, in his own words,

> heard more about my new superior. As a person, he was said to be bad. That dampened my enthusiasm completely, so that I wanted to turn back.

Part II. Greenland

When Balto finally met Nansen, 'it was indescribably pleasant', as he put it.

> He was a stranger to us, but his face beamed at us like the faces of the parents we left behind. A feeling of warmth streamed through me, both because of the meeting and because of his welcome to us.

Nansen, in fact, was hiding disappointment. For one thing, Balto was 27 years old and Ravna, 46. He had wanted his companions between the ages of 30 and 40 because, he thought, people were then in their prime. He himself was the same age as Balto. Furthermore he had asked for mountain Lapps, who were nomads, following the reindeer. Only Ravna was such a one. Balto belonged to the river Lapps, who lived a settled life. To cap it all, Ravna had a wife and five children, and unmarried men had been specifically requested. In Nansen's own words, he 'had the strongest wish to send them back, but it was now too late to find anyone else'. Barely three weeks remained before departure.

By now the enterprise had achieved some public recognition, with a reception held in its honour. The Lapps were reluctant to attend because, as Balto touchingly put it, 'we did not know the way that fine people ate and drank'. Nansen, however, persuaded them to go. There were, said Balto,

> many well-decorated gentlemen [and] to begin with we thought it was difficult to mix with them, because we had never done it before ... But that soon passed over, as they showed by their kindliness that they had not gathered to show their superiority, but ... to honour us ... we who were going to the strange and unknown and cold island Greenland.

Balto was less impressed when the whole expedition – except Kristiansen, who had not yet arrived – camped out in Nordmarka for a day to test the equipment. The tent passed muster, but not Nansen's carefully designed cooker. It was 'filled with snow. Then we lit it, and let it burn for a couple of hours, but it did not come to the boil, so we had to drink the tepid water to which coffee extract was added. It didn't taste much.' In the last-minute rush, Nansen would now have to modify the cooker also.

Meanwhile, to talk to the isolated inhabitants of Eastern Greenland, he was learning Eskimo as well. It so happened that in Christiania at the time lived Hinrich Rink, a retired governor of Southern Greenland. His wife, Signe, had been born in Greenland and spoke Eskimo fluently. To her Nansen had applied for lessons; but originally she shrank from teaching him, in the belief that he lacked the ability. Somehow he overcame her objections, confounding her by the sheer intensity with which he attacked a language so utterly alien to his own.

In between these activities he also had to take his degree. There yet remained his doctoral disputation, a mediaeval custom which survives in

Scandinavia still. Like all candidates for a Ph.D., he was required to defend his thesis in public debate against two opponents nominated by the University.

Doctoral disputations took place in the ceremonial auditorium of Christiania University; a marbled, Germanic simulacrum of a Greek theatre. Here, on 28 April 1888, exactly four days before he was due to depart, Nansen underwent his ordeal.

On the rostrum, in the obligatory dress suit, Nansen's tall, commanding figure suggested elegance but seemed somehow out of place. The stereotype of the age required that academics wear beards, and spectacles too. Nansen had neither. He gave the impression of being more at home on a ski jump than in the lecture room. His overwhelming personality hinted at both arrogance and charm. He needed all the powers he could command, for to be a scientist who looked like a sportsman was disconcerting enough, and on his argumentation hinged the question of whether he passed or failed. The outcome was far from certain.

In a lengthy disquisition, the First Opponent, Dr Axel Holst, bitterly attacked Nansen for contradicting what was generally accepted, fuelling an atmosphere that was heated and censorious. Although the Norwegian condensation of Nansen's paper had been formally presented, it was the original English version that was in reality on trial. What particularly enraged Holst was that the central (and most controversial) assertion: 'We are obliged to abandon the theory of the direct combination between the [nerve] cells' was graced by a haughty footnote: 'We cannot change the reality according to our ideas but we can change our ideas according to the reality.'

Dr Holst declared that 'one ought to eschew theories until one clearly saw that all the experimental facts were consistent'. He did in fact have a point. Strictly speaking, Nansen was ahead of his experimental evidence. Also, in the light of later knowledge, he had made certain mistakes. But these were subsidiary, and had no bearing on his central thesis. As he vigorously protested, 'any theory ... that is probable, will benefit science'. The disputation had degenerated into a *dialogue des sourds*.

When the Second Opponent, Professor Hjalmar Heiberg, rose to join the fray, in the words of a newspaper reporter, he

> expressed his conviction that the hypotheses the Candidate had presented will certainly share the fate of so many others: they will be forgotten. The anatomical discoveries, on the other hand, will remain significant.

What is certain is that Nansen had found that nerve fibres, on entering the spinal cord, bifurcate, like a T-joint, into ascending and descending branches. They are known today as 'Nansen's fibres'. It was a discovery of fundamental importance, for it provided the foundation for the understanding of spinal reflexes.

To Nansen, all this was secondary. He probably took comfort in the Ibsenesque thought that if the accepted local authorities disagreed with him, then he must be right. To ensure that the world would know, he had taken the precaution of publishing in the *Anatomischer Anzeiger*, a noted German anatomical journal, a condensation, in German, of *The Structure and Combination of the Histological Elements of the Central Nervous System*, with the categorical essence unimpaired. This had appeared in February. Nansen remained unshaken in his theory of the independence of the nervous cellular unit. To him – quite rightly as it turned out in the end – this was his main achievement.

Perhaps this was dimly glimpsed even by the disapproving and mystified audience before whom Nansen stood that day. In the words of one reporter, Professor Heiberg brought the proceedings to a close by saying:

> There was something bold and 'sporting' about Herr Nansen's science, which the Professor was certain would bear fruit.

All this took place on a Saturday; the following Wednesday, Nansen left for Greenland, 'happy to have everything behind me', as he wrote in a farewell letter to Dr Danielssen.

> In the end, there was such a confusion of one thing on top of another … that I believe that had it continued any longer, I would have had a nervous breakdown … There was hardly a second to spare; we finished precisely as calculated, but no more.

He was now Dr Nansen; he had passed, after all. He liked to say that this was out of charity. It was generally believed that he was heading for disaster – and unlikely to return alive.

'I Let Them All Prate'

Nansen had arranged with *Jason* to fetch the expedition in Iceland. Leaving the others to follow by another route, he went on ahead, via Copenhagen. There, among the canals, coppered cupolas and spires, he met Augustin Gamél for the first time, and was able to thank him in person.

Face framed in straggling side-whiskers, Gamél turned out to be a characteristically amiable Dane, albeit of French descent. He was a coffee importer and wholesaler but craved wider recognition. He was a dedicated Maecenas. A few years previously, he had paid for a Danish attempt to reach the North Pole.

Underneath Nansen's gratitude there lurked, to begin with, a suggestion of constraint because, like most of his compatriots, he saw Greenland as 'Norway's old colony', having been discovered and first colonised by Norwegian Vikings. It was a national grievance that, on separation from Denmark, Norway had not taken Greenland with her, but been forced to leave it as a Danish possession. Gamél's view was that 'since the expedition concerns Greenland, I hope that Norwegians and Danes can unite in its exploration'. He certainly wanted no outsider to make the first crossing from coast to coast. He fêted Nansen now with a dinner party and an evening at the theatre.

Nansen had not come to Copenhagen merely to thank Gamél. He had to make arrangements with *Den Kongelige Grønlandske Handel*, the Royal Greenland Trading Company. It had a monopoly of all trade in Greenland, and was the virtual ruler of the country. There were no banks in Greenland, so Nansen needed a letter of credit from the Company – familiarly known by its initials KGH – for its trading stations. To this, and more, the KGH agreed – but only on the strength of Gamél's guarantee.

In Copenhagen, Nansen also finally met those to whom he had written for advice; Gustav Holm in particular. Holm now reiterated his warnings; backed by his own experience of pack ice barring the way to land. Holm was a man with whom it was impossible to be offended. More vehement and offensive were some of the comments in the Danish press. There was, for example, an article by Peter Eberlin, who had been with Holm in Greenland. Nansen, Eberlin predicted, would never get through. He would have to be rescued by the Eskimos and taken down the coast to the Danish colonies on the west coast – 'and no one,' he continued, 'has any right to plunge East Greenlanders into a long, and in many ways corrupting, journey to no purpose at all.'

Nansen was not deterred. 'I let them all prate,' he wrote to a friend, 'and follow my own straight or crooked path.' In a cheerful, or at least a confident, mood, after three busy days, he hurried on to London. Here he made his way to the Royal Geographical Society. Its home, at No. 1 Savile Row, with porticoed entrance on the corner, a stone's throw from Piccadilly, suggested a gentleman's club of a particularly somnolent kind. Through quiet corridors, Nansen was ushered in to see John Scott Keltie.

Keltie was nominally the Librarian, though a deputy did the actual work. Behind a courteous, bland exterior, enlivened by a pointed, auburn beard, there lay a sharp-witted and discerning Scot. Keltie presided over a clearing house of geographical information. He was a born journalist. He made himself easily accessible, and found plenty of time for lunch. He was geographical correspondent of *The Times* and an informal publicity agent of the first rank – which is why Nansen had come to London to seek him out. At home, he was no more than a big frog in a small pool. Keltie, with his access to the rolling vistas of the Anglo-Saxon Press, offered a path to fame and fortune in the wider world outside.

Keltie's response – as with any untried hopeful – was encouraging but non-committal. At least it was a start. Next day Nansen took the train to Scotland to rejoin the other members of the expedition, who had sailed to Leith, near Edinburgh, with all the expedition's impedimenta. 'The strangest thing,' said Balto, 'was that the Scotsmen gathered round us simple Lapps in such great numbers.' The reason was what a local newspaper called 'their peculiar dress'. So great was the crowd that the police actually had to break it up.

From Leith, the expedition transferred to Granton, another port near Edinburgh, to join *Thyra*, a Danish mailboat, waiting to sail for Iceland, still at that time a Danish possession. *Thyra*'s owners had given Nansen a 25% discount on all his fares. Around midnight on 9 May, from a lonely quayside, *Thyra* cast off and headed out into the darkness.

On his way to the ship, Nansen had stayed in Edinburgh with Minnie and William Hoyle, Marion Sharp's married sister and brother-in-law. It was with the Hoyles that Marion was living when Nansen had visited her eighteen months before. Nansen had grown to know them well, and was vividly remembered by their daughter Muriel as 'Mr Viking'. They all came down to the docks to see him off. 'We have good news from our friends in Japan,' Hoyle himself slyly observed; and from Hikone, near Kyoto, where she was now living with her mother, Marion had sent a farewell letter, reminding him of Naples:

> Does a dark robed procession with flying hair still wind its way down that rock-hewn staircase to the bathing beach, & do fair haired barbarians still

dance with laughing English girls ... to the accompaniment of guitar & mandolin?

Her mother also sent a farewell letter, complete with a photograph of herself in her best lace cap. Marion's own last words were

If it should be that we are not to meet again ... Then until God wills – perhaps in The Happy Hunting grounds of Walhalla we may tell each other the story of our lives! ... *Addio mio caro.*

Confined to a small ship for a long voyage, Nansen and his companions were able finally to take each other's measure. They made a notably heterogeneous party. Sverdrup and Kristiansen had been to sea, Dietrichson was a professional army officer. Each in his own way therefore was accustomed to working in a group. Nansen was a moody individualist and the only academic among them. As the ship pitched and tossed over an uneasy sea, he was frantically writing, in English, a scientific paper on hermaphroditism in *Myxine glutinosa* that he had long promised his mentor Dr Danielssen.

As for the Lapps, Ravna was uneasy on board. First he was seasick; then he refused to sleep below. Instead, as Nansen put it, he 'drew himself into his reindeer fur doublet, curled up like a dog in a corner of the deck, and undoubtedly slept as well as us'. Perhaps Ravna simply felt like another of his kind who once said that outsiders 'don't really understand our life and circumstances ... When a Lapp gets into a room his brains go round ... they're no good unless the wind's blowing in his nose.' At all events, he now observed that, as the ship sailed north and the air grew colder, the Norwegians froze, but not the Lapps. In Nansen's own words,

Balto came to us and announced: 'Ravna says, what has made us follow these people, they have such thin clothes, they're already shivering here; they'll die in Greenland, where it is so cold ... and then we two Lapps will also die, because we don't know the way back to other people.'

Ravna, as a rule, was taciturn and passive. Balto, by contrast, had a ready tongue. Unlike Ravna, who could scarcely speak Norwegian, he spoke the language with a thick and comical accent. He was lively and unselfconscious. By the end of the voyage, and in spite of his hot-tempered outbursts, he had become what Nansen called 'the expedition's minister of humour'.

On 20 May *Thyra* dropped anchor in Isafjord, in north-west Iceland, after a voyage of eleven days. Here they were meant to rendezvous with *Jason*. Pack ice, however, lay menacingly near, so Nansen decided to sail back with *Thyra* to Dyrefjord, a little to the south, which was known never to be closed by ice. At Thingeyri, the main settlement on the fjord, they were warmly welcomed and hospitably housed by Christian Gram, a convivial Dane, who combined the rôles of shopkeeper and Norwegian vice-consul, and settled down to wait for *Jason*. While doing so they repacked their equipment in smaller loads that could be stowed in a small boat and manhandled over the ice.

Always Nansen carried a pocket sketchbook and stopped frequently to draw. More rarely, he took with him instead a 'portable' camera, bulky but embodying nonetheless the latest technical advance. Instead of glass plates, it used the first roll film commercially available. This was probably the first time such a piece of equipment had been used on a polar expedition.

One day, Nansen took his companions skiing on Glámujökull, a snow-clad escarpment at the end of the fjord. From the top, some 1,000 metres high, there was a long steep downhill run over packed snow. Before starting, Balto discussed with Ravna whether they should put on heel bindings, like the Norwegians, or depend on toestraps alone, in the traditional Lapp way. The advantage of the latter was safe ejection in case of a fall; it was a primitive safety binding, in other words. Against all their instincts both Lapps felt that, out of politeness, they had to do like the Norwegians. Ravna saved the honour of the Lapps and did not fall. Balto, however, in his own words,

> was going full speed ... suddenly I was faced with a dip. The skis slid sideways, because I was not used to Norwegian skis, which are flat underneath.

Lapp skis had convex soles, which made them easier to control. Whatever the explanation, Balto fell awkwardly, pulling a tendon.

It was now 28 May, and the rest of the stay at Thingeyri revolved round the condition of Balto's leg. As it remained swollen and resistant to treatment, Nansen considered leaving Balto behind, to be replaced by one of the local Icelanders. But Ravna was afraid of being the only Lapp in the party, and in any case none of the Icelanders would volunteer.

On 3 June, a local whale catcher steamed into Thingeyri. On board was Mauritz Jacobsen, captain of *Jason*, which he had left in Isafjord while, to save time, he went ahead to fetch Nansen and his companions. As a result, the expedition had to pack up and embark in haste. Meanwhile a Danish warship, *Fylla*, had been lying at anchor and offering the party the hospitality of her gunroom. Nansen made a final quick visit aboard, was plied with champagne, and left to the strains of a stirring march played by the ship's band. In the bleak surroundings of Isafjord, the expedition was greeted by *Jason* with bunting overall, much cheering and a salute of many guns.

Next day, 4 June, there was more champagne, this time at the postmaster's, and *Jason* put to sea. It was all a notable contrast to the muted farewells at home. The weather played its part. *Jason* steamed off into a perfect northern summer's night, under the red afterglow of twilight blazing from a cloudless sky, and playing against dark undertones on smooth, gently rolling waters. Kittiwakes, raucous and inquisitive, swarmed round the ship, as if to see her off. They were rewarded by being used as target practice on the wing.

The following day, *Jason* found the ice. As previously agreed, she immediately made for Greenland and, after a week, the coastal mountains hove into sight. Land seemed tantalisingly near; but heavy, broken pack ice lay in between. 'Too risky to attempt landing,' Nansen wrote succinctly in his diary. *Jason* put about. Balto for one was relieved. He was surprised to be on board at all. Dietrichson had appointed himself masseur and, somehow, got his leg almost to heal before sailing. But Balto still needed convalescence and for that he now had ample opportunity. For his part, Nansen now saw the force of Gustav Holm's warning that 'you cannot count on reaching the East Coast by ship before the end of the summer'.

Jason withdrew and Capt. Jacobsen, as his contract with Nansen allowed him to do, started sealing; in company, as it happened, with other ships. 'I am willing to serve as marksman, being not inexperienced,' Nansen had told the owners. So now he joined *Jason*'s crew in shooting the not too abundant seal dotting the floes.

Eventually, the pack ice began to slacken and Capt. Jacobsen shaped westwards once more. On the afternoon of 15 July, after more than a month, land was raised once more. Nansen was below at the time. He rushed topsides and, in his own words,

> ahead, not more than 70 miles off, lie Greenland's wonderful line of peaks north of Cape Dan ... This landscape has a rare, wild beauty, more broken than anything I remember having seen.

Jason started to close land. Nansen hurried round making, as he thought, final preparations. But, once more, pack ice barred the way. Past eerie, green-glistening icebergs, *Jason* nosed her way in retreat. Two days later, on 17 July, she came within 20 kilometres of the coast, before reaching the edge of the ice. It was the closest yet. Ahead lay the Sermilik Fjord, one of the more promising routes up to the ice cap.

The ice was slack, with plenty of open leads. *Jason* had passed through worse ice before unscathed. But that was out to sea; this was up against land, in uncharted shoals. Jacobsen dared not sail any closer in; it was uncertain whether he would get that close again. Nansen decided to seize the moment.

After all the waiting, the expedition finally prepared to disembark. For the last time Nansen clambered up into the crow's nest, to spy out the way ahead. Compulsive correspondent that he was, he put the finishing touches to his mail. To Augustin Gamél he wrote that 'just behind the mountains, for the first time we can see the edge of the ice cap. It is here, within a few hours that we will leave *Jason* and say a last farewell.' To Nordenskiöld, his mentor, he wrote: 'Dear Herr Baron, Time is short ... but I cannot leave without sending you a few words of farewell.'

Captain Jacobsen, bearded and patriarchal, was concerned for the expedition. Nansen had with him a specially made boat with metal runners on the bilges to pull over the ice if need be. Because of the risk of being crushed by the ice, Jacobsen felt that one boat was not enough. He offered one of *Jason*'s whalers. So two boats were now put into the water. Nansen got into the whaler, with Balto and Dietrichson. Sverdrup was put in command of the original boat, and under him were Ravna and Kristiansen. It was raining a little. There was some cheering, and a salute from *Jason*'s signal cannon.

'At 7 p.m. on 17 July, the expedition left *Jason* in good spirits and with the highest hopes of a fortunate result,' Capt. Jacobsen reported later to Augustin Gamél, after *Jason* had returned to port.

> We watched ... the expedition ... until midnight, when the fog came down. They had by then covered about half the approximately ten mile broad belt of ice, and were then in open water. At 6 in the morning, the fog lifted, and we could see nothing more of them, and I take it as certain that the expedition reached land some time in the evening of 18 July.

'While rowing through the belt of ice,' Jacobsen went on, 'the expedition members climbed up onto a height several times and waved us their last farewells.'

13

Threatened by Ice

It was an eerie scene. Under leaden skies, among ice floes glinting white against grey waters, the two boats followed close upon each other into dark twilight filtered by thickening curtains of rain. Bent over the oars were silent, monk-like figures, clad in dark brown oilskins with cowls drawn over their heads. The only touch of colour was the red and white Danish ensign at the stern of the leading boat, and the red, white and blue of the Norwegian flag at the prow.

Except for a brush with floes where the current swirled past an iceberg, it was plain sailing at the start. The rain lifted. In a brilliant sunset, the mountains around the Sermilik Fjord rose up high ahead. Nansen could already see open water along the coast. There was talk of evening coffee somewhere on the fjord.

Meanwhile the ice, driven possibly by the tide, began ominously to close. Nansen, in the van, turned into a lead that rapidly contracted. Both boats were hastily dragged up onto a floe to avoid being crushed. A lead soon opened out again but, as Nansen's boat was being relaunched, she stove in a strake. Luckily it was *Jason*'s whaler and not the specially built boat, which was the bigger of the two. All the same, she had to be pulled up onto the floe again for repairs. Unfortunately, proper equipment had not been brought along. Sverdrup and Kristiansen improvised with a loose bilge board, a few stray nails, and the back of an axe as a hammer. By the time the work was done, the ice had closed yet again, and there was no open water within reach.

Nansen made camp. For the first time in earnest the tent was pitched, unexpectedly, on a floe. Dietrichson volunteered to keep watch, and the remainder tumbled into their sleeping bags to make up for fifteen hours unabated effort. By then, it was the morning of 18 July. During a break in the weather there had been a last glimpse of *Jason*, now a distant smudge of smoke, before she finally disappeared from view.

Next day, 19 July dawned dull but hopefully with slackened ice and a promising open lead. The boats were stowed and launched. The current was now setting to the south but, in Nansen's own words, 'all we need is to work our way across with unremitting determination'. Yet again he was mocked by the caprice of the pack. He soon underwent the sequence, growing all too familiar, of ice bearing down on either side, and the boats being rushed out of the water to safety. At a certain point, the floe of refuge started rocking, the muffled roar of breakers grew louder. They were drifting out to sea.

There was nothing to do but make camp, and wait on events. In the evening, the weather lifted. Long after the others had crept into their sleeping bags, Nansen sat up gazing wistfully at the line of the inland ice between the peaks, growing ever smaller as the floe drifted away from land, and the sea surged more strongly underfoot. By the following day, the floe had split across. It shuddered intermittently as neighbouring floes crashed into it, heaving on the swell. Nansen tried hauling boats and sledges towards land, but soon found that the drift out to sea was too strong, and settled down instead on the most substantial floe within reach. Meanwhile, as he jotted in his diary, 'the surf grows closer, the noise increases, waves hurl themselves towards us and break over the floe from all sides.' The situation was beginning to be critical.

'The poor Lapps are not in the best of spirits,' Nansen went on. 'They disappeared during the morning, but were found in the bottom of a boat, where one was reading aloud from the [New] Testament. They are preparing for the end.'

So far as they let it be known, none of the Norwegians were praying – yet. They were, however, planning for survival. Their folklore pointed that way. Years ago on *Viking*, for example, Nansen had heard of a ship's boat that became separated from another sealer in the pack ice, not far from where he was now, and rowed safely across the Denmark Strait to Iceland. That was one of the great unsung open boat journeys. Nansen, at any rate, was planning how best to load his boats and launch them when the moment came. 'The annoying consequence,' as he wrote, 'would be that the outcome of our expedition would no longer be in doubt.'

By then, the breakers were only a few hundred yards off and 'none of us doubt that within a few hours we will find ourselves either sweeping over the sea, or sinking to the bottom.' After a long day the sunset, when it came, 'was wonderful, not a breath of wind stirs ... we could not ask for a finer hour to end our lives.'

So, when all was said and done, Norwegian and Lapp were equally fatalistic. Whatever happened, rest was vital. They crept into their sleeping bags once more. Balto, however, declined to sleep in the tent, and lay in one of the boats instead. Sverdrup remained on watch.

To the sound of the floes grinding against each other Nansen fell asleep. He woke to violent rocking, the roar of the surf louder than ever, and the hiss of spume now sweeping past the tent. At any moment, he expected Sverdrup to rout them all out; but nothing happened, so he simply dozed off again.

Sverdrup, meanwhile, had been on the verge of waking them up several times. He got as far as loosening the first fastening of the tent door. Crisis or not, he was still reluctant to disturb his companions. Sleep, as he well knew, was a key to survival. Leaving the fastening undone, he calmly took another turn, as if he were the officer of the watch on the bridge of an ocean liner, and strolled to the end of the floe. By now it was at the edge of the pack. The surf was swilling over. The boat in which Balto was sleeping soundly through it all threatened to roll over as each wave washed by. Holding it upright, so as not to disturb the occupant, Sverdrup surveyed the scene. Just as the floe seemed about to sail out into the breakers, it suddenly turned, and started moving into the pack again with unexpected speed.

So after all, Sverdrup was saved from interrupting his companions' sleep. When they finally woke up they were already far from the open sea, and only a distant rumble of the surf could still be heard.

The men on the floe felt as if they had lived through considerably more than the three days since they had left the ship. From another point of view, they had simply been involved in an insignificant whorl of the great current sweeping the ice down from the Arctic along the coast of Greenland. They were unmistakably at the mercy of impersonal, overpowering natural forces. Nansen returned to the overriding theme:

> Only one thought seems more and more ominous, and that is the prospect that the expedition will fail this time. Well, we will have to do what is allowed to us, but otherwise comfort ourselves with that great virtue, patience.

Like many truisms, this one was surprisingly hard to live up to. Opening and closing, like the slow pulsation of some primordial organism, the ice several times persuaded Nansen to make for the land glimpsed tantalisingly, far off, through shifting veils of rain and mist. Alternately rowing through grudgingly opened leads, and dragging the boats over the clinging mushy surface of ice mouldering from fog and thaw, Nansen finally accepted that, as he put it, 'the sea works faster than we'. He resigned himself to waiting on a suitable floe.

Finding one, said Dietrichson, was 'no easy matter'.

> It has to be solid and strong ... and on its edges admit of rapid handling ... of the boats. It must have good drinking water.

Given time, sea ice leaches its salt, turning into fresh water. So, above all, an old floe was required. Eventually one was found that fulfilled the specifications. It was now 26 July. Gustav Holm's warnings no doubt came back suitably to haunt Nansen.

To find his way across the ice cap, Nansen had learned navigation; but it was now, imprisoned on his floe, that he first put his knowledge to the test. Getting out his sextant and tables each noon when the sun was pleased to shine, he discovered that he was drifting south, away from his goal, at almost a mile an hour. 'Must encourage the Lapps,' Nansen wrote in his diary, 'they are losing hope, they are afraid we will be swept out into the Atlantic in the end.' Was that the fear preying on his mind too? Anyway, it was the Lapps who, unconsciously, enlivened the ennui that settled on the floe.

In Iceland, Nansen had bought a pony to help haul the sledges. The fodder brought along on *Jason* was soon exhausted, demonstrating the folly of bringing a grass eater where no grass grew. Long before the end of the voyage, the pony, to general regret, was put down. His flesh now eked out the rations of the men on the floe. When, to save fuel, it was served raw, a Lapp taboo was unwittingly broken, and Nansen would 'not easily forget the expression on Balto's face'.

Early one morning, the camp was roused by the watchman announcing the arrival of a polar bear. In the ensuing commotion, it rapidly decamped. Balto then confessed that he was terrified by the mere thought of bears, so that when he was supposed to be on watch he hugged the wall of the tent and dared not move an inch. He vowed never to drink again if ever he survived. He had only promised to join the expedition, so he said, because he was drunk at the time.

At least the sojourn on the floe allowed six highly different human beings to come to terms with isolation, and with one another. Kristiansen was emerging as taciturn but dependable. Dietrichson was the most loquacious. By common consent Sverdrup, solid, intermittently reserved and idiosyncratically conversational, was quietly confirmed as second-in-command.

Only Nansen stood apart, noticeably a prey to moods. His diary mirrored the constantly changing weather. On 28 July, the southwards drift had ceased; the sun shone again after a bitter taste of winter. Nansen paced up and down the floe, gazing at the sharks-tooth coastal peaks of Greenland in the distance, with the edge of the ice cap plainly visible in between. 'It entices one far, far, into the unknown interior,' he wrote wistfully. 'Oh well, our time will come yet.'

14

Eskimo and Lapp

'What a difference between the scene that now surrounds me,' ran the next entry in Nansen's diary, 'and that when I last wrote.'

> Then, it was ice, loneliness, and the roar of the sea; now howling dogs, heathens in droves, boats, folded tents, bespeak life, activity, and summertime, but above all, the solid rock of Greenland underfoot.

Intervening events had dowsed all thought of diaries. On the morning of 29 July, Ravna was coming off watch. Diffident, as usual, about waking his relief, he poked his little round, bearded face through the crack of the tent door and waited for someone to stir. He then announced that the ice was open and the land, as he put it in his broken idiom, 'too near'. His companions tumbled out to find the coastal mountains indeed looming up the closest yet. Like a jigsaw puzzle that had come apart, the pack was interspersed by a maze of open leads. Camp was quickly struck; the boats were rushed into the water and, almost unimpeded now, escaped from the ice at last.

When finally they pulled ashore, they had been rowing without food, rest or drink for five hours. The actual landing place was a grotesquely glaciated, rocky island called Kekertarsuak. It was futile to cross the ice cap there, since it was too narrow and near the end. Temptingly close to the south hovered Cape Farewell, the southern tip of Greenland, and the settlements of the west coast. In that direction was safety, but the failure of the expedition. It was northwards that the chance of success lay. But to reach a proper starting point now meant a daunting boat journey up the coast.

The dilemma had already been debated on the floe. The Lapps clearly wanted to cut their losses and go home. In varying degrees, the others wished still to carry on. Dietrichson advocated wintering on the east coast and crossing the ice cap the next summer. Other things aside, Nansen was afraid of being forestalled. He insisted on making the attempt that year, as planned. He was in a minority of one, but he prevailed.

Meanwhile, upon landing, Dietrichson was more concerned with the 'special meal which, by previous agreement' was to mark the event.

'Chocolate, biscuits, cheese, jam and other delicacies,' he lovingly enumerated:

> In a little creek, on a mountainside, we huddle round the cooking apparatus [and] a hissing sound reveals that the chocolate is boiling.

Nansen was now 380 kilometres south of the point where he had left *Jason*. It would take a fortnight to make good his distance. The short Arctic summer was well advanced; he was already more than a month late. He grudged every moment of delay. After exactly three hours' rest, the expedition got into the boats again.

They were not yet finished with the ice. 'It was very difficult to advance,' as Balto recorded. 'We had to push the floes aside with the boathooks ... Some places, we had to hack our way ahead with axes ... And we who rowed became tired, and we had to land on a little promontory to rest our tired bodies.' By then it was around noon on 30 July and they had rowed through the night.

They had covered 30 kilometres to the north at least, and reached another offshore island called Karra Akungnak. There Nansen called a halt, and took up his diary again.

> While we were eating ... a frugal meal [he wrote], once or twice, among the shrieks of the gulls, I heard another kind of cry that bore an amazing resemblance to human voices ... but people were so unlikely in these parts, that for long we talked about loons, and similar birds ... The cries approached steadily.

Balto seized the expedition telescope, ran up a knoll, scanned the horizon, and shouted to Nansen. Nansen came up and, in his own words,

> soon had the telescope focussed on two black dots darting ... among the ice floes ... see how the paddles go; they are two people (small) in kayaks.

By then the others had joined Nansen and Balto. They all shouted and waved: the kayaks turned and made for where they stood. Balto, as Nansen put it, 'had an expression of half amazement, half fear. He says he is almost afraid of these peculiar creatures.'

> There they come [Nansen continued], the one bending double over his kayak, as if in greeting ... they lay to with a single stroke of the paddles, creep out of their kayaks ... and they stand in front of us, the first representatives of these much discussed heathens.

For both Nansen and Balto, it was a pregnant moment. Greenland was still mostly unknown. To Nansen, the pair of Eskimos stood for an exotic tribe still living its own life, uncontaminated by civilisation.

Balto's feelings were ambivalent. At home he was conscious, as a Lapp, of belonging to a weaker tribe succumbing to a stronger one. But here he saw himself as someone civilised, encountering savages, from whom it behoved him to keep his distance. 'Was the first impression favourable?' Nansen, for his part, wrote in his diary. 'Unquestionably Yes; certainly somewhat wild but friendly faces smiled at us.'

'If we had not met these people in Greenland,' Dietrichson remarked,

> one would assume that their sunburned, chestnut-coloured complexions and full jet-black hair, belonged to the burning sun of the tropics, and not to inhabitants of the polar regions ... But it is not alone in their appearance that these men resemble Southerners; their loquacity and liveliness remind one of them.

When the two kayak rowers approached, 'they lowed like a cow, "Moo, Moo" ', as Balto recalled the scene.

> So then we began to talk to them ... Nansen got out a phrase book and tried to speak with its help, but it was of no use, because we didn't know how the letters were pronounced in their language.

The encounter dissolved into a welter of gesticulation. The Eskimos, it appeared, were going north, facing nameless peril in a nearby glacier front, called Puissortoq. Nansen knew it by reputation; four years earlier it had held up Holm and his companion Garde for seventeen days. In the Eskimo language, Puissortoq simply means 'something that sticks up' but, by the Eskimos, it was regarded with religious awe. A complex ritual was prescribed for its safe traverse. Its very name, for example, was not to be pronounced aloud; or even thought of.

Puissortoq was six miles broad. Glaciers in this part of Greenland are usually confined to the inner reaches of the fjords. This one was unusual in then thrusting out from the coast. Moreover, outside there was no archipelago, so the crossing was exposed to the open sea. Under the glacier's sinister, greenish, crevassed overhanging front there was an appreciable risk from pieces falling off, or even the calving of an iceberg.

The two Eskimos soon departed. Early in the evening of 30 July, after a few hours' sleep, Nansen and his companions followed. Like the Eskimos, as Dietrichson put it, they had

> considerable respect for this glacier ... It is true we do not follow the [Eskimo] rules for a safe passage, for not only do we observe it carefully – and talk on the way – but we even dare to name it by name. Nonetheless, we get through unharmed.

On the other side of Puissortoq, a rancid reek of seal blubber hung upon the air. It was accompanied by a distant chorus of human voices and howling dogs. This all emanated from what Dietrichson called 'a heathen encampment' on a rocky foreland called Cape Bille. It was still early evening. Nansen was naturally anxious to cover his distance. But after his encounter with the kayak rowers, he could not, as he phrased it, 'withstand the temptation to visit these strange people, totally unknown to us'.

Nansen disembarked with approximately the same sensation of discovery that he had felt on peering at nerve cells through the microscope. 'On all sides,' he wrote, 'there stood long rows of wild and unkempt people … pointing and staring at us, making the same cow-like noise we had heard that morning.'

> If to this is added the glacier, drift ice, and a sky glowing red, and finally the two boats with the six of us, who were also not exactly distinguished by a tame appearance, there emerges a picture of a quite peculiar kind.

At first sight, these Eskimos seemed innocent of contact with civilisation. They were dressed in sealskin clothes. Along the shore were scattered kayaks, made in the traditional way out of driftwood covered with sealskin. There were also four umiaks, even more exotic: big, frail-looking craft, also made of sealskin and driftwood. They might have come out of the Stone Age. When some of the Eskimos spontaneously drew the Norwegians' boats up on land, they acted as if they had never seen such vessels before.

The impression of something primitive and untouched was enhanced when Nansen and his companions were conducted to one of the big sealskin tents pitched on the rocks. The inner door was made of seal gut, thin and translucent. Inside, the light came from blubber lamps made of soapstone. The sights and smells – especially the smells – unmistakably suggested men in a state of nature.

Kristiansen and Sverdrup found the foetid aromas overpowering, and soon escaped into the open air. Balto and Ravna were transfixed by what seemed a gruesome caricature of their own, customary Lapp life in the *kåta*, or skin tent, at home. They were prepared – just – to tolerate the fact that the Eskimos went about naked indoors. They even swallowed their revulsion when it emerged that their hosts washed in urine – chemically a sound idea, incidentally, because urine dissolves fat; and soap, here, was still unknown. But when a nursing mother entered the tent, completely disrobed, and proceeded to suckle her child on all fours, like an animal, that was too much even for the Lapps, and they too hurried out into the open air.

Nansen and Dietrichson, possessing a higher degree of stamina and curiosity than the rest, remained longest in the tent. The first impression of primitive, unspoiled people was modified by wooden packing cases used as seats of honour for their guests. Glass beads, moreover, were present in head-dress and elsewhere.

There were about seventy or eighty people in the encampment. Some, it appeared, were travelling south, the others, north, and had met here by chance. They were evidently on trading voyages to and from the Danish settlements around Cape Farewell. Tobacco was what they mainly wanted. Rolls of shag were exhibited as the greatest treasure.

Ravna and Balto found themselves the objects of particular scrutiny. To begin with, it was their high, four-pointed caps – the so-called 'cap of the four winds' – that attracted attention. The next wave of chattering curiosity came when the Norwegians finally pitched their tent and the two Lapps appeared in their sleeping garments of reindeer fur.

By the way the Eskimos fingered the garments the material was clearly a mystery to them. In puzzlement, they pointed to their dogs, or indicated seals. Balto tried to mime a reindeer. That only deepened mystification. The reindeer – itself a polar creature – was obviously unknown to these Eskimos. Their world was profoundly circumscribed. In their own language, Eskimos called themselves 'Inuit', which means simply 'people'; as if no one else existed.

At least one thing Lapps and Eskimos had in common: 'The Heathen,' noted Balto, 'used sennegrass in their footwear, like us Sami' – as Lapps call themselves. Sennegrass is a kind of arctic sedge that absorbs moisture. It is used to keep feet warm and dry in deep cold. What surprised Balto was that Eskimos only gathered enough for the day; the Lapps liked to have a good supply in reserve.

In any case, Balto was grateful when the Eskimos offered him sennegrass, for his own stock was sadly depleted, and sennegrass gradually loses its insulating properties unless renewed.

Fending off the Eskimos' insistent curiosity, the expedition finally managed to retire. But, in Balto's words, 'from midnight the dogs began to howl and bark like wolves'.

> And the heathen got up very early … The women [rocked] the children, who are carried on their backs … to stop them crying … by standing and swaying from side to side, and chanted horribly: 'Hi, hi, hi.' That night, we did not get much … sleep.

The next morning, like the nomads they were, the Eskimos quickly folded their tents. In a parting ceremony, the four umiaks and about twelve kayaks gathered in line abreast, and horns of snuff were passed around.

The Norwegians, meanwhile, had also struck camp and, in Nansen's words, 'the place was soon deserted as, before, it had been full of life'. He wanted to travel with the Eskimos going north, so as to make use of their local knowledge. They too wished to profit by the chance encounter. Soon after starting, they firmly sent the Norwegians on ahead, with their wooden boats, to break a way between the floes. Neither umiak nor kayak, being made of hide, are really robust enough for ice.

The women in the umiaks, using short paddles, moved in spurts of accelerating tempo. The Norwegians, by contrast, plied their oars slowly and steadily. In the event, their overall speeds were much the same.

A few hours later, it began to rain. The Eskimos put into land. Nansen, against their advice, pushed on – a decision he soon had cause to regret. Ice and swirling currents turned the crossing of a nearby fjord into a hazardous adventure. Two days later, on 2 August, the same Eskimos appeared again. Giggling, they indicated that they had passed Nansen while he slept. Thereafter, the Norwegians rowed on alone.

To port, they had the land; to starboard, a shield of scattered islands and a still solid belt of pack ice. Along the sheltered waters in between, the two boats steadily moved each day another sixteen nautical miles or so to the north.

The coast, slowly drifting by, was wild and intimidating and indented by endless fjords. The shores were steep – sometimes with hardly a ledge wide enough to camp, or a haven for the boats. Occasionally, abandoned Eskimo settlements were found, once with human bones strewn about, sinister and enigmatic.

Drift ice, heavy tides and winds rushing down like torrents from the hinterland made even the coastal lead periodically difficult. All the time, Balto, Ravna, Dietrichson and Kristiansen at the oars were rowing against the East Greenland Current, which sweeps along the coast at the rate of half a knot. That meant the boats were pushed back anything up to six or seven miles a day before any distance was made good. One day, off an island called Skjøldungen, Dietrichson 'fell into the water and broke an oar. It was the last whole one we have', Nansen noted in his diary. That meant rowing extra hard, with shattered blades or shortened shafts.

Glaciers now ran from the heights down to waters riddled by grotesquely weathered icebergs from which, in Nansen's words, 'pieces drop down in our neighbourhood ... every day, often so close we could easily be hit'. But on 6 August: 'Woken this morning by *mosquitoes*,' he incredulously recorded. They 'pursue us far out to sea'.

Soon after, the smell of blubber on the wind told of Eskimos again. They were camped on an island on Nansen's course, but reacted very differently to the party previously encountered. 'The heathen had seen us coming,' as Balto told the tale. 'Therefore they fled.'

> Then two men appeared from behind a knoll and ... approached us like the other heathen, saying 'Moo, moo, moo.' One was about a metre tall. We went up to them and asked for dried meat, because we saw some hanging out.

It had, in fact, been highly recommended by Gustav Holm. 'We gave sewing needles in exchange,' Balto continued. 'Then we continued on our way.' Very soon, seven kayaks materialised, and formed up as an escort. One of the kayak rowers 'was handsome,' Balto observed.

14. Eskimo and Lapp

We did not know for certain whether it was a man or a woman, because the person concerned had a chest so big that he seemed to have breasts.

The kayak rowers eventually turned, leaving the expedition to carry on alone. Balto and Ravna were visibly distressed. They had left Norway convinced that Eskimos were cannibals but, having seen the truth for themselves, now clung to them as companions in a barren world.

There never seemed enough to eat, especially after hours of hard rowing. Nansen explained that the food was really adequate but, being concentrated, gave the illusion of an empty stomach. The Lapps especially remained unconvinced. Ravna was silent, but Balto repeatedly voiced their discontent – and not only about food. Eventually, Balto's grumbling reached such a pitch that Nansen, in his own words, 'gave him a dressing down for his miserable cowardice'.

And then the storm broke. He wanted now to tell me everything he had been brooding over ... they had had coffee exactly once in 3 weeks, and as far as food was concerned, they received a miserable helping ... And in addition, to be treated like a dog ... compelled to slave away from early morning to late at night ... he remained inconsolable at having fallen 'among people with such foreign habits'.

Nansen considered that it was 'the Lapps' nomadic instincts and unfamiliarity with submission to discipline' which had broken out, and 'despite a pleasant exterior, often reappeared'. Whatever it was, Balto's outburst subsided and like a galley slave he resignedly returned with his companions to their oars.

On 8 August, the party reached the huge Bernstoffs Fjord. It was choked with icebergs and they had to sheer off to seaward. Finding one berg that was easy to climb, Nansen landed in order to spy out the way ahead. He was surprised by the iceberg itself which, as he noted in his diary, was 'interminably flat, like the ice cap (cannot understand how the ice can reach the sea so evenly)'. It resembled the tabular icebergs of the Antarctic; it was not at all like the shattered forms of the Arctic version. It took a quarter of an hour to cross at the narrowest point. From the edge, two hundred feet high, Nansen saw clearer water, with open leads straggling to the north.

That night, precious sleep was disturbed by what Nansen called the 'horrible musical academy' of gulls nesting in a cliff above their camping place. Nansen and his companions needed all the rest they could get. They had rowed between icebergs so close that the sky was a thin ribbon far above, framed by walls of ice on either side. Once they actually had to go through a tunnel in a weathered berg. Water dripped on them. An eerie light filtered through the ice. Next day, the whole expedition nearly came to grief when part of an iceberg toppled into a channel through which the boats had just passed. That evening, at the edge of Colberger Heights,

93

there was no room to pitch their tent. Instead, they had to lie in the open air and sleep was disturbed again, this time by the thundering of a glacier above. But the ordeal was coming to an end.

The landscape was changing from mountain ramparts to something gentler. They were now in a part of the coast where the ice flowed down to the sea, and it could be approached anywhere. Nansen, however, wanted to go still further north because it would bring him closer to Christianshåb, his destination on the west coast.

On 10 August, clear waters and a favourable wind allowed sails to be set and, for the first time, the team had a comfortable run. They were now in the vicinity of Umivik, at the mouth of a long fjord that conveniently penetrated the land. There Nansen decided to disembark. It was still somewhat short of his originally intended landing place at Sermilik; but time was running out. He was already two months late, and three weeks behind the date on which he had expected to get ashore from *Jason*. Shifting swirls of mist rolling in from the sea helped him to make up his mind. Square sails gently billowing, like Viking ships stealing up on their prey, the boats slid up an inlet and, as Nansen wrote in his diary, 'arrived early in the evening (about 8 o'clock) at our *final boat harbour*' after 'twelve days' rowing'.

> As soon as I set foot ashore, a flock of snipe flew up and sat on a stone; I downed 4 with one shot [and] while the boats were drawn up on shore I started making coffee. (This was the 2nd warm meal in all the 12 days ...)

In Eskimo, Umivik means 'Where the umiak is drawn up on land'. That met the case now. 'Coffee and supper,' Nansen wrote, 'were savoured on the rock down by the boats in the happiest mood; even the Lapps seemed content.'

Since leaving *Jason*, Balto had been pointedly reading a New Testament in Lappish, borrowed from Ravna. Here, on the beach, he grandly returned it, on the grounds that it was no longer needed since all peril was now past.

The expedition had landed on a patch of rounded, weathered rock, with just enough level space to pitch the tent. In Nansen's own words:

> The rock on which we rested was grey gneiss, and then glaciers on either side that ran right into the sea ... In the water swam ... pieces of broken calved ice. It was a mixture of grey and white, the whole broken here and there by blue-grey sky, lead-grey sea [and] a little blue in the crevasses of the glacier overhead. [But we] all had the feeling of having reached a destination ... Of course the most difficult part of the journey remained, but there was something more solid underfoot, not drifting floes and boats which could be crushed at any moment. Inside us there was no grey now.

15

'So Much Suffering'

The boat journey had told both on the men and on their equipment, and first there had to be a pause for rest and reorganisation. To save food, they ate only sea birds, shot along the way. Rain, thaw and leaden cloud supervened, sparing them at least the restless urge for an instant start that clear skies and sparkling snow would have brought on. They concentrated on the work.

Boots, for example, already showed signs of wear. To prepare for the ice cap, protective soles had to be sewn on. Squatting on the rocks like cobblers in a folk tale, the men stitched away with long tarred threads. Each attended to his own boots – except Balto who, as he carefully noted, did the work on Nansen's as well.

In the boats, water had got in everywhere. The steel sheathing on sledge runners and skis had rusted, and now had to be scraped clean. Some sledging rations were encrusted in mould. Nonetheless, to quote Dietrichson, the day might come 'when we would bitterly regret having thrown food away because it did not look appetising'. It was decided, therefore, that all should be taken along.

For five days, the party remained in their camp. On 14 August the weather lifted and Nansen decided to start. On the day of their arrival, he and Sverdrup had reconnoitred the heights. Ruefully, they observed that the ice had gone out, and open water now swept up to the horizon; the whole boat journey seemed to be for nought. More to the point, they found tongues of ice sloping down to the water's edge, giving an approach to the ice cap which, as Nansen put it, 'was so simple that we had never hoped for anything better'. He was perturbed, however, by the abundance both of crevasses and nunataks – bare pinnacles of rock eerily protruding through the ice, like skerries in a frozen sea. To the Eskimos, nunataks were the abode of people who had fled society and acquired supernatural powers. To Nansen and his companions, they suggested, more practically, that the ice cap was anything but clear of the underlying coast, and that hence there would be a long climb before the summit was attained.

During his reconnaissance Nansen had seen what appeared a particularly easy way up, accessible, however, only by sea. The boats, accordingly, were stowed once more and rowed two miles across a bay, but the short cut turned out to be an illusion. From above, Nansen had not seen that the rock beneath was too steep to climb. The crews had to row all the way back to their camp site where, for the last time, the boats were unloaded.

Next day, 15 August, the sledges were packed, having been moved to a nearby ribbon of snow which led to the heights, ready for the start. The boats were hauled a few hundred feet to a sheltered cleft among the rocks, where they were secured with their keels in the air. Underneath, a small depot was concealed. It contained chiefly ammunition for the expedition's two sporting guns. If Eskimos stumbled on the depot it was, as Nansen put it,

> uncertain what they would think of us, who had left all this on the coast; presumably we would have the honour of appearing in their legends as Kivitokker, Inland People, or similar supernatural creatures.

In search of lower temperatures and better going, it had been agreed to travel at night, and sleep during the day. At 65°N they were still short of the Arctic Circle, and therefore without the Midnight Sun. Nonetheless, even at this season of the year, it was never completely dark. At 9 p.m. or thereabouts, Nansen and his companions finally sauntered over to their sledges and started on their ski tour to – as they thought – Christianshåb, in Disko Bay, on the other side of Greenland. It was a distance of at least 600 kilometres.

'Firm going, smooth snow,' Nansen was able to record at the start. Riding on their broad ski runners, the sledges glided with unexpected ease. The climb up from the shore was too steep to haul on skis, so they had instead to trudge drearily on foot; the sledges so heavy that three men were shackled to each. Since there were five sledges, that meant relaying, with the same ground having to be covered twice at least. Even Dietrichson, who had skied the length and breadth of his native land, so chatty under normal circumstances, was silent. At the first camp, nonetheless, he volunteered to go back and fetch a piece of cheese which had been left behind at a resting place. Before turning in, he said, he could do with a morning stroll. By then, they had been ten hours on the march, having climbed around 200 metres and advanced all of five kilometres.

For two days, the drudgery continued. Eventually the gradient eased, and only two men were needed at the traces. The snow, however, became loose; the going harder. Crevasses appeared. On his reconnaissance, Nansen had roped up with Sverdrup, in best mountaineering manner. But now he trusted instead to the harnesses and the weight of the sledges as a belay. Occasionally someone fell through a snow bridge across one of the wider chasms, but saved himself by holding a ski stick horizontally to stop his fall. The sledges, laden as they were, cleared all the crossings without mishap. It was graphic proof that skis really did mean safety in the snow by distributing weight.

15. 'So Much Suffering'

Rain on snow is the ultimate in gloom, and on the morning of 17 August it began to fall. In Dietrichson's words,

> most of us are ... soaked through when, at noon, we creep into the tent, having reached an altitude of [300 metres]. We therefore change clothes ... and have a cup of tea.

The tent lay between two large, gaping crevasses; and they had to wait for their tea. For all Nansen's development of his spirit cooker, it was still maddeningly slow. That partly explained why, since leaving the previous camp sixteen hours before, their only warm food had been lentil soup and a cup of hot chocolate each.

Meanwhile, they found themselves weatherbound. 'Now, while the wind howls ... and the rain whips the wall of the tent,' Nansen wrote on the second day, 'it is an excellent opportunity to repair the gaps in my diary.' That brought him to the end of one volume. He opened the next one by rewriting what he had just written:

> How strange, while I lie here in my sleeping bag and only long for the rain to stop, and the wind to howl a little less, and not tear so strongly at the guy ropes, that I think of ... that distant time when we were drifting in the ice and every day only longed for a storm from land and for the ice to scatter.

Balto and Ravna, together with Kristiansen – 'we three of lower rank', as Balto phrased it – lay together in one sleeping bag. Nansen, Sverdrup and Dietrichson shared the other. For the sake of warmth and saving weight, Nansen had decided against single sleeping bags. Except to cook, or go outside to relieve themselves, they remained packed in their bags, all day long, while hunger gnawed.

When not working, so Nansen thought, a man needed little food. So, as long as they lay cooped up in the tent, he allowed just one meal a day. Kristiansen felt his stomach screaming with hunger, as he put it; but like Sverdrup and Dietrichson, was prepared to suffer in silence. The Lapps continued to complain. Finally, on the morning of 20 August, when the weather lifted, and travel could continue, Nansen granted 'a large meal which would atone for the previous days' starvation cure'.

An all too clear view of Kiatorq, a domed mountain, – 'The trunk' in Eskimo – that like the sleeping body of some monster loomed over the inlet where they had started, showed how little progress they had made so far. Even more depressingly the day, in Nansen's words, began with a 'tour in vain up the nearest rise'. There he 'found too many crevasses; had to turn, rode down on the sledges'.

All day they continued picking their way through a honeycomb of chasms. Then, around 4 o'clock next morning, they found that they had passed the fissured edge of the ice cap, and reached the unbroken surface of the interior. The ice, Balto said, was 'rough as waves on the sea'.

Part II. Greenland

Near midnight on 22 August, the ice cap settled down to long, regular, frozen waves like the everlasting swell of the ocean even when at rest. The weather 'was wonderful, with moonlight and a splendid aurora', Nansen reported. In the small hours, when they stopped for coffee and a little rest, the going had become 'wonderful, the like of which we had not yet seen'. That is to say, there was not a grain of loose snow, and the surface was polished hard and even.

While they huddled round the cooker under the shimmering curtains of the aurora, Nansen proposed to lighten the sledges. By now relaying had almost ceased; however, the load was over 100 kilograms per man. Balto suggested abandoning their Canadian snowshoes, which now were of no use. No use on the present surface, Nansen agreed. But no one knew what lay ahead. He had prudently brought snowshoes, in case of meeting loose, deep, powdery and uncompacted snow, on which skis would helplessly sink. But then, in Nansen's words,

> Balto said: 'Damn and hell, he Ravna is a mountain Lapp, and he has lived for 45 winters in the mountains, and he has never used anything like that, and nobody is going to teach him, old man either; and the same say I also, and I am a Lapp and no one is going to teach us Lapp anything about snow.'
> … these snowshoes, no, he swore a mighty oath, he would never put them on his feet.

This outburst struck a chord in his companions. They had overcome the crevasses, alien dangers that belonged to mountaineering. The view of Kiatorq and the coast had disappeared. They were all once more in familiar terrain. They were longing once more to be running on their skis. Where was the giant ski tour, with which Nansen had lured them on this enterprise?

At Umivik, underneath the boats, Nansen had left a note with a résumé of his experiences so far, and the prospects ahead. All would go well, he had written, 'if only it is cold enough, so the snow is firm'. Those words came back to mock him now. On the evening of 23 August, the thermometer showed 8 degrees of frost. The polished crust gave way to snow which was decidedly not firm. It was fine, crystalline and abrasive. The iron-shod sledge runners slid sluggishly. Hauling became too heavy for comfort. Soon after starting, Nansen stopped and made camp again. After a short discussion, he decided to move instead by day, when the snow ought not to be so cold, and therefore let the sledges slide.

But the change made little difference, for the mechanism of sliding on snow was not yet really understood. Certain remote Eskimo tribes could make their sledges slide even in cold, clinging drift by coating the runners with a thin layer of ice. But that knowledge was still hidden from Europeans. As things were, their sledges would run freely in moderate conditions alone. Nansen could only rue the delay that had condemned him to travel so late in the season.

15. 'So Much Suffering'

On 24 August the new régime began. 'The going was miserable,' Nansen reported.

> The snow became stickier and stickier and deeper and deeper; we sank 4 inches. Besides which, we had to work our way up a stiff incline.

To measure his distance, Nansen carried a pedometer, an instrument for counting steps. That day, it registered 17,550. Each step was half a metre; making the day's run nine kilometres at most. Such figures mocked them all with a vivid equation of drudgery. They stopped at 5 o'clock to eat: on this occasion what Nansen called a 'good dinner with an abundance of chocolate, cooked with the ash tripod, splints and oilskin covers', some of the equipment they were abandoning to save weight.

Now that the rain had given way to frost, every drop of water had to be made by melting snow. Because the spirit stove was highly inefficient, it was impossible to make enough. They were all suffering chronically from thirst, the true plague of polar travel. When he camped on 24 August Nansen tried to assuage thirst with a concoction of snow and lemon juice, which to him evoked memories of *granita*, a kind of lemon sorbet, that he had tasted in Italy. It was, he wrote in his diary,

> strange to sit outside the tent and eat ... *granita* and look at the moon shining over the even, monotonous surface of the snow and think of the summer evenings in Naples when one also ate *granita*.

At five o'clock they stopped as usual to eat. During the meal what Nansen called 'a raging blizzard' blew up. In plain figures, as he also recorded, a 'gentle breeze' of around four knots had become a 'moderate breeze' blowing six knots. In summer, this means what it says: small branches stir on trees; light pennants stream. When the thermometer drops, and the fine, needle-sharp grains of drift snow lash the skin, it is like a sandstorm in the Sahara.

Next morning everything was covered in fine snow, which had penetrated all openings in the tent as it had earlier penetrated their clothes. Outside, the sledges were half buried and huge drifts reached up over the tent walls. A bitter gale-force wind – which at sea means spindrift driving off white-topped waves – hissed over the snow. Because of the drumming of the wind on the tent the general effect was that of a minor hurricane.

'Nonetheless,' Nansen noted in his diary, 'we had a cosy Sunday morning with breakfast in bed.' He was then formally presented by Balto with a pair of finneskoe, or Lapp boots made of reindeer fur. They were 'fantastically warm', he gratefully recorded. They eased the irksome plod that day, through loose drift, in the teeth of the same old wind, and up an interminable climb. For some time, they were faced with a slope of 1 in 4. Again, they had to relay. The sledges seemed gripped by glue. Thirst raged. At one point Kristiansen who, in Nansen's words, 'rarely opened his mouth',

> turned to Dietrichson and said: 'My God, how can people wish so much suffering on themselves that they do this.'

Yet 'good humour reigns', as Nansen recorded that evening after making camp. For one thing, he dug the tent well in so that, as he put it, they had 'a comparatively calm nest here in the middle of the wilds'.

> And the tea kettle hisses over the spirit flame, which casts a strange weak light on our property, but where snow dust whirls round, and settles on everything, and where the moon strives to shine through the tent walls.

They had now reached an altitude of 2,000 metres and after the spurt that caused Kristiansen's *cri de coeur* found themselves on a gentler gradient altogether. After twelve days on the march, they seemed at last to be approaching the summit.

Next morning, the blizzard was just as strong. The time had come, said Nansen, to rig sails on the sledges. He was faced with much 'difficulty and discontent', as he put it. Balto 'swore unbelievably'. Nansen and his friends could no doubt teach him, Balto, something about sailing on water, but only a madman would think of sailing on snow. Less vehemently, the others agreed. Nansen's continued reluctance to try skiing played its part in their sulky mood. For all that, two 'rafts' were improvised out of sledges lashed side by side; three in one and two in the other. One of the sails had to be sewn together out of two pieces of canvas. Yet still, in the end, Nansen found he could not beat to windward. A northwester was blowing, as it had done from the start. It was impossible to sail in the direction of Christianshåb. So on 27 August they changed course westwards towards the Godthåb district, 'tired', as Nansen put it, 'of struggling against the wind in appalling snow'.

16

Eye of the Storm

When Nansen announced the change of course, there was 'general satis-faction', as he said. 'It seemed as if everyone was already beginning to have enough of the ice cap.' He had asked the Danish authorities to send Eskimos in kayaks weekly, within a certain period, to search for him near Christianshåb. He was not expected at Godthåb. Christianshåb however was still at least 550 kilometres off. Their average daily run now was seven kilometres. At that rate, they would be lucky to arrive by the end of October. To Godthåb, on the other hand, it was only 400 kilometres. That far outweighed the risks of finding a way down from the ice cap, with no one to help at the other end. Going to Godthåb would still mean achieving their aim, but without heroics, and well within their power. To the whole party, this made sense.

Nevertheless, as they slewed their rafts round to the west, it was soon obvious that the most they could sail off the wind was when it was on the beam. That meant actually heading well south of Godthåb – a price worth paying as a respite from their toil. Sails straining at crude masts and rigs, heaving over endless billows of snow, the craft seemed like primitive catamarans on a storm-lashed sea.

The snow was so loose that they still had to be hauled; but now with only a fraction of the effort. 'The steps I take,' Nansen now jotted in his diary, 'are gargantuan.' Most of the work was to stop the craft making leeway, so two men pulled each one at the front, while a third pushed and steered from behind. The day's run rose to twelve kilometres, or more, but at the cost of too many thousand troublesome steps. Until they were on skis, nobody could be quite content.

On the afternoon of 29 August, the wind dropped; it was time to haul in earnest again. The catamarans were dismantled. One man was now harnessed to each of four sledges; but Nansen and Sverdrup together hauled the fifth, because it was almost double the weight. At least they could now head directly towards their goal.

The terrain continued steadily to rise; drift snow now lay deeper than before. After a whole fortnight on the way, it was depressing still to be plodding along on foot. It was also exhausting. Nansen, however, still felt that the conditions were not quite right for skis. He decided to begin with Canadian snowshoes instead.

No one had tried them yet and, in Nansen's words, 'the first steps remorselessly sent us flat on our faces'. The technique was the diametric opposite of skiing. For one thing, it involved stepping, not sliding. For another, it involved a completely different posture, with legs wide apart, instead of close together, to prevent the snowshoes, wide as tennis rackets, tangling with each other.

Fairly soon, however, they succeeded in acquiring the knack – with three exceptions. Kristiansen had injured his knee the day before. He quickly gave up and, in a fury, put on Norwegian snowshoes instead. Round and small, they sank somewhat in the snow, but he was used to them. The Lapps refused for different reasons. These were alien contraptions, and they stubbornly declined to have anything to do with them.

Next morning, the snow had undergone a characteristic, bewildering transformation. A thin wind-crust had formed on the surface. Balto tentatively put on his skis. The crust gave, but underneath lay only a few inches of loose snow above a firm foundation. The skis held up; they gripped the snow; the sledge followed uphill on the trace. Balto was vindicated. More, he had become the first member of the whole expedition to use skis on the ice cap. After some hesitation, Ravna followed his example. Then around midday Kristiansen who, in Nansen's words, had been 'mulish' and 're-duced our speed somewhat … finally put on his skis; now things are better'.

Nonetheless, Nansen, Sverdrup and Dietrichson still stumped along on their snowshoes. 'The skiers (Balto, Kristiansen & Ravna),' Nansen smugly observed next day, 'are groaning … especially during the stiff climb towards the end.'

While Nansen was preparing the expedition, he had received a letter reporting a solution for the fundamental inability of skis to climb steep slopes. Waxing, as everyone knew all too well, was still too rudimentary to help. The writer described a ski based on a traditional model, swathed in sealskin, the hairs of which, by the direction in which they are pointed, slide one way, and grip in the other. In the adaptation, a strip of sealskin was let into a broad groove the length of the sole and fastened by threads passing through holes drilled through the ski. This had

> the immense advantage that one can climb straight up any slope … up to a gradient of 1 in 1 without … the use of sticks … Moreover, [in] conditions where you want to advance quickly, it is a simple matter to remove the skins from the skis, and later, if you want, to sew them on again.

Nansen adopted this then novel idea, with modifications. He had skis made of birch, the soles of which, to ensure glide in wet snow, were lined with thin iron plates. A strip of elk fur was let into a short slot in the middle of the ski. This proved an uneasy compromise. Balto, Ravna and Kristiansen found they could neither slide uphill easily, nor secure a proper grip. They struggled, using herringbones, to stop themselves slipping back. It was hardly surprising that they 'groaned'.

That same day they had their last sight of land, which Nansen omitted to record but Dietrichson did. About 10 a.m. on 31 August, he wrote, 'on the crest of a wave',

> we had a glimpse of a little nunatak which, for many days, had been the only dark point, besides ourselves and our sledges, to which we could turn our eyes. Now, this also disappeared. [It was eventually called Gamél's Nunatak, in honour of the expedition's patron.]

What Nansen did note was the appearance, an hour later, of 'a snow bunting [that] came from the west, chirped a little, hopped cheerfully around, and then, with a few merry chirps, flew off again to the north'. And that was the last intrusion of a living creature from the outside.

Their camp that night was the sixteenth since leaving Umivik and, as Nansen wistfully put it, 'very near the summit, I hope ... Our time must come; disappointment has been our lot. May nothing worse befall us.'

They were now at least 2,500 metres up. The following day, the terrain continued to rise in long, gentle waves, the crest of each tantalisingly just higher than the one before. Dietrichson went over to skis at the start, leaving only Nansen and Sverdrup to persevere on snowshoes. In the afternoon they faced yet another stiff climb but, Nansen wrote in his diary, 'there was now a distinct improvement in the weather'. That evening they celebrated with a party. 'That is to say,' added Nansen, 'a modest increase in rations.'

Next morning, 2 September, Nansen and Sverdrup abandoned their snowshoes, and finally put on their skis. After seventeen days they had started their much-promised ski tour at last. An 'endless unchanging snow surface', Nansen wrote in his diary,

> now ran on and on, still [slightly] climbing, like some diamond-studded blanket, soft and fine, in gentle, almost imperceptible waves.

The skiing was 'good [with] good glide, and skis sink hardly at all'. It was 'a real Paradise'. Nonetheless, it was 'quite frankly a little hell to haul'. The others, following in his tracks, 'found it comparatively easy'. Together with Sverdrup, he was out in front, breaking the trail. From cross-country ski racing, Nansen knew all too well the strain of being a pacemaker. As the leader, he felt he had to take the whole burden on himself.

They were all, incidentally, skiing with two sticks, where a single stick was still the fashion. This pleased Balto and Ravna especially. For one thing, two ski sticks had always been common among Lapps. For another, Lapps skied mostly with their legs, because it was there that their strength lay. As a result, they chiefly used their sticks as anchors. A

Norwegian, on the other hand, got most of his thrust from his torso, making him appear to haul himself along on his sticks.

Like a caravan in the desert, the sledges straggled over the snow. They were high and cumbersome, for most of their loads were bulky. The sleeping bags were at least five times the volume of modern ones when packed.

Hour after hour there were no voices heard. The only sounds were the familiar ones of skiing: the shifting scrape or rustle underfoot that told of a changing surface; the squeak of sticks levering in deep cold; the sough of the wind, the hiss of drift sweeping over the snow.

As they drove deeper into the interior, the cold remorselessly increased. But late in the afternoon of 4 September the sky cleared and the thermometer dropped to −18°. At the same time a headwind – WSW – force 6 blew up. On the Beaufort Wind Scale this is classified as a 'strong breeze'. In fact it blows at around 20 knots. Norwegians call it a 'little gale'. At sea, waves are whipped up 3 metres high; in the snow, on skis, the wind is physically tiring to fight. More to the point, the so-called 'wind chill factor' depresses the effective temperature. Nansen was actually facing the equivalent of −50° that day. 'First, nose froze,' he jotted in his diary.

> Noticed it so soon, I massaged it, believe no danger; then throat was about to freeze off around larynx, was numb, but massaged and wrapped in wolfskin mittens + hood; next p. was in the process of freezing.

To ward off this last consequence, he 'was compelled to use felt hat' over his fly; 'then everything was all right'. Such is the distress from which the invention of the zip fastener eventually saved mankind.

Nonetheless, as long as the wind did not blow from an awkward quarter, Nansen and his men were untroubled on the march. The anorak broke its force, as Nansen had intended. Underneath, the layers of wool maintained warmth and allowed sweat to escape, keeping everybody more or less dry.

In their own way, Balto and Ravna coped serenely too. They stuck to their familiar winter garb of reindeer fur. Thus native lore and a modern approach each provided a solution. At night the sleeping bags of reindeer fur – Nansen's own design – kept everybody warm, even when the temperature dropped below 30° of frost. Nobody lost any sleep in the cold.

Ski bindings, ever the weak link in skiing, had much perplexed Nansen. There was now on the market a rigid design with stout leather toestrap, and heelstrap of a thick double cane loop. It gave impeccable control. But it was adapted to ski-jumping and downhill skiing. It was less suited to skiing across country.

Nansen had therefore reverted to a military binding, in use for a quarter of a century at least. It consisted of a leather loop for the toe of the boot, and a pliant leather heel strap with a buckle to keep it in place. This allowed unrestricted movement up and down; also, unfortunately, from side to side. Since most skiing was expected to be on the flat, however, that was a price worth paying. The gain was lightness and comfort.

All this added up to a notable advance on what had been endured on previous polar expeditions. Blisters there were none. The boots themselves complemented the bindings. Sverdrup, Dietrichson and Kristiansen were shod in the Norwegian tradition with lauperskoe, light ski boots with soft leather uppers and thin, pliable soles, turned up like moccasins. Balto and Ravna wore their finneskoe, always used for skiing among the Lapps. Nansen wore his too. As he had discovered, since receiving them from Balto, they had extraordinary advantages. On the march either kind, at any rate, formed with the bindings a unit which, for freedom of movement, it took almost a century for technology to match.

Rhythmically, these men were skiing ten, fifteen, perhaps twenty kilometres a day; but always within their powers and without obvious exhaustion. All around was an endless flat field of white, broken only by the furrowed forms gouged by the wind, and their own tracks in the snow. It was a skier's promised land.

Thirst remained the flaw. Ravna alleged that, because of thirst, he could not eat all his food. He would save his meat biscuits and then produce four or five at a time, slowly nibbling them in front of his companions, who showed unconcealed annoyance.

The days nonetheless passed smoothly, one very much like the other. The huge difference between air temperature in and out of the sun became a conversation piece. One day, for example, the sunny side of the tent was +40° – hot as the tropics. The other wall was –40°, burning cold to the touch. But even that was soon reduced to commonplace. Then came the first real blizzard.

The day, 6 September, began with a 'moderate breeze' betweeen south and east. It was the expedition's first favourable wind for a week. Nansen proposed setting sail but, in his own words, 'that met with so many objections from everyone else that I unfortunately had to give up the idea'. So instead he concentrated on exploiting the wind with his back as a sail. He also thought that the terrain had begun to fall very slightly. When they finally stopped for the day he was sure they had covered 30 kilometres at least.

By then a gale had swept down, turning the plateau into a seething cauldron. It was impossible to discern where the ground ended and the driving snow began. Visibility was barely ten yards. Pitching the tent was a martyrdom. It finally came up but 'there was no cooking', as Nansen said. 'Snow crept in through all openings.' Of those there were many, where the five separate parts of the tent were laced together.

We took some biscuits [Nansen's account continues], liver pâté & pemmican and were glad to creep into bed as quickly as possible and eat it [cold] there and sleep and so let the storm rage as it might.

Next morning they woke to the curiously muffled roar of the wind, and the crack of the weather guy parting. The wall of the tent ballooned spectacularly inwards. Nansen told Kristiansen to reinforce it with various bags. However, he observed that the bulging wall faced east. The wind had backed to precisely the right quarter for sailing, and 'today we will sail like anything'.

So Nansen got the spirit cooker going and, as usual, served breakfast in bed 'which, in spite of the wind, tasted excellent. Then we rigged ourselves ready for sailing.'

> *Balto* was ready first, and crept out of the door ... It wasn't a minute before he came in again, face and clothes full of snow ... almost unable to breathe; the first thing he said when he recovered enough to draw a breath, was: today there'll be no travel.

In this Balto was correct. The tent door was blocked by a snow drift, and in his own words:

> The storm was as strong and thick as running water ... I took a few steps from the tent to look for the sledges. But I couldn't see a single sledge because they were all drifted over, and I couldn't see the tent any longer, so I had to shout to the others in order to find my way. They answered immediately. The tent was ... almost completely buried in snow.

At least that broke the force of the wind. Kristiansen was told to brace the tent externally with extra storm guys; he had to creep on all fours to avoid being blown over. Inside, the tent was reinforced with skis and sticks. Nansen himself went outside with Balto to fetch in food 'so that we could withstand a siege, even if it lasted several days'. Then they all settled down to wait while the wind drummed overhead. For Ravna, used to sitting out storms in Lapp tents on the tundra, it was almost like home. The familiar sweet and sour smell of reindeer fur made it even more so. Sverdrup had by now come out of his shell, and quietly entertained them with a flow of dry anecdotes.

In the afternoon, there was an eerie moment when the wind suddenly dropped and silence supervened. It was the eye of the storm passing over. Then the gale surged from the other quarter – this time right against the door of the tent. Inside, the air was now filled with swirling snow. Somehow the opening was barricaded so that, as Nansen recorded in his diary, 'it was bearable'.

> Now we were really caught like rats in a trap. We couldn't get out if we wanted. Anyway, we made coffee and creep into our sleeping bags, while the wind rages and little by little buries the tent more and more.

17

Quite the Wrong Diet

Next morning it was still snowing, with a bitter wind from the west, but the blizzard had spent itself. They dug themselves out and, at a convenient hour, set off. During the day, the wind dropped, the weather brightened. The snow had the scoured look that comes after a storm. There was a ring round the sun and, repeatedly, in air glittering with ice-crystals, the elaborate cruciform of a parhelion. But the going was the heaviest yet. 'To say that it was like dragging through potter's clay is not saying enough,' Nansen wrote in a dirge-like wail.

> We had to struggle for all we were worth for every single step, and in the evening, when we stopped, Sverdrup and I were thoroughly worn out.

Snow is the arbiter of the skier's world, not distance. Simple at first sight, it displays a promethean capacity for metamorphosis. Its quality runs the whole gamut from silk to sand.

Crystalline when formed, snow must preserve that structure if it is to offer a properly sliding surface. Driven sufficiently by the wind, it is soon ground down to particles which, under the microscope, look like grains of sand. Such is the drift snow, and such the explanation, of Nansen's lament. It was familiar from his own mountains. He was not prepared for its sheer extent, swept from end to end on the wind-scoured, cold Sahara of the Greenland Ice Cap.

Nor was he prepared for the discovery that his own sledge was mysteriously a dud. As a result he and Sverdrup took over Balto's sledge instead, Balto's load being transferred to Ravna's, which those two now hauled together. 'In that connection,' Nansen blandly noted, 'considerable unpleasantness with Balto and the others.' But for Sverdrup and himself 'it was like coming from hell into Paradise & we are now advancing quickly'. And next day: 'Wonderful weather, good going, splendid humour.' This last observation did not apply to Balto who about this time, according to Nansen, had another outburst:

> 'When you asked us two Lapps in Christiania how much we could pull, we answered we could pull 50 kilos, but now we are pulling over 100 each, and I'll say one thing, if we can pull this load to the West Coast, we are stronger than horses.'

Behind this tirade lay a grouse about skis. At 2.3 metres, all were much longer and, with a breadth of 8 centimetres, more cumbersome than those in use today. Balto's and Ravna's skis, however, like Dietrichson's and Kristiansen's, ran more sluggishly than Sverdrup's and Nansen's. This was partly due to the soles; smooth in the one case, with three longitudinal grooves, making for greater stability, in the other. But Sverdrup's and Nansen's skis were also distinguished by being broader at tip and heel than in the middle. This was the Telemark pattern, like a modern ski in fact, which floated on the snow instead of tending to dig in.

Nonetheless, the whole party were now manifestly skiers in their element. Skis and sledges – *pace* Balto – were really skating along. When they stopped for the storm, they had covered over 200 kilometres since leaving Umivik; when Nansen changed sledges, and jettisoned the dud, they were almost half way over.

Various hitches were fading into memory. For one thing, Kristiansen wrenched his knee by catching a ski against a sastrugi. Dietrichson helped it with frequent massage in snowdrift and biting cold. The Lapps – alone of the party – suffered from snowblindness. Nansen had to relieve Balto's pain with cocaine drops in the eye – an early use for this purpose of the drug, first suggested as a local anaesthetic a few years earlier by Freud. Otherwise, they protected themselves against snowblindness and the glare of the sun on snow by red-tinted goggles – and red silk veils, like some grotesque fashion parade.

Periodically, Nansen stopped to fix his position with a pocket sextant; for greater accuracy using an artificial horizon of mercury, squatting down awkwardly to line up the reflection of the sun on its surface. To Ravna, it was hocus pocus.

> You may think I am mad [Balto reported him as saying]. And ... I must have been mad in the first place, because I sold myself to come here for money, but I tell you that we will never get over alive, for you don't know how far it is across because no human being has gone across.'

In the featureless white desert Ravna certainly disbelieved Nansen when he announced that his observations suggested that the terrain was now slightly sloping down towards the west – a fact confirmed by something in the behaviour of the skis themselves. The rhythm of a ski tour settled on the party. On stopping for the day, someone automatically cleared a camping site; others raised the tent, digging it into the snow, and reinforcing with a piece of canvas the windward wall.

Ravna's work was to fill the saucepans with snow. As an old mountain Lapp, he knew what to look for. So off he went, to dig down to the old, compacted grainy snow, which yields far more water when it melts than the loose fresh kind. Afterwards, he crept into the tent, squatted down, and waited passively for the evening meal.

17. Quite the Wrong Diet

It was only after I had set him to this task for many days [said Nansen,] that
Ravna showed so much initiative as to do this sole work without being asked;
but then he seemed to think that his mission in life was accomplished.

The divide between Lapp and the rest, besides all the other cross-currents, dissolved in the ambience of the expedition. It was not only the
touch of melodrama in 'death or the west coast of Greenland', as Nansen
had proclaimed. They were united now by the peculiar spirit of skiing. The
day's run was around 15 kilometres. They felt they were making ground.
More to the point, they were animated by a real sense of being in command
of themselves and their surroundings. Not even the heavy hauling could
quite reduce the days to drudgery, or quench the characteristic exhilaration of a man on skis. Nor could the sensation of never being quite satisfied
with their food that still constantly assailed them.

Nansen blamed this on a craving for fat. He had ordered his pemmican
from Beauvais on the assumption that it would be half dried meat, half
fat, as usual. Through Gustav Holm, Nansen was told that Beauvais made
his pemmican according to 'the recipe of an American manufacturer'. Too
late, Nansen learned that this meant without any fat at all.

Nansen had tried to calculate his diet analytically; the first polar
explorer to do so. Nutrition as a science, however, was still in the cradle.
Nansen based his figures on the experiments of Carl Voit, a German
physiologist who, stimulated by the necessity of feeding the Prussian
Army properly, was one of the great pioneers in the field. With pemmican,
Swedish crispbread, butter, chocolate; pea, lentil and bean soup, liver pâté
and biscuits, Nansen's food seemed to have enough variety. About 1
kilogram in all, the daily ration provided about 4,000 calories per man. By
modern standards, this is between 500 and 1,000 calories too little for hard
work in the cold.

More to the point, the proportions were wrong. It is now accepted that
energy should be provided by about 10% protein, 30% fat and 60% carbohy-
drates; Nansen's diet had respectively 40%, 10% and 50%. This is far too
much protein and too little fat. The body needs more essential fatty acids for
proper functioning; but fat also gives a sensation of satiety which nothing else
can match. Of this Nansen had ample proof as he skied over the ice cap.

He carefully and openly weighed out rations for each man on a pair of
letter scales – even at lunch, in the open, with a bitter wind blowing. He
doled out the butter ration weekly: 250 grams. The greatest pleasure, as
he said, was 'to eat butter in big pieces, without anything else'. Kristiansen
ate all of his the first day which, Nansen primly remarked, 'was very bad
housekeeping'. Sverdrup considered drinking the expedition's shoe polish,
which was simply old linseed oil.

Food had, quite simply, become an obsession. This was exacerbated by
Nansen's belief that, to save fuel, anything could be eaten uncooked; even
pemmican. Still, he took some trouble with the day's hot meal. This was

109

generally after making camp for the day. It might be lentil soup, or just tea, or a stew of pemmican, pea soup and meat biscuits. Understandably, the evenings in the tent, 'when we sat round the stove watching the weak stripes of light from the spirit flame ... and waited for our supper', as Nansen put it, were the 'high points of our existence'.

The worst moments were 'to turn out in the mornings an hour before the others to be cook'. It was not exactly the purgatory of emerging from a uniformly warm sleeping bag into a glacial enclosure where breath froze upon the air, and where from each wall, except the windward one, hung stalactites of rime, easily dislodged, to start the day with an all too bracing shower. Nansen's discomfiture lay in the spirit stove itself.

This was the glaring technical defect of the expedition. Nothing better was available yet. It was as demanding as a piece of laboratory apparatus. So, as the leader, Nansen took all cooking on himself. Because the burner used wicks it needed constant attention and precise adjustment. If the flame was too low, cooking took too long; too high, and there was the danger of explosion. Here, on the Greenland Ice Cap, where the thermometer drops below $-20°$, even petrol will not ignite. But at those temperatures alcohol still vaporises and remains inflammable. The wicks, on the other hand, all too readily absorbed moisture, which made them difficult to ignite. So Nansen carried them in his pocket to keep them warm and dry.

Another serious drawback was that the pure alcohol needed by the stove could also be drunk. That, as Nansen put it, was 'a strong temptation even for the best of us'. Therefore he added methyl alcohol, turning the fuel into methylated spirits and making it supposedly undrinkable. All the same he preferred not to take any chances, which was another reason why he did all the cooking.

Nansen in fact deprecated 'the use of narcotic stimulants, whether it be coffee, tea, tobacco or alcoholic drinks'. He banned drink from his party but, regretfully, not tobacco because 'most people are ... used to it'. So he rationed it mercilessly instead. 'There was no more than a pipeful for each of us on Sundays,' Balto recalled. 'It was a horrible punishment to work without tobacco.' Sverdrup, Kristiansen and Dietrichson felt the same way.

> Sometimes [said Balto] we cut up tarred rope and put it in our pipes and lit up to stay our tobacco hunger. When we were on the move, we chewed a piece of tarred rope as a substitute for tobacco.

Nansen had little sympathy with them. Normally he drank in moderation, but neither he nor Ravna smoked or chewed tobacco. Nansen now felt that, on an expedition, 'too enthusiastic smokers ... ought not to be taken'. His own habit, when skiing, of chewing a bit of wood, had a reason behind it, however. It was an old nostrum for slaking the sensation of thirst.

Nothing now, however, could dim the even days of skiing. Suspended between snow and sky, the expedition drove on. 'Quite good going,' Nansen noted in his diary on 16 September.

Downward slope stronger than ever, 3 big waves down: Notice also by the temperature that we are going lower and more to the West, as the temp. this afternoon is only −17.8°, which is really mild compared with the previous few days, when it was often under −30°. Have had a good, fast march today, estimate it only 20 kilometres, however.

The note of contentment was pervasive. The skis were sliding well; conditions were almost perfect. Even the purgatory of man-hauling was somehow mitigated. The essence of it all was that, whatever the distance, they were never exhausted, and always felt within their powers.

Next morning, Nansen served a special breakfast in bed, with butter and 'good tea with [condensed] milk and sugar'. It was in honour of the day, 17 September, exactly two months since leaving *Jason*.

While they were eating, Balto and Sverdrup said they heard the chirrup of a snow bunting. Outside there was nothing to be seen, but early in the afternoon, one actually appeared. It was the first living creature that they had seen since the other bunting, so far behind, at the end of August. It 'flew over the sledges several times as if it wanted to settle', Nansen noted in his diary.

[It] then flew off in a ... north-westerly direction. Caused general satisfaction, since it was taken as a ... sign of bare land.

They had now come something like 300 kilometres; but he was not at all sure now of his position. Next day, as they skied along, there was a steady and appreciable rise in the barometer. It was the very first so far. In the course of twenty kilometres, they seemed to have dropped about 100 metres. Now they must truly have been on the downward curve of the dome of the ice cap. They needed no instruments to sense this, as the rhapsodic skier's idiom of Nansen's diary suggested:

Went wonderfully today: very much downhill, going excellent, fine soft and absolutely smooth fresh snow, a few inches, and absolutely hard underneath.

Like any skier, Nansen knew exactly when he was fighting gravity and when he was not. The drag on his harness that day was now inspiringly small; on some of the great standing waves in which the terrain was descending, the sledges actually seemed on the verge of overrunning. Meanwhile, a breeze started weakly from the north and west but, by 7 p.m. when they made camp, it had veered round to the east. That evening, for the first time since the beginning of the month, the aurora was seen. Next morning, 19 September, the wind had risen to 20 knots, blowing directly from behind.

Nansen now had no difficulty persuading his companions to set sail – although the work of lashing the sledges two and two 'in the cold was not very pleasant', as he put it in his diary. He was 'extremely worried over how it will turn out'.

> Sail is set; the sledge, which is snowed in, gives a jerk, but does not move; we [Kristiansen, Sverdrup and I] harness ourselves, we give a heave, but the vessel is hardly loose before it is on our legs, and over we go; try again, but that way, no use.

'One man must steer,' he eventually discerned. 'The others will have to try moving under their own power, and keep up as best they can.' A bamboo pole was lashed to the bows as a tiller. It also prevented the craft overrunning the helmsman. Sverdrup took first trick at the wheel. His great passion had always been sailing small open boats in stormy weather off the north Norwegian coast and of that he now had a nostalgic simulation. The slope suddenly dipped downwards even more, the sail billowed full and, to the roar of the wind, the craft behind him swooped over the snow in wild career.

The terrain, said Dietrichson, at the helm of the craft behind, soon became

> very uneven, and the higher the speed, the more the sledges jump, bend, twist and yaw, so that at any moment they seem about to be torn apart; but they stand up to the most incredible shocks. They are light and flexible, and bend to each violent shock, without showing any marks.

That was a triumph for Nansen's design. The sledges were turning out to be the great innovation of the whole enterprise; and Sverdrup was thoroughly enjoying himself. As was his wont, under those circumstances, he liked a little chat; he was pained at getting no reply. Nansen was normally talkative; even Kristiansen answered when spoken to. The sail hid the view astern; Sverdrup shouted to make himself heard above the wind. Still there was no reply. So he luffed his helm, brought the vessel to, and went round to investigate. He assumed his companions had been riding abaft the sail. But nobody was there.

In fact, Nansen had clung to the superstructure for some unofficial ski-jöring, but was soon knocked off balance. Disaster was completed when the edge of one ski was caught in a sastrugi, and he found himself flat in the snow. Kristiansen had more prudently preferred to ski under his own steam, and came loping after. The vessel was a tiny dot in the distance. Dietrichson was astern, somewhere, out of sight.

Nansen and Kristiansen found that with the wind as it was, they were literally blown along on their skis, and soon rejoined Sverdrup. Dietrichson's craft eventually arrived too. Meanwhile, various items had fallen off the sledges, involving miles of backtracking on skis up wind for their retrieval. So now, in the middle of the morning, the little squadron halted, while all the lashings were reinforced.

17. Quite the Wrong Diet

Ropes were fixed to the stern of each craft, so that now those not steering could comfortably hitch a lift on skis. In Nansen's words, 'now it was in truth a happy ski run.'

> After a while Sverdrup had enough of being ahead, and I changed places with him. Now we had several long, steep drops, together with a good wind. We tore on ahead, as if running down a steep ski slope, and it lasted hour after hour.

'It was exciting,' Nansen observed, 'to ski ahead and steer.'

> Above all, one simply must not fall; because if that happened, the whole contraption would sweep with lightning speed over one, and one would fall under the runners, and be ground downhill, and would be lucky not to be broken on the rack ... one had to take care of every movement; every muscle was tensed, skis were kept close together, hands firmly gripped the tiller, eyes gazed unceasingly ahead, one bore off the worst sastrugi, but otherwise one simply tore on straight ahead, while one jumped on one's skis over the tops of the sastrugi.

Balto's view, from the rear craft, was that 'we didn't even have time to eat. It was such fun to ski.'

> It was also fun to see all the slopes we ran down ... As evening was falling, I caught sight of a black mark to the west.

'I gazed and gazed until I saw it was bare land,' Balto went on.

> Then I shouted to Dietrichson that I saw bare land. And immediately he was ready to shout to the others that Balto had seen the bare land of the west side, and he shouted 'Hurrah, hurrah'.

Nansen recorded 'a howl of pleasure' from the vessel astern. It was Balto's voice in particular that was shouting 'Land ahead!' When, through a gap in the seething veils of snow, Nansen glimpsed with his own eyes the tell-tale dark elongated shape, he called a halt, and handed out two pieces of chocolate all round. 'It was our habit,' Balto carefully observed, 'to eat the best food together when we reached a place we had been waiting for, like when we reached land from the driven ice floe ... And now that we could see the west side.'

'Happiness settled on us all,' as Nansen put it. That 'for which we had fought so long was at last in sight.'

> Now we were happy [observed Balto for his part], because there was hope at last of getting over the cold desert of ice, safe and without injury. That was really best of all. If we had been any longer in the desert of ice, I really think something would have gone wrong with one or two of us.

Although night was falling, they tacitly agreed to carry on. They swept downhill, enveloped once more in driving snow. At a certain point they each took a piece of bread 'to chew and stay our hunger while we were skiing', in Balto's words. 'We had no time to stop and eat. We had found a means of transport which carried us faster than we could have hoped.'

> At half past six in the evening, when it was quite dark, we saw Nansen waving wildly to us. And he shouted: 'Don't sail, this is a dangerous place.' And we who were at full speed, found it hard to stop. We had to swing the sledge across, and throw ourselves sideways, for we could see the huge chasm in the ice right in front. It was at least a hundred metres deep.

Nansen dismissed any concern now about going further in the dark. He gave the tiller to Sverdrup, and went ahead on skis, alone, to find the way. The wind rose; sails were reefed so that Nansen was not overrun. Darkness was eventually pierced by moonrise. It was an eerie sight to see the two craft sweeping along, 'with broad Viking-like sails', in Nansen's own words, 'against the big disc of the moon, over the monotonous white surface'.

Even in the light of the full moon, it became harder to distinguish between ghostly shadows and chasms looming up ahead. Probing snow bridges with a ski stick to gauge their strength, Nansen sometimes let the sledges sail over places where the snow broke away under the runners. He was like someone driven now by fear. He had within his grasp the first great geographical goal since Stanley settled the sources of the Congo and the Nile eleven years before. He was about to achieve exactly what he had intended, something granted to very few and for which a price is always exacted. It was almost as if he imagined Nemesis somewhere in the howling of the wind, already in pursuit.

18

'We Are Norwegian!'

In the end, Nansen was brought up by an abyss, looming, ghost-like, out of the shadows. By then, he had crossed the snow line and was menaced by loss of control on bare ice. Even by the light of the full moon he grasped that there was no longer any safe way through. Regretfully, he gave the order to camp.

It had been a memorable day's skiing. They had covered 70 kilometres – as far as the four previous days together. They had touched, perhaps, the limit of what they could safely ask of themselves.

It was the following morning before they struck camp and finally set off once more. The terrain was now transformed from a sweeping snowfield to a labyrinthine, ice-bound chaos of gulleys and greenish gaping chasms among leaning pinnacles, high razorback ridges and eerie overhanging walls, like some viscous cataract. This was one of the outflows of the ice cap, where it fell over the edge in a frozen stream that seemed fixed in time, but which moved imperceptibly and inexorably down towards the sea.

Through this sinister cascade Nansen proceeded to lead his men. Tempted by a long downhill run apparently safely surfaced with hard névé, he and Sverdrup, in the van, threw themselves unconcernedly over. The sledge runners, however, were by now neatly rounded by weeks of wear, and sharp metal keels originally fitted to hold a course had long since disappeared.

In the end [said Nansen], we had to resign ourselves to taking our skis off. So now we went straight downhill, and held onto the [sledges] while we scraped and braked as best we could to avoid the crevasses.

The ski tour was over. What remained was the tedium of getting safely off the ice and down to terra firma. They were back in the nightmarish borderland between skiing, mountaineering and glacier travel.

Twisting and turning, they drove on blindly; on the second day in thick falling snow, hemmed in between overhanging walls of an ice cañon. Nansen was lost, and more worried than he cared to admit. Calling a halt, he took Sverdup and Kristiansen to scout a way out of the maze. A foul filigree of sharp slabs and fissures opened up ahead. Nansen soon 'noticed a little dark patch down below, amongst some snow covered ice ridges'.

> It looked remarkably like water but might be ice, so I said nothing. But when I reached it, stuck my stick in and saw that it was soft, our joy knew no bounds.

Like desert travellers at an oasis they flung themselves down, buried their faces in the water, and drank endlessly in compulsive bursts. As they rapidly discovered, after a whole month of deprivation, they would now have enough to drink.

Even with the imperfect map at his disposal, Nansen eventually identified the mountains round Kangersunek, a fjord running north of Godthåb. At last he knew where he was; and that was considerably north of where he had intended to arrive. So he altered course to the south and, for the next two days, continued arduously to pick his way through the assorted devilries of an ice fall. Sometimes the sledges had to be carried bodily over obstacles and round crevasses. At least the expedition was spared the torrents that had impeded earlier explorers. Because it was late in the season the watercourses were frozen and had turned into highways that simplified travel.

In the early afternoon of 24 September the party emerged onto the final slope. It was steeper than anything they had met before. Driving their crampons with particular care into the ice they painfully inched their way down, straining to hold the sledges in check, and after an unconscionable time were safely down on the frozen tarn at the foot of the glacier tongue. It was a vaguely anticlimactic end to an historic ski tour. In any case the ice cap, as Nansen stoically put it, 'lay behind us for ever'. The crossing had taken exactly forty-one days.

On the other side of the tarn, they finally shook off the dead world of the ice cap and reached bare ground.

> Words [said Nansen,] cannot describe what it meant just to feel earth and rock underfoot, the sense of wellbeing that rippled through us when we felt the heather give under our soles, and to smell the wonderful scent of grass and moss.

Ravna showed his feelings most vividly of all. On his small, weatherbeaten face there was, to quote Nansen, 'at last a happy expression; poor devil, many a time he had given up hope of ever feeling solid earth underfoot again'.

But now there followed the disagreeable burden of back-packing. What could not be carried was put on the sledges and dumped by the side of the tarn to be fetched later. Nansen divided the remainder into six equal loads. Ravna shouldered his, but then added his own duffel bag, containing the

New Testament from which he refused to be parted. His diminutive form almost disappearing under the huge load, he unconcernedly trotted off.

It was a notable contrast to his behaviour on the ice cap. There, he had hauled the lightest load, but complained the most, and always trailed behind. In retrospect, it could be seen that he had merely been conserving his strength. In this he was wise. They still had to reach Godthåb, and that was at least another 100 kilometres further on. Their journey was not finished yet.

They had arrived in a valley called Austmannadalen, which they first had to follow all the way down to the head of the Ameralik Fjord. Over the moraines of glaciers in retreat, through subdued but gradually thickening northern vegetation, they picked their way down the terraced valley floor.

On 26 September, after three long days of hard tramping, they reached the end of the valley; but not quite the head of the fjord. Several miles of sand flats still separated them from open water, but there Nansen decided to camp. They were all considerably uplifted to see old tracks of Eskimo *kamiks* in the sand along the river bank a little upstream – the first indisputable trace of human beings they had seen on the west coast.

They were now once more at sea-level, the realisation of which finally brought home to them the fact that they had crossed Greenland. In his diary Nansen recorded his own characteristic satisfaction:

A difficulty, considered by many ... to be insuperable, was now overcome – was it any wonder that our mood was one of unrelieved wellbeing?

The mood was enhanced by an evening as mild as a September night at home. Some foliage was still green; only the osier leaves had yellowed. In a few days they had rolled back the seasons from mid-winter to the frontier between autumn and late summer.

They were now in a familiar landscape, very much like the Norwegian fjords. So they were hardly surprised when Nansen, having climbed up on a height to survey the way ahead, reported steep mountainsides dropping down sheer into the water. Out of sight, an arm of the fjord was known to cleave the northern shore. To Godthåb there was no practicable way overland. It would have to be by water. Nansen now announced that he and Sverdrup would go ahead alone to fetch help, while the others stayed behind – a course of action for which he had long since prepared.

First, a boat had to be built. That, too, Nansen and Sverdrup had decided in detail up on the ice cap. But unfortunately the sledges, which had intended to use for the frames, were still, with much else, up at the head of Austmannadalen. Early in the morning of 27 September Dietrichson, Ravna and Kristiansen started back up the valley to fetch what had been left behind.

Nansen could not afford to wait for their return. The descent had taken far longer than he had anticipated, and he still hoped to catch the last ship home. He would have to improvise with what lay to hand.

First the tent groundsheet, which would be used to cover the boat, had to be sewn to shape. Unfortunately the expedition's sewing palm had been left behind at Umivik, so the needles had to be pushed through the tarpaulin with bare hands. Worse still, the sun brought a plague of small biting flies. They were even more unpleasant than the gnats on the east coast.

Nansen, meanwhile, had started suffering from a bad headache, which became so acute that he found he could not sew. So he left the work to Sverdrup and Balto who, as he put it, 'were sheer masters [in sewing] as in so much else'. He himself went into the osier brush to cut the frames. Eventually, he found enough branches roughly grown to shape. By evening, the boat's hull was finished.

Next morning, Balto left to rejoin the others up the valley. Nansen and Sverdrup stayed behind to finish the boat. Oars were contrived from bamboo they had brought down with them. The blades were osier forks, across which canvas was stretched. By noon the work was finished. The boat was carried down to the river bank, launched and loaded, and Nansen and Sverdrup embarked with the intention of rowing down the river to the fjord.

But the river was too shallow. Nansen, as the heavier of the two by far, got out to walk along the bank. But even then the vessel would not float. Sverdup accordingly had to get out and wade, pulling it along. Further on, the river branched out into a delta, and there the boat would not float at all. To reach the fjord a portage was required. Nansen and Sverdrup were walking now through mud that sucked their feet down at every step like quicksand. By the time night fell they were utterly exhausted and still had not reached open water, so they crept under a bush to rest. They had left their sleeping bag behind, borrowing instead the Lapps' reindeer fur *peske*. Each wrapped himself and soon both men were fast asleep.

Next morning, after diverse setbacks, they got everything down to the water's edge and finally launched their vessel. Elegant, or even sturdy-looking, it was not. Its lines were those of the upturned carapace of a turtle. It was all of 2.5 metres long, but 1.4 metres in the beam, and 60 centimetres deep. With that stunted length and those proportions, together with a truncated stern, it gave the impression of having been cut off in the middle. Looking like two men in a half boat, Nansen and Sverdrup started down the fjord.

They did not get far that first day of their voyage, 29 September. For one thing, they were following the north bank of the fjord, which turned out to be steeper than appeared at a distance. Landing places were rare, and they stopped at the first one to be found.

'Words cannot describe the contentment of the two savages who sat on the ... shore of the [Ameralik Fjord] that evening,' Nansen wrote, 'while the glow of the camp fire was nearly eclipsed by ... the Northern Lights ... it was as if a gigantic whirlwind broke out over the heavens [driving] flames before it into a spinning vortex of fire overhead.'

Nansen had not dragged his sporting gun all the way over the ice cap in vain. From the boat that day he had shot six large gulls. Two were cooked over the camp fire – the spirit cooker had been left behind for the others – and consumed for supper when they landed, head, feet, half the crop and all. After 46 days' fasting on dried rations they could have fresh food and eat their fill. Better food, said Sverdrup, he had never tasted.

Perhaps in reaction to all that had gone before, they seemed to have lost all sense of urgency. They were, in Nansen's words, 'content just to be sailing on the sea again'. Their voyage resolved itself into a lotus-eater's progress. On 1 October, having covered about 30 kilometres, nearly half way to Godthåb, they were detained by threatening weather at a point burgeoning with crowberries. These they ate raw, as a sweet, after supper.

They rowed on, in a state between a dream-world and a gluttonous stupor. The boat had turned out to be unexpectedly seaworthy, but hopeless against the wind, so when it blew head on they stopped to rest and eat. Also, water seeped in constantly through the fabric covering. It was necessary to bail out every ten minutes, and the only receptacle was one of the drinking cups. Nonetheless, on 2 October, with a following wind, the two men rowed for 20 hours at a stretch.

That evening Nansen and Sverdrup finally emerged from the mouth of the fjord. The following day, 3 October, they rowed up a sound and, late in the morning, were off New Herrnhut, a Moravian Brotherhood mission station just south of Godthåb. A sudden headwind persuaded them to put in there, and finish the last mile or so overland. On the beach they were met by a swarm of Eskimos, 'especially old women', as Nansen said; the first human beings from the outside world since the other Eskimos they had met on the east coast.

Meanwhile, a young man approached. He was dressed in a kind of Eskimo outfit, but had a fair complexioned, most un-Eskimo appearance, topped by a tam o'shanter.

> He came up to us [Nansen recorded], shook hands, and then he asked: 'Do you speak English?' His accent betrayed the Danish tongue.

His name was Gustav Baumann. He was the acting Governor of Godthåb, and turned out to have been in New Hernhut purely by chance when, in his own words, 'The Eskimos shouted Europeans,' and he went down to investigate.

> I first addressed ... the two men in English because I thought they were shipwrecked Americans, but then Dr Nansen introduced himself, and so I was the first of the Danes he greeted here on the West Coast.

119

In Nansen's version, Baumann actually said:

'Are you Englishmen?' To which I could safely reply in good Norwegian: 'No, we are Norwegian.' 'May I ask your name?' 'My name is Nansen, and we come from the ice cap.' 'Ah, I thought as much. May I congratulate you on – your doctor's degree.'

19

Out of Paradise

Having been congratulated on his doctor's degree, Nansen walked into Godthåb with Sverdrup, to be greeted by the boom of cannon. To the sound of gunfire, Nansen had parted from *Jason*; by gunfire he was now being welcomed back to the civilised world. As he came over a rise, all Godthåb spread out before him, shrouded in rain – the first he had encountered since starting up the ice cap on the other side.

From a flagpole on an eminence limply flew the swallow-tailed Danish ensign – a white cross on a red ground. Beneath it small figures bustled round the single cannon of the place to continue firing the salute. Lower down were four or five small European houses, a number of Eskimo ones, and a modest cupola'd church, all lying in a bouldered hollow at the water's edge. The backdrop to the whole tableau was the Godthåb landmark, a humpbacked mountain called by the Danes *Sadlen*, The Saddle.

Such was this outpost of civilisation, the capital of South Greenland, the whole population of which now appeared to have turned out to witness this great event. Most were Eskimos of more or less mixed blood; but their dress was pure Eskimo. 'In their picturesque costumes,' Nansen observed, 'they were splendid, especially the women.' He also noted, among the European spectators, 'the colony's four Danish ladies ... It was odd to see petticoats again amongst all these fur and trouser clad beauties.'

Then the two men were conducted to the Governor's house and there, for the first time since leaving *Jason*, they saw themselves in a mirror. A pair of filthy savages stared back – hair lank and unshorn, faces black with two months' accumulated grease and dirt. There had been no chance of washing since the party had disembarked from *Jason*.

Everything was overlaid by irony. They had hurried all the way over the ice cap to catch the last boat home; only to be told now that it had left before they had even started the crossing.

*

There was no telegraph in Greenland, no cable to the outside world. The first news of Nansen's achievement, reported in a leader in *The Times* over a full column and a quarter, was based on a single letter from Nansen to Gamél, hastily summarising his journey, amplified by one from Sverdrup to his father. Both letters had been rushed by two Eskimos in kayaks 500 kilometres southwards down the coast to Ivigtut, where a ship called *Fox* was waiting to sail. *Fox* belonged to a company engaged in mining a deposit of cryolite, an early source of aluminium, at Ivigtut. She had only stayed on to extend the working of the mine as late as possible in the season.

Nansen's intention, as his letter to Gamél explained, was to have *Fox* wait for him 'so that instead of this letter you may see our sunburnt faces'. Nansen's eloquent note to the captain was in vain. Any further delay would have been dangerous for the ship. *Fox* left for Denmark as intended, without the men, although with at least their mail. According to *The Times* even that was a piece of good fortune. For, the paper reported, the kayaks arrived 'just in the nick of time, as the [ship] was weighing anchor ready to start'.

Homeward bound, *Fox* ran into violent storms and had to put in unexpectedly to Farsund, a Norwegian port at the entrance to the Skagerrak. There she arrived on 9 November, and thence her master telegraphed to Gamél in Copenhagen the news that Nansen was 'over the Ice Cap All Well'. 'At 2 o'clock,' Gamél carefully noted, 'I ... posted it myself at the Stock Exchange. Great jubilation!' From there, as he later wrote to Nansen, 'the news of this achievement of will power was cabled all over the world'.

By 'carrying ... through ... his perilous undertaking', commented *The Times*, Nansen had 'acquired world-wide fame'. Thos. Cook, the travel agents, asked if he would 'kindly favour' them with particulars of his journey, for the benefit of an enquirer who was contemplating the same thing. Alexander wrote to his brother from London, where he was now staying to learn English: 'Here in England, your name is also known. But for me it is not quite so bad as in Norway, for there I was no longer Nansen, only "Nansen's brother".'

In the New Year Marion Sharp, having been travelling in the Far East, wrote that 'only within these last few days I read of the ... successful accomplishment of your great undertaking'.

This joined all the other letters in limbo, waiting for the first ship of the season to depart.

*

While Nansen was sending his and Sverdrup's letters to *Fox*, arrangements were being made to fetch their companions. They, meanwhile, had fetched their loads from the foot of the ice cap, and were waiting at the camp at the head of the Ameralik Fjord, gnawed by creeping doubt whether Nansen and Sverdrup had got through.

At Godthåb, weather delayed the rescue party. To remove uncertainty two Eskimos, Terkel and his brother Hoseas, were sent ahead in kayaks

from a nearby settlement. But more or less simultaneously, and quite
independently, two other Eskimos, called Silas and Peter, were sent out,
also in kayaks, and on the same errand, by the brothers of a Moravian
mission station at Umanak, some thirty miles from Godthåb. Silas was
literate, and later wrote down his experiences. In his own words, he had
just returned from hunting and 'had no wish to go out again'. On 6 October,
after a rain-sodden journey, the pair reached the camp. Having assumed
that all depended on them, they were not best pleased to find themselves
forestalled.

Terkel and Hoseas soon started back to Godthåb. Silas and Peter,
however, stayed behind – chiefly, it would appear, at the instigation of
Silas, who was curious to inspect the Lapps at close quarters.

> We were puzzled by their costume [Silas later wrote down], because it was
> not at all like the costume we are used to seeing on Europeans, their shoes
> were like skates, the toes were bent up ... in their jackets ... the whole lining
> was used as a hiding place.

He further observed that both Lapps and Norwegians were obsessed
with food: they gorged themselves on delicacies sent from Godthåb and
Umanak. So he took his rifle and went hunting for wild reindeer. It was a
Sunday and at home he would 'never do any work on that day'. But, he
said, 'I had such a desire to get some meat for the four strangers.' So he
said the Lord's Prayer, brought down a large bull, and returned with as
much of its meat as he could carry. Balto cooked it over a camp fire.

> As soon as the saucepan began to boil [said Balto,] we started eating. We ate
> until it was empty, then we filled the saucepan again ... We began to forget
> the hard journey, where we had to suffer so much hunger, thirst, difficulties,
> cold and loneliness up on the ice.

Silas received 50 kroner for his work. He spent the money on a new rifle
and hurried off home – by his own account, not at all content:

> I was constantly nagged by the expedition's members to sell the fur of the
> reindeer I had shot, as I really wanted to keep it myself, because it was a
> lovely thick-haired fur, good to lie on in winter when it is cold ... But when
> they came 3 times and asked to buy it, I didn't think I could say no any
> longer.

On 11 October two boats arrived at last to fetch the four men waiting in
the camp. Next day, they reached Godthåb. Nansen was down by the shore
with his camera to photograph their arrival. Towards the end of October
the two kayak men returned from Ivigtut confirming the news that *Fox*
had indeed taken Nansen's and Sverdrup's letters, but could not wait for
the men themselves. They were now, in a way we can no longer conceive,

cut off the world until the spring. For the next few months they would have to make the best of Godthåb.

With the same division of the sleeping bags, Nansen, Sverdrup and Dietrichson were lodged with the Governor, Laurits Bistrup. Kristiansen, Balto and Ravna were given a room together in another house. All except Ravna contrived to make themselves at home. In his broken Norwegian, he complained that

> 'I old Lapp.' [Nansen recorded] 'I not always like those many people.' [Which was] understandable, when one considers that he was a venerable old patriarch, while Balto and Kristiansen were young and full of life.

Like the other Norwegians, but not the Lapps, who stuck to their native costume, Nansen adopted Eskimo dress. That meant sealskin trousers and *kamiks* (high boots), a *timiak*, or short under-coat of birdskin, and an outer anorak of cloth. It was all that was available as a change from the garments in which they had made their crossing.

For his part, Nansen went further than merely adopting local dress. He became 'more and more completely Eskimo'. As he wrote in his diary:

> I live their life, eat their food, learn to appreciate their delicacies, like ... rancid blubber etc. I talk to them as best I may, work with them ... shoot [and] fish ... with them.

In the end, Christian Maigaard, the Dane who had been with Peary on his attempt to cross the ice cap, told him:

> I have now been in Greenland for 12 years, but I cannot say that I know the Greenlanders better than you seem to know them ... after one winter.

In one way, Nansen was merely following the example of the Danish officials. They stood out, among colonial rulers, in admiring those whom they had been sent to govern. They also dressed like the Eskimo, whom they regarded as the one authentic example of Rousseau's 'noble savage'.

Appealing though that was, Nansen also had ulterior motives. His crossing of the ice cap had turned his thoughts to more polar exploration. In his own words, there was a temptation to believe that 'the progress made every day ... raises the gifted white race high above all others'. It was therefore a healthy corrective to

> observe closely the ... inventions which [the Eskimos] have made to secure the necessities of life in surroundings where extremely small means were available.

Put another way, Eskimos were highly adapted to their environment, and therefore must have lessons to teach.

19. Out of Paradise

The waters round Godthåb were open all year round. Consequently there was no sea ice that required dogs and sledges for travelling, which was the case further north along the coast. As a result, the Godthåb Eskimos were specialised hunters of the sea and masters of the kayak. So from them Nansen proceeded to learn the use of this craft.

'As a one-man vessel,' in Nansen's own words, 'the kayak [is] unexcelled.' It was also highly dangerous and unstable. With the temporary help of small outriggers, he learned how to keep his balance.

> Once one has mastered the kayak [he said], one can paddle it against storm and waves without fear for almost any seas. In a storm, it is most thrilling. Like an arrow, one cuts through the breakers ... one is buried, the sea rolls over one, and like a water bird one shoots up again ... not a drop of water finds its way in.

Round the cockpit was a coaming, or raised rim, over which the bottom of the occupant's short, specialised waterproof anorak of sealskin was lashed. Cuffs and hood fitted closely. Man and kayak formed a watertight entity, almost like a submarine. It was a formidable piece of design and, as Nansen concluded: 'If you want to know the Eskimo in his element, you must follow him in a kayak.'

Dietrichson, Kristiansen, Sverdrup and Balto – but not Ravna – all followed Nansen's example. Dietrichson turned out the best kayaker, and the quickest to learn. Kristiansen and Balto actually built their own kayak frames, getting Eskimo women, who traditionally did the work, to put on the sealskin covering.

Nansen absorbed the Eskimos' hunting technique, even learning how to throw their ingeniously designed harpoon. Two Godthåb Eskimos, Arkaluk and Wêleme, recorded that 'He found our language extraordinarily easy to learn.'

> He understood most things ... he would be down on the shore to greet the homecoming kayaks ... we always ... thought of [him] almost like our own kind.

That did not prevent the Eskimos from calling him *nalagak*, 'chief', or sometimes *umitormiut nalagak*, 'the Norwegians' chief'. Nansen took this as a compliment, but it was a sly dig at a hint of vanity. *Nalagak* is always ironic.

The winter wore on, and finally came to an end. The first ship of the season materialised dramatically out of a blizzard on 25 April 1889. She was *Hvidbjørnen* – The White Bear – the regular Danish mailboat, breaking an isolation of eight months. That meant the intrusion of the outside world and, for Nansen, a mound of mail.

'That you got across Greenland wasn't bad,' ran a letter to Nansen from Axel Huitfeldt, his half-sister Ida's husband. 'But if you can survive with equal health the deluge of letters ... newspapers, honours, etc., etc., which is now pouring over you, you will have done even better.' Since the arrival of the news in the autumn it had been

> Nansen here and Nansen there, Nansen, Nansen, nothing else but Nansen, Nansen caps, Nansen cakes, Nansen cigars, Nansen pens, a Nansen March, and so on *ad infinitum*; the only things I haven't seen are Nansen handker-chiefs ... But seriously, when one idiot after the other comes up and asks 'Have you heard anything from your brother-in-law Nansen?' 'Why of course,' I answer, 'we talk over the telephone every day.'

Thus, in his humorous and idiosyncratic way, Huitfeldt was warning Nansen to be on guard against the streak of vanity which had long perturbed his family, and which the Eskimos also had perceived. Ida joined the chorus of concern. 'Please don't be ruined,' she wrote, 'by all the adulation which will be yours when you arrive home.'

But first Nansen had to cope with departure. When on 25 April *Hvidbjørnen* finally began the homeward voyage it was with strangely mixed feelings that the expedition embarked. 'Although we will be glad to return home,' wrote Dietrichson, 'it is also with melancholy we leave the many friends we have made, both among Greenlanders and Danes.' Nansen, he added, 'had long dreaded the moment.'

In Anna Bistrup, wife of the Danish Governor of Godthåb, Nansen had found another female confidante. She was one he would miss. He also recorded the touching words of an Eskimo hunter:

> 'We enjoyed ourselves, we lived together like brothers; but now you will travel to the unknown world out there, you will possibly forget us among all the people, but we will never forget you.'

Such were the concerns of a simple and isolated people. To Nansen, his sojourn among them had been a kind of Eden, where he was protected from the wiles and pressures of the world.

As for Balto, he had fallen in love with an Eskimo girl called Sophie and she with him. But she was already engaged. As the ship drew away, he was on the verge of tears.

20

Nansen Fever

On 21 May, after a voyage of twenty-seven days, *Hvidbjørnen* was nearing Copenhagen. As she approached the Narrows under the ornate silhouette of Hamlet's castle at Elsinore a lone steamer came out to meet her. On board was a small party, led by the Chief Magistrate of Elsinore, a certain Høst. In elided Danish syllables, as the vessels closed, he intoned across the waters to the 'bold Greenland explorers' what he called 'the first speech of welcome' back to Europe.

This was a piece of cheek. Augustin Gamél came out with the quarantine boat from Copenhagen to be the first to greet Nansen, only to find himself forestalled. By this and other pinpricks he was, however, undeterred. The expedition had cost far more than the 5,000 kroner he had originally given but, as he insisted now, 'all extra expenses fall on me'.

> From the day the expedition sets foot on the coast of Greenland, and until it lands in Norway, I hope that you and your men will consider yourselves as my guests.

From Greenland, Nansen brought back a bill for his upkeep of 4,049.60 kroner (£10,000 or $16,000 in present terms) due to the KGH on his letter of credit. Gamél quickly settled the whole account in full. He was hankering for honours. Through his connections he managed to obtain for Nansen the Order of Danebrog, the leading Danish decoration; but for himself, so far, nothing.

Nansen, 'the tall, slim, but powerfully built Norwegian', as one journal put it, 'was the lion of the moment'.

> Journalists poured into his hotel, and subjected him to an embarrassing cross-examination ... telegrams of admiration piled up; he went from party to party.

By coincidence, the Eiffel Tower had just been completed in Paris. Bizarre, sensational and the tallest structure ever built, it was, with its form and design of open lattice work, an emblem of man's growing mastery over space. By crossing Greenland, Nansen was a symbol of that process too. Hence in part the applause.

On 29 May, after a week in Copenhagen at Gamél's expense, the expedition left on the Danish mailship, *M.G. Melchior* – in a cloudburst. At Christiania next morning, in fitful sunshine after rain, she laid to at the quayside. 'Even on Ravna,' in Nansen's words, 'it made an impression.'

> As we approached [the] harbour, and saw the castle walls and quays on all sides absolutely black with people, Dietrichson said to him: 'Look, isn't it wonderful to see all those people, Ravna?' 'Pretty, very pretty,' Ravna replied. 'If only they had been reindeer.'

On shore a Christiania schoolboy, who does not appear again in this tale, was preparing for the day's events. 'During the morning a flotilla of steamers sailed out [with] papa and mama [on the leading ship]. As papa was on the reception committee, they went to meet *Melchior*,' he wrote in his diary.

> A little before 1.30 … I went down to the [waterfront]. Soon the whole fleet came sailing into the harbour with flags on all masts and staffs, and with hundreds of sailing boats round about.

Nansen, he went on, was expected to drive in an open carriage down a certain street.

> I, poor devil, positioned myself there in good faith, but when I asked a constable I was told that plans had been changed.

This was because the restive crowds on the quayside threatened to push people into the water, so a safer route was required.

> I ran as fast as I could down there but pulled a long face, as Nansen had already gone past. Finally, I walked to the [hotel] where Nansen was staying. A huge mass of people was gathered outside. They screamed and clapped for Nansen and his companions. They appeared several times at the windows, so I could properly look at them all. Nansen is quite a tall, handsome man with a rather big face and a pair of white-blond moustaches; Dietrichson is however the best looking of the 6, a dark, energetic chap; there is nothing special about the others. There were huge crowds, I have never seen anything like it; estimated at 40 to 50 thousand.

In other words about a third of all the inhabitants of Christiania.

All this was the consequence of what Oscar II, Bernadotte's grandson, and the reigning monarch of Sweden-Norway, half despairingly called 'the ultra-Norwegian mania for a "great man" '. But, said one newspaper, the expedition had 'brilliantly represented their fatherland' and Nansen had accomplished 'a great national deed'. Like it or not, 'Nansen fever' was sweeping the country from end to end. There were even Nansen fly-buttons. Never mind that those who had pooh-poohed him on departure were now loudest in his praise. He was the first contemporary Norwegian to bring home a popular triumph. The quest for national independence had reached an impasse, and Nansen's success in the snows offered welcome consolation.

After ten days of cheers, oratory and banqueting, Sverdrup, Dietrichson, Kristiansen, Balto and Ravna left by train together, heading north, and finally homeward bound. Their first stop was Trondheim, where they were fêted all over again. But before they finally went their separate ways they telegraphed to Nansen:

> As we shake hands today for the last time in parting, we are united by thoughts of our dear chieftain with thanks for each unforgettable moment from our memorable journey.

In Christiania Nansen was left alone to cope with protracted adulation. From all the rodomontade there did emerge some grains of sober sense. A group of academics seized the moment to found the Norwegian Geographical Society.

Meanwhile, with the expedition disbanded and the plaudits dying down, Nansen had to consider the direction of his life. Dr Danielssen wanted him back at the Bergen Museum – not for his science, but because 'your now famous name ... could help to make [the museum] even more famous than it is'. Nansen declined the invitation as tactfully as he could. 'For the moment I cannot bind myself to any post,' he politely wrote.

A week later he had to break the news that he had, after all, bound himself – to the University of Christiania. He was to be curator of the zoological collection. 'I told them the same as I wrote to you,' he explained to Danielssen.

> But then I was told I could do exactly as I liked ... no work would be required of me ... So in the end I agreed to take the post, at least in name, but I will never be any use, and I have told them so at the outset.

No more than Danielssen were the professors concerned with Nansen's scientific work. They too were more interested in the 'extraordinary journey across Greenland' which had 'spread his name all over the civilised world', as they put it when asking the government to raise the salary offered to Nansen. They got the money, and for Nansen that decided the matter.

The arrangement brought satisfaction all round. The university shared in Nansen's prestige while he himself acquired financial security. Even after Gamél had paid his share, the bill for crossing Greenland ran to about 10,000 kroner (£25,000 or $40,000 in today's terms). Nansen said he was prepared to pay it all himself, but in the wake of 'Nansen fever' a public collection covered it. So Nansen was clear of debt, with an annual allowance of 3,000 kroner (£7,000 or $12,000) into the bargain, and freedom to devote himself to writing the book of the expedition.

But he was not yet prepared to bury himself (as he chose to put it) in the academic life. Three weeks after returning from Greenland he left expectantly for London.

There he found no welcoming parades. He was just one more drop in the ocean of humanity. But unnoticed he was not. The *Pall Mall Gazette*, a sort of jaunty proto-tabloid, reported that he was 'dressed in his light grey tight-fitting suit and the small hat so well known from the pictures published of him'. In a sober throng of top hats and frock coats he 'created a deal of attention as he walked through Piccadilly and Regent Street'.

He had come to address the Royal Geographical Society. 'I need scarcely remind you that in some respects [this] is the most important Geographical Society in the world,' Scott Keltie had written when issuing his invitation.

> Its honours are, as you know, much sought after by explorers ... and while we should be greatly gratified if you would come to us first of all to tell the story of your journey, probably you yourself might reap some advantage.

And indeed the RGS, the oldest institution of its kind in the world, really did possess unique prestige. Travellers were usually flattered when invited to tell their tales at its Monday evening meetings. On 24 June it was Nansen's turn.

The audience assembled in the lecture theatre of London University in Burlington House, next to the Royal Academy. Conveniently across the way from the RGS in Savile Row, it was used as the Society's auditorium. With a capacity of one thousand, it was nearly full that night. One of Nansen's sledges was parked on the platform. The audience was not so much fashionable as earnest, in keeping with the premises. But when Nansen appeared on the platform he was greeted by uninhibited cheering instead of the usual decorous applause.

After what the gossip columns had said, it was no surprise to hear Nansen speak English well. He had a nice turn of idiomatic phrase and a firm, well-modulated voice, in which his native sing-song lurked. A suspicion of vanity might be detected as he surveyed the assembly; also something a shade awe-inspiring. With his height, powerful build, blond hair, blue eyes and evident physical strength he was every inch the marauding Norseman.

The last official British Arctic expedition had gone out thirteen years before. A naval enterprise under Captain George Nares, it was an incompetent attempt on the North Pole from which was salvaged a modest new Furthest North of 83°20′, some 32 miles beyond the one before. Since then, the record having passed out of British hands, British polar exploration had as good as lapsed. It was like an omen of decay. And now this half-tamed man in his Jaeger suit came bursting in, hauling his country into the limelight with himself.

Shortly before Nansen arrived in London, Ibsen's *A Doll's House* had opened at the Novelty Theatre, ten years after its original production in Copenhagen and the entry of Ibsen onto the English stage. 'It was amusing to see the representatives of the British public sitting astounded ... before [its] sublime audacity,' the drama critic of the *Pall Mall Gazette* waspishly remarked. Much the same might have been said of the gathering in Burlington House.

Nansen's listeners had come expecting to be thrilled by a dramatic recital of setback and suffering, as usually presented by explorers. They found instead someone who minimised his difficulties; who wished to appear in control of circumstances; who brought every one of his companions through a hazardous journey without a scratch. That alone was enough to set him apart. What is more, he paid no lip-service to higher motives, so beloved of the Victorians and their immediate successors. To an audience schooled in the Romantic ideal of suffering as accomplishment, all this was distinctly puzzling.

At home there were those who had tried to invest the expedition with a scientific sheen. Nansen energetically disclaimed this protesting that he had simply returned from a ski tour. Or, as one Christiania newspaper cogently put it: 'In the Greenland expedition skiing has scored its greatest triumph.' So it was altogether appropriate that, on 12 June, the Christiania ski clubs gave a dinner for Nansen at a newly opened restaurant on the banks of the fjord. Something sober distinguished this occasion from all the others he had been obliged to attend. The speaker who proposed his *skål* touchingly thanked him for the honour conferred on the clubs in being able to call him 'one of us'. Nansen replied that 'there was no sport in the world – despite the kayak – which could compare with skiing, and there were no circles in which [he] felt more at home than among skiers'.

Ludvig Schmelck, a Norwegian analytical chemist who had helped Nansen to prepare his expedition and was a skiing pioneer in his own right, further amplified the point. Nansen, he said in an article in a Christiania newspaper, had launched 'a new method' in polar exploration which he called 'the sportsman's method'. By this he meant not only the use of skis but also the choice of men. 'Previous foreign expeditions have gathered a large number of heterogeneous ... participants,' Schmelck explained.

> The principle of the new method consists in limiting the number of participants and selecting ... a small, trained group, in which all keep pace with each other.

This authoritatively defined the revolution that Nansen had accomplished. He had sounded the death-knell of the large, cumbrous expeditions of the past. He had demythologised polar exploration.

When Nansen sat down at Burlington House to rapturous cheers, Dr John Rae, his inspiring model, spoke from the floor. He nursed an unconcealed contempt for the cumbrousness and ineptitude of official British polar exploration. He pointed to the evident superiority of Nansen's sledges to those used on the great English government Arctic expeditions. Nansen's lecture, he told him, would 'furnish food for discussion ... among those who have made snowclad mountains, glaciers and icebergs their special study'.

Admiral Sir Erasmus Ommaney concurred. A distinguished 'old Arctic', and one of the British naval explorers excoriated by Dr Rae, this venerable figure, now seventy years old, was nonetheless not cast in the usual mould. He had first gone to the Arctic in 1836, visited the west coast of Greenland, and had often wondered whether any human being could traverse the ice cap. He was, he now said, 'happy in having lived to see the man who had accomplished the feat'. And Sir Mountstuart Grant-Duff, the affable President of the RGS, declared when he closed the proceedings: 'At the age of twenty-seven, to have taken a foremost place amongst northern travellers was to have done enough for fame.'

Away from the lecture hall, Nansen distinguished himself by appearing in his Jaeger suit when presented to the Prince of Wales, later King Edward VII, to the horror of the Swedish-Norwegian Ambassador, Count Piper. 'I told my dear friend and cousin Fridtjof,' in the words of Fritz Wedel Jarlsberg, then a Secretary at the Swedish-Norwegian Legation,

> that to behave in that way was simply not done in England. But he would not listen to me, and only after he had appeared in the same way at a garden party given by the Archbishop of Canterbury, and the newspapers made comments, was he a little chastened.

But this would do no harm to the publicity for his book, when it finally appeared in English. Keltie was acting as his informal agent for this, and introduced him to Longmans. They were the first publishers to take the book.

After briefly visiting Edinburgh to keep a promise to lecture to the Royal Scottish Geographical Society, Nansen returned to Christiania, and a voice from the past. A letter came from Emmy, whom he had last seen five years before when he left her at the health resort to make the mountain crossing to Bergen. Emmy was Caspersen no longer, but Endemann, and living in Königsberg, East Prussia.

> I am only sorry not to have been able to be an eyewitness of my old friend's triumph [she wrote]. However, I have become a German professor's wife, thoroughly domesticated, and the happiest creature on earth.

Another who wrote to him was Emma Gamél, the wife of his benefactor, Augustin, who, with her daughters, had joined the ranks of his female admirers. 'Today it is four weeks since you left,' Emma wrote; 'to me it seems like a whole year.' This was a reference to a visit Nansen had paid to her at her house in the country outside Copenhagen, on his way back to Christiania. 'Shame on you for thinking that I would dream sweet dreams because you were passing by,' Emma wrote, asking him mysteriously to send his reply 'like the last time' so that she could 'enjoy it alone'. This letter she was going to post herself because 'it cannot be entrusted to anyone'. Especially, she implied, her husband.

Her letter was written on 11 August. On the same day, in Christiania, Nansen became engaged.

Part III

Fram

21

'A Hot Affair'

A university professor once told Nansen: 'All great men have had a strong sexual drive.' Certainly a way with women enhanced his new-found fame. Yet he himself once said that he 'never understood women, or rather they never understood me'. In fact, they understood him all too well. Few were bamboozled by the self-confident façade. The rest saw straight through to the little boy within. To the right women that was what gave him his appeal.

Such a person, evidently, was Dagmar Engelhart, brown-eyed, much sought-after, and one of the reigning beauties of Christiania. With her, before his departure for Greenland, Nansen had been having what Professor Amund Helland, his original sponsor for the expedition, described as 'a hot affair'. On his return, he rushed back to her arms. But soon he found himself besieging someone else.

At some point before the expedition left, while skiing in Nordmarka, near Frognersæteren, a haunt of the Christiania *beau monde*, Nansen had met a young woman called Eva Sars. At first he appeared to be not greatly attracted to her. He did, however, take her out skiing once or twice. She joined the women to whom he wrote farewell letters on the way to Greenland with, in her case, the rider, 'as I promised'. She, by contrast, and by her own account, was 'hopelessly infatuated' from the start, and on his return lost no time in playing the old game of pretending to flirt with somebody else.

Before very long, it was Nansen who was infatuated with her. 'What have you done to me?' he plaintively asked in a letter he wrote to her when they were unavoidably apart.

> I don't understand it; everything which had attraction, the beauty of Nature, the sea, work, reading, everything is equally uninteresting ... I am thrashing about like an impatient child.

Perhaps the answer was that she had dazzled him on the ski slopes, one of the few settings in which Norwegians come fully to life and present to each other the best aspects of their divided selves. For he recalled, with touching sincerity, the first time I saw you, on skis, so bewitchingly fresh and forthright. You acted on me like a fresh wind from a new world I did not yet know.

Eva knew all about the affair with Dagmar, nicknamed *Klenodiet*, 'The Treasure', and, by Eva, never called anything else. Eva was 'mortally jealous', as she eventually confessed to Nansen. She felt 'a stab in the heart' whenever she heard the old gossip maliciously repeated. 'That my own, beautiful property should ever have thought of anyone except poor little Eva is so disgusting.'

It was a whirlwind affair. There was a short respite in the middle of that summer of 1889 while Nansen went to give his lectures in London and Edinburgh. When he returned, by way of his visit to Emma Gamél in Copenhagen, he took Eva off alone to stay at a mountain farm outside Christiania. Around midnight on 11 August, he appeared before his half-sister Ida's house and woke her and her husband up to announce that he had that day become engaged to Eva.

Balto was one of those to whom Nansen personally wrote announcing his engagement. 'I hope she will be really kind to you,' Balto replied. 'I know you well, you are a fine man.'

Eva was small, with dark brown eyes and black hair; scarcely Nordic, in fact, and not exactly beautiful. Nansen had never met anyone quite like Eva before. Behind a cool gaze and a forbidding air of reserve, there lurked a veiled glimmer of passion to which he was unaccustomed, and a hint of something else, mysterious and more disturbing still. Most important of all was her independence of spirit. In that she resembled both Dagmar and Emmy. Without exactly being feminists, each was challenging female subjection and asserting her individuality in a more or less conscious way. Ahead of the rest of Europe, Norwegian women were well on the way to emancipation.

Eva, as Nansen appreciatively put it, was 'the best woman skier in Norway'. That was pardonable hyperbole, but certainly Eva was another skiing pioneer. Like Nansen's mother a generation before, she was defying the old moral rescript that reserved skiing among adults to men alone. All women skiers still faced grouchy opposition. In that company, Eva was distinguished by daring to ski alone. As she hauntingly wrote in a Christiania newspaper: 'When I look back on the years since as a sixteen or seventeen-year-old girl I began skiing, the many brisk tours out in the Norwegian winter are the happiest and most precious memories that life has given me.'

When, as I often do, I think about this, I am always glad to see how much better off the girls of our age are in that respect. [I remember] how a few years ago ... young girls, ... often pale and miserable, dragged themselves from one dance hall to the other – it was about the only way young people of both sexes could meet. [But now] young girls ... can move freely through the forest, unhindered by the many prejudices we had to defy.

21. 'A Hot Affair'

In Norway, it could be argued that the emancipation of women owed as much to skiing as to the plays of Ibsen and the feminist movement proper.

If skiing was not in Eva's youth a ladylike accomplishment, music definitely was. The tinkling of a piano was heard in her home, as in middle-class homes all over Norway and elsewhere. Eva, however, took her music more seriously than most. She was a singer; a mezzo-soprano of some talent. She had her voice trained.

By now, Edvard Grieg had been recognised abroad as one of the great composers of the age. Nonetheless, musical life in Norway, like much else, was embryonic still. Christiania had no opera company, no permanent symphony orchestra, no musical academy, and no dedicated concert hall. Eva shared her compatriots' historic urge to break out of a provincial environment and fulfil herself abroad. In 1886, at the age of twenty-eight, she finally realised her ambition, and went to Berlin.

There she was coached by Désirée Artôt, a celebrated operatic singer to whom Tchaikovsky had once proposed marriage. Eva made the most of her stay in Berlin – going to operas and concerts, polishing her German, revelling in café life. In a letter to a cousin she lingered over a students' party, 'where we carried on until 3 a.m. I drank 3 *seidler* of beer – what about that?' It was daring behaviour for a woman in the context of the times. A girl with her 'had a hangover next day, but I was all right. The devil looks after his own.'

Before going to Berlin, Eva had already made her public debut. Soon after her return, on 21 May 1887, she gave her first solo recital. So, by the time she made Nansen's acquaintance, she was an established singer, with a name better known than his.

Eva came from an extraordinary family. Her father, Michael Sars, was a pioneering marine biologist with an international reputation. Of mixed German and Estonian descent, he was by profession a clergyman, but only because it was the one way he knew of supporting himself while still being able to pursue his scientific vocation. To that end also he held a parish on an outlying island off the west coast near Bergen, his birthplace. His wife, too, was remarkable. Also from Bergen, she was born Maren Welhaven, a sister of Johan Sebastian Welhaven, the first poet of consequence in the Norwegian language. Out on the islands, with no doctor or midwife, she gave birth to nineteen children, of whom only seven survived infancy.

Eva was the afterthought. She was born on 7 December 1858 in Christiania, where her father had moved on being appointed professor of zoology at the university. Her mother was then in her forty-eighth year and at first dismayed by this decidedly unwanted pregnancy.

Eva's father died when she was eleven. He had always lived cheerfully beyond his means, and left nothing for his dependants. There was an international collection to help. Two of Eva's brothers were also university professors. Ernst taught history. Ossian, like his father, was a marine biologist, another pioneer in the field, and an early Darwinist in Norway.

Both helped with the upkeep of the family. In fact, both remained unmarried and contined to live at home.

Their mother, who had been forced by her husband's easygoing ways to rule the household with a strong hand, was more than just another dominating matriarch. Among other things, she presided over the only authentic salon in the country. John Paulsen, a Norwegian poet and friend of Ibsen, was astounded, on a visit home, to find 'such a product of refined culture and polished intercourse in my dear fatherland, with its frontier conditions'. Paulsen, who lived abroad, frequented the Parisian salons, so he felt qualified to comment. Maren Sars' home, he said, was 'the influential centre in our young, unfinished capital'.

Yet she herself was a homely, not to say dumpy, figure, swathed artlessly in lace but possessed of a quick and earthy wit. Nor were there servants handing round refreshments. It was Maren Sars who presided behind her coffee pots and cakes. Men and women were segregated in their separate rooms. But there, every other Sunday, Maren Sars, with humour and authority, entertained anyone of note in politics and the arts – with one reservation. The Sars household was Liberal; Conservative dissent was not willingly admitted.

The youngest in her family by a long way, Eva seemed a happy child; the household's 'little sunshine', it was said, and shamelessly spoiled with it. Childhood turned to womanhood, and still she stayed at home. She had various flirtations; possibly an affair with an older man. But until Nansen appeared she had never been seriously in love.

Somebody said of her that she was 'one of the very few people ... who never had a childhood faith to grapple with, and that [gave] her a heathen innocence ... which acted like a refreshing bath'.

> Her laughter was easily aroused, so fresh and healthy behind that unassailable row of strong, shining teeth. What her nature might lack in intimacy was richly compensated by simplicity.

Her music, however, suggested a darker side. A pianist who knew her well said of her singing of *lieder* (her voice was too light for opera):

> Most singers know how to sing light-hearted songs – very few completely manage the dark and the gloomy, those that paint the innermost seriousness and horror of ... the soul. But was it not here that Eva ... was strange and unforgettable.

Some months after returning from Berlin, making a rare appearance in a choral work, Eva sang in Schumann's *Scenes from Faust*. This is a setting of the final part of Goethe's work – less celebrated than the first, but equally profound. She sang Margareta's solo near the end where she is waiting for Faust in Heaven, having been betrayed by him on earth:

21. 'A Hot Affair'

Der früh Geliebte,
Nicht mehr Getrübte,
Er kommt zurück.

'The one I loved,
Oppressed no more,
Is coming back to me.'

To one critic at least, Eva exuded an atmosphere of startling eeriness. For her part, Eva was more than capable of acting out in cold blood a Margareta to match Nansen's Faust.

Although Nansen could not play an instrument himself he was profoundly affected by music. He was also, as someone said, 'seriousness itself':

He could be cheerful among cheerful people [but] behind the happiness sounded a heavy undertone of melancholy.

These, then, were the two people proposing to marry; both passionate, both physical, both melancholy and grappling with careers. Nansen was now the more famous of the two. Eva was three years older, but in some ways less mature.

Marriage was presaged by a conflict of Nansen's making. When he went to Greenland he was a typical agnostic of the age. But his experience among the Eskimos hardened his attitude. He blamed their undeniable ills on the interference of the missionaries and returned to Europe a virulent anti-clerical, not to say an anti-Christian, to the point where he objected to getting married in church.

However, in another of his contradictions, Nansen betrayed the religious temperament. It took various forms. At this point it was expressed in a pagan Nature-worship. He believed in Fate. He denied the existence of an individual soul, but eventually subscribed to the idea of some kind of universal world-spirit shared by all living creatures.

He told his bride-to-be of his wish for a civil wedding. 'By all that is holy, Eva,' he declared, 'I could do anything for you except give up the real me.' And that, he added, he would 'have a feeling of doing' if he submitted to a church wedding.

To Eva, this was consistency taken to extremes. Bigots, she and her family most emphatically were not. Michael Sars, clergyman though he had been, was at heart a genial sceptic. Faith, in his view, was a matter for the individual. In his own case, when faced with the conflict of the age between Darwin's theory of evolution and the tenets of the Church he was supposed to defend, he came down on Darwin's side when his own work left no alternative. His duty, as he saw it, was not to guard religious dogma but to play his part as a pillar of society, keeping the forms of observance and upholding respect for tradition. Eva told Nansen that if her brothers,

Ernst and Ossian, were to get married, '[they] say they would cheerfully [do so] according to the old customs, despite their agnosticism'.

That seems to have decided matters. On 6 September 1889, after an engagement of less than a month, Nansen married Eva, in church, before a packed congregation.

When Otto Sverdrup first heard of Nansen's engagement, he wrote that he 'was so bloody surprised, I thought at first I had read wrongly'. He was not alone in this feeling, for Nansen's dogmatic hostility to marriage was a by-word. But, as Sverdrup wistfully reflected:

> One must take care to drop anchor in good time, as in the long run it is dreary to be like a vessel that drifts about without a course. The thing is to be as happy as possible.

22

The Married State

The day after his wedding Nansen left for England once more, accompanied by Eva. He had to lecture on Greenland again, this time to the British Association meeting at Newcastle on Tyne. There, 'that promising young traveller' or 'great Viking', as *The Times* variously called him, 'attracted crowded audiences, eager to see and listen to the hero of the year'.

Home again, the couple had nowhere to live. There had been no time to set up house. So Nansen began his married life with a return to times past, lodging at an hotel run by Marthe Larsen, the housekeeper of his childhood home. He then moved to a flat in a new and much-admired building in the fashionable western district of Christiania. He had not been there long before both he and Eva discovered that they did not wish to live in a city. Nansen decided to build his own house in more countrified surroundings.

But before his book on Greenland was published, that was more than he could afford. Before the end of the year, to save money, he moved yet again – this time to a wooden shack at Lysaker, just outside Christiania, on a promontory by the fjord where, as a boy, he had hunted wild duck, and where the building of his house had already started.

Nansen's new abode was primitive, and barely habitable. On winter mornings, the water in the pitchers on the wash stand was frozen solid. Icy draughts whirled from one wall to the other. Nansen maintained that this promoted mental and physical health. He was both making a virtue of a necessity and displaying the streak of asceticism that was part of his makeup. In the same spirit, he now imposed a frugal – and repellant – diet of mainly gruel.

For Eva, this was a trying contrast to all she had known before. She had lived sociably among a large circle of family and friends; now she found herself sharing a sudden, self-imposed isolation. Her musical career seemed somehow in abeyance. She also discovered that when, during their engagement, Nansen had written, 'Now you know what you have in prospect; a gloomy, moody man,' it had been no self-dramatisation, but the all too literal truth.

Greenland would not release Nansen from its thrall. Balto had written his own story of the expedition. It was an entertaining little saga from which, after its translation from the Lappish, Nansen liberally quoted in his book for the humour it injected.

Balto, however, was melancholy and restless. Like Nansen, he had been changed by Greenland. At home in Karasjok, Balto complained

> many boys had not been really good to us [Ravna and himself], because we got across Greenland alive, and we have had so much honour out in the world. ... I haven't much desire to stay here in Lapland.

At least when Nansen put on his skis his depression lifted, and he seemed to come alive. The same might be said of Eva. In after years, she talked wistfully about 'our happy days on skis'. Skiing was what they truly had in common. Both somehow appeared at their best loping along on skis, through the sharp winter air.

That first winter, so the story goes, Nansen put Eva through her paces. One day, out skiing in Nordmarka, without warning and without looking back, he suddenly threw himself straight down what in those days appeared a fearsome slope on the Holmenkollen escarpment. 'And dammit, she was on my heels at the bottom,' he would say proudly, when he told the tale. It was then she probably passed her test as his wife – and he, perversely, as her husband.

Some of Nansen's moodiness came from the agony of writing. 'Where language is concerned,' as he put it, 'I feel all too clearly that I suffer from many defects.' There was the sheer effort of forcing himself to drive pen across paper for page after page as quickly as he could. The rush turned out to be unnecessary. Henry Morton Stanley had returned from yet another African expedition to write yet another book. Longmans did not want the two to clash, so Nansen found the English edition of *his* book postponed from the spring of 1890 to later in the year.

It was just as well. Nansen was copious; too much so, in fact, for his Danish-Norwegian publisher in Copenhagen who, expecting a concise narrative, was horrified to receive the head-waters of a long, discursive tome. A new firm had to be found. Eventually, in April 1890, he placed the book with Aschehoug, the leading Christiania publishers. There were to be no royalties, but a fixed payment of 7,000 kroner (£17,000 or $28,000 in present terms) – by Norwegian standards, a sumptuous amount.

The book, which began by being published in parts, was completed by the end of the year, to coincide with its simultaneous publication in English and German. To mark the moment Nansen took Eva out on skis on New Year's Eve to Norefjell, a mountain outside Christiania. The winter's day was short, the snow loose and deep, but Nansen declined to turn back, so the light was failing when they reached the top. They had to ski blindly down in the dark for seven miles without the vestige of a track. The snow had begun to thaw and cling. Where it was too steep to ski they were reduced to sliding on their rumps, and lost each other more than once. Eva was not amused.

Before then, in November, they had visited Germany on a lecture tour. In Berlin, Nansen had an audience with Kaiser Wilhelm II, to whom he presented a copy of the German edition of his book.

To Marion Sharp Nansen remembered to send *The First Crossing of Greenland*, as the English edition was called. Before then, he had persuaded Eva to write to her, so that there should be no misplaced jealousy.

Marion in Japan was still living with her parents, now in Kyoto. 'The outside was so attractive that I looked for great things within the cover,' she wrote, once having read the book, '& I was not disappointed ... You have fulfilled your name of "Viking" more thoroughly than I ever anticipated when I gave it you.' She also wrote: 'I wonder whether you would know me again with the crop of curls gone, & in their place a neatly coiffed head.'

The First Crossing of Greenland ran to two volumes and a thousand pages – this was not an age which subscribed to the ancient Greek dictum that 'a long book is a great evil'. Only about a third of it concerned the expedition itself. The rest covered the winter in Godthåb, the historical background, a disquisition on the Eskimos and, above all, a history of skiing.

In almost two whole columns, *The Times* praised Nansen as a 'book-maker of the best type' who 'cannot be dull'. Moreover: 'Unlike some other expeditions, that of Dr Nansen left behind it nothing but pleasant memories.' That was the theme running through the many extensive reviews. 'We are spared ... the painful interest that attaches to many Arctic narratives ... the horrible details of a timely or just-too-late relief,' in the words of the *Spectator*. As for the *Pall Mall Gazette*, it declared that Nansen told his story 'with a modesty and simplicity which appeal strongly to us after a surfeit of Stanley's Salvation Army style'. This was not only a literary judgement. It also heralded the changing of the guard. Once again, Africa was seen to taint anyone it touched. The Arctic purified. Nansen was a healthy contrast to Stanley's flashy ways.

In England, *The First Crossing of Greenland* was regarded as an uplifting tale of discovery. Elsewhere it was more accurately seen as the chronicle of a sporting achievement and an apologia for skiing – which, after all, had been Nansen's intention. *The First Crossing of Greenland* was really a misnomer. The original Norwegian title, *Paa ski over Grønland*, and the German, *Auf Schneeschuhen durch Grönland* – literally 'On skis across Greenland' – were much nearer the mark. In 1892, a year after the German translation had appeared, it was noted that the book

has quickly ... spread this sport [skiing] in Germany ... Those clubs which propose to organise races for schoolchildren in the course of the ski season must not forget that nothing is more suited to a prize than Nansen's book.

At about the same time a Norwegian ski manufacturer told Nansen that he had just exported his first skis – to Styria, in Austria. In short, *The First Crossing of Greenland* was the stimulus that brought skiing to the attention of the outside world, and launched it as a universal sport. And in Norway itself, it inspired a whole generation of skiers to open up the mountains in winter.

In the spring of 1891, Nansen and Eva moved into their new home at last. It was in high Norse romantic style – all logs, high-pitched roof, and deep overhanging eaves. Surrounded by trees, through which glinted the waters of the fjord, it was called *Godthåb* – 'Good Hope' – after the place where Nansen had ended his crossing of the ice cap. It seemed exactly what he and Eva both wanted.

Eva's mother, however, had shrewdly warned her that in marrying Nansen, she would be marrying only half of him. Indeed, when he proposed to Eva, or so one story goes, he said (casually) that he 'would have to go up to the North Pole'. He was also harbouring another ambition.

In London, at the RGS meeting on Greenland in June 1889, Admiral Sir Erasmus Ommaney had wanted to see Nansen 'attempt the exploration of the Antarctic regions, where a far more glorious field for research was open to his power and skill than he could find in the Arctic'. Nansen needed no prompting. The crossing of Greenland had convinced him that, for skiers, the conquest of the South Pole would be a simple matter. Nobody had yet penetrated the interior of Antarctica but he believed that it too was covered by an ice cap. He expected skiing there to be even easier than in Greenland, because the flat-topped southern icebergs hinted at a smoother surface. Nansen's desire was now, quite simply, to be the first man at both poles of the Earth.

146

23

Planning for the Pole

With the first crossing of Greenland out of the way, it really was now the turn of the Poles of the Earth. Nansen had in fact been asked by a group of Australians to lead an expedition to the Antarctic. He tactfully declined. 'For the moment,' he explained, 'the North Pole [is] of the greater interest to us Scandinavians, and [therefore] it would be best if I went there first.'

To Dr Danielssen, his fatherly and faithful friend, Nansen explained some of his complicated motives. 'I am young,' he wrote,

> and as you once said, there is possibly some of the aspiring Viking blood in me; a too quiet life attracts me not at all, and perhaps in this way I can also serve my country.

To anyone prepared to listen, Nansen had for some time been airing new polar plans. 'According to what I have read in the papers,' Balto had written to him in November 1889,

> you are going ... to the North Pole ... I want very much to be on that trip ...
> It is possible I was disobedient to you, dear Nansen, but I hope it will be better with me this time.

What Balto read emanated from Stockholm, where Nansen had just received the Vega Medal, the main Swedish geographical decoration, named in honour of Nordenskiöld's famous ship. This belonged to the harvest of awards for the crossing of Greenland. It was an early occasion when Nansen's intentions were picked up by the press.

The reports that made Balto write also elicited a letter from Baron Oscar Dickson, a Swedish philanthropist who had financed Nordenskiöld. Dickson asked about Nansen's plans because, as he put it, he might conceivably 'secure the financial side of such an enterprise'.

'My plan for the North Pole,' Nansen explained to Dickson in reply,

> is to build a ship as small and strong as possible ... and of such a construction that it could not easily be crushed by the ice ... With this vessel, we go through the Bering strait ... We sail ... in ice-free water as far as possible, then go into the ice until we are beset [and] drift towards the Pole.

Once more, Nansen was standing a reigning concept on its head. The race for the North Pole had so far been a saga of struggle against the elements. Nansen decided instead to 'take note of the forces of Nature', as he put it, 'and try to work *with* them and not *against* them'.

By Nansen's own account, the germ of the idea sprang from a newspaper article in November 1884. This concerned the discovery on an ice floe off Julianehåb in South West Greenland of relics from the *Jeannette* expedition. That was an American enterprise, financed by James Gordon Bennett, owner of the *New York Herald Tribune* and sponsor of Stanley's search for Livingstone.

Jeannette was the name of the expedition ship. She left San Francisco on 8 July 1879, bound for the North Pole via the Bering Strait. *Jeannette* was soon beset off the Siberian coast, drifted for eighteen months, and, in June 1881, was crushed in the ice near the New Siberian Islands. Of her crew of thirty-three, eighteen perished, including the expedition leader, Lt. George Washington De Long, of the U.S. Navy. It was one of the great polar disasters.

The article was the report of a lecture on the subject by Professor Henrik Mohn, one of the founders of modern meteorology. Speaking to an audience at the Norwegian Academy of Sciences, Mohn persuasively argued that the *Jeannette* relics must have been carried by a current that flowed from Siberia right across the Arctic ocean towards Greenland, skirting the North Pole on the way. 'It immediately struck me,' Nansen said, 'that this was the way ahead. If an ice floe could cross the unknown, then such a drift could also be used in the service of exploration – and my plan was born.'

The idea probably also owed something to Carl Lytzen, the Danish Governor of Julianehåb when the *Jeannette* relics were discovered. 'Those polar explorers who wish to force their way towards the Pole from the Siberian sea,' Lytzen wrote in a magazine article at the time, would be

> beset in the ice. But these masses of ice would be carried by the current along the coast of Greenland. Therefore it would not be impossible that such an expedition, if its ship could survive the pressure of the ice for an extended time, might land in South Greenland.

For his faith in a current flowing past the Pole, Nansen did not depend entirely on this evidence. An Eskimo throwing-stick from Alaska found later in the same area; also driftwood from Siberia – both these phenomena pointed in the same direction.

The *Jeannette* expedition had foundered on the illusion of an open polar sea. Nansen accepted that the Arctic was probably frozen from shore to shore. Hence, as he explained to Dickson, the need for a ship specially built to withstand the pressure of the ice.

23. Planning for the Pole

Nansen proposed 'going right over the Pole from the one side to the other', he went on to tell Dickson.

> In my opinion, it is of little use to try from the side where one has the current against one ... One has to seek a point of departure where the current heads for the Pole, and here one works one's way forwards, without thought of retreat.

In other words, he was once again applying the doctrine of burning his bridges that had got him across Greenland. Starting off from the coast of Siberia, and if 'no unforeseen obstacles supervene', he believed that

> finally (after $1\frac{1}{2}$ years?), we will arrive with the polar current in the sea between Spitsbergen and Greenland. There, as long as the vessel is still undamaged, we will work it free as soon as possible; otherwise we will take to the boats we have brought along.

The plan was 'both grand and brilliant', Dickson admiringly replied. He himself was animated by a kind of idealistic Scandinavian expansionism, in which industrial advance, scientific research and polar exploration would match the wars and colonisation of the Great Powers. Together with another Swede he offered to pay for Nansen's expedition.

The result was a broadside of displeasure from the Norwegian press. For the honour of the country Nansen was advised to spurn Dickson's offer and accept Norwegian support alone.

At heart, Nansen also disliked the thought of sharing national honour again. In late November 1889, the Norwegian Prime Minister, Emil Stang, told Nansen that if he cared to apply, the government would recommend a state grant for the expedition. The following spring, Nansen did as requested. He estimated the cost of the expedition to be 300,000 kroner (£750,000 or $1,200,000 in present terms). For political reasons, Nansen could not be seen to depend wholly on the state, so he only asked for 200,000 kroner, the remainder to be raised privately. That was the limit of what could realistically be expected. There were few wealthy men in Norway, with too many calls on their liberality.

Nansen had publicly launched his plan on 18 February 1890, in a lecture to the Norwegian Geographical Society. The text was the core of his application for a grant. It began by elaborating the ideas he had sketched out to Dickson. It presented a long and plausible justification on the grounds of scientific benefit. The true motive peeped out nonetheless. 'Many people believe ... that the investigation of such inaccessible places as the polar regions ought to be postponed until the development of new means of transport,' Nansen declared in his peroration to the government.

> I have even heard it said that one fine day we will reach the Pole in a balloon and until [then] it would therefore be so much wasted effort to try and reach

the goal. [But] among the nations, at this time, there is a noble contest for that goal ... May Norwegians show the way! May it be the Norwegian flag that first flies over our Pole!

On 30 June 1890 the Storting, the Norwegian parliament, finally debated the affair. Inside their grim, grey building, the deputies talked on for most of the afternoon. Nansen's left-wing opponents oozed social conscience with habitual ease. 'It would be far greater [to] bring happiness into a single poor, miserable home,' declared one notably radical speaker, 'than anything mentioned here.' His supporters on the right-wing, minority government side played on national aspirations.

National honour [as one of them put it] is of the greatest importance for a small country. [It] reinforces a feeling of independence.

And it was unashamedly to patriotic fervour that the Prime Minister appealed, when at last he rose to wind up the debate. Did his listeners really want to share national honour again if Nansen returned in triumph as he had from Greenland? The division, when it came, cut across faction. The Opposition press had been excoriating those, even of the left, who did not support a grant. The good deputies got the point. The grant was approved by 73 votes to 39.

Nansen meanwhile had begun his preparations. His ship was his first concern, for on that hinged the whole enterprise. Unlike previous polar explorers, he could not simply use an existing vessel. As he had told Dickson, one would have to be specially built. What he wanted was a ship with sloping sides and rounded bilges, completely smooth, rather like an egg cut in half. In this way the ice could not get a grip, and instead of being crushed by the floes she would rise safely under pressure. But to reach the ice the ship would first sail via Suez to the Bering Strait, across the Indian Ocean and the North Pacific, so she would have to be a good sea boat too. Also, to navigate the coastal waters of Siberia, she would have to be of shallow draught.

Nansen was told by a shipbuilder specialising in sealing vessels that his specifications were mutually exclusive. Undeterred, he commissioned a drawing embodying his ideas, and sent it to a well-known naval architect called Colin Archer for his opinion. He received in reply a letter of four pages. 'With respect to seaworthiness,' Archer wrote, there was 'no reason to fear that the ship will lack anything in that direction.'

And there, for months, the matter rested, while Nansen pursued his parliamentary grant and finished his book on Greenland. In December 1890, he finally went to visit Archer at Larvik (then called Laurvig), a port on the Skagerrak, five or six hours by train from Christiania. He was met by a pillar of local society. A dignified, patriarchal figure with long flowing beard, Archer at fifty-eight was exactly twice Nansen's age. Like various distinguished Norwegians, including Edvard Grieg, he was of Scots descent.

When Archer was a young man his father, a timber merchant, fell on hard times. To save his sons from penury he sent them to relatives in Australia. In 1850 it was Colin's turn. He travelled via California, unsuccessfully joining in the gold rush. In 1861, after nine years' sheep farming in Queensland, he returned to Larvik a wealthy man and started building wooden sailing ships. Although he turned out a merchantman or two – there was still a niche for bulk cargoes in sail – he concentrated on small craft. They were yachts in the main, but notably a new kind of pilot boat; a gaff-rigged, carvel-built, double-ended vessel, stiff, dry, and quick to answer the helm.

So far, Archer was like any other shipbuilder, responding to demand. What distinguished him was his grasp of theory. In the shipyards up and down the coast tradition and rule of thumb prevailed. In all of Norway at the time, Archer was one of only three men able to produce a design according to specifications. He had a penchant for mathematics and an ability to extract underlying principles. On returning to Norway from Australia he devoured all the shipbuilding literature he could lay his hands on, mastering the wave line theory, a method of designing hulls to minimise water resistance. Using this theory, Archer turned himself into a distinguished naval architect.

When Nansen first approached him, Archer, through his pilot boat, was widely known for a hull design that was fast, stable and seaworthy to a degree, with a capacity to weather any storm. In his larger vessels, he had mastered the art of combining seaworthiness with shallow draught. That was of course precisely what Nansen needed. Understandably, he now wanted Archer to design and build his ship.

Archer was curiously reluctant. For one thing, nothing like it had been attempted before and, as he said, it would be 'a task of great responsibility, whoever takes it on'. Eventually, however, he was persuaded to start the work, and thereafter – the wrong way round – the two men signed a contract. This was dated 9 June 1891. By then, Archer had drawings and the first model ready. 'As far as the construction itself is concerned, I have few reservations,' he told Nansen. 'The worst part is the purchase of material, for which there is little time if the ship is to be ready in a year.'

The ship had to be as strong and elastic as possible. Wood, however, is a living substance, not to be treated cavalierly. The right kind, properly grown and seasoned, was essential. Archer found the pine he needed from a local forest. But the ship would be largely built of hardwoood, and much of this was only to be found abroad.

Summer was nearly over when the rasp of the saw and the tattoo of hammer and axe rang out over the water from Archer's yard at Rækkevik. It was September before the keel was laid, and the frames started to rise on the stocks, like the skeleton of an upturned whale. It was a scene from a forgotten world. Alone among the rocks along the fjord, the slipway might have been the cradle of a Viking ship. The workmen had all sprung from the native soil, with no alien faces to intrude.

In every conceivable way the ship was armoured against the menace of the ice. The keel was of American elm, imported from Glasgow, through a nephew of Archer's in the timber trade. The frames were of oak, grown to shape, and seasoned for thirty years. They were double; each fifty centimetres thick, and closely spaced. Weak point of any ship, the stem was made of three massive oak timbers, one inside the other, giving one and a quarter metres of solid wood fore and aft, almost forty centimetres wide.

'I fear my cash will not stretch to the wage bill on Saturday,' Archer wrote to Nansen one Monday in November, 'and it would therefore give me pleasure to receive a small remittance before then.' The building of the ship was punctuated by such appeals, due partly to lack of capital and partly to the fact that Archer, like too many boatbuilders the world over, did not actually make much money from his yard.

Archer had stipulated that he was to receive a fixed fee of 5,000 kroner (£12,000 or $20,000 in present terms) for designing and building the ship. Everything else – material, wages, and so forth – was to be paid by Nansen as it fell due. It was an unusual arrangement; but Nansen was an unusual customer. Archer felt it prudent to limit his financial liability.

So besides all his other preoccupations, Nansen had to secure instalments on the government grant, arrange the payments for which Archer was politely clamouring, and deal with the minutiae of everyday finance. The ship was to have auxiliary steam power and Nansen also had to order the engines, acting as intermediary between Archer and the makers. That, too, was part of the deal. But above all Nansen was desperate for his ship to be finished and the expedition under way before anyone else could set out on the same quest.

24

'My Lovely Boy'

'You remember always that I will be coming with you to the North Pole? Otherwise, it'll be all up with me.' Thus Eva wrote in February 1892 to Nansen. His answer seemed to imply that she would have her way.

Nansen had gone to England on a lecture tour. He grudged the interference with his preparations; as it was, he had been forced to postpone his departure until the following year. He was driven by dire necessity. He had funds for his expedition, but needed to earn money for himself. Beyond his university stipend, he had no income, and he was living beyond his means.

It was the first occasion since their marriage that he and Eva had been apart for any length of time. Eva had had a miscarriage; and then, at the end of December 1891, a stillborn child. She was still recovering from the ordeal when, after a month, Nansen set off on his tour, perforce leaving her behind.

At the age of thirty-one, Eva was old to be giving birth for the first time. Partly on that account she was prey to violent changes of mood. She missed Nansen terribly, as she repeated in the stream of anguished letters that now passed between them. She was uncertain of her hold on him. Various encounters fuelled her insecurity. She met the man, she frankly wrote, who – rightly – reproached her with having used him as a foil to catch Nansen; she faced resurrected gossip about Nansen and 'The Treasure'.

Eva was sorrowing for the little boy she had lost: 'Why must I be punished so hard?'

> Write to me a little and comfort me ... Tell me if you think we will ever have little living children we can go skiing with ... we *must* have children, otherwise it will all be meaningless.

Nansen was scarcely in a better frame of mind. Without Eva, he was 'like half a human being', as he wrote. He too was stifling twinges of unease. 'The Treasure', in his own words, he had 'treated shamefully'. And then, although he subscribed to the idea of female emancipation, where Eva was concerned, he respectfully conceded, the love that he 'demanded

153

was that of a slave, rather than that of a proud, independent human being like you'.

But that was later. Uppermost now in Nansen's troubled mind was the irksome futility of his lecture tour. Nobody knows the sheer extent of the human misery the modern media have saved. Now, a session or two on television captures both audience and fees. But in the closing decade of the nineteenth century, only a personal, face-to-face appearance would do. Nansen earned fees of over £400 (that is, £19,000 or $30,000 at today's values). But to do so he had to deliver twenty-one lectures in twenty-nine days. 'You toil and moil just for my sake,' Eva wrote to him, only half in jest. 'For if you hadn't married me, you would have had no financial worries ... Now ... you have a wife who wants to go with you to the North Pole, and who you are mortally afraid will die up there.'

Eva had detected the conflict within her husband. He wanted to be free. But an overwhelming need for inner security forced him to be bound, or at least have a woman bound to him. Since leaving Eva on this journey, from the moment he tumbled into the train in Christiania and scrawled a pencilled note, he had started signing his letters to her with 'your boy'. Eva responded by addressing him as 'my lovely boy' and the like.

From Cardiff, after his seventeenth lecture, Nansen wrote despairingly to Eva about 'this smoke-filled prosaic country I have now roamed for so long, and all these dismal modern people without two words of poetry, without dignity'.

> I dream back to the time when Norwegian Vikings [and then] William of Normandy came here and then I dream of myself as a knight in one of these castles, fighting for honour and freedom, and you my lovely Eva are my châtelaine, sitting in a tower.

In Manchester, a businessman called Henry Simon gave a dinner for 'that splendid fellow Nansen'. For his part, Nansen told Eva that he found Simon 'an unusually pleasant and cultivated man'. Simon was actually of German origin. With a commanding presence the equal of Nansen's own, he had made his fortune by, among other things, inventing and manufacturing the first roller mills for flour. He was also a philanthropist who made notable donations to the Halle Orchestra and Manchester University. Altogether, he was one of the Germans who contributed so much to the technological supremacy of mid-Victorian England. He had a grand residence outside Manchester which aroused Nansen's admiration.

Simon was enthusiastic about Nansen's new expedition. 'The most touching thing, however,' in Nansen's words to Eva, was that Simon's children, '12-14 years old, are determined to contribute some of their savings. I really don't know what to say ... it seems to me almost like robbery to accept.'

And just think, [Simon's] oldest son is at school in Edinburgh ... but he sent for him, and he travelled the whole way ... to Manchester, just to see me for a few hours, and then go back to school the same night again ... Verily, verily I say unto ye, such faith found I not in Israel.

By the middle of February Eva had more or less recovered from the shock of the still birth, physically at least. Nansen pleaded with her to join him now. She adduced plausible reasons for not doing so. For one thing, she had started to take singing pupils again which, as she proudly wrote, helped with the housekeeping.

Perversely, it was almost as if they could only converse frankly now when apart. Face to face, they seemed to hide their thoughts; only on paper could they reveal what they truly felt. 'It is a wonderful home [your family] has,' Nansen wrote to Eva from Bristol.

I am so grateful to have become a member. Nowhere else in the world have I felt at ease among people as I do there.

To Eva, this came out of the blue. She replied: 'It was so lovely to read what you wrote about your pleasure at having become a member of our family.' That was after nearly two and a half years of marriage.

And then I am so glad that you are so fond of Mother ... I had to say a little about this to [her]. She became so radiantly happy, she nurses a great love for you, and considers you far above all other people.

Maren Sars' attitude was in reality not quite so simple. At the outset, Eva's mother had privately disapproved of the match. Nansen's unbounded self-assurance, his eccentricity of dress – the Jaeger suit was still much in evidence – his argumentativeness, his dislike of compromise, had caused his future mother-in-law great concern. Added to which, she had disliked the idea of the new expedition from the start.

But gradually her attitude had mellowed. To begin with, Nansen turned out to be an ornament to her intellectual gatherings. When Edvard Grieg met him at one of these functions, he 'acquired a great admiration for Nansen', who was, as Grieg put it:

something entirely different from a mere sportsman and adventurer. He must have gone through a unique development. Which one can see immediately from his look – strange as that may sound. He is a considerable philosopher, and has a store of knowledge which is quite rare. But what is particularly rare is that these qualities are to be found in a man who, despite all his obvious self-confidence, is nonetheless of a sound, frank, undemanding and modest character.

Eva's brothers, Ernst and Ossian, had begun by sharing their mother's reservations. Ernst had gradually warmed to Nansen. Ossian never did.

'Ossian is so good,' Eva now pleaded with Nansen in one of her letters, while he was still in England, 'I could wish that you would like him really well.'

By early March, Nansen was home again. Together at Easter, they went skiing across Hardangervidda. It was Nansen's old playground, but Eva had not been there before. 'Shall we not be newly married,' Eva had written at the prospect, 'and have our honeymoon [there]?'

With this trip Eva became one of the first women to go ski-touring. Earlier, while Nansen was still in London, she had devised a revolutionary skiing costume, made out of grey material, which she inaugurated on a local ski track. One of the young men who witnessed the event was, as Eva put it, 'a little horrified. [But] he thought I was a martyr to the good cause.' His 'horror' was caused by Eva's trousers. Up to this moment, women were generally allowed to ski in trousers, but were expected to wear long skirts over the top. Eva now appeared wearing a short skirt, like a Lapp, with her trousered legs protruding free. This made skiing easier, but it required temerity to appear in public thus clad. But her friend 'believed that in 10 years the ladies would follow my example'.

Up in the snows Nansen and Eva enjoyed a rare moment of unalloyed contentment. Easter was celebrated late that year, shortly after the middle of April. But on the heights of Hardangervidda it was still full winter, and the skiing was good.

25

A Most Peculiar Hull

In London, meanwhile, Clements Markham, C.B., a past Secretary of the RGS and soon to be elected Vice President, proposed that '£300 be granted towards ... Nansen's expedition into the unknown polar regions'. Markham was campaigning to renew British polar exploration, then in the doldrums, and this was partly a ruse to shame his own countrymen into action. Nansen, whom he had first met three years earlier in Copenhagen, after the crossing of Greenland, and who struck him as 'a very fine young fellow ... in his travelling dress, tall and handsome', was exactly the icon to exploit.

The RGS Council agreed, and on 11 April 1892 made the grant. But the news, which Markham wrote the same day to convey to him, put Nansen in a quandary. He was greatly touched, and certainly still needed every penny he could get. But foreign money might offend nationalist sentiment. He replied that he would first have to consult the Norwegian government and the Expedition Committee – a small fund-raising and accounting body recently formed at his own urgent instigation.

In the end, nobody minded a modest donation from abroad and Nansen, with a clear conscience, was able to accept the RGS grant. Markham, an inveterate traveller and a considerable Scandinavian scholar, came across from England in the middle of July to view the ship. Nansen took him down to Larvik for the day: 'Nine hours of railway,' in Markham's words, 'rendered pleasant by ... Nansen's unflagging conversation the whole way.'

What Markham saw, now nearing completion, was a most peculiar hull. To begin with, it was stubby; 128 feet (31.5 metres) overall, and 36 feet (11 metres) beam; a ratio, in other words, of little more than three to one. Even odder were the lines. When complete, the vessel was to be around 400 gross register tons. Yet the structure on the stocks seemed curiously not that of a full-sized ship but a scaled-up model of some small boat. The causes of this singular illusion were the round bilges, the equal sharpness of stem and stern making the craft a double-ender and the curved, cockleshell shape. All these features were to prevent the ice from getting a grip, but also characterised Archer's pilot cutters. A further oddity was a long half-deck and an extended poop, hinting at the shape of a shoe.

157

As Colin Archer himself put it, the purpose of this vessel 'was so totally different to that of any ordinary ship' that 'the established rules and regulations for shipbuilding' were of no help, and he had been thrown on his own resources.

The deck was of Norwegian pine, with pitch pine for the inner lining of the sides. The outside planking was double and of oak. Extra protection was provided by a thick outer ice sheathing of greenheart – a South American hardwood (*Nectandra rodiaei*) specially resistant to splintering, and hence to abrasion by the pack ice. To prevent decay the space between the inner and outer planking was filled with a witches' brew of coal tar, pine pitch and sawdust, boiled up and poured in hot to set in place. That gave the ship's sides a massive, compact thickness of around 30 inches (75 centimetres). A spiderweb of diagonal braces reinforced the hull internally. Elasticity, however, was as important as sheer structural strength. The cross beams, for example, were fixed to the ship's sides by white pine knees, each made from the root and stem of a single tree, grown to shape.

In the pack ice, a ship's stern is the weak point. To overcome this, Archer had contrived a double sternpost, with a well in between, through which rudder and propeller could be easily raised to safety, and as easily replaced, as ice conditions required. Markham, untroubled by the vessel's eccentric appearance, returned to London full of admration. The ship, he said, was 'strengthened in every way that can be devised'.

Other aspects of the design were preoccupying Nansen. The ship was to be the expedition's home for years in a polar climate. Proper insulation was vital. Only natural materials were then known. Nansen finally settled for triple insulation of all living space, achieved by three layers of light panelling, with gaps between. Two of the gaps were filled with cork shavings, reindeer hairs and thick felt; the third was left empty as an air jacket. Doors were insulated with reindeer hairs, and the sills were 15 inches (40 centimetres) high, to stop cold air pouring in.

It wasn't only the ship that had to be considered. To reach the Pole, or merely to survive, Nansen had to plan for snow and ice travel too. Polar equipment was still not available ready made. Again, Nansen had to order what he wanted specially, and himself deal with the design. The lessons from the crossing of Greenland he faithfully proceeded to apply. He modified his sledge, for example, by having convex runners to reduce drag and make turning easier. Much, however, had to come from abroad, and Nansen profited from the rapid technical advances of the age.

In late September 1892, meanwhile, Robert E. Peary returned from another expedition to Greenland. Josephine Peary had gone with him; the first polar explorer's wife to accompany her husband in the field. Peary himself had crossed the Greenland Ice Cap to the north. His journey from McCormick Bay to Independence Bay and back – a distance of over 2,000 kilometres – was almost four times the length of Nansen's one-way crossing. It was, by any standards, an historic performance. Nansen wrote off to Peary with a barrage of enquiries.

To begin with, Nansen was interested in Peary's sledge. He also wanted to know if Peary had any experience with aluminium, then just coming into use; also what food he had used. New concentrated foods were beginning to appear, the result primarily of advances in chemistry and a medical fad for a high protein diet.

Peary eventually replied that he stuck to pemmican as his staple diet and that his sledge was based on Nansen's model. His letter was curt and reserved. He saw Nansen as a deadly rival. He was consumed by resentment towards the man who, as he considered, had forestalled him in the first crossing of Greenland, and robbed him of his rightful due. According to one story, when Nansen's news came through, Peary 'shocked his wife by coming home looking, as she said, "as if he had just seen someone die" '. Peary believed that his reconnaissance of the ice cap in 1886 had given him a prescriptive right to priority in crossing. That brought about a lasting bitterness which turned Peary's life into a polar obsession and hence changed the course of history.

Peary had crossed Greenland with dogs and sledges. It was about that which Nansen wanted, most of all, to know. Nansen was determined to use dogs this time on any sledging of his own. Still, he had not yet driven dogs himself. As it turned out, on 1 November, long before Peary's letter arrived, Eivind Astrup came home.

Astrup had been Peary's sole companion on the crossing of the Greenland Ice Cap; without him, the journey would probably have ended in disaster. Just turned twenty-one, Astrup was a Norwegian from Christiania. He had been visiting America, and happened to be in Philadelphia where his elder brother lived, at the same time as Peary was fitting out his expedition there. He applied to join Peary on a whim. He was among the five candidates finally selected, another being the later so controversial Dr Frederick A. Cook.

From Peary's point of view, Astrup was supremely qualified. Though short, he was well built and athletic. Footballer, oarsman and speed skater, he was pre-eminently a skier. When Astrup came home to an ecstatic, patriotic welcome Nansen made it his business to meet him and, among other things, hear what he had to say about sledge dogs.

From the Eskimos themselves, Astrup had learned how to deal with dogs. The 'hardiness and toughness' of the North Greenland Eskimos, he once said, 'applies in even a higher degree to their faithful dogs'.

The fatigue and the privation that they can endure really borders upon the incredible ... That there is no lack of intelligence in the [Eskimo] dog is especially apparent in their capacity as thieves ...

'Were it not for these remarkable animals,' he summed up, he and Peary 'would never have completed [our] journey.'

Wednesday 26 October 1892 meanwhile was set for the launch of Nansen's ship, and on the eve he arrived in Larvik to oversee the final details. Next day, by train from Christiania, came the specially invited guests. There were more than a hundred, among them one of Nansen's old colleagues in neuroscience, Gustav Retzius, a dishevelled-looking Swede who touched life at many points. He was also a considerable journalist. In a piece for *Aftonbladet*, the Stockholm newspaper of which he once was Editor, he wrote that he had arrived in Larvik in the 'pleasant company [of] doctors and professors, consuls and businessmen, artists, journalists and sportsmen'. They were met at the station by Nansen and, almost in an echo of Clements Markham, Retzius continued:

> [He] welcomed us in his open, unaffected and winning manner, dressed as usual in his peculiar dark blue casual [Jaeger] suit, and characteristic small, low-crowned hat.
>
> Yes, there he stood before us, Fridtjof Nansen, that typical, youthful representative of the Nordic race [with his] tall, manly, slim yet lithe figure, his blond hair, and his blue, strangely flashing and charming, thoughtful eyes.

Snow had fallen during the night. A 'thin, white veil' covered the rocky, undulating banks of the fjord. The sun shone 'with the strange, subdued gleam that belongs to clear winter days'. All the guests hurried on board a whalecatcher, complete with crow's nest, chartered to take them across the fjord to Archer's yard. On the slipway, Nansen's ship hove into sight, 'black below, all white above'.

> It was an appealing sight that met our eyes. Thousands of people had gathered here ... to be present at the solemn act about to he performed. Thousands had ... climbed on to the surrounding snow-clad heights, forming by their ranks, as it were, garland upon garland.

'From the vessel's deck rises a trio of flagstaffs, from two of which are flying the [Swedish-Norwegian] Union Flag. The middle one is still empty, but on that, during the act of launching, will be raised the flag with the ship's as yet unknown name.' At 2 p.m. Nansen and Eva 'mount a stand erected at the bows'.

> Mrs Nansen steps forward to the stem and as, with a powerful blow, she breaks on it a bottle of champagne she holds in her hand, she – a well-known singer – declares in a loud, clear voice: '*Fram* shall be her name!'

Fram means 'Forwards'. The usual Danish-Norwegian form was *Frem*. *Fram*, however, was a very Norwegian variant, more sonorous than *Frem* and unexpected into the bargain. White letters on a red ground, *Fram*'s name pennant was broken on the empty flagstaff.

Now the final blocks and chains are quickly loosened [Retzius went on,] and ... to the accompaniment of a cannon salute and resounding cheers from the crowd ... the big, heavy vessel glides down ... the steeply sloping slipway ... stern first. She dives into the water, deeper and deeper. For a moment we fear she will sink to the bottom ... But as the stem approaches the water, the stern rises, and the whole vessel is soon swimming over the waves, within a few minutes to be moored to the quay.

It was, as Retzius put it, 'an unusually moving occasion'. It was also somewhat homely, like a birthday or a wedding. In the shipyard, a temporary wooden shelter had been erected. Inside, at a long table, after the launch, the specially invited guests sat down to eat, drink and listen to speeches. One notable absentee was Nordenskiöld. Nansen had particularly wanted him because, in his own words, 'it is essentially your fault that my life has taken the turn ... it now has', and 'in one way it is your own child that is to go into the water'. But Nordenskiöld was in Spain for the anniversary celebrations of Columbus' discovery of America four hundred years before, almost to the day.

Archer solemnly praised what he called 'Nansen's constructive sense' in helping to design the ship. When Nansen spoke, he 'turned to me', as Retzius put it, and

declared that in the field so important to both of us, neurobiology ... it was also a matter of penetrating unknown regions.

And then followed the now almost ritual protestation which, somehow, seemed less convincing each time that it was uttered:

For the sake of his polar exploration he had to interrupt that work, but hoped that after achieving his aims ... he would return ... to biology.

The oratory eventually ceased, and the guests were ushered out, to make way for a second sitting at the same table for the sixty or so workers who had built the ship.

When Eva strode up to baptise *Fram*, she was manifestly pregnant. On that account, a fortnight later, when Nansen again visited London to address the RGS on his new expedition, he went alone. As usual, a stream of letters passed between them. 'If it isn't a living child this time,' Eva wrote in anguish, 'I don't know what will happen to me.'

Nansen tried his best to console her. 'Everything which is great and beautiful takes on your form,' he declared, in a note dashed off on returning to his hotel one evening from a performance of *King Lear*. 'You were naturally Cordelia.' More cheerfully he regaled her with an account of his lecture, delivered to the Society on 14 November.

> The hall was packed [and after] my lecture ... those old veterans came, one after the other and did their best to ... pour cold water over me.

Admiral Sir George Nares, who had commanded the last British Arctic expedition in 1875-76, a saga of ineptitude in itself, particularly irritated him. Other critics doubted the existence of a trans-polar current. In particular they objected to Nansen's concept of deliberately freezing his ship into the pack ice and cutting off his line of retreat. That contradicted all their received ideas.

In spite of this carping, which Nansen made much of to Eva, the audience was basically well disposed. Two members spoke up robustly in support. One was Joseph Wiggins, a merchant captain who knew the Siberian waters well. The other was Captain William Wharton, of the hydrographic (surveying) service of the Navy. Wharton stated plainly that Nansen was 'quite justified in supposing there is a drift from [Siberia] to Greenland'. What is more, unbeknown to Nansen, Clements Markham had long since postulated a current across the Arctic. Hugh Robert Mill, now Librarian of the RGS in place of Scott Keltie who had become Secretary, saw Nansen off at Victoria Station when he left for home, and gave him a pocket edition of Browning's poetry as a memento.

Throughout his life, though he could not endure criticism, Nansen nursed a perverse, deep-rooted feeling that he could only be right if others disagreed. Yet now a scintilla of genuine doubt did intrude. He had previously sent for analysis in Sweden specimens of mud he had collected from ice floes during his drift along the east coast of Greenland before landing in 1888. Professor Theodor Cleve, of Uppsala University, and an authority on diatoms, unequivocally identified the diatom flora of Nansen's material with one, 'of the many thousands of specimens I have examined ... namely one ... collected ... during the voyage of the *Vega* ... near the Bering Strait'. That was surely proof positive of a trans-polar current.

Nonetheless, for at least a year, Nansen had been debating whether he really ought to go through the Bering Strait as he originally announced. Because of what happened to *Jeannette*, and other stray evidence, Nansen had begun to fear some sort of trap that way. He considered instead following Nordenskiöld's route in *Vega* along the Siberian coastline from the west. When Nansen addressed the RGS, that is what he had finally decided to do.

The change set off a string of consequences, from the refusal of an invitation to give a lecture in San Francisco to the question of where now to obtain sledge dogs. Originally, Nansen had intended doing so in Alaska on the way. In vain he now tried Canada and Greenland. Finally, towards the end of 1892, he asked Baron von Toll in St Petersburg to help obtain dogs from Siberia. A geologist in the Imperial Russian geological service, a polar explorer in his own right, Eduard von Toll knew Siberia well. He had been a friend and supporter of Nansen's since they met in Berlin in 1890 – actually helping to persuade Nansen to change his route. An Estonian by birth and a 'Baltic Baron' – that is, one of the German-speaking aristocrats who were part of the backbone of the old Russian Empire – he was perfectly willing to find Nansen his Siberian sledge dogs. But this being Russia, and a profoundly bureaucratised autocracy, official sanction was desirable first. So Nansen asked the Swedish-Norwegian Foreign Ministry to intervene.

In St Petersburg, the capital of the Russian empire, the Swedish-Norwegian Ambassador, a Swede called Lennart Reuterskiöld, consequently had his comfortable routine disrupted. Finding dogs for an explorer was scarcely part of the diplomatic round. Reuterskiöld nonetheless 'met with the uttermost interest and accommodation from the [Russian] Foreign Ministry', as he reported to Count Lewenhaupt, the Foreign Minister in Stockholm, 'especially on the part of Baron Osten Sacken' – a senior official and another 'Baltic Baron'.

> After a few days, the Baron told me that letters concerning Dr Nansen had immediately been sent to the authorities in East and West Siberia, besides the Government of Archangel.

Unfortunately for Reuterskiöld, however, when Nansen's official request for dogs arrived, von Toll was about to leave St Petersburg for Siberia on an expedition of his own. He thus had little time to spare and departed, pursued by telegrams from Reuterskiöld. One of these gave him news unconnected with either his or Nansen's polar exploits. 'I have received the satisfying news,' he telegraphed back to Nansen, 'that you have become [a] happy father ... and that all is well with your wife.'

In Christiania, on 8 January, Eva had given birth, finally, to a living child. Unlike Mrs Peary before her, she would not now, after all, be going north with her husband.

26

'Burns Without a Wick'

To Nansen's home at Lysaker came, after Eva's confinement, Ethel Brilliana Tweedie, an English woman journalist, one of the earliest of her kind.

> What a strange contrast the Nansens are! [Mrs Tweedie wrote.] He, a great, big, tall, fair Norwegian, [she] a jolly, bright little woman, with dark hair, and all the merriment ... of a more southern people ... He is very fond of joking and chaffing her.

Such, at least, was the outward show. Like all other visitors at this time, Mrs Tweedie was taken down by Nansen to see *Fram*.

At the end of November, *Fram* had been towed round from Larvik to Christiania for fitting out. At a shipyard on the waterfront, her ungainly lines became a landmark while her masts were stepped and her engines installed. At the same time, she was open to the public, every weekday, for a modest entrance fee, in aid of the expedition fund. When Mrs Tweedie arrived, *Fram* was in dry dock. She found Otto Sverdrup 'examining the keel ... then coated with ice', as she reported.

> Nansen ... told him in English [I was] from London and he must come and show himself. Almost shyly, a small man ... of thick stature, and with very red whiskers, emerged from under the keel, his hands deeply embedded in the pockets of a thick pea jacket. 'Dr Nansen can show you everything better than I can,' he remarked, with a very Scotch accent; perhaps acquired when he was wrecked off the Scotch coast some years ago ... 'But I want to show *you*,' laughed Nansen ... It was a shame to tease the little man, for he seemed quite shy, although he laughed.

Nansen might well wish to show him off as much as *Fram*. Sverdrup was vital to the expedition. By his own account, he was torn between a 'burning desire' to go and the creeping thought that it was time to settle down. In October 1891, he had got married – to a cousin as it happened – and his condition for joining Nansen was that the latter should sign an agreement – in addition to ship's articles – guaranteeing his wife financial security. Despite the added burden this imposed, Nansen eventually did so. Sverdrup was the one man he had known that he wanted from the start. Indeed, so important was he that in the parliamentary debate on the grant for *Fram* one waverer was prepared to vote in support if Sverdrup really was willing to go. Sverdrup, he percipiently argued, was

> No. 1 on the Greenland expedition because of his practical ability and presence of mind, and because on the whole it seems that it was he who really managed the Greenland affair.

For the rest of the party it was a different story altogether. Impelled by newspaper coverage, a cosmopolitan shower of unsolicited applications had been descending upon Nansen's head. One of the more entertaining was from a French lady in Algiers, calling herself 'un petit homme manqué', who liked 'tough things which ... lead to death or glory', not to mention 'blue skies ... love and springtime'.

Once the too obviously escapist or unbalanced had been eliminated, a trickle of realistic candidates was left. Balto, the first of all applicants after Sverdrup, had tactfully to be rejected; so too Ravna, who was longing to escape from the rural poverty of Northern Norway into which he had relapsed after the crossing of Greenland. From the problems of people Nansen was, as always, relieved to turn to those of equipment. He profited from the rapid technical advances of the age.

One of these was the Primus stove. It was a Swedish product, invented by a Stockholm mechanic, and just now coming on to the market. It was the first device efficiently to burn liquid fuel, vaporising paraffin under pressure to produce a gas flame of intense heat. 'A litre of water brought to the boil in 3 or 4 minutes,' ran an early advertisement. 'A hitherto unknown fuel saving ... *Burns without a wick*.' 'Explosion impossible,' was another of the manufacturer's claims; intended no doubt to offset the unfamiliar roar of the burner and the fears of pumping up a fragile-looking brass tank. For a given weight of fuel, the Primus developed five or six times more heat than anything before. It was also compact, much lighter, and eminently portable, thus vastly increasing the range of unsupported travel. Market women were said to put a Primus stove under their voluminous skirts to keep them warm in winter. However that may be, Nansen adopted it, the first explorer to do so.

The Primus stove was merely one of a bewildering array of new products of potential use. Most came from abroad. Nansen did all the choosing himself, ordering samples and calculating quantities. From Germany and Switzerland came new kinds of dried and concentrated rations. Nansen had these and all other foods analysed. From London Edward Whymper, the conqueror of the Matterhorn, who had had ambitions on Greenland himself, wrote to suggest an aluminium pocket aneroid barometer that was light in weight and much used now by mountaineers. Nansen duly ordered a supply.

Since Nansen expected possibly to live by hunting, he had to look at guns. He finally chose a combination sporting model, made by Holland and Holland, the celebrated London gunsmiths. It had two barrels; one for bullets, the other for shot: rifle and shotgun in one and enabling the user to shoot game and birds with the same weapon. To be absolutely sure of what he was getting, Nansen had the muzzle velocities tested.

He was also preoccupied by what skis to take. Like much else, skiing equipment was then undergoing the transformation into its modern form. This included bindings. At a meeting in Christiania in December 1892, Nansen laid it down that 'iron and steel on skis are a monstrosity', advocating instead a return to a primitive Lapp binding, made entirely of untanned leather. This opinion caused great offence. Nansen was roundly accused of 'not following the development of our skiing over the past 12 to 15 years'.

For his expedition, Nansen abandoned the Telemark ski, which he now scorned as an instrument of downhill 'acrobatics'. Instead, he needed something adapted to moving over flat terrain. So he chose a model based on the ski from the district of Selbu, in central Norway. This was long and narrow, with a deep, broad groove in the sole. Nansen's version was at least 350 centimetres long, almost a metre longer than modern jumping skis. (He bought most of his skis from Fritz Huitfeldt, his half-sister Ida's brother-in-law, a Christiania dealer, and one of the great skiing pioneers. Huitfeldt invented the first modern downhill binding.)

When negotiating with manufacturers, Nansen tried hopefully for discounts. Wolter & Reuter of Hamburg, suppliers of dried vegetables, sternly declined: 'We only supply the *finest* wares [unlike] our competitors.' Cadbury's, on the other hand, were so taken with Nansen's praise of chocolate on the crossing of Greenland that they now offered to give him all he needed, free.

For Eva, all the bustle and clutter about the house intensified the dull throb of dread at the impending separation. Mrs Tweedie made things worse by sending patterns of curtain material to keep draughts out of cabins. It was the kind of womanly concern that Eva knew she lacked.

Others offered gifts. Henry Simon sent works by Schopenhauer:

They are for me in many parts what to a fervent Christian ... the Bible is said to be, and if you ... take them with you to that point where the axis of the earth pierces the surface, I have no doubt that you and the friends that go with you will find many a sentence for pleasurable discussion during the possibly long hours of confinement.

Fram, completed, finally left the yard, and early in April 1893 Nansen wrote to tell Archer about her trials:

She behaved splendidly; did 7 knots and turned on a sixpence. I have never seen a ship that turns that way. We went round in a circle, the diameter of which was not much longer than the ship. She will certainly be excellent to manoeuvre in the ice.

For that, Sverdrup could take some of the credit. His experience in America had taught him that schooners were highly manoeuvrable and easy to handle with a small crew, notably because the fore- and aft-sails could be worked from the deck, with little going aloft. In consequence, from the start, he had wanted a schooner rig, and he quietly got his way. *Fram* was actually the first polar ship to be rigged as a schooner; all others had been square-riggers of one kind or another.

But *Fram* was not simply a sailing ship. She was a highly adapted machine. Her engines, specially designed, were the latest thing in triple expansion – the apex of steam power, before the advent of the steam turbine. She carried a motor pinnace, one of the earliest craft powered by an internal combustion engine.

While spring turned to summer, and preparations gathered way, Eva was burdened by the sense of time running out – a sense accentuated by the farewell letters and telegrams which were now beginning to arrive. Adolf Ónodi wrote to Nansen from Budapest not only to say goodbye but to dwell once again on 'the unforgettable, wonderful days in Naples', when they were hopeful neuroscientists together, in those now distant arcadian times.

Another echo of Naples came from Marion, now Mrs Ure, married and living in Yokohama. On 30 March, with an hour to spare, she rushed to catch the mail, sending her own 'affectionate farewell' together with that of her husband and her mother, and adding, in her old manner: 'All good go with you, brave Viking.'

Oscar II, the King of Sweden-Norway, tall, dignified, every inch the amiable monarch, had given 20,000 kroner (£50,000 or $80,000 in present terms) to the expedition. On 12 May, while in residence in the Palace in Christiania, he visited *Fram*. About three weeks earlier he had seen a performance in Christiania of *The Master Builder*, Ibsen's latest play and his first since returning to live in Norway in 1891 after a quarter of a century abroad. One of its themes is that of a man expected to do the impossible once more; another, how his ambition is paid for by the suffering of others, especially his wife. It was an apt if unintentional reflection of Nansen's own life.

The days passed and *Fram*, moored at her berth, became the scene of a frenzied rush. Tradesmen and messengers stalked the ship. 'Down in the saloon,' as one journalist reported, 'Nansen himself is working under high pressure from early morning.'

He has to see things for himself, so that he knows what has to be done ... Nansen talks with a notebook in his hand, making notes now and then ... He does not leave this notebook in peace, even at night, so we are told. He lies in bed and notes down things that must not be forgotten.

Sailing day loomed up, and there was a ball in honour of the members of the expedition. All too soon Nansen and Eva found themselves at a farewell dinner on the eve of departure. It was given by an artist friend called Christian Skredsvig in his home at Fleskum, a few miles from *Godthåb*. One of Eva's sisters was there; so too was a leading Norwegian writer called Arne Garborg and his wife Hulda, a founder of the folk-dance movement. It was a small, sympathetic and very private affair. But it was Midsummer's Eve and, outside, the traditional bonfires pierced the evening sky. In an atmosphere of forced jollity Nansen and Eva were sick at heart.

At half past ten next morning, 24 June, in what Nansen called 'a dismal parting atmosphere', he walked out of the house, across the garden, and down to the water's edge, where he boarded *Fram*'s motor pinnace. He had said goodbye to Eva in their bedroom. She refused to follow him across the threshold. The pinnace now took him to where the ship lay out of sight, behind the headland, on the Christiania waterfront.

Fram had only finished lading the afternoon before. She then left the quayside, and was now moored to a buoy, waiting to depart. A crowd of several thousands had gathered to see her off. Even the Storting had suspended its proceedings for parliamentarians to go down to the docks.

By 10 a.m., *Fram* had steam up. At eleven o'clock, she was due to sail. All beflagged, a fleet of small boats and steamers carrying well-wishers (in return for a modest fee) was waiting to escort her out of the harbour. There were last-minute deliveries to *Fram* including Russian roubles from the bank for expenses in Siberia. But the morning passed; there was no sign of movement. Nansen did not appear. He had been hard put to tear himself away from home. On land, the spectators lost patience and drifted off, leaving the waterfront half deserted.

Nature had perversely set the stage. After a long bright spell the day had dawned with sombre clouds and intermittent curtains of rain drifting over the fjord.

It was already past noon when *Fram*'s motor pinnace appeared out of the haze with a sailor, standing, boathook in hand, at the bows and Nansen sitting in the stern.

The pinnace came alongside. In a deathly silence Nansen came over the side, and soon afterwards *Fram* slipped her moorings. As she got under way, salutes thundered across the water from the cannon in the Christiania forts. Nonetheless, said one reporter, 'there was something dismal about the departure ... The grey air and the bitter, cold weather did not help the spirits of a public tired of waiting.'

27

How to Choose Dogs

'Your trust in me in the vital matter of the dogs is a heavy burden on my soul,' Baron von Toll had written to Nansen on 7 January. He was then in Moscow, having started from St Petersburg the day before on the long journey to Siberia. Only now, while changing trains, was he able to write about the matter. The sledge dogs could not be delivered from Siberia in time to catch *Fram* before she sailed. She would have to pick them up at Khabarova, on the Yugor Strait, at the entrance to the Kara Sea.

Until von Toll left Zlatoust, where the railway then ended, crossed the Urals, and reached Tyumen, the gateway of Siberia, he was confined to good intentions. 'Everything turning out well,' he wrote triumphantly from Tyumen, nearly a fortnight after leaving St Petersburg, 'thanks to a succession of happy accidents.'

His first piece of luck was that when he received Nansen's plea for dogs there happened to be in St Petersburg one V.A. Troinitski, the former Governor of Tobolsk, of which Tyumen was the capital. Von Toll asked Troinitski to help, and Troinitski instantly wrote and telegraphed; not, oddly enough, to a local Russian, but to Robert Wardroper, an English trader in Tyumen.

When von Toll set off, no reply had yet arrived. But when he entered the shabby snowbound sprawl of wooden houses liberally stocked with petty officials that was Tyumen, he found that everything had been arranged. The crux had been to find a man who could be trusted both to buy the dogs and convey them to Khabarova. Von Toll could write to Nansen that Wardroper had found someone 'made for the job'.

This was Alexander Ivanovitch Trontheim, a German-speaking Latvian from Riga whose father was actually a Norwegian sea-captain from Trondheim – hence his son's adopted surname. And indeed Alexander Ivanovitch himself looked Norwegian, with his high cheekbones, red-gold beard and middling height. He had been exiled to Siberia, but not as a hardened criminal. His class of exiles, known as *Sibni*, were at worst venial offenders, who might be banished for political reasons, for vagrancy, or quite simply by mistake. At all events, after completing his seven-year sentence (for whatever offence) Trontheim stayed where he was, married, and settled down. By the time Wardroper called on him he had lived in Siberia for twenty years. The whole basin of the River Ob was his home. He had mastered the technique of Arctic travel and was a fisherman, dog driver, trapper and hunter. He knew the local tribesmen.

Trontheim had been trusted to guide the son of the British Ambassador in St Petersburg on a journey through the tundra. But, von Toll told Nansen, 'the best guarantee for Trontheim [is] his burning desire to take part in your expedition!'

Most important of all, Trontheim had been to Khabarova several times, and therefore knew the way. Before von Toll continued on his own journey he could write to Nansen that Trontheim had signed a contract – for 50 roubles a month (£100 or $160 in present terms), plus 200 roubles for his return – and had already left Tyumen for Tobolsk to start the work.

This was a particularly fortunate piece of timing, for when Troinitski's original request arrived, Trontheim was on the point of leaving with one of the Wardropers on a journey. 'A few days later,' von Toll wrote to Nansen, 'and Trontheim would have slipped through our fingers, and with that the possibility of carrying out the task.'

For all that, von Toll, as he made his way to Irkutsk, another 2,400 kilometres eastwards on from Tyumen, felt that for safety's sake a second team of dogs ought to be sent further along the coast. The dogs from Eastern Siberia and Kamchatka were well known to be bigger and stronger than the West Siberian breed that Trontheim was going to buy. But, more important, in von Toll's own words,

> the thought occurred to me that in case the *Fram* suffered the same fate as the *Jeannette*, it might not be without value if, to save the survivors, depots could be laid on the New Siberian Islands.

In Irkutsk, von Toll had his crowning stroke of luck. There he met a certain Nikolai Kelch who, though Russian, was 'of German descent', von Toll was once more careful to explain to Nansen. (All other traders were considered more reliable than Russian ones!) Kelch owned a goldfield and spontaneously offered to pay both for von Toll's proposed depots and for a second team of dogs for Nansen. Kelch put 1,500 roubles (£3,000 or $4,800 in present terms) at von Toll's disposal. A thousand miles later, after a crossing of the snow-covered tundra and a journey down the Lena river, von Toll reached the coast. Along the way, in the person of a Norwegian called Johan Torgersen who had lived in Siberia for fifteen years, he found someone he could trust to buy the dogs and take them to a prearranged point in the estuary of the Olenek river to await Nansen. Von Toll himself made an adventurous little side trip of another thousand miles or so across the frozen sea to the New Siberian Islands to put out the depots.

Meanwhile, at the end of January, ten days after signing his contract, Trontheim had reached Berezov, a town almost 1,500 kilometres from Tyumen, down the River Ob to the north. This was where Russian colonisation gave way to the wild outlands of the Siberian tribesmen. He had come to visit a market frequented by Ostyaks and Samoyeds – Uralic tribesmen of vaguely Mongolian aspect, whose languages he spoke. There, mainly from Samoyeds, Trontheim bought the best-trained sledge dogs he could find. Conscientiously, he reported to Reuterskiöld, at the Swedish-Norwegian Embassy in St Petersburg, that all was well. 'I will be waiting at the place on the sea where I should,' he wrote, in his native German, the edges rubbed off by decades of contact with foreign tongues.

Two months later he was writing again to Reuterskiöld, this time from a settlement called Muzhi, 150 kilometres to the north, on the west bank of the Ob, to reassure him – and through him Nansen – that the dogs were in good condition. He also explained that, although his contract called for thirty dogs, for safety's sake he had bought ten extra. 'With God's help I will deliver them all healthy,' he concluded.

In Muzhi, for 300 roubles, Trontheim hired a reindeer nomad called Terencheff to take him to Khabarova. On 16 April, they set off – Trontheim, with his dogs and baggage, Terencheff with his reindeer drivers, their families, forty sledges and a herd of 450 reindeer.

Leaving behind in the wilderness a depressing swathe of mangled snow churned by reindeer hooves, the caravan wound its way northwards up a tributary of the Ob and across the Urals. It was more of a nomadic migration than travel in the normal sense. The drivers had to follow their reindeer, which in their turn followed the twisting line of the lichen on which they fed. More profoundly, the nomad wandered without goal or sense of time. Settled man relied on both.

On 5 May, the caravan reached the River Usa, its first goal, having taken nearly three weeks to cover 150 kilometres in a straight line. The crossing of the Urals had tired the animals so, for a fortnight, the expedition halted to let them rest. Trontheim, ever anxious about his dogs, wanted to give them fresh food. There was no question of slaughtering Terencheff's reindeer, so Trontheim went hunting, though game was scarce. At last, on 19 May, the caravan started off again, crossing the Arctic Circle but having to slow down again as the reindeer began to calve. The forest meanwhile thinned into scrub, and finally gave way to the tundra, bleak and disturbing to those who know it not.

Towards the end of May, the caravan had to struggle through a low-lying flooded labyrinth of bogs. Thereafter came a violent change in the weather. Deep frost descended, killing two reindeer calves. Three adult animals were devoured by wolves. To add to the general misery, firewood, which had been collected before entering the tundra, and which was the only fuel, gave out.

At last, on 10 July, six months after leaving Tyumen, Trontheim reached Khabarova. He paid off Terencheff and his men and sent them back. In his last letter to the outside world, written from Muzhi, he had promised to meet Nansen by the end of June. He was already ten days late. Cross-examination of various people in the vicinity reassured him that no ship had yet appeared. The Yugor Strait was still choked with ice. So too was the whole sea, as far as the horizon. Trontheim settled down with his dogs to wait for *Fram*.

28

Fram Sails Off

When *Fram* sailed from Christiania she carried on board an English journalist and explorer called Herbert Ward, who had been in Africa with Stanley. As *Fram* rounded the headland, Ward keenly observed Nansen straining for one more lingering glimpse of his home beside the water. In his own words:

> It was hazy ... but while Dr Nansen ... stood upon the bridge ... the sun, struggling through the rain clouds, cast a faint beam upon the shore, a mile distant. Upon the rocks stood Mrs Nansen, clad in a conspicuous white dress. The view lasted only a few moments, the brief sunshine vanished, and the distant shore became once more but a blurred shadow without outline ...

> I shall never forget the pathos of it all ... Nansen was very brave, but one could see he was suffering terribly, struggling with himself.

This indeed was the literal truth. 'I thought that everything was black,' Nansen wrote to Eva. 'Within me I was torn apart, as if something would break, and at that moment if someone had given me the choice of going or not, I could not have trusted myself.'

At Drøbak, where the fjord narrowed, about 30 kilometres down towards the sea, Herbert Ward, with some other visitors, transhipped to escorting vessels to return to Christiania, leaving on board for the moment, Colin Archer and – in an echo of times past – Marion Ure's sister Minnie and her husband, William Hoyle. They had been the last people to bid Nansen farewell when he sailed for Greenland; they had insisted on coming over specially to say goodbye now. With the remaining visitors they disembarked next day at Larvik, where *Fram* had put in to fetch from Colin Archer's yard two large half-decked lifeboats, specially strengthened for the ice; also to rig davits, and complete ship's stores. When she sailed Archer himself, as if saying farewell to his creation, was at the wheel to take her out of harbour. A cutter – also of his own design – took him off, leaving Nansen to glimpse his patriarchal figure at the helm, scudding out of sight behind a skerry.

Out into the Skagerrak, the sea began to rise, and *Fram* started rolling out of all proportion to the swell. Her movement was highly individual: more like a cradle rocked by an inconsiderate hand than a ship in a seaway. Though in part this was a consequence of her rounded bilges, it was also a result of deliberate design: a safe ship, as every seaman knows, is an uncomfortable one. But just how safe was put to the test when she nosed out of the Skagerrak and into the North Sea.

Here, in heavy weather, she heaved and tossed and pitched. Because of her stubby proportions, she yawed biliously as well. Heavily laden, with little freeboard, and down by the bows, sluggish in answering to the seas, she took green water over the foredeck; there was not a dry place on the ship. The deck cargo shifted; some had to be jettisoned; all hands grappled through the night with confusion. Empty paraffin drums intended for blubber had to be thrown overboard, together with precious timber. Thus distressed, *Fram* passed a barque with sails reefed, primly riding out the gale as if nothing untoward was in progress. Finally, on the last day of June, having been delayed by fog, she put into Bergen, there to load dried fish, both for dogs and men.

Besides the agony of parting from wife and child, Nansen had had another reason, when he boarded *Fram* in Christiania, for looking what Ward called 'haggard and half dazed'. He was hounded by financial worries. His brother, Alexander, was now a lawyer in Christiania. For some reason they had become estranged, but Alexander looked on with mounting concern until at last he felt that he had to intervene. Nansen clutched at the extended hand. Alexander uncovered a deficit of around 100,000 kroner (£250,000 or $400,000 in present terms). The government was once more approached, and at the last minute an extra parliamentary grant of 80,000 kroner (£200,000 or $325,000) was reluctantly agreed. The rest had to be found privately.

Among the well-wishers to sail from Christiania on *Fram* had been a wealthy local businessman called Axel Heiberg. When he turned back with other visitors down the fjord, Heiberg found himself on a steam launch belonging to Charles Dick, an Englishman long resident in Norway. As a fellow-member of the Christiania Ski Club, and the first private donor to the expedition, Heiberg was one of Nansen's staunchest supporters. Being on the expedition committee, he was aware of the finances. On the way up the fjord back to Christiania Heiberg, as he recorded, told Dick that Nansen 'had a shortfall of 12,000 kroner' (£30,000 or $48,000).

> To which [Dick] answered: 'Shouldn't we two share it?' The 12,000 kroner was thereby out of the story; I will never forget the pleasant manner in which Mr Dick made the proposal.

Alexander, now the expedition's agent as well as its unofficial accountant, hastened to transmit the news. Bergen was the first point at which he could get in touch with his brother. There Nansen found a telegram explaining how his financial predicament had been so unexpectedly resolved. In the face of his difficulties he had planned to make up at least some of the deficit by giving lectures along the coast. Bergen was the first booking and it was too late now to cancel it. But providentially there would be no need for any more. In comparison with this stroke of luck, Scott Keltie's less palatable news from London – that he had failed to persuade *The Times* to buy the expedition's story – appeared hardly a pinprick.

It was consequently in a somewhat better frame of mind that, on 2 July, Nansen sailed out from Bergen. He had other consolation too. 'I cannot say how tremendously happy I am ... to see how well you are managing,' he wrote in reply to letters pouring out from Eva to catch him along the coast. 'The waiting will not seem as long as you imagine,' Nansen went on. 'Our Heaven-sent little Liv, how nice that we have her ... What does it matter if distance separates our bodies ... Whether it be a long or short time, and even if we don't come after 2 years; even after 3 years, you will wait with undaunted courage.'

Past the islands Nansen sailed out, through the waters where he had once collected zoological specimens. It was a poignant reminder of one parting present. This was the latest volume of *Biologische Untersuchungen*, Gustav Retzius' record of his research. It was dedicated to 'my friend Fridtjof Nansen, the bold and distinguished explorer of the ... central nervous system, and the polar regions'. The dedication, as Retzius gently, but pointedly put it in his farewell letter,

> concerned that Fridtjof Nansen, who has contributed so fundamentally to dispelling the obscurity [surrounding] the so little known regions of the central nervous system. [I] long for the day when that Nansen, after the accomplishment of his North Pole expedition may return to his former field of research ... and once more break new trails [in] the great mystery of the nervous system.

To return to the central nervous system, Nansen replied as usual, was his ultimate aim. But that protestation sounded hollower with the years. Each heavy dip of *Fram*'s prow carried him further from what once had been the goal of his desires.

29

One Over the Eight

Out of Bergen, *Fram* entered the Inner Lead. This is the coastal channel shielded by a natural breakwater of windswept islands which runs along most of the western seaboard of Norway. Here, in sheltered waters, *Fram*, her engines hissing and stamping, steamed slowly north. After only fleeting individual encounters, Nansen was now becoming acquainted with his men as a crew within the crowded confines of his ship.

Since the Greenland expedition, he had changed his concept of the kind of follower he sought. No longer did he look for plain and simple Norwegian countryfolk. Now, the ship's officers aside, he wanted his men to be university educated, if only to provide him with intellectual company in the long, dark years ahead. Then he wanted good skiers with some knowledge of the sea. His idea was to carry scientists who could also work the ship, thus keeping the numbers down.

The difficulty was that he was asking men to bury themselves in the Arctic for an indeterminate period of time. For the short, circumscribed crossing of Greenland, the well-educated had been fired by enthusiasm. Now such people were reluctant to risk their careers, or face the likely long absence from home. For example, in September 1890, a certain Birger Pedersen volunteered. He was a Norwegian chemist working at a dynamite factory in Belgium. He was also an accomplished skier who probably invented the first safety binding, in the form of a rubber heel strap. His father was a ship's captain with whom he sometimes sailed, so his qualifications seemed ideal. In the end, however, he withdrew. 'I cannot overcome the thought,' as he put it, that 'my mother and other relatives would be uncertain of my fate probably for years.' Adventurers there were aplenty, but academics resolutely abstained. Nansen could not even find a geologist abroad.

A doctor did at least appear. Henrik Greve Blessing was the son of a clergyman. He was a few years younger than Nansen, and still a medical student when, late in 1892, he applied to join the expedition. Nansen paid him an allowance 'for the preservation of my modest existence', as Blessing put it. This enabled him to qualify – which he did in the nick of time – and was mainly what had induced him to join. He did take his finals in time; but it was a close-run thing. Having grown up in Telemark, he was also a practised skier.

176

Hjalmar Johansen was an altogether different case. Born in Ibsen's birthplace, Skien in Telemark, he was the son of the town hall janitor. In 1886, he began reading law at the University in Christiania. After two years, he was forced to abandon his studies by the death of his father and the loss of all financial support. Thereafter he returned home and drifted from job to job. In 1891, however, he managed to enter the military academy in Christiania. For some reason he was not allowed to complete the course and therefore did not get a regular commission, as he had hoped, but was put on the reserve as a lieutenant. It was after this setback that Johansen first wrote to Nansen. Then on 28 November 1892 – the very same day that *Fram* arrived in Christiania for fitting out – having received no reply, Johansen waylaid him near his house as he was walking home.

'I think I could be useful either as storekeeper or stoker,' Johansen had written in his letter.

I was once ... a prison warder ... and as such had to organise the feeding of the prison's inmates, as a result of which I have acquired practice in dealing with food.

Finally, after five months of waiting, he was signed on as stoker, as he had proposed. Nansen warned him, as he had to warn everybody else, that he could only guarantee pay for three years, even if the expedition lasted longer. Johansen was unconcerned; he cared only that he had found a way out of the dilemma of what to do with his life.

Of medium height, well built, quiet and modest, Johansen was an all-round sportsman, but especially a skier and, above all, a gymnast. In 1889, he had been a member of the Norwegian national team at an international gymnastic tournament in Paris.

This impressed Nansen, as did technical ability. As general handyman, he hired Ivar Otto Irgens Mogstad who, born in 1856, had trained as a forester, become a good mechanic and, amongst other things, patented a potato picking machine. Appropriately or not, for the past eleven years Mogstad had been employed as a warder in a lunatic asylum.

Otto Sverdrup was Captain of the *Fram*. He had, however, taken his wife home to see her settled, and would only come on board further up the coast. Until then Sigurd Scott Hansen was in command.

Scott Hansen was a naval sub-lieutenant who, thirsting for escape from stultifying routine, had already approached Nansen at the end of 1890. After Sverdrup, he was in fact the first to sign on. Small, dark, anything but Nordic looking, he was born in 1868 at Leith in Scotland, the son of a Norwegian seamen's chaplain. Time passed, while his application hung fire; in the meanwhile he got engaged, but by early 1892 had nonetheless joined the expedition. His main perplexity had been arranging naval leave.

'Up and down in this world,' he wryly noted in his diary when Sverdrup boarded *Fram* on 5 July at Beian, on the coast outside Trondheim, and finally assumed command. 'From skipper to glorified deck hand.'

On board with Sverdrup came Professor Waldemar Brøgger, the good-humoured geologist and, since the Greenland expedition, friend of Nansen's, who was sailing as far as Tromsø. Also on board was Kristian Kristiansen, who had been on the crossing of Greenland and half wanted to join this expedition too; and Nansen's secretary, Ola Christian Christofersen, who definitely did want to join the expedition but was supposed to leave at Khabarova.

Other polar expeditions, when they sailed, made a clean break with their homelands. *Fram*'s progress so far had been one long lingering farewell. From the coastal towns steamers came out, beflagged, with sightseers to stare at the ship as she passed; rowing boats emerged from the islands. It was all highly unsettling. But when Sverdrup came on board he brought with him a air of steadiness. He provided the strong, calm personality that was needed at the helm.

A fortnight after starting, *Fram* crossed the Arctic Circle. Threading her way through narrow sounds she was now, in Northern Norway, among the most spectacular scenery of the whole wild, mountainous coast. The midnight sun cast its eerie glow upon the scene; half-tamed country, with little wooden houses clinging to windswept islands.

On 12 July, after coasting for 1,500 miles, *Fram* finally reached Tromsø, sealing and whaling port. It was the home of Theodor Claudius Jacobsen, the tall, dark, bearded, talkative and Mephistophelean-looking Chief Mate, and under Sverdrup the senior professional seafarer on *Fram*. Now thirty-eight years old, Jacobsen had been at sea since the age of fifteen. After ten years on foreign going ships he returned to home waters and, out of Tromsø, went sealing and whaling as a skipper. For the past two seasons he had sailed as ice pilot to Novaya Zemlya in a yacht belonging to the Austrian Prince Heinrich of Bourbon. Somewhere along the way he had picked up a wife and child; nonetheless he urgently asked to join *Fram*. He had the very best references for dependability – at least when afloat. He signed his contract on 15 December 1892.

Also from the environs of Tromsø, and typical of another kind of North Norwegian seafarer, was Peter Leonhard Hendriksen, born in 1859. Nansen wanted 'experienced arctic people who are also skilled harpooners and shots', as he wrote to Hendriksen, and in this last respect, Hendriksen more than filled the bill. As a journalist picturesquely put it, he was 'one of the best known mass murderers of the Arctic fleet'. Together with Sverdrup, he was alone in having been approached by Nansen, rather than the other way about. He had sailed in sealers since he was nineteen.

At Tromsø, polar clothing was delivered to the ship. As far as he could, Nansen had stayed faithful to Jaeger and the comfort of wool. But more than this would now be required. From the Lapps of Northern Norway, he had to obtain finneskoe, ski boots, fur garments, sennegrass and reindeer furs for sleeping bags – all part of ancient cold weather lore for which there was still no modern substitute. These were produced for him by a lawyer called Daniel Mack, his agent in Tromsø, who had also helped in choosing the crew. Frantic telegraphing preceded the ship's arrival. But in Tromsø Nansen found waiting for him everything that he had ordered.

Each member of the expedition reacted in his own way to the approaching departure from civilisation. Scott Hansen went to a dentist and had eight cavities filled. He also saw his fiancée, who had sailed all the way in a passenger ship to be with him until the last moment. Eva Nansen, had she wished, could have done the same. She did not, and Nansen felt increasingly isolated and forlorn.

On the day that *Fram* berthed in Tromsø, Brøgger sailed south on a waiting passenger ship. 'Sad to part from him, the last good friend,' Nansen laconically noted in his diary. Kristiansen took the same ship home. Having had the opportunity once more to inspect Nansen at close quarters, he had finally decided he could not serve under him again. This hurt Nansen more than he cared to admit.

After two days coaling and scaling salt from boilers (because of using sea water), Nansen proposed leaving Tromsø on 14 July, at 8 a.m. This proved impossible because, in his own words, he 'made the unpleasant discovery' that the crew 'had got thoroughly drunk during the night'. Meanwhile, at half past eight, a man called Bernt Bentsen appeared, anxious to join the ship. The departure of Kristiansen had left a vacant berth. A qualified mate, who had sailed the Arctic for years, Bentsen was so keen to go that he signed on before the mast for Khabarova, with 50 kroner (£125 or $200 in present terms) in advance. This, he said, was to buy his gear. In fact, he went drinking round the harbour with Jacobsen and Hendriksen. Eventually all three staggered back on board. *Fram* finally sailed at 1 p.m.

For an ordinary voyage it would have been ordinary behaviour. But as Johansen, for one, wrote in his diary: 'I regret what I have done.'

> As we come further north, and leave all that is known [he continued], the thought occurs to me that it is a serious journey we have ahead [and] the thought of my loved ones brings the thought: 'Perhaps you will never see them again?'

Another member of the crew was Bernhard Nordahl, the electrician. *Fram* was fitted with electric lighting, uncommon at sea at the time, and equipment could still be temperamental. Yet Nordahl, with his vital rôle, was on board only by chance. He had joined in Christiania on an impulse, after meeting Johansen, an old crony, down at the docks, about a fortnight before sailing. Small, well built, a good gymnast and a skier, he was now thirty-one years old, and had worked in America. When he joined *Fram*, he was a foreman in an electrical firm. He sailed away, leaving behind a wife and five children; ostensibly only as far as Tromsø, to give instruction in the use of the electrical system. By his own admission, he really intended going the whole way from the start.

Because of a pattern of insobriety among the crew, Nansen already saw cause for disquiet. He secretly decided to send two men back from Khabarova, replacing them as best he could. One was Adolf Juell, part farmer, part seaman and, although at the age of thirty-three an experienced merchant captain, now mustered on *Fram* as cook. Blond, blue-eyed and moustachioed, with a wife and four children, he came from Kragerø, on the south coast. Unfortunately for him, his humour and chattiness, characteristic of that part of the country, were marred by alcohol, and not at all to Nansen's taste.

The second was Anton Amundsen, *Fram*'s Chief Engineer, who had come fully trained from twenty-five years in the navy. No relation of Roald Amundsen, who was to feature so prominently later in Nansen's life, he had been passed over for promotion because, as Scott Hansen charitably told Nansen, he was

> prone to take one over the eight, but this can possibly be explained by the unhappy conditions of his domestic life.
> He did not get the one he wanted, and a wife was forced on him who is anything but pretty, and with whom he has nothing in common.

Nansen accepted Amundsen despite an adverse medical report, but wrote to him ominously:

> Your organism has been severely injured by the use of alcoholic drinks ... I am writing to you immediately, so that not a single hour more than is necessary passes before I inform you that the *only* condition under which there can be any possibility of coming along is *absolute abstention* from *all alcoholic drinks* ... This must be observed from the moment you receive this letter [and] if on *one single occasion* you taste alcoholic drinks of any kind, *any possibility* of your coming along will be forfeited.

Heedless of this warning, and ignorant of Nansen's intentions, Amundsen, like a true mechanic, continued to dote over his engines in the face of all discomfort, even after *Fram* emerged from the Inner Lead and turned east along the unprotected Arctic coast of Norway.

The second engineer who, with Amundsen and Johansen, made up the staff of the spectacularly cramped engine room, had actually sailed under false colours. His name was Lars Petterson, and although for several years he had been working near Christiania for the Norwegian navy, he came from Landskrona, in southern Sweden. Nansen believed him when he pretended Norwegian parentage, but his shipmates soon rumbled him. He was, however, so good at his job, and so transparently keen to go north on *Fram* that, although a dyed-in-the-wool Swede (and therefore, it might be argued, rather brave to embark on a ship full of Norwegians) no one bore him much ill will, even those who most keenly shared Nansen's patriotic desire for an expedition of Norwegians only.

There was also a dog on board. She was a cross-bred bitch from Greenland, part Greenlander, part Newfoundland, called Kvik, which means both 'brisk' and 'quick-witted'. She was a present to Nansen from the Dane, Carl Ryder, who had forestalled his plans, before making for the Pole, of returning to Greenland in 1891-92 to cross the Greenland Ice Cap by his originally intended route. On *Fram*, after some difficulty getting her sea legs, Kvik appointed herself watchdog. Johansen maintained that she was everybody's favourite. To Scott Hansen, she was 'that bloody dog that eats up anything it finds'. Such, then, was the motley company sailing out into the unknown: not quite explorers, nor ordinary ship's crew.

Along the coast, *Fram* met her second gale in open waters. She performed *da capo* her little playful trick of rolling like a cranky tub. Despite a persistent leak, she was seaworthy, but still wrongly trimmed. She scooped the seas with her bows. In a convenient fjord, she was restowed so as to settle by the stern.

At last, on 18 July, *Fram* reached Vardø, the eastern outpost of the country, her last port of call on Norwegian soil, and the last haven of civilised amenities for no one knew how long. Here divers were sent down to scrape off the barnacles and plant life now fouling *Fram's* bottom and slowing her down. Also, in Nansen's words, 'our own bodies needed a last civilised cleansing before the life of the wilds began'.

Lying close to Finland, Vardø was partly populated by Finns. The town therefore had a sauna, to which, early on sailing day, 20 July, Nansen, Sverdrup, Blessing and Scott Hansen repaired. It was their first taste of the full Finnish ritual: lying stark naked in the sauna's hellish heat and steam, while being beaten with fresh cut birch branches by two young girls.

Thereafter the local worthies gave a lavish farewell party. *Fram* was supposed to sail in the evening, but when the crew were finally all rounded up on board, they were once more comprehensively drunk. Nansen himself took the watch, which he spent finishing his post. In the small hours, having sent it ashore, he roused Scott Hansen (himself suffering with a headache caused by drinking doubtful champagne) and Sverdrup to weigh anchor 'since the others needed to sleep it off', as Scott Hansen put it.

Nansen was not so charitable. The day after *Fram* put to sea he ordered the crew to the half deck. There, in the afternoon watch, framed by a clammy grey Arctic fog enveloping the ship, he 'remonstrated with them over their drunkenness', as he summarised in his diary,

> [Also] their going ashore without permission [was] bad enough, but worst of all was the theft on board from their shipmates, in that they stole beer and also food ... All in all, their behaviour on board was bad.

Had the expedition not come so far, Nansen thundered at one point, he would undoubtedly have taken on a new crew.

All this was far outside the experience of the men. Earlier in the day, Nansen had seemed in the best of moods. Something other than their own behaviour, they shrewdly guessed, must have triggered off the outburst.

And indeed it had. Since the start of the voyage, Nansen had been bottling up a wretched turmoil of longing and remorse. At every turn, he was reminded of what he had left behind. In his cabin were photographs of Eva. The letters and telegrams with which they bombarded each other along the way, for all their protestations of love, seemed somehow a frenzied attempt to construct at the eleventh hour a dialogue that perversely continued to elude them when they were at home together, face to face.

In Vardø, about to leave the last cablehead astern, Nansen was hoping against hope for a final telegram from Eva. Just in time, one did arrive. 'I kiss it and you a thousand times,' he wrote with unwonted ecstasy, 'and depart thinking of you with bright, cheerful thoughts.' But at other times he feared that he might return to find Eva dead; and wrote to tell her so.

The castigation of the crew had been one way of relieving the gloom and tension which had been building up in him to an unbearable extent. Its upshot was a dismal atmosphere on board. The crew felt genuinely hurt. The Dionysian orgy before sailing was the accepted solace of their kind, and on this occasion they had greater need of it than most. All too many well-wishers, whether blurting out the truth or uneasily hinting at it, in their cups or not, clearly thought that neither ship nor men would ever be seen again.

'I would rather this had not happened,' Johansen remarked in his diary, on being told of Nansen's tirade. Alone among the crew, Johansen had not been on deck, having been ordered to stay below in the engine room on watch. 'Of course [Nansen] was within his rights, but that makes it all the more regrettable.' And, by contrast with his reaction after getting drunk at Tromsø: 'I do not feel particularly guilty.' But: 'Everything will be all right when we are really on our own.'

30

From the Siberian Plains

In Khabarova, Trontheim was waiting with his dogs. Uncertainty was growing with each passing day. At last, on the afternoon of 29 July, a smudge of smoke appeared on the horizon, and *Fram* hove into sight. Trontheim, now about to see Nansen in the flesh for the first time, rowed out in a small boat to meet her as she came in.

Trontheim recorded his impressions of that encounter. Nansen was 'dressed in a greasy working jacket' – quite a shock for someone accustomed to uniforms as the badge of authority of every grade:

> He is still a young man ... His every movement, every word, bespeaks energy, willpower and steadfastness. His relations with his subordinates – all picked young, healthy men – are characterised by friendliness and kindness. It [was like] a family.

Trontheim was hardly to know that Nansen's tongue-lashing of the crew had left a lingering, unpleasant aftertaste.

Fram's baptism of the element for which she was designed took place in the fog-ridden waters off Novaya Zemlya. In a few hours, she easily slipped through. Then she ran into more ice, older, heavier, more tightly packed, and for the first time she was put seriously to the test. Now she made up for all her wallowing in a seaway. Turning on the proverbial sixpence, minutely sensitive to the helm, she snaked through the twisting labyrinth of leads between the floes. Where there was no lead, she rammed her way ahead with barely a shudder, not even disturbing the chronometers.

Running happily out into open water again *Fram* sailed on, unhindered, to Khabarova. Her hull had proved itself. But the engines were another story. Steam pipes leaked. The injector for filling the boiler failed. So too did the bilge pump. All this had to be repaired before putting to sea again. One decision was thereby taken out of Nansen's hands.

He had ordered *Urania*, a Norwegian coaster, to Khabarova with final coal bunkers for *Fram*. But *Urania* had not yet arrived. Now, Nansen, however anxious to press ahead, was forced to wait.

As an outpost of civilisation, Khabarova left much to be desired. It turned out to be a small, squalid settlement lying, half-forgotten, on a flat, dreary strand, at the western entrance to the Yugor Strait, inhabited in summer only by a few Samoyed tribesmen and Russian traders. Its principal features were two small wooden chapels, both in an equal state of disrepair. Harbour, there was none. *Fram* was gingerly worked through shoaling waters as close in as it was safe to go. At 7 p.m., she dropped anchor a few cables from land.

Nansen, Sverdrup, Blessing and Christophersen immediately went ashore with Trontheim to inspect the dogs. They were tethered well away from habitation on a level piece of ground. Trontheim had been justified in buying more than the thirty originally ordered. Of the forty who started off from Berezov in January, thirty-four remained. By their coats and clamour they appeared in good condition.

For the moment, however, Nansen was more concerned with the state of the Kara Sea. That, after all, was what would decide the outcome of the expedition. As it was, in Northern Norway there had been stray warnings of bad conditions. Moreover, *Fram* had found the first ice too soon for comfort. So, the day after arriving, Nansen took Sverdrup and Hendriksen to probe the waters to the east. They went in *Fram*'s motor pinnace; the same craft that had borne Nansen away from his home.

The three men in their boat, with Nansen at the helm, made their way through the Yugor Strait, the motor banging, spluttering, backfiring and periodically stalling. Each time Hendriksen, the strongest of the trio, comically (to the others) cranked it back to life it somehow responded. It was a marine caricature of motoring on land – except that the very word 'motor car' did not yet exist – the term was still 'horseless carriage'. This was the infancy of the internal combustion engine, and Nansen's pinnace was probably the first motor-powered vessel in the Arctic.

It moved – *when* it moved – in Nansen's words, 'like lightning' – all of six knots, in fact. When he returned to *Fram* he had been away nearly twenty-four hours. In that time, for all the breakdowns, he had chugged the whole length of the Yugor Strait to the eastern end, where the Kara Sea began, and back, a total distance of over forty miles. He had seen with his own eyes that the strait was navigable, although partially filled with floes. On the horizon, the Kara Sea displayed a menacing band of heavy ice, but there was open water along the coast. The way was clear. Nansen wanted to be off.

But the repairs to *Fram*'s engines were still far from finished. Also, the boiler had to be chipped free of salt again. Nordahl used the delay to install electric signalling between the crow's nest and the engine room. This was to give the lookout direct control of the engines while navigating in the ice. It was probably the first of its kind.

Trontheim meanwhile had made himself ship's agent, interpreter and general factotum. He was invited to take his meals on board and was profoundly impressed to find 'no difference between the ordinary sailor, the Captain, and the Expedition Leader himself. [Nansen] sets a good example everywhere and in everything.'

30. From the Siberian Plains

Nansen returned from the Yugor Strait at five in the morning. The same evening, he went ashore for his initiation into dog driving. Even in Greenland he had had no opportunity. Trontheim harnessed ten dogs to a summer sledge. It differed from the winter kind in having a high ground clearance to avoid damage by rocks. After preliminary murderous confusion the team was eventually untangled and persuaded to pull. In wild career, before an appreciative audience of Russians and Samoyeds, they hauled Nansen and Trontheim effortlessly in a terrifying, bumpy sprint over grass, clay, moss and stones.

Given the anything but frictionless going, Nansen was impressed by the power of the dogs. He was less pleased to find that, with three or four exceptions, they were all castrated. Trontheim was taken aback. It was, he said, what he had explicitly agreed with von Toll, because it was a well-known fact that, for sledge driving, castrated animals were better. The explanation for that unusual view lay in the Siberian harness. This was a primitive device, much inferior to that of the Greenland Eskimos, consisting of a band around the belly, with the trace running underneath between the legs. As a result, with testicles in place, constant rubbing led to inflammation of the scrotum. Nansen, however, had hoped, as he wrote in his diary, 'for an increase in the family'.

That day, 31 July, Nansen began what he assumed would be his last letter to Eva before disappearing into the void. 'I think of you day and night,' ran his now familiar phrase. Eva's last telegram in Norway had left him 'relieved and happy'. He was certain she would 'not be rash, but calmly wait'. He invoked, too, his now familiar, Faust-like faith in some grand, elusive passion whose fulfilment lay always just over the horizon:

I so look forward to coming back to you again ... The [expedition] will go like a dream, now the prospects are so bright ... It is all just a little interruption, so that we will appreciate our life together all the more.

Nansen had implied to Eva that he would return within two years or so. But with considerably more frankness he had written to Alexander that he did not 'believe we will come home before 3 years ... perhaps 4 or even 5'. However, Nansen went on, 'I do not at all want to write this to Eva now, because it will only make her miserable.'

What Nansen did proceed to tell Eva now was what he had seen at the end of the Yugor Strait:

It was strange, low country, you know, just green plains; on and on, the whole great Siberian tundra undulates endlessly. It does not seem dreary, on the contrary, I think it is quite inviting, the open plains where the Samoyed roams freely with his reindeer, pitching his tent where and when he feels like it. I half want to follow him; half wish that you and I were nomads that could travel south with our reindeer in winter and north in summer again.

185

Part III. Fram

In their tribal garb of reindeer fur, the Samoyeds may at first glance have seemed unspoiled. But in fact, as Nansen well knew, they had long since become addicted to the vodka with which the Russian traders plied them to facilitate their deals.

By 1 August the repairs to *Fram* were nearly finished and she was ready to take on fresh water. Help was needed ashore, but it was the feast of St Elias, a Russian religious holiday, and the population was unwilling to work. There was a special service in one of the churches, after which, by custom, the vodka flowed. Priest and churchwarden became as drunk as the rest. Staggering about in their furs, fighting, sometimes driving crazily on sledges behind their reindeer, the Samoyeds resembled figures on a vase painting of some primitive bacchic train. At last, the screaming died down and Khabarova was shrouded in an alcoholic haze. Earlier, Trontheim had managed to round up a quorum in need of the wherewithal to get drunk. For one rouble, a bottle of beer and a biscuit each, these worthies shuttled water in boats to the ship.

Nansen, meanwhile, was still waiting for *Urania* with her extra coal. In any case, before *Fram* could sail, coal had to be humped from the hold to bunkers in the boiler room. It was filthy work but, in Trontheim's admiring words, 'all members of the expedition took part, with Nansen in the lead' – because help from shore was precluded by a communal hangover.

At the dinner table in *Fram*'s saloon on the evening of 2 August, Nansen held a small parting ceremony for Trontheim, and presented him with a gold medal which Baron von Toll had obtained for him from the Swedish-Norwegian Embassy in St Petersburg as a reward for the safe delivery of the dogs. 'Medals, of gold,' as von Toll had written, 'are the greatest ambition of the simple souls in the North.' And indeed, when Nansen made the presentation Trontheim's eyes, as he put it, 'shone at the sight of the ribbon and the gold'.

So that his men could sleep, Nansen took the middle watch, and used the time to finish his letters. To the sounds of *Fram* riding at anchor, the scratch of pen on paper and the creak of the rigging, he sat writing through the night. Besides his medal Trontheim wanted a testimonial. So now in the small hours, Nansen obliged. Trontheim had 'shown rare conscientiousness and intelligence, and' – was this a rebuke to Nansen's own bookkeeping? – 'it has been a pleasure to see the accuracy and order in which he has kept his accounts.'

As the crew began to stir, Nansen started a long letter to Alexander. 'Even at the risk of being sentimental,' Alexander had written in the last letter he sent off to catch his brother along the coast, 'I want to say [that] I am very fond of my brother Fridtjof, more than you have ever understood.'

So much has come between us ... which has meant that I, at any rate, would have wished that much had turned out otherwise. But if you count your

186

friends, you would with difficulty find one who really cares for you more than I do.

It seems that their estrangement had had something to do with Alexander's wife, an Englishwoman, formerly Lilian Emma Peyton, nicknamed 'Eily'. There was 'something in her expression', he once told Eva, 'which absolutely revolts me, I cannot help it'.

Nansen now told Alexander that he had 'reprieved' Amundsen and Juell. They had 'been very good since we left land', as he put it, echoing Johansen's prediction at the time, 'so I feel more charitable towards them'. Nansen had divined that they were all, perhaps, outcasts of one kind or another, at home only on the deck of a ship or somewhere else away from the mortal bonds of society.

In his letter to Eva, Nansen gossiped about the dogs, and Kvik in particular. She 'reminds me of you', he had written a month earlier. 'She is the only living creature I have from ... home.' Now he added:

> She is quite like a human being. When I sit or stand next to her and take no notice, she nudges me with her snout repeatedly, until I pat her, exactly as you do sometimes.

Nansen snatched a little sleep. By noon, all coal had been humped and fires were lit. A fair wind was blowing, from the south, to keep the ice off shore. Of *Urania*, there was still no sign, but Nansen was determined to wait no longer. He judged he had enough coal in any case. Yelping and happily rioting, the dogs were ferried on board.

Bernt Bentsen, who had mustered at Tromsø originally for Khabarova, had meanwhile decided to sign on for the whole voyage. This meant yet another wage to finance, as Nansen told Alexander in the course of yet another letter. Finally, on that afternoon of 3 August, Nansen concluded his letter to Eva:

> The hour of parting strikes. Let my last word to you be: don't worry about me, whether I am away for a long or a short time. You must know that I will not expose myself to any danger, *there is no danger*, absolutely none at all, and I will come back to you safe and sound and strong.

With his letter, he enclosed some dried flowers. They were, as he put it in a pencilled postscript, a greeting 'from the Siberian plains ... these are the first flowers I found here'.

With that, Nansen made up the post and gave it to Christofersen to take home. Christofersen could not after all, as he so ardently desired, sail on. Everything, from accommodation onwards, was calculated for twelve. With Bentsen they were already thirteen. Food had been reckoned to last for nearly six years; one extra man alone significantly reduced the margin of safety. Sadly, Christofersen got into the boat with Trontheim to row ashore.

Among the post carried by Christofersen was a last minute farewell note from Nansen for Nordenskiöld: 'as I am about to follow in your wake'; also one to a compatriot: 'if only I return to find Norway a free country.'

At Christmas that year, 'The North Pole Game' appeared in the Christiania shops. It was all about whether Nansen or Peary would be first at the Pole. While *Fram* was heading north, Peary had sailed on his third expedition to Greenland, originally to extend his exploration there, but also, if the conditions were right, as he now issued his challenge, to make his own attempt on the Pole.

But it was to Nansen that drama and attention clung. In London, he was apotheosised, inimitably, by *Punch*:

> So Dr Fridtjof Nansen's off!
> Cynics will chuckle and pessimists scoff,
> What a noodle, that Norroway chap,
> Who'd drift to the Pole to – complete our map!

On 8 January 1894, Baron von Toll returned to St Petersburg bringing news that Torgersen with his East Siberian dogs had waited for *Fram* at the mouth of the Olenek River in vain. It all somehow seemed part of a twilight world.

At Khabarova, when Christofersen and Trontheim had started rowing ashore, *Fram* was enveloped in a clammy, stagnant fog. After a few strokes of the oars, she was swallowed up and lost to sight. Next morning, like a phantom ship, she had disappeared.

31

Towards the Kara Sea

At last, around midnight, the weather lifted sufficiently for *Fram* to weigh anchor. Nansen went ahead in the motor pinnace, himself at the helm, with Scott Hansen standing in the bows with the lead, continually sounding. They first brought *Fram* to the north side of Yugor Strait, under the low shore of Vaigatch Island, and then turned eastwards, close to land.

In the glow of the midnight sun scattered by the stagnant swirls of fog Nansen and Scott Hansen led the way through the shallows of the strait. At one point the motor caught fire. Nansen's old, greasy jacket, which he was still wearing, ignited too. The flames were extinguished and the slow stutter of the motor rose once more. By 4 a.m., *Fram* had been safely piloted through the Yugor Strait, and emerged into the Kara Sea.

Nansen was aiming for the waters north of the New Siberian Islands, where *Jeannette* had been crushed, and where he hoped to find his current. According to the map, such as it was, he ought first to make a beeline for Cape Chelyuskin. But this being the Arctic, ice dictated the actual course. *Vega*, fifteen years before, had been able to strike out across an open sea. Now, a tight-pressed mass of floes, like a patchwork of giant, barren white and green-tinted fields, immediately forced *Fram* to turn aside and follow the shore of the Kara Sea in an open lead running south-east along the land, until she was able to cut across to the Yamal Peninsula. There, on the evening of 6 August, off Cape Mora Sale, she was stopped by fog and ice, and lay to. Nansen, Sverdrup, Scott Hansen, Blessing, Hendriksen and Johansen rowed ashore.

The coast here was flat, shelving gently, so the boat was stopped some distance out in shallow water. In Johansen's words,

> Only Scott Hansen and I had sea boots, Hendriksen as well, so we had to carry the others in and out of the boat, and I looked quite peculiar with Nansen on my back, his long legs barely clear of the water.

A day or two later, with *Fram* still stuck, there was another trip ashore. Johansen discovered another side of Sverdrup. On board, as if conscious of command, his companion had seemed humourless and taciturn. Now, on the bleak strand of Yamal, round a camp fire of driftwood, Sverdrup 'was in his element. In his calm way he uttered the one priceless joke after the other.'

Eventually, the ice slackened, and in the evening of 9 August, *Fram* was able to get under way again. Ashore, a record of her call was left. During her stay, two Samoyeds had come out in a boat. They were afraid to come on board, but before rowing off again were given food and a box of matches.

Through straggling floes of slack drift ice *Fram* now sailed unimpeded and, on 12 August, near the end of the Yamal Peninsula, ran out into open water. Free of ice, the Kara Sea rolled on to the horizon. An easterly breeze had freshened. Fires were banked, the funnel lowered, and for the first time, *Fram* was under sail alone.

With every inch of canvas set, *Fram* made five knots. She now displayed an unexpectedly violent taste for griping to windward, which made her difficult to steer. Nonetheless, as Johansen put it, 'everyone is in a good mood, because we are under sail alone'. There is always a sense of exhilaration when engines fall silent, leaving undisturbed the hiss of spume and the moan of wind through rigging. Now even Nansen seemed finally to relax and took his turn with gusto, hauling at the shrouds when the ship had to go about.

By 16 August, *Fram* had rounded the Yamal Peninsula. She was already half way to Cape Chelyuskin, eastern boundary of the Kara Sea and the northernmost point of the Old World. Danger lurked in its approaches, reinforced by a quality of demonic myth. Nansen soon withdrew into himself again, walking alone and manifestly worried. The whole atmosphere on board became subdued.

Although a thousand miles from east to west, the Kara Sea is mostly shallow, and now the pack ice pressing down from the north, still unseen, gave it all the unlovelier features of narrow waters. A nasty, choppy, jumbled sea was soon whipped up. *Fram* headed north, until she providentially found a stream of ice. Smoke pouring from her funnel in a dark plume over a uniformly bleak grey Arctic sea, she hauled and tacked, hugging the quieter channels where the ice floes calmed the waves.

From the crow's nest Sverdrup, early on 18 August, sighted an unknown island, position 74°35′N. 80°10′E, level with the delta of the Yenisei River, a mere seventy miles or so off shore. This was the first discovery of the expedition.

At breakfast, there was a general discussion about what to call the island. Everyone, from Nansen downwards, messed together in the saloon aft: an elaborately carved and decorated place, with dragon's heads on the furniture, giving the popular idea of the hall of a Viking chief. In the end, since Sverdrup had first seen the island, it was by common consent named after him.

Over the next week or so, there was more naming. Russia had been marching eastwards for two hundred years, but the Siberian coastline and its inshore waters were still imperfectly charted. As *Fram* zig-zagged to the east, constrained by the edge of the pack ice to the north, she stumbled upon a forlorn, unknown archipelago – one cluster of which was eventually called after Clements Markham.

On the afternoon of 27 August *Fram*, once more enveloped in fog, was brought up by heavy ice. Nansen was now following the track of the *Vega*. He knew he was somewhere off Taimyr Island, but not exactly where. So *Fram* was put about to turn a few offshore islands charted by Nordenskiöld. The islands proved to be the outliers of another undiscovered archipelago – which Nansen named after Nordenskiöld – along which *Fram* cruised, first westerly, then north, before being stopped by ice again. She had to go about, and on 30 August she was back more or less where she started. She was still baffled by heavy ice ahead. After 1,500 miles of Arctic navigation she had met her first setback.

That was mirrored by events on board. In the engine room, an experimental auxiliary oil burner, intended to save coal, nearly melted the boiler and had to be discarded. The dogs were permanently tied up on deck, because otherwise they fought. 'If only they would make peace, they could come below decks,' Johansen whimsically remarked. 'But they don't know what is best for them – exactly like human beings.' Bedraggled, miserable and sick, they were exposed to cold, damp and wind. Two of their number had died.

For four days, *Fram* was stuck at her anchorage while the stokehold gang crawled into the boiler and scraped it free of salt once more. In September, which opened with a heavy snowfall, Nansen indulged in some gloomy stocktaking. Winter had already come; the short summer was long since on the wane. The ever-present comparison with Nordenskiöld was depressing. By 20 August, *he* had passed Cape Chelyuskin.

At last the engine room repairs were finished, and the boiler was filled with fresh water lying on the surface of the sea. This came from the outflow of the Siberian rivers, and the thawing of ice floes leached of salt. It also clutched like some monster at *Fram* when she tried to steam off southwards in search of a way out of the impasse. She was a victim of 'dead-water' – the excessive friction caused by a shallow layer of fresh water on top of heavier salt water, where the boundary between the two lies near the ship's bottom. Early in the morning of 3 September she reached some sludge ice, the dead-water lost hold, and with a noticeable bound she returned to normal speed.

In the afternoon, she was brought up once more by heavy ice floes. The prelude had been a highly disorienting search for the Taimyr Sound, the known passage to Cape Chelyuskin, passing strange islands not marked on any maps. That, together with the dead-water, caused a doleful shift of mood on board. It was not helped by the dawning realisation that the Samoyeds who had visited them off Yamal were probably the last human beings they would meet for a long time. When anchor was dropped, Nansen remained far from certain where he was. '*Is* this Taimyr Sound?'

he asked in his diary, 'Can we perhaps get through? A whole year is at stake.'

This was actually written somewhat later, for Nansen had neglected his diary since finishing the first volume. Now he had to start by casting his mind back all the way to 22 August, but meanwhile another crew member had also been keeping records. 'A month ago today since the speech from the throne was read out,' Anton Amundsen had written in *his* diary at the appropriate time – in a sarcastic reference to Nansen's tirade against the crew's drunkenness. He also observed that on the occasion of that anniversary, Nansen, for some reason, 'was in a bad mood'. Nansen's moods were becoming a feature of various diaries kept on board.

By 6 September, Nansen's wedding anniversary, *Fram* was under way again. A gale from the south-west had finally spent itself. The passage east towards Cape Chelyuskin was choked with ice, but a channel between two islands to the north had been swept clear. *Fram* started steaming up the sound. But where exactly she was heading, remained an enigma.

At this crisis in his fortunes, nervous and exhausted, Nansen turned in, leaving the ship gratefully to Sverdrup. Next morning at six o'clock Sverdrup woke him with the news that Taimyr Island was astern. Ahead, once more, lay heavy pack ice and an uncharted promontory marking the eastern end of Taimyr Bay. But now, at least, they had found their bearings once more. Between the land and the pack ice pressing in from the sea there was a narrow open lead. With Sverdrup and Nansen alternating in the crow's nest, and sounding constantly, *Fram* was nursed through shallow, foul waters until, in the evening, the lead closed, and she was brought to again. All the following day, she stayed where she was, hemmed in by ice against a low, shelving shore.

Next morning, 9 September, easterly winds had slackened the ice. From the crow's nest, Nansen saw a lead some way off, running out into an open sea. He decided to try and break out. The weather was ominous; the barometer preternaturally low. For the safety of the ship, Sverdrup wanted to wait; captain though he was, he yet bowed to Nansen. With all sail set, and steam raised to bursting point, *Fram* forced her way through the floes and found open water. 'Today we sail for King and country,' wrote Nansen. '*Fram* knows what is at stake.' It was a race to double Cape Chelyuskin before the ice closed in again and barred the way ahead.

Making eight knots, more than she had ever done before, *Fram* swept along a low coast, with islands out to sea and, to landward, features not yet on any map. In the deepening twilight, she crawled the last few miles against the turn of the tide. The sun set, but at that season in those latitudes, the nights were not yet dark. The sky was clear, iridescent, and around the horizon burning with the gold of the afterglow. Jupiter gleamed 'in lonely majesty', as Scott Hansen recorded, 'and was shot by me for a longitude fix.'

Nansen also observed Jupiter, but from a different point of view. In the crow's nest, atop the mainmast, high above the deck, alone and apart, he waited all night for 'the solemn moment', as he put it, 'when we would reach the goal which for so long had haunted us'. Swaying and dipping as the masthead swung lazily in the breeze, Jupiter seemed to hang over Cape Chelyuskin. In Nansen's own words, 'it must be my star, it was Eva's'. Eva, with her birthday on 7 December, was a Sagittarian, and therefore, in astrology, ruled by Jupiter. In the planetary cycle, Jupiter was then closest to the Earth, and hence burning bright.

At last, at 2 a.m., Cape Chelyuskin, a low promontory with a range of unnamed mountains rising up behind, was on the starboard beam. An hour later it had unequivocally been doubled. All hands were called. *Fram* put in close to land. At eight bells in the middle watch, flags were hoisted and from the ship's signal cannon a salute thundered across the waters. As if on cue, the sun broke the horizon and, as it did so, said Nansen, 'the Chelyuskin demon, which had bewitched us for so long, was shattered'.

Except for one man at the helm, and another in the stokehold, everyone now sat down at the table in the saloon, decorated with lanterns, round a hot bowl of punch. That proved what the moment meant to Nansen. Under his regime, spirits were a rarity. He came down from the crow's nest a different man and, to much cheering, proposed Cape Chelyuskin's *skål*.

A party that begins at 4 in the morning at the northenmost tip of the Old World [as Scott Hansen put it], belongs to the rarer events in a man's life. The party lasted until 5 a.m. ... and must absolutely be classed a success.

Nansen was in high good humour now. Jacobsen, the mate, an inveterate gambler, had bet Johansen they would not pass Cape Chelyuskin that season and was delighted to have lost. As usual, Jacobsen had laid off his bet, so financially he was safe too.

This outburst of relief overlaid the solemn consciousness of an historical event. Only one ship – the *Vega* – was known with certainty to have doubled Cape Chelyuskin before. *Fram* had become the second. More to the point: *Fram* had escaped being trapped for the winter, and perhaps for good.

In a broad band of open water, broken occasionally by floes loosely clustered, *Fram* headed south-east across the Laptev Sea for the mouth of the Olenek River, where Torgersen was waiting with the East Siberian dogs sent by Baron von Toll. The waters, however, ill charted as they were, shoaled ominously, and there was every chance of grounding. More sinister still, the ice was behaving in an unexpected way. Instead of the northerly current he had predicted, Nansen saw the threat of being trapped off the Taimyr Peninsula by a gyre from which there would be no escape. Badly though he wanted the extra dogs, the risks in consequence had grown too great. On 15 September, about 100 miles short of the Olenek, Nansen, regretfully, decided to sheer off to sea.

Heavy pack ice to the north drove *Fram* eastwards, over towards the New Siberian Islands. On 17 September Nansen, as Scott Hansen recorded in his diary, 'insisted on shaping north today, but S. [Sverdrup] is not particularly keen'. This time, Sverdrup prevailed – luckily, as it turned out. Next day, the waters were open to the north. *Fram* was off the delta of the Lena River, a mighty Siberian drainage system pouring warm water out into the Laptev Sea. Even where *Fram* was, 100 miles offshore, the sea was tinted brown by the silt borne along by the outflow.

Under full steam, with all sail set, *Fram* now headed north, unhindered. A loom over the eastern horizon probably marked Kotelnoi, at the western edge of the New Siberian Islands. From the crow's nest, all day on 19 September, there was open water all round, right up to the horizon, without a speck of ice, and there was music in the bubbling of the wake. Johansen tellingly recorded that 'we are in a good mood because our luck has turned'. Nansen himself was noticeably cheerful, chaffing Sverdrup for his half-serious belief in an open polar sea, and expectations of sailing to 85°N. For his part, Nansen saw his theories being fulfilled. To him, the open water was proof positive of a current across the Arctic from east to west. Nonetheless, he would be content to reach a latitude of 78° before finding the ice. That day, bottle post was thrown overboard.

In Nansen's own words next morning, 20 September: 'Now all my dreams are shattered.'

> At eleven o'clock ... as I sat looking at the map, and thinking that my cup of joy was full to overflowing, the 78th parallel would soon be reached, and if I added another two degrees, that would make as far as 80° sailing in open water, when we hauled off, and I ran out – ahead lay the edge of the ice, massive and tight-packed, gleaming in the fog.

The sun broke through in time for a meridian altitude: 77°46′N. was the result. Nansen was now faced with a dilemma. All along, he had planned to make enough northing before turning east to clear the New Siberian Islands. He was already on a level to do so. Unfortunately, eastwards the ice seemed to sheer off to the south. That way held the threat, perhaps, of being trapped up against land. Westwards would take *Fram* further from Nansen's predicted current. But at least in that direction, there seemed a chance of reaching further north, and perhaps even of eventually turning east. So, as the lesser risk, *Fram* was put about. Following the edge of the ice, she now sailed in a north-westerly direction, so she did in fact continue to gain latitude.

'Now we are entering the absolutely unknown,' in Johansen's words, 'here all charts stop, now our real voyage of discovery begins. Still we have seen nothing but ice and water,' he continued, 'but we have seen birds [migrating], both big and small, and' – prophetically – 'we believe that perhaps there is more land nearby.' To the north-west, opposite Cape Chelyuskin, still hidden in the Arctic mists, lay another archipelago. Known today as Severnaya Zemlya, it was almost another two decades before it was discovered.

On 21 September, late in the morning, *Fram* reached the end of a bay in the ice, which then started running south. Fog once again descended. Nansen gave orders to lay to and wait for the weather to clear. They were now well above the 78th parallel of latitude so, as he put it, 'my wishing-cup has done its job'. In the evening, the fog lifted. Around midnight, with a clear sky, Nansen recorded 'wonderful Northern Lights'.

> In an intensely glowing band of light, yellow-green and reddish, it wound its way from the horizon … upwards through the zenith and a little to the west, made a northwards turn. The sky deep blue alongside, the stars burning clear, and Eva's star (Jupiter) shone through the bands of colour, reddish and with greater power than ever.

Again the hint of the Zodiac and astrology: in Nansen's otherwise so rational mind.

Meanwhile lice were found on board. 'The cause of this charming entertainment,' to quote Johansen, 'is ascribed to the Samoyeds at Khabarova.' All day on 22 September there was what he called 'a grand louse war'. The ship was fumigated with steam hissing from a hose; clothes were boiled; heads were washed in disinfectant.

The following day, *Fram* still lay at the same ice floe. So Sverdrup seized the chance to have coal humped from the hold to replenish the engine room bunkers. In the surroundings, it was an even more grotesquely filthy business than usual. Black grime and coal dust settled on every available surface, a mordant contrast with the clean expanses of ice glinting in the autumn sun.

The days passed. *Fram* had to stay where she was. The silence was broken only by the periodic yelping of the dogs. No one formally announced on such-and-such a date that now *Fram* had been committed to the ice, but at some point it was tacitly accepted: perhaps already on 22 September, when fires were drawn; perhaps a few days later when the slush around the waterline began to congeal. 'The sun is beginning to sink now, 9 degrees above the horizon at midday,' Nansen observed on 26 September. '8 degrees of frost this evening at eight o'clock.' And, he continued, with an abrupt and characteristic change of mood after a walk out on the ice:

> Anything more wonderfully beautiful than the polar night does not exist. It is a dream-like sight. It is a light poem of all the finest and most delicate tones of the soul.

Two days later the dogs were moved from the ship out onto a floe, on 5 October the rudder was raised out of its well to safety.

'So now,' as Scott Hansen put it, 'we are well and truly moored for the winter.'

32

Frozen In

Fram was soon properly beset. On 9 October, after dinner, 'a great commotion began', in Nansen's words, 'and the whole [ship] trembled. Everybody rushed on deck to watch. *It was the first pressure in the ice.*'

> She allowed the ice to move cleanly beneath her, and lifted a little. The screwing continued during the afternoon, sometimes so strongly, that *Fram* was raised a few feet, but then the ice held no longer, and she broke through.

A day or two later, *Fram* was put more forcibly to the test. There was a

> creaking and groaning ... the gamut of tone colour ... like all the registers of an organ ... the ship trembles and jumps up ... or slowly rises.

Meanwhile, 'the ice is pressed up against the ship's side,'

> the floes split, pile up, are forced under the heavy hull, and we lie as if in a bed. Soon the noise begins to drop, the ship sinks down, and everything is quiet as before.

Fram had indeed shown that she could rise to the pressure of the ice. The rounded bottom, giving no purchase, could not be gripped, and functioned exactly as intended. The great unspoken fear had been laid to rest. Nansen's original idea and Colin Archer's design had been vindicated.

Nansen's birthday, on 10 October, coincided with the dawning of this discovery. He was anything but elated however. For one thing, he was now thirty-two and overwhelmed by the sense of the passage of time; for another:

> So far far away from Eva [he wrote in his diary.] Eva, Eva, you are thinking a lot about me today, I feel that, and you are miserable. Why should we be separated ... but what is the point of all this – don't complain, in time, we will meet again, but how long will it last?

Moreover, Nansen was ill.

> He has a fever, [wrote Johansen] but that man won't give in. He staggers

197

about, weak in every joint, his commanding eye is veiled, the winning smile is absent.

Dr Blessing simply diagnosed 'rheumatic pains and stiffness in right side of body. Treatment: massage with olive oil ... 23/10 Pain and stiffness disappeared.' Perhaps latitude was the real cause. *Fram* had laid to at 78°49′N and 132°53′E. On Nansen's birthday, her position was 78°22.5′N and 136°5′E. They were therefore drifting south, and continued to do so. That eventually provoked Nansen to a demonically nihilistic wail, of which the essence was that 'Nature knows no purpose', as he put it, and that science was probably an illusion.

> Here I sit among the drifting ice floes in the great silence and stare up at the eternal courses of the stars, and in the distance I see the thread of life becoming entangled in the complex web which stretches unbroken from the gentle dawn of life to the everlasting silence of the ice. I see the febrile race, soap bubbles form and burst. Thought follows thought, everything is picked to pieces, and becomes miserably small and worthless.

In more measured terms Scott Hansen, at about the same time, recorded a dialogue with Johansen about predestination and chance; in particular whether they were fated to discover new land. From the ship herself came intermittent rumblings 'like an angry man who cannot control himself', observed Johansen, coinciding with the periodic disturbance in the ice. Twice a day the floes were forced together and then eased, as if the movement were due to the tides. In a huge viscous wave of greenish-white, the ice would raft remorselessly in slow motion, throwing up hummocks on the way. Nansen carefully measured these, the tallest of which were around twenty feet high. Scornfully, he dismissed the claims of previous explorers to have seen hummocks fifty feet high.

On 14 October, Nansen ordered the rudder shipped again. For a day or two, *Fram* had floated in a pool when the pressure eased. From the crow's nest could be seen, beyond a band of ice, a lead running northwards to a horizon above which loomed a 'water sky'; the dark tint that meant open seas ahead. Nansen believed that possibly there lay the boundary between the pack ice that seized *Jeannette* and the southerly drift in which *Fram* was caught. *Jeannette* was much on Nansen's mind at this time, when *Fram* was 200 miles west of the point where she had been beset. Perhaps at a turn in the tide the ice barrier would open and allow *Fram* to slip through. But the expected opening never came. *Fram* had finally become a hulk embedded in the ice. Hummocks piled around the floes, rime clustered on the rigging, making a truly arctic scene.

Seaman's gear, meanwhile, was replaced by the expedition polar suits. These were designed by Nansen, and based on Eskimo clothing. Made of vadmel, like the garments on the Greenland expedition, the outfit consisted of breeches, leggings, and an anorak with the hood trimmed with fur. Footwear was a low boot made of sealskin.

One day, about a fortnight after *Fram* found her winter station, Kvik, the bitch Nansen had brought from home, mated with Barabbas, one of the uncastrated dogs fetched at Khabarova. In Scott Hansen's words: 'Kvik looked absolutely smug, and sneered at all other approaches.' The event had been widely looked forward to: now there was hope of pups before Christmas.

The dogs had become the great diversion. Nansen himself, soon after his failure to break out and steam further north, made his first attempt at driving dogs solo. He harnessed six animals to a Samoyed sledge brought from Khabarova, and proceeded to apply the lessons learned from Trontheim on dry ground there.

To begin with, he felt quite the accomplished dog driver. 'Prrr! – Prrr!' he mouthed, as he had been taught at Khabarova, and obediently the dogs loped off. Sitting on the sledge, Nansen was pulled sedately more or less in the right direction. But then the way was barred by a high tangle of hummocks marking the limit of the floe. The dogs made for the ship in wild career and, having gained this first victory over their new master, proceeded thoroughly to humiliate him. Back and forth, from one side of the ship to the other, they ran, sweetly ignoring the stream of Nansen's utterances which Scott Hansen observed 'were not to be expected of an educated man'. 'In the end, I gave up trying to get [the dogs] to go where I wanted,' Nansen recorded in his diary. There were no brakes, so he tried to stop by holding on to the sledge, and literally digging his heels in. 'It was of little use. In my smooth sealskin trousers I was dragged ignominiously over the ice, either on my belly, back or side ... Such was my first attempt at trying to drive dogs on my own.'

Part of the trouble lay in the system of harnessing. These dogs were arranged in a fantail – that is to say their traces were individually attached to a point on the sledge. It gave each animal the maximum freedom as distinct from being harnessed in tandem. But it also gave free play to the creative devilry that lurks in the mind of the dog. Nansen was appalled at their habit of fighting, and their ruthlessness in battle. One day a dog called Job was killed by his companions. 'There is not a grain of decency in these curs,' Nansen fumed in his diary.

> Like wild beasts the whole pack throws itself on the loser when they fight. – Stop – might it not be natural and healthy that the strong and not the weak are protected? Is it perhaps only we human beings who have defied the order of Nature by protecting all the weak?

On 25 October, the sun appeared for the last time before the polar night set in. Its farewell was a melancholy red segment above the edge of the ice around midday, shining weakly, without warmth, as if on a lifeless outer planet. 'We are exceptionally comfortable in every respect,' Amundsen wrote in his diary on that day. 'But sometimes the thought of home rises up, and deep down one longs for its protective atmosphere ... But that is impossible. There is not even a letter to look forward to, nothing else to see but icebergs round about and darkness.'

Suspended between sea and sky, *Fram* was isolated in a way beyond our own conception. Even the first men on the Moon, more than a century later and nearly a quarter of a million miles away, were in touch with their friends on Earth. *Fram* could not move much more than a thousand miles from human habitation, but when she passed out of sight, she had vanished from the world, and the world from her. Nordahl expressed that feeling in his diary when he wrote: 'Nansen is painting a picture of his home. I think of mine and paint with my memories.'

The day before the sun disappeared, the electric lighting was tried for the first time since the drift began. Current was provided by a German generator, one of the first models specially designed for marine use. It could be coupled to the engines, but also driven by a windmill, or by men turning a capstan on deck, or by a combination of both these methods. The windmill was used on its own.

Since early in October, Nordahl had been struggling with the assembly of a complex mechanism. The windmill was a bulky affair, with four great sails, reaching half way up the mainmast, and linked by an awkward contrivance of shafts and gears down to the generator in the engine room. The friction was such that a wind of at least 12 knots was needed to turn the machinery. Nordahl dubbed it a 'windmill breeze'. The day of inauguration was the first time that one had blown after a fortnight of near calm.

An aurora flickered across the sky; there was a ring round the moon; the ice glowed by reflection from below. Bathed in this ghostly light, the dark vanes of the windmill slowly began to turn, the grinding of its machinery breaking in upon the silence. It was, in Nansen's words, 'an eerie atmosphere – civilisation suddenly intruding into this frozen spirit world'. But when the lights came on, there was 'such pleasure', declared Nordahl, 'that at dinner *skåls* were drunk to me and the light'. There was another *skål* for Baron Oscar Dickson, who had paid for the lighting equipment and made this near-miracle possible. The light, said Nansen, raised everyone's spirits 'like a glass of good wine'.

After a decade or more of technical advance, the incandescent light bulb had become reliable. By modern standards the bulbs on *Fram*, giving a mere sixteen candlepower each, were unimpressive. But the fact remained that there was electric lighting throughout the ship. Besides, in the saloon there was a blazing arc lamp of 400 candlepower suspended beneath the skylight. To the men on board, it seemed a passable simulacrum of the sun.

During the first week of November *Fram*'s southward drift finally seemed to halt. As in other crises, Nansen had neglected his diary for a spell. He recommended on 19 November, after Scott Hansen had taken an observation that clearly showed they were moving north again. They were now at 78°27′N, having covered 44 miles in ten days. 'Hell and damnation,' Nansen exuberantly wrote, 'drive on in that direction.' Within a week, he was in the grip of depression again, as the drift slowed and threatened to reverse. But on the last day of November *Fram* was well past 78°30′. That suggested movement away from land but was not yet proof positive of the wished-for current. They were also moving east and might well be trapped in a gyre, merely swinging round to the outward spiral. But, in Nansen's words, 'hope rises, and life becomes brighter once more'.

33

A Flailing of Fists

'Ah, how I love that star,' Nansen was writing on 5 December – which he recorded as Eva's birthday, two days before the event – after seeing Jupiter once more through the haze. 'It shines over our journey, it is your eye, no evil can befall us as long as I have it.' The midday observation put *Fram* at 78°50′, which meant that after another check, she was drifting north respectably again at two miles a day.

Soon afterwards, there was an attack by a polar bear; the third since *Fram* was frozen in. It was the worst so far, chiefly because most guns were out of action. One or two misfired, because their mechanisms were clogged with vaseline made sluggish by the cold. Johansen eventually shot the bear – Nansen giving the coup de grace – but not before it had mauled Hendriksen and killed two dogs. One of these animals was called 'Johansen's friend' because it snarled at him as long as he was outside, even if far off on a floe. 'Instead of avenging myself on "my friend" for its fury against me,' Johansen wrote in his diary, 'I now had the satisfaction of being able to avenge its death by killing its murderer.' And:

> The dogs seem to get on better since being threatened with death and destruction by their common foe, the bear.

The day of the bear's attack, 13 December, was also marked by Kvik's much anticipated whelping. 'She is an amiable creature,' Scott Hansen recorded, 'and is now addressed as Fru' – Mrs in Norwegian. She had produced thirteen pups, of which she had been allowed to keep five bitches and three males.

Such were the mixed heralds of Christmas; celebrated, when it came, in true Scandinavian style with the elaborate, childlike semi-pagan ceremony of the eve. Behind the presents, the over-eating and the ritual washing each man was hiding homesickness. Probably Blessing alone was glad to be where he was.

The waning of the old year was marred by a push towards the south. Symbolically, too, *Fram* had been swung right round, so that she showed her stern to the north and was pointing the wrong way. At the best of times, behind the New Year's festive mask, often lies a darker undertone.

33. A Flailing of Fists

In those distant days before radio and the programmed ease of satellite systems, fixing position involved tedious squinting through telescopes at heavenly bodies followed by much arithmetic and looking up of tables. There were also no time signals: finding the right time, essential for navigation, required complex observations. Scott Hansen, *Fram*'s chief navigator, upon whom sole responsibility lay, used the occultation of Jupiter's moons. This meant timing the precise moment when one of them disappeared behind the planet's rim.

To help him by timing sights and booking the readings, Scott Hansen had Johansen. Each swathed in wolfskin outfits, noses barely protruding, they spent hours out on the ice with their instruments and pocket chronometers. Over the New Year Scott Hansen found Johansen 'not really in form now, but it is not possible to understand why, and I am unwilling to ask'. In the interior monologue of his diary, Johansen revealed precisely what was mirrored in the outward view:

> It is chastening to consider life at home and one's own past life from one's present standpoint. How many things do I not wish undone? I wonder how many mistakes my life is teeming with? ... And now I regret it all.

Constant yearning for Eva made Nansen equally despondent. He had a habit of walking alone out on the ice, a pack of dogs at his heels. 'The stars are good company,' he wrote of one such midwinter promenade. 'One can confide all one's longings to them, and they listen quietly.' He stayed outside until Jupiter appeared through shifting clouds. 'Parted, parted,' he was then moved to write, 'for no one knows how long from the only one I love.' His dreams also troubled him, and his reaction became more volatile.

On 8 January, after dinner, Hendriksen came and asked him to come up and look at a peculiar star that had just appeared over the horizon. In Nansen's own words:

> I came up on deck, and saw a strong red light just over the edge of the ice to the south ... It was *Venus*, which we saw today for the first time ... Strange that it should appear exactly today.

It was his little daughter Liv's first birthday. 'You have long since forgotten me,' he wrote, 'and you don't know what a father is.' Venus, Nansen went on, 'must be Liv's star, as Jupiter is Eva's'. In this he was wrong. Liv was a Capricorn, and therefore ruled by Saturn. But still he wrote:

> A good day to you on this your day, little Liv ... Perhaps Liv's day will be the start of our luck in our northwards drift ... under [her] star.

What Nansen's companions saw was a shifting and elusive personality. Scott Hansen wrote:

He is an odd character, sometimes serious, scientific and aggressive in discussions, and then one fine day extravagantly cheerful and pleasant, almost to the point of puerility. He wishes to dominate, which is quite natural, but he sets himself up too often as an authority ... In argument he is dogmatic when he is in the mood, which he is now for the most part ... so dogmatic that he gives the impression of not trying to understand his opponent's point of view, but only trying to overturn his arguments.

He also recorded that Nansen 'has a sheer mania for interfering in everything, and taking work out of the hands of people'. Nansen's presence brooded over the ship. His companions lived in apprehension of his next change of mood. As on Greenland, however, and luckily for them all, between them and him stood Otto Sverdrup.

Sverdrup and Nansen were a study in contrasts. Nansen was talkative. When the spirit moved, he could radiate an irresistible enthusiasm. Sverdrup very definitely could not. He rarely smiled, but behind a stony face he was, in Johansen's words, 'strangely funny, a really pleasant chap', who 'moved on board quietly and unobtrusively – saw everything, said little, but accomplished all the more'.

Sverdrup understood his fellow-men, which Nansen unfortunately did not. Nansen, on the other hand, as someone once said, had 'a certain quality, a force of character, an air of high distinction which he wore to a degree unmatched in all my experience of men'. In a word, he had presence. Unfortunately, however, he was unable to mask his emotions, or prevent them affecting his companions' state of mind. Sverdrup could. It was the distinction between personality and leadership, the one too often mistaken for the other. Nansen was the man with drive; Sverdrup had the talent to command.

On the face of it, this ought to have been an ideal partnership, but from the start Sverdrup had been in an invidious position. He was the captain of the ship. But Nansen was designated 'Expedition Leader' whom the essential clause in each man's contract required that he 'promise on my faith and honour to obey'. For the seamen, it was a worrying division of authority. In their world, a captain was the god-like figure astride the deck, whose word was law, and subject to no other mortal. 'In case ... the Expedition Leader decides to abandon the ship,' the contract further stipulated, encroaching yet more on the captain's prerogative, 'my obligations remain unaltered and in such an eventuality I also agree to ... blindly obey the orders of my commander and other superiors, and completely submit to the Expedition Leader.'

Nansen was haunted by the fear of mutiny, one of the ghosts of Arctic exploration. The classic cautionary tale was that of Private Henry's execution by Greely in 1884 for stealing food. Nansen had hoped that by invoking an element of democracy he could obviate such horrors. He therefore introduced the curious provision that the sole punishment for insubordination – and, marginally less heinous, incompetence – was to be loss of pay. This would be decided by Nansen 'in consultation with the Captain and 2 of the best men of the crew'. In one way, this was good psychology. Norwegians were not built for blind obedience. Nonetheless, when *Fram* was frozen in, the upshot was that Sverdrup had been reduced to an uncertain status in a decommissioned hulk.

Like most skippers in sail, Sverdrup commanded by sheer force of character. Nordahl tellingly remarked that he 'arouses confidence and a sense of security like no one else'. Scott Hansen agreed: 'In the hour of need, we will be better served by Sverdrup.' One way or another, Sverdrup found the psychological leadership thrust upon him. For his part, he had to admit that he found Nansen

> difficult to deal with in everyday contact. He was rather surly and overbearing, and in the long run that contributed to a less good atmosphere on board.

Sverdrup also realised that he had, at all costs, to avoid making Nansen feel that his authority was threatened.

There was, for example, wide discontent because Nansen, who was afraid both of fire and of burning too much fuel, banned all heating in the living quarters. It was only at the end of December, with the thermometer outside steadily around –30°C that Sverdrup, after the exercise of much patience and tact, finally persuaded him to light the stove. Thenceforth, at the cost of one bag of coal every three days, eked out by fuel oil burned as well, the temperature was tolerable for human beings below deck.

With the temperature, the mood on board changed too. 'We get on very well with one another now,' Johansen observed after New Year's Day. Nansen was now behaving 'not like the chief, but just like one of ourselves'. Round the table, after dinner, he was 'entertaining when he talked about his trips in summer and winter'. One day, for example, he told a story of how on a ski tour, Eva in her trousered outfit had been mistaken by the locals for a little boy.

One way or another, all were at last settling down. Amundsen pottered about his beloved engine room. Nordahl had his hands full keeping the electrical lighting in order. Blessing and Johansen were glad to escape the strains of being misfits in civilisation. Scott Hansen planned what he would do after returning home. His ambition was to open up the northern sea route to Siberia, via the Arctic, and up the Yenisei and Lena rivers into the hinterland. He found in Sverdrup a willing accomplice. 'Wild schemes', Scott Hansen said candidly early in the drift, but as the winter wore on he wrote: 'We immerse ourselves so deeply, that [the plan] must become reality.'

This happy scheming invariably took place in Sverdrup's cabin. Sverdrup deliberately arranged it so. Behind the camaraderie, he believed it vital to give relief from the presence of the captain. For that reason, he kept out of the way much of the time.

Despite the improved atmosphere, there had in fact been three fights on board. They all happened in the galley – the only place on the ship where smoking was allowed and where, after dinner, the smokers naturally congregated. One of these clashes involved Jacobsen and Juell. Jacobsen, the Chief Mate, was a good seaman; practical and ingenious. He was also rich in idiosyncracy. He was nicknamed 'In Short' because, in Scott Hansen's words, 'he says it all the time, especially when he delivers yard-long explanations'. Jacobsen also became a bit of a joke for 'wanting a book that someone else had borrowed. He always wants what others have.'

Norwegians are generally slow to anger and accustomed to isolation, but *Fram* posed special strains. For one thing, nobody on board had quite grasped what they were letting themselves in for. How could they, since nothing like it had ever yet been contemplated? While *Fram* was sailing over open seas, there was still the stimulation of an ordinary voyage. But what now lay ahead was an indeterminate time of waiting, a state to which the Norwegian psyche is particularly ill suited.

The ship, moreover, was cramped. There was only one saloon, onto which all the living quarters opened. There were four single cabins; two on each side. Nansen and Hansen had the starboard ones, Sverdrup and Blessing, those to port. Aft were two larger cabins intended for four men each, crowded quarters in themselves. Amundsen, Petterson, Juell and Johansen shared the one to starboard. Because of the unforeseen hiring of Bernt Bentsen, he, Jacobsen, Mogstad, Nordahl and Hendriksen were crammed into the one to port.

Apart from these general strains, there was also an insidious fear of disease. Every month, Blessing carried out a medical examination. He took blood samples – earning him the soubriquet of 'Vampire' – to test for anaemia. Beyond all else, he was looking for signs of scurvy. No longer, as on the first crossing of Greenland, could it be ignored. Blessing failed to find the apathy, swollen limbs, and other mental and physical symptoms of the disease.

Scurvy was the bane of polar exploration. Untreated, it is always fatal. Against all prognostications, Nansen had apparently kept it at bay. He provided a classic example of being right for the wrong reasons.

When *Fram* sailed, the cause of scurvy was still far from clear, but it was associated with prolonged lack of fresh food. Nansen had to feed his men for up to an estimated five years, cut off from regular supplies.

Scurvy is now known to be the result of an acute lack of Vitamin C, but that was only identified in 1932, the first vitamin to be isolated. In fact, at the end of the eighteenth century, well over a hundred years before the concept of vitamins arose, the Royal Navy had identified scurvy as a deficiency disease, virtually eradicating it by the use of lime juice. Much earlier, the Vikings had learned the same lesson, although their preventative was the arctic cloudberry (*Rubus chamoemórus L.*), from the

Scandinavian heathlands, an even more potent source of Vitamin C. On their long ocean voyages, they loaded their ships with vast quantities of the berry.

In the nineteenth century, however, orthodox medicine, not for the first time having failed to learn from history, was off on a wild goose chase. It succumbed to the fashion of seeing everything in terms of bacteriological infection. Since scurvy was prevented by fresh food, this neatly fitted the preconceived pattern. It was the theory uncritically accepted by Nansen's chosen expert on nutrition, Sophus Torup, the Danish-born Professor of Physiology at Christiania University.

Torup therefore advocated tinned foods, preserved with clinical cleanliness. However, he also believed in variety. Nansen took him at his word. He had samples analysed; that too, a piece of pioneering, and ordered about fifty different kinds of tinned food.

Vitamin C, besides not being synthesised by human beings, is highly unstable, destroyed by oxidation and prolonged cooking. The canning process, based on quick heating, and storage under vacuum, counteracts this to some extent. In the interests of variety, among Nansen's tins were vegetables like red cabbage, kohl rabi, and savoy; all rich in Vitamin C. Nansen also had another stroke of luck. Nordenskiöld, on the voyage of the *Vega*, had taken cloudberries preserved in rum, because knowledge of its preventative powers had been handed down in Nordic folk medicine, and this became one of the few polar expeditions free of scurvy. Nansen copied Nordenskiöld to the extent of loading *Fram* with half a ton of cloudberry preserve. Thus, by accident, on the basis of a false assumption, he fed his men in the right way to prevent scurvy.

Paradoxically, for all the care he took in selecting the right food Nansen was cavalier over its preparation. He declined to hire, or could not obtain, a professional cook. He assumed that anyone could take his turn in the galley, especially since much of the cooking would merely be heating tins. In the end, by natural selection, Nordahl, Petterson and Juell took charge. The passage of time was marked by the changing of the cook; each served four weeks in turn. Juell at least was a find. Having learned from his wife, he turned out to be, amongst other things, a passionate baker. When he reigned in the galley, there were fresh rolls for breakfast. Thus, again by luck, the food served was healthy, and at times even quite appetising.

Despite all the planning, there were hitches in the order of things. There was unexpectedly little wind. Consequently, the windmill often stopped, the electric lighting failed, and only the wan gleam of paraffin lamps remained. There was also the feeling, well summed up by Scott Hansen, that *Fram* was drifting on an unknown sea, and that

The screwing of the ice tells us that forces are at work here, which it is impossible for us to master, but only avoid.

Of all those on *Fram* it turned out to be Nansen himself who found it hardest to settle down. Partly, of course, this was because he missed Eva, but the cause went deeper than that. It was not mere sexual deprivation. Nansen was incapable of making a proper friend among men. He needed the companionship of women. He also felt the lack of intellectual conversation. In the end, he seemed to have most in common with Peder Hendriksen, the harpooner from Tromsø. Hendriksen became Nansen's favoured crony, and the only one whom Nansen addressed, or even referred to, by his Christian name, or allowed to accompany him on his otherwise solitary walks out on the ice floe. Nansen might have stepped out of a novel by his extraordinary fellow-countryman, Knut Hamsun; the embodiment, as Nansen himself once said, of 'that irredeemable old tragedy – the conflict between ... the primitive man ... in us ... and an all-powerful civilising culture'. Hendriksen played the part of his alter ego, regaling his chief with a fund of stories from his years sealing round Spitsbergen. Nansen found them vastly entertaining, even the unlikeliest, the grossest, and those involving the wildest characters with a touch of bestiality.

The only really unpopular member of the crew was Mogstad, the handyman. He had turned out to be an exceptionally quarrelsome character who played the therapeutic rôle of scapegoat. The dogs had theirs as well. But, as Johansen wryly noted, in their case the ritual unfortunate was condemned to death.

Their fighting apart, the dogs offered general solace. The chartroom was converted to Kvik's maternity ward, and when her pups grew to the entertaining stage, beating each other with their little paws, they became furry things to cuddle.

At Nansen's instigation, an expedition magazine was started. Called *Framsjaa*, 'Fram Review', it was edited by Blessing, but folded after eight issues due to flagging contributions. *Fram* also had a library of some six hundred books including the works of Ibsen, Zola, Dostoievsky and Goethe. As the polar darkness gathered, Sverdrup was reading *Trætte mænd*, 'Tired Men', a pioneering novel in the 'decadent' style, by Arne Garborg, who had been at Nansen's farewell dinner – an odd choice, at first sight, for a practical seaman. But a Norwegian archetype is the rough exterior hiding cultivated interests. Nansen himself returned at one point to Byron, the love of his youth, copying quotations into his diary from 'Childe Harold' to match his mood. For example:

> 'Upon such a shrine
> What are our petty griefs? let me not number mine'

followed by the comment:

Is there more pain than pleasure in life, more suffering than enjoyment?

The library also contained the chronicles, frequently consulted, of previous polar expeditions. Soon after Christmas, Nansen was reading *Arctic
Explorations* by Elisha Kent Kane, the American explorer who, forty years
earlier, had tried for the Pole. 'I feel that we are fighting the battle of life
at a disadvantage, and that an Arctic night and an Arctic day age a man
more rapidly than a year anywhere else in this weary world,' Kane at one
point had written in his journal. Nansen copied the passage into his own
diary, with the observation: 'Those were dismal experiences [and an]
exceedingly discouraging ... view of the matter.'

> Luckily, I believe I can say that it is completely false. For my own part ... I
> believe I have never felt physically so healthy and so balanced as I am now.

This protestation was a little too fervent. Even to those who live above
the Arctic Circle in Northern Norway and are accustomed to winters
without the sun, the darkness seems oppressive. Even more did it seem so
to Nansen and his crew. It was not that it was pitch dark. There was light
from the stars, in season from the moon, from meteorite showers and,
above all, from the aurora borealis, shimmering in luminescent veils
overhead. There was an eerie beauty in the scene, with *Fram* silhouetted
like a ghost ship against the sky and the ice. 'The windmill revolves
periodically,' said Johansen, 'and shows that there is life amongst the
isolation.' Nonetheless:

> When the sun arrives, we will have a sun festival, just like other heathen –
> it will be a kind of religious service, and the only one to be held here on board.

But whatever the tensions on *Fram*, they were softened by a sense of
cohesion and security. In Nansen's words, this was largely due to 'the life
together in the same mess, with everything in common; certainly the first
time it has been tried'. Above all, there was the comforting knowledge that
this expedition was designed to avoid the historical sagas of disaster. As
Nansen himself recorded after a bout of disturbance in the ice:

> It is strange, this pressure, which has caused many previous polar explorers
> so many worries. We virtually ignore it.

There was also the comfort of routine. Regular watches were kept,
meals arrived on time. Sometimes the silence was broken by sentimental
melodies from an automatic organ (like the electric lighting, also presented by Oscar Dickson) usually with Nansen tramping at the pedals.
From the dogs periodically came mournful, wolf-like howls. An air of
almost unreal normality descended on the ship. Only a distant clamour in
the ice and creaking of the ship's timbers sometimes obtruded with their
reminder of reality. As Nansen recorded one day, 'life is fundamentally

pleasant ... Fate has allowed one ... to escape being ground down by the tedium of everyday life'.

> Amundsen [says] 'we are the happiest people on earth ... we have no troubles; everything is given to us, without having to think about it'. [And] Juell thought that what was especially attractive was that there were no court cases or creditors.

34

Mood Swings and a Secret

It was transitory contentment. On 10 October 1894, Nansen's thirty-third birthday and his second on the ship, he was out alone on the ice with Sverdrup, when the latter blandly suggested that next October Nansen might no longer be on board. Nansen laconically agreed, and left it at that.

The origins of this enigmatic exchange went far back. In the middle of January that year, Johansen recorded what he called 'a cheerful chat after dinner' about

> a sledge expedition towards the Pole, when we had gone further North, and then to Franz Josef Land, while the old tub would try to break loose and hurry there to meet the sledge party that would not count more than 3, but have all the dogs.

The following day, Nansen went for a long walk across the floes with Hendriksen, as was his wont; this time in a northerly direction. 'There was splendid flat ice and excellent conditions for sledging, better as we proceeded north,' Nansen observed.

> The more I see of this ice ... the more that plan begins to mature that I have long been brooding over. It must be possible after all to reach the Pole with dogs and sledges over this ice, if one left the ship for good, and headed for Franz Josef Land or the West Coast of Greenland.

This was a mental somersault. Nansen seemed to be abandoning his own principle of working with natural forces, not against them. But he evidently no longer believed that the drift alone would get him to his goal.

The facts spoke all too plainly for themselves. It was only on 22 March, after four slow tantalising oscillations about the invisible line, that *Fram* at last cleared the eightieth parallel for good. She had taken six months to cover a single degree of latitude. At that rate, it would take five years to reach the Pole.

Nansen's doubts could be traced to the very beginning of the drift. When *Fram* entered the ice the previous autumn, soundings had so far shown 50 fathoms at most. Then suddenly, there was no bottom at 200 fathoms; likewise on succeeding days. Finally, bottom was found at 800 fathoms. The first southerly setback towards land brought a return to shoal waters.

But when the ship began moving north out to sea again, the lead ran out more and more until, on 21 December, there was no bottom at over 1,000 fathoms.

It was a startling sequence of events. 'There goes the shallow polar basin,' was Nansen's lugubrious remark. Nobody had recorded such soundings in these latitudes before. If he returned safely home, he would have with him the momentous discovery of a deep Arctic sea. The immediate implications were less comforting. 'My plan lies smashed to pieces,' Nansen lamented.

> My theories, my palace, where I esconced myself self-confidently, and looked down on the many ridiculous criticisms; at the first breath of wind, everything collapses like a pack of cards. You may construct the most ingenious theories, and you may be certain of one thing, and that is that reality will defy them. Did I really believe with such certainty? [It was] self-delusion. An inner doubt always lurked behind all reasoning. It was as if the longer I defended myself, the closer I came to doubt.

What Nansen really meant was that the whole concept of his drift had been based on the circulation of shallow waters. In calmer mood:

> These depths overturn all my deductions of a current. Either we will find no current, or an extremely small one.

But the nub was this. *Fram* had deviated from the predicted course. It was becoming clear that she would miss the Pole by a disconcerting margin.

'Columbus discovered America by a miscalculation that was not even his own,' wrote Nansen. 'God knows what my miscalculation will mean for me.' At least it meant a logical justification for wanting to set off for the Pole:

> It is after all in order to traverse the unknown polar regions that one has gone out ... and therefore one's duty is first and foremost to do what one can to attain that goal.

But he was honest enough with himself to raise other, less rational motives. One was a characteristic Norwegian craving for action at almost any cost. The passive waiting on *Fram* had quickly reduced him to a dismal moody fluctuation between restlessness and boredom.

There was also another, more insistent theme. *Fram*'s masts and rime-filled rigging dimly silhouetted against a starlit winter sky conjured up images of a forest, and Eva and ski tours at home. He wrote tellingly in his diary of 'a burning desire day and night' for Eva. And: 'My thoughts have circled round this one thing; the possibility of going to the Pole and then home.' He recorded a dream to that effect. And in this revealing passage:

> One would be home by the autumn, if one set off now, immediately in the spring. I can hardly bear to think of it, it is almost *too* early ... Am I afraid, perhaps to risk my life? No, it cannot be that, it must be something else that holds me back, and inhibits my happiness. Perhaps a secret doubt over the feasibility of the plan? I can no longer control my thoughts, everything melts together. I am an enigma to myself ... It has never been like this before.

It would be too simple to say that Nansen wanted to go home, and the quickest way happened to be via the Pole. But he was jealous of Eva, and wanted to return to her as soon as he could. Everything else began to look like rationalising that desire.

Parallel with his emotional turbulence, Nansen preserved a thread of logical thought. He decided to wait and see what the summer would bring in the way of a drift. Every mile towards the Pole would lessen the distance to be covered over the ice. Longitude, however, was more important than latitude. Nansen wanted to be so far to the west, that he was due north of Franz Josef Land, and hence as close as possible to the nearest shore. But:

> Nothing can stop a journey northwards to the Pole [he wrote in his diary] and then homewards with all sail set.

While Nansen was ruminating, Johansen emerged from his depression one day 'to do somersaults and handstands on the ice next to the ship', as he said. Partly, this was a celebration of light returning. As January ebbed, darkness began yielding around noon to the muted glow of early dawn. Even Nansen, so Scott Hansen observed,

> is in brilliant form these days, and has been extremely pleasant recently, so I am inclined to admire him again.

But behind the good humour, Nansen was still torn by conflicting emotions:

> I laugh at scurvy [as he put it], I laugh at the power of the ice. We live as if in an impregnable fortress, I also laugh at the cold, that is nothing. But at the wind I do not laugh, for that is everything, and that, no effort of will can command.

With uncertainty clouding his predicted current now, Nansen had transferred his faith to the wind. 'I say once again that the Siberian driftwood off Greenland cannot lie,' he reiterated. Through a hole in a thin patch of ice, a plumb line was rigged to show the apparent drift. Nansen became prey to its behaviour. When the line streamed southwards in the

213

water, and *Fram* was therefore moving north, Nansen was elated; otherwise, he relapsed into despair.

His own plans for the Pole he kept entirely to himself. To conceal what was really in his mind, he pretended that the preparations he now set in train were both for a *possible* polar journey, and precautions for abandoning ship.

Ambivalence undeniably tinged the activity with which, towards the end of January, *Fram* began to stir. The homely tramp of a sewing machine was heard: Sverdrup was making sails for the boats. This was actually against the day the ship might have to be abandoned in open water.

On 10 February, Nansen tried driving dogs on the ice for the first time since his ignominious performance the previous autumn. Since then new harnesses had been made. Instead of the original Siberian type, they followed the more sophisticated Greenland Eskimo design, and now the traces, instead of lying under the belly between the legs, ran freely above the back.

Nansen had also realised that running dogs was not like driving horses. He sat on the sledge as before, but now someone went ahead to show the way. The dogs followed, and things went considerably better.

Somebody had once remarked that Nansen was not very good at training his hunting dogs; he was too impatient. Nor did he have the touch needed to make a good dog driver. Johansen and Nordahl were far better. Both had an empathy with the dogs and both, from time to time, preferred their society to that of human beings.

Meanwhile, there was the perennial question of ski bindings. Nansen was having yet another model fitted for everyone. It was the so-called Finnish type, consisting of a single tough leather strap wound through a lateral slot in the ski, then over the toe and round the heel of the boot. It differed from the binding used by Nansen on the first crossing of Greenland, in that it lacked buckles of any kind. Suppleness, and hence economy of effort, was its great quality.

One day in February, Nansen was the first to go out skiing in winter quarters. He went alone and far away. The winter had been arid, with little snow. All around, until recently, had lain the dead surface of bare ice. At last snow had come, to bring life to a barren world. In his diary, Nansen rhapsodised:

It's quite bracing at −42° to −44° and a biting north wind. Nature is so beautiful and clean, the ice sparkling white with blue shadows on fresh fallen snow, set against the growing daylight [and] the glittering blue sky.

Preparations continued all the while. Petterson – 'Lars the Smith', so called – made the air ring out with his anvil as he forged various gadgets, including small nails, which had given out. Hauling at their single sticks, figures ambled across the scene, testing different skis.

The level surface of the ice made an ideal nursery for running dogs. For skiers, it was less inspiring. Where the floes had rafted at the seams lay rudimentary gradients. Near the ship, the process had thrown up a hummock that offered a miniature slope.

It was on Sunday, 18 February, that Nansen felt for the first time that he was making real progress in the art of dog driving. He went out on the ice with a team of eight dogs, himself sitting on the sledge. The animals were not only beginning to respond to his commands, but pulled away at a proper pace. The real event of the day, however, lay elsewhere.

Scott Hansen, Sverdrup and Johansen accompanied Nansen on skis. In Scott Hansen's own words:

We can say that skiers and dog sledge kept up with each other.

Such was the almost casual record of an historic discovery: *the natural speed of a cross-country skier was the same as that of dogs pulling a load.*

The consequences were profound. A skier could move under his own power, instead of riding on the sledge. This meant in turn that the useful load was correspondingly raised. That is what distinguishes the combination of dogs and men on skis. On the ice floes around *Fram*, Nansen spent long hours developing this method. He was launching what amounted to another revolution in polar travel.

On 20 February, the sun returned; according to the almanac at least. Clouds obscured the horizon, so the disc could not actually be seen. Nonetheless, the event was celebrated by a special dinner, and target shooting out on the ice. In Johansen's words: 'The horrors of the polar night, as so often described, have gone like a dance for us.'

Nansen, however, was less inclined to brag. 'I stand and gaze over this desolate landscape of ice, with plains and heights and valleys formed by screwing during the changing tidal currents of the winter,' he wrote, awed yet again by the helplessness of what he called a 'human insect' before the might of natural forces toying with anything in their path.

In March, the first sounding since midwinter was tried. Expecting shallow waters, Nansen had brought no deep-sea sounding apparatus, so he was reduced to improvisation. A steel hawser was unwound, the strands spliced together, and added to what hempen rope there was. The lead was hauled up by a party marching over the ice with the line over their shoulders for a hundred metres or so, laying it down, and then returning to the hole for the next pull. The outcome was 1,860 fathoms, no bottom. There was an eerie sense of floating on the edge of the abyss. Amundsen suggested they had found the hole through which the earth's axis ran.

Meanwhile, on the shifting crust of ice, plaything of wind and water, floe grinding remorselessly against floe, the seasons maintained their contradictory advance. On 8 March, Scott Hansen took the first meridian altitude of the sun after the long winter depending on the stars for navigational fixes. A few days later, Nansen went skiing in –50°C, the coldest yet. For the first time in his life, his thighs were frozen. Nonetheless, despite a breeze in his face, he claimed he felt less discomfort than skiing at home in temperatures thirty degrees higher. Nearly a month later, on 7 April, after a long absence, polar bears reappeared: 'our herald of spring,' as Johansen put it, 'like the first blue tit at home.'

On *Fram* the saloon was washed to remove the winter's grime. Yet another harbinger of spring came from the nostalgic acrid scent of Stockholm tar. Skis were being impregnated with the hot, black and sticky substance, the usual method of waxing then. The skis were then stacked along the side of the ship, like a mountain restaurant at home. Good snow and lengthening days enticed everybody out skiing as far as they could still see *Fram*'s masts over the horizon. The dogs, lolling in the sunlight as it increased, completed the picture of contentment.

Blessing, pleasant and universally liked, continued meticulously to examine his charges. He detected obesity and had some well-chosen words to say about over-eating and lack of exercise. Once he had to treat Petterson for an injured eye after fisticuffs with Mogstad; for them, being cooped up together was still too much of a trial. Of scurvy, however, there was still no obvious sign – although the fighting might have been partly due to vitamin deficiency.

Mirror of what would be happening at home, a solemn procession round *Fram* on the ice (dogs included), marked the Norwegian national day on 17 May. Nansen, in an oration from the bridge, 'opined that we would do much to rouse the Norwegian people's self confidence', to quote Scott Hansen.

> I did not actually have the feeling of anything so damned uplifting in the fact that we lie here and laze about and eat well.

On 24 June, the first anniversary of their departure from Christiania, Blessing recorded: 'Everybody sound in mind and body – to an even higher degree than at our departure last year. If only the same can be said next Midsummer's Day!'

Some time between 13 and 19 May *Fram* had crossed the eighty-first parallel. (Clouds prevented daily observations.) She had taken less than two months to cover this degree of latitude – three times faster than for the one before. She was moving north now at roughly a mile a day. This acceleration promoted good humour on board, even in the face of continuing monotony; each day a repetition of the other.

The summer dragged on, the air temperature hovering just above freezing point. It was a time of ennui. The Midnight Sun was one thing.

The drab, churned and thawing floes were something else. Worst of all was the slush underfoot, like some everlasting late spring. There was no skiing now. Much of the time, men moped around the ship. Blessing tried to enliven the proceedings by wearing a light frock coat, as if on a boulevard, when collecting algae.

Meanwhile, cracks appeared in the ice; leads opened and closed. Near *Fram*, a sizeable lake of fresh melt water formed on the surface of the floe. There, one day in June, Nansen supervised the introduction of the crew to rowing in a kayak. He had brought some specimens along, originally acquired in Greenland. Having discoursed on his own ability, he hoped to enjoy the sight of tyros capsising in these unstable craft at their first attempt. That at least was the impression when, after various people in fact managed rather well, their leader quickly left the scene.

As the season turned, and the midnight sun began gently spiralling down again, Nansen displayed another of his bewildering changes of mood. He had become notably talkative, buttonholing anyone in his path. Paradoxically, at the same time, he seemed to be growing more isolated and had now withdrawn to a private work cabin. 'It is basically pleasanter down here when he is absent,' Scott Hansen commented. 'He is too overbearing in his judgment, and his opinion must take precedence over everyone else's.'

But behind the arrogant persona so obvious to his companions, Nansen was secretly consumed by another of his waves of self-disgust. He now recorded in his diary what he called his 'life's account, and found it bankrupt'. Besides a change of the drift to the south, this particular outburst was precipitated when, leafing through a popular magazine one evening, he stumbled on the potted biographies of great men. 'I have a bitter feeling that while they concentrated on a single task [and] achieved something, my life has been divided and wasted.'

It was a long outpouring, page after page. Two themes were intertwined. One was his despair – 'the sin against the Holy Ghost, that which is never forgiven', as Nansen put it, agnostic though he was. The other was his old Faustian sense of possessing hidden powers that he was unable to release.

'I have never lacked great thoughts about my own intellectual worth,' Nansen wrote. 'Why was I given a Titan's longings and then formed like an ordinary worker ant?' 'Homunculus', 'vain', were some of the epithets he now hurled at himself.

Nansen catalogued the interests he had run through, from mathematics as a schoolboy to neuroscience, art, geology, and now oceanography. All his life he had waited for 'the great idea that ... would hit me like a bolt of lightning'. Youth was when 'the bolts of lightning come, if they are ever to strike ... But now ... I am hardly really young any longer ... and the future is unlikely to bring any.'

Oddly enough, Nansen found that his own subject, neuroscience, was the one that attracted him least now. In it he had found contentment for the only time in his life. He had tried to 'trace the origin of thought, investigate the innermost structure of the nervous system ... I thought I glimpsed new paths, and views opened that seemed to lead further on ... and I feel the whole burden of my sin at having deserted ... the microscope.' Yet once he had established the principle, in his own revealing words, 'the charm had vanished'.

That was a pity. Some time before he sailed on *Fram* it was being said of Nansen that he 'knew how to handle the microscope as well as ice axe and snowshoes'. Wilhelm Waldeyer, a German anatomist, wrote those words.

Waldeyer was concerned with Nansen's research into the central nervous system, but felt that even he had to work in a topical allusion. Waldeyer was writing in a Berlin medical journal on recent neurological research, and especially 'those authors who do not accept a continuous network'. Their ideas could

> easily be summarised in a simply expressed principle of great significance. This would be:
> 'The Nervous System consists of innumerable units, not connected ... anatomically.'

That unit, wrote Waldeyer, 'I propose to call [a] "neuron".' The independence of the cellular unit is the cardinal tenet of what came to be known as the neuron theory, which, in its turn, is the foundation of modern neurology.

Waldeyer claimed no part in the research. He was only gathering up the threads. Nansen was one of six pioneers whose work he was summarising.

Almost in the same breath, Nansen had become a pioneer both of modern skiing and of neurology. For the one, he obtained ample honour, but for the other, despite Waldeyer's mark of recognition, he never received his rightful due.

Waldeyer published his formulation of the independence of the neuron in December 1891, having defined the term in print – from the Greek word for 'sinew' – about six months earlier. Besides Nansen, among the figures whom he invoked was Santiago Ramón y Cajal.

Cajal was a provincial Spanish doctor with an heroic vision of himself, and a monumental capacity for self-advertisement. He was not over-scrupulous in acknowledging his predecessors. He built himself up as the discoverer of the neuron theory, and the sole founder of modern neurology. To this day, Cajal has been taken at his own valuation, although in fact, he was relatively late in the field. Nansen became one of the pioneers whose work, in the process, was eclipsed. He suffered the treble disadvantage of having published few papers, of being a lone invertebrate zoologist among medical men, and of having left the field, so that he could not keep his name to the fore. However, by the very act of definition, his work is implicitly commemorated in a celebrated medical term.

It is not an academic question. The neuron theory turned out to explain the workings of the central nervous system. It lies at the heart of modern medicine. From the development of new anaesthetics onwards, its practical consequences have been incalculable.

Nansen could likewise have balanced his exercise in self-loathing with a book he had written about the Eskimos of Greenland. As *Eskimoliv* ('Eskimo Life'), it appeared in parts in 1891. A distillation of his own experiences in Greenland, this book was a highly personal blend of ethnographic record and a paean to a threatened way of life. It proclaimed Nansen's now unshakeable conviction that Western civilisation, and Christianity in particular, only ended, for all its incidental benefits, in corrupting the Eskimos and any other primitive culture with which it came in contact.

While the book was appearing – on 29 October 1891 to be exact – Nansen formally left the Norwegian state church. This was a step of considerable significance in those days. Eva, though virtually without belief herself, declined to follow him. Nansen had been meditating his action for years. Very likely his contact with the Eskimos helped him to make up his mind. In a highly personal variation of the worship of the noble savage, he was greatly attracted by their mythology, and their particular form of animism.

Gustav Retzius, Nansen's Swedish scientific colleague – whom he had probably inspired with the idea of the neuron – was, for one, ecstatic about the book. 'My wife [is] now … reading your "Eskimo Life" aloud [while I am] working on the nervous system of the lamprey,' he had written to Nansen.

But no amount of applause seemed to enable Nansen to find pleasure in what he had undoubtedly accomplished so far. He foresaw even less pleasure in what he might yet do. 'Let me attain the North Pole,' he wrote, looking through a porthole on the midnight sun gleaming over the ice, 'or even the very South Pole, how will that help?'

> I now feel the justification in my father's constant warning against dividing myself too much … Too late I feel the gravity of that warning, now I sit here like a hopeless dilettante.

Thereafter, Nansen changed attitude again. He was, Scott Hansen recorded towards the end of August, 'unusually pleasant … approximately as he was in Christiania. Reasonable and accommodating … If only it continues, it will soon be as pleasant here as it was miserable before.'

But the next reversal of mood predictably arrived. It reigned for most of September, as snow, proper frost and hence good skiing conditions returned. Towards the end of the month, Nansen decreed that everyone, excepting duty cooks and meteorological observers, should ski for two hours a day, between 11 a.m. and 1 p.m. The order was resented by some, because regimentation was not to their taste. But Nansen wanted his men fit in case, after all, a retreat over the ice to safety was required. There were clear signs of unfitness, as also of clumsy technique, as evidenced now by various broken skis in the rough terrain of the Arctic pack.

The men on *Fram* were now suspended in limbo, waiting for Nansen to announce his intentions. By the middle of October, the sun disappeared again, and the second winter night was upon them. That further depressed the mood. The dogs at least provided entertaining gossip. Later in the month Scott Hansen heard 'confidentially', as he noted, 'that Freja has had a little encounter with Bielki, so against the regulations there will be pups again during the winter'.

The denouement came on 16 November when, on a moonlight ski tour alone with Sverdrup, Nansen finally revealed his plans. Little contained in them came as a surprise. 'It is now almost certain,' Scott Hansen had already noted long before, 'that if we drift to around 85° by the spring, two men will go off with the pack of dogs to bag the Pole ... It will probably be Nansen himself and, as his companion, Johansen will be the obvious choice.'

That in broad outline, was what Sverdrup now heard from Nansen himself, as their skis rasped over the snow. There was this difference, however: Nansen would settle for 83° instead of 85° as the lowest latitude from which he was prepared to start.

Three days later, on 19 November, Nansen, in the presence of Sverdrup, formally asked Johansen to accompany him on a journey towards the Pole. It was 'a red letter day in the story of my life', Johansen began his diary that day, even though Sverdrup had long since forewarned him. 'To which,' as Johansen put it at the time, 'I naturally declared myself willing – all as a hypothetical question, naturally.' Also, in his own words, Johansen now told Nansen that 'there was talk about the matter among my shipmates'. Consequently when

> Nansen asked me to think the matter over ... I replied that I needed no time for consideration, but had already thought it over, and declared myself willing to go along. I naturally considered it a great distinction that the choice had fallen on me.

Nansen had chosen Johansen because, as he succinctly put it, Johansen was 'unquestionably best suited in all respects; an accomplished skier, certainly a stayer like few others, and a splendid fellow, both physically and mentally.'

This opinion was widely shared. Johansen, modest and unassuming, was (when not in a fit of gloom) probably the most popular man on board. He was at any rate the best available companion for Nansen in the isolation and danger that lay ahead. For one thing, each was in some ways a mirror of the other. Johansen, like Nansen, was plagued by recurrent regrets over his past life. Both were uneasy over the woman they had left behind. Nansen needed an unquestioning follower; Johansen was looking for a leader, or at least a stronger figure to whom he could attach himself.

Having spoken to Johansen, Nansen unfolded his plan before the whole company. Departing from the ship was, he said, the greater risk; therefore, as leader, he himself had to go: Sverdrup, the old sea-dog, was needed to bring the ship safely home. Then he explained how he proposed to reach the Pole, continue on to Franz Josef Land and finally make for Spitsbergen, where he would be sure to meet sealers who would take him home.

On 12 December, an observation put *Fram* at 82°30′N, thereby breaking the record of 82°27′ set by the English vessel *Alert* on the Nares expedition in 1876. This feat made little impression, however, because the real glory of the enterprise seemed now destined for Nansen and Johansen. They, so Scott Hansen wistfully recorded, 'are now in a good mood, but they after all have their thoughts ahead, and the prospect of home to look forward to'.

His companions were thinking along the same lines. 'To whichever of us Nansen might have asked the question ... he put to Johansen,' declared Nordahl, 'he would have received the same unqualified "yes" [because] we were quite convinced that they ... would be home long before us.'

Sverdrup, Scott Hansen and Blessing had all made it plain to Nansen that, whatever the risks, each of them would gladly go. As Scott Hansen put it, what otherwise remained was 'to stay in the same old rut, and crawl along to the sea in the West'. Sverdrup noted in his diary that 'we are all very pleased that Nansen and Johansen are going, so we can send letters home'. Some felt that Nansen, taking with him his oppressive moods, would not be missed. But that was the only crumb of comfort. Amundsen, noted for his black moods and extreme opinions, took the news particularly hard. To him *Fram* was now 'this cold prison of loneliness in which we are confined'. He still felt acutely the stigma of drinking with which he had been branded by Nansen at the very start, and was still affected more than most by Nansen's tirade against drunkenness on the way to Khabarova. Nonetheless, here, in the ice, he had found some self-respect. He had once stayed out for hours in a temperature of −40°C to repair the windmill (the gears of which were wearing out), so the electric light could come on again. Also, craftsman that he was, Amundsen had helped Nansen with his oceanography by ingeniously constructing, to Nansen's design, a vital water sampler and a current meter.

His reward was to be treated by Nansen like a little child. Yet this 'odd character', to quote Scott Hansen,

> says it will be horrible when Nansen leaves, because it is better to be ruled by one king than by many petty kings.

35

'The North Pole Kayaks'

With the eye of a skier, Nansen was worried only by 'impossible snow', as he put it. 'I am not afraid of the cold.' He was prepared to risk much for the going to be good. That meant winter snow and an early start. He hoped for late February, as soon as the light returned. That left three months to prepare. As soon as he announced his decision the whole ship was shaken out of its torpor and all efforts were devoted to the enterprise of the Pole.

To concentrate exclusively on the preparations, Johansen was absolved from all other duties. For the first time in the complex little society of the ship, he found himself directly under Nansen's command. That very soon provoked an uncharacteristic outburst, echoing what Scott Hansen had frequently observed. Nansen, as Johansen put it in his diary, was

> not always the best person to work for, especially when he says how every little thing has to be done, which he now does constantly. For he thinks he knows everything, and his word is law. But it is the prevailing opinion on board that N. is not particularly skilful with his hands.

Perhaps this irritation had something to do with Nansen's sudden order to ration coffee: after dinner on Sundays and Wednesdays, and for breakfast on Mondays and Fridays. Only 100 kilos of coffee had been brought – enough for a year at most without economising. Sugar was also short, because Nansen ignored Juell's advice when ordering. What is more, only three pairs of mittens per man had been taken for a voyage expected to last five years. These were mere aberrations in otherwise splendid equipment. But they were irritants nonetheless.

Nansen at first wanted Johansen to help him finish their kayaks. Together with Mogstad, Nansen had in fact already begun construction towards the end of September. Their purpose was not then revealed, but they had soon been slyly dubbed 'The North Pole kayaks'.

Based on the Eskimo model that Nansen and Sverdrup had known in Greenland, these kayaks were altered to suit different circumstances. Nansen had made what was probably the first European adaptation of the native craft.

The original Eskimo kayak was a highly specialised hunting machine. It was long and slender, and therefore fast, easy to paddle, adapted to cut the waves. By the same token, it was unstable. Nansen, on the other hand, needed something to cross open leads in the pack ice, or to help him along land. His kayaks might have to carry supplies for three months, and were to be hauled on sledges for much of the way. Capacity was therefore more important than speed; so too were weight and stability. Also, too much overhang on the sledges would expose the kayaks to damage when travelling over rough ice. Nansen, therefore, designed a short, stubby craft. It was 3.7 metres long, 70 centimetres beam amidships, around 30 cm deep, and with very full lines. By comparison, a typical Eskimo kayak from Godthåb was $5\frac{1}{2}$ metres long, 45 cm beam, and perhaps 20 cm deep.

Instead of the traditional Eskimo materials of driftwood and sealskin, Nansen built the frames of his kayaks out of bamboo, covering them with canvas. There was another departure in small hatches fore and aft, to give access to food and equipment. But in other respects, the basic Eskimo design was preserved. The frame followed the same principles. There was a coaming round the cockpit, over which an anorak could be fitted in a watertight seal to make man and kayak one.

Waterproofing the kayaks was the main difficulty. In the end, Nansen impregnated the canvas with a melted concoction of tallow and stearine devised for the provision bags. This also had the advantage of facilitating repairs, and Petterson forged a neat little soldering iron for the purpose. When finished, each kayak weighed around eighteen kilos. Both were ready by the first half of December.

Sverdrup was making sleeping bags from reindeer fur. He was about the only one capable doing so. At the end of November, however, he fell ill with what Blessing diagnosed as gastro-enteritis. All along there had been a trickle of minor ailments, possibly due to vitamin deficiencies; but Sverdrup now became the first man on board to retire to a sickbed. For three weeks or more he was incapacitated, with all work on the sleeping bags consequently suspended.

Meanwhile, equipment had to be tested. Nobody, for example, yet knew whether the Primus stove would function outside at low temperatures. So, in a tent pitched by the side of the ship, Nansen and Johansen found out for themselves. They practised the still unfamiliar technique of starting the Primus by heating with a spirit flame, then working the pump until the right pressure was built up, and the characteristic roar of the burner was achieved. At the first attempt they proved that the Primus did indeed work in deep cold. Using the insulated cooker Nansen had designed for Greenland, they found that, at a temperature of $-36°C$, starting with compacted snow, they were able to melt eight litres of water, of which three were brought to the boil, in an hour and a half, using no more than 100 grams of paraffin. It was spectacularly more efficient than the spirit stove used on the crossing of Greenland.

These experiments were finished early in December, and thereafter Nansen and Johansen began trying out their travelling clothes. The moon having returned, it was again light enough to ski. On 9 December, they went skiing in their wolfskin outfits. A combination of fresh snow polluted with leaching sea salt made the going ominously sticky. The temperature was –40°C. Nonetheless, Nansen recorded, 'We sweated so that ... we could have driven water mills under our backs ... Still too mild. God knows if it will ever be cold enough.'

Oddly enough, this problem had long since been solved. The previous February, at a temperature of nearly –50°C, Johansen had gone out 'with only a wind jacket over Iceland sweater' and noted: 'It is extraordinary how warm these wind clothes are.' Where clothing was concerned, Nansen had originally stuck to the layer principle he had successfully tested in Greenland. Now, however, he wanted better windproof cloth. This was supplied to him by an English manufacturer, Thomas Burberry of Basingstoke, who had developed a close woven, water resistant cotton gabardine, proofed in the yarn, which 'breathed', thus inhibiting condensation. It was the first modern weatherproof material. Nansen had stumbled on it in London while preparing this expedition. He had ordered fifty yards of this 'Burberry cloth', specifying that it must be of the light tropical weight – for during extreme exertion in Arctic temperatures sweating was the constant fear, not cold.

Nansen's moods continued to swing; one moment cheerful and talkative, the next silent and morose. Observing a notably brilliant aurora, 'waving bands of light twisting in rapid bows', he tellingly wrote:

> I often think how faithful an image of the Northerner himself lies in this contradiction: in this heavy, silent landscape, in this barren cold, this dance of sparkling rays of light; for me it is like his ... surge of mental power deep down behind his frozen facade.

Counterpointing this introspection, the dogs howled like wolves every other night in a gloomy fugue, badly disturbing sleep.

When Boxing Day came round, Johansen remarked that the dogs

> know nothing about any Christmas out on the ice. But they also have their part to play, and perhaps not the least. It will be the heaviest part of our forthcoming journey, to take the lives of these animals, who will have done what they can to bring us forwards.

That indeed was the plan: as the journey progressed, to slaughter the dogs and feed them to each other.

Despite mock champagne brewed by Blessing and Nansen, 'a champagne mood was missing nonetheless' from the festivities, Johansen sadly wrote of Christmas Eve. The dynamo was out of order, and the only light came from the yellowish subdued flames of a few paraffin lamps; a gloomy contrast to the white incandescence of the arc lamp. Also, Johansen himself was visited again by his own enigmatic shadow:

On an evening like this, we dwell on ... Christmas at home, amongst our nearest and dearest ... home!... The energy or listlessness of my youth took place there.... If only I could remember it all happily! But there were dark moments ... I will atone for the dark events. Although I have not always given pleasure to those at home, I hope that they send me a kind thought ...

'Christmas again, far from home,' as Nansen put it in his diary, speaking for them all, 'and at home they send thoughts and wishes, and no one knows where.'

New Year's Eve was more cheerful. For one thing, it was free of agonising nostalgia. Each man in his own way was now looking ahead. Besides, after dinner, there appeared a hot punch devised with absolute alcohol and essence of cloudberry. To toast the arrival of 1895 Blessing conjured up out of his seemingly inexhaustible private cellar, a bottle of genuine aquavit.

As he liked doing on such occasions, Nansen made a speech. His theme was the good atmosphere on board; due, he said, to the excellent companionship. He would remember with longing the many happy times he had had. About that, 'opinions were divided', as Scott Hansen put it; 'not a word that he might have done anything wrong, no attempt to put things to rights'. No one was prepared to follow custom and reply with a speech for 'Himself', as Nansen had by now been dubbed. Prompted by Blessing, Sverdrup, now recovered from his illness, saved the situation. He 'raised his glass quietly', as Scott Hansen recorded the scene, 'and said to Nansen approximately the following: "So I toast the New Year and success to the sledge expedition, *skål*." And that was that.'

In the dying days of 1894 pressure in the ice, so long a part of life on board, seemed somehow to become more menacing. The new year opened with groaning and creaking, subsiding into eerie calm; then, early in the morning of 3 January, a Thursday, violent and prolonged tremors tossed the ship about as if in an earthquake. The diarists duly recorded these events. 'There you see how safe we are, lying in thick ice,' remarked Amundsen. 'Here ... Bentsen and I drilled last year and found a thickness of 20 feet, but still it has been shattered to pieces. Nature's work is millions of horsepower.'

A line of rafting ice close by to port was slowly bearing down on the ship. The floe in which *Fram* lay cracked across, but leaving a remnant in which she was still securely gripped. Not all the shipbuilder's art could save her unless she broke free. Even if she did, she might still be crushed by the ice breaking over her and forcing her down into the trap again.

That Thursday, for the first time, serious preparations were made for abandoning ship. Sledges and kayaks were made ready, supplies brought on deck, and some moved out onto the ice. Intermittent creaking in the hull told of pressure building up. After dinner, while most were diverting themselves by playing halma, Hendriksen burst into the saloon to say that the dogs were drowning. There was a stampede topsides. Through a new crack in the ice water was flooding the kennels. The dogs were hastily brought to safety.

For two days, accompanied by ghostly creaks and groans, the wave of ice to port inched ever closer to the side. Early on Saturday everyone was roused to continue preparing to abandon ship. As the day wore on there was a lull in the grinding of the ice. After dinner, the disturbance recommenced.

Troubled by a sinister, unfamiliar note, almost like thunder, Nansen raced out. What he saw was the arrival of the wave of ice to port. Like a frozen sea breaking in a storm, it was tumbling slowly in shattered pieces bathed in snow high over the bulwarks amidships. It was held back only by the winter awning, which had been rigged as a kind of airlock to improve the insulation. If the canvas gave, the ice might block the exits. The men below would be caught like rats in a trap.

Nansen raised the age-old sailor's alarm – 'All hands on deck!' – and hurried back to save the dogs. They were penned on deck to port, whining beneath the awning as it bulged under the advancing wave. Nansen opened the barrier. The dogs scampered out and were left to their own devices. The men came tumbling out on deck; all except Johansen, who had started to take a bath and first had to get dressed again.

Suddenly the tremors in the ice seemed of cataclysmic proportions. Nobody was giving orders. Scott Hansen 'heard Nansen ... say: "We'll never manage this." Then I realised it was best to hurry ... I asked someone if we were to abandon ship and he answered that such appeared to be the case.'

Whereupon, in the best traditions of the sea, he dived into the charthouse to save the logs. Each man had duffle bags ready packed with personal belongings. In a frenzy, these were now heaved up on deck and over the side. Scurrying back and forth, without directions, men instinctively grabbed anything else that might be useful when marooned on the ice. The choice was revealing. Scott Hansen and Sverdrup took extra guns and ammunition; Jacobsen, the mate, a gaggle of cups lashed outside a duffle bag. Over man and beast there was an air of *sauve qui peut* – with two notable exceptions. One was Hendriksen, who quixotically tried to save the ship by attacking the breaking wave of ice with a shovel. 'He was a hell of a chap,' to quote Scott Hansen:

> Afterwards he said, 'bugger me, [the ice] heaved both me and the spade, ha ha' ... in the same tone of voice he tells about how many Russians the Norwegians killed on such and such an occasion on Spitsbergen.

The other hero was a dog called Suggen ('Thug'), who perched himself atop a dump shifted a safe distance from the ship and, snarling and snapping, proceeded to guard it against all comers.

35. 'The North Pole Kayaks'

Nansen and his men were now all waiting resignedly on the ice. Happily the temperature was only around –20°C and the moon had risen to illuminate the surroundings, its pallid gleam accentuating the forlorn sense of isolation. They were after all on an uncharted sea, with the nearest known land at least 250 miles away.

By now *Fram* was half engulfed by ice and snow, and listing perceptibly to starboard. Yet so far she still showed no sign of disintegrating, so it was decided to spend at least one more night on board. A watch was set. Everybody lay down, fully clothed, ready to abandon ship at a moment's notice, and tried to get what sleep they could. In case the pressure resumed, this time deforming the hull, all doors were left open to prevent their being jammed shut by buckling frames.

Next morning, Sunday, 6 January, under a moon now shining round the clock, all was quiescent still. Scott Hansen profited by the lull to level his theodolite and take an observation. What he found was that since the New Year, *Fram* had actually been pushed thirteen miles closer to the Pole. She was now at 83°34′N and had finally broken the record for the Furthest North, by ten miles. But when Scott Hansen hurried over to tell his shipmates, now starting to clear the hummock that had spilled over the ship, 'there were no cheers', as he recorded. 'The most notable demonstration that accompanied the news was that I received a spadeful of snow ... down my neck.'

Perhaps, Nansen suggested in his diary for that day, 'the ice has [simply] discharged a cannonade for the high latitude ... Let it do its worst, as long as we move North.' And he decreed a party in honour of the record. The mood was hardly festive, despite unstinted drink. The men were too shaken by events. Sverdrup disgorged a precious stock of honey cake he had carefully been husbanding, as if he wished to enjoy it while there was yet time. Nansen, on the other hand, was convinced that all danger was past.

He was right. *Fram* had lifted a foot or two, and safely slipped astern. In other words, she had broken free, and ridden the turmoil as if it had merely been the buffeting of a choppy sea. The rounded bilges had, after all, worked precisely as intended. The ice had been unable to get a grip. Yet after the crisis, he wrote in his diary, surveying the frozen inferno:

We are like tiny dwarfs in a struggle with Titans; one must save oneself with cunning and ingenuity if one is to escape from this giant fist that rarely lets go what it has once seized.

The following days went by undisturbed except for a rumble or two, like the dying aftershocks of an earthquake. Was it, in Nansen's own words, 'just to remind us not to feel too self confident?'

It was now 8 January, and his daughter Liv's second birthday. As usual on such occasions, Nansen tortured himself with thoughts of home. 'You

227

are thinking of me, oh Eva mine,' he wrote with his customary hopeful-ness. 'Your thoughts fly northwards in the great desolation. They do not know where to look for me ... In the highest northern latitudes, in the deepest polar night yet experienced.'

36

Working All Hours

The same day, preparations for the polar journey recommenced. 'It is quite odd,' Johansen wrote:

> For many years, Nansen has been considering this expedition, and sledge and ski equipment is supposed to be his speciality, but still right up to now he has constantly made changes.... He is always fiddling.

In fact, Nansen was urgently still searching for the perfect sledge. The mechanics of sliding on snow were still barely understood, yet reducing friction might be a matter of life and death. Snow is infinitely variable, and the surface of the polar sea was a world away from the heights of the Greenland Ice Cap. There, Nansen had revolutionised the sledge. Now he wisely avoided the trap of being hostage to his own success. On the floes around *Fram*, he started from first principles again.

H.W. Christiansen, the carpenter who had made Nansen's sledges for Greenland, had once more been called upon, and this time, to cope with the unpredictable circumstances, had produced different models, mostly of Nansen's 'Greenland' pattern with broad ski-like runners. He altered the profiles of some runners and varied the material. Because wood absorbs moisture it is sluggish in wet snow, and to provide further alternatives, Christiansen also made false runners: some of aluminium, others of German silver.

Christiansen was a remarkable man. He was the first on record to manufacture laminated skis, which came on the market towards the end of the century, decades ahead of their time, and were only flawed by the fact that the sole glue then obtainable could not withstand the damp. But he was dilatory and wayward. The upshot was that the sledges had been delivered to *Fram* at the last moment, with no chance before sailing of a final inspection, and most of the lashings now had to be replaced. As on Greenland, Nansen eschewed metal fastenings. He still insisted on supple leather lashings to make the sledges flexible and avoid breakage.

Already, during the first winter in the ice, Nansen had started experimenting afresh. He began with a Samoyed model obtained at Khabarova but, slow, heavy and crude, it was soon discarded. In another trial, with the temperature around $-40°C$, and the snow crusted hard, the easiest sledge to haul turned out to be one with relatively narrow runners, shod with thin steel plates. In soft snow, however, the best type was definitely one of Christiansen's 'Greenland' ski sledges with aluminium false runners. A model to meet all conditions thus still had to be devised, but Nansen for the moment let the work lapse in order to concentrate on learning to drive dogs. Scott Hansen observed acidly:

> [He] cannot work evenly and constantly with anything, but makes a spurt, working far into the night; then at other times he can fritter away half the day by sitting and preaching endlessly.

The rest of the winter and all the next summer passed, and only in the autumn, after privately deciding on his polar journey, did Nansen resume his experiments.

On 1 October 1894 – a Monday ('like most Mondays', as Scott Hansen lugubriously wrote), there was a trial of man-hauling on skis. Various men were hitched up singly and in turn to a sledge with a load of 120 kilos. Amundsen was one of them. Afterwards, he declared that, faced with such loads, one might as well lie down, one would get just as far that way.

And indeed it was easy enough on the flat. But at the slightest incline skis flailed helplessly backwards. When three dogs were harnessed to the same sledge, however, they trotted off unperturbed. More trials in December, while the moonlight was strong enough, proved that the average useful load was 40 kilos for each dog, a result which catapulted Nansen from a trough of depression to an almost manic crest of hope. In his own words: 'it is almost as if the Pole is already in the bag.'

Nonetheless it was now imperative to devise a sledge that slid efficiently in all sorts of snow, from the delicate crystals of midwinter to the mushy grains of spring and from the dreaded, rough sand-like drift snow at low temperatures to every other variant. It was eventually found that maple wood, impregnated with a hot melted mixture of Stockholm tar and candlewax, slid best on even the most abrasive drift down to –40°C and below. For everything else, German silver turned out to be the best compromise. So the sledges for the polar journey were to be shod with German silver, and false impregnated maple runners attached on top. The idea was that Nansen and Johansen would start off in winter conditions and then, as the season advanced, with rising temperatures and changing snow, they could remove the wooden runners to expose the proper running surface.

But that was only half the story. Most of the sledges stuck at even modest bumps in the ice. Adapted to the smooth sweep of the ice cap, their clearance was too low. Nor were they robust enough to survive the hideously broken terrain of the pack ice at its worst. Moreover, none was long enough to carry the kayaks. So Nansen was forced to have new sledges built. They were to have much higher clearance. Also the runners, although still broad, were to be slightly convex in cross-section. Various experiments had showed that this made for easier sliding, and turning too.

Mogstad did the critical work of cutting and shaping the parts. He was only told to start in the week after the great pressure in the ice. Nansen wanted four sledges. He proposed starting on 20 February, which left barely six weeks for completion. Johansen was now prompted to observe that the year before he had recorded in his diary 'a number of unflattering remarks' about Mogstad, the scapegoat of the expedition. Gracefully making amends, he conceded:

> Now circumstances have changed, and it turns out that [Mogstad] is exceptionally skilful at everything conceivable, and he has shown his shipmates, who were unpleasant to him, that he is a very capable man.

For example, because of strength and flexibility, ash was to be used for the sledges' frames and fixed runners. But the stock was running out. Mogstad ingeniously spliced and glued various bits to make up the necessary lengths. Others, meanwhile, were bending the runners. That took place in a forge built out on the ice for Petterson, and housed in an igloo. The ends of the runners were heated over the fire, sprinkled with water and, thus made pliable, bent up by main force like the tip of a ski.

The skis were even more troublesome than the sledges, because they not only had to slide but also to grip for the kick-off. Nansen had brought about fifty pairs – of different types, made variously of maple, birch and hickory, because which wood functioned best was still a matter of debate. Tirelessly, Nansen experimented. The long, narrow Selbu ski he had originally favoured now seemed unwieldy. He was veering round to Finnish skis, because they ran best on the flat. He had with him a supply, but the wood was poor.

The best-made skis were some supplied, half finished, by Christiansen. These, Nansen proceeded to refashion. Working stoically in the ship's hold at a temperature of $-20°C$, he planed the skis down so that they resembled the Finnish type. That is to say, the upper surfaces, excepting the space for the foot, were well rounded, with all edges blunt. The groove in the sole was shallow and square. The advantage was that it was light and supple, following the contours of the snow. Also, without sharp corners, and hence lines of weakness, it was supposedly less liable to break.

In the end, for running properties, Nansen chose skis of maple and hickory. Each being a hard and close-grained wood, they did not easily soak up water. By the same token, they were hard to wax, since ski wax needs a porous surface. Johansen spent many a back-breaking hour in the forge, coaxing the skis to absorb a simmering witches' brew of Stockholm tar, tallow and candle wax. 'This must be done many times, and thoroughly,' Johansen recorded, 'if it is to last on a pair of skis constantly in use for 100 days from morning to night in all kinds of snow.' As yet there were no commercial waxes; out in the field there would be no second chance.

Except for the men in the galley, the whole ship was now immersed in preparations. 'The saloon looks like a whorehouse,' Scott Hansen observed, 'what with sledges and sledge parts strewn about.' Juell was making the dog harnesses. On 7 February he finished and exhibited the outcome. Solid, light and practical, his workmanship excited general admiration. On each harness – made carefully to measure – the animal's name was prominently painted. 'Perhaps, like the *Jeannette* relics,' Johansen sadly noted, the harnesses would

> drift ashore on Greenland and reach people, because we will presumably abandon them as we slaughter the dogs.

'I am not free of travel fever, now that they are about to leave,' Scott Hansen observed that same day. Sverdrup, by contrast, seemed impervious to any emotion. To support the kayaks on the sledges, he had the ingenious idea of making chocks out of pemmican so as to save weight. The pemmican was taken out of its tins, softened by heat and kneaded to shape. Then, imperturbably treading away at his sewing machine, Sverdrup, like a born sailmaker, quickly ran up strangely formed bags to cover the chocks.

With the altogether different skills of a furrier, he was also deftly sewing new sleeping bags of reindeer skins. On 14 February – a bare week before their planned departure – Nansen and Johansen slept out for the first time in a tent to test the result. The temperature was –43°C. When Johansen woke in the morning he found that Nansen had decamped – and spent the night in his warm bunk on board. Because of the cold, he had been unable to sleep. It was the outcome of insisting on thin pelts in the sleeping bags to save weight. Johansen had managed to sleep – just – because his bag was marginally thicker. This provoked him to an outburst in his diary:

> It proves [he wrote] that we must have other things to lie in, and that N[ansen]'s boast about light bags has been exploded. It touches him to the quick that he has been wrong. He is one of those people who will never admit a mistake ... What he says goes, be it never so silly. If he sees that something would be far ... better if it is done as someone else says ... he takes no notice but carries on his own sweet way.

Nansen now decided that it would be warmer to share the same sleeping bag, and Sverdrup uncomplainingly started all over again. Having measured Nansen and Johansen lying down on the deck, he proceeded to contrive a double sleeping bag out of two single ones – the best he could find, made of the thickest reindeer pelts.

Nansen was 'one of those people who make a great fuss over the least thing he does,' Johansen also wrote. 'My friends on board predict it will be a miserable tour with him.' One day, alone in the forge, Sverdrup confidentially told 'stories about the Greenland expedition that nobody outside the participants know about' – and, continued Johansen darkly, 'they gave me much food for thought'.

Nansen was chastened for a spell by the great onslaught of the ice, but he had soon reverted to his overbearing behaviour. As the day of departure loomed, he seemed more tense, and the atmosphere on board grew correspondingly more oppressive. The diary of Johansen, for one, was filled almost daily with criticisms, the main burden of which was that Nansen was often 'unpleasant' and that 'he interferes in everything, presumably he imagines he must do so because he is the chief'.

Nansen's interior monologue gave a slightly different perspective. 'My head [is] full, day and night, with everything that must be done and not forgotten,' he wrote in his diary.

> Oh, this incessant tension of the mind that allows not a moment's rest, when one can put aside one's responsibility ... Nerves taut from the time one wakes up in the morning until one closes one's eyes late at night. Ah, how I recognise this state of affairs from every time I have been about to depart, and the line of retreat will be severed, and never has it been more intense than now.

Another violently contradictory aspect of Nansen's self-searching scarcely mirrored what his companions saw. 'I see that we will be ready in good time,' he wrote in his diary on 9 February, 'and I am in a happy mood.' Yet he was simultaneously gripped by a tortured longing for Eva.

> I can think of nothing else day and night [his diary recorded] ... I see you vividly before me as you sit at home, waiting, waiting, but soon, soon, we will have each other again for ever, and I am so light of heart, just burn with impatience to start off. I believe that if everything was ready I would leave tomorrow.

'I long for home,' Johansen wrote in *his* diary. 'I want to live my life in the future in a safe harbour, by a beloved creature's side, God knows if I will succeed.' And again: 'I will lead a better life ... what happiness if everything goes well! And thou, my old mother, will be proud of your boy.'

But he soon switched back to his commentaries on men and dogs. To prepare for the polar journey, he noted one day in February, the dogs were now being given as much food as they wanted. The carcasses of their dead companions, which had been hanging up at the yard arm all winter, 'went like hot cakes'. Polar bear blubber was unstintingly provided. Between meals, dog biscuits were on offer but hardly touched. The dogs, Johansen added, 'are in a better mood now, as the light begins to appear; the darkness has its effect on them, as well as on us'.

Irritability punctuated much of the preparation. This was under-standable, given the crowding of the saloon table with men at work. Nansen had promised to carry mail; each letter to weigh no more than 15 grams. That meant laborious, microscopic calligraphy to cram as much as possible onto a sheet of tissue paper.

To Nansen, wrapped up in his own private world, this was 'a peculiar time'.

> It is just as if I were preparing for a summer excursion, as if spring were here. And still it is midwinter, and the nature of that summer excursion might be rather mixed.

To make sure he had missed no scrap of knowledge of his first intended haven, Nansen was re-reading, yet again, Julius Payer's book about the discovery of Franz Josef Land. 'The land that [Payer] depicts as the kingdom of the dead, where they would inevitably have perished if they had not found their ship again, that is what we see as our salvation,' he commented, even adding: 'It might seem reckless, but I cannot believe that a land teeming with bears ... where the seal basks on the ice, is anything but an excellent food depot ... for our journey on to Spitsbergen.'

Payer, with his polyglot companions from Austria-Hungary, had discov-ered Franz Josef Land in 1873. Since then few had followed his tracks. The archipelago was still largely unexplored, and the mapping uncertain.

In the last few weeks before departure Nansen was afflicted by another wave of doubt. But he remembered Carlyle's words: 'A man ... must march forward ... trusting imperturbably in the appointment and *choice* of the upper Powers.' 'Well,' he now commented, 'I have no "upper Powers", they would be useful in these circumstances, but in any case I have to go.'

To his companions, this strain of philosophical detachment was very far from being apparent. 'Himself dithers as usual,' Scott Hansen observed. And Johansen remarked: 'If someone comes and asks [him] about any-thing (he must be asked about everything, down to the tiniest detail), the answer often given is "Well, I don't really know." And then, after babbling a bit, something emerges in the end.' Nansen could 'also be not a little unpleasant towards some poor devil who perhaps has a comment on something or other'.

Under other circumstances, all this might have been unbearable. But everybody knew by now how well off they were materially by comparison with other expeditions, and that they owed this to Nansen's exceptional foresight. Besides, it was a well-known fact that men were different ashore and afloat, and those on *Fram* curbed their resentment accordingly. Yet as Johansen could not refrain from pointing out: 'He must understand that things would be incomparably better if he let Sverdrup do everything.'

Sverdrup at least did his best to set the tone, unobtrusively getting on with his work; lightening the mood here and there with welcome glimpses of his idiosyncratic humour. Petterson, too, was a well-liked character, with his constant prediction of 'a bloody big push northwards'. He kept out of the way in the forge, making gadgets for the polar journey. First there was a lightweight axe, next pointed iron spikes for the ski sticks to let them double as harpoons.

As 20 February approached, Nansen was reluctantly forced to concede that he would not be ready in time. There now followed a highly unsettling period, in which departure was constantly postponed, and Nansen seemed more contradictory than ever. Attending to detail, as it was necessary that he should, he was driving himself to the limit and suffering badly from lack of sleep, usually not getting to bed until between 4.30 and 5.30 in the morning.

Alongside dogs and skis, hunting guns were to be the vital instruments of survival. Once more, Nansen experimented with different models, finally deciding on the same composite weapon that he had taken to Greenland. With two different barrels, a rifle and shotgun in one, it could deal with any game likely to be found. It had turned out more reliable than similar guns ordered for this expedition, and saved weight into the bargain.

Johansen complained that he had to remind Nansen to let him test fire his gun. That was on Friday, 22 February; two days after they were supposed to have left. That same day, the four polar sledges were finally ranged up alongside the ship, loaded and ready to go. On recording the loads, Johansen discovered that they weighed 100 kilos too much. That entailed further changes, and 'does not show precise calculation', he querulously commented.

The day before, Johansen had lashed the pemmican chocks on the two sledges carrying the kayaks; a trying job with bare hands outside at a temperature of −45°C and a breeze to boot. It was also dark, and the paraffin froze in the lamps. Winter was technically on the wane, and there was already twilight for a few hours around noon, but the return of the sun was still some way off. Scott Hansen, for one, was convinced that he would 'lose by leaving so ridiculously early ... in the worst cold.... If not for the sake of the men ... then for the dogs at least.'

Every night, the whole company sat up working into the small hours, as if it really was the eve of departure. Scott Hansen, having asked about maps, reminded Nansen that he needed some of Spitsbergen, and had to turn to and make copies; he finished at 6 a.m. on 25 February. Likewise Mogstad, against his better judgment, had been slaving away at an invention of Nansen's for a sledgemeter to measure the distance travelled. In the end, it refused to work. Mogstad was then given a free hand. He quickly rigged up an outlandish but serviceable contraption from a wheel, together with a revolution counter improvised from a discarded anemometer, all mounted behind a sledge. Blessing gave a quick course in setting broken limbs. Scott Hansen taught Johansen essential navigation.

The mail to be carried by Nansen had naturally been finished by his original starting date. Amundsen used the delay to add a letter to the Norwegian naval authorities, requesting an extension of leave 'for an indefinite period'. He was supposed to be back on duty by 1 December the same year but, as he explained, 'it seems that the time for my return will extend beyond that date'.

Johansen, meanwhile, was debating whether he ought not to leave behind a letter for Hilda Øvrum, the girl he wanted to marry. 'If I open my heart to her and I do not come home, but she gets my letter, it might not be a good thing, supposing she has banished me from her thoughts,' he reasoned pessimistically. 'But if she has not done so, she would be glad to get my last words.'

Similarly, on 17 February, Nansen began a farewell letter to Eva in case he never came home. It was a long apologia about his decision to leave *Fram* and 'go home via the Pole', as he tellingly phrased it. 'If it were not for you,' he wrote, trying to probe his own motives, 'my longing to start off would not be so intense.'

> Now it seems a journey towards the sun and summer; towards the only thing that life holds for me ... all the time the image rises up before me vividly and beautifully where you receive me when I arrive ... And if it should happen that this journey is no bridal dance, you will know that your image will be the last I see ... when I go to the eternal rest, where we will meet some time and rest for ever safely in each other's arms. Ah Eva, my Eva, if it should happen, do not cry too hard. Remember no one escapes his fate.

He quoted Dostoievsky: 'The most difficult thing in life is to live and not to lie – and not to believe in one's own lies.' Writing by fits and starts, he only finished in the final hours before departing. After a last profession of love for Eva, he ended:

> But no, it's no use writing, I can't say anything the way I want to, I am tired, I need some sleep before I start on the long journey early tomorrow morning.

37

Eva's Songs and Sorrows

'Long after you were gone, I lay in bed, and was miserable and wept and wept,' Eva had written to Nansen almost two years before, the day after he departed.

> But then little by little such peace came over me that I got up, made myself decent, and went downstairs ... and looked over the water to see if you were coming soon and quite right all the ships came sailing slowly out past Godthåb and your Eva stood calmly looking through the small telescope.

'Was it not strange, for the rest of the day, I couldn't cry, I was so cold, so cold.' She was gripped by a ravenous hunger. For dinner, all by herself, she devoured a whole lobster. It had been sent by Marthe Larsen, the housekeeper of Nansen's childhood home. Eva never forgot Marthe's tact in sending the lobster but not coming out herself. Until she had mastered her feelings, she wished to be left alone.

'I went to bed as if nothing had happened, and got up today calmly,' she went on to tell her husband. 'But now while I am writing this I am crying ... but nobody will be allowed to see the tears.'

Thus began the torrent of letters from Eva, in her dark sitting room overlooking the fjord, to Nansen in his cramped cabin, sailing up the coast. In a jumble of inconsequential domestic details, stoic resignation, anguish and despair, Eva let the words pour out. One moment, it was to describe how she read in a newspaper 'that you stood motionless with your telescope glued to your eye, gazing towards [our house] when you departed'.

> and then the comforting weeping came over me. I don't have much of that, you know, I'm quite cold, and that tortures me.

Then, Eva wanted Nansen to know that after a few days she finally went visiting. But 'nobody could see that I had lost the dearest one on earth. I laughed and joked as usual.' And yet: 'if only the horrible years would hurry past, think if one could lie in a sleep or turn oneself into a mummy and suddenly wake in your arms – (Your Eva is ranting.)'

More soberly, Eva also wrote about a visit by Alexander, Nansen's brother. He 'is very fond of you', Eva said. 'Look, it's something quite different when I can talk to someone who is fond of you, it warms my heart.... That good, kind Alexander; you must like him. He is so touching, and I will also be fond of him. After all he is your nearest and dearest, and he will be a great help to me on many an occasion.'

Eva had grieved to see the brothers estranged. In the midst of her own distress, at the eleventh hour, she was still trying to have them truly reconciled, though her feelings on the subject were mixed. On the one hand, while Nansen was away Alexander, the lawyer-turned-accountant, would be in charge of her finances, and so she would do well to keep in with him, her natural feelings of affection for him apart. On the other, she shared Nansen's dislike of Eily, Alexander's wife. Yet grudgingly she had to admit that Eily knew how to make her husband happy, something she believed that she had signally failed to do for Nansen. A sense of inadequacy was the result. Nevertheless she wrote: 'I bless the fate that brought me together with you, I would not change places with *anyone.*'

'You little idiot,' she replied when among the letters soon streaming back from Nansen appeared the fear of returning to find her dead. 'I won't give up the ghost so quickly. I want to have many happy years before I give up. And then I want to be burned together with my beloved boy, and the pyre will be down on our strand, bright and beautiful, and Liv can hide our ashes where she wants.'

But in the farewell telegram that caught Nansen at Vadsø, just before he vanished out of reach, her final words had been 'ALL WELL. GOOD LUCK MY OWN BOY! I AM SURE YOU ARE SAILING TOWARDS A HAPPY REUNION.'

Only when that was despatched, and her last letters were returned, having missed Nansen along the way, did Eva finally feel that the last link had been broken. 'Come back in 2 years,' she had written in one of the letters that did reach her husband, 'but don't worry if you can't manage it so soon, your Eva is strong; she has the courage to wait much longer.'

Among the farewell letters that arrived from Nansen had been one to Eva's mother. 'Dear good mother,' he had written, recalling 'the wonderful hours in your bright home, where life met me in all its beauty'. He repeated to her what he had insistently told Eva, and everyone else for that matter, that

> you must not worry about us, we will come home safe and sound, just as certainly as it is I who am sitting and writing in my cabin.

Maren Sars remained unconvinced. She still disapproved of the expedition and was angered by the distress that it was causing her daughter. She still nursed a scintilla of reserve towards Nansen as a son-in-law.

In one of her letters Eva told Nansen that she had moved her piano to the centre of the room, and was soon practising hard. 'If we are ever rich,' she had added, 'you'll build a proper music room for me, won't you?' In fact, her impresario, a genial, avuncular and shrewd figure called Peter Vogt

238

Fischer, wanted her to start giving recitals again. Eva needed little persuasion. For one thing, Nansen had told her that her music might help to fill the void when he had gone.

There is a story that after Nansen had sailed away, Eva started singing Schubert's *Gretchen am Spinnrade* – 'Margareta at her Spinning Wheel'. This is a setting of a song from the first part of Goethe's *Faust*. Margareta, hopelessly in love with Faust, is pining for him while he is away:

> *Wo ich ihn nicht hab,*
> *Ist mir das Grab,*
> *Die Ganze Welt,*
> *Ist mir vergällt.*

> 'Him gone, my room
> Is like a tomb,
> Him gone, all
> The world to me is gall.'

It is entirely possible that the melancholy strains of Schubert's *Lied* did indeed permeate the Norse log-built house in the shadow of the birch trees. The piece was in Eva's repertoire. Those who heard her sing it were always struck by the almost frightening way she seemed somehow to turn into Margareta before their eyes.

On 21 October 1893, Eva gave a recital in the Freemasons' Hall, Christiania's main auditorium. It was her first public performance for two and a half years. Thereafter, plainly dressed in the fashion of the day – though she did not really care about clothes – Eva, with her enigmatic dark brown eyes, her black hair drawn back like a schoolgirl, was regularly to be heard on the concert platform.

To the outside world, she presented an appearance of great calm, and seemed able to talk about her husband with serene detachment. Underneath, she was slowly becoming embittered. Brooding on her predicament, she grew less and less willing to believe that her husband really loved her, if he was prepared to leave her for no one knew how long. By her own account, she reached the stage of contemplating suicide. 'At any rate, I went round and thought out the easiest way of killing myself', she truthfully recorded – only to discover that 'as a result', the memory of Nansen 'vanished more and more for me'. Miserably, she noticed that her 'longing itself had waned'.

Her singing was her salvation. One critic was waspish enough to point out that her 'own fate undoubtedly facilitates the success that [she] is now enjoying everywhere'. He admitted, none the less, that 'she possesses a rare talent as a *Lieder* singer'. Another critic wrote that 'she need not exploit her husband's name in order to arouse interest, but she is fully able to do so by virtue of her own abilities'. And indeed she was soon enjoying an undoubted success.

It was a galling situation all the same. It was widely assumed that Nansen would never return. Nor was Eva allowed to forget that she was a public figure by the fact of being Nansen's wife. Yet paradoxically it was only when Nansen vanished on *Fram* that Eva was freed from his dominating shadow and able resume a career of her own.

She last performed *Gretchen am Spinnrade* at a concert in February 1891, and thereafter ceased to sing it in public. As if in compensation, the distinctive, spontaneous melodies of Grieg became prominent in her repertoire. A concert programme without some work by this celebrated fellow-countryman, then going through a creative burst in his strangely spasmodic and uneven career, would at the time have been unthinkable. On 9 February 1895, at a recital in Christiania, Eva actually gave some of his *Barnlige Sange*, or 'Children's Songs', their first performance. Grieg himself was not present; he was in Germany, conducting his own orchestral works. But King Oscar II of Sweden-Norway, then on a visit to Christiania, attended, along with one of his sons, Prince Eugen. The prince, a regal and handsome figure, was much taken with Eva, and she in her turn audaciously flirted with him from the platform.

Eugen was a considerable artist in his own right, and he understood music too. Like the rest of the audience, he was evidently touched, especially by the new Grieg pieces. Their simple melodies and simpler words acquired a magical quality in Eva's warm mezzo-soprano. For her, there was a thunderous roar of applause.

38

Off at Last

With another roar, the cannon on *Fram*, a little over a fortnight later, on 26 February, signalled that Nansen and Johansen were off at last.

It was only late the previous night that the announcement of departure came. As Johansen ironically noted in his diary: 'It is official; we will start our expedition to the North Pole tomorrow.' The day before, they had had their farewell dinner, in the belief that this would have been the day of departure. At midday photographs had been taken out on the ice.

Staying up late had taken its usual toll. Departure was enveloped in a sleepy, subdued atmosphere. Last minute delays had also supervened. The morning was well advanced before the four sledges, two monstrously topped by a kayak, were finally lashed, loaded and marshalled by the side of the ship. Twenty-eight dogs, seven to a sledge, were lying down in their traces, patiently waiting on events. From the gangway Nansen delivered a farewell oration, the point of which was publicly to confirm that Sverdrup would henceforth lead the expedition, with Scott Hansen second in command.

Around midday Nansen at last gave the order to start. To the accompaniment of men shouting, whips cracking and dogs howling, the caravan surged into action. Nansen loped along on skis in front. Behind him trotted Kvik, the lead dog of the first sledge, and a memento of home.

It was a dull day, overcast, with a bitter easterly breeze, biting snowdrift, and the temperature hovering around $-30°C$. Nansen found that on level floes the dogs streaked along like the wind, so that he was hardpressed to keep clear of Kvik, panting at his heels. At moderate obstacles, however, the sledges stopped dead, and needed much shoving to restart. There was help to hand. For the first day, Sverdrup, Scott Hansen, Blessing, Hendriksen and Mogstad were following in support. And then, in Johansen's words: ' "The great expedition" had gone about 500 metres from the ship, and the salutes from the cannon had barely died away, when one of the sledges was completely shattered by a rather small hummock. That was a magnificent outcome of years of experience ... and after so many grandiloquent pronouncements of daily marches of so and so many miles.'

There was no alternative but to turn back for repairs. On the way, there was more damage when Nansen's sledge, now hindmost, rammed the one in front, cracking its own forward bow. In all this the kayaks, fortunately, were unscathed.

The sledges were clearly overloaded. Nansen now decided to take two more, making six in all. With a total weight of around 1100 kilos, that would decrease the load from around 280 kilos per sledge to just under 200 kilos. This would not only reduce the strain on each sledge but also make it easier to lift.

Despite the setback, Nansen was 'in a strange, victorious mood', as he wrote in his diary the evening of his return. 'The sledges seemed to glide easily, even although the load was about 100 kilos greater than originally intended.' What is more, *Fram* had that day passed 83°50′. She was drifting happily north again. 'Eva,' as Nansen put it, harping on an old refrain, 'I am being carried to you, to you.'

Johansen was in less lyrical mood: 'The same rush began all over again,' he wrote. The lesson to be drawn was that the sledges were exposed to damage from even moderately uneven ice. Besides repairing the broken ones, Nansen therefore decided to protect them all with boards fitted along the underside of the superstructure.

By now, wood of any kind was running out. However, some odd planks were found, and lashed in place on the sledges with steel wire. Once more, *Fram*'s saloon became a workshop. Johansen was happy to find himself together again with Sverdrup outside in the forge, impregnating the runners of the extra sledges with pine pitch.

It was on a Tuesday that Nansen had set out, and returned. All the work was done on the Wednesday. On Thursday, 28 February, with only two days' delay, he started off once more.

As soon as Nansen put on his skis, half the heel of one, unbeknown to him, broke off. Nordahl, who was following as far as the first hummocks, drew his attention to the mishap. Nansen indicated that it was not enough to make him turn back yet again. Pride was involved. Nansen had on his Finnish skis, about which, in the face of compact scepticism, he had often boasted.

Six sledges now seemed infinitely more cumbersome than four. The dogs were somehow dispirited. For one thing, they were more efficient in larger teams. Only four or five were now harnessed before each sledge, where previously they had been seven. The second procession did not start with the verve of the first attempt.

It was soon clear that, despite redistribution, the total load was still too great. After about a kilometre, Nansen ordered a halt and jettisoned two kayak chocks and a bag of pemmican, weighing 150 kilos altogether. These were dumped in the snow, and marked with Nansen's broken ski – he having by now put on a spare one. At this point Bentsen and Jacobsen, who had followed a little further than Nordahl, turned back. They were to come out next day with a sledge to fetch the pemmican.

Once again, Sverdrup, Scott Hansen, Blessing, Hendriksen and Mogstad continued for the first day in support. Even with their help, the sledges moved sluggishly and often stopped. Restarting them needed much heaving to break the friction before the dogs could trot off. At four in the afternoon, having covered no more than six kilometres, Nansen decided to stop for the night.

It was the first time that he had camped in earnest on the pack ice. He now had a foretaste of what was in store. Admittedly there were now two tents, where soon there would be only one; but it took a long time to pitch them both, and longer still to unharness and feed the dogs. At least the Primus, with its confident roar, was a great improvement on the temperamental spirit burner used in the crossing of Greenland.

In the distance a bright light was shining. This was *Fram*'s arc lamp, moved from the saloon to the crow's nest. It was, as Nansen observed, the first time that electric light had shone over the polar wastes. Other, weaker glows picked out a pattern of bonfires, lit in further farewell. Sverdrup had ordered a light at the masthead every evening until he returned, so that he had a beacon to guide him.

Breaking camp next morning involved more confusion and delay. Running dogs requires practice; so too does caring for them at rest. Here, everyone was still learning. It was half past eleven before the caravan set off again. Sverdrup soon decided to turn back. He shunned the slightest risk of getting lost. The final moment of parting came early in the afternoon.

'It was certainly a cheerful farewell, but it is always sad to part ... and a tear glistened here and there,' Nansen recorded in his diary. 'The weather was gloomy, and gloomy was our mood,' as Johansen chose to put it. 'We shook hands for the last time, not without emotion on both sides.'

And then they were alone in the ice, and forlorn. 'The weather was gloomy,' Johansen reiterated. 'The sun had not yet come back to us, our polar night was not yet over.'

There was the hint of a hangover too. In Sverdrup's tent the previous evening, Blessing had concocted out of rectified spirits a heady farewell punch. Nansen abandoned his scruples for the occasion, and they had all tumbled into their sleeping bags in a haze of alcohol, tobacco fumes and the afterglow of yet another recital of Hendriksen's rich store of yarns. Nor had there been much sleep, because the dogs had kept up a howling chorus through what remained of the night.

All this would have been bearable if only the going had been reasonable. Instead, it was nightmarishly heavy. First of all, there were only two men now to six sledges and six dog teams. This meant much shuttling back and forth. In practice it fell mostly on Johansen, since Nansen went ahead to find a passable trail through the maze of hummocks and massive, rafted floes. At the slightest incline, the dogs all stopped, intentionally or not. Nansen then had to retreat and help start the sledges all over again. It was physically tiring and, far worse, mentally wearing.

The outburst came while making camp. Johansen was offended when Nansen ignored a suggestion for simplifying the routine of tethering the dogs. 'I was outraged at the unnecessary work, and told him so in no uncertain terms,' he recorded.

> I considered that we had enough work without wasting time and energy on so simple a piece of work as tethering a few miserable dogs. 'What are you saying,' he said, apparently most surprised to hear this from my quiet person. I repeated it again in the same words. And then he said: 'I would willingly hand over command to you, if I could, but it won't do,' and he maintained that he had such great experience in travelling.

It was one of Johansen's faults, which might yet cost him dear, that he said things impulsively which he regretted almost as soon as the words were out of his mouth. But on this occasion he restrained himself.

> I could easily have replied convincingly merely by referring to the equipment of this sledge expedition ... One of the sledges had broken again and so had his splendid sledgemeter, but I confined myself to replying approximately thus: 'You need not hand over command to me, but you might entrust so elementary a matter as tethering some dogs to a person that you found worthy of going on this trip with you.'

Probably this was the first time on the whole expedition that anyone had spoken thus frankly to Nansen. He replied, according to Johansen:

> Oh well, let us not begin quarrelling the first evening, [and he did] what I suggested.

Johansen was still seething with months of pent-up resentment at being treated, as he thought, like a child. He made some cutting rejoinder, which Nansen chose to ignore. Thus, with tension between them, they shared their double sleeping bag to try and get some rest.

Next day, Saturday 2 March, the going was not much better. Some time after starting Nansen, in Johansen's words, 'condescended to ask my opinion'. This abrupt change from hauteur to humility unsettled Johansen. In his diary he continued to brood sarcastically over Nansen, as an exemplar of fallen pride.

Whatever the cause, Nansen now frankly admitted a succession of mistakes. As Johansen concisely summed up, there were too many sledges, too much weight in the loads, and too few people. Nansen also said that he had started too early in the season. The days were too short. The temperature was too low; forty degrees of frost. The dogs were freezing at night. 'He didn't say that he was freezing himself,' wrote Johansen in the sub-text of his diary. 'Without boasting, I stand the cold better.'

Very soon, Nansen decided to scout ahead, leaving Johansen behind to make camp and feed the dogs. Again, to quote Johansen:

38. Off at Last

'If the others had not yet left us,' said [Nansen], 'he would definitely return to the ship to reorganise.' That is what this man said, who is so experienced a traveller. 'Aha,' I thought, 'you'll go back anyway,' but I said nothing.

Nansen then went off and, in his own words:

I had not gone far before I again reached fine, broad and level expanses where there was good going, so as far as that goes, everything was all right, but the load had to be reduced and the number of sledges limited. So it would be best to turn back yet again and make the necessary changes on board.

It was not until the next morning that Nansen actually announced his decision. He set off alone for the ship to fetch help, leaving Johansen to stay behind or start back, as he saw fit. The weather was now bright and clear, and *Fram*'s masts luckily still broke the horizon. Even after all the struggle, she was only eight miles away.

Nansen had taken one sledge but a double dog team. That is to say, he had eight animals instead of four or five before each sledge as hitherto. Skiing as hard as he could, Nansen now had his work cut out to keep pace with the dogs. But, as he put it, 'In a couple of hours I had covered the same distance which had taken us three days on the way out. The advantage of a lighter load was all too obvious.'

Nansen arrived noticeably crestfallen, to be blandly greeted with the news that *Fram* had just crossed the eighty-fourth parallel, an achievement the party intended to celebrate that evening. The sun had returned that same day, 3 March, so that would be celebrated too. Johansen, however, could only be fetched on the morrow and, as Nordahl said, 'we thought it was dismal that a companion, instead of taking part, would be lying alone out on the ice'. So he and Scott Hansen, with Nansen's consent, took an empty sledge and dog team and sped out to keep Johansen company. They arrived in an hour and twenty-five minutes.

Johansen meanwhile, without Nansen's presence, had been, in his own revealing words, 'in a good mood all day, despite having to labour alone with the dogs in the fields of ice'. He had had to shuttle back and forth, hauling the sledges in relays. When Nordahl and Scott Hansen arrived he had just pitched camp and was settling down for the night. He was careful to explain that with five sledges and four dog teams he had driven further by himself than he had done with Nansen the previous day when they had *six* sledges and *six* dog teams.

The visitors had brought tobacco and a bottle of aquavit, both thoughtfully sent along by Sverdrup from his 'secret' store. Over the Primus stove a hot punch was once more brewed, and the three men in the tent had their own party. At a certain stage of the proceedings Johansen and Nordahl started singing but, to quote Scott Hansen, 'the dogs began to provide an accompaniment, so they had to stop'.

Next morning, understandably, they rose rather late, but were almost ready when Nansen, Sverdrup and Hendriksen, they too coping with a modest *katzenjammer*, arrived to help on the homeward way. The dogs knew where they were heading, so they trotted with considerably more verve than on the outward run. They were only stopped by a lead that had opened in the few hours since the relief party came out. The sledges were parked in safety while men and dogs were ferried across on loose pieces of ice, to get back on board for the night. Two days later, the lead was frozen over well enough to bear the sledges, and they were finally brought back to the ship. It was now 6 March. For the third time Nansen reorganised.

'There has been much criticism of the preparations,' Scott Hansen recorded, 'and for the most part it is justified, but ... one becomes sick and tired of listening to this chatter.' All the same, it was odd 'that a journey like this, which could have been prepared quietly and steadily, with trials beforehand, should take place head over heels, and have such a start'.

This obscured Nansen's considerable accomplishments so far. After all, he had already broken the record for the Furthest North. He had yet again changed the face of polar travel. In *Fram* he had provided a comfortable home. He had conquered cold and avoided scurvy. He had eliminated danger and fear. And beyond all this, he had shown that skis could be used in the pack ice too. Under favourable circumstances, as the rapid comings and goings had proved, skis took the drudgery out of travelling. Above all, he had established the combination of running dogs with men on skis.

Despite his overbearing attitude Nansen, as he had proved to Johansen out in the tent, was actually quick to learn from his mistakes. He was innocent of hubris, punctilious in acknowledging his predecessors. He now hastened to apply the lessons forced upon him by his two false starts. So much had gone wrong that virtually every aspect of his equipment had to be overhauled.

The trouble went deeper than material preparation. Nansen had been going against his own nature, an infallible recipe for self-destruction. He and Johansen were essentially both skiers who happened to have taken to polar exploration, and the skier is attuned to running uninterruptedly. He puts his trust in speed and mobility.

Misled, perhaps, by historical examples, Nansen had sought safety instead in plentiful supplies, at the cost of a morose plod. He now renounced this aberration and reverted to his natural instincts. In his diary he wrote:

> I will now calculate the journey on the assumption that it will happen as quickly as possible. With light sledges we will forge ahead as fast as legs and skis will carry us. If we do not meet too many hummocks and open leads it will scarcely be the worse for that.

To begin with, it was now clear, after the debacle with the preposterous flotilla, that there ought to be one man to a sledge. Because of the kayaks, this was not actually possible. So Nansen settled for three sledges. He chose them from among those that Mogstad had built, but now he wanted them thoroughly reinforced.

The false starts had shown that in the rough terrain of the pack ice, sledges had to be robustly constructed. The difficulty was to strike a balance between strength and excessive weight. To begin with, all joints were reinforced with iron angle-brackets. The transverse ribs were strengthened with slats of ash. The underside of each sledge was now completely protected with boards taken from the other sledges. Underneath each sledge, too, a spare pair of skis was then fixed. Still, to preserve elasticity, no metal fastenings were used. Everything was lashed together using rope yarn, the most resilient fibre available.

Jacobsen, helped by Johansen, lashed the sledges together down in *Fram*'s hold. Johansen perceptively noted in his diary:

> There is much feeling in Jacobsen, despite his verbosity, and he is touching when he begins to talk about the longing of the seaman for peace in a good home with a faithful wife. I am sure that we will all appreciate our homes much more when we finally see them again.

Whether or not as a result of his setback, Nansen suddenly appeared to have learned how to delegate. He kept to his cabin and no longer interfered with the details of the work. As a result, the atmosphere notably improved.

In a few days, Johansen and Jacobsen finished modifying the sledges. One ended up weighing around 20 kilos; the other two, for carrying the kayaks, weighed 35 kilos each. Admittedly this included spare skis, but it was heavier than Nansen originally wanted. But he had quickly learned that the Nordic skier's obsession with the pursuit of lightness in weight at any cost was a fatal mistake.

Nansen now chose stronger but heavier skis. One spare pair was made of solid hickory, a particularly tough and resilient hardwood, and tipped the scales at 5 kilos. By comparison, a modern pair of plastic touring skis, including bindings, weighs about $3\frac{1}{2}$ kilos. Where strength and safety were not jeopardised, however, Nansen pursued his goal of lightness.

His travelling tents were made of raw silk which, before the advent of synthetic fibres, was the strongest known material, weight for weight. Nansen had originally taken a four-man tent. Instead, he now took a two-man model. It weighed about 2.8 kilos, a saving of $1\frac{1}{2}$ kilos. Moreover, the previous tent had a sewn-in groundsheet, which the new one did not. By soaking up moisture, the groundsheet increased in weight, which outweighed the other advantages.

This tent was another innovation in polar travel. Previously, ridge tents had been used; cumbersome, with several guys, and difficult to pitch, with a pole at either end. Nansen had chosen a pyramid model, supported by a single pole, and held down by small pegs round the edge. It was easily pitched, with few guys, and was stable in high winds.

Given his forethought when originally equipping *Fram*, Nansen had been strangely casual in preparing for the polar journey. The loads, for example, were not properly weighed. Consequently, it was impossible to say exactly how much the dogs had been pulling, except that it was rather more than 1,100 kilos. All that was now changed.

Nansen began by weighing all the dogs carefully, to ascertain the meat each might provide. From this he calculated that by feeding them on each other the dogs could be kept going for 50 days. In addition, dog food for 30 days would be taken. That meant that the dogs could be expected to haul for 80 days – 'and in that time', as Nansen put it, 'we must be able to achieve something'.

For himself and Johansen, Nansen proposed taking supplies for 100 days. The food had been bad, in Johansen's estimation, during their first abortive days out on the ice: 'We ate chocolate, bread and butter morning and evening ... on just one evening we had a stew made of pemmican.'

Nansen now went to the other extreme. He carried out meticulous dietary calculations. He wanted sufficient nourishment according to the best knowledge at the time. Scurvy was his one fear. But he assumed that because he had avoided it so far, he would continue to do so.

Weighing everything now to the nearest ten grams, Nansen began pruning his load. One outcome of putting his faith in speed was to reduce fuel for the Primus stove to twenty litres. After repeated calculations and, to the exasperation of his companions, much agonising indecision, Nansen finally brought the total weight, including sledges, down to 763.8 kilos. The weight to be hauled by each dog had been reduced from perhaps 42 kilos to 27 kilos, a decrease of 35%. On a trial run the dogs now hauled the sledges, Nansen exultantly observed, 'as if it was nothing at all'.

Sleeping arrangements proved to be another disastrous shortcoming. Nansen had taken wolfskin outfits to wear inside the reindeer fur sleeping bags. He had not tried them out before leaving. What he discovered was that the wolfskins rapidly became sodden with condensation and, in the deep cold, froze stiff. On the march, they were impossible to dry. He now decided to leave them behind. Instead, he reverted to his old favourite, wool.

As a sleeping garment, Nansen designed a kind of nightshirt made out of a blanket. It had a slit, so that it could double as a cape to keep warm while resting on the march. Yet again, the sleeping bag was radically altered. Hitherto, the hair had been outside; now it was reversed. But with the hair inside there was less space, so Sverdrup had to turn to again, and enlarge the bag.

To test the new equipment, Nansen and Johansen again slept outside in a tent one night, lying fully dressed inside their outer sleeping garment.

They slept well in forty degrees of frost, and in the morning everything was remarkably dry.

Other pieces of equipment required tedious alteration. In little more than a week the work was all done – to the accompaniment of the by now usual complaint, *sotto voce*, that 'Himself' did everything in a rush. Sverdrup, as was his wont, worked quietly in the background to avoid panic and make things go smoothly. Nonetheless, so many changes were upsetting, reported Johansen and, 'some of my shipmates predict little good of the journey.'

So, on the morning of Thursday 14 March, Nansen and Johansen were drawn up by the side of the ship for the third time, ready to go. Their equipage looked altogether more businesslike. What is more, when they had first set out, sixteen days before, *Fram*'s latitude had been 83°48′N. Now it was 84°4′. They were sixteen miles further north. Besides which, there was the uplift of beginning their journey beyond the eighty-fourth parallel. And the sun was now above the horizon.

Flags were flying and there was a tense but festive atmosphere, rather like the start of a ski race. It had been another late night – not this time, on account of a last minute rush but of a party. Sverdrup had repeated his laconic benediction. Nansen, as usual, inspired by relays of hot punch, had responded with an elaborate and optimistic oration. As usual, too, the aftermath was a slight hangover.

As they lined up for their departure, Nansen positioned himself in front. Behind him waited the sledge with his kayak, and nine dogs harnessed. Next followed sledge No. 2, holding chiefly food and the bulky sleeping bag, with another team of nine dogs. And finally came Johansen's sledge with his kayak, and ten dogs in the traces. Blessing photographed the scene. Nansen assumed a dramatic pose of spying out the land ahead.

Otherwise the two of them looked anything but heroic. Each was, after all, a Nordic skier, that quintessential anti-hero, and each had on two thick woollen Jaeger shirts, with a camel hair vest on top. Outside this Nansen wore a woollen Iceland jersey and Johansen an Eskimo-like anorak made of thick vadmel. On their legs, starting on the inside, they wore woollen underpants. Next came thick vadmel breeches, and knitted woollen leggings made by cutting the tops of long stockings. The purpose was to keep the socks as small as possible, because they would have to be dried at night in the sleeping bag next to the skin. The woollen leggings were covered by outer ones made of vadmel. There was no need, yet, for the Burberry wind clothes. For one thing, the thermometer showed no more than thirty degrees of frost. For another, only a gentle breeze was blowing, and from the south-east at that, which meant a following wind. The only remnant of the wolfskin clothing lay in large outer mittens, worn over inner ones of wool.

On their feet, Nansen and Johansen wore finneskoe filled with senne-grass, incontestably the softest ski boots available, exactly suited to the loose Finnish leather bindings, and warm, light, and unrivalled in low temperatures.

Lolling in the snow before the sledges, the dogs were resigned to waiting yet again for the start. These were their names, lovingly catalogued by Johansen: Kvik, Baro, Little Fox, Strumpet, Narrifas, Freia, Barbara, Potifar, Rattlesnake, Thug, Child, Hare, Yellow and Flint; Caiaphas, Block, Bielki, Sultan, Barabbas, Beldam, Perpetuum, The Cat, The Lifeguardsman, Big Fox, Polar Bear, The Russian, Pan and Ulenka. Each reflected something in the character of its bearer. They were the twenty-eight animals on whom the whole enterprise depended.

At 11.30, Nansen finally gave the order to start. Once more *Fram*'s signal cannon roared over the ice in salute. Once more the dogs lunged ahead. The caravan sprang into motion. Several men, including Sverdrup, set off as well, to follow Nansen and Johansen a little way. Sverdrup was the first to turn back – so as not to be late for lunch on board at one o'clock, or so he said.

Soon after, repeating Nansen's mishap on the second start, Johansen broke a ski. He received a new one in exchange from Mogstad, who ambled homewards on a ski and a half leaving Scott Hansen, Hendriksen and Petterson accompanying the departing Nansen and Johansen a little further. 'They were undoubtedly glad of our help', Scott Hansen wrote:

There was much pressure and other misery in our path [although] now the dogs managed lesser obstacles without a trace of difficulty. [All afternoon] we travelled through hideous broken terrain. At one point we had to haul and lift the sledges over a horribly tangled ridge, about 40 metres. At 6 p.m. however, we emerged from all this, and before us we had a huge level plain that stretched without interruption as far as the eye could see.

They halted and made camp in the lee of a huge weathered old pillar of ice overlooking a whole dune of loose drift snow. For Scott Hansen's party, the latter was essential. They had no tent, and were going to sleep in a snow cave. Petterson and Scott Hansen dug one out. Caustic as usual, Scott Hansen observed that Nansen took half an hour to pitch his tent 'which at the table in the saloon [on *Fram*] was accomplished theoretically in less than a minute'. Also, 'with his usual grandiloquence', Nansen had promised to have the Primus going, ice melted, and a hot drink ready within twenty minutes, but it took more than an hour.

Next morning, Nansen was handier with the Primus, and breakfast was quickly served. Soon it was time for the final handshakes. Not many words were exchanged, but while Hendriksen was helping to harness Johansen's dog team The Child and Pan, mortal enemies, began fighting. To keep order, Hendriksen had to give The Child a hiding. It hurt him to part in this manner. It was not that The Child was particularly lovable – the day before, by way of farewell, he had bitten Nordahl in the leg – but he was foredoomed to sacrifice as part of the plan, like all the other dogs.

38. Off at Last

During the battle, and the subsequent chastisement, Nansen started off with the leading sledges. The two belligerents thereupon hauled away together with the same enthusiasm they had devoted to fighting each other, and then, without warning, the whole team careered off, leaving Johansen behind. He had to lunge forward on his skis with all his strength to catch up.

Scott Hansen and his companions stood and watched until the polar party dwindled into little dots upon the snow. Then they put on their skis and headed homewards as quickly as they could. *Fram* was out of sight, and although they had a compass bearing they could not shake off a sense of unease until the mastheads reappeared through the haze. They were back on board after four and a quarter hours, not having stopped once to rest.

Nansen was half expected to reappear. Scott Hansen, however, believed that '*Fram* is so distasteful to [him] now, that he would risk anything rather than come here again.' The days passed, and it eventually became clear that he was indeed not coming back.

'They have now presumably put 85° behind them,' Scott Hansen was writing in his diary on 23 March, ten days after Nansen and Johansen had left.

It has been fine clear weather ... so [they] have had good travelling weather [although] rather cold, but little wind, and what there is has been behind them, so they ought to be comfortable ... I wonder – and others as well – how Himself's nose is getting on.

That meant the frostbite to which Nansen's nose was thought to be prone. There was actually more concern for Johansen. He had to cope with Nansen's temperament and that was felt to be rather more burdensome than the worst the Arctic could do. In Scott Hansen's words:

I hope that all will be well with them, and that it will be reasonably pleasant for Hjalle [Johansen].

39

85th Parallel

When Nansen parted from his companions at the camp out on the ice, he skied ahead with Kvik, his devoted lead dog, hard on his heels. At a certain point, he stole a glance behind. In the distance, Peter Hendriksen stood atop the big serac, gazing out in silent farewell, the last figure to vanish out of sight.

Men and dogs sped over the level plain which had been the vista from the camp. But all too soon advance was barred once more by a deformed upheaval of twisted seracs and rafted floes. Taking off his skis, Nansen plodded ahead on foot to pick a way through the chaos. At the same time he had constantly to turn back and help Johansen manoeuvre the sledges, which had sometimes to be lifted bodily over obstacles. Often, in the convoluted passages winding through the hummocks, the sledges capsized, which meant yet more struggle and delay. 'Stopped at 6 [p.m.] rather worn out,' Nansen laconically noted in his diary. The sledgemeter showed a mere five nautical miles for the day.

Camp was made as quickly as possible. Johansen unharnessed the dogs, fed them, and tethered them for the night. Meanwhile Nansen raised the tent, crawled inside, and, having filled the cooking pot with ice, began preparing supper – a tacit recognition of each man's aptitude. Johansen had long since proved to be the better dog driver. Nansen preferred the technicalities of pitching the tent and working the Primus stove.

When Johansen had finished with the dogs he joined Nansen inside the tent. They spread the sleeping bag and got in together to keep themselves warm while supper was cooked. All told, it took about an hour before the ice was melted and the soft bubble of a boiling meal was added to the comforting roar of the Primus flame and the occasional click of the pump.

In the morning it was Nansen, too, still half in the sleeping bag, who made breakfast. On 16 March, waiting for the pot to boil, he now wrote up his diary for the first time since leaving the ship two days before.

Johansen also kept his diary. 'If only the cold would relent, it is miserable,' he wrote on 19 March. It was an effort even to keep a diary, pencil clasped clumsily in a wolfskin mitten. Since the very start, the temperature had obstinately hovered around –40°C. This is below the freezing point of mercury; only spirit thermometers continued to function in such cold.

Nansen's blind faith in wool seemed now to have been misplaced. 'Our clothes are turning ... into frozen armour by day and wet wrappings at night,' he was soon recording. Polar Eskimos knew the cure: large garments, with plenty of space for air to circulate inside and keep surfaces dry. It was a lesson Nansen had not learnt. His clothes were quite simply too tight. Cuffs as hard as steel sawed into his wrists, leaving permanent open wounds exacerbated by frost.

Nansen now bitterly regretted leaving the wolfskin outfits behind, for there were no extra clothes to keep warm in while standing still. Their best friend was now their sleeping bag. Even so, there was no question of peeling off the rigid outer clothing with frozen fingers. At the end of each day, the two men crept into the sleeping bag as they were. Made of reindeer fur as it was, it had soon nonetheless iced up. Daily it grew stiffer and heavier and more encrusted with ice. Clinging to each other for extra warmth; shivering with cold, teeth chattering, Nansen and Johansen waited for clothes and sleeping bag to thaw. They were further burdened by the overriding need to keep their feet unharmed, for upon that depended their survival. Finneskoe were turned inside out. Together with sennegrass, socks and leggings, they were distributed over bare belly and chest to dry out reasonably by morning. But that in itself was yet another drain on the heat of tortured human frames. It was probably an hour and a half before a sensation of clammy warmth appeared. 'We suffer more and more from the cold,' Johansen recorded in a dismal succession of diary entries. 'It is growing worse and worse ... I do not know how long we can hold out.'

But these were also reasons for confidence. Nansen had based his calculations on a daily run of around eight miles. After the setbacks of the first few days, he was covering closer to nine. Moreover, he had left *Fram* a whole degree further north than he originally assumed, and that offset the delay in starting out. Even better, on 16 March, the day after parting with his companions from the ship, Nansen once more left broken ice behind. Flat or undulating snowfields returned for good, or so it seemed. It was terrain made for skiing.

Various mishaps punctuated the passing of the days. On March 18th, for example – the fifth day out – one of the sledges rammed a jagged piece of ice. As a result, a sack of fish meal was ripped open. There was a long delay while the contents were gathered up and the sack mended. The whole sledge naturally had to be restowed and lashed. But against all this and more could be set the familiar, rhythmic comfort of skiing. With the lopsided gait of the skier with one stick, Nansen and Johansen loped comfortably along. All around was an endless field of glinting snow crust running to the horizon. They were in their element. Before that single fact, all difficulties paled.

The dogs meanwhile had established a modus vivendi with their masters. That is to say, under favourable circumstances, they obliged by hauling. With level backs, bushy tails held high like pennants, heads at attention and puffed out coats, they trotted at their characteristic gait. Meanwhile, Nansen and Johansen on skis comfortably kept pace. This too was history in the making. The combination of the skier and the sledge dog was being proven on the pack ice.

Periodically, the dogs stopped for a little mayhem. They would jump over each others' traces so as to produce an unholy tangle. Some dogs took advantage of the confusion to bite through their traces. The worst culprit was one called – appropriately enough – The Russian. He was known of old, so had steel wire in his harness but, finding it impossible to bite himself free, he playfully bit through other dogs' harnesses instead.

This devilry was calculated. It is in the nature of the dog that, although his stamina is limitless, he needs frequent and regular rests. That is wholly against the instincts of the skier, who loathes interruption of any kind. But men are usually better served by adjusting to their dogs, and not the other way about. This was what these animals were trying to convey – and what neither Nansen nor Johansen grasped. Sometimes, instead of wasting more time rounding up the rogues, they drove on in their impatience with depleted teams. The loose dogs followed the caravan at a respectful distance, having the last laugh, as dogs very often do.

By and large, however, the dogs hauled obediently ahead. They were pulling roughly their own weight, having started off with a load of 27 kilos each, while the average weight was 25 kilos. For sledge dogs, this was a reasonable burden. But also, these animals were fed when camp was made and thus, in Johansen's words, 'they have something to long for, and exert themselves in the course of the day to arrive where they know that food is to be had'.

The men too yearned only to creep into their sleeping bags at the end of the day, and feel the lifegiving comfort of their hot evening meal.

As cook, Nansen had no sinecure. In the end, survival depended on his skill. His housekeeping was surprisingly elaborate and he considered variety essential to good diet. Besides the staples of pemmican and biscuits fortified with protein he carried butter, liver pâté and fish meal, There was also chocolate, a selection of patent concentrated foods, and some dried soups – but neither coffee nor tea. Since Greenland, he had maintained his opinion that they were harmful stimulants, and therefore wasteful ballast.

To ring the changes, he had prepared a set of menus. There were three supper dishes: a stew of pemmican and dried potatoes; so-called 'fish gratin', made of dried fish meal, flour fortified with concentrated protein and butter; and pea, bean or lentil soup with pemmican. Breakfast alternated between porridge and hot chocolate. Nansen arranged the permutations over a five-day cycle.

Lunch was a hasty meal, snatched during a halt before the cold penetrated too far. It consisted of Swedish rye crispbread and butter, a kind of chocolate fortified with meat, cold pemmican, or other concentrated food.

All this Nansen had noted in one of his diaries, with the nutritional values carefully tabulated. The total allowance of food was one kilo per man per day. Nansen had calculated that this gave about 200 grams of protein, 220 grams of fat and 450 grams of carbohydrate, which was the way food was then exclusively analysed. This gave about 4,700 calories, which was probably enough. Anyway, the men were well fed, so that they merely faced the cold and lack of sleep. To be cold, tired *and* hungry is to invite disaster.

In Nansen's own words: 'The ice seems to become better and smoother the further north we go.' It was not only the contours that counted. The very same temperatures that made camping a misery also enhanced the going. The ice was covered by firm, granular, compacted snow, and under those conditions, the colder the better. Sledges moved easily over a surface that hardly gave, where dogs' paws found comfortable purchase and, as a familiar rasp of wood on snow crust confirmed, where the skiing was good.

What is more, the Finnish bindings were exactly suited to the terrain. The link between skier and skis, the critical aspect of equipment, had turned out an unmitigated success. Simple, light in weight, and supremely supple, these bindings allowed heels to lift unhindered, and were noticed hardly at all. That saved energy and reduced fatigue. Also, circulation was unimpeded, so that feet at least were warm. This in turn was profoundly comforting. Freezing feet are not only physical torture; they also induce a particularly loathsome kind of depression.

'Lovely weather to travel in, with beautiful sunset,' Nansen wrote in his diary at one point. 'The ice seems to become smoother the further we advance.' Johansen wrote:

> We travel in this way. Nansen goes ahead on ski with one sledge, and it is then up to me to follow with the two other sledges, and that is not always so easy, since the loads are heavy and they often capsize. In uneven ice it is naturally worse, since the dogs often stop, and there is nothing for it but to go from the one sledge to the other, and give it a shove ... so my hands are full.

Nonetheless, the whole enterprise, as Nansen had hoped, was settling down to a kind of ski tour. Circumstances were harsh, but these men were not struggling. This echoed the first crossing of Greenland, and distinguished them from all those who had trudged across the pack ice and tried to reach the Pole before.

In another way, Nansen was making history as he skied along. Previous explorers had been plagued by the so-called Arctic thirst. This was due to inefficient cooking apparatus, and hence an inability to melt enough ice. The Primus, with its minute fuel consumption, changed all that. Nansen could produce unlimited drinking water. Sometimes flavoured with Lactoserin, a kind of dried milk protein, it was drunk in huge quantities. They gulped down as much as they could manage morning and evening, and still had to throw some away. The effect was to prevent the menacing dehydration that paradoxically accompanies exertion in deep cold. Such was one outcome of a small technological revolution. To be thirsty *and* freezing is horrible.

The seventh day out, the sledgemeter fell off. When this was discovered, it was somewhere out of sight. Neither Nansen nor Johansen could be bothered to fetch it. They had, moreover, already been delayed when The Lifeguardsman, one of Johansen's dogs, had collapsed; he was now being dragged along as fodder for his friends. The sledgemeter was, in fact, a misleading device since, although it correctly registered the distance run, it ignored the drift of the ice. The only reliable arbiter of progress was the astronomical observation, which meant in practice the meridian altitude of the sun. Nansen finally took the first one on 22 March, after the sledgemeter was lost. The outcome was 85°9′N.

The observation was taken before starting out, so it only covered the distances up to March 21st. It had taken eight days to cover one degree of latitude. That meant a sixth of the outward journey already done. In exact figures, Nansen had started 356 miles from the Pole, and was now only 291 miles off. The average daily northing was eight miles – Nansen's original estimate – and evidently rising. At a conservative estimate, Nansen could now count on reaching the Pole around 27 April, a week later than anticipated. He had, however, allowed fifty days for the distance; now it looked as if he would do it in about forty.

'It's going gloriously,' Johansen happily observed. Not even the inevitable rider, 'If only the cold would lift,' could quite dampen their spirits. As they headed north, small Norwegian flags, red ground picked out against the blue-white snow, were flying on the kayaks atop their sledges in honour both of the eighty-fifth parallel and of a goal now seemingly within their grasp.

40

Sverdrup in Charge

On *Fram*, meanwhile, two views of Nansen were being expressed. 'It is extraordinary how the atmosphere has changed since [he] left,' Sverdrup wrote in his diary.

> Everybody is content, and in a good mood, and the work goes like a dance. All his crowing has caused an unbelievable amount of bad blood ... I think everybody hates him. Worst of all was the arrogance with which he always treated his subordinates, and then he was always unpleasant to everyone.

Sverdrup usually kept his diary like a ship's log; mostly a restrained record of wind and weather. Very rarely did he make personal comments. This was his first outburst on the whole expedition so far. It was out of character; he must have been deeply provoked.

Scott Hansen, as second in command, reflected differently: 'Now that they don't have Nansen to blame, they'll take it out on the Captain and myself.'

In short, feelings towards Nansen were thoroughly ambivalent. On the one hand there was relief among these men, cooped up in an isolated little community, at being spared his oppressive moods, his aristocratic assumption of superiority. On the other, he had taken away with him a sense of purpose. It was he and Johansen who would be tackling the Pole. The rest had been left behind in what Scott Hansen gloomily called 'the monastic life we lead in this dead zone'.

All this Sverdrup had to resolve with sheer willpower and his gift for leadership. He avoided Nansen's obvious shortcomings. To begin with, he knew instinctively how to deal with small groups. He never permitted himself the slightest airs. He made his subordinates feel as if he were one of themselves. Nonetheless, he had to tread warily at the start, tactfully transferring allegiance to himself without provoking disloyalty to Nansen. For that, there was fertile soil. 'Nansen had no idea about running a ship,' wrote Jacobsen in his diary, 'although he ... certainly understood how to make the Captain powerless in those matters which concerned him ... and thus undermined discipline ... so that the matter has not been settled yet.' Nansen was also resented because he was untidy. He had left the ship in a mess. The first thing that Sverdrup did on taking over command, therefore, was to have everything cleared up.

The departure of Nansen and Johansen also left the ship less cramped – the effect of which was an almost disproportionate sense of relief. Without Johansen, only Amundsen, Juell and Petterson were left sharing the starboard cabin. Meanwhile Sverdrup moved into Nansen's berth, cleaned his typewriter and sat down to learn how to use it. Jacobsen then took over the berth vacated by Sverdrup, bringing the numbers in the big port cabin down from five to four. It was, wrote Nordahl,

> fantastically roomy and pleasant in our cabin now; you would not recognise it since we got Jacobsen out, with all his mess.

With the return of a sense of order, and hence a raising of morale, Sverdrup's next concern was for the safety of the ship. She lay embedded in about eight metres of ice. Along the port side ran a broken pressure ridge, level with the half deck. Sverdrup feared that it might topple over and force *Fram* down. He now did what he had wanted to do for months. He set the whole crew to dig away the ridge. The work lasted until the end of March. He did his full share. He worked with Blessing, which led to a quite piquant contretemps. Blessing, recorded Sverdrup,

> suspected me of being angry and I, him.... It so happens that I do not like to gossip when I am [working], while the opposite is the case with the doctor. When now, as is my wont, I kept quiet, the doctor thought that *I* was angry, and similarly I thought that *he* was angry, because he had stopped talking. But the misunderstanding was soon cleared up, and we had a good laugh.

Fram now seemed unlikely to come to any harm. Sverdrup therefore now turned his energies to overhauling the sledges and kayaks. The work here was hampered by a shortage of wood – a problem once again put at the door of Nansen, this time by Nordahl. To overcome it, Sverdrup had the motor boat broken up and the windmill dismantled (it was now damaged beyond repair) so that its wooden parts could also be used. By these and other expedients all the sledges and kayaks were finally put in order. They were then slung on the davits, ready, like lifeboats, to be lowered at a moment's notice.

At the same time, supplies were prepared for a six months' stay on the pack ice, and a sledge journey of 70 days to the nearest land. Everything was packed in loads that could be carried by one man, and stowed up on the foredeck, ready to be heaved overboard. One of the big half-decked boats from Colin Archer's yard was put out on the ice, ready for sea.

All this was fairly straightforward. More serious was a shortage of dependable skis. Without them, snow travel was unthinkable. Sverdrup required at least one serviceable pair for each man. New ones had to be made. Unfortunately, the only acceptable wood was in a solid beam of oak.

Worse still, there was no proper ripsaw to cut it up. Amundsen improvised one out of an ice saw. Mogstad and Hendriksen did the sawing. Amundsen constantly had to sharpen and set the saw. In five days, nonetheless, the Sisyphean task was done. The beam yielded blanks for six pairs of skis, which were then hung out in the saloon to season.

In the meantime, there were enough practice skis to go round. When the month of May arrived, Sverdrup ordered everybody out onto the ice to ski for two hours every day. If he were ever faced with an emergency, he wanted practised skiers in good condition.

Nansen had left seven dogs behind; a bitch called Susine, from Kvik's first litter on board, and six young animals from her second. Towards the end of April, Susine had twelve pups, of whom eight survived. Under favourable circumstances, there might now eventually be enough dogs for two sledges. But if there were ever to be a retreat over the ice it would be mostly man-hauling.

In hauling heavily laden sledges over the broken surface of the pack ice, Sverdrup had the heretical idea – for a Norwegian – that snowshoes were superior to skis, because they did not slip. So he got Mogstad to make snowshoes out of some maple laths on board.

By elaborately preparing for the worst, Sverdrup showed once more that he had the measure of his men. They were, after all, heirs to yet another Norwegian dichotomy. In certain circumstances, they would notoriously trust to luck. But where the powers of Nature were concerned, they were imbued with everlasting caution.

'Your duty,' Nansen had told Sverdrup in his letter of instruction, just before he left,

is to bring home in the safest possible way the human beings hereby confided to your care, and not to expose them to any unnecessary danger, either for the sake of the ship and its contents, or the outcome of the expedition.

Sverdrup obeyed this command to the letter, and in his quiet way was quickly earning the undivided respect of his men. While approachable to anyone individually, he had the knack of keeping his distance from the crew as a whole. Now and then, he made solitary excursions far out on the pack ice, for days at a time. His pretext was hunting polar bears. In reality, he wanted to remove himself, to allow everyone the seaman's time-honoured therapy of cursing the skipper.

At intervals, Sverdrup continued sounding, as Nansen had instructed. Depths of between 1,500 and 2,000 fathoms persisted, thus confirming the discovery of a deep polar sea.

The seventeenth of May, the Norwegian national day, arrived for the second time on *Fram*. Once more, there was the obligatory procession on the pack ice round the ship, varied now by cheers for Nansen and Johansen, sadly thin in the silent air. Mogstad gave the first performance on his violin of a march he had composed in honour of Nansen. The sun shone from a cloudless sky. Nonetheless, it all lacked the spirit of the year before. The mood lifted during the evening when, in Scott Hansen's words

> we all became well and truly drunk ... Juell took the opportunity to challenge Mogstad to go out and fight on the half deck [but] we separated them.... Today neither of the participants in this little comedy remembers anything of what had happened, and so all's well that ends well ... The whole of the 18th we went round with hangovers, every one of us ... and now there is goodwill all round, and I heard things which suggest that the worst of our bad spirits are over, and henceforth our life together will be pleasant.

Yet the fact that this was the second summer in the ice irredeemably depressed the atmosphere on board. Once more the snow turned to coarse grained slush; leads opened and closed. In the wider channels, whales occasionally blew. A few Ross gulls and other hardy birds sometimes flew overhead. These were the only signs of life in an arid wilderness. Once more, the midnight sun spiralled round the horizon to its zenith, and then started its descent. Late in August, the open leads started freezing over again. Another winter was on the way.

Feelings, as usual, were dictated by the drift. And the drift, all that summer of 1895, made spirits low. Nothing, it seemed, could abate a forlorn sense of isolation. Sometimes for days on end, only monosyllables were exchanged. Fights flared up over trifles; like one, for example, between Mogstad and Nordahl, the reason for which, in Jacobsen's words, was that Mogstad tried to point out to Nordahl that his way of blowing his nose or disposing of the snot was not correct.

Blessing, the Captain and Hendriksen managed best, according to Scott Hansen, but quite soon Blessing became unaccountably ill. The cause, hidden from the rest of the crew, but dispassionately recorded by Blessing in his medical journal, was that 'during the last days of July I began injecting myself daily with morphine *ut experimendum fiat* [as an experiment]'. Blessing wanted to test a theory that laxatives would help withdrawal. Or so, at least, he said. After about six weeks, he began weaning himself off the drug. His mysterious illness was really the onset of withdrawal symptoms.

Five months had now gone by, and some time in August Amundsen was writing: 'I suppose that now Nansen has reached home and brought news from us.'

And Jacobsen reflected:

> If only things go well with [Nansen] and he and Johansen return home having achieved a good result, then everything will be all right after all.

Before Nansen left, Sverdrup had asked him whether he still proposed making an attempt on the South Pole after coming home. If so, would he wait for *Fram* to return? Nansen had been freely discussing an Antarctic expedition, for while with one half of himself he was longing only to return to Eva, with the other half he was still consumed by his ambition to be the first man at both poles of the Earth, and was already planning to leave again soon after coming home.

Sverdrup was keen to join, if the expedition took place, and so was Scott Hansen, but on certain conditions. The plan would be to take two ships, one of which would winter in the Antarctic while the other would be sent back to civilisation. 'I will go on that expedition if I can have the command of one of [the ships],' Scott Hansen told himself. Tellingly, he would have to be 'liberated from anything to do with [scientific] observations, and then of course good pay'.

> Besides, I want the ship which sails out during the summer, and returns to Australia or New Zealand for the winter. *Voilà mes conditions.*

But he was not quite convinced that Nansen was 'all that keen'. 'If he comes home with his attainment [of the North Pole] his name is made, and he can leave the South Pole to others.'

41

A Dog's Life

'In some places it is like travelling over the [Greenland] Ice Cap,' Nansen had exultantly written in his diary out on the pack ice, on 20 March, around 85°N. He had just covered more than eleven miles, the best daily run so far. 'If it continues this way, the whole thing will go like a dream.'

Meanwhile Johansen, becoming more like Nansen's shadow side with each passing day, was giving events another interpretation. 'We did a proper job,' he conceded. Nonetheless: 'We suffer from the cold more and more. During the night temp. −42.7°, today −40.2°.' On the trail, the cold was held at bay; at rest, it remorselessly advanced. Johansen's diary was turning into a canon of misery:

> We don't sleep at all because of the cold, work a lot and suffer much ... my God! My fingers are all destroyed. All mittens are frozen stiff.... It is becoming worse and worse... Tuesday −45° ... icy sleeping bags, heavy loads, but onward we must go ... God alone knows what will happen to us.

The dogs mocked their masters by sleeping soundly, curled up in the snow. Since the enterprise rested on their wellbeing, they had to be waited on hand and foot. It was a moot point who were really the servants and who the masters. After the day's run, the dogs merely lay down and waited to be fed. That was a miserable procedure with frozen fingers in the biting cold. First, pemmican had to be removed from the chocks underneath the kayaks. Then it was divided into twenty-eight suitable portions and dealt out. Thereafter the loads on all three sledges had to be rearranged so as to keep the kayaks on an even keel. Nansen, moreover, insisted that the dogs had all the sleep they needed.

In the meantime, the men had to cook and eat their own meals, make and break camp, and carry out running repairs. When to this was added their own need for rest, and making sure of doing the distance, there were not enough hours in the day. But now, as the vernal equinox went by and the midnight sun approached, it was continually light. Nansen abandoned the clock, simply marching and resting as it pleased him. The diaries began to take on the undertones of a dream play.

'Yesterday I had to be butcher for The Lifeguardsman, who met his end by the bear hunting spear.' Thus Johansen, on 24 March, a Sunday, blandly recorded the killing of the first dog. Also the day before,

> sharp [head] wind from N.E., very bad ice and a hard grind. It is not pleasant to be a human being here but there must surely be an end to it some time. – Today hazy, raw fog ... –40° ... the same wind, gruesome weather. One of the worst Sundays I have known.

The Lifeguardsman was divided and served up as supper for the twenty seven animals remaining. Hungry as they were, many glumly refused to eat their old companion. Nansen also noted in his diary:

> This interminable lifting of heavily laden sledges is calculated to put one's poor old back out of sorts.

The good going had ended two days after crossing the eighty-fifth parallel. To drive them on, Johansen started shouting at the dogs so much that he no longer recognised his own voice. He shouted at them even when he slept, waking Nansen in the process.

The long, flowing plain had given way to crumpled floes like a choppy frozen sea. There were occasional stretches of bare ice, decidedly not suited to skis. Nansen mostly had to plod ahead on foot, picking a way through the hummocked maze, then turn back to lead the waiting caravan as far as he had scouted.

On 25 March, Nansen took his second observation for latitude. It was a meridian sight, the result of which was 85°20′N. This was surprisingly low, but discarded as unreliable. When Nansen got his first shot of the sun, it was descending after noon. The accuracy of this observation depends on finely judging exactly when it is hovering at the zenith. It is a demanding procedure, even with ideal instruments under good conditions. Nansen was blessed with neither. Admittedly he had an almost continually clear sky, but by the same token that ensured low temperatures which turned squinting through an eyepiece into a form of torture. Fatigue inhibited judgment. In the harsh daily routine, it was hard to find time for observations.

Above all, saving weight had forced Nansen to compromise. He had brought the same kind of pocket sextant that he had used in Greenland, but without the artificial horizon of mercury, bringing a lighter one of silvered glass instead. And in place of the standard theodolite used on that occasion, he now had with him a light portable model of aluminium, specially made for the expedition.

So far, Nansen had only used the sextant. On 29 March he took the next observation, using both sextant and theodolite as a check against each other. The advantage of the sextant is ease of use; the procedure being to line up the lower limb of the sun with the image of the horizon. Also, being designed for ships at sea, it takes account of movement. The theodolite is, theoretically, more accurate, since it measures angles by directly sighting through a telescope, but it has to be meticulously levelled. The same objection applies to the glass artificial horizon. With one exception, Nansen ignored it, climbing up on a convenient hummock, as he did on this occasion, to be clear of the disturbance of the ice and find an acceptable natural horizon. What he now worked out was that, by the theodolite, his latitude was 85°15'N. The sextant gave 85°56'N.

Either way, the result was depressing. Even the higher figure only gave 47 miles northing in a week. That in turn implied now arriving at the Pole around 4 May, a fortnight later than Nansen had envisaged. The theodolite reading suggested a whole month in addition, which did not bear thinking about. Worse still, there was no way of telling which observation was correct. On top of all, no sights for longitude had been taken since leaving the ship. Nansen, and especially Johansen, had an uneasy sense of not quite knowing where they were.

By the calendar that day, 29 March, was the sixteenth out from the ship. In his diary, Nansen registered it as the fifteenth day on the march. In effect, he was now working to a thirty-hour day. Added to the febrile disorientation of light round the clock, with day and night melting into one, and to the uncertainty of position, all this combined to generate a sense of confusion in time and space.

As usual, the animals echoed the feelings of their masters. That same day Nansen recorded that

> the dogs are becoming rather slow and sluggish and almost impossible to drive ahead. And then there is the interminable untangling of the traces, which become worse and worse to deal with the more tangles and knots and other devilment appear in them.

It was in the fantail harnessing that the weakness lay. Without proper discipline, the dogs continually jumped over the traces. They continued to bite themselves free, and the traces were crudely knotted together again. There was neither the time nor the inclination to make proper splices. The dogs had long since ceased fighting amongst themselves. They had to concentrate on dealing with their masters. To save time harnessing and unharnessing, they were now left constantly in their traces. Nansen candidly admitted

> maltreating the poor animals, [driving] them forwards with thick ash sticks when they were stopped by fatigue ... it made one's heart ache to see them, but one had to avert one's eyes and harden oneself. We *had* to go forwards – all other considerations had to give way. It is sad that on such a journey one must systematically kill all finer feelings, and only the hard-hearted egoist remains.

The day which began on the afternoon of 29 March Nansen called in his diary 'ill-starred'. At one point, there was a stretch of even ice with the first proper skiing for at least a week. It rapidly ebbed out into the worst disturbance so far. 'To advance, we had to cross a crevasse that completely resembled a glacier crevasse'; so Nansen almost wistfully wrote, with a hint of nostalgia for the certainties of the Greenland Ice Cap. The first dog team fell into the crevasse and were hauled out one by one. In the process The Rattlesnake wriggled free of his harness, scampering hopefully out into the distance. He returned soon enough to the devils he knew. The second sledge fell in bodily, escaped damage, but had to be restowed and lashed. The third got across safely. At last, despite all obstacles, the men were in their sleeping bags – and then the Primus leaked and would not burn. At long last Nansen discovered that the fault lay in ice under the burner washer – the temperature was –43° – and soon he had the healthy comforting roar of the flame once more. 'When the pea soup was finally ready at 5 a.m.,' to quote Nansen again, 'it tasted indescribably good.'

The next day, straddling 30 and 31 March, a Saturday and Sunday, 'the much longed-for change in the weather finally arrived, with SE wind (about S.true) and rising temperature. Early today it had climbed up to –30°, which we welcomed as pure summer.'

This was practically the first time on the whole journey that the temperature had risen above the freezing point of mercury which, at around –40°, happens to coincide with a kind of cold barrier. Just as important, it was the first time since leaving the ship that a harsh easterly side breeze had dropped. Even Johansen's mood momentarily lightened. 'The journey during the night went well at the start,' he recorded, 'we had a following wind … I am sitting now in the sleeping bag in peace and quiet and writing this with light gloves … What I have otherwise written in my diary during this trip has been written at the moment before leaving camp on my kayak with huge wolfskin mittens on my hands, so that the pencil nearly disappeared.'

The veering of the wind had coincided with palpable movement in the ice. Some time after starting, Nansen and Johansen came up against a lead in the process of opening. They nonetheless all safely crossed. At the next open lead, soon after, they were not so lucky.

Nansen had barely got across with his dog team when the gap widened so rapidly that Johansen and the other dogs had no hope of following. Then the ice collapsed beneath Johansen, throwing him into the water. He managed to extricate himself before sinking further than his legs. Nonetheless, although it was *relatively* summery, the air temperature still showed over thirty degrees of frost. So, in Johansen's own words, it was 'a less than warm pleasure … naturally the garments immediately froze stiff', and he had no change of clothing. And there he stood, or rather moved up and down at the double to keep warm while Nansen with his sledge and, incidentally, tent and Primus stove, receded ever further on the other side of the lead.

There was no question of using the kayaks to ferry across, because they had been holed in the various capsizings and collisions along the way. The only alternative was to find a place where the lead was narrow enough to be crossed. After much trouble and a long detour, Nansen did so. He got the whole party to the north side of the lead, but then had immediately to make camp. Johansen needed to get into the sleeping bag to get warm and dry out. Also, his wind trousers had become brittle after their ducking and freezing and were badly torn. Before proceeding, they had to be repaired. This involved thawing them with body heat in the sleeping bag, sewing a little before the material froze up, then pushing it under the fur to warm up again, and so on. It was, said Johansen, 'the worst sewing I have ever known … I think it was worse than sewing canvas at –40°, which we have also done'.

There was no camp on 1 April, and the men only tumbled into their sleeping bags in the early hours of the following day. By then, Nansen had realised that it was a long time since they had wound their watches, and Johansen's had actually stopped. Nansen's watch was still going, so Johansen's could be reset, but now there was no independent check on each other.

Of the march on 1 April, Nansen wrote: 'Desperate work to plod between these newly formed hummocks, and find a way through.' This was the first overt hint of lurking distress. For one thing, Johansen's ducking and the movement of the ice had shattered the illusion of geological certainty underfoot. More profoundly, the broken upheaval of the terrain inhibited skiing. Existence had degenerated into a jagged shuttle, back and forth, probing a way through the seracs. Rhythm was denied. All pleasure had disappeared. Both went against the whole nature of the skier.

On 2 April, Nansen finally took his first sights for longitude. For some reason, he did not work them out. In his own words, he was 'beginning to have reservations over continuing northwards for too long'. This was Nansen's first unequivocal admission that the Pole might be beyond his reach.

'All these seracs make one despair,' he repeated on 3 April. And again: 'Beginning to have serious reservations over continuing northwards much longer.'

This was prompted by a latitude sight at noon that day. The result was 85°59′. Twenty-one days after starting, this was only the second reliable observation so far. The midnight sun had just returned. The top of the orb ignited the sky with flames of red and orange and the ice beneath turned into a sea of fire. It was an eerie accompaniment to sobering arithmetic. Nansen and Johansen had covered 115 miles. It was probably 370 miles or so to Cape Fliguely, the closest known part of Franz Josef Land.

The North Pole, meanwhile, was 240 miles off. That meant that Cape Fliguely, and hence terra firma, was now more distant than the Pole itself. This was the reverse of the position when the two men had left *Fram*.

How, Nansen asked himself in his diary, would conditions turn out on the way to Franz Josef Land?

41. A Dog's Life

We can hardly count on an improvement.... And in addition, the form and extent of the country are unknown.... We ought not to wait much longer.

The mood was further darkened by the slaughter that same day, 3 April, of the second dog, The Russian. He, said Johansen,

gave up his life to feed the other dogs, all of whom nonetheless were not keen on him. They preferred the flesh of those dogs they themselves had torn to pieces in the halcyon days on board 'Fram'.

That was an attempt to hide emotion. Johansen had done the slaughtering but, with his feeling for dogs, it had felt like murder. Ideally, The Russian ought to have been cleanly shot. But only about 180 rifle bullets and 150 shotgun cartridges had been taken. None could be spared. All had to be husbanded for hunting and survival. Instead, Johansen had to cut The Russian's throat. It caused both Johansen and Nansen great distress.

Next day, 4 April, Nansen took another succession of longitude sights. He spent the following morning in camp working them out – a tortuous procedure before the era of electronic calculation – 'to discover exactly where we are', as he put it; the first time, incidentally, since leaving the ship. The outcome was 98°47′E. Nansen also recalculated the latitude sight of two days earlier, making it now 86°2.8′N.

Even so, that was deeply disappointing. Both men believed they had long since crossed the eighty-sixth parallel. The wind had backed north again, so the ice was probably drifting south. That alone intensified a discouraging sense of fighting the elements. Besides, even although the thermometer kept a relatively humane level of around –30°, life was riddled with discomfort. Without a change of clothing the men had to alternate between frozen and mushy garments. They had forgotten what it was like to be warm and dry. In Johansen's lugubrious words: 'It is simply a matter of holding out.'

Soon Nansen was writing: 'I have become more and more convinced that we ought to turn before time.' He meant before the thirty days he had allowed for travelling north. It was now the twenty-third day out. And in fact, rather more was pulling Nansen back now than driving him on.

When leaving *Fram*, he had started a new volume of his diary. It was a small leather-bound sketchbook, in which had been pasted a photograph of Eva and their daughter, Liv. This was the memento with which Nansen was confronted each time he opened the covers to jot down the record of his days. On the fly leaf there was a message in Eva's own handwriting: 'My beloved boy, God grant that happiness, health and good luck will follow you.'

An ironic wish! 'The ice is growing worse and worse,' Nansen wrote on 6 April. 'Yesterday it brought me to the brink of despair. And when we stopped in the early hours of this morning, I was about ready to turn. I will continue one day more, to see if the ice really is the same northwards as it seems from on top of an almost 30 foot high serac under which we have camped.'

'We advanced hardly a mile or two yesterday,' he was soon adding. Then:

> Open leads, seracs, and endless upheaval – the whole surface of the ice looks like a moraine – and this interminable lifting of the sledges over every single unevenness; it tells on the arms, and we were undeniably worn out.

Under the midnight sun, in the small hours of 7 April, a Sunday, they set off once more. 'Nearly time to turn out,' Johansen finished his diary for the day, 'that's the worst thing of all, I think.'

When they camped again, a few hours later, they had advanced very little. In Nansen's words:

> I went ahead a good distance northwards on skis, but saw no reasonable way ahead, and from the top of the highest serac no other kind of ice could be seen right up to the horizon; it was like looking over a snow covered moraine. There seems little sense in carrying on any longer, we sacrifice the precious days for too little, and if there is much ice like this between us and Franz Josef Land, we will really need them. Therefore I decided to stop and set a course for Cape Fliguely, to Johansen's great relief.

'It is my considered opinion that we ought not to tempt Fate by continuing much further north,' Johansen had actually written in his diary several days before. So now, in the small hours of 7 April, they retraced their steps to a good camping site and raised their tent in the lee of a large serac.

That evening, they celebrated with what Johansen called a 'party' and Nansen a 'banquet'. Both agreed on the menu: lobscouse, a piece of chocolate, with cowberry pudding as a sweet, and a hot Serin drink afterwards. It was hard to know whether they were marking 'this northernmost camp', as Nansen phrased it or, in Johansen's words, 'the day for changing course'. Either way, 'replete and over-fed', to quote Nansen, 'we crept into our beloved sleeping-bag' which, frozen and moulting though it was, nonetheless remained 'our dearest friend'.

The dogs lay in their traces with resignation. They were preoccupied with survival. At least the occasion was not marred by the slaughter of another of their companions.

Nansen took a meridian sight for latitude. He waited until the following day to work it out, arriving at a latitude of about 86°10′N. He had broken the record for the Furthest North by 146 miles, the biggest single advance for nearly 400 years, but was still 230 miles from the Pole. He was, however, considerably further north than he had any right to expect. But that suggested that the ice was drifting north again and that once they turned they would be fighting nature more than they had feared. In Johansen's words: 'We can have our work cut out to find our way to Franz Josef Land from where we are, in the middle of the drifting ice.'

Their intended landfall at Cape Fliguely was three times further away than the distance they had made good so far. Unfortunately, its exact position was not known; nor indeed the precise extent of Franz Josef Land – that 'cold, congealed, frozen land', as Julius Payer, its discoverer, had called it. In fact, Nansen did not know exactly where he was even now. He took a longitude sight, but did not work it out. It was Monday, 8 April, the day that he was to turn, and he wished to avoid wasting time on tedious calculations. Dead reckoning since the last known longitude three days earlier put them at around 96°E, to within a degree or so. Greater precision was meaningless. At that latitude, a degree of longitude is only four miles. It hardly affected their compass course, which was what mattered now.

Before setting off, what Johansen called 'the most northerly camp site in the world' was decorated with two small flags: one 'pure' Norwegian and one with the Union mark. After much photographing, the dogs rose stiffly to their feet, and they all finally turned south, towards Franz Josef Land, homeward bound at last.

42

Chronometric Chaos

'To our surprise,' in Nansen's words,

> we had not gone far before we ran out onto good ice, which constantly became better, and we drove on unremittingly with few interruptions. We did meet seracs, but they were easy to circumvent.

And Johansen, amplifying the record of that first day homeward bound:

> I could ski after the sledges, where otherwise I have had to plod along on foot and lift my two sledges.

Instead of the frozen tumult on the northwards march, flat or gently undulating terrain stretched away gleaming to the horizon. The going was well-nigh perfect. Harsh, crystalline snow gave purchase for the thrust off the back ski, yet allowing the forward one to slide. Nansen and Johansen were skiers back in their element. The nostalgic scrape of skis on wind-packed crust, the happy rhythm of loping along and heaving on the stick were enough to lighten any mood.

Probably the improvement was due to the change of course. It was parallel to the lines of disturbance, where before it had been athwart. The main obstacles now were open, or newly frozen, leads. Here too, Nansen was broadly running parallel, so that only occasionally was he forced to find a crossing.

Nor did the dogs now need to be driven on. They too thought they were homeward bound. Thick furry backs undulating, tails held high like banners in the breeze, they loped wolf-like along, cheerfully heaving on the traces. The muffled patter of their paws over the snow accompanied the creak and rasp of sledges evenly following in their wake. This was at least an interlude of dogs and skiers working properly together in even terrain made for both. To complete the picture, still air, glittering snow, and constant sunshine conjured up recollections of spring skiing at home.

'Day and night the same marvellous ice,' Nansen rejoiced in his diary. Johansen, as usual, saw the shadow side:

> It is cold and raw at night. Luckily neither of us is sick. It is not easy to know

whether we can hold out. I have no idea how much a human being can stand under these conditions.

Although the sun was now circling and dipping round the horizon from midnight to midnight, it still did not warm. What is more, the same clear skies and calm air that enhanced the skiing also depressed the temperature. The thermometer still hovered around −35°. The men continued waking to rime frost hanging from the tent walls and showering them when they moved. But after a day or two, Johansen was suddenly writing:

Last night was the best we have had so far. It was warm in the sleeping bag, and the sunny side of the tent was free of rime frost ... it is the best morning we have had.

And revealingly: 'We are in a good mood, we talk about home, and when we are hungry (which we are almost always) we talk about how we are going to guzzle when we finally get home.'

From Nansen's diary on 13 April came this exultant echo: 'We sweep over plain after plain ... If it continues like this, the journey home will be shorter than I thought.'

In the same breath, he had to record what he called 'the unfortunate accident' that punished this touch of hubris. For the second time, Johansen's watch had stopped, but now his own had as well. Johansen ascribed this to what he called the 'confusion of letting day and night melt into one'. They had camped at half past five in the morning after a run of ten hours. Concerned only with driving onwards both men had forgotten to wind their watches. If, 'like others', Johansen pointedly wrote, they had marched in regular stages, 'I don't think this would have happened.'

Next day, the going remained good, but uncertainty now gnawed at the pleasure of skiing. As the implications sank in Nansen was aghast. The stopping of the watches was an unmitigated disaster. Upon accurate time depended reliable navigation. They were now unable precisely to fix their position. Cape Fliguely, their goal, from the meagre information at their disposal, appeared to be a low spit of land, difficult to sight from seaward even under favourable circumstances. Now the difficulties were appreciably compounded. A landfall suddenly seemed problematic.

When open leads took an unfavourable turn, blocking the way ahead, Nansen seized the opportunity to stop and rectify the situation as best he could. He broke his camping routine of immediately starting supper, retiring instead into the sleeping bag to start his calculations. In his own words:

To lie and thaw out a frozen bag, frozen clothes and frozen boots and simultaneously work out observations ... with tender, frozen fists is not pleasant, even if the temperature is not lower than −30°. Nor is it very quick.

It was Easter Sunday, 14 April, and exactly a month since they had left *Fram*. Nansen had to interrupt his calculations to cook. They celebrated the feast day with a copious meal. To a Norwegian, Easter is one of the holiest days in the calendar, not so much because of its Christian meaning as because of its much stronger underlying connection with an ancient pagan festival of sun-worship. It was to be marked, even in the wastes of the pack ice; and appropriately too. Given a knowledge of the right time the sun would tell them where they were. Now he circled round the sky, mocking them with the secret they could not unlock.

As soon as he could, Nansen returned to his calculations. He was thrown on his own resources in a way we, with instant communication and satellite navigation, are increasingly unable to comprehend. He did not have the view from space which has given us a picture of reality. His view was bounded by the horizon; exactly like that of the earliest men. He depended on an act of faith in abstract figures on a scrap of paper.

His problem was longitude. In classical navigation this could only be fixed by precise timekeeping, because it was measured by the rotation of the earth past a fixed point, with one degree corresponding to four minutes by the clock. Nansen believed that his watches had stopped for about half an hour, but he could not be sure. He solved the dilemma by assuming a longitude of 86°E, and setting the watches accordingly. This placed him further west, by a generous margin, than he was likely to be. The idea was to bring him east of Franz Josef Land, thus making sure he would not miss his landfall and be swept out into the ocean to the west. But guesswork it remained.

In their isolation, nothing could now erase the nagging sense of being lost. It was like passing some kind of divide.

Unlike longitude, latitude at least was unaffected by time, but that offered no consolation. It placed them at 86°5′N, whereas dead reckoning suggested that they ought already to be well below the eighty-sixth parallel. Other figures were equally discouraging. In three days of uninterrupted skiing they had only made five miles to the south. They were evidently now fighting a strong northerly drift, 'which is good for *Fram*,' as Nansen tersely put it, 'but less so for us – now.'

Next day, Nansen suffered more irritation. On the march, he discovered he had left his only compass behind somewhere after setting the course. He had to turn back to look for it, leaving Johansen with the dogs. For Johansen, in his own words, 'it was strange to sit there alone in isolation', waiting for Nansen's return.

Never have I felt anything so still. Not the slightest sound of any kind disturbed the silence near or far; the dogs lay as if lifeless with their heads on their paws in the white snow, glistening in the gleaming sun. It was so frighteningly still, I had to remain where I sat, I dared not move a limb; I hardly dared to breathe.

42. Chronometric Chaos

He dozed off on his sledge in the sunshine – to be woken by a puff of wind. Such are the contradictions of the polar world. The air temperature was actually –26°C. But the reflection from the ice and snow of the sun's rays was like the scorching of desert sands. After a while, one or two dogs pricked up their ears. The silence was broken by the comforting scrape of skis on crusted snow, and soon after, Nansen hove into view.

For the first time on this journey, Nansen was troubled, not by cold, but by the heat of the sun. He now talked about avoiding the middle of the day and travelling at night. He might have been in the tropics instead of a thousand miles above the Arctic circle.

On 16 April came the longest march so far. It lasted thirteen and a half hours. At the same time, the terrain deteriorated. Instead of even snow-fields, now there was rough going over rafted floes, between piled up ice ridges and menacing seracs. The skiing was less glorious too. Instead of easy crust, there were bouts of sticky loose snow. But at least the dogs continued pulling without being driven.

Nansen guessed that they had advanced at least sixteen nautical miles. Best of all, the weather continued to hold up. In all the five weeks since leaving the ship, they had not once been stopped by the elements. 'The same glorious sunshine the whole time,' as Nansen put it.

> Life becomes lovelier and lovelier; the cold period is past, we go on towards land and summer; it is wonderful to turn out in the morning, in the certainty of a good day's march, and ... dream bright dreams of the future, when we come home, home at last.

An observation on 18 April gave a latitude of 85°37.8′. This meant that since turning homewards, they had made about 40 miles to the south. Cape Fliguely appeared now barely 250 miles off, the North Pole more than 290 miles. For the first time on the homeward journey, they were closer to land than the Pole – and, did they but know it, only about 100 miles from *Fram*.

A few days later, Nansen was checked once more by broken terrain, with upturned floes like icebergs and, even more disconcerting, by a broad jagged open lead zig-zagging its way to the horizon, choked with fragments of ice. On the other side, flat expanses once more swept tantalisingly on into the distance.

The sight was more than Nansen could bear. He drove the whole caravan back and forth until finally he found a crossing. They hurried over while the floes were grinding together under their feet.

Once across, they were again in 'the land of Canaan', as Nansen liked to say when the skiing was good. They pressed on until the dogs began to wilt. By then, they had all been on the march for sixteen hours, but the poor beasts had not been fed for almost two days.

At one point a large piece of driftwood was found sticking up out of a

273

floe. It was probably a Siberian larch. This was the first object from the outside world spotted by them since they had entered the ice more than eighteen months before. Johansen carved his and Nansen's initials on the log, together with their latitude – in case of accidents, as it were. 'Once more we have level plains, lovely and broad ahead of us,' Nansen finished his diary for that day.

> It is glorious to glide off [on skis] over these flat fields, ever closer to land and home, and while one glides one's thoughts incessantly speed ahead to all that is beautiful.

This was a world away from the language of others who had preceded Nansen over the ice. It was an historic shift to men at ease in the polar environment, physically at least. But emotionally:

> My friends on board predicted an awful trip with him who is not made for friendship [Johansen at the same time was writing in his diary]. It is true. He is too self-centred to be anyone's friend, and one's patience is sorely tried. It is silent in the tent; no fun, never a joke ...
> The fellow is unsociable and clumsy in the smallest things; egoistic in the highest degree. On the march he goes ahead with his sledge, which is somewhat light in weight. I follow with my two [sledges].... On the other side of [an] obstacle, he simply goes on as if he were alone. He doesn't care how I manage with my two sledges; I have got to keep up anyhow.

At the beginning of the sixth week on the march, only a few days' dog food remained. Nansen decided to save it, using the weaker animals as fodder instead. The first victim of the new regime was Perpetuum, so called because he was always wagging his tail. He was only the fourth dog to be slaughtered in almost a month. As usual, he was taken behind a hummock, so that the proceedings were hidden from the other dogs. Nansen and Johansen were revolted at having to cut the poor creatures' throats. They now tried strangling instead. In Nansen's words, 'that was even worse'.

> We put a rope round the animal's throat, and each hauled at his end, so that we were lying flat on the snow, but the dog squealed and breathed nonetheless ... and there was no alternative but to stab it this time as well.

On 25 April, fox tracks appeared in the snow. Since the arrival of three polar bears at *Fram* the previous November, this was the first trace of a living creature from the outside. The spoors were fresh, coming from the south-west. Nansen at first saw in this a sign of land, but quickly recognised the danger of making the wish father to the thought. The foxes were probably scavengers 'staggering in the wake' of polar bears, the presence of which was no guarantee of the vicinity of land. 'But still, mammals as far north as 85°.' When more fox spoors appeared over the next few days, all coming from the same quarter, he finally began to believe that land really might be in the offing.

The passage of time was now marked by the regular slaughter of a dog every other day or so. Each was tersely listed: Block, Bielki, Freia, Potifar, and so forth. But towards the end of the month, Yellow had a special mention. On the day before, 26 April, Nansen had taken the first observation for over a week, and found the latitude to be 84°46′. The sacrifice of Yellow marked the crossing of the eighty-fifth parallel and a milestone along the way. But also, Yellow was one of the pups born on *Fram*. Nansen wrote:

> Poor creature, it has tried devotedly and hauled until it could no longer manage, and now all the thanks it gets after it is completely worn out is to be slaughtered and eaten. It would never see anything but snow and ice; a true polar child. It was a good and kind dog.

Johansen, though also saddened, matter-of-factly recorded: 'The dogs are hungry now, so they like the flesh of their friends.' Both men were appalled at the ease with which they themselves accepted the alien harshness forced upon them by necessity.

The arrival of what Johansen called 'the wonderful month of May' conjured up a change of mood: 'Life seems brighter, and home appears during the march in many enticing forms. It will be wonderful to come home again!' Open leads now began seriously to impede progress, but still Nansen could write in his diary:

> Repulsive as it is to be stopped in the midst of glorious flat ice by ... a lead, when one is hungering to advance, nonetheless it was a strange feeling to see the open water stretch out ahead, and watch the sun playing on the ripples raised by the wind. Open water and glittering waves after so long, and one's thoughts sped homewards, towards summer.

And then abruptly: 'In vain, I searched for the sight of a seal's head in this lead or a bear along the edge.' It was high time to begin living by the hunt, as originally intended.

For the dogs, at least, food was running short. It was becoming harder to drive them on. In camp on 29 April, Nansen was roused by an unusual rustling and gnawing. He dived outside the tent to discover a dog rummaging among the sledges. One of the pemmican chocks underneath a kayak had already been gnawed. This was the first time the dogs had stolen food. The culprits were unidentified, but the fact remained that hunger was beginning to overcome training. That might herald the collapse of the dog teams. Seventeen of the original twenty-eight animals now remained. The spectre of man-hauling rose up. Nansen doled out that day an extra ration to the dogs.

On the last day of April a long, wide open lead finally barred the way ahead. Nansen skied along the edge long and vainly in search of a crossing. He finally resigned himself to waiting for circumstances to mend. The upshot was the first rest day since leaving *Fram*, seven weeks before.

It was also the first time they had been stopped by open water. The kayaks were still unseaworthy, the little accidents of travelling having holed them even more. Nansen was postponing repairs as long as possible, so as not to waste time while the ice was still passable by any other means.

The rest day Nansen actually spent repairing his finneskoe. They had been damp from sweat all along, which was causing the reindeer fur to moult. Nansen now half-soled them with canvas. Every stitch was a kind of torture to frostbitten fingers at temperatures still below –20°C. But the reward was two whole pairs of finneskoe which would allow one each day to dry out, more or less. For his part, Johansen was happy just to rest; and so, for that matter, were the dogs.

In the evening of 1 May, the lead closed up. Nansen struck camp and, at 10 p.m., set off once more. The rest day had spanned 30 April and 1 May, a Tuesday and Wednesday. The midnight sun had long since disrupted clock and calendar, and disorientation was compounded by a sky now veiled by heavy drapes of cumulus so that there was no sight of the sun circling round the horizon to signal the passage of time.

On the other side of the lead, in Nansen's words, 'we found a flat plain and good going'. Once more they were reasonably content in the skier's world with the comforting scrape of wood on crusted snow; the swing of ski-tip overtaking ski-tip, set off by the panting of the dogs and the creak of the sledges, all generating a sense of the miles falling away. It was merely an interlude. After four hours, they again ran into a shifting system of open leads. Dodging about, they managed to find crossings here and there.

In the meantime, out of the south-east, a good stiff headwind blew up, with driving snow as well. Sky and clouds and snow boiling into one put paid to what visibility there was. It was the first blizzard since leaving *Fram*. Also for the first time, Nansen had to give the weather best. He camped at the first opportunity and, while the Primus roared and the wind tore at the tent to build up snowdrifts along the walls, he comforted Johansen and himself with another hot 'fish gratin'.

By the next day the wind had eased and they were able to continue on their way. But they had passed another divide. Conditions abruptly changed. Open leads were more frequent; travel was constantly interrupted. Where the floes were unbroken they were often completely smooth, in Nansen's words, 'almost like an ice cap'. He wrote:

> It is strange the effect of atmosphere. A little while ago, when I moved along a hellish open lead between seracs and rafted floes and could not glimpse a way ahead, I was so exhausted that I thought I could simply lie down at every step, and no pleasure in the world could compare with creeping into the

sleeping bag, and now that fortune is smiling again, and one can advance once more, all fatigue has vanished at a blow.

A perverse southerly wind was in part to blame for the growing disturbance in the ice. Spring was clearly on the way, with its cruel ambiguity of warm air but bad snow and heavy going.

Nansen and Johansen were now treated to another of the assorted devilries of the Arctic. At intervals, instead of high ridges, the ice was crumpled on a different scale like mountain ranges on a miniature planet. The sledges had to be helped up steep little passes, and then held back from dwarfish precipices on the other side. Neither men nor dogs found this enjoyable.

Among the animals, Flint eventually objected so much that, on 8 May, he squirmed out of his harness, and was only recaptured in the evening, when he was slaughtered, as Nansen tersely noted. Johansen observed that Flint had been condemned beforehand to slaughter that day as the next one to feed his companions. 'He was continually morose and vicious towards the other dogs.'

> He was a lazy devil, fat as a pig. It is peculiar that he has managed to keep his fat so long on the meagre food he has had.

His diary was hardly more charitable towards Nansen:

> When I have eaten, got myself ready and written up my diary, I naturally have to get out of the tent as quickly as possible, for in that way things go more quickly as N. says ... He himself stays inside long after I have done the duties around camp that I can. I have got to loaf around outside in all kinds of weather without anything to do, and that is not pleasant.

Soon after, the temperature rose to –8.5°; the highest so far, and the first time in single figures. It brought even closer the prospect of heavy going. On 9 May, an observation by Nansen yielded a latitude of 84°3′N. That was far less southing than they had expected. They felt the frustration of fighting wind and drift.

Nansen, noted Johansen, 'has more trouble with the dogs now, since they are more tired, he has only four, we have 12 in all. Perhaps now he will understand that I have not had the best time with two sledges with which I have followed at his heels.' He himself was being worn down by having had to drive two sledges and two dog teams all the way; for sixty days and more than 350 miles so far, while Nansen only had one.

The dogs' strength was waning; their number dwindling to the point where they were too few for all the sledges. Finally, on 13 May, to Johansen's inexpressible relief, Nansen agreed to jettison the third sledge. Loads and dog teams were redistributed. There were now six dogs before each sledge. Johansen was vastly less resentful now with only one sledge to drive, but progress was no quicker. Either the dogs were too worn out or there was something wrong with the sledges.

15 May was Johansen's birthday. In his own words, 'It was as if Nature herself was celebrating it,'

> she had put on the most beautiful garb there is up here; blinding sunshine ... and little or no wind. 28 years is a great age for me, I think.... We had a little party in the tent ... with a large helping of lobscouse ... N. skåled with me, and wished me in the coming year 'many a happy surprise and many a happy hour'.

But next day Nansen was 'in a very bad mood'. Johansen put this down to 'the poor hauling of his dogs ... He is angry with me, as if it is my fault that he has beaten his dogs too much, that is what is the trouble.... When he said that my dogs were the strongest ... I suggested that he change his worst dog, The Rattlesnake for my best one, The Polar Bear. No reply. Pleasant travelling companion!'

How different it would have been with Sverdrup, he continued. 'There's a real man for you. We would undoubtedly have reached land many happy days ago, but God knows what we will do now. It looks rather bad.'

Nansen was doubly irritated because of Johansen's talent for dealing with dogs. With a word and a gesture he could coax his team in a way that Nansen, with all his ferocious beating, could not. Johansen was consistent, the key to the dogs' devotion, and they responded by accepting him as the leader of the pack. Nansen, by contrast, was moody with dogs as with men showing sympathy one moment and anger the next. That was alien to their mental landscape, and forfeited their trust.

But in the end Johansen decided that the dogs could not be the main reason for Nansen's bad mood. The underlying cause was probably 'the land we never reach'.

43

Miseries of Spring

Johansen was right. Towards the end of April, Nansen had recorded:

> For a long time now, I have noticed a dense bank of cloud over the horizon between S. and S.W., and I thought it must be over land. Now it began to grow suspiciously.

Ten days later, during a snowfall, he observed, in the same south-westerly quarter, a persistent strip of clear blue sky which, as he repeated, 'must have something to do with land'.

Nansen was hoping for Petermann Land. It had allegedly been sighted by Julius Payer and was marked on his map. It seemed to lie at about 83°N, around 65 miles away. Cape Fliguely, the nearest land that Payer had actually trodden, was now about 120 miles off. The possible loom of land covered both, and each therefore fitted the circumstances.

Uncertainty was compounded by an observation Nansen took on 9 May. 'I let Johansen sleep on,' he wrote in his diary next morning, 'and calculated my longitude, which I found was 64°20′E.' In four days, they had drifted 2° to the west, which at that latitude meant three miles a day. To compensate, Nansen held more to the east. A week later, nonetheless, the next observation apparently showed a longitude of 59°55′E. That meant another 26 miles to the west, nearly four miles a day. At that rate, they were on the verge of sweeping past the meridian of Cape Fliguely. That was bad enough. The latitude was 83°36′N, which was equally discouraging. After all the moil and toil, they had made exactly 27 miles to the south; less than four miles a day. They were still fighting wind and drift.

Worst of all, Nansen was nagged by the everlasting uncertainty of his longitude. He irritated Johansen by interminably recalculating his observations, with the fidgeting that implied while they were lying together in their sleeping bag. 'It is strange that we still see no sign of land,' Nansen wrote yet again. He pursued the theme in his diary before getting up next morning, which was 17 May, the Norwegian national day: 'Certainly I thought that on this day of all days we would have been on land somewhere or other.'

I lie in the sleeping bag ... and dream that I am among the ... crowds who at this moment are parading through the streets.... See how the flags wave with their red bunting ... and the sun is gleaming wonderfully through the first light green shoots of spring. And here we lie on the drifting ice and do not know where we are.

Nansen kept this for the pages of his diary. All that Johansen saw was a morose and taciturn companion. The lead which had stopped them the day before no longer held them up. In honour of the day a small flag was hoisted on each sledge but, as Johansen put it: 'We began the march ... both of us in a bad mood.'

It was not helped by the behaviour of Johansen's dogs. Nansen had been leading all the way so far. As a relief from the drudgery he wanted Johansen now to go ahead. Johansen's dogs, however, had become accustomed to following Nansen's. After sixty-five days on the march they saw no reason to change. *They* knew what it meant to break the trail. They simply stood and stared back at Nansen's team in pained surprise at this disruption of their routine, waiting for the others to go ahead. In the end, of course, they won. The caravan set off in the familiar old order of running.

As they prepared to cross the lead, Nansen was surprised by a sound exactly like a whale blowing. The dogs had clearly caught the scent of something. Then, in Nansen's words:

A whale's head broke the water, and the body followed in the familiar arc, and then the same sound. There was a whole school.... All the leads around were full of narwhal.

The prospect of food for the dogs and a change of diet for the men rose up. Nansen dug out his rifle and harpoon from the sledge and scurried off on the hunt. But the narwhal were too shy and he had to return empty-handed. Nonetheless it was an uplifting encounter. For one thing, on the whole journey this was the first sight of living creatures from the outside.

Meanwhile, a fresh breeze, force 5, had sprung up from the south-east, bringing thick snow drift. The temperature was only –10°C which, under the circumstances, felt relatively spring-like. But the sledges became depressingly more sluggish. Eventually, Nansen called a halt, and removed the false runners. The wood was by now roughly scoured after a good 400 miles over abrasive snow. Besides, the waxing no longer suited the conditions. And in any case, the wood had by now absorbed so much water that it no longer slid properly. The German silver covering the main runners quickly proved to slide freely on the coarse-grained spring snow laced with drift. The sledges ran without compare. The dogs took on a new lease of life, and as Johansen put it: 'We finished in a considerably better temper than we started.'

In the tent, they celebrated the national day with what Nansen called 'a thundering great banquet'. It was a four-course menu, the main dish being lobscouse of pemmican. 'With distended bellies,' in Nansen's words, 'we crept into the sleeping bag.' Johansen wrote: 'The banquet suited us down to the ground, and ditto the ensuing sleep.' Thereafter, apparently none the worse, they continued on their way.

But the little column winding southwards over the ice under the midnight sun was one dog less. Barabbas had been slaughtered to feed his companions. Of the 28 animals with which they had started, ten now remained.

On 19 May they passed another milestone: the first bear tracks on the whole journey. They were fresh, which promised game and a change of diet. On the march, Nansen climbed a particularly high hummock to look for land, but once more in vain. He also, incidentally, measured the hummock, and found it to be 30 feet high; one of the tallest so far.

Soon afterwards the terrain drastically changed. Instead of ridges and hummocks and brutal disturbance, the ice became relatively even, gently folded here and there into low broken blocks like rock strata on a plain. At the same time, the conditions began rapidly to deteriorate. One maze of open leads after another encroached upon the trail. The snow was beginning to crumble; the deepening of a sinister greenish tinge suggested an alteration in the ice. 'It is incredibly hard to advance,' Nansen observed on 26 May.

> The snow is loose, and if one steps off one's skis ever so little, one sinks in right up to the crotch. It is no use having skis fixed on [He meant with heelstraps tightened and in place. They were skiing with loose bindings, only using toestraps.] because we must everlastingly [get off our skis] to help the dogs. If it is hazy, like yesterday, one runs into the biggest heaps and sastrugi without seeing them, everything is the same whiteness, mantled in fresh snow, and head over heels one goes, and then one has to heave oneself up with one's fists, and find safety on skis again.

This is a heart-felt record of a whiteout; the teasing little trick of the snows when clouds scatter sunlight so that it comes from all directions, casts no shadows and, combined with the glare from underfoot, eliminates all contours.

> And thus [Nansen wrote] it goes on interminably, and the longer it carries on, the worse it becomes, and in the end one staggers on one's skis from fatigue as if one were drunk. But we creep forwards, and that is the main thing, be one's legs never so tired and tender. It is particularly hard on the ankles, because of the constant unsteadiness and twisting on the skis, and many a day they have been badly swollen.

All rhythm had vanished. The pleasure of skiing had gone. Nonetheless: 'A pleasant Sunday morning in the tent,' Nansen wrote the same day. His latest observations, taken on the Friday, showed a latitude of 82°52′N, an advance of 44 miles to the south since the last fix ten days before, and now level with the enigmatic Petermann Land. More to the point, the longitude was 61°27′E, a good degree and a half more, which meant that the westwards drift had been checked and with it the immediate risk of being swept past Franz Josef Land out into the open sea. 'These observations,' in Nansen's own words, 'put me in such a good humour, I thought life lay ahead so bright, soon we must be winging our way homewards with good speed over open water.'

Johansen's record showed a wary undertone of relief, quickly dissolving into sympathy. That evening, Kvik had to be put down. 'Nansen was miserable,' wrote Johansen. 'I took her out of sight and killed her almost before he knew what was happening.' In his diary, Nansen tersely wrote: 'It hurt me to part from her.' She was the last living link with home, in what now seemed the distant days in the house beside the fjord. She had become a pet and he had grown fond of her. He consoled himself with the thought that 'she was big, and would provide 3 days' food for the remaining 8 dogs'. Johansen recorded factually:

> She was completely worn out and starved. Lately, she destroyed her harness as soon as we put on a new one … I found in her stomach pieces of canvas; the poor creature probably thought she could stay her hunger with her harnesses. We wear our dogs to shreds, like articles of clothing.

An atmosphere of disintegration and turmoil was descending. The ice, which for so long had been thick and old, was giving way to a younger kind, probably frozen during the previous winter, smoother and thinner. Open leads were changing from clearly defined channels into a confusing mesh like the delta of a meandering river. The heavy crust of the compact, floating polar ice cap was turning into the fragmented pack around the edge.

When Nansen shot the sun at noon at his furthest north, it hovered barely 10° above the horizon; now it was closer to 30°, and an altitude familiar from home. Other signs of change came crowding in. Because the ice was young, there were no more layers leached of salt. At each camp, now, drinking water had to be made from snow, which required more effort to garner, more fuel to melt. As the month waned, the first bird, a fulmar, appeared and, better still, the first seal, basking on the ice.

The real milestone came on 28 May. On that day Nansen changed from finneskoe to *komager*. Finneskoe, being made of fur, were adapted to the dry cold of deep winter, but had started moulting and soaked up dampness like a sponge. *Komager* were specialised soft ski boots, which had evolved to cope with the transitional conditions of spring. They were made of rawhide, with sealskin soles, thoroughly waterproofed with pine pitch and tallow, and reindeer fur round the ankles for warmth.

43. Miseries of Spring

It was a pleasant change [Nansen wrote], now one's feet are warm and dry, and then one is spared all the trouble with finneskoe ... having to lie with wet rags on one's chest and thighs at night [to dry them out].

This was a momentary consolation. Nansen's diary had lapsed into a dirge of the assorted miseries of spring. Conditions were deteriorating by the day. To inch their way southwards, men and dogs were often wading now through a degenerate, metamorphosed slush halfway between snow and granular ice. The season was closing in. Nansen longed for March, with all its cold, for the sake of good skiing. 'It was precisely this period at the end of May I feared so much,' he wrote in self-reproach,

and by when I considered it extremely important to have reached land ... and we are going to feel the consequences more than is perhaps desirable.

At least, however, rests along the way no longer meant crawling into the sleeping bag; it was now comfortable just sitting on a sledge. During one of these interludes, at the end of May, Nansen unfolded the bellows of his Kodak snapshot camera. He had neglected it for too long, was only on his third film, and now clicked off a string of pictures.

For the first time, Johansen was allowed to use the camera, taking a picture of Nansen shooting the sun. This last gave a latitude of 82°21′N. They were now well within latitudes previously trodden by other men. What is more, this observation put them *south* of Petermann Land, and barely fifty miles from Cape Fliguely, 'and still no glimpse of land', in Nansen's words. Once camped, he and Johansen together pored yet again over their map.

This is becoming more and more perplexing [as Nansen put it]. What would I not give to be walking on terra firma now, but patience, always patience.

The end of May also brought the slaughter of Pan who, 'in his day hauled for three', as Johansen wrote, 'but now was a wasted shadow. He has worn himself out for us to the last.' Pan had been the best of the dogs; now for the next three days he would feed the seven that remained. They were a bedraggled remnant of the spirited cavalcade that had left *Fram* two and a half months before. The same might have been said of the men, their clothes torn, their faces scarred by frost and wind and sun.

For all that, they were no longer moving through an uninhabited desert. The ice now echoed to the blowing of whales, the distant barking of seals, and the screech of gulls overhead. 'It is fun to see life, it cheers one up,' wrote Johansen. 'It persuades one that it is not too far to land.' Over the south-west horizon the shifting signs persisted; now in the form of a blueish loom which, to Johansen at least, seemed to retreat as they advanced, like one of the islands of myth.

On the last day of the month, the ice suddenly flattened out. Men and dogs threaded their way with unaccustomed ease through the network of open leads. After a few hours all progress stopped. Try as he might, Nansen now found no escape. They were marooned on a floe in a dark labyrinth of rippled water on every side.

Nansen had gloomy forebodings about spending another winter in the ice. 'Oh my Eva, you will have to wait yet another year,' he wrote in his diary on the first day of June; the first reference to his wife since the journey began.

Next day they were still marooned. It happened to be Whit Sunday which, together with a sense of being trapped, triggered the same nostalgia in the diaries of both men. 'Whitsun; ah, there is something so wonderfully good and summery about that word,' Nansen wrote.

But the open water had become a barrier, and Nansen realised he could no longer postpone repairing the kayaks – indeed they had virtually to be rebuilt. The tent was moved to the lee of a large hummock, and the work began.

Firstly the covers were removed and patched. The joints of the frames had loosened, and had to be relashed. But there was little spare thread, so each lashing had to be carefully unwound and used again, forty or fifty in each kayak. Also, various ribs were broken, and had to be repaired with what material was to hand. By now the air temperature was creeping up towards zero, so that it was warm sitting still in the sun. Fingers were unhindered by cold and the work went on, sometimes for twelve hours or more at a stretch.

To Johansen's relief, Nansen was returning to a routine by the clock. He also started rationing food, for the first time on the whole journey. So far, he and Johansen had eaten as they wished. They turned out to have kept, more or less, to Nansen's original estimate of half a kilo each per day. Nonetheless, Nansen realised he had been improvident. Until a landfall he would have to eke out supplies. He immediately reduced breakfast to 50 grams of butter and 200 grams of bread.

But at least they were in good health, with no trace of scurvy yet, and on 3 June Johansen shot a seagull, the first game on the whole journey. Two days later he shot another gull, and that evening both birds were served for dinner; the first fresh food for months, and the first fulfilment, at last, of the promise of living by the hunt.

However, by the time Nansen and Johansen finally started off again, on 8 June, both men were in a miserable state of mind. For one thing, another of the dogs had been slaughtered, The Rattlesnake this time, leaving only six. For another, Nansen had used the rest to get a precise fix with the theodolite. The result was 82°17.8′N and 61°16.5′E. That put Cape Fliguely now about 25 miles off, but the observation was illusory. Only the latitude was precise; the longitude was guesswork. The contrast merely intensified the nagging of uncertainty.

Moreover the thermometer now rose above freezing point for the first time, and the going was unspeakably foul. The sledges constantly stuck, the snow balled up under the skis. 'The collapse of skiing is in sight,' reported Johansen succinctly on 11 June, 'the snow is wet through to the bottom.' What was approaching was the twilight world between spring and summer. The snow would not bear up; the floes were crumbling at the edges, filling the leads with treacherous feathery brash that likewise neither bore a load nor allowed safe passage. The substance underfoot was being transmuted into something between sea and ice, but was not exactly either. It was a boundary zone, almost like another state of matter, and the interlude was fast approaching that would bar advance of any kind. It was simply too late in the season. It did not help Nansen's state of mind that he was being overtaken by the conditions which he had foreseen, and had done everything in his power to avoid.

'It would be hard for the dogs, even if they were not so miserably worn out as they are,' so he summed up one day. 'They stop constantly, and have to be helped or driven forward with the whip. Poor creatures, they have a horrible time.'

By now the five surviving dogs were so hungry that they devoured anything remotely edible: one day, for example, the toestrap and some of the wood of one of the skis. The men were not much better off. Nansen had drastically reduced the rations. Sometimes they did not eat for a whole day at a stretch. Their insides were screaming with the pangs of hunger. Still they crept forwards at a crawl, making perhaps three miles a day.

On 14 June it was exactly three months since leaving *Fram*. 'For a quarter of a year we have wandered around this desert of ice,' reflected Nansen, 'and still we remain here. Certainly I believed that by this day we would have reached Spitsbergen, or at any rate long since have landed on Franz Josef Land, but one cannot escape one's fate.'

One evening, after their meagre dinner, Johansen wrote a vivid description of the scene:

> Now and then the sun broke through dark, fantastic clouds which were almost black, while others were light, down on the horizon; the snow-covered ice blinding white, the water in the leads dark and black, and the horizon towards the south, yellow and red, while dark cumulus clouds came constantly driving from the ESE and now and then darkened the sun. It was strangely beautiful, and we enjoyed it and got into a good mood.

Nansen was inspired to take photographs but not to become cheerful.

> It is no pleasure to turn out for the day's struggle. I lie here and think of how everything is lovely in June at home ... what would I not give to exchange this ice to be there, and there Eva goes round and longs for me.

During the march on 15 June, a Saturday as it happened, Little Fox, one of the last remaining dogs, had to be put down. Slaughtering was now exclusively Johansen's concern. He had become so adept, Nansen observed, that with a single stroke of a long Lapp knife he could 'finish off an animal, so that it hardly gave a sound'.

What Nansen failed to grasp was the sensitivity underlying Johansen's impassive shell. For while Nansen simply remarked that Little Fox 'could not keep up', Johansen recorded: 'Poor creature, its sufferings are finished, I am glad I could do it. It has not had an easy time lately. Worn out as it was, nonetheless it was whipped by Nansen, who wanted it to pull when it couldn't, poor devil.'

At the end of the march that day, Big Fox also had to be slaughtered. Nansen made dinner out of his blood. 'If I say that it was good, I lie,' as Johansen put it, 'but it went down, and that is the main thing.' It was the first time the men had eaten any of their dogs. They felt like cannibals. But they were on the verge of despair.

Only three dogs now remained. They were Caiaphas, which belonged to Nansen, and Johansen's last dogs, Hare and Thug. By now, the men had had to start hauling the sledges in tandem with the dogs. At first, they did so with the primitive improvisation of a rope hitched over the shoulder. Discomfort quickly forced them to make out of discarded dog harnesses proper ones for themselves. These took the form of braces attached to a belt, so that the strain was evenly distributed. Nonetheless there was something uniquely dispiriting about the whole process. The mood was not helped by a heavy, overcast sky, and the only fitful emergence of the sun. Nansen took observations when he could, but the outcome only compounded the enigma of the absent land. To cap it all, both men were enmeshed in the dual depression of chronic hunger and the gloomy ambivalence of spring.

There was a crumb of comfort one day when Nansen tallied the ammunition. He found nearly 350 cartridges, which was more than he expected. That promised plenty of game, when once it was within reach. In fact, streams of little auks soon began flying overhead with irritating quacks. But they were too small to be worth shooting.

For a few more days men and dogs dragged themselves through wet, crumbling snow. In the hope of frost, Nansen switched once more to travelling at night. That produced another kind of misery in breakable crust which clutched at skis and sledge runners, while open cracks threaded the ice in all directions like a spider's web. The going was so treacherous that Nansen had to scout ahead, leaving Johansen to wait on tenterhooks behind, until he returned to lead them on – in the process covering the same ground three times. Exhausted and undernourished though they were, they periodically had to bridge cracks by heaving ice fragments into place, sometimes leaping like acrobats over open leads to pioneer a way across. By 21 June, their misfortunes reached the point when they were sinking deep in the snow even with skis on.

That was the ultimate degradation. After a quick discussion, Nansen and Johansen agreed that they could not carry on as they were. Less than forty days' food remained for the men, ten days' perhaps for the dogs. Fuel for the Primus was running low. Ringed seals occasionally appeared in open leads but they were comprehensively elusive. Nansen shot at one now but missed, the third time he had done so in a short while.

It was agreed that the only sensible course of action would be to jettison everything they could and then, with lightened loads, push on as fast as they could, to try and reach land before their food finally gave out. Also, to avoid constant loading and unloading, everything was to be packed in the kayaks so that they could be launched as they were and then drawn up again with the least delay. Since he had not yet ferried his equipment, Nansen wanted a trial before actually making the changes. The opportunity soon presented itself. After a short but notably depressing struggle, they arrived at a wide open channel, unencumbered with brash.

A kind of catamaran was improvised by loosely lashing skis athwart the kayaks fore and aft. On top of this, the sledges were laid, also athwart; and on top of them again, an unruly mound of impedimenta. The dogs embarked, surprisingly, as if they had been used to nothing else. Where the sledges went, they went too. They settled down quietly for the voyage where they could find space. Caiaphas sat in front, peering ahead like a captain on the bridge. The men pushed off and, manoeuvring through the deck cargo, wriggled into the cockpits to start paddling the top-heavy contraption. In an all too rare flash of wry humour, Johansen likened the spectacle to a ragged gipsy baggage train.

The kayaks were still leaky and had frequently to be pumped out, while because of the constrictions of the deck cargo paddling was awkward. Nonetheless, in Johansen's words: 'We both thought it was fun to advance over water for a change.'

'This is a miserable time I would unwillingly go through again,' wrote Nansen. 'We don't know where we are, not a glimpse of land [and] supplies dwindling by the day.... At night I lie for hours without being able to sleep, racking my brains for the best way out.'

Thus ended his diary at the last camp on the frozen morass now slowly receding across the sombre grey water.

44

A Feast of Seals

'How a little chance is all that is necessary to change our whole life,' Nansen continued in the next entry. On the other side of the channel, he sprang ashore with his camera and, in Johansen's words, 'took some entertaining pictures of the raft, while my kayak continually filled with water and I drifted away from the edge of the ice. Then I heard a mighty splash behind us. I asked what it was – It was a seal, said Nansen.'

Twice the seal dived and reappeared before vanishing, as it seemed for good. But it bobbed up once more, inspected the raft, and began swimming towards the edge of the ice. Johansen, still in his kayak, seized his gun where it lay on the deck and, just as the seal was about to submerge, loosed what he called 'the best and most useful shot of my whole life'. The bullet entered the head at precisely the right point. The seal gave a little leap, and floated motionless, its back just visible above the surface of the water.

Nansen, meanwhile, had finished his photography. When the bullet went home, he was in the act of beaching one of the sledges. He dropped the sledge, raced like the wind along the edge of the ice and, having seized a harpoon, which Johansen with foresight had already flung ashore, drove it into the seal. The carcass stirred. Nansen grabbed a knife, leant over the water's edge and, with a stab in the neck, gave the coup de grace. He thrust another harpoon into the carcass and started to haul it in.

While this was happening, the sledge that Nansen had dropped began sliding back into the water. Johansen tried to haul it back on board. He could only get it halfway up. As a result, the vessel listed over. Water streamed into Johansen's kayak between himself and the cockpit coaming. The dogs were becoming decidedly concerned.

This scene of utter confusion competed in Nansen's mind with a ferocious desire not to let the seal escape. For what to Johansen, sinking helplessly below the waves, seemed far too long, Nansen was the image of a man suspended between two desires. It was only a moment. Dropping the harpoons and lines, he hauled the sledges ashore, followed by Johansen in his kayak. Johansen was then able to get out, and together they rushed over to the seal.

But now Nansen's kayak was drifting off across the waters; so too was a little flotilla of skis together with the box containing the Primus stove and the cooking gear. So the two men had to scurry back, salvage their equipment, and then finally return to the seal. After much struggling, they heaved it onto the ice and – according to Nansen – did a war dance round the carcass.

What they had at their feet was a bearded seal, one of the largest Arctic species, big, fat and blubbery. By comparison, the fact that most of their equipment was soaked hardly seemed to matter. After calming down, they started to count the cost. There was the fate of their matches and ammunition to consider. Most of their matches were soldered in watertight tins and by firing off a shotgun cartridge towards a pair of gulls that had arrived to share the bag, Nansen satisfied himself that the ammunition, although wet, was unscathed too. The essentials had survived. They made camp, flensed and cut up the carcass and, in Nansen's words, gorged themselves 'on a sumptuous breakfast of seal meat, liver, blubber and soup'.

Their luck was not just that the bearded seal is much bigger than the ringed seal but that it is easier to catch. Its leading trait is an almost suicidal curiosity, which was probably this specimen's undoing. Released from the distress of hunger, Nansen found it easier to make rational decisions. He decided to stay where he was, feeding up men and dogs, while he waited for the going to improve.

This sequence of events took place on 21 June; exactly one hundred days since leaving *Fram*. 'We are now living like veritable Eskimos,' wrote Johansen, contentedly marking this somersault of fortune. They were now living off the land, feeding exclusively on seal meat. And they were cooking like Eskimos too.

To save paraffin for the Primus, Nansen had changed to seal blubber as fuel, in the Eskimo fashion. He also improvised a blubber lamp on the Eskimo model, consisting of a shallow bowl with a ring of wicks. Although applying what he had learned of Eskimo lore he did not stick to Eskimo dishes. With more sophistication, he cooked seal cutlets. And, in Johansen's words, he served 'a delicate seal steak of sirloin, which tasted better than any Chateaubriand'.

'We dared not use blubber to fry it in,' Johansen's diary continued. 'We were afraid that there would be too much oily taste, and the meat was therefore fried alone. But when we were nearly finished … we discovered that after being rendered in the frying pan, the blubber had no oily taste at all.' Inspired by this discovery, Nansen proceeded to cook a special little late night collation. This consisted of pancakes made of seal's blood, fried in plenty of blubber.

Now Nansen had made the bowl of his blubber lamp out of German silver intended to repair the false runners of the sledges. The wicks, he contrived out of bandages from the first aid kit. In the Eskimo original, the wicks were made of moss. More critically, the Eskimos make the bowls out of soapstone or, sometimes, wood. This controls the temperature. By using metal, Nansen incurred the risk of overheating. The upshot was a cloud of flame and smoke and sizzling blubber which drove the men outside, with streaming eyes and half asphyxiated, and finally blew itself out with a small explosion.

It was Midsummer's Eve, and at home bonfires would assuredly be blazing in honour of the day. So far as it went the misbehaving lamp was, as Johansen put it, 'a suitable illumination'. But a hole had been burned in one of the silken tent walls. With an interval for temporary repairs, Nansen – more carefully this time – continued the cooking and served the second helping of blood pancakes, with sugar strewn on top as a sauce. It was, said Johansen, 'the most wonderful meal we have had during the whole trip'.

The rest of Midsummer's Eve passed in a haze of sleep and gorging on seal meat. Nansen rounded off the proceedings by concocting with warm lime juice a simulacrum of the punch served at home on such occasions. They drank a toast which, as Johansen put it, was that 'just as the seal was at a turning point in its life, so might we also now be at a turning point, leading to better times'.

The carefree gluttonising, the reappearance of civilised amenities in the formality of the *skål*, suggested an altogether happier frame of mind. What is more, an observation that Nansen took earlier in the day gave a latitude of 82°4′. That meant that in five days they had made another 14 miles to the south. In Nansen's own words, this alone was 'more than enough ... to put us in a good mood'.

The sun meanwhile circled round the horizon. Midsummer's Eve glided into Midsummer's Day, 24 June, the second anniversary of the departure from Christiania. 'When I think back to this day, two years ago, dismal and grey as it was, it does not seem long since,' Nansen characteristically wrote. And, with another familiar echo of regret: 'I would not go through that day again for anything in the world.'

Just as characteristically, Johansen harked back to the mysterious shadow he felt hanging over him:

> I have learned that one must work in order to be happy ... I have learned that my whole existence has been a bad existence, and I have also learned to appreciate the advantages of home and the civilised world. It is now necessary to profit by these lessons and not to forget them.

Next day, Nansen shot their second seal, both he and Johansen having each missed once. It was only a small ringed seal, but the meat was a relief from the everlasting bearded seal. What is more, Johansen found a fresh water pool nearby, doubtless formed from melting snow. For the first time on the whole journey, they had drinking water without having to melt ice. It was like finding an oasis in the desert.

The dogs also were enjoying a Heaven-sent break. Their first meal under the new regime had been the entrails of the bearded seal, but they brought it all up and were thoroughly miserable. Their diet was then changed to the meat from their old companions, Big Fox and Little Fox, with seal blubber for dessert. That suited them better. In reasonable contentment they lolled around, watching their masters toil for a change.

On Midsummer's Day, Nansen and Johansen had started preparing for the next stage of their journey. Johansen sewed a rifle cover out of canvas and, with a sledge sail, started repairing the fire damage to the tent. He cut up seal meat and hung it out to dry for travelling rations.

Nansen, meanwhile, was waterproofing the kayaks. They were now leaking like sieves, and no spare proofing had been brought. After some experimentation, he improvised a hideous but effective mixture of soot and rendered blubber. To collect enough soot he had to sit long hours over his blubber lamp, holding an empty paraffin tin over the flame, and laboriously scraping off a slowly accumulating deposit. Eventually, he produced enough to impregnate the covering of both kayaks. To caulk the patches and seams he sacrificed his pastel crayons, grinding them up and mixing with blubber. When that gave out, he contrived a viscous blend of bitumen (intended for shoe repairs), resin (taken as flux for soldering) and candle wax.

It was not exactly a frenzied scene. 'We take the view,' in Johansen's words, 'that time is on our side.' He did not mean improvident slacking. He meant resisting the urge to rush, which is a very different thing. He was expressing an instinct, characteristic of his kind, that any living organism has a natural pace which must not be exceeded. That way lies self-punishment, exhaustion and disaster.

Nansen and Johansen worked deliberately, keeping well away from the perilous border zone between panic and impatience. They followed a regular routine. At a certain point every day, Johansen put down his work and went out to fetch drinking water. Nansen thereupon began cooking dinner. By an unspoken agreement, each at his self-appointed time went for a little walk to escape from the presence of the other and seize a moment of privacy.

It was the very picture of calm, with both men apparently adapted to circumstances. In part that was an illusion. It would be more correct to say that they controlled what was in their power, and submitted to what was not. Underneath, the tensions smouldered. 'Life has become monotonous in every way,' Johansen was writing at one point.

> We are both silent most of the time, and when we do speak it is naturally mostly about travelling on, about home, and how wonderful it will be to arrive there.

Johansen called his longings 'building castles in the air'. Nansen qualified his daydreams more ambiguously. 'I almost dare not think how wonderful it will be,' he wrote in one of his periodical outpourings.

Such musings each man kept for his diary alone. But they could read each other's minds. As both by now had realised, longing for home was all they really had in common. They coined a nickname for their temporary resting place: 'Homesickness Camp'.

Their appearance had now spectacularly deteriorated, and they longed to be clean again. Smoke from constant cooking with blubber had made their faces black and filthy, with grease ingrained in every pore. Of villainous aspect, they were soon unable to recognise each other. After a rare glance in the mirror of an artificial horizon they could not even recognise themselves. Their clothes were sooty and greasy too. Reindeer hair moulting from their sleeping bags penetrated everywhere, even to the charred, greasy stratified remains of accumulated meals encrusting the cooking utensils. Both men clung to some niceties of civilisation. 'I eat with sticks like the Chinese,' Johansen recorded, 'instead of biting the meat or blubber and cutting it off next to the mouth like the Eskimos.' Seal meat and belongings were strewn about the ice. Gulls impertinently attacked the mounds of blubber. Even when Johansen shook his fist at them, they barely deigned to budge.

The days passed somehow, the one very like the other. 'Nothing else of note happened,' Johansen, with bitter irony, observed of 3 July, 'except that The Hare was slaughtered.' Despite all the extra food, the dog was wasting away with no signs, it seemed, of recovery. Johansen felt even more like a murderer than usual:

> Poor creature, I think it has been the very best of the dogs, the way it has kept at it from beginning to end, and still it hauled, although its back was somewhat twisted, and it hurt me when I cut its throat, especially as I could not do it as cleanly as I wanted, because I could not find the jugular at once.

Only Thug and Caiaphas now remained of the twenty-eight dogs that had started. Nansen and Johansen were left with a sense of melancholy even deeper than before.

The weather, meanwhile, hardly helped their state of mind. For a whole fortnight, they had waited for the right conditions to melt the snow. Day after day, they were depressed by leaden skies; relapsing into a downright bad mood when a clammy fog came crawling in, to paint the snow with a protective crust. Finally, in the small hours of Saturday 6 July the much longed-for change arrived. Rain poured down in torrents and continued through the day.

Most of the time, Nansen and Johansen had to huddle in the tent for shelter of a kind. The fabric leaked and everything was wet. Nonetheless, in Nansen's unwontedly cheerful words, 'we gloried in hearing the rain outside'. This was what was needed to wash away the snow. It was being visibly depleted. To celebrate what Nansen called 'the beatific rain', a cup of cocoa was decreed. This had become a rare occurrence in the now monotonous diet of seal meat. While the cocoa was being prepared the dogs, who had remained outside, started barking in an unfamiliar way. Nansen tumbled out of the tent, followed closely by Johansen. A huge polar bear was sniffing at Caiaphas.

Nansen grabbed his rifle, waiting ready by the side of the tent, ripped the cover off, and shot the bear in the chest. It staggered under the impact, then swung round and made off. Before Nansen could send off another shot, the bear was down among the hummocks, and out of the line of fire. Nansen set off in pursuit, with Johansen still behind. After a few steps, they saw two bear cubs reared up and looking for what was clearly their mother, who was now staggering towards them issuing a trail of blood. 'As soon as she reached them, they gathered round her,' Nansen recorded in his diary. 'And there was confusion in all their behaviour. They did not know, poor devils, what was wrong.'

The three animals turned to flee. They made off across an open lead with Nansen in pursuit. He fired again at the she-bear, but without dropping her this time either. It was his last bullet; for a moment he stood nonplussed. Then Johansen caught up. He had remembered to bring ammunition, and handed over some. 'There now began a wild pursuit over open leads ... and hummocks and all kinds of gruesomeness,' Nansen's diary continued.

> There is something strange about the fever of the hunt. It is like igniting gunpowder. Where in everyday circumstances, advance would be slow and cumbersome ... just let the fever of the hunt flare up and one flies over everything as if it were smooth, flat ice.

Nansen dared not waste cartridges. He had to continue the chase until finally he had the she-bear facing him at point-blank range, and dropped her with a single shot. He sent another bullet after one of the cubs, which dropped with a howl. The other cub, in Nansen's words, 'stood in perplex-ity'.

> As I approached, he turned his head listlessly towards me – what did I matter to him now? Everything he loved in the world lay there maimed and destroyed, and he did not know where to go.

Nansen killed him with a single shot, and he fell by the side of his mother. It was, said Nansen, with the ambivalence of the hunter towards his prey, 'a bloody sight to see the 3 bears lying in a heap'. The mother and the first cub were not yet dead. Nansen did not have a proper knife with him to finish them off, but the ingrained rule of the hunt, even here in the pack ice, allowed no delay. He spent three of his precious cartridges on the *coup de grâce*. When Johansen arrived, having been held up by an open lead, it was all over. At their feet lay a superabundance of food. Once more the men knew the atavistic exhilaration of the hunter. It took two days to skin the bears and haul the carcasses back to the camp. The bearskins were brought into the tent as a soft undermattress for the sleeping bag. The upshot was that Nansen and Johansen slept twenty-two hours at a stretch. It was their first proper night's sleep for a long time.

What is more, both men were now growing accustomed to eating meat and fat alone. Originally, their abrupt change to a purely carnivorous diet had produced constipation, which added to depression. Their digestion was at last settling down. They had lost their craving for farinaceous foods.

The hunting of the bears had been a kind of watershed. The dogs now had all the fresh meat they could manage. 'They are enjoying halcyon days,' our two veterans,' Johansen recorded, himself cheered by the sight. Thug, who had been half paralysed, began to convalesce. Caiaphas strutted about, bedraggled no longer, his coat shiny and fluffed, bright of eye, a thoroughly respectable figure once more.

That was more than could be said for his masters. Unrelievedly tattered and dirty, they were becoming 'more and more like savages', as Johansen pointed out. Nonetheless an air of expectancy how hung over Homesickness Camp. The thermometer kept above zero. The weather obliged with continual overcast skies, oppressively holding in the heat and acting like a slow cooker – good circumstances for devouring the snow. There was even rain now and then. After the weeks of measured work there was a rush to get ready in time for a swift departure.

Nansen aimed to start on 19 July but, in a repetition of leaving *Fram*, it was postponed day by day. Finally, at half past ten in the morning of 22 July, they left Homesickness Camp, a whole month since they had arrived.

Behind them they left a pile of meat and bearskins. Spare skis, rope, bamboo, part of the cooker, first-aid kit, a comprehensive selection of what originally had been considered indispensable, also lay strewn about the ice. Barely a scrap of wood or spare rope for repairs was taken. Lightness and mobility were all. The reindeer fur sleeping bag was abandoned too. It was now worn out but heavy with accumulated damp. In its place, out of blankets, Johansen had sewn another, lighter sleeping bag. To save another pound or two the men had even considered jettisoning the tent, but one attempt at sleeping in the open or sheltering in the kayaks had demonstrated the folly of such a course.

As they set off, both men were in an unusually good mood. After so long in stagnant stillness, to be on the move again in itself meant a lift to the spirits. But also this seemed the start of the last lap home. The snow had finally settled, so the going was humanly tolerable at last. Pulling the lightened sledges was child's play for each man in tandem with his dog. At the first open lead Johansen launched his kayak, put Thug on the foredeck, while he himself knelt aft, and paddled across. Nansen could not match Johansen's gymnastic sense of balance, so he towed his kayak round, with Caiaphas smugly resting on board.

Next day, 23 July, about noon, Nansen had gone off to find the way ahead. Johansen, as usual, stayed behind. As was his wont, he climbed a convenient hummock to see what he could see. Over the horizon, he observed a dark stripe which he mentioned to Nansen on his return.

Nansen took scant notice. Much later, after covering considerably more ground, he himself climbed a hummock to spy out the way ahead, and noticed the same dark stripe over the horizon. It ran diagonally across what he took to be a bank of cloud. He fetched his telescope.

45

'We Have Seen Land'

'At last the great miracle has happened, which we had nearly ceased to believe in,' began Nansen's record of that day. Through the telescope, the black stripe resolved itself into a line of rock, the bank of cloud into a glacier domed against the sky. 'Both of us,' in Nansen's words, 'were overcome by a wonderful happy mood.'

> At last we have seen land! Land! Oh wonderful word! After nearly two years, we can see something raise itself once more over that everlasting white line out there on the horizon. And this white line, which has spread over this sea for thousands upon thousands of years, and which for thousands of years will continue to spread in the same way – now we will leave it, and all that has happened is the trifle that the narrow track of a little caravan has been drawn in the snow over the white surface; a track which has long since vanished. Now a new life begins for us, because the ice is and always will be the same.

Nansen really did write all that in his diary, on the ice, under Arctic skies, the pencil moving firmly and and evenly across the page.

It was the 132nd day since leaving *Fram*.

Both Nansen and Johansen now realised that they had long seen land without recognising what it was. What now stood out as a glacier over terra firma was the same formation observed from Homesickness Camp as a bank of cloud. 'It is a shame that we have lain [still] for a whole month with land as our neighbour, so to speak,' Johansen characteristically wrote. 'But what could we do?'

Nansen started out once more to pioneer the route. The going was easy, but it was late. He decided that they had done enough for one day, and returned to make camp where they had stopped. He celebrated the sight of land in the usual way by serving a special meal. 'Lobscouse of [dried] potatoes [with] pemmican, dried sliced bear and seal and bear tongue. Dessert of bread crumbs fried in bear fat,' Nansen lovingly listed. 'A piece of chocolate to finish off.'

The only malcontent was Johansen's dog, Thug. That day he escaped, to scamper off back in the direction whence they came, 'presumably remembering all the meat he abandoned in "Homesickness Camp" ', as

Johansen put it. Or perhaps, with the instincts of a dog, he had forebodings over what lay ahead.

> I really had to use my legs to catch him, since he started galloping as I started to overtake him, but he wasn't quick enough to escape, the old gentleman.

Next morning, 24 July, leaden skies gave way to gleaming sunshine. Johansen tumbled out and rushed up a nearby hummock to reassure himself that the land was still there. In Nansen's words, it had 'long haunted our dreams', and it still appeared 'as a dream, a goblin landscape ... like white clouds you fear will disappear the next moment'. But the land *was* still there, in the same south-westerly quarter. Then the fog came down and swallowed it.

At the end of the march the fog lifted and once more land seemed appreciably closer. Johansen at least was certain they would arrive the following day. In celebration or not, he noted before setting out: 'I changed underwear for the first time since we left *Fram* 14 March this year.'

That was written around noon on Thursday 25 July. On the Saturday, Nansen could pick out an ice front stretching westwards in the distance, and believed they might arrive before that day was out. But Sunday came and Monday too, and land seemed as far off as before.

Meanwhile, the going spectacularly deteriorated. 'The ice is now as horrible as possible to advance over,' Nansen wrote, 'broken up so that it seems like a single massive frozen surf.' Hauling their sledges, Nansen and Johansen had to jump warily across from one ice fragment to another. Sometimes they trod blindly over the treacherous froth of brash ice blended with mushy snow. Somehow they negotiated these treacherous causeways without mishap. Not so the dogs who had many an icy salt water dousing. The ice meanwhile was constantly grinding and shifting in a turgid chaos.

All this hinted that the edge of the pack was, at long last, approaching. So too did a dark loom suggesting open water ahead. More land started to appear. But it shifted tauntingly round the horizon to show they were still at the mercy of wind and current. 'And anything is better than fighting those two enemies,' Nansen wrote, his high spirits once more driven out by gloom. 'I fear that all struggle against them will be in vain.'

Obstacles seemed deliberately to pile up in their path. For one thing, their new blanket sleeping-bag, although relatively light, was cold and uncomfortable. On that account or otherwise, Nansen was virtually crippled one day by a sudden onset of lumbago. In his own words, 'it was only by summoning up all my willpower that I was able to drag myself forwards'. He was not helped when, soon after, they were held up for a whole day by streaming rain. Before they could find a proper camping place they were thoroughly wet through.

Johansen had to take over all camp duties, nursing Nansen into the bargain. He also had to break the trail. That meant he had to cope with Thug, who was unused to going ahead and made it crystal clear that he preferred to run behind. Finally, on the first day of August, despite all the dampness, Nansen could record that his back was better.

> In the meanwhile, I have had a little taste of what it would mean if one us should be seriously ill. I fear definitely that in that case our fate would be sealed.

After over a week with land in sight, both men were forced to accept that arriving was going to be harder than they had been willing to believe. Food for the dogs ran out. It was Johansen who, out of sympathy, spent precious cartridges on shooting birds for them. Caiaphas at first spurned Johansen's offering; after bear meat, sea birds were beneath his dignity. Hunger, however, eventually overcame fastidiousnes. In any case, both dogs hauled like Trojans in tandem with their masters. Even Thug, now in his appointed place behind once more, with Nansen and Caiaphas going on ahead, did his part valiantly.

At the end of July, for the first time, the distant murmur of the surf could be heard. But land seemed no closer yet, and both Nansen and Johansen plunged deeper into gloom. They were further depressed by the broken rhythm of their advance. On the one hand, they were relieved now for the most part to be able to walk through broken ice where skiing was a pain. On the other hand, to be in a landscape of snow and ice and not to be able to ski went against their nature. The ultimate humiliation was that they were actually dragging their skis on the sledges. Both Nansen and Johansen were further depressed by the nagging uncertainty of where they really were.

Probably the flattened domes pushing up over the horizon were part of Franz Josef Land but, because Nansen did not know his longitude, he could not be absolutely sure. He might have stumbled on another archipelago to the east or west. Even assuming that this was Franz Josef Land, Payer's sketchy map was of little help. Because Nansen had no surveyed altitudes on land to guide him, he could not fix distances. And given the notorious distortion of perspective in the ice, it was difficult even to judge reliably. When land was first identified, it seemed between five and ten miles off. In reality, it was closer to twenty miles.

There was a kind of climax on 4 August, a notably trying day. The ice, as Nansen feelingly put it,

> was as if a Titan had thrown the heaviest blocks of ice together pell mell, and strewn deep, wet snow in between with water underneath, where one sank in up to one's thighs. There were deep pools interminably between the blocks. We had to struggle over hill and dale, up and down over ridge after

298

ridge with deep clefts in between. There was not even a level stretch big enough to pitch a tent.

To complete the picture, there was a dense and clammy fog through which it was scarcely possible to glimpse a hundred yards ahead. Progress was reduced to an enervating crawl. When the fog seemed thickest, and the hummocks highest, the little caravan was stopped by an open lead. To reach the other side meant ferrying across. Nansen and Johansen cleared broken ice away from the water's edge preparatory to launching the kayaks. Nansen hauled his sledge forward, while Johansen went back to fetch his. The ice sloped downwards, and Nansen stood holding his sledge, with the kayak on top, to prevent it sliding into the water, while he waited for Johansen. Nansen heard a sudden commotion behind him and, in his own words, Johansen

> shouted 'Grab your gun!' I turned round, and saw a huge bear throw itself over Johansen, and he was flung on his back. I let go of the kayak in order to seize my rifle, which lay in its holster on the foredeck, but simultaneously the kayak slid into the water. My first thought was to throw myself out into the water onto the kayak and shoot from there, but I immediately saw the danger [of hitting Johansen], so I hauled the kayak up as quickly as I could, grabbed my gun ... cocked one of the triggers, which happened to be on the shotgun barrel, and let [the bear] have the whole charge in its neck. It sank down on the spot. For safety's sake, I also let it have a bullet from the other barrel. It lay there dead between us. It was all over in a moment.

'I thought it took a long time,' was Johansen's recollection. 'But I lay under the bear.' He said to Nansen (remembering to use the polite form of address), 'Now you must hurry, otherwise it will be too late.' In his diary he recorded:

> The bear raised itself on its hind legs and forced me backwards ... It gave me a cuff on my right cheek with its giant fore-paw, so that my head rang with the blow, and then I was on my back with the bear over me. It was about to bite my head. In defence, I stretched out my arms, and with my left hand got hold of its throat, and held on as hard as I could. At that, the bear hesitated, and that saved my life, or at least saved me from a severe mauling. The bear now became aware of our two dogs alongside, and turned its attention to them.... In the same instant ... I squirmed out of its grip, and scrambled to my feet, completely unhurt.

Then the shots rang out. Almost immediately, two young bears then peered round some nearby hummocks. Once again, the fallen bear was a mother foraging for her cubs. Johansen seized his gun and sprang to the attack. Nansen tried to stop him, since now they had plenty of fresh meat again, and he wanted to waste no more cartridges. Johansen disobeyed. He was seized with an atavistic desire for revenge. The cubs fled, then returned, and Johansen loosed off a shot, hitting one of them. They ran off again, the wounded one lowing plaintively like a cow.

By now Johansen had calmed down. The dogs were all but unhurt. The only marks Johansen himself bore were a scratched hand and a white stripe on his cheek where the bear had scraped away the epidermis together with the encrustation of blubber and soot that had built up at Homesickness Camp. 'We could joke about that now – luckily,' as Johansen put it. 'We were in a brilliant mood, everything had gone so well.' In his diary, he could even afford a touch of understanding for his attacker. Polar bears, he wrote,

> very rarely attack in this way, at least where human beings are concerned. Usually, they are very shy. But this one must have been very hungry.

The upshot was an uncovenanted addition to their supplies. Having cut up the carcass, Nansen and Johansen loaded fresh bear meat onto their sledges and fed their dogs to their heart's content. Thereafter they finally crossed the lead. By now the fog was clearing and they were moving once more under leaden banks of cumulus. Some time later, from a hummock on the other side, Nansen, for the first time, through his telescope, saw the open water along the ice front on the land ahead. At last journey's end was in sight. Not even the persistence of abominably broken and chaotic ice could mask the uplift that gave.

By now, it was in the small hours of 5 August. When they emerged from the tent that evening, they could see from the tracks in the snow that another bear had been right up to the camp while they slept. More to the point, land loomed up closer than ever. Also while they slept, the wind, after backing and hauling for days, had swung right round to the north, and evidently driven them on.

They struck camp more quickly than usual and set off with a faint hope of arriving before another day was done. But, in Nansen's own words, having

> suffered so many disappointments, we were all too prepared for more set-backs. This pack ice has trained us well in two virtues: patience and frugality; admirable virtues for anyone, but especially for a polar explorer.

Eventually the going improved. Soon after, it became clear to the naked eye that the land was appreciably closer. The men were galvanised into hauling away at the sledges in something like a sprint. The dogs reacted to the mood of their masters. The men were in such spirits now that they ceased to mind stumping along on foot instead of sliding on skis. 'Everything went like a dance,' wrote Nansen exuberantly, 'And little did we care that we sank into water high above our gaiters so that our legs were soaking wet. What did it matter to us, as long as we went forwards, forwards?'

Soon the snow was criss-crossed with the spoors of polar bears, but neither Nansen nor Johansen were interested in game. Soon they could see the open water under the glacier front. Their strides grew longer.

45. 'We Have Seen Land'

Johansen who, as usual, was following behind suddenly saw Nansen stop and swing his hat. Johansen swung his in return, and the first cheer on the whole journey rang out. At last they stood at the edge of the ice.

It was early in the morning of 6 August. It was the 146th day since leaving *Fram*. They had travelled over 600 miles. It was the longest journey so far over the Arctic pack.

At their feet lay the sombre grey waters of an open sound. On the surface dull white floes swam. In the distance, like an upturned shield, lay the domed silhouette of the glacier front. A dismal misty light illuminated the scene, but, as Nansen recorded:

> It was a flood of happiness that filled one's soul at this sight, and which it was impossible to express in words. Behind us lay all our troubles, and ahead the waterway lay open all the way home and light and happiness.

Instant celebration was called for. So, in the usual way, Nansen doled out a small piece of their precious chocolate each.

But there was no time to waste. The wind was still fair, and they wanted to reach land before it turned foul. As quickly as they could, they made ready for sea. They detached the sledges and fixed them athwart the kayaks once more, with the skis, to improvise a catamaran.

For the dogs, lying patiently in the snow, this was their death warrant. On the fragile craft they would be a dangerous encumbrance. 'To part with them hurt us both,' Nansen wrote in his diary. 'We had become so fond of these last survivors.' 'Poor Thug and Caiaphas,' ran Johansen's farewell, 'You were faithful to the last, and if you come to another world, may you enjoy yourselves in the eternal hunting grounds.'

Neither man had the heart to slaughter them like the others. They spent a cartridge on each. To make things easier, they took each other's dogs. Nansen shot Thug and Johansen, Caiaphas.

Both men were close to tears. The pack ice had become doubly hateful now. Hurriedly, they launched their vessel and got under way.

46

Food for the Taking

'It was a true pleasure to let the kayaks dance over the water, and listen to the wavelets lapping against the sides,' wrote Nansen. 'For two years, we had not seen such a stretch of water.'

Nansen and Johansen had begun by rowing, but the fair wind held. With a breeze almost dead astern they quickly rigged their bamboo mast, raised sail and shipped their oars. In Nansen's words:

> Effortlessly we glided before the wind towards the land for which we had hungered so long. What a change from having to struggle inch by inch and foot by foot over the broken ice.

And Johansen recorded:

> We sat at our ease, and approached the glacier with respectable speed [while] we ate breakfast in the kayaks. It was an abrupt change from the struggle over the pack ice and we were happy as children at the thought of having finished with it.

For a while, fog veiled what lay ahead. At a certain point it parted to reveal the glacier looming up. At the same time, the sun broke through, bathing the scene with a gentle glow. Nansen could 'scarcely remember a more beautiful morning'.

Soon, they were under land and had to take in all sail. They started rowing westwards along the glacier front. A strong tidal set began running in the same direction. So they shipped oars once more and drifted with the tide.

To port, the glacier front passed by. It rose straight up from the sea in a high precipice, tinted eerily with pale emerald. The waters had undercut the base, but there were no crevasses, nor was there the sound of avalanches or calving nor any other sign of movement. As if cut by a knife, the ice cliff exposed the strata of annual snowfall like the growth-rings of a fossilised tree. It was an image of sterility. Such was the mythic shore that had haunted the imagination of both men for so long.

To land on the sheer face was impossible. So they had to camp yet once again on a drifting floe. Next morning a short haul brought them to open water again. In the meantime, both men had agreed that they needed new oars. Their first day in open water had shown that their existing ones, made of canvas blades lashed to long bamboo sticks, were clumsy and ineffective. So before launching their kayaks they made paddles with blades cut from a broken hickory ski and lashed to their ski sticks.

Alternately sailing through open channels and hauling their kayaks over the ice, they followed the land, first west, then broadly south. They still had to camp on the sea ice, because the shore remained glacier-bound. It was only intermittently visible, because of clinging fog. Other drawbacks were that the temperature stayed in the dismal regions just above freezing point, and that it periodically rained. Nonetheless, Johansen recorded that now 'I for my part sleep well every single night'. Nansen, however, 'had a hard time now and then where going to sleep was concerned'.

Finally, after three days of constant fog, the weather lifted. They were then camped off a small island entirely capped by a glacier which, instead of ending abruptly, ran gently into the ice foot on which their tent was pitched. So they got onto their skis and climbed the ice dome. The slope was so slack that, on the return, they were deprived of a downhill run because the skis would not slide of their own accord even on the polished, wind-blown crust.

In any case, the view from the top only intensified Nansen's confusion. Three other ice-capped islands dotted a leaden sea. They were in an archipelago, and not off a continuous coast, as they had hitherto assumed. Their guide was still Julius Payer's map; the only one of Northern Franz Josef Land yet published when they left civilisation, but what they had seen bore no relation to it. That implied that they must have traversed an extensive country called Wilczek Land. Nansen could only assume that he had discovered new land. He had, but he was unelated. He wanted to know where he was.

Nansen was sure of his latitude – 81°37.7'N on 9 August. His longitude was still bedevilled by uncertainty. The last observation that he had actually worked out was on 1 July. This gave 57°59'E. Their course since then had brought them even further west. Although in guessing his longitude when both watches stopped more than three months before, Nansen had generously allowed for westerly movement, it now seemed that he had not allowed enough. He could only reconcile Payer's map with what he saw by assuming his margin of error had been an illusion and, after all, he was on the western limit of Franz Josef Land, or beyond. In that case, as Johansen hopefully recorded, 'we are fairly certain to reach Spitsbergen in time to find a ship', and thus still reach home that year. So now they struck out in a westerly direction, following the edge of the ice.

The land was sterile but its surface was boiling with life. The sea-ice was criss-crossed with the tracks of polar bears. Overhead, fulmars, kittiwakes and little auks swooped and dived; gulls intruded with their raucous screech. In the open water seals regularly surfaced. On a floe, now and then, walrus basked. All this meant food for the taking. Whatever the other uncertainties the debilitating fear of starvation was held at bay.

Sunday, 11 August, marked the sixth anniversary of Nansen's engagement to Eva. 'Ah, my Eva,' he wrote in his diary before starting off on that day's stage, 'today you are surely longing grievously. If only you do not have to wait yet another long, long year.'

This was the first time that Nansen recorded his doubt over reaching home that year. He had grounds for his pessimism. The temperature had fallen again below zero. Where the sea was calm, it was starting to freeze over. The midnight sun hovered barely above the horizon. Suddenly, that day, winter seemed uncomfortably close.

After Nansen and Johansen had been under way for some time, a walrus, heavily tusked, surfaced close by their vessel, glaring inquisitively, or menacingly, at them. They ignored the obese monster. They had food enough, and merely wanted to advance. The walrus objected. And when Nansen and Johansen tried to drive it away with their oars, it became enraged. Puffing and snorting, it threatened to hole the kayaks with its tusks. Reluctantly, Johansen, in self-defence, had to waste a bullet full in its pompous face. Then they rowed off as fast as they could, while the creature's howls died away in the distance.

Soon after, another walrus attacked the kayaks and one more precious bullet had to be spent. This time the animal was killed instantly, and floated conveniently close by. Cutting off a few strips of meat from the back, Nansen and Johansen rowed on, considerably warier now. The walrus is without exception the most aggressive Arctic beast.

All too soon the tide turned and the ice closed up, barring the way ahead. Instead of dismantling the catamaran yet again and hauling the kayaks over the floes, Nansen decided to stop and wait for the turn of the tide. He wanted urgently to rectify more defects in his equipment.

The catamaran was a cumbersome device, necessitated by the long sledges, which could only be carried athwart. Now Nansen and Johansen cut the sledges in half, retaining one part each. These were now short enough to be lashed aft on each kayak, which could henceforth sail separately. Also the oars had been found wanting. Once again the men changed all that and made proper narrow double-bladed paddles like the Eskimos.

Still the fog hung heavy over the ice. One could barely see a mile ahead. But late in the evening, while they were still working, it once more lifted. In the forlorn autumnal glow of the waning midnight sun the surroundings emerged like a stage set. What they saw was 'land, a lot of land, in a circle from SE to WNW' – which, as Johansen put it, they believed was the east coast of Franz Josef Land. 'With that,' he added, 'disappeared all hope of a homecoming this year.'

Neither man could yet contemplate another polar night and clinging to a wisp of hope, they continued on their way.

46. Food for the Taking

There was a memorable occasion on Thursday, 15 August, when, in the evening, they landed on an island partly free of ice. Once more, at long last, they felt dry land underfoot. It was five months since leaving *Fram*, and the first time they had trodden mother earth since going ashore on Cape Chelyuskin almost two years before. As land went it was not much: a half-submerged moraine jammed around a skerry. But, said Nansen, it was 'an indescribably beautiful feeling [to jump] from one granite boulder to the other'. They were profoundly moved also to see among the stones the first flowers since leaving Khabarova: saxifrages and little yellow Siberian poppies. In honour of it all, especially the flowers, they hoisted the Norwegian flag and celebrated in the usual way with another special meal – their first hot meal for more than twenty-four hours.

The day before, their paraffin had finally run out and the Primus stove was a closed chapter. Now Nansen had to light the blubber lamp, an altogether more trying procedure. He made a lobscouse of pemmican with the last remnants of their dried potatoes. The steaming hot concoction, eaten while sitting on dry gravel after so long in the ice, was a memorable sensation.

The following day, they pursued their course through an ever more baffling archipelago. After a short spell paddling along a lead, they struggled for some time hauling their sledges over uneven ice, then reached what appeared to be an open sea. They launched their kayaks, and continued paddling westwards.

By their latitude, the glacier front passing by to port must have belonged to Payer's Karl Alexander Land. Again however, it was difficult to reconcile the trend of the coast with Payer's map and with a bleak promontory jutting out westwards into the sombre waters under a heavy sky tinged purple by the dying midnight sun in the north. 'We became more and more tensed as we approached the promontory,' Nansen recorded in his diary.

> Did the land bear south? And was there no land further west? That would decide our fate – whether we would winter in this land or not. Closer and closer we moved along the sheer wall of ice ... At last we rounded the promontory and our hearts jumped for joy to see only water to the west, and the land soon ran away to the SW.

A short way off, a peculiar razorbacked rock ridge broke through the glacier. Nansen identified it as Cape Felder, the limit of what Payer had charted as land certainly sighted. Nansen and Johansen climbed up a cliff to a gap on the skyline to spy out the way ahead. They were accompanied by the din of thousands of nesting sea birds. Both men recorded meeting two screeching foxes squabbling on the edge of the abyss over a little auk that one of them had caught.

After the descent it was time to camp. But a fair wind was blowing and tired though they were instinct drove them to profit by the circumstances. Snatching a meal of raw pemmican and blubber, they once more fixed their kayaks together as a catamaran, rigged their mast, hoisted sail, and ran south-west before the wind. They were now so weary they dozed off in their cockpits, but did not stop sailing until the wind dropped. In the small hours of 17 August they finally camped on the ice off an unknown promontory. Nansen dubbed it Brøgger's Headland in honour of his friend.

This seemed to mark a turning point at last. On the other side, the coast fell away to the east. An open sea ran on to the horizon. Karl Alexander Land was an island, after all. 'Happy as a child at the thought that we are on the west coast,' Nansen jotted in his diary.

> have open water free of current and ice ahead of us ... once more hope of reaching home this year.

Johansen elaborated:

> We will try as hard as we can to reach Spitsbergen and find a ship this year. Think of coming home this year, after not too long a time perhaps. What happiness! That will be a change from everything that we have suffered!

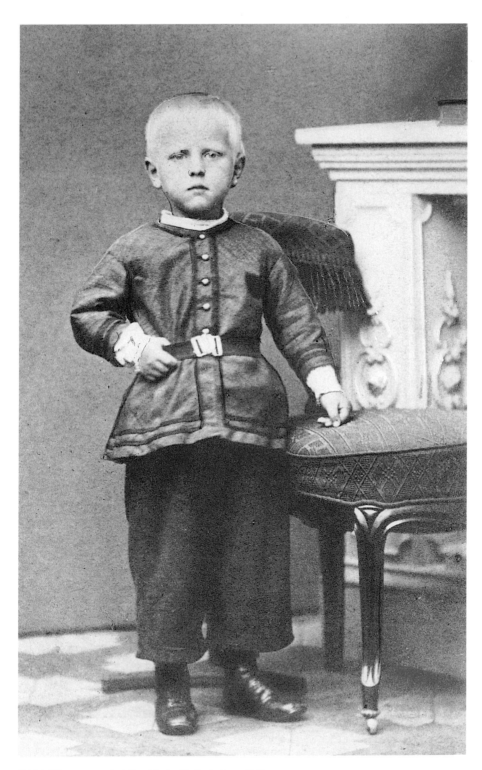

Fridtjof Nansen as a toddler. Photo: H. Aschehoug & Co.

At his home at Lille Frøen, Nansen had hunting and skiing in Normarka on his doorstep; first with his older half-brothers and later with his younger brother, Alexander. Photo: University of Oslo Library.

The Nansen family at Lille Frøen. Standing, left to right: Harald, Hjalmar, Einar and Ida Bølling. Seated, left to right: Sigrid Bølling, Alexander Nansen, Adelaide and Baldur Nansen, Fridtjof and Moltke Nansen. Photo: H. Aschehoug & Co.

Studio photograph of Nansen demonstrating the Telemark landing, used in an exhibition in Germany in 1881 to illustrate skiing. Photo: University of Oslo Library.

Nansen looks up from his microscope in the Bergen Museum to gaze at a specimen of the hag fish preserved in formalin. This was one of the species on which he based his ground-breaking research into the central nervous system. Photo: University of Bergen Library.

A gathering of research workers at the Bergen Museum. From left to right: J. Brunchorst (who carried out one of the earliest investigations into the effects of electricity on plant growth), Armauer Hansen (who discovered the leprosy bacillus), Nansen, T.C. Thomassen, J. Grieg, A. Lorange, and the Museum director Dr Daniel C. Danielssen (author of one of the first systematic studies of leprosy). Photo: University of Bergen Library.

When Nansen embarked on his Continental study tour in 1886, he had this photograph taken in Copenhagen - decked out in Dr Jaeger's patent 'Sanitary Woollen Clothing'. Photo: H. Aschehoug & Co.

The first sledges ready to start on the Greenland Ice Cap. The ski sticks were without baskets and wrist straps, and some of them were fitted with ice axe heads. Photo: H. Aschehoug & Co.

Members of the Greenland expedition: (left to right) Ole Nielsen Ravna, Nansen, Otto Sverdrup, Kristian Kristiansen, Oluf Dietrichson and Samuel Balto. This photograph was taken after they returned home. Photo: H. Aschehoug & Co.

Both drift ice and calving glaciers caused difficulty and danger while rowing up the east coast of Greenland. Photo: H. Aschehoug & Co.

When the Greenland expedition was approaching Christiania on the ship from Copenhagen, they were transferred to the Norwegian coastal express ship, Kong Carl ('King Carl') and cheered by a large reception committee. Photo: University of Oslo Library.

When Eva Sars married Nansen in the autumn of 1889, she had been a well known lieder singer for several years. Photo: H. Aschehoug & Co.

Studio photograph of Nansen and Eva in skiing gear after they were married. Photo: H. Aschehoug & Co.

Fram in Bergen on her way to the Arctic during the summer of 1893. Photo: University of Bergen Library.

Building sledges - for a thrust towards the North Pole? Photo: H. Aschehoug & Co.

During the summer of 1894, Nansen doubted more and more whether the drift of the ice would carry *Fram* far enough to the north. Photo: H. Aschehoug & Co.

Scott Hansen (right) responsible for navigation and scientific observations, with his assistant, Hjalmar Johansen. Photo: H. Aschehoug & Co.

Fram smothered in ice and snow following violent pressure from the ice early in 1895. Photo: H. Aschehoug & Co.

Nansen (second left) and Johansen (second right), ready for the third and final start of their sledge journey towards the pole on 14 March 1895. Photo: University of Oslo Library.

On the last lap over the pack ice, Nansen and Johansen had to haul their sledges themselves, with only one dog each to help. Photo: H. Aschehoug & Co.

With a following wind, Johansen (nearest the camera) and Nansen sail with their kayaks lashed together as a catamaran. (Reconstruction photographed off Cape Flora on Franz Josef Land.) Photo: H. Aschehoug & Co.

The winter hut (left foreground) lay half underground. The heat from the blubber lamp has melted the snow to expose the roof of walrus hide. In the background, a sledge has been parked vertically so as not to be buried by snow. Photo: University of Oslo Library.

Interior of the winter hut, with a saucepan on the rock floor. All boiling, frying and melting of ice was done over blubber lamps made from false metal runners from the sledges.
Photo: H. Aschehoug & Co.

Before over-wintering on Franz Josef Land, supplies of meat and blubber were secured by slaughtering walrus. On dry ground walrus are helpless, but in the water, they attacked the kayaks several times. Both marksman (Johansen) and photographer (Nansen) really are as close to the animals as they seem to be in the picture. Photo: H. Aschehoug & Co.

Captain Sverdrup puts his men to work clearing snow and ice from *Fram*. Photo: H. Aschehoug & Co.

Posed photograph of Frederick Jackson welcoming Nansen to his base at Cape Flora. Photo: H. Aschehoug & Co.

(Left) Nansen outside Jackson's hut. Photo: H. Aschehoug & Co. (Right) Johansen outside Jackson's hut. Photo: University of Oslo Library.

Captain Brown between Nansen and Johansen, on *Windward* on the voyage south from Franz Josef Land. Photo: H. Aschehoug & Co.

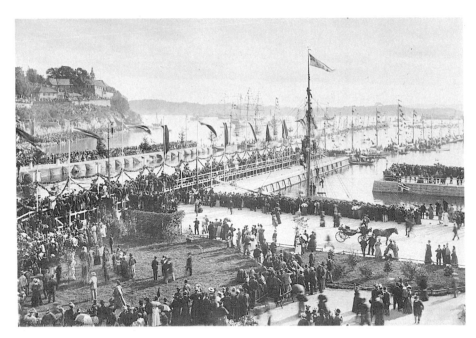

The inlet of Pipervika in Christiania decorated for the return of *Fram*. Photo: H. Aschehoug & Co.

Gymnasts formed an impressive triumphal arch for *Fram's* return. Photo: H. Aschehoug & Co.

Nansen's new home at Lysaker, *Polhøiden*, subsequently Norwegianised as *Polhøgda*. Photo: University of Oslo Library.

Nansen with visitors at Sørkje in 1901. To his right, in front: Irmelin on the nursemaid's lap, Eva, Kåre and Eva's brother-in-law Thorvald Lammers. Behind, from left to right: Lydar, the groom, Eva's friend Anna Schøtt, Janette Myre, the cook-housemaid, Eva's sister Mally Lammers, Dr Jens Jenssen (the family doctor) and Thea Halvorsen. Photo: H. Aschehoug & Co.

Caricature of Nansen replacing King
Karl Johan on the equestrian statue
in front of the Royal Palace in
Christiania (by Andreas Bloch in
Korsaren, 1905). Photo: H.
Aschehoug & Co.

As Ambassador in London, Nansen was a devoted horseman, both in town and riding to hounds.
Photo: H. Aschehoug & Co.

The Norwegian Royal couple and Roald Amundsen (behind, to the left) being received by Nansen and his children at *Polhøgda*. Photo: H. Aschehoug & Co.

The Duchess of Sutherland by Charles Lallie. Photo: Courtesy of the National Portrait Gallery, London.

Marie Lewis was one of Nansen's many interesting female friends while he was Ambassador in London. Photo: Courtauld Institute of Art.

After the First World War, Nansen resumed contact with Kathleen Scott, the widow of the Antarctic explorer, Robert Falcon Scott. Photo: H. Aschehoug & Co.

Left to right: Sigrun Munthe, Anna Schøtt and Eva, c. 1900. A few years later, Nansen started an affair with Sigrun Munthe. Photo: University of Oslo Library.

Philip Noel-Baker, agent of Nansen's international activity and winner of the Nobel Peace Prize in 1959, pictured here with Nansen at *Polhøgda* in the 1920s. Photo: H. Aschehoug & Co.

Nansen and Amundsen at an open air meeting arranged by the Fædrelandslaget at the Akershus Castle in Oslo on 16 July 1926 - Amundsen's birthday. On the extreme left, partly obscured by Nansen, stands the chairman of the Fædrelandslaget, Joakim Lemkuhl. Photo: Cappelens Billedarchiv.

Nansen as national politician, delivering a speech in 1928 at an open air meeting as part of a campaign to stem the advance of communism. Photo: H. Aschehoug & Co.

47

From Storm to Calm

At midnight on 17 August, they set off again. Nansen lyrically depicted the scene:

> The sky was overcast ... but along the whole horizon to the north lay the most wonderful crimson, with gold tinted clouds, like a sunset...A wonderful night ... the water smooth as a mirror, not a piece of ice to be seen and ... the kayaks glided ... to the silent strokes of the oars. It was all like a trip in a gondola.

But not for long. They were making for another uncharted promontory to the south-west before striking out to sea and heading for Spitsbergen. The barometer was falling. The stillness turned eerie. After an hour or so, they were brought up by ice. Meanwhile, a headwind had sprung up. They went about, and ran for safety under land. On the way, they were attacked by another walrus. The pack ice came crowding in. Open water was not to be seen on any side and, as Nansen put it, 'all our hopes of a homecoming this year finally sank'.

They found a kind of haven on the ice at the eastern end of a gulf, also decidedly not on their map; and there they were stormbound for the best part of a week. To seaward, ice now crammed up against where they lay. Overland, there was no escape either. They were trapped. 'Courage is still there,' wrote Nansen in his diary, 'but hope, the hope of soon being at home, has long since vanished, and all that remains is the certainty of a long dark winter in these surroundings.'

'How the south coast of the country with Eira Harbour now seems a Land of Canaan,' Nansen ruefully declared. He meant a harbour discovered by Benjamin Leigh Smith. In 1880 and 1881 Leigh Smith, one of the wealthy, unassuming and enterprising English Arctic travellers of the age, had led (and paid for) expeditions to Franz Josef Land. Since Payer made the original discovery, Leigh Smith was the only one so far to have visited the place. He had done some exploration and considerably extended the survey. Nansen had his map of south Franz Josef Land. At Eira Harbour, Leigh Smith had built a hut – 'Eira Lodge' – and left supplies. Nansen was caught on an unknown coast, with food beginning to run out again.

Around midnight on 21 August, a Wednesday, a polar bear obligingly wandered up to the camp, was shot by Nansen, half asleep, through a tear in the tent wall, and thus once more removed anxiety about food. Meanwhile, however, they were still trapped by the wind, and haunted now by the spectre of being forced to winter where they were.

On the Friday, they finally went ashore to reconnoitre the coast off which they were camped. They found yet another ice cap, from under which a small patch of bare boulder-strewn earth escaped. It would make a passable wintering place. But the approach was through a chaos of floes rafted one upon the other in a geological upheaval. Neither man wished to set foot again on that particular shore. Ironically or not, Nansen dubbed it Helland's Foreland, after his patron on the first crossing of Greenland. Eira Harbour, as Nansen wistfully put it, 'has become the goal of our desires'.

Then, on the Saturday, the wind, having blown from the south-west for a week on end, hauled right round to the north-east. This was the much desired change. Now the wind was blowing off the land and there was the prospect of escape.

Nansen and Johansen moved over to another floe and a camp site closer to where open water might appear. Soon after, a lead did open, but on the landward side. Rapidly the dark band of open water widened. The wind rose to a gale, in a rough cadence roaring, shrieking, tearing at the ice, whipping up sheets of hissing spume high over the edge of the floe. There was no question of launching the kayaks. They were driving helplessly out to sea, in the clutches of the pack again.

They paced up and down the floe, talking through the clamour of the storm. But the wind was raging far more violently than ever before, and in the end they saw the futility of discussion. It was time to rest. But now when they yearned for hummocked ice as lee for the tent, there was none. They tried pitching the tent unprotected, but as quickly struck it when the storm threatened to tear its already ragged fabric to shreds. Finally, they lay down in their sleeping bag, with the tent spread over them, and snatched a few hours rest.

They were roused early on Sunday morning by a slight easing of the gale. Immediately they turned out and, leaving their camp site, beyond the range of the spray, hastened to the edge of the ice. A heavy sea was running, with high, white-topped waves. During the night they had driven far out to sea. Land was now well down on the horizon, perhaps ten miles off. The storm rose again with the same, or worse, violence than before. With the stirrings of despair, Nansen and Johansen felt they had to try and escape, come what may.

Driven by the wind, a stream of broken ice was crashing against the floe. For hours, Nansen and Johansen moved restlessly along the edge, seeking a safe place to launch their kayaks if they dared. Eventually they did. But the kayaks were down by the head because of all the bear meat.

47. From Storm to Calm

What is more they griped to windward. The combination meant that headway by paddling was minimal. So Nansen and Johansen returned to the ice, rigged up their old familiar catamaran, and put out under sail once more.

By now the storm was easing again. The wind was still north-easterly. Clasped in the kayak up to the waist, his eyes close to the waterline, Nansen could not see far ahead, but now and then to the south west, over the crest of a wave, through the driving spray, he glimpsed the headland he had been trying to reach for the past week. He had dubbed it Cape Athos, presumably after the first of Dumas' Three Musketeers. Anyway, it lay conveniently almost dead to leeward, so the catamaran could run before the wind.

There was a small difficulty when Nansen crowded on too much sail, and the vessel was almost dismasted. Eventually, he found the right amount of canvas. With a single reefed squaresail straining at a bamboo spar, the catamaran heaved through the spume over the choppy waves.

Nansen steered, with sail and oar: he had added small craft handling to his other acomplishments. Johansen was the lookout. He had to give warning of approaching seas, so that Nansen could let the vessel fall off, to avoid broaching-to and probably capsizing. It was, in Johansen's words, 'an entertaining voyage, and I must admit I was a little seasick'.

Nausea at least kept fear at bay. Between the men and the abyss was nothing but a frail film of canvas. The raucous sough of the wind, the hiss of the spume, the drumming of water on the hulls, the staccato flapping of the lee sheet; the whole cacophony of a gale seemed to mock the fragility of the craft. But all sailing is an act of faith. This was the hardest test so far. The kayaks were cramped but seaworthy even, as it turned out, *in extremis*. They were also spectacularly wet. Both men were very quickly soaked through. Neither cared because, as Nansen put it, 'at last we could say farewell to the ice where we had to leave our hopes of reaching home this year'.

Hour after hour under heavy low grey billows of scudding clouds, they sailed on, running before the wind. At last, on Sunday evening, they rounded Cape Athos. The wind also eased. Nansen kept on coasting through the night. Finally, in the small hours of Monday, the wind dropped altogether. In the deep twilight, Nansen and Johansen went ashore, beached their kayaks, and pitched their tent. After a hot meal – the first for over twenty-four hours – they crept into their sleeping bag, still dripping wet. Somewhere on a nearby cliff a bird colony kept up an incessant commotion, but Nansen and Johansen quickly fell into a deep sleep.

When they turned out in the morning, the weather had cleared. The view still bore no relation to Payer's map. That insisted that they had sailed over terra firma labelled Zichy Land, which was patently absurd. They were evidently among a string of islands. In the distance, to the south-east, yet another uncharted headland jutted out to sea. It lay in the general direction of Eira Harbour. Nansen and Johansen launched their kayaks and set off, first paddling, then sailing, then paddling again. To the south, the sky was ominously dark and stormy. The wind veered right round and they found themselves paddling in the teeth of a fresh, biting breeze. To seaward, they were threatened by the pack. The land ahead seemed thoroughly hostile. It was encased by a glacier with no haven in sight.

Astern lay a more promising strand. They went about and, in the evening, reached the shore at a point about ten miles south-east of their previous camp, on the same or an adjacent island. On landing, they were met by a polar bear – which they shot, flensed, and then cooked some of the meat for their dinner.

The date was 26 August. Eira Harbour was still at least a hundred miles off. The next day, and the day after that, contrary winds, and pack ice driven on shore, continued to block the way ahead. On 28 August, Nansen took a meridian altitude. That startled him into realising how low the sun was sinking. The season was on the wane. The prospect of Eira Harbour faded like a mirage in a dream. That day Nansen decided to stay where he was and start preparing for what Johansen called 'the third and worst polar night'.

It was a logical decision. What lay ahead was shrouded in uncertainty, but here they had stumbled on a good wintering place. Even if a better one was lurking round the corner, time was running out.

Nansen and Johansen needed food, fuel and shelter. They were on a narrow bridgehead of bare earth exposed by the ice. It had the form of a cove facing south, shut off on three sides by a glacier, and nestling on a fjord or sound. Stones and moss strewn over the ground offered building materials enough. There was plenty of game: polar bears prowled along the shore; walrus were basking on the ice; off shore the waters were seething with whole herds.

The same day that Nansen decided to winter where he was, a bear with her cub unsuspectingly came ashore off the ice and were quickly shot. Next day, Nansen and Johansen went hunting walrus. They began by doing so from their kayaks. What Nansen had learned in Greenland did not include that art. Tyros both, their dubious efforts descended into farce. The upshot was a carcass that sank and nine wasted bullets, including one that Nansen accidently discharged through the deck of his kayak. There was no more hunting from kayaks that day. Instead, they went after two walrus that had just climbed onto the ice foot.

Out of their element, the creatures were defenceless. One was instantly killed; the other merely wounded. In Nansen's words:

Despite the huge body and deformed appearance ... there was something gently pleading and helpless in the round eyes as it lay there, that one forgot both the devilish appearance and one's own need, and only sorrowed over it. It seemed mostly like murder. I put an end to it with a bullet behind the ear. But those eyes pursue me even now.

A wind now sprang up, breaking off the ice, and they were once again driven on a floe out to sea. Nansen had wisely insisted on bringing the kayaks along so that, after a battle with a maelstrom of ice, they were able to get back to land. But the carcasses had to be left behind.

Next day, however, they shot three polar bears. These animals had flung the kayaks around but luckily without serious damage. Two tried to escape by swimming, but Nansen and Johansen chased them in their kayaks, and drove them back on land. Better still, floating by the shore, they found the walrus that, the previous day, had cost so many bullets and been given up for lost. They towed it round to safety in a narrow open channel. Finally after a few days, on 2 September, they began the business of flensing.

The walrus was berthed where the glacier sloped gently down to the water, forming a natural ramp. Nansen proposed using it to bring the carcass ashore. That meant hauling a ton deadweight up the slope. A primitive block and tackle was improvised by running a rope under a strap cut in the hide of the walrus, and belaying one end to a small piece of wood from an old sledge driven into the ice. The other end of the rope was attached to half a discarded sledge runner which was used as a lever, pivoted in a socket hacked out of the ice some way up the slope.

While trying out the tackle, Nansen and Johansen were interruped by a lone walrus swimming up the channel driven, so it seemed, by curiosity. A bullet or two finished it off. They then returned to their lifting tackle. They found that they were not strong enough to haul the huge blubbery carcasses ashore. The only solution was to do the flensing in the water.

This was quite the most horrible work on the whole journey. Walrus hide may be inches thick. It is nature's armour plate. Proper tools were not available. Worse still, instead of simply peeling off the hide, they had to hoist the creature up. For that the lifting tackle came in useful. While one man lay on the carcass and cut away the hide, the other hauled at the lever to pull it off.

But at low water the walrus was grounded, and impossible to move. They had to wait for high tide to roll the carcass over and get at the other side. But the physical effort was not the real distress. Nansen and Johansen were quickly drenched in blubber and blood from top to toe. Their clothes soaked up the grease to add to the clammy detritus already absorbed, and cling to their skins, with the only prospect of a change in the indeterminate future.

The gulls meanwhile, in Nansen's words, 'had halcyon days'. In large flocks interminably screeching and squabbling, they descended on the offal strewn over the rocks. It was 'one of Nature's unpredictable caprices', he added, 'to make these birds so beautiful but give them such an awful voice.'

On the last day of August came the setting of the midnight sun, with premonitions of winter and an acute sense of the seasons passing by. Flensing the walrus never seemed to end. But after the best part of a week it was finally done. The reward was two walrus hides, a mound of meat and, most importantly, blubber enough for a stock of fuel.

With six bears and two walrus, there was the nucleus of a winter larder. Nansen and Johansen could now turn to the urgent question of shelter. Even before finally deciding to winter there they had thrown up a small stone shelter, roofing it with the silken fabric of their tent, spread over skis and bamboo sticks. By now the tent was threadbare and tattered, but this structure at least would not blow down. It was, however, horribly cramped. Johansen could just about lie full length, but Nansen's legs stuck out of the door. Nor could he even sit up properly. The wind whistled through the walls. They were half blinded by the smoke from their blubber lamp. They quickly called it The Hole. It was a very temporary shelter. At last, on 7 September, having finished flensing the walrus, they began on their proper winter hut.

They chose a place on level ground, with earth and moss, and close to their building material at the foot of a steep scree slope where the rock emerged from the glacier. In Nansen's words: 'From now on, every morning we could be seen going to our site like other workmen, with water can and gun.'

Both men understood that survival demanded balance and rhythm to their days. They could not afford physical or mental exhaustion. 'We learned patience,' in Johansen's lapidary words; 'it was what was required.' Instinct told them to work well within the limits of their strength. They had schooled themselves to eat regularly and, more important still, to drink enough. Even here, hunger was less deadly than thirst.

Above all, Nansen and Johansen gave the curious impression of being somehow at home. They knew now that they could truly live off the land. What is more, in building their shelter, they were not exactly improvising. They were following ancient lore, copying the primitive dry stone huts of the Norwegian uplands.

Again, they had hardly any tools. That merely seemed to enhance the impression of being masters of their surroundings. With their bare hands, they prised stones loose from the frozen ground. Their only implement was the same broken sledge runner which had done duty as the lever of their lifting tackle, and now served as an occasional crowbar. They then carried the stones painfully down the slope, one by one, and piled them up to form a rectangular wall about a metre high. They also dug down the same amount. A pick was made out of a walrus tusk lashed to a slat from a discarded sledge; a spade from a walrus shoulder blade fixed to a broken ski stick.

The walls were relatively simple. The roof caused rather more concern. For one thing, there was a dearth of driftwood. What is more, the land consisted of weathered basalt, a volcanic rock, with no convenient slabs to build a vault. The only alternative was to roof the hut with walrus hide. Providentially, soon after landing, Nansen had found a solitary log for a roof-tree.

The log was frozen solid among the scree a little way up from the beach. Its roots were still attached, and deeply embedded in the ground. It had to be cut free. The work fell to Johansen's lot. His only implement was what he called 'a microscopic little axe'. With that, he had to chip his way through a foot of close-grained fir. The work took him all day on 11 September. Next day, he and Nansen somehow rolled it up to the hut and, when the walls were finally finished, hoisted it into place.

Putting the roof on was even worse. The walrus hides had been cut in two, but were still heavy and cumbrous. Moving them up to the hut was difficult enough. But by now they they were frozen solid. Flattening them into shape was like trying to unbend steel.

Well into the second half of September, the work dragged on. The sun was low at midday now, quickly and forlornly sinking, by more than its own diameter every two days. The first snows had fallen. The birds were going south in droves. Winter was truly on the march. Even the polar bears had vanished. That worried Nansen, because he did not yet feel that he had stored up enough food and fuel.

This changed notably at the equinox. On that day, two polar bears appeared, one of which, with every sign of gastronomic glee, stood up against the hut and proceeded to nibble at the walrus hide on the still unfinished roof. It was felled for its pains. So too was its companion, which had fished up a walrus hide suspended in the sea water beneath the ice foot in order to thaw it out. Within the next few days, Nansen and Johansen shot three more bears; also two walrus, on the ice foot this time, so they were spared the misery of flensing in the water. All in all, they now had eleven bears and four walrus. That meant a ton or so of meat and blubber. It promised to last the winter.

Amongst other things, the new walrus meant extra material for the hut, as the hides were all long enough to reach from one side of the hut to the other. With generous overlap, they were stretched across the roof tree, then anchored with thongs attached to heavy stones lying on the ground, like the guys of a tent. In this way, the hides were drawn over the outside edges of the walls, and then fixed with stones laid along the top.

By 28 September the roof was finished at last. That same day, pausing to shoot an intrusive polar bear and add it to their winter store, Nansen and Johansen finally moved into their new home.

48

Like Robinson Crusoe

'One would not think that this was a human habitation,' Johansen observed in his diary.

> It is absolutely like [the] adventure books I read as a boy, and never had I thought that I would ever live a life like this, à la Robinson Crusoe, for that is what it is.

The new hut was exactly ten feet long and six feet wide; windowless and dark. Compared with the cramped little shelter from which they had just moved, it was palatial nonetheless. There was space to move about. Above all, under the roof-tree there was headroom. For the first time since leaving *Fram*, six months before, they had a place out of the wind where they could stretch their limbs.

Meanwhile, the sun was sinking lower and lower. On 15 October, it vanished beneath the horizon for the winter. Twilight lingered around the middle of the day, quickly dwindling to darkness at noon. The cold returned. Their third polar night had begun.

Driving snow piled up against the walls of the hut. Soon only the roof remained exposed, at about the level of the snowdrifts round about. Nansen and Johansen appeared to be living underground. There was no door to be seen, but a bearskin overhead in the snow like a hatch. It covered a shallow well that led down to an entrance in one corner of an end wall, closed on the inside, to form an airlock, by a bearskin curtain hanging from the roof. This entrance was so low, it was necessary to crouch in order to go through; the approach well was so constricted that one also had to squirm up or down virtually in the same movement. For Nansen, with his long back, it was notably inconvenient.

At the front of the hut, in the angle of the wall away from the entrance, they arranged their cooking corner. They built up a raised platform for blubber lamp and saucepans and, in the walrus hide of the roof above, cut a hole to let out the smoke. From bearskin, they made a hood to lead the smoke up to the hole. Clouds of lachrymatory smoke billowing back quickly showed the need of a chimney. On top of the roof, they built one out of snow and walrus bones. That drew splendidly, making thenceforth breathable the air within.

48. Like Robinson Crusoe

When the hut was built, the gaps between the stones had been plugged with moss and snow and strips of hide. At the start, it was draughty just the same. This was soon cured when the hut was mantled in snow, and the wind had packed the sand-like grains of drift into the finest crevices. On the floor, nonetheless, a cup of water froze. Rime frost encrusted the walls. To Nansen, however, it was 'warm and cosy'. For one thing, the radiant heat from the flames of the blubber lamps gave him a sensation of warmth. What he really meant was that, whatever the conditions, the lamps kept the air at the centre of the hut around freezing point. That was up to forty degrees warmer than outside.

The weak point in the hut was the roof. The heat from the blubber lamps naturally rose straight up, to thaw the walrus hides. As a result, they sagged and came apart at the edges, letting water drip down from the snow packed outside on the roof for insulation. The hides were stretched out again; but the only lasting solution was to line the ceiling with bearskin.

The bearskins that hitherto had served as a mattress were to be used. Before that, new pelts had to be brought in from the store outside and prepared as a replacement. That involved hanging them up to thaw, then scraping the blubber off; all inside the hut. Thereafter, the old sleeping furs were scraped clean. In Johansen's words:

> It was a swinish job to manipulate these ill-smelling furs, which were moulting ... from constantly lying on them.... It took a long time before we lined our ceiling, and it was intricate, but we managed somehow.

At least they had the satisfaction of securing food and shelter in good time. What they ate was manifestly nourishing. Of scurvy there was not a trace. The fresh meat saw to that. Their physical survival had been simple to prepare. Their sanity was another matter altogether.

They could not expect to continue their journey before April at the earliest. That meant dark months of concentrated boredom. The work on the lining of the roof had mercifully prolonged physical activity. Thereafter, the two men descended into a torpid routine.

Twice a day, they ate. The menu was invariable: boiled bear and soup in the morning, fried bear steak in the evening. Each man cooked alternate weeks. Over the blubber lamps hung a container cut from an old paraffin tank: it was the main task of the man off duty to keep this filled with ice in order to ensure plenty of drinking water. (Physical needs aside, thirst has various mental consequences; amongst them fretfulness and hence friction too.)

The man off duty also had to tend the lamps, to make sure that they never went out. The only other recurring work was reading barometer and thermometer outside, together with drying bearskins for clothes and a new sleeping bag. Inside the hut, along the top of each side wall, a ski was fixed by a pair of thongs; between these skis, the pelts were stretched after laboriously scraping off all blubber. It was a slow business; each lot had to remain for weeks before being taken down, and replaced by the next one. All this could not fill their days. 'It is not often that one writes in one's diary, in spite of our having little to do,' Johansen tellingly remarked, 'and for the most part we sleep to make time pass.'

That was not as easy as it sounds. When they moved in, both men had looked forward to sleeping on their own again. With blubber lamps burning, they expected the hut to be so warm that they no longer needed a double sleeping bag. At the back of the hut they had built up two raised single sleeping platforms. They split their sleeping bag into its two component blankets and used one each as a cover. The upshot was a miserably cold and sleepless first night. They quickly sewed up their double sleeping bag again and merged the separate sleeping platforms into one.

Their building material for these platforms consisted of big, knobbly stones. With the means at their disposal, it was a surface impossible to make smooth. They twisted and turned to find a comfortable position between the bumps. But they hurt all over, and eventually got bedsores. Nonetheless, with bearskins under them, and the return to animal warmth, they did contrive to sleep once more; sometimes halfway round the clock.

Like hibernating animals, they became dozy and lethargic. The only mark of the passage of time was each Tuesday, with the changing of the cook. Day and night coalesced into one. Outside was only the darkness of the polar night. Inside, the lamps burned without pause, casting a soft, yellow, oddly comforting light, in which the rime frost on the walls glittered like crystals in a cave.

It was not only in the torpor of the hut, week following monotonously upon week, that the diaries became irregular. Both Nansen and Johansen had ceased keeping one towards the end of August, when they were busy enough, but they finally realised that they would not get home that year. Since then, Nansen had kept a brief log; Johansen nothing at all. Eventually both men recommenced their diaries – Johansen on 17 November, Nansen ten days later.

While they were still building the hut, at least they had a new subject of conversation. They expatiated on how nice and comfortable it would be when they finally moved in. After they did so, there was little more to discuss. Nor did they have anything to read; their only printed matter was part of the Norwegian nautical almanac.

Cooped up in their lair, Nansen and Johansen recognised with greater force than ever how little they had in common. At home, they would never have come within each other's ambit. Here, despite all his tatters and grime, Nansen had maintained his awesome dignity. Nonetheless, they were saved from getting on each other's nerves. Obvious friction was absent from their diaries. Nansen continued studiously to avoid criticising

316

his companion; although sometimes there were obscure hints of self-restraint. One day, for example, when Johansen snored, Nansen wrote that

> the hut trembled. I am glad his mother can't see him now. She would certainly bewail her boy, black and dirty and ragged as he is, with sooty grime all over his face.

For his part Johansen, since his outbursts all those months before in the pack ice, now confined himself to only the most oblique of complaints, if indeed he voiced any at all.

Between repairing the gaps in their diaries, both men succumbed to bouts of philosophising on their predicament. 'What are we striving for? Immortality?' Nansen wrote one day, while the wind piped eerily outside. They also seized gratefully on anything, however trivial, that broke the monotony. There were, for example, the foxes on the roof.

They were arctic foxes, grey and silver, whose pelts, in civilisation, were much prized. They had a lair somewhere up near the glacier; much of the time they spent around the hut, padding over the roof, screeching, scuffling, gnawing away at bear carcasses so that the sound rang out in the hard, resonant, wind-packed snow; even cheekily peering down the chimney now and then. So far as they could, Nansen and Johansen preferred to live and let live, because this was company of sorts. Nor did they grudge the foxes a share of their plentiful meat. But when the blubber was attacked they were less amused, because they had none to spare. 'The fox plays us every trick he can,' so Nansen opened an impassioned chronicle of villainy.

> Blast it, he has made off with the harness we use to fix the hide that serves as a door and, believe it or not, we hear him at it again. Today, he made off with one of our sails, in which we kept salt water ice [for cooking] ... we plodded round in the darkness ... searching everywhere, but no sail was to be seen. In the end, we had almost given up hope, when Johansen ... found it down on the beach. But what did he want to do with it? To line his winter lair?... If only I could find that lair and retrieve the thermometer, ball of twine, harpoon line, and all the other precious things he has taken, the beast.

Early in November, when heavy footfalls on the roof, very different from the usual pattering of foxes, turned out to be the last bear of the season, Johansen wrote:

> When we emerged into the open, there was no bear in sight ... From the tracks we could see it was a little bear ... He was in a hurry, that fellow, when he saw that there was life underground.

Even Johansen's tolerant understanding was exhausted by the brazen depredations of the foxes. One or two were shot, but there were not enough bullets to spare for all. Johansen improvised a trap; first with a flat stone, then with a frozen walrus hide. In both cases, the trap was sprung, but the bait had vanished, together with the enterprising fox, or foxes. Johansen gave up.

During the first half of December, a particularly obnoxious gale swept out of the south-east, off the frozen fjord. With the personal malevolence peculiar to the wind, it blew one of the kayaks up into the scree, where it was luckily retrieved, and forced its way through the packing between the stones of the hut walls so that, in Johansen's words, 'the lamps flicker, and a breath of cold grips our haven'.

He wrote this while cooped up in the hut. Whenever the wind blew, they stayed inside, sometimes for a week or more, going out only when driven by necessity. Their windproof outer garments had to be saved for their journey onwards in the spring; their other clothes, being greasy, threadbare and torn, let the wind cut right through to the skin. When the wind dropped, they roused themselves sufficiently to go outside and stretch their cramped limbs on a short track beaten in the snow outside the hut. Under favourable circumstances, when the air was still, and the sky clear, 'one never tires of going up and down ... while the moon changes the whole of this world of ice to a fairytale', Nansen wrote.

> There lies the hut still in the shadow under the cliff, which looms up dark and menacingly overhead. But over the ice and the fjord the moonlight flows, and is thrown back gleaming from all the snow ridges.... A strange, Nirvana-like beauty, as if from another, extinct planet made of shining white marble ... and everything so silent, so frighteningly silent, like the great silence that will arrive one day, when the world will once more be desolate and empty, when not even the fox will move in this broken scree, nor the bear roam the ice out there ... still, still as the flames of the aurora.

On 21 December, with the dead months of autumn past, Johansen provided surrogate domesticity by a thorough housecleaning, scraping the ashes from the cooking platform and throwing out an accumulation of bones and scraps of meat left over from their meals since they had moved in. Best of all, he removed a thick layer of ice on the floor, congealed with a rich assortment of dirt.

This traditional Scandinavian pre-Christmas clean-out brought a sense of occasion. The sun was at its lowest, over the tropic of Capricorn. It was the winter solstice, the turn of the year. 'How well do I not understand the old custom of our forefathers in holding a grand celebration for the winter solstice, when the power of winter darkness is broken,' Nansen noted in his diary.

He had climbed out of the hut to allow Johansen to get on with his cleaning while he himself paced back and forth in a still and burning starlit night. The constellations intensified a sense of human insignificance and awe. 'There was a wonderful aurora,' Nansen recorded.

318

48. Like Robinson Crusoe

Is it the fire-Titan Surt himself that plucks at his mighty silver harp, so that the strings shiver and glitter? ... Here is the kingdom of the giants, here Surt rules the heavens, and the frost giants rule the earth. But some day they will sweep southwards, when Surt's hordes, circled by the flames of the aurora will sough through the air and in roaring winter storms the frost giants will ravage all countries – that will be the twilight of the Gods, the end of all things.

Seeing Jupiter, low over a ridge, Nansen at first called it 'Odin's shining eye', but then remembered: 'It is Eva's star, as if she is smiling at me. I feel as if my guardian spirit is around me.'

Have I become superstitious? This life and these surroundings almost make one so. When all is said and done, everyone is superstitious, each in his own way. Do I not have an impregnable faith in my star.... Do I not believe in a ... mission in the world? and I can never believe that death can approach before it is done – and just as well ... Superstition strengthens one's work ... perhaps it also has a mission in the world. Why eradicate it, we have scarcely anything else except a new superstition to put in its place.

So Nansen could write, in terms of Faustian striving. And so he could also write, sitting soon after in the hut:

Christmas is on the way, the season of joy. The meat cauldron is bubbling cheerfully on the stove. I sit here and stare into the flickering flames.... What is the strange power that fire and light have that all creation seeks them, from the microscopic piece of slime in the ocean to the wandering human child that stops ... to make a fire in the forest?

Pagan fire worship and the Nordic Christmas are easy to confuse. 'Involuntarily these piercing tongues of flame seize one's attention,' Nansen continued. 'One stares into them as if one could read one's fate.' He pursued a fantasy of Eva and their daughter, Liv, at home:

In the lamplight [Eva] sits on winter evenings and sews a child's dress. By her side, a lovely little girl with blue eyes and blond hair.... She looks tenderly at the child ... but her eyes become moist and heavy tears fall on its hair.

49

The Nordic Penelope

Less than a month before those words were written Eva had gone on a concert tour of Sweden, and the previous year she had wrenched herself away from her home by the fjord to give recitals in Copenhagen – her first public performances abroad. On each occasion, she showed no compunction in leaving her child behind.

Liv had turned out sickly. It seemed to be a matter of keeping her alive until Nansen returned. Eva left her in the care of a girlhood friend, demanding a daily telegram with a bulletin on the child's health. Without this, she would not sing.

Her repertoire included a Swedish folk song, one verse of which ran:

> I do not wish to pine away,
> But just the same I do.
> Surely he'll come back to me,
> In a year or two.

This was blatantly playing to the gallery; but except when it suited her on the concert platform she took care not to act the romantic, sorrowing steadfast wife. Even before her own mother, she exercised self-control. She entertained regularly, almost in defiance of the seclusion forced on her while Nansen was at home.

Hardly surprisingly, she was rumoured to have a lover. One candidate was a certain Herman Major Schirmer, an old friend from her past whom she continued to see regularly. His appearance as a guest in 1895 at her Midsummer party, one of her regular events, probably helped to stoke the fire. Another was Eivind Astrup, who came home prematurely from Peary's Greenland expedition in the autumn of 1894 and in January 1896 was found dead at the start of a lone ski tour in the Rondane mountains in Central Norway. The circumstances were mysterious, but hinted at suicide. At his funeral in Christiania there was a wreath from Eva, or so it was said in the press and out of this was spun a story with the element of folk tale, that Astrup killed himself because he had dared to make love to the wife of a national hero.

Publicly Eva tolerated the journalists who now regularly turned up to interview what one of them – a German – called 'the Nordic Penelope'. 'I believe in my husband's return,' she told him, 'but not now. It's too soon.' Privately, Eva was irked by the rumours now beginning to circulate. The first had appeared in April 1894 via the Paris newspaper *Figaro*. It suggested, with a touch of circumstantial detail, that Nansen had actually reached the Pole. So too, the next month, did a telegram from a telegraph official in Finland to King Oscar II:

NANSENS BALLOON LANDED TAMMERFORS ATTAINED NORTH POLE 14 JULY 94 ALL WELL GOOD STATE OF HEALTH

That was quickly unmasked as an April Fool's trick. Then another telegram was sent to Eva from a police chief in Northern Norway on 11 September 1895:

HAVE SENT TWO NOTES DISCOVERED SIGNED NANSEN EX-TRACTED FLOATING BOTTLE SENT FROM NORTH POLE FIRST NO-VEMBER HOPE GENUINE CONGRATULATIONS

Away in the Arctic that same day, *Fram* was finally crossing the 85th parallel. It had taken more than six months to cover this last degree north. Since Nansen had left, however, latitude no longer counted. Getting home was the concern. Longitude was what mattered now. It was not the slow northing that had made the summer hard to bear but the lack of movement to the west, for that way was escape. Since late June, *Fram* had hovered around the eightieth meridian east.

Appropriately or not, Nansen's birthday on 10 October proved to be the turning point. Soon thereafter *Fram*, as if given a push by an unseen hand, arbitrarily resumed her westwards drift. Scott Hansen's sorties every other day to squint through his theodolite at this star or that became more than mere routine. On 27 November there was an air of expectancy. During a brief gap in falling snow he managed to get an observation. His shipmates were waiting impatiently in the saloon for the result. There was cheering when it came, followed by a salute of guns, and a round of celebration.

The reason for all this was that they had passed what Scott Hansen called 'the epoch making' longitude of 60°E. For one thing, that was the meridian of Khabarova, *Fram*'s last port of call, two long years before. With hot punch, Sverdrup proposed a *skål* for the meridian and, as Amundsen recorded the proceedings, 'welcomed us back to the domains of civilisation, which he assumed he could say, since Khabarova ... had both houses and churches'.

In little over a month, *Fram* had covered twenty degrees of longitude. The log line hanging through a hole in the ice (constantly kept open) showed that she was still drifting to the west. What is more, she was now on her way south as well. Nonetheless, leaving aside the bout of rejoicing, the atmosphere on board was peculiarly subdued.

Sixty degrees east was also (roughly) the meridian of Cape Fliguely on Franz Josef Land. That meant in turn, to those on *Fram*, that they had covered the unknown Arctic quadrant, of which the New Siberian Islands were the eastern limit. 'Our task has been accomplished,' as Nordahl wrote in his diary, 'now it's just a matter of getting home safe and sound.'

Any vestigial feeling of adventure had long since disappeared. Early in September, the last narwhals vanished, followed by the last birds which, as Sverdrup put it, 'had swarmed around us during the short summer and awaked our longings. Now they fled towards South, towards sun and light and pleasant coasts, while we remained up in the ice for yet another winter.'

The sun set for the winter at the beginning of October; by now continual darkness had descended once more. The men were settling down to their third polar night with a sense of resignation and routine.

All along, Sverdrup had demonstratively been improving preparations for the worst – in case, after all, they had to abandon ship. Most recently he had reorganised the supply depots put out in readiness on the ice. He split them up into small circular mounds, so arranged that, even if the ice split under one, the loss would be confined to two packing cases. Thus Sverdrup banished any lingering sense of insecurity. The air temperature dropped once more to twenty and thirty degrees of frost, but inside the ship it remained pleasantly warm. Scurvy still being absent, there was no fear of disease. After two years these men were still healthy, well-fed, comfortable and safe. In the tortured history of Arctic exploration, that in itself was an achievement.

But nobody on board any longer saw it in those terms. Few gave a thought to the fact that they were about to break a record by wintering at a higher latitude than anyone else before and, with the sun absent for a full five months, undergoing the longest polar night. Spared the necessity of having to fight danger, the men on *Fram* found themselves fighting monotony instead.

Sverdrup attacked ennui where he could. In that respect he was confronted with a distasteful problem. When Blessing, as he noted in his medical journal, began injecting himself with morphine after Nansen's departure, he thought that he had gone undetected. Such turned out not to be the case. On 17 November, Sverdrup recorded in his diary that Blessing had become an addict. That it was the doctor himself, made it doubly worrying. 'I have taken charge of all morphine,' Sverdrup wrote, but added: 'This evening he was so bad that I had to let him have a little dose so that he could sleep.'

> It is horribly irresponsible of [Blessing] to start this sort of thing under the circumstances in which we are living. If anything should happen to the ship,

he could bring ... the expedition ... into dire straits. He will no longer have access to morphine, except in cases of illness, but always under my supervision.

Sverdrup was now extra vigilant. Soon after, on 20 November, he ordered daily exercise: two hours of skiing, or walking round a circuit on the ice. Amongst other things, it got everyone out of the confines of the ship. The dogs, however, of whom there would soon be eighteen on board, were the principal diversion. On 20 October Susine had her second litter, two dogs and nine bitches. She was allowed to keep both dogs and one bitch; the rest were put down. For men deprived of the company of women the act of parturition, and small furry pups to fondle, were once more a grain of consolation.

Nothing however could remove the dead weight of boredom and isolation. The men longed for the sight of life from the outside, even the company of polar bears. But except for one distant sighting in August there had been none for a year. There was no longer even the break in routine with the changing of the cooks. Juell and Petterson had been alternating every fortnight, but on 10 September Petterson, at his own request, took over permanently. For one thing he liked the galley as a refuge from his shipmates.

This third winter was a parody of those that had gone before. As then, the men sat round the saloon evening after evening, but now without even the intermittent solace of electric light. What remained was the yellow flame of paraffin lamps. Without the windmill, no longer was there the cheerful grinding of the gears to turn the generator. Silence had descended, broken only by the eerie creak of the ship's timbers, the periodic clink of cutlery, and the subdued sounds of men trying not to irritate each other.

At least, with a library of six hundred volumes, there was plenty to read. There was also escape in skiing off away from the ship. But underlying all, there ran the oppressive sense of not being masters of their own fate. Wind and current were the arbiters of this world.

The men on *Fram* were prey to shifting moods, dictated by the drift. 'You cannot conceive how fed up we are with each other,' Scott Hansen was moved to observe. 'It has got to the point where we can hardly stand the sight of each other.'

Alone among them, Sverdrup displayed no moodiness and, despite periodic grumbling, notably over his insistence on saving fur clothing for an emergency, continued to command the respect of all his men. One way or another, he managed to reconcile them to the need to wait patiently on natural forces and to prevent ennui spilling over into something worse. For months there had been none of what Amundsen called 'Viking battles'. As Christmas approached, Scott Hansen, probably the most articulate of the men on board, wrote:

Everything is running more smoothly since Nansen left, and some of the spirit of division which we suffered in the beginning has died down.... It is strange how bitterness fades with the passage of time, giving way to the preservation of memories of pleasanter things. There was a time when I hated Nansen to such an extent that I almost dare not think of it, but now that feeling has faded to a memory, vague as a fog, of a dark period, and has given way to an ordinary, polite sympathy, which makes me concentrate on the good aspects.

A week or so later, in the winter hut, 250 miles due south, Johansen was blandly writing in his diary: 'On New Year's Eve Nansen proposed that we begin to say [the familiar] "you" to each other. Which was gratifying.' These were men who had shared the same sleeping bag for three quarters of a year and still did not use Christian names. Even now, it was only a half-way house: surnames combined with the familiar 'you'. Until Nansen unbent they had continued with the polite form of address.

50

Onward to Spitsbergen

Nansen, writing on that same New Year's Eve, felt that 1895 had brought 'both success and setback, but when all is said and done it was really a good year'.

And the next day:

> Now 1896 has arrived, the year of happiness, the year of homecoming. In bright moonlight 95 went out; in bright moonlight 96 begins.

But on 8 January, his daughter Liv's third birthday, he was reporting:

> A violent storm outside ... so that one nearly loses one's breath as soon as one puts one's nose out of the door.... One throws oneself from the one side to the other, stretching one's legs to get a little warmth in one's frozen feet, and wishes just one thing, to be able to sleep. Thoughts turn incessantly homewards, but my long, heavy body lies here and I try in vain to find a tolerable position between the stones.

The tables in the Nautical Almanac showed meanwhile that the sun was now appreciably retreating from the tropic of Capricorn, and thus really on its way back. The homeward journey moved from imagination to reality. By their own efforts, Nansen and Johansen would have to move. Fatalistic brooding receded.

The change began at Christmas. On Christmas Eve, they celebrated by varying their everlasting diet of meat with some of their sledging rations: 'Fish meal, a little bread, chocolate,' ran Johansen's catalogue of the feast. 'Two portions of Knorr's dried soup, it's not so bad after all.' And again on Christmas Day: 'We are content with what we have, and are pleased with life to the point that many a social eminence at home might envy us.'

He also recorded their walk on the occasion, 'in weather we will long remember and which we will never see again another Christmas.'

> The whole sky was on fire with the Northern Lights that, like a whirlwind, flew over the zenith in all possible colours.... To the South, the Moon was shining ... the wind had fallen.... The temperature was reasonable, around –30°C. I felt quite uplifted as I walked up and down in this wonderful weather. Ah moonlight, this wonderful Arctic moonlight that makes everything so soft and peaceful, as if it is caressing Nature.

On Christmas Eve he had put his outer shirt innermost, and the inner one outside. Nansen followed his example. He also cut off some of his hair, sitting up awkwardly in the sleeping bag. Nansen, however, let his now dark, greasy locks hang down to his shoulders and grow on. However, he changed underpants and, as he wrote in his diary, 'put on the other, which I had rinsed in warm water, and I have also washed myself with $\frac{1}{4}$ cup of warm water using the discarded underpants as sponge and towel'.

On Boxing Day Johansen patched one of his trouser knees with bear-skin. Then, over the New Year, enough bearskins had finally been cured for work to start on a new sleeping bag. Nansen did most of the sewing. Thread there was none so, like the Eskimos, he used sinews taken from bear carcasses. In the third week of January, the sleeping bag was finished.

It was notably warmer than the thin blanket bag with which they had been making do for the past six months. That meant that they could now sleep without trousers. They could also dispense with most of the wrappings on their feet. After nearly a year with all clothes on day and night this was a great step forward. For Nansen, it was a considerable relief. He – but not Johansen – had open sores from the constant clinging of greasy underclothes. Now he treated them with moss as a sponge dipped in a drop of warm water.

After Liv's birthday, Nansen's diary became sporadic once more. For weeks he kept the barest of logs. It was hardly more than a record of the weather. Johansen alone persevered with a regular, comprehensive, although not exactly a daily, journal. On 1 February, Nansen interrupted a long hiatus with a short, single entry:

> Outside, little by little, it is becoming lighter; day by day the horizon is growing more strongly red over the glaciers to the south.... Spring is on the way.... Often I have found Spring melancholy ... but there is no melancholy in this Spring. Its promise will be kept. Otherwise it would be too horrible.

Nansen also recorded that he was now crippled with lumbago. For a fortnight he was bedridden. Johansen became cook, attendant and nurse, night and day. On 11 February, Nansen was well enough to take over the cooking once more. That day Johansen, in his own words, 'shook the dust of the hut from my feet.' Taking his rifle in case of bears, he walked over the hard, wind-packed snow to climb a hillock under the glacier hanging over them, in order to see something else than 'the hut's four ice-bound walls'.

Though Nansen's illness had delayed preparations for the homeward journey, Johansen nonetheless had managed to make a start. He had dug out the meat store, which had been buried in a hard, wind-packed snow-drift, so as to establish what was left. To make new mittens and leggings he had also dug out a suitable bearskin, scraped it clean, and hung it up inside to dry.

By now, they were seriously debating their journey and had, once more, a subject of genuine conversation. The question was whether to continue south, or strike out westwards towards Spitsbergen. Or had they been on Spitsbergen all the time? They wistfully talked of the comfort of being on *Fram* and knowing precisely their position. They knew how far they were from the Equator to within a mile or two – 81°17'N – but their distance from the Greenwich meridian remained a matter of perplexity. Nansen had taken observations for time, but without the proper tables, he could not work them out. After ten months, the running down of their watches out on the pack ice was haunting them still.

On 25 February, the first birds reappeared. They were little auks winging their way over the ice to the south on the way northwards up the coast. Two days later, the sun appeared again for the first time after five long months: the upper limb of the orb breaking the horizon, albeit briefly, at midday, and veiled by clouds of snow. The sight perversely threw Johansen into another dark outburst about 'spending the best days of one's life up here'.

> One feels bitter and depressed now and then, it is not easy to be happy all the time. Monotony has told on both of us ... we both have our dark moments – If we did not have the certainty of returning to the world, this existence would be unbearable.

But Nansen, was cheerful. He had

> discovered that it was possible to get 12 threads from a piece of string, and I am happy as a young god, now we have enough sewing thread, and our wind clothes will be whole again. We can also unravel the cloth in our bags.

On 8 March, a Sunday, Johansen decided on a further spring cleaning. He gathered the detritus strewn about the hut, including the skull and backbone of a bear, preparatory to throwing them out. Then he crawled into the entrance well, and began opening the trapdoor overhead. As usual, it had been jammed by drifting snow. As usual, too, much heaving was needed, before the frozen hide was finally dislodged.

When Johansen got his head into the open, he was met by the sight of a huge polar bear, blinding white after the gloom inside. There followed a hectic sequence of events. Johansen tumbled back, seized his rifle – which hung loaded from the ceiling – and dashed out into the well again. He took aim, but forgot to cock the hammer, and then found the muzzle choked with old bear fur. The bear, meanwhile, evidently astonished by the sight of movement from underground, was trying to get in. Its paws were already halfway down the well. Johansen held out his rifle, pointed it upwards, like an artillery piece, and, at last, fired a shot. A howl announced he had found his mark. The bear hastily withdrew and lumbered off, leaving a trail of blood, with Johansen in hot pursuit. Eventually he got within range, down on the beach. He fired and the bear fell. Having no more ammunition, he started back towards the hut.

Nansen, meanwhile, who had been contentedly sewing in the sleeping bag, tumbled out with rifle, ammunition and knife (with a file for sharpening). Along the way, he met Johansen, who continued back to fetch the sledges. Nansen went on, as he thought, to begin the flensing. He found the supposedly dead bear making off into the distance. There followed a long chase, the bear periodically turning round and stretching its neck to observe its pursuer. Nansen was hampered by deep soft snow and no skis. At one point, he found himself on a glacier tongue, falling up to his waist in a crevasse. Finally he drew level. By now the bear was high up under a cliff, at the head of a steep scree, none too sure-footed, and out of range. Nansen fired nonetheless. The bear was evidently startled, fell, and, frantically clawing, tumbled down the scree, coming to rest, lifeless at last, close by. Eventually Johansen returned with the sledges. In the fury of the chase they had gone far from the hut, impervious to a violent southerly wind. Luckily it was relatively mild – only –2°C. Their bag was a huge male bear, too heavy to drag back against the wind in one go. So they took half, leaving the remainder to be fetched later. By now the short Arctic spring day was past. It was a long haul back to the hut in the dark over the sea ice, and they finally arrived at midnight, worn out after twelve hours of unwonted exertion. But, in Nansen's words,

> how good was it not … to stretch out in the sleeping bag and savour one's supper of fresh bear meat and warm soup. We haven't done that for a long time.

About a week later, on 14 March, came the first anniversary of leaving *Fram*. It was, as Johansen put it, 'a year full of deprivation, exertion, trouble and suffering; a year that will mark one for the rest of one's life'. But, he went on, it had also been 'an instructive year [which] has been good for my future life'. Each in his own way, both men were considerably uplifted.

For one thing, the hunt had enabled them to wash their hands properly for the first time since the previous autumn. For want of soap, the specific was fresh bear's blood and blubber dried off with moss. What is more, there was now plenty of fuel for 'Primus the second', as they called the blubber lamps. With unsticky fingers, and lamps burning as long as they wished once more, Nansen and Johansen were full of rising zeal.

Among other things, they seriously started laundering their underwear by boiling it (in their saucepans) over the blubber lamps. After various frustrating trials, the only way of removing the grease turned out to be scraping it off with a knife while the garments were still warm. As a measure of economy, the detritus was added to the fuel in the lamps. Then they turned cobbler and resoled their ski boots. They used walrus hide, pared to the right thickness, and dried over a blubber lamp. The windproof garments, ragged, weatherworn and rotting, were painstakingly repaired; patch upon patch.

Above all, they desperately needed new outer clothes to replace their greasy rags. After much measurement and juggling, it appeared they could get a pair of breeches and a smock each out of the blankets from the discarded sleeping bag. It was a nerve-racking moment when the scissors were applied. But the cutting succeeded. Week after week, Nansen and Johansen sat up in the sleeping bags sewing with increasing dexterity. At times it was quite enjoyable plying the needles in and out, while the wind whined outside.

Thus the months passed, the sun rising higher every day. In the middle of April, the midnight sun returned. The birds had also come back in force. Silence was dispelled once more by incessant cackling and twittering. The foxes had deserted the hut for the lusher fields of the nesting cliffs nearby. They were replaced by the considerably more annoying gulls, drumming on the roof at all hours. Polar bears, the true harbingers of spring, regularly appeared. After shooting the third one early in May Nansen and Johansen had to drive them off. By now they had plenty of meat and blubber. Wanton killing, besides wasting ammunition, was repugnant to both. At one point a she-bear intruded, with a tiny cub suckling her. Nansen had great trouble persuading her, with warning shots, that he would prefer her elsewhere. His reward was a long bout of snarling and hissing but eventually she disappeared, pushing her cub before her to safety.

Meanwhile the weather moderated, and the temperature crept up until, by the beginning of May, it reached the spring-like levels around –10°C. On the twelfth of the month the new suits were finished, the breeches lined with old underpants and shirts.

All too human, Nansen and Johansen were involved in a last-minute rush. Nansen, now adept with needle and thread, was furiously sewing a light travelling sleeping bag of thin bearskin. Johansen's kayak had to be repaired and waterproofed with blubber. The stumpy sledges posed a problem. In rough pack ice, they would pitch like a cranky ship, damaging the kayaks. Out of scraps of driftwood and bearskin, Johansen improvised high cradles to keep the kayaks clear. Lashings were raw thongs of bearskin and walrus hide. Food for the journey was another obstacle. Most of the sledging rations had turned mouldy. It was too cold and damp to dry meat. Fresh meat would have to be taken and cooked along the way. So blubber was rendered down; three tins full, a long and disagreeable process. A light travelling blubber lamp was contrived out of the tank of the Primus stove. The rifles were overhauled and lubricated with rendered blubber. Ammunition was tallied, to reveal that they still had 100 rifle bullets and 110 shotgun cartridges, so that in Nansen's words: 'We could winter for several more years, if necessary.' Sails were scraped clean of blubber and soot.

At last, on 19 May, after many a postponement, they were finally ready to start. Their skis, sticks and kayak oars had been kept in the hut; now they opened the roof, and extracted the precious implements. Once more they stood on their skis down on the sea ice, harnessed to their sledges. In their homemade clothes, with long, greasy hair and white eyeballs staring out of soot-grimed faces, they more than ever resembled savages. As backdrop to their departure lay the tumbled scree, the domed glacier, the basalt cliff weathered like the pinnacles of a grotesque Gothic cathedral that had been the wild scene of their wintering. The interminable chattering of sea birds made a farewell chorus.

Their last act was to photograph the squalid lair that had been their home for nearly eight months of their lives. From the roof tree, Nansen hung the pump from the Primus, containing a short résumé of their journey since leaving *Fram*, and their further plans: 'We are going south west, along the land, to cross over to Spitsbergen.'

At seven in the evening, Nansen and Johansen heaved on their ski sticks and, with few regrets, set off.

51

Lucky Escapes

The sledges seemed grotesquely hard to haul. A winter of inactivity had left Nansen and Johansen out of condition, and that first day, therefore, to avoid overstraining themselves, they only travelled for an hour or two.

Among other things, they wanted to try out their new camping arrangements. Their tent had long since disintegrated. Their idea was to place their sledges, with kayaks, parallel to each other a man's height apart, pile snow underneath, lay skis and bamboo poles across the kayaks as a roof support, and then drape their sails over the top, so that they hung down on both sides to the ground, like the end walls of a tent.

This proved now to be a usable shelter. Well content, they crawled into their sleeping bag. It was, in Nansen's words, 'such a happy feeling to know that we were at last once more on the move and that now we were really homeward bound'.

They were making for the headland to the south-west that they had been trying to reach the previous August when forced to turn. Ever since, that spit of land had haunted them. They called it the Cape of Good Hope, because on the other side they believed in better things. Late in the evening of 21 May, they finally arrived. The Cape of Good Hope turned out to be a bare rock ridge jutting out of a glacier. They had taken three days to cover a mere twelve miles, but they were still limbering up and, as Nansen put it, 'hope did not fail us, we have open water straight ahead'. Next day, he expected to launch the kayaks and sail on.

Instead, a blizzard roared out of the south-west, and they had to stay where they were. While they were lying in the sleeping bag making breakfast a polar bear passed by, a few yards off, hardly giving them a second glance. It was up wind and could not get their scent, even helped by the fragrant reek of cooking. It was an easy shot, but the men did not need the meat, so they let the animal go in peace. This was the one incident all day that either Nansen or Johansen deemed worth recording.

Hopefully, they prepared for sea, restowing the kayaks and caulking the seams with candlewax. Around noon on 24 May, the third day weatherbound off the cape, and a Sunday, the wind fell and hauled to the east. Nansen broke camp, heading for an island off Hope Point to the west, and open water beyond. They rigged sails on the sledges, and skied off merrily before the wind. It was a deceptive lull. After an hour or two, the wind backed west again, until it was almost dead ahead. Dirty weather was in the offing. They had to furl sails, unstep the masts and, by main force, haul up wind on skis for land. Nansen was ready first and impetuously set off alone. At a certain point he found himself slowly sinking through mushy snow like quicksand that masked a crack in the ice. He had left his bindings closed, so that he could neither kick off his skis nor lift them up through the clinging brash. He could not move. He was trapped. Luckily for him, he managed to drive the spike of his ski stick into solid ice and stop himself sinking further than his waist. Patiently he waited for Johansen to catch him up and help.

Johansen, meanwhile, was securing his mast and sails preparatory to setting off. He did see Nansen stop and fall, but assumed it was a familiar case of skis slipping backwards on a hummock. He finished his work, and put on his skis but, in his own words:

> Nansen lay on the same spot. How strange that he did not get up and carry on! Now I heard him shout. So I rushed off … and quickly reached him and found that he … could not move, but was sinking deeper into the mushy snow … I placed myself gingerly on the edge of the crack, got a good grip of his Iceland jersey, and pulled him up … Thus we learned not to go with ski bindings closed in such ice.

Somewhat shaken, and wiser, they carried on with extra care. In the small hours of Monday, without further mishap, they reached land under a glacier front at the northern tip of the island. There they camped – just in time, as it turned out. Dirty weather laced with sleet and rain blew up from the south, and kept them camp-bound for day after day. For company they had herds of walrus – 'those hateful beasts', Johansen called them – basking on the shore. Wherever they went around the camp, tusked heads popped up grotesquely through cracks in the ice to glare at them, almost inducing a sense of persecution.

On 28 May, during another short-lived lull, they moved their camp a mile or two round to the southern end of what Johansen called 'this accursed island' in order to be closer to open water. But foul winds kept them weatherbound still. One day, Nansen walked over the island, which turned out to be flat, with gravel plains. He found traces of geese, so dubbed it Goose Island, having first loosely called it Hope Island. In the same way, on rounding the uttermost point of the land opposite, across a narrow sound, and finding it to be of basalt pillars, the shape prompted him to call it The Citadel.

Nothing fitted Payer's map, so Nansen was bound to name what he took to be his discoveries. Gathering signs of islands sweeping south, added to perplexity over longitude, confirmed Nansen in his old nagging doubts over whether this was really Franz Josef Land. He veered round to the belief that all the time they had been on an unknown archipelago between Franz Josef Land and Spitsbergen. In the message left behind at the winter hut he suggested he had been on Giles Land (now White Island, at the north-eastern tip of Spitsbergen). All this only served to intensify the feeling of uncertainty that had been gnawing at them for so long.

For once, under this cumulative strain, Johansen was the more emotional in his diary. Thus on 2 June:

> The month of May is past, and we have got nowhere. [For] about 2 weeks we have been pinned down by storms at the start of our journey. It is miserable. Our stock of meat is used up, and we have only a little cooked meat left. It is bad enough to lie in a wet sleeping bag day after day in a miserable tent and melt one's way deeper into the snow ... while the storm forces drift snow through the tiniest opening, so that it sweeps like ocean spray over the bag ... But to know that one cannot advance, while time passes, and summer goes by ... to feel imprisoned here in the unknown, while longing causes one's heart to thump in one's chest – that feels heavy after having lived in this desert of ice for over a year like beasts, and not like human beings.

Nansen for the moment had a different cause of worry. 'If only I need not worry about Fram,' he wrote on that same date. 'If she arrives before us, then poor Eva.'

By now, in fact, the wind was easing and hauling round from the south. Next day, 3 June, it was blowing northerly. The fair wind had arrived. Nansen and Johansen could finally escape the dismal promontory – but not by sea as they had hoped. The storms had driven the pack up against land. They had to travel over the ice as usual.

It was not exactly a punishment. They rigged sails on their sledges, lashed bamboo poles to steer, got on their skis and drove off southwards, more or less effortlessly, before a following wind. The going was of an undesirable spring type. That is to say, the weight of the snow depressed the thawing ice beneath to the point where water was forced onto the surface. That meant clinging wet snow and skis disinclined to slide. Nothing, however, could destroy the violent relief of being on their way again or, for that matter, the exhilaration of skiing. Following a low coastline to the east, they skied for some hours and finally camped off a high basalt cliff, loud with nesting guillemots. It was the first time on the whole tour that these birds had appeared in quantity. To both men, it suggested the approach of familiar territory.

Meanwhile, they were running out of food. They wanted a bear. But bears, perversely, there were now none. Walrus, however, continued littering the ice. So as a last resort they shot one near their camp. There followed a little black comedy. The demise of one of their number disturbed the herd not at all. Nansen and Johansen tried to drive them off; the walrus merely showed their displeasure by hacking with their tusks on the ice. By dint of much screaming and beating, they were finally persuaded to move, and sluggishly humped themselves into the water. 'But while we proceeded to carve up their companion,' wrote Nansen, 'they popped up again in a row along the crack, grunted, and crept half up onto the ice, as if demanding an explanation.'

After a long diet of bear meat, the much loathed walrus was even more repulsive than either Nansen or Johansen remembered from their earlier sampling. After so long with meals the high point of the day, they had entered a gastronomic wasteland.

Their travel, by contrast, happily improved. By the following day, 4 June, the wind had veered round to due north. The going got better. They swept off merrily before the wind, skis and sledges skimming over compacted snow. Their sole concerns were to keep the wind exactly astern, to hold their skis together and, because it was misty, which flattened contours, to look out for obstacles and unexpected dips in the snow. Most of the time they simply leaned back effortlessly on the bamboo tiller to stop the sledges overrunning. All night they swept along until, in the small hours, open water appeared. With great relief they launched their kayaks for the first time since leaving the winter hut. With flotillas of seabirds bobbing on the wavelets for company they rowed on.

After an hour or two, they were brought up by ice barring their way to the south. By now it was well into the morning, and they had advanced ten miles at least. It was time to rest. They landed on the ice and camped under a peculiarly uninspiring table land jutting out into the sea ice.

In the early hours of 6 June, they were ready to continue. Westwards, open water ran on into the unrelenting mist. That way – perhaps – lay Spitsbergen. The temptation, therefore, was to turn and sail on. Both men, however, were now gripped by doubt. For one thing, the still northerly wind was whipping up an unattractive sea. They argued too that, southwards, they might find a short cut to Spitsbergen. Beneath the rationalising some obscure instinct probably made up their minds for them. Whatever it was, they decided to return to the ice and carry on southwards.

The fair wind held. Day after day they drove on. Loose squaresails on single spars suggested Viking ships in the half-world between land and sea. The air was full of the chattering of sea birds. The going ran the gamut from the coarse-grained slush of spring mush to hard winter crust. In the squalls, the equipages wafted along like feathers in a breeze. In the shifting kinds of snow the men had their work cut out to keep control of their skis. To complicate matters, each had only one whole ski left.

They presented a striking contrast: Nansen, tall and heavy, with a wide-brimmed felt hat turned down the wrong way like a sou'wester; Johansen, short, compact, head always covered by the hood of his anorak. It was usually Johansen, the lighter in weight and the better gymnast by far, who sailed far ahead. For a whole week, they swept continually on, time disjointed by the midnight sun filtering through clouds. Over the horizon to starboard loomed a glacier-covered land; low promontories punctuated by skerries and frozen sounds drifted by to port.

On 12 June, they were crossing a wide strait. Early in the morning, having travelled all night, they came to open water for the first time since their short crossing eight days before. Without hesitation, they launched their kayaks, contrived their familiar catamaran and drove on, their sails billowing in a fresh breeze dead astern. It was a wet passage, but neither man cared. They rounded a promontory for which they had been steering and found themselves sailing westwards along a low, undulating, ice-bound shore to starboard. The weather had now lifted. To port, there was no more land in sight. In Nansen's words, 'at last we are on the south coast of the land we have been in for so long'.

Still they did not know where they were. Nansen had for some time begun to suspect that they were on Franz Josef Land after all. He was now confirmed in his belief when the coastline along which they were running seemed to agree with Leigh Smith's chart. Johansen invoked Payer's map and begged to disagree. Goaded by uncertainty they sailed on, without any desire to rest. Towards evening the wind dropped. Finally, after nearly four hours on the way, they lay to at the ice foot, in order to stretch their limbs and spy out the way ahead.

They moored the vessel, and climbed a nearby hummock to look around. As they stood there, they suddenly saw the kayaks starting to drift off. They raced back as fast as they could, but it was too late. The catamaran had broken its moorings. It was already some way out to sea, and rapidly receding.

Nansen gave Johansen his watch, then tore off some of his clothes as quickly as he could, jumped into the water, and started swimming after the kayaks.

'There went all our possessions,' Johansen recorded.

Food, clothing, ammunition ... our lives depended on retrieving the kayaks. I could not keep still, paced back and forth ... could do absolutely nothing whatsoever, watched Nansen, who rested now and then by swimming on his back; was afraid that he would get cramp and sink before my eyes.

'The water was icy cold,' Nansen wrote in his diary,

and it was exhausting to swim with clothes on. The kayaks drifted further and further away. It seemed more than doubtful whether I would manage it. But there drifted all our hope, and whether I stiffened and sank here, or returned without the kayaks, the result seemed much the same. So I pressed on with all my strength, and when I became too tired, I turned round and swam on my back ... Then I saw Johansen pace restlessly back and forth. Poor fellow, he couldn't do a thing ... But when I turned round again and found that the kayaks were closer my courage rose, and I carried on with renewed strength. Little by little, however, I felt my limbs become stiffer and unfeeling, I understood that I could not manage much more, but now it was not all that far, and if only I could hold out we were saved. So I forced myself on. My limbs became weaker and weaker the shorter the distance. I began to believe that I would get there. At long last, I could stretch out my hand and grasp the ski that lay aft across the kayaks, and haul myself alongside, and we were saved.

I tried to haul myself up, but now my whole body was so stiff from the cold that it was an impossibility. For a moment I thought that it was too late after all, that I would get so far, and no further. After a while, however, I managed to get one leg up on the deck, and then swung myself up.

With an Arctic breeze blowing through his wet clothes as if they were open gauze, Nansen was now completely numbed. He could hardly grip one of the paddles. One way or another, he summoned up the strength to row – up against wind and current. This was far worse than the swimming itself. But the shore painfully crept closer. Then a brace of guillemots floated placidly on the water across the bows. The fever of the hunt rose up. So did the soul of the gastronome, embittered by a repellent and unrelieved diet of walrus. Nansen stopped rowing, seized a gun, shot both birds with one shot, and managed to pick them up as well. Eventually he reached the edge of the ice but, driven eastwards by the current, at a point where it was too high to clamber ashore.

Johansen, inexpressibly relieved, jumped down into the other kayak and rowed the vessel back to their original landing point. Nansen 'looked horrible when he arrived', he recalled. 'Pale, with long hair and beard soaked, frothing at the mouth, he had difficulty speaking, and could hardly stand, shivered incessantly.' He helped Nansen out of his wet clothes, put something dry on him, even giving up his own trousers, and got him into the sleeping bag. Quite soon, Nansen fell asleep. Johansen meanwhile got their belongings ashore and prepared supper. When Nansen woke after a few hours, 'We ate the guillemots which had been shot under such unusual circumstances.'

'Guillemots and warm soup,' added Nansen, 'eradicated the last traces of the cold swim.'

But now a northerly breeze blowing offshore caused a further delay, and it was not until around 10 p.m. on 13 June that they were able to resume their voyage. Through the small hours, under the cloud-dimmed midnight sun, they paddled their kayaks separately, the catamaran dismantled, sledges lashed astern in ungainly deck cargo, while the land drifted by to starboard with exhilarating speed. In the meantime, the smell of walrus grew upon the air. At a certain point a herd appeared upon the ice. Nansen and Johansen put in. It was now five o'clock on the morning of 14 June.

The encounter was providential. Except for a few guillemots shot along the way, their food was exhausted. They were still hoping for a bear, but in vain. Walrus would have to do. This was the biggest herd they had yet seen; there were hundreds strewn about, luckily with plenty of young. Nansen shot two calves; their mothers pushed them into the water with their tusks, and disappeared. Taught by experience, Nansen shot another calf and its mother too. It was, he wrote in his diary, 'a moving sight to see her bend over the dead young one before she was shot'. Her blubber supplied the lamps. From the calf there was plenty of meat. They set off again at the next turn of the tide, at half past one in the morning of Monday 15 June, with the double comfort of knowing that they had food and fuel for a long time to come.

Driven by the current, Nansen and Johansen paddled on westwards along the greenish edge of the chaotic land ice. Mist and cloud still clung to the coast behind, obscuring features and distorting perspective. In Nansen's words, 'it was impossible to decide whether there were sounds or glaciers between the mountains'. He very much wanted to know. By now, he was almost convinced that they were in the vicinity of Leigh Smith's winter quarters at Cape Flora. That would have put them in Franz Josef Land, coasting along Northbrook Island. Johansen still disagreed. Against Leigh Smith's map he continued to cling to Payer's, which told a different story altogether.

Meanwhile, the wind completely dropped; the overcast sky brightened from its midnight hue as the sun dipped, rose and circled. It was a splendid Arctic summer's morning. But walrus heads broke the dark, gently rippled waters. Nansen and Johansen, wary of attack, moved in closer to the edge of the drift ice lining the coast. By 6.30 a.m., they seemed to have left the beasts behind. Then a single specimen rose up from the depths next to Nansen. Glaring balefully, it drove its tusks into the kayak, simultanously dragging it down, so that it listed to port. Desperately Nansen leaned over the other way, at the same time beating the walrus on the nose with his paddle. After a short scuffle, the creature disappeared.

Nansen was luckily unscathed, but dampness round his limbs told him the kayak had been holed and was rapidly sinking. Frantically, he headed for the shore. It so happened that the attack took place precisely where an ice foot jutted out underwater like a sloping shoal. Nansen drove his kayak there and, just in time, saved himself from foundering. Johansen, meanwhile, had gone ahead. He was able to return and haul Nansen round to a point where the ice edge was so low that the kayak could be beached. And in the vicinity, they camped. The whole affair took place with a minimum of risk. It was almost as if the walrus had wanted to drive them ashore at that particular place.

For two whole days they remained where they were, drying the gear and repairing Nansen's kayak. They were finally ready to move on 17 June. Exhausted by events, they only got up at midday. As Johansen recorded:

It was N[ansen]'s turn to cook ... While he was cooking, he went up onto a hummock nearby.... After a moment he said to me, as I was lying and dozing: 'I hear dogs barking inland.' I jumped up quicker than quick [and] listened, but was not certain whether it was dogs I heard or noise from the bird cliffs over there.

337

Nansen was in no doubt. He decided to investigate. Hurrying through breakfast he set off, alone, over the ice.

Johansen was now jotting down events as they occurred: 'N. has gone off, while I am not allowed to leave the kayaks.' They had no wish to repeat the previous episode. Now the fear was not that the kayaks would break their moorings but that the ice might split and the whole camp drift out to sea.

52

'I Am Devilish Glad to See You'

Leaving the camp, Nansen skied off across the ice towards the bleak slopes of what looked like a truncated volcano melting into the mist. He had one ski of his own; the other belonged to Johansen. Both agreed that Nansen ought to have a whole pair, so that he might appear respectable before strangers. Over his shoulder Nansen carried his telescope and, in case of polar bears, a gun.

'I started off in doubt,' Nansen said. Try as he might, after the first faint volley of barks, he had heard no more. All that came to him was the old insistent cacophony of birds borne upon the breeze. But soon after starting he noticed on the ice fresh tracks as of a dog.

> With strange thoughts hovering between doubt and certainty, I went on [Nansen wrote in his diary], and out of the misty land of doubt, certainty began to dawn – a stream of dogs' barks reached my ears, more distinctly than ever, and I saw more and more tracks that could not be from anything but dogs ...
>
> Then a long time passed; nothing to hear but the noise of birds. Again doubt rose up ... I made my way over towards the land through this maze of hummocks and irregularities. Suddenly I was certain that I heard a strange voice, the first for three years; what a stream of emotion flooded the soul; how my heart hammered. I jumped up on a hummock and shouted with all the power of my lungs. Behind that single human voice in the middle of this wilderness of ice – this single message from the south, with its pulsating life – lay home and she who was waiting at home for me, and I saw nothing else as I forged ahead between floes and hummocks as fast as my skis could carry me. Soon I heard a shout again, saw a dark shape moving between the hummocks. It was a dog, but further off there was another form. It was a human being ... We quickly approached each other, I waved my hat, he did the same. I heard him speak to the dog. I listened but could not hear whether it was English or Norwegian. I came closer, and then I heard that it was English, and believed that I recognised Mr Jackson.

It was a scene fraught with irony. By an odd twist of fate, Nansen himself had set in train the events now unfolding on the ice.

*

When Nansen visited London in November 1892 to lecture on his expedition, he received a letter, signed F.G. Jackson, declaring 'I am very desirous of accompanying you', and requesting 'a few minutes' interview'. To that, Nansen agreed but, in Jackson's own words: 'He at once told me that my proposal was quite out of the question, as I was not a Norwegian. However, he was very nice and quite sympathetic at my disappointment.'

Frederick George Jackson stood apart from most of the unbidden hopefuls pestering Nansen. Behind a mildly foppish exterior, there lay a man of action. In his own words:

> The effect of this friendly rebuff was to make me determined to 'run my own show,' and forthwith I set to work to organise a Polar expedition of my own.

Jackson was the quintessential Victorian gentleman adventurer. Born at Alcester, in Warwickshire, in 1860, of thoroughly English landowning and sporting stock, he fled the hedgerow for the wider vistas of the British Empire. At the age of twenty, he went out to Australia. In 1887, after a spell in Florida, he was to be found on a Scottish whaler off the east coast of Greenland. By his own account, that was what originally turned his attention to the Arctic.

Jackson was a man in a hurry. In February 1893 he publicly announced his expedition. In the words of an acquaintance, he was 'overmastered by the idea of being the first [at] the North Pole and exasperated at the thought of the probable success of Dr Nansen depriving him of the glory in view'.

But money, and hence the enterprise, hung fire. Jackson, however, had a devoted supporter on his side. This was a certain Arthur Montefiore, another gentlemanly wanderer and believer in Britain's imperial destiny. Montefiore knew Alfred Harmsworth, later Lord Northcliffe, the celebrated newspaper magnate. Notably by appealing to patriotism and imperial sentiment, he persuaded Harmsworth to donate the money required. On 12 July 1894, a year after *Fram* vanished into the mist, Jackson sailed down the Thames, the leader of what was called the Jackson-Harmsworth expedition.

On 17 June 1896, Jackson was at his base. His diary for that memorable day recorded that after dinner someone 'came in to tell me that he could see a man on the floe to the southward towards the open water.'

> I could hardly believe it but having got a glass I could see that he was correct and I could also see a staff or mast with a man standing near it at the water's edge.
>   I ... started off to meet the man coming across the ice ... As he approached I saw a man on ski with roughly made clothes and an old felt hat on his head, covered with oil and grease and black from head to foot. His hair was very long and dirty.... At first ... I ... imagined that he was a walrus hunter who had come to grief in some sloop ... His complexion appeared to be fair but

dirt prevented me being sure on the point. I, having examined his features, came to the conclusion that it must be Nansen.

Nansen recorded: 'I raised my hat, we shook hands heartily. "How do you do?" – "How do you do".'

Jackson elaborated. Their 'exact conversation', according to him was:

J. 'I am damned glad to see you.' (And we shook hands.) 'Have you a ship here?'
N. 'No my ship is not here.'
J. 'How many are there of you?'
N. 'I have one companion at the water's edge.'
J. 'Aren't you Nansen?'
N. 'Yes I am Nansen.'
J. 'By Jove, I am devilish glad to see you.' (And we shook hands again very heartily.)

Nansen, in a few words, told his story. Thus Jackson, for his part, continued his account:

[I said:] 'I congratulate you most heartily, you have made a deuced good job of it, and I am awfully glad to be the first person to congratulate you.'

Shades indeed of Stanley and Livingstone, for in concluding his greeting ('I congratulate you', etc.) Jackson, whether consciously or not, was repeating Stanley's exact words.* As for Nansen, he was moved to observe in his diary:

Surely the desolate, frozen regions of ice have never witnessed such an encounter.

In the meantime, all Jackson's companions, seven in number, had come down on to the ice. Jackson made the introduction, announced the new record for the Furthest North, and called for three cheers.

Jackson had wanted immediately to fetch Johansen. Nansen explained that it would be difficult for them alone to haul the load over the broken ice. So Jackson, staying behind with Nansen, now sent off a party to the camp at the water's edge. There Johansen had his own private reception. Over the forlorn ice, cheers once again rang out. What is more, Jackson's second in command, Albert Armitage (the man, incidentally, who had

---

* The exact interchange, as recorded by Stanley in words which have passed into the nation's folklore, ran: 'I ... walked deliberately to him, took off my hat and said: "Dr Livingstone I presume?" "YES" said he, with a kind smile, lifting his cap slightly. I replace my cap on my head, and he puts on his cap, and we both grasp hands, and then say aloud: "I thank God, Doctor, I have been permitted to see you." He answered, "I feel thankful that I am here to welcome you." [I said] "I congratulate you most heartily, you have made a deuced good job of it, and I am awfully glad to be the first person to congratulate you." '

spotted Nansen first), pulled out a hip flask and hospitably proffered a welcoming glass of wine. 'That,' Johansen drily observed, 'was some change in a short while.'

Now all riddles are solved ... It was Franz Josef Land we were on, after all.

They were at Cape Flora, on Northbrook Island – more or less as Nansen had begun to surmise during the last few days of their journey.

About a mile away over the ice Jackson, in the meantime, was leading Nansen up on shore to his base. This was a group of about half a dozen huts on the banks of a tarn, under an arid, ice-capped cliff, and named by Jackson Elmwood, after Harmsworth's country house. When Nansen crossed the threshold of the living quarters he saw 'a warm, welcoming refuge in the midst of these wintry surroundings'. The interior was covered with green baize. Books and pictures lined the walls. A small stove radiated the heat of a coal fire. But civilisation was brought home to Nansen by something else. For the first time in fifteen months, he abandoned primitive posture and sank into a chair. That precipitated a flood of feeling. 'At one stroke of a fickle fate,' he wrote, 'responsibility and sorrow were swept away from a spirit they had oppressed for 3 long years.'

Ever since arriving on Franz Josef Land, Nansen had half hoped that he and Jackson would meet. Jackson all along had half expected them to do so. He was actually carrying letters for Nansen. In March, it now turned out, he had come within forty miles of Nansen's winter hut before being stopped by open water. Now he was finally able to deliver Nansen's post. It was packed in a tin, soldered tight. 'With almost trembling hands and beating heart,' Nansen said, 'I got it open.'

From Eva, there was nothing, 'at which', Jackson observed, Nansen 'was very downcast'. Alexander, however, had written. His letter explained that 'she would not write by Jackson', but that she and their daughter were both well. Jackson was able to reassure Nansen that this was the case when last he heard. That in fact was two years ago, but Nansen seemed not to mind. It was the illusion of contact that counted. Despite Eva's perversity, he recorded that at that moment 'a blessed feeling of peace and quiet settled on my soul'.

When sending his men off to fetch Johansen, Jackson had considerately kept back the cook. So food followed hard upon the mail. 'Was it not wonderful,' observed Nansen reverently, 'to have bread, butter, milk, sugar, coffee, and everything that the long months had taught us to do without, and yet yearn for!' Thereafter, at Jackson's prompting, Nansen went out, got onto his skis, and was photographed before the hut in the state in which he had been found.

At that point Johansen arrived and was photographed too. The kayaks and other equipment had been loaded onto two sledges brought down by the welcoming party. 'They are all full of admiration for our journey,' wrote

Johansen in his diary. He had not been allowed to touch the drag ropes. He skied back alongside the sledges, unencumbered, as a mark of the welcoming party's deep respect, while the others did the hauling.

After food and photography Nansen and Johansen began their transformation from the savage state. They had their first hot baths since leaving *Fram*. They removed as much of the ingrained dirt as they could in one operation. They had haircuts and shaves. Jackson found them clean clothes. At long last, they were free of the clammy sensation of greasy cloth clinging to their skins. Out of the sooty troglodytes from the long winter in the half-buried hut there emerged two fresh-scrubbed, barely recognisable Europeans.

Jackson gave up his own private room to Nansen and himself went to sleep with the others in the main body of the hut. Johansen was put in with Armitage in the other private room. But that first night Nansen could not sleep, 'he felt so happy', as Jackson said. 'Nansen, the doctor [Koettlitz] and I ... sat up for 48 hours at a stretch talking.' The Midnight Sun, as usual, was playing havoc with their time sense.

After barely another forty-eight hours Jackson was recording that

Nansen and I went for a walk after we had breakfast and we discussed his plans for the South Pole.

For Nansen, the North Pole was no obsession. It was already just one more discarded goal. Even the image of Eva faded now before the vision of the Antarctic, with limitless skiing fields of powder snow on terra firma beckoning, like the next mirage of unattained contentment, at the other end of the earth. And so he settled down at Elmwood to wait for *Windward*, Jackson's expedition ship. But the weeks passed, and no ship arrived.

It was probably just as well. Before facing the drumbeat of acclaim there was time to adjust in isolation. In a world without universal, instant communication, this was still a possibility.

On the one hand Johansen found it 'pleasant here among these Englishmen, they are as kind and attentive as humanly possible'. Johansen was indeed, from the start, notably content. When he arrived at Cape Flora his only foreign languages were French and German. He quickly saw the stay at Elmwood as a heaven-sent opportunity to learn English. In that, literally from the first day, he was happily employed. Encouraged by Armitage, his room mate and self-appointed tutor, his progress was astounding.

On arriving at Elmwood, both he and Nansen seemed eminently fit. Since leaving *Fram* each had put on weight. The only blemish was Nansen's piles. But that was an occupational hazard of Arctic explorers. There was no sign of scurvy, or any of the privations that were the hallmarks of previous expeditions.

In contrast to Johansen, however, Nansen appeared somewhat

strained. He had, after all, borne the burden of command. Now, about ten days after reaching Elmwood, he fell mysteriously ill. He suffered what amounted to a collapse. Physically this was manifested in uncharacteristic shortness of breath. He had crossed the watershed between healthy exhaustion and overpowering fatigue.

It was not only that he had broken the record for the Furthest North. Since leaving *Fram* he had travelled seven hundred miles, and accomplished the first great journey across the polar pack. He had proved that dogs and skis could be used there as well. For over three months he had made his fuel last – an unheard-of achievement at the time. Through giving the Primus its first trial out in the field he had spectacularly extended the range of unsupported travel. He had once more revolutionised technique.

Jackson had come to Franz Josef Land because, misled by the same map by Payer that had grievously confused Nansen, he believed that it was the southern edge of terra firma, allowing him to romp all the way to the Pole. Instead, he found himself marooned on an archipelago, barely able to exceed 81°N. He explored the islands, and added new land to the map. But now he had suddenly been reduced to the rôle of the man who saved Nansen. Nonetheless, he ungrudgingly wrote in his diary, 'Nansen has done a marvellous, unheard of performance and licks hollow all other feats of daring I have heard of.'

From a certain point of view, Nansen and Jackson were reflections of each other. Both had the indefinable quality of realising intentions and making things happen. Neither was a good leader of men. Johansen was treated by various of Jackson's expedition members to recitals of complaint, the burden of which, by his own account, was that Jackson 'was no use at all, that he was an autocrat, much worse than the Russian Tsar'. He commented characteristically:

> I can't be bothered to tell them that our leader also has his shadow side; that on board *Fram* nobody liked him.

Nansen himself let slip the first recorded hint that he was aware of his subordinates' feelings when, in Jackson's words, he 'made the remark ... that some of the *Fram* people would have plenty of faults to find in him'.

Pioneers are bound to be uncomfortable creatures. By definition they are at odds with the majority. And Jackson too was a pioneer. Inspired partly by Nansen's crossing of Greenland, he introduced a string of innovations to English polar exploration. He abandoned the disastrous old English faith in numbers. He prepared for his expedition in the field, notably by a long training journey through northern Russia, and was experimenting, unsuccessfully as it turned out, with North Russian ponies. He had brought sledge dogs, in defiance of the English tradition of man hauling. Above all, his was the first English polar expedition to use skis – supplied, ironically enough, by Nansen's brother Alexander. Likewise, Alexander had provided Jackson with sledges. Thus Jackson became the first foreign explorer to use the Nansen ski sledge. He had every intention of still trying to outdo Nansen.

Disabused of the belief in continental land leading to the Pole, Jackson decided to strike out across the pack. To negotiate the channels among the islands he had contrived an aluminium boat that could be dismantled into manageable loads. It was ingenious but impractical. Seeing Nansen's kayaks, he decided to copy them, follow in his footsteps, and set his own record for the Furthest North.

Johansen was sceptical. As he wrote in his diary: 'Skiers, the Englishmen are not.'

> I do not believe that they will reach as far as us; in fact I am certain, from what I have seen of them. We can be sure of our 86°14'.

Of course, sooner or later, that record was bound to be broken. Both Nansen and Johansen merely wanted time to enjoy the fruits of their attainment. As soon as Nansen also realised, again in Johansen's words, that 'the Englishmen will not be in a position to accomplish much', his mental and physical troubles went away.

53

Fram Breaks Free

On 15 November 1895, meanwhile, *Fram* had reached 85°55.5′. After a fortnight, it was clear that this was going to be her furthest north. There was no recorded celebration. Of Christmas and the New Year, in Scott Hansen's words, 'all there is to say is that they passed quietly, with the usual hot punch and consequent hangover'. (He had made a resolution 'to be a fairly abstemious character when I come home, because I am getting more and more disgusted with drunkenness'.)

By the middle of March, *Fram* was around 84°N and 25°E. In the four months since her furthest north, she had lost almost two degrees of latitude, and moved 240 miles to the south-west. Her course was now a curve dropping down homewards from its apogee.

Fram, as usual, lay safely in her berth, cradled by ice ten feet thick; disturbed only by occasional tremors. Once more, a rising alpenglow, over an arid plain of rafted floes, heralded the end of yet another polar night. But now the ice was working differently. Cracks and open leads were appearing in a rich, confused pattern that hinted at the edge of the pack. Precisely on that account, the atmosphere on board was tense. There was still no trust in a current. Every little setback might mean the entrance to a gyre from which there would be no escape, on *Fram* at any rate. The nagging fear, as Jacobsen put it, was that 'we will have to celebrate a fourth winter up here'.

That was enough to explain why tempers were short. On two occasions, a check to the drift coincided with men coming to blows, both involving Jacobsen. Salvation was seen only in the wind. The men disliked clear skies and still air. They were happier under heavy scudding clouds and a northerly wind blowing homewards.

On 4 March, the sun returned after yet another winter night. Next, on 14 March, came the anniversary of Nansen's and Johansen's departure. After dinner, Sverdrup proposed their *skål* and, in Jacobsen's words, 'said that in the worst case, they would remember us by a glass of mead ... in Valhalla'.

By the middle of April, the Midnight Sun returned. When skies were clear, the dogs basked outside in the rising warmth. The floes began breaking up. The boats and supplies kept out on the ice in case the ship was crushed were brought on board again.

53. Fram Breaks Free

On 19 May the funnel was shipped and steam raised for the first time since October 1893. The day before, the crew had started hacking away at the ice to free the propeller in its well. On 21 May, with aid of a steam hose, the job was finally done. At 1.30 p.m. precisely, Amundsen started the engines for a spell.

An odd coincidence can be recorded here. 19 May was the very same day that Nansen and Johansen left their winter hut. It was also the date of a letter sent to someone at the University in Christiania, in which the writer explained that early that morning he had dreamt that he met Nansen 'and he told me that he had been near the North Pole ... and was now on his way home.... It will be interesting to see what this might mean. Surely we can expect to hear something soon.'

On 3 June, *Fram* was blasted clear of the ice, and floated free in a pool. Ten days later, a lead opened, and she was warped a few hundred yards into a larger basin. After three years, *Fram* was no longer a hulk, but a living ship once more.

It was another fortnight before she moved again. On 27 June, the ice slackened enough for Sverdrup to order steam up, and make some two miles to the south-east along an open lead. Over the next ten days, the ship barely made another three miles. The way ahead was barred. The trouble was a malicious southerly wind that jammed the pack together. Simultaneously there were violent, shifting tidal currents. Floes, grey green on dark waters, flurried and whirled in the lead as if possessed. To make matters worse, the ice was now drifting north and *Fram* was pushed back further than she had steamed. On the last day of June, her latitude was down to 82°57.8′N; a week later, she was over the 83rd parallel again, and further back towards the east as well.

Like a huge creature breathing, the ice slowly opened and closed. Sverdrup prudently held back. He needed to save coal until the time was ripe. Jacobsen spoke for his shipmates when, as he recorded, he 'told the Capt. that it was better to know that he had burned some extra coal than to have a fourth winter on his conscience'.

An added worry for Sverdrup was Blessing's deterioration, but whether from his morphine addiction or withdrawal symptoms was unclear. On one occasion, Blessing was overheard at the dinner table explaining to Mogstad with slurred speech that he was so dizzy that he found it difficult to find a vein for injection. On 15 July, Sverdrup noted in his diary that

A deputation came to me and asked to talk [privately] in the charthouse. They were Juell, Bentsen, Mogstad, Amundsen, Nordahl. They said that Blessing was fuddled on watch during the night and that they had noticed it several times. They suspected it was abuse of some medicines ... I thought that ... he no longer took morphine [although] when I checked the medicines in my custody, I thought that the level of morphine had sunk.

Sverdrup faced all this with his usual imperturbability. He believed in

347

hunting as a cure for depression, and the pack was now teeming with game. Various polar bears were shot, usually with the joyous help of the dogs. One day Sverdrup and Scott Hansen downed 23 guillemots from among the migratory stream overhead.

On 10 July, Sverdrup left the ship on a solitary hunting foray. While he was absent, the ice opened. Scott Hansen seized the opportunity to have *Fram* warped by hand into a convenient basin ahead. He had to argue with some of the crew before they would obey.

They only warped the ship a few hundred yards, but the move was critical nonetheless. A week later, after lying inertly, the ice opened on the *far* side of the basin. Steam was raised and, in the small hours, *Fram* forced her way through a press of brash and broken floes like a stopper in a bottle, and emerged into a broad open channel running south east. Around 3 a.m., she was brought up by fog, and moored to the ice. But by then she had steamed freely for three miles at least. It was her longest run so far.

Zig-zagging through a fluid web of shifting open leads, *Fram* continued tortuously to thread her way south between the floes, engines beating, and thick smoke belching from her funnel, black against the ice. By 27 July, she had made good 75 miles and dropped her latitude all the way from just over the eighty third parallel to 81°32′.

For the next fortnight, *Fram* was held back by wind, fog and the closing of the ice. In the engine room, fires were tantalisingly drawn and lit. Meanwhile the proliferation of seals and birds and, from 4 August, a dark water sky announced open seas ahead.

The ice was in confusion. Broken floes, thawed underwater and unstable, capsized at the least pretext, sometimes ramming *Fram*. Jerking and jolting, she inched her way through narrow bottlenecks jammed with brash. Through it all, Sverdrup imperturbably conned the ship from the bridge or crow's nest and, when the opportunity arose, descended onto the ice to shoot a polar bear for yet another pelt.

On the afternoon of 11 August, the ice arbitrarily opened. Instead of the pack, there was suddenly an archipelago of separate shifting floes. Steam was raised again, and *Fram* made her way unhindered down a lead that widened to a channel running on to the south, dark grey and rippled, encumbered only by fragmented ice. When Scott Hansen came off watch next morning, he wrote: 'Perhaps we can soon celebrate with the classic greeting Tallata Tallata. Don't know if it's written correctly, but what the hell.' He meant 'Thalassa! Thalassa!' (The Sea! The Sea!), the famous cry of Xenophon's Greeks. At 3.45 a.m. on 13 August, just before the end of Scott Hansen's watch, the last block of ice was left astern. *Fram* ran out into the open sea.

The change of fortune brought an abrupt change of mood. All the drab ennui of the years fell away. Watch above and watch below were on deck.

53. Fram Breaks Free

The crew cheered. Nordahl got out a signal cannon and, as the receding line of ice was swallowed by the fog, he fired off a salute.

After a few hours, a ship under sail appeared to port through a gap in the haze. Sverdrup altered course towards her. She then put about and began approaching too. As they closed, what appeared to be the whole crew of the other ship could be seen crowding the rails. 'We saw a human being,' Nordahl succinctly wrote in his diary.

It has been 3 years since we last saw human beings. Three Samoyeds off Yamal, the coast of Siberia.

In sheer exuberance, Nordahl fired a thunderous salvo of salutes with both cannon. There were cheers in reply. The stranger was flying the Norwegian ensign at the masthead. When she came within hailing distance, the first thing that Sverdrup did was to ask whether Nansen had returned. The answer was No.

The other ship was the sealer *Søstrene* ('The Sisters') of Tromsø, commended by Captain Botolfsen. He now rowed across in a boat with some of his men. As they came over the side, everybody shook hands. There were tears of joy among *Fram*'s crew – they felt as if they had returned to the land of the living. But time seemed truly out of joint. They had lost three years and suffered a disorienting necessity to know what had happened in the world while they were away.

War, insurrection and political confusion apparently still held the stage. The Turks were slaughtering Christians in Crete; Nicholas II was Tsar of Russia instead of Alexander III; the French had conquered Madagascar. But in the end, from the point of view of Sverdrup and his men, the vital news was that Andrée, a Swede unknown to them, was trying to reach the North Pole by balloon. He was even then in Spitsbergen, preparing to take off.

Having heard *Fram*'s saga, Captain Botolfsen immediately wanted to sail with her back to Norway, bringing with him two live polar bears. Tactfully he was told that he himself was welcome, but that the dogs on board would object to the bears. He cheerfully left the bears behind. Handing over command to his mate, he moved over to *Fram* as a passenger, bringing with him his own collapsible bed, some coffee, fifty bottles of beer and almost a whole bottle of whisky.

Around midday, *Fram* got under way once more. All along, she had been heading for Spitsbergen to take on water and make ready for sea. Sverdrup continued on his course, with one small variation. He decided to visit Andrée in case he had news of Nansen.

*

Salomon August Andrée was like a character out of Jules Verne. Tall, blond, big-boned, with a drooping walrus-like moustache and a distant gaze in his eyes, he was obstinate and self-controlled, and believed invincibly in technology alone. He was an engineer working at the Swedish patent office in Stockholm. He was forty-one years old, convivial, and a bachelor with one known mistress and one obsession: to accomplish a great balloon journey as part of the conquest of the air. As in Jackson's case, it was Nansen's departure on *Fram* that drove Andrée to try for the North Pole. He chose Spitsbergen for his take-off, to be as close as possible to the Pole. On the island of Danskøya he set up his base, erected a striking octagonal hangar, inflated his balloon, and settled down to wait for a favourable wind.

On the morning of 14 August *Fram* dropped anchor in the forlorn surroundings of the bay. Andrée, together with Nils Strindberg and Nils Ekholm, who formed the balloon's crew, went off in a steam pinnace to visit her. They gave three cheers and waved their caps. 'It was like a dream,' Strindberg – a cousin of August Strindberg, the author and dramatist – wrote to his father,

> to see these men, who have spent 3 long years on this ship, on the deck that we are now treading, surrounded the whole time by ice ... ice, ice, on all sides. It is strange, moving, magnificent. It seems almost sacred ...
>
> We took them ... to see the balloon. When they came ashore they were absolutely fascinated! It was the first time for 3 years that they had set foot on solid earth and they had to pick up stones and play with them.

But back on *Fram*, as Nordahl put it, all resentment gone, 'we are in low spirits now, because Nansen and Johansen aren't home'. Andrée had post for Scott Hansen, but of Nansen there was no news at all. They hoped, however, that he and Johansen were on Franz Josef Land with Jackson, news of whose expedition they had also just absorbed.

Fram was quickly made ready for sea, and in the small hours of 15 August got under way. Sverdrup had decided first to make for Norway to hear the latest news and then, if necessary, sail for Jackson's base at Cape Flora in search of the two absent men.

54

Reunion All Round

'During the time we were together in the winter hut, and on the journey thence,' Johansen wrote in his diary at Cape Flora on 1 July,

> Nansen ... was different from what he was on board the ship. He was more like another person; sociable and not arrogant, not egotistic. We were equals. Now he has changed again – now, so to speak, that he has saved his bacon, now that he sees that the Englishmen will not be in a position to achieve anything.

This was all too obvious. When Johansen first appeared at Elmwood, Jackson pointedly noted in his diary that 'I looked after him in the same manner as I had Nansen.'

Jackson's own verdict on Nansen was that 'I know him to be very touchy.' And, echoing Johansen: 'One thing I notice ... is that he runs down all explorers without exception.' Nansen shocked (or amused) Jackson and the other Englishmen with his brand of fiery republicanism. He 'can't understand our loyalty to the Queen', Jackson wrote. Nonetheless, he added, 'I like Nansen immensely, and we get on A.1 together.' Politics aside, it was 'pleasant to have one of similar tastes to talk to'.

Jackson was a big game hunter, devoted at Cape Flora to bagging polar bears beyond the necessity of shooting for the pot – and incidentally testing a new kind of ammunition for the War Office. He was also the first English polar explorer to take dedicated scientists on an expedition. There was a qualified biologist, a certain Harry Fisher; and a mineralogist, J.F. Child. In this respect, Jackson was ahead of Nansen.

Johansen wrote down in his diary a long soliloquy on the inner meaning of his and Nansen's journey. They had challenged the might of Nature and, in his own words, learned that 'humankind is a miserable insect'. 'And yet,' he decided, 'it is wonderful to be a human being!' He ended with a paean to what he called 'that power which has saved us from destruction so often on this journey!'

Jackson's opinion was rather more down-to-earth. 'On learning the full details,' he wrote, 'it strikes me forcibly that great luck has attended [Nansen's] daring trip.'

But whether ascribed to luck or divine power, a quite extraordinary concatenation of circumstances had been required to bring about this meeting on the ice. If Nansen's kayaks had not drifted off, and delayed him exactly as he rounded Cape Barents and made Northbrooke Island, and if the walrus had not attacked him at that particular point off Cape Flora, he would not have landed precisely where he did, and therefore, in all likelihood, he would have missed Jackson. What then might have followed is another matter altogether. Nansen told Jackson that, given the condition of the ice, he now thought he could not have reached Spitsbergen.

In the meanwhile, against the day when he should land back in civilisation, Nansen was preparing his telegrams and his newspaper reports. The latter he first had to write out in Norwegian, and then translate into English for simultaneous publication at home and in the English-speaking world. Jackson helped him to turn them into correct English.

Between the two men there reigned the ambiguous undertones of rescuer and rescued. They trod gingerly round the subject. They went hunting together. Jackson unselfishly shared a favourite, and secret, spot for shooting loons sportingly on the wing, high up on the cliff overlooking Elmwood.

Nansen, for his part, developed an intense concern with geology, being particularly interested in signs at Cape Flora of the rising of the land, presumably after the last ice age – at the time a new and contentious subject. He now prowled along the shore, up and down the basalt cliffs, contentedly geologising. His companion was usually Dr Reginald Koettlitz, the expedition doctor, a born wanderer, dogged by the melancholy fear of never quite succeeding. To this Nansen's overwhelming personality supplied an uplifting antidote, while the excursions themselves provided a much needed escape from Jackson and his bursts of temper. Others also appreciated the break in routine. Armitage, the errant son of a Harley Street specialist and a merchant officer from the P&O, called Nansen and Johansen 'our companions, most welcome ones'.

> Nansen talked well on all topics ... Notwithstanding, he always listened with interest to anything we had to say, and was wonderfully broadminded, although, obviously, somewhat impatient towards ignorant foolishness ... I have never met anyone who had such a magnetic personality, and such a profound confidence in himself.

In between geology and journalism, Nansen was working out his observations. Armitage rated his watches and discovered that he had only been about 26 minutes slow, after all, which meant $6\frac{1}{2}°$ east of his true longitude. This had a bearing on the delicate situation of intruding on Jackson's preserves. Where Nansen had made discoveries in the northern part of Franz Josef Land, it was agreed that he could name them. So where he spent the winter he called Frederick Jackson Island. The islands where he made his landfall he named after Eva, Liv, and his mother Adelaide. The

whole cluster he called Hvidtenland, 'White Land', after the title of a
Norwegian fairy tale, *The Three Princesses in Hvidtenland.*

That hinted at eerie undertones. The tale is about a fisher boy who is
carried off in a magic boat to the mythic Hvidtenland. There he finds three
princesses, buried up to their necks in the ground by three trolls. The boy
releases the princesses by allowing the trolls to torture him, before killing
them. He then marries one of the princesses. Nansen evidently identified
himself with the boy, as he had openly adumbrated in a speech on *Fram*
just before departure, and the princesses with his wife, his mother and his
daughter. (Eventually Eva and Liv islands were found to be one, and that
called Adelaide disappeared from some maps.)

The weeks dragged on, the ice packed up against the shore, and still no
ship appeared. Nansen and Johansen began to fear yet another winter
marooned in the Arctic. At last, in the small hours of 26 July, *Windward*
finally appeared. Jackson hurried on board to enquire, among other
things, about Nansen's family. Hearing that Eva was well Jackson, in his
own words, 'sent [someone] to tell Nansen the good news, as I knew the
poor chap was anxious about his wife'. When he approached the ship
Nansen was greeted by cheering from the whole crew lined up on deck by
the Master, Captain Brown.

Windward also brought news that was only a few weeks old. Peary had
returned from Greenland the year before, his expedition a fiasco, so
Nansen now knew that his record was safe so far. Yet in the welter of alien
events that he had to assimilate in order to fill the void of years what stuck
in his mind was the discovery of X rays: 'that they could now photograph
people right through doors that were several inches thick.'

Jackson was staying for another year, and before sailing *Windward* had
to discharge her cargo. That took about a week. Then foul winds and
swirling ice drove her off shore, nearly sending her aground. Nansen now
wrote the first letter he had written for three years – excluding the last
message to Eva which he had left behind on *Fram.*

The addressee was Otto Irminger, the President of the Danish Geographical Society, who had helped so greatly in his crossing of Greenland.
It was a surprising but logical choice. In the sense of achieving his stated
goal, Nansen had then succeeded, as now he had failed. Irminger was a
suitable person to whom to unburden himself of the ultimate stigma, to a
Norwegian, of an unaccomplished errand.

> Even if a journey like ours has been comfortable and far better than any
> other expedition before [his letter ran], nonetheless it has not been exclu-
> sively a bed of roses.... By and large I am satisfied with the trip, it has
> fulfilled my expectations, and what more can one ask ... but nonetheless in
> my heart of hearts there is a thorn which is difficult to remove; I can do
> nothing but regret that we could not go in and fetch the dogs sent to us at
> the mouth of the Olenek! If we had them, it is my belief that we could have
> covered the distance we left between our highest latitude and 90°. I know

that this is nothing but absurd vanity ... for what would its significance
really be?... But in spite of all, we are no more than human beings [with]
human failings, and it would have been so pleasant to have taken the Pole.

Nansen's next letter was to Gustav Retzius, his old colleague from the
now distant days of exploring the central nervous system. 'I don't want you
to be without a line from me,' he wrote,

> even though I feel convinced that you will not think 3 years in the ice have
> been enough to cool our friendship. When I sat in our low stone hut and
> stared out into the darkness and made plans for the future, I longed to sit
> down at the microscope again, and thought about you and your work, and
> what you had accomplished.... It seems as if I have sat still for 3 years ...
> while you and the world have advanced ... and I have been left far astern in
> the darkness; I who would so like to have been up alongside.

About this time, Johansen wrote to his mother: 'I knew that my future
would be secured if all went well. And everything has gone well!... It will
be a long time before anyone makes a better journey than we have done.'

Finally, on 7 August, *Windward* managed to come inshore, pick up her
passengers, and shape for the south. Johansen embarked with the satisfaction of now speaking English passably well. Both he and Nansen were
missed at Elmwood.

Two days after sailing, *Windward* left the pack and found the open sea.
Nansen summarily recorded the ice blink over the horizon,

> the last greeting from the world which has been our home, seen our pleasure
> and our sorrows for 3 long years – how strange that all this lies far behind
> us and ahead – it is like a wonderful dream, my thoughts fly on golden
> clouds.

Johansen, reverting to Nansen's shadow side, wrote sombrely:

> Now when I think of how wonderful I thought it would be to say farewell to
> the ice and to all suffering, and compare that feeling with my reality now –
> I find that reality, after all, is not so wonderful as it appeared to me in the
> midst of our hard life.

*

On 13 August *Windward* made the Norwegian coast and, early in the
afternoon, dropped anchor inside the mole at Vardø. Before the chains had
stopped rattling in the lockers, Nansen and Johansen were over the side,
into a boat and heading for the shore, on their way to the telegraph station.

Nansen had literally dreamt of this moment. 'I can still clearly remember with what trembling joy I approached my homeland and longed for the
first telegraph station,' he had written in his diary two and a half years

before. But in that dream he had reached the North Pole. Now he had to face reality.

A cow stared out at Nansen and Johansen from a side street as they hurried by. Some passing cyclists stared as well. The one so tall, the other short, both dressed in obviously borrowed clothes, they were conspicuous but unrecognised. But when they entered the telegraph station and Nansen dumped his pile of telegrams on the counter the manager first of all turned his back and went over to the telegraphists (all women) sitting at a table to reveal the identity of the mysterious stranger, whose signature he had spotted. Then he turned round, came up to Nansen and, wreathed in smiles, formally welcomed him home.

The telegraph keys instantly began to click. Nansen's first telegram was to Eva: HERE YOU HAVE YOUR BOY AT LAST ALL WELL EXPEDITION SUCCESSFUL AS EXPECTED. Thereafter came his English newspaper report. This was addressed to John Scott Keltie, now Secretary of the Royal Geographical Society in London and, as far as Nansen knew, still acting as his literary agent. Thereafter, in a loose order of priority, followed a long string of telegrams to monopolise the lines for several hours to come.

In Vardø on that day happened to be Professor Henrik Mohn, the man who first brought to Nansen's attention the postulate of a transpolar current and hence became the father of the expedition. He was staying in the town's hotel. 'I was lying on the sofa and was just about to rise from my siesta,' Mohn wrote in a letter to his wife.

> Then there was a hammering on the door. 'Come in.' The door opened, and there stood Fridtjof Nansen as large as life. Well, that was a surprise, and there was hugging, and ... thanks to God, who has heard my daily prayer ... I had to ask whether this was reality or a dream ... Immediately I ordered a bottle of champagne.

A total eclipse of the sun had brought Mohn to the Arctic. He was now on his way home, and only chance had kept him in Vardø. The town had been Nansen's last port of call in Norway on his way out, and the place where Mohn had bidden him farewell. 'What an encounter', Mohn added in his letter. With a small interval for his guests to go out and buy new clothes he entertained them well into the night. In the small hours, after what Mohn called 'a strange dinner party that I will never forget', Nansen saw him on to the coastal steamer in which he was about to sail and then, at 3 a.m., himself finally returned to *Windward*.

Vardø was on the frontier, still a thousand miles from home; an enclave at the north-eastern extremity of Scandinavia, cut off overland and accessible only by sea. Nonetheless when *Windward* sailed, after a day or two, Nansen stayed behind. She was too slow, he said, and he preferred to wait for the weekly mail steamer. In reality he shrank from appearing in the ship which might be said to have rescued him. He also had to stay close to the cablehead. Meanwhile, in the local sauna, he and Johansen finally rid themselves of the last vestiges of ingrained dirt from the winter hut.

Before sailing on Nansen needed to settle arrangements with Eva. In stilted telegraphese he declared: STILL CANNOT GRASP HOW WONDERFUL TO MEET. The quickest way was for Eva to meet him up the coast. She appeared to hesitate. Finally, they agreed on Hammerfest, still facing the Arctic.

On the afternoon of 18 August Nansen arrived there in the mail ship, a modest little black-hulled steamer called *Thor*. At Vardø, there had been informal and haphazard greetings. During Mohn's little dinner party the local brass band had assembled outside the hotel, and earlier a gaggle of schoolboys had been the first to recognise Nansen and Johansen in the street. Hammerfest provided the first organised reception.

The town was awash with Norwegian flags. What appeared to be all its few thousand inhabitants were waiting round the quayside. As *Thor* berthed, guns fired and a band played patriotic airs. A civic deputation came on board. According to an Englishman in the crowd, there were 'cheers and such enthusiasm as a reserved Norwegian multitude considers it not undignified to manifest'.

The man who wrote those words was Sir Martin Conway, a distinguished mountaineer who had surveyed uncharted regions of the Himalayas. He had just returned from the first crossing of Spitsbergen, and thus may be said to have succeeded in his aims where Nansen had not.

Also in Hammerfest was a friend of Nansen's, Sir George Baden-Powell. Sir George was, in that order, a Conservative MP, a political pamphleteer and a scientific amateur. He had come to the Arctic in his yacht *Otaria*, also for the solar eclipse. He was about to sail for Franz Josef Land to look for Nansen when Nansen reached Vardø. Sir George now invited Nansen to stay on *Otaria*, an invitation willingly accepted. *Otaria* was a luxurious schooner with an attentive crew, and rather more attractive than a local hotel. From *Thor* into this much needed refuge he now disappeared, greatly to local chagrin, and there he kept all visitors at bay.

Meanwhile *Windward* sailed in, followed, at half past ten in the evening, by the regular coastal ship bringing Eva. She too had a quasi-royal welcome, down to a salute of guns as the steamer berthed. Nansen was the first on board, pursued by a jostling crowd. At midnight, there followed a civic reception in the courthouse. Anyone who was anybody in the little town was present, and foreign visitors as well.

In Hammerfest also that day was a German journalist called George Wegener, who had once met Nansen in Berlin. 'At this ecstatic moment,' he wrote, 'there was a wonderful expression of happiness in Frau Eva's flushed cheeks and in her gleaming eyes.' But, he added shrewdly, 'how far husband and wife had already conquered the natural shyness which unquestionably must have overcome them at the beginning after so long and absolute a separation, how far they also had inwardly already found each other again, escaped my judgment.'

Eva was unreserved. 'It is all like a dream, and I am in the seventh Heaven,' she wrote to a friend. 'Who could ever have dreamt of such happiness? My man looks wonderful, well-fed, fat and strong. I had expected to find a skeleton.'

Nansen was supposed to leave immediately after the reception in the ship that had brought Eva. Instead he returned with her to *Otaria* and stayed in Hammerfest. That meant a delay in seeing his daughter, Liv, because Eva had left her at home. *Fram* was preying on his mind. After the first flush of excitement stray voices were beginning to hint that he had deserted his men. What is more, Andrée in his balloon might yet turn Nansen's saga to ashes.

On the morning of 20 August, the manager of the local telegraph station appeared on board *Otaria* with a telegram for Nansen he wished personally to deliver. Nansen was still dressing. He controlled himself to the extent of completing his toilet before bursting out of the cabin. 'With slightly trembling hands,' as he put it, 'I tore open the telegram.'

It had been handed in that morning at Skjærvø, between Hammerfest and Tromsø. It was from Sverdrup:

FRAM ARRIVED HERE TODAYS DATE SAFE AND SOUND. ALL WELL ON BOARD. LEAVING IMMEDIATELY FOR TROMSØ WELCOME HOME

Sverdrup had put in to Skjærvø, because it was the closest telegraph station after his landfall. Sir George ordered steam up immediately. Well might Eva say that she was 'staying ... with two sweet people [Sir George and his wife] who stand on their heads for us'.

Next day, *Otaria* sailed into Tromsø, which was beflagged, *en fête*, like Hammerfest had been before. *Fram* was already anchored in the roadstead, her old inimitable self, all funnel and halfdeck, like a clumsy child's toy. The whole crew rowed over to *Otaria* for an uninhibited, emotional reunion.

Nansen had to wait three days more to end his suspense for good. On 24 August, Andrée arrived in Tromsø on board his expedition ship, *Virgo*. Foul winds had stopped him taking off. He had no alternative but to deflate his balloon and sail for home. Now on board *Virgo*, for the first time, Nansen and Andrée came warily face to face. On deck, Andrée made a little speech of welcome. Nansen replied with the courteous hope that Andrée might succeed the following year.

After a few hours, Andrée sailed on homewards, a disappointed man, with a bitter winter to face. Nansen stayed behind, knowing now that he had at least a year to profit by his achievement. His relief overshadowed the ironic news that all his enterprise had merely taken him nineteen miles further north than had he remained on *Fram*. She had reached a latitude of 85°55′N. Nor did the public seem to care. On 26 August Nansen on *Otaria* sailed from Tromsø on a triumphal progress down the coast, towed, with *Fram*, by an ocean-going tug.

At Trondheim, he experienced the most elaborate, patriotic reception so far. Trondheim was the railhead, and Nordahl, having tired of *Fram*, hurried home by train. At Trondheim too *Otaria* left to sail back to England. Nansen and Eva transferred to the tug for the remainder of the voyage; 'because *Fram* is a pigsty', so Eva said. Johansen was less fussy. He had already transferred from *Otaria*'s 'elegant saloons', as he blandly put it, to a cabin on *Fram* 'full of reindeer furs and sleeping bags'.

At last, on 9 September, *Fram* sailed up the fjord to Christiania, with Nansen and Eva now on board. It was a repetition on an even grander scale of the return from Greenland seven years before. *Fram* was escorted by a squadron of warships. As a welcoming armada, the banks of the fjord seemed to have disgorged anything that could float. *Fram* anchored out in the roadstead and Nansen was ceremonially rowed ashore.

In a procession of carriages, past the largest crowds the city was said ever to have mustered, Nansen and his men made their way to the Royal Palace to be received by the King. As King of Sweden *and* Norway too, Oscar felt it his duty to be present on that day. Nansen was treated something like a king himself. On the way, he passed through a triumphal arch on which two hundred men and women, in white gymnastic outfits, formed a living *bas relief*, and at the palace came out onto the balcony to receive the homage of the crowd. What is more, by Royal invitation his daughter, Liv, had been staying at the Palace, so that they could be reunited early there and not have to wait until he got home.

On that day in a Christiania street, according to one story with all the ring of truth, someone happened to meet Henrik Ibsen. The street was deserted. What appeared to be the whole population was strung out along Nansen's processional route. 'You here?' the passer-by, in all innocence, apparently asked Ibsen, 'and not down at the quayside?' Ibsen's face darkened. 'No,' he is supposed to have replied, almost in a fury. 'It's a Red Indian deed, and it's being celebrated by Indian war dances, and I don't belong there!'

55

A Tumult of Applause

'If amid the tumult of applause,' began one of the letters with which Nansen was deluged, 'you should care for the welcome of an old friend, be sure you have mine.' The writer was Marion Ure, his old flame and faithful correspondent from the now distant days in Naples. There was another voice from that corner of the past. Adolf Ónodi, his Hungarian companion at the zoological station, also wrote. 'With indescribable happiness I read the news of your ... return, and that same evening, from sheer excitement, I could hardly shut my eyes,' his letter ran. 'I know with what fantastic jubilation the civilised world has greeted your return.' And Edward Else, steward of the *Windward*, touchingly wrote: 'How proud we were to have brought [you] back to Home sweet home.'

I am astonished at the interest taken in your journey by English people....
You would be surprised to see the great number of people who come aboard
the *Windward* to see the Ship and the Stateroom in which you slept, I have
had your Coat & Trousers hung up there since arrival and I am continually
refusing offers for them.

The original news was a front page sensation. Thereafter the world's press was filled with reportage, column after eulogistic column. *Punch* marked Nansen's return, as it had his departure, in verse:

You ask how it comes that I sing about NANSEN,
His pluck, and his craft and his crew?

– began the first of its four stanzas. A German journalist tellingly wrote about the 'heroic romanticism of his journey'.

In short, Nansen mania had also broken out abroad. At home, it 'went to the nation's head', King Oscar remarked, joining Ibsen in a rare dissenting voice, 'and ... it ... encouraged the already more than sufficient very Norwegian megalomania.' The Norwegian novelist Alexander Kielland thought it, however, 'a blessing for the whole country'. In their quest for independence from Sweden the Norwegians had suffered a succession of humiliating reverses. Kielland elaborated the theme. It was 'a great and unexpected help in our tribulations that [Nansen] came home and in such a manner, – to the point where even the Swedes had to add to the glory with their 3 gasbags' – that is Andrée and his companions – 'who came back with their balloon between their legs'.

Then the crowds departed, the cheering died away. Besides his other trials, Nansen was burdened with responsibility towards his men. Whatever the tensions on board *Fram*, he was loyal to them now. Their pay contractually ended with the expedition, but almost single-handedly he persuaded the Government to continue it for another year for those with families to support.

Meanwhile, he had to profit while there was yet time. His failure to attain his goal seemed strangely not to count. For the moment, he was the man who had come closest to either pole of the earth. And his adventure of the sledge journey and the winter in the hut had somehow touched a chord. In London the *Daily Chronicle* had splashed his first telegram in a special edition. For the full story, they paid him £2,250 (£100,000 or $160,000 in present terms). This was all very well, but he now had to write the book of the expedition. He had to do so quickly, before being overmastered. To do so he swallowed his restlessness and retreated to his study at *Godthåb* on the banks of the fjord. 'Good Lord, it is easy to organise good expeditions,' he ruefully told Armauer Hansen, another of his faithful correspondents from the days of working on the central nervous sytem. 'It is very difficult to write a good book about them. I don't think anyone has yet managed it.'

What Nansen now needed above all was peace of mind. Instead he faced corrosive domestic strife. After the first ecstasies of reunion, he and Eva had returned to their old predicament of dealing with each other from day to day. 'You saw me working hard, and it was all I could do to get everything done,' he plaintively accused her once. 'But you did not make any particular effort to help me.'

> I had so looked forward to reading my book to you, but it was hard to make you sit and listen, and I always had a feeling that you did so out of a sense of duty.

There were other reproaches, but this was the one that expressed the deepest hurt.

Eva had her own purgatory which, in a moment of percipience, Nansen understood:

> You talked about your singing and everything you had done while I was away and ... I understood that in some ways it was a good thing for you that I left, you could ... devote yourself entirely to your art. Then I understood that in one way you were afraid that this would finish when I came home.

With nursemaid, domestics and a once more reclusive and taciturn husband, Eva soon felt superfluous. In the middle of November she went off alone on a concert tour to Stockholm and Helsinki. There followed the now familiar exchange of amorous and tortured communications, like adolescents unhappily in love. The culmination was a semi-hysterical letter from Eva about arranging a long distance telephone call to her in Stockholm:

For God's sake don't forget, otherwise ... I'll think you no longer care for me, and so I won't come home but go directly on a concert tour to America or accept a booking for St Petersburg offered me in Helsinki by a Russian impresario.

She did come home, of course, early in December, but the bickering had been an untimely distraction. By late November, the stipulated date, Nansen had nonetheless finished the original Norwegian text followed, in January, by the all-important English translation. Somehow, in barely two months, Nansen had produced a book of 300,000 words.

Following the custom of the day, Nansen largely reproduced his journals, with linking passages where required. He had not exactly kept his diary for the purpose of publication, but what he had written possessed the quality of saga; unforced, with considerable literary power. Essentially he cut repetition and the private, uncomfortably revealing, psychological passages; also anything that hinted at the tensions on *Fram*.

Even as a piece of editing against the clock (not to mention translation, done by others), the book was an impressive performance. So too was the reward. From Aschehoug, his Norwegian publishers, Nansen received the then unheard-of advance of 88,000 kroner (£220,000 or $350,000 in present terms). The bargaining was hard but straightforward. This was scarcely the case in London for the English edition. Alexander Nansen and Scott Keltie acted as intermediaries. Neither was versed in the arcana of popular publishing, and the upshot was confusion and bad blood. In the end the book went to Constable, the contract being signed on 20 October, with publication on 15 February 1897. The advance was £10,000 (£470,000 or $750,000 in present terms). This was a quarter of what Stanley had received for *In Darkest Africa* some years before. But even today it would be a respectable amount. It was the highest price put on a polar explorer yet. The outlay proved justified. *Farthest North*, as Nansen's book was called in English, became an instant best-seller. Published in two heavy volumes though it was, the first printing of 40,000 quickly sold out.

For both book and author there was a universal acreage of acclaim. Across ten whole pages, in the *Review of Reviews*, of which he was the editor, W.T. Stead (one of the founders of modern investigative journalism) analysed what he called 'The Secret of the Nansen Boom'.

Two things were very prominent. One was the indomitable faith of the man in himself, and the other the unanimity with which most of the best authorities believed he was going to a living grave. Hence, when a man has backed himself at heavy odds against all comers ... and has come off in the end victorious, there is no need to look any further for ... the popularity of *Farthest North*.

Men of wildly different backgrounds joined the chorus of admiration. Prince Peter Kropotkin, a Russian anarchist living in exile in Britain, wrote in an English periodical that 'Nansen and Johansen [are] true heroes of our century'. Sir Leslie Stephen, editor of the *Dictionary of National Biography* and the father of Virgina Woolf, as well as being an accomplished mountaineer in his own right, said:

> Nansen's performance [is] a kind of play [which] includes a very large part of the most valuable and elevating human activities. Play, that is, may be taken to mean every variety of energy which is delightful without reference to any ulterior end.

Edward Whymper, the conqueror of the Matterhorn and a climber of a different type, pointed out that Nansen had

> made the most conspicuous advance towards the Pole that has ever been made, and almost as great an advance as has been accomplished by all other voyages in the nineteenth century put together.... He is a Man in a Million.

Or, as Stead tellingly summed it up: 'Nansen is for the moment our popular gladiator.'

Reviewers also liked what one of them called his 'simple, vivid unassuming narrative', which they contrasted favourably with the florid style and heroic posturing then the fashion in books by explorers. There was, however, something else. 'This modern Viking', as the *Daily Chronicle* in an echo of the first crossing of Greenland called him, was an antidote to *fin-de-siècle* preciosity and an overpowering feeling of decadence.

Nansen was the first of the Pole-seekers to return without loss of life. He had adventure but no martyrdom. By his journey on skis over the pack, he had tamed the Arctic and, incidentally, advanced the spread of skiing abroad. He had completed the demythologising of the polar environment that he began on the first crossing of Greenland. On that account alone his expedition took on a wholly new significance from any that had gone before. Above all, he had finally discredited the traditional idea of large, cumbersome official expeditions, and proved the essential virtues of the small party in polar exploration.

All these things were separately admirable. Nansen had the mysterious gift of transmuting them into the elements of fame. For one thing, he was eminently photogenic. The half-tone process of reproducing photographs was then being applied to periodicals and newspapers, and Nansen's brooding visage stared out of many a printed page. His crowning talent was to appeal to the popular press, precisely as it was coming into its own, and the popular press sensed, in its turn, that he had opened an era.

Already at Cape Flora, when first he heard news from the outside, Nansen had remarked that 'not the least strange is the interest the whole world now seems to have acquired for the Arctic regions'. There had been a change while he was away, and it was due to himself.

Africa, the Dark Continent, was burned out as an arena for discovery. Nansen had supplanted the African explorers in public esteem. He had brought polar exploration to the centre of the stage.

56

The Hero as Orator

Early in February 1897 Nansen arrived in England for the first of the lecture tours by which he hoped to profit while the going was good; also incidentally to promote *Farthest North*. He had a more than willing ally in Sir Clements Markham, newly knighted and, for the past four years, President of the RGS.

In Christiania, the previous September, when Nansen returned in *Fram*, Sir Clements happened to be among the guests at a banquet given by King Oscar at the Royal Palace. Over coffee and cigars, Sir Clements noted in his diary, 'the King made me sit down with him, on a small sofa … and said that "any honour our Society could confer upon the great Norwegian explorer, he should look upon as a favour to himself".' The King emphasised the hint by pointing out that he had just decorated both Nansen and Sverdrup with the Norwegian Order of St Olaf.

Sir Clements had a number of claims to originality. Among other achievements he brought the cinchona tree, the main source of quinine, from South America to India, was instrumental in having flogging abolished in the Navy and had been the first person to publish a serious work of history in defence of Richard III. Now, for his own purposes, he was only too happy to agree to the King's request, fully realising that Oscar was clearly hoping that through Nansen he might propitiate Norwegian political discontent. Sir Clements was a philo-Scandinavian who understood Norwegian and an inveterate genealogist who had already contrived to adorn a page of his diary with Nansen's family tree. He foresaw that 'Nansen mania', judiciously exploited, might finally enable him to achieve his old ambition of reviving British official polar exploration – but this time to the Antarctic.

Two months later Sir Clements was in fact received by Mr George Goschen, the First Lord of the Admiralty. After over a decade of trying, it was the first time that Sir Clements had managed to overcome official obduracy even to this modest extent.

Nansen had single-handedly diverted attention to the south. By his discovery of the deep polar basin he had finally shown that the Arctic was a sea encircled by land, and that consequently there could be no easy route to the Pole. He had also scotched two lingering, contrary illusions. One was that of an open polar sea; the other, of a floating but solid stable frozen cap of ancient ice. What remained was the shifting and changeable pack.

56. The Hero as Orator

In the Antarctic, meanwhile, as Nansen himself had already observed, everything pointed to land encircled by sea. The idea of a mysterious sixth continent beyond the Southern Ocean, like another Atlantis, was beginning to grip the imagination.

Over the Arctic there hung a pall of growing disillusion. Too much money had been spent; too many lives lost for small returns. The Antarctic promised a whole coastline, merely waiting for a ship to sail within sight. Above all, instead of the grinding horrors of the northern pack, there was the prospect of *terra firma* all the way to the other Pole.

Sir Clements Markham arranged to open Nansen's English tour with the kind of grand occasion that would further his own ends – an evening lecture under the aegis of the RGS on 8 February at the Albert Hall, by invitation only. The place was packed with what Sir Clements, as chairman, in his opening address, swelling with characteristic orotund phrase, called 'a vast assembly' of 7,000. He implied that anyone who was somebody was there. It was pardonable rhetoric. This was the year of Queen Victoria's Diamond Jubilee, the zenith of Empire, with a public mood self-certain and benign.

On the flower-swathed platform that evening were the Prince of Wales, later King Edward VII, and the Duke of York, the future King George V, flanked by the great and the good. 'Nansen is an old friend,' so *The Times* reported Sir Clements as saying, 'and I for one never doubted that he would return safely and … successful (loud cheers).' That was a not so sly dig at Nansen's former critics, present on this occasion almost to a man.

When Nansen came to speak, without any acoustic aids, his voice and foreign diction carried clearly to the furthest recesses of the cavernous arena in some directions, less so in others. There were lantern slides as well. For an hour or more Nansen held his audience, and when he sat down he was rewarded with rapturous cheering.

A gold medal, specially struck for Nansen by the RGS at Sir Clements' instigation, was now presented to him by the Prince of Wales. The Prince also presented a special RGS silver medal for Scott Hansen who, alone of *Fram*'s men, was with his leader on the platform. Other medals were being sent to his absent companions: bronze for most, but silver for Sverdrup, and also Colin Archer as designer of the ship.

There were silver medals for Blessing and Johansen too. For both, it was timely consolation. Blessing was struggling with morphine addiction following his experiments on board *Fram*. Johansen was pursued by the mysterious shadow that had haunted him all along. The expedition had not been the door to fame and fortune that he had hoped. He had no work, little money and few prospects. Nansen had already helped both men after urgent appeals: Blessing with medical treatment, Johansen with a loan, or gift.

Gerald Christy, Nansen's lecture agent, who represented many famous men, once said that he had greater drawing power than anyone else, with the later exception of Winston Churchill. Nonetheless, something had changed in him since the day he embarked on *Fram*. 'Perhaps none of us can go unpunished through three years like those,' he once told Eva.

> And there is no doubt they have changed me. I see it in many ... respects. Much of what I previously found attractive ... no longer seems of any worth.

A terrible melancholy had settled on him. He was prey to swings of mood between depression and elation more manic than he had ever known. Sometimes he seemed not quite to belong to the land of the living. Perceptive observers, journalists among them, divined the change. But to the world at large, Nansen preserved his mask. In London he was gloriously lionised. Then he set out on the money-making segment of his tour.

It was a harried rush of forty-one lectures in forty-two days, covering the length and breadth of the United Kingdom. Everywhere he drew full houses, but he paid a heavy price in ennui and exhaustion. For Eva, who had accompanied him from the start, it was even worse. By nature, she had a cold exterior; it was an effort for her to put on a friendly face. Jaded but relieved, they finished this purgatory on 24 March and the following day left for Paris.

Behind him, Nansen left a singular impression. As a result, or otherwise, within a fortnight the Admiralty wrote to Sir Clements Markham promising the loan of instruments for a putative British Antarctic expedition. This was the first official endorsement of any kind. A few days later, on 12 April, the RGS council, after all their hesitation, finally decided to organise an Antarctic expedition after all. Thus far had the 'Nansen boom' helped Sir Clements to get his way.

In Paris, meanwhile, Nansen was also making an impact. The French being more acutely aware of the creeping decadence of the age, their commentators articulated another facet of his appeal. Nansen belonged 'to a different race', as one of them put it. 'He spends on actions what we spend on words.'

> We make our journeys round the world in the books of Jules Verne, as we learn the history of France through the novels of Alexandre Dumas. And when one fine day ... we are brought face to face with a Nansen we are just as surprised as if we were to pass Captain [Nemo] or d'Artagnan in [the] street.

Nansen was also compared to Yan, the hero of Pierre Loti's novel, *Pêcheur d'Island*, a favourite of the times. Yan, as someone said, was 'the soft and primitive sailor ... affianced to the sea, the distant sea of Iceland which one day, perhaps, would want to keep him for herself'. In other words, Nansen represented the romantic, half-civilised hero from the outlands. He was an antidote to creeping regimentation and over-refinement. 'I present my homage to the illustrious Norwegian navigator,' Jules Verne himself wrote to Nansen,

> to the hero of the North Pole ... who, at the risk of his life, with a superhuman effort, has realised the dreams of the old French [explorers].

Nansen's visit to France was purely ceremonial. From the Gare du Nord he went to a dinner given by Charles Rabot, his French translator, a glaciologist and considerable Scandinavian scholar. There he was introduced to a circle more aristocratic than he had encountered in London. It was headed by Prince Roland Bonaparte, President of the Société de Géographie, a rarefied institution compared to the RGS with its Victorian intent of popular improvement. Nansen was an instant social success. It was here, for the first time on their tour, that Eva emerged from the shadow of her husband to be recognised in her own right. After dinner, by invitation, she sang at a recital which included singers from the Paris Opera.

On 26 March, the day after his arrival, Nansen gave his obligatory lecture – to the Société de Géographie in this case – followed by the presentation of what was becoming the obligatory gold medal. It all took place at the Palais du Trocadéro, Paris's exuberant answer to the Albert Hall. Again it was a full house, with all five thousand seats taken. Unpractised in the French language, Nansen took the precaution of rehearsing his lecture with Jean Hoss, a journalist on *Le Figaro*. Hoss reported the fact, which was met with much approval, and doubtless helped to increase the adulation. Through Ibsen, Norway had already become known in France to an intellectual coterie; it was Nansen who now, by a *coup de foudre*, brought his country to the attention of the wider French public.

From Paris, Nansen went to Berlin where, on 3 April, there was another lecture to another geographical society – Der Gesellschaft für Erdkunde zu Berlin – and yet another gold medal. Finally, about a week later, by way of Copenhagen, he and Eva returned home. Then Nansen continued on to Stockholm, this time alone. Here he again met Andrée, in whose person he faced a reminder of the transience of his own record for the Furthest North.

Andrée was still committed to another Arctic flight in his balloon. The two men swallowed their rivalry. When Andrée wrote to Nansen asking for magnetic and meteorological observations from *Fram*, Nansen courteously obliged. 'On your banner,' he added sombrely,

> there could well be Macbeth's golden words: 'I dare do all that becomes a man, who dares do more is none.' It is in finding that limit that true intellectual strength is revealed.

'Since I have proved that I am able to turn back,' Andrée replied, 'I am much tempted to go the other way.' It was an enigmatic farewell. He had already started by sea for Spitsbergen. On 11 July, once more at Danskøen, he finally took off in *Örnen* – 'The Eagle' – as he had named his balloon. The wind was fair, but of Andrée's two original companions of the year before Nils Ekholm had refused to follow him again because he considered that *Örnen* leaked too much and that in consequence the flight was doomed from the start. At take-off *Örnen* lost most of its drag lines, and therefore almost any capacity to manoeuvre.

Nansen, meanwhile, on 19 May, received a telegram from Marie Elizabeth, Princess of Saxony:

TODAY ON THE FIRST ANNIVERSARY OF YOUR DEPARTURE FROM THE WINTER HUT I THINK OF YOU SINCE I HAVE JUST READ THE WONDERFUL DESCRIPTION OF YOUR EXPEDITION WITH THE GREATEST AND LIVELIEST INTEREST AMAZEMENT AND RESPECT

It was a gratifying proof of unabated hero-worship, but at the same time a disturbing hint of already belonging to the past. Nansen felt uncomfortably in limbo. Besides Andrée, Jackson was still hidden in the Arctic, attaining no one knew what latitude. But Nansen had no need to worry yet.

On 3 September Jackson returned to London in *Windward*, not having made any appreciable progress northwards. In the meantime, on 15 July, the captain of a Norwegian sealing vessel had shot a carrier pigeon with a message from Andrée. On 19 September the Stockholm newspaper for which it was intended finally received it and, the following day, published the text. It was dated 13 July, at latitude 82° 2′N. It was a whisper of things to come. In two days, Andrée had made as much to the north as *Fram* in eight months.

But this was the last heard of Andrée and his companions. They had been swallowed by the Arctic and were never seen alive again.

Hard Pounding in the States

His record still intact, Nansen was hastening to consolidate his finances, while his social standing was being built up.

In England, early in 1897, he had bought a yacht. That was a sign of wealth and class then even more than now. Sir George Baden-Powell (a relation of the founder of the scout movement), a devoted yachtsman and Nansen's constant admirer, had been an intermediary, or probably the instigator of the affair. It seemed a bargain at the time. For £1,000 (£47,000 or $75,000 in present terms), Nansen obtained an ocean-going schooner, 30 tons Thames measurement, 57 ft overall, newly-built in Teignmouth in Devon, with the latest Swedish Bolinder auxiliary motor running on paraffin.

Nansen took delivery of the vessel on 3 June. A fortnight or so later he sailed her out into the Skagerrak with Eva and Liv on board. Eva was six months pregnant and, not on that account alone, somewhat out of sorts. Nansen was more concerned with *Belgica*, a barque in port at Sandefjord, waiting to set sail.

Originally *Patria*, a Norwegian bottlenose whaler, *Belgica* had been bought and renamed by a titled Belgian naval lieutenant, Baron Adrien de Gerlache. He had won the race to organise the first Antarctic expedition – as distinct from a whaling cruise – for half a century. Inspired by *Fram*'s romantic aura, and hence by Nansen's example, de Gerlache's ambition was to be the first man to winter above the Antarctic Circle.

Neat, slender and refined, de Gerlache was an unlikely figure to open modern Antarctic exploration. Belgium was engrossed in colonising her part of the Congo, and wholly unconcerned with polar matters. Somehow de Gerlache nonetheless persuaded the Belgian Royal Geographical Society to lend him their support. Somehow he raised the money and bought his ship. He spent months in Norway learning to ski and collecting equipment. Because of their experience in the ice, he even signed on a number of Norwegians among his crew.

Nansen's yacht put into Sandefjord on 19 June, the date on which *Belgica* was due to sail. He was shown round the vessel by de Gerlache himself, and thereby had the ambiguous experience of facing a man whom he had inspired to act. He had come expressly to see *Belgica* off, but last-minute hitches delayed her departure by a few days, and he could not or would not wait to watch her cast off and sail down the channel to the sea. He returned home, and made do with a farewell telegram: 'MAY THE EXPEDITION ... CAST NEW LIGHT ON THE MOST MYSTERIOUS PART OF THE EARTH.'

Meanwhile, two months earlier, on 12 April, without his asking, he had been created professor. The chair was *ad hominem*, with no duties. This was a device on the part of others to give him both title and position – in Norwegian society, a professor enjoyed huge prestige – and a stipend from the State. Also, it was hoped, once more, that the University of Christiania would benefit by the lustre of Nansen's name.

His chair was in zoology. When Armauer Hansen, like others, wrote urging him to return to the central nervous system, Nansen replied, with familiar disingenuousness, that 'if only I were there again, but it will have to wait a little'.

On 16 September Eva gave birth to her second child: a son, Kåre, a name derived from an old Norse word meaning 'strong' and also identified with a god of wine. Nansen called him 'a young polar explorer'.

A few weeks later, on 12 October, he hurried off alone on a lecture tour of the United States, while the going was still good. By way of London, Liverpool, and a stormy Atlantic crossing on a Cunard liner, he arrived in New York on 24 October.

His tour began in Washington, two days later, at the White House. There (in the Blue Room) the President, William McKinley, received him. This was followed by a reception at the Arlington Hotel, arranged by the National Geographical Society. According to the *Washington Post*, 'Nearly every prominent resident of the city whose coming and going does not hinge on the sessions of Congress ... met to do [him] homage' – including the future President, Theodore (Teddy) Roosevelt.

Someone observed that Nansen hid 'the rarest refinement under the most rugged exterior'. He was decribed as

> considerably taller than most American men, light in complexion, and almost boyish in manner.... His voice is deep and full and he talks with an accent slightly foreign, but which is the more marked because of his inclination to let his voice fall at the end of every sentence.

His lecture was greeted with the now familiar applause, varied with much waving of handkerchiefs. This was tempered by an uneasy meeting with an ambiguous figure from the past. Among the audience was Rear Admiral George W. Melville, Engineer-in-Chief of the U.S. Navy. Melville had been on the *Jeannette*, whose relics all those years ago had led Nansen to the idea of a transpolar current and the drift of the *Fram*. In his own words, Melville now told Nansen that he had 'simply finished our drift and [taken] hold where [we] let go'. And Robert E. Peary, absent from the function, was smouldering with resentment at his own failure and Nansen's success. Mrs Peary was angry too. She 'was said to be furious with me', Nansen wrote to Eva, once back in New York to start the main part of the tour,

> because of my dedication [of *Farthest North*] to you [who] 'had the courage to remain behind' ... She thinks ... this is aimed at her. What self-delusion.

Critical acclaim had also been showered on the American edition of *Farthest North*, which had appeared in the spring. The praise was not only for the content. Nansen might 'lay some solid claim to being a man of letters', the *New York Times* declared in the course of two whole pages. He was freely compared to Columbus – and also, by one surly Irish-American clerical reviewer, to Frankenstein (not the monster, but his creator), on the grounds of his alleged 'oppressive ... superiority to the forces of nature'.

Such pinpricks were rare, and hardly worth consideration. Yet despite the atmosphere of general acclaim in which his tour started, Nansen was restless and unhappy as never before. He was oppressed by the complex tensions continuing to rage between Eva and himself. These had resurfaced almost as soon as he had left Norway.

'I wonder if you will ever find peace,' Eva wrote almost at once, 'or whether your life will be restless to the end.' A family friend had just told her that

> one of the reasons you have gone to America was to raise money to go on an expedition to the South Pole ... Is that true? You might tell *me* how matters stand.

It was indeed true. Nansen had not been exactly open with Eva because, in his own words, after the *Fram* expedition, 'you said that if I went away again, it would be all over between us'.

'If you are thinking about the South Pole,' Eva continued in another letter,

> you must not let me stand in your way ... I understand that a man like you cannot rest until he has done what he feels he has the strength and ability for.

The conflict erupted again after Nansen was jolted by another figure from the past. At New Haven, Connecticut, he had met Professor Marsh, the man who, some fifteen years earlier, had offered to appoint him his assistant. Marsh 'congratulated me on not having taken the post', Nansen told Eva. 'He believed that, as it had turned out, I had found a greater goal in life. I am not so sure ... It is not we ourselves who determine our own fate.'

That's horrible to contemplate [wrote Eva in reply]. Do you mean to say that if Fate has intended you for the South Pole, you will have to go there?

'If it has to be, neither you nor I can avoid it,' was Nansen's gloomy answer.

This was written on 19 December. For nearly two months now he had been living on trains, criss-crossing the Eastern States and the margins of the mid-West, rushing from one lecture to the next. He was jaded and, to add to his discontent, after his opening reception his audiences had shrunk. Often he was faced with half-empty houses. In Europe he was everywhere a great man. But in America he felt somehow just one of the crowd, all competing for attention.

He was lonely and dispirited, hounded by a stream of letters from Eva pursuing the tortured dialogue between them, reflecting, as she herself confessed, a variety of black moods. She too had been disturbed by a figure from the past, this time in the shape of 'the other woman', 'The Treasure', Nansen's old flame Dagmar Nicolaysen, whose shadow continued to haunt Eva still. The day after Nansen landed in New York Eva wrote to say that a family friend had told her that, according to the latest gossip,

you and I are going to be divorced, because you are so in love with The Treasure that we can no longer hold out. What is more, you two have been seen alone.

Desperately she continued:

I feel as if we were no longer man and wife, and as if I can only be unhappily in love with you, exactly as I suffered in the old days, when I was nothing to you.

'We two are made for each other [yet we] are made to destroy life for each other,' Nansen miserably observed. A succession of letters composed over a month or more in trains and hotels between New York, St Louis and Chicago pursued this unhappy theme. One moment he was hurling accusations: 'You have not always been quite frank with me.... You have not wanted to let me see what you really are.' The next he was wallowing in self-reproach: 'It was my own fault, my unreasonable demands, my narrow-minded egotism ... I scarcely understand myself.... What dark genie has come between us?'

One answer, to his shame, was their daughter, Liv. When he sailed off on *Fram*, he wrote to Eva, Liv

had not yet begun to form such an important part of your life. I was still unquestionably the midpoint.... While I was away, I thought of you only as you were, and not as a mother ... I did not think that mother love, according to the law of Nature, had to grow in you and partly overshadow your love for me, and it would be different from before ... I came home and discovered [that] Liv had to be closest to your heart, but I found it hard to accept.

He visited his resentment on Liv. He rejected her. When he spoke it was only to be harsh. 'My trouble in life,' he now wrote in exculpation, 'is that I have never been able to compromise. I have always demanded *all* or *nothing*.' But also with Faustian overtones, conscious or not: 'I understand all too well that my desires ... can never be fulfilled, and *ought never to be so*.'

Eva responded with an equal flood of remorse. 'It has all been my fault ... I have wronged you,' she wrote. But:

> Perhaps you know that when a woman is pregnant she is often abnormal and unpredictable.... You will find me a different person when you come home. [I will] live only for you.

Nansen also promised to turn over a new leaf. 'If you will show some tenderness to me and not just violent emotions,' he revealingly declared, 'that will be enough to make me happy. It is tenderness I have missed.'

Nansen was missing her, if he was to be believed, more than on *Fram*. Soon he was pressing her to join him in America, with or without the children. On medical advice, or for other reasons, she declined.

Nansen made things worse when he crassly explained that he had indeed been seeing Dagmar Nicolaysen 'and discovered that my old feelings were not quite dead'. But this, he claimed, was 'a means of forgetting' that now he had to share Eva's attention with their children. 'No longer [was I] the only one [and it] tortured me.'

'DO YOU LOVE ME OR THE TREASURE', Eva frantically cabled back. 'LIFE DEPENDS ON REPLY.' A cable or two, remorseful letters, mutual protestations that it had all been the product of sickly sensibility combined to restore a calm of sorts. 'I am too firmly trapped in another web,' Nansen declared, 'and however hard I try, I can never escape. '*Du bist die Hexe Lorelei*' – 'Thou art the siren Lorelei.' (In the circumstances, an ambivalent quotation from a romantic German poem about meeting a woman in a dark wood: '... God give me strength/Thou art the siren Lorelei/"Thou knowest me well – atop a crag/In the flowing Rhine my castle lies/Late it is, it will soon be cold/This wood you nevermore will leave!" '. Set to music by Schumann, it was in Eva's repertoire.)

Filtered or amplified by distance (for letters to or from the United States took a good fortnight to arrive), there still remained the conflicts of two fierce, mutually destructive characters, each the other's shadow side. Once more they seemed intent on proving that, face to face, they were incapable of showing their private selves. In order to be frank they had to be apart. 'I got out my old skis, those I had on the day you and I first met,' Eva wrote artlessly after the worst was over. 'Do you remember how we became good friends immediately ... ah, that was a lovely day.'

This was the outer dialogue; the inner one, echoed in Nansen's diary, revealed other cross-currents. It was, he wrote, 'strange to hear all these people assure me that it has "given them so much pleasure to read my book".' He met one woman who assured him that he had 'saved her in the darkest moment of her life.' Her husband had committed suicide and she herself was on the edge of the abyss.

Is it not sad [he commented] to be able to help others but be so helpless oneself; it is a trick of Fate to pour wine for others, but lose the capacity to drink oneself.

And all too typically, on a train in Canada as it happened:

I see two female forms out there in the dark, but cannot distinguish the one from the other. Both are looking at me unhappily and reproachfully – Oh my God, I love them both, each in her own way, and I would give my life not to make either unhappy.

On 15 November he received a letter from a certain MacAlister, who was forming The Great Klondyke Corporation Limited to develop Alaska and the North Western Territory. MacAlister invited Nansen – as he frankly said, because of his fame – to become what he called Governor of the Court of Directors. 'It is unquestionably a wonderful civilising task to open a whole new country for humanity,' Nansen wrote to Eva. He wished she was by his side to help him make up his mind: 'You know ... I can never make a decision without your help.'

In the event, his mind was made up for him. He had written to Sir George Baden-Powell, who had been quoted as one of the directors. Sir George urgently cabled him to have nothing to do with the company – his own name had been used without his knowledge. MacAlister, whom both Nansen and Sir George had met, was a plausible crony from the Savage Club in London, and like many another flotation The Great Klondyke Corporation existed only in the imagination of its promoter. It was, after all, the height of the Klondyke gold rush. Nansen backed off, protesting to all the world that he had never taken the proposition seriously.

Meanwhile, he was being pursued by echoes of *Fram*. Letters from home reported that books on the expedition by both Johansen and Nordahl were appearing – in parts, following the custom of the day. Johansen's – called *With Nansen in the North* when it appeared in its English translation – was a simple but moving account, which followed Nansen in discreetly suppressing personal conflicts and overt unpleasantness. Nordahl's book – *Framgutterne*, 'The Boys on Fram' – was another matter altogether. It included the incident of the stolen beer and Nansen's dressing-down of the crew and gave Nansen most of the blame. 'It cannot harm me much,' Nansen wrote to one of his correspondents.

and even if it does it is nonetheless better than if the story were to be told as it really happened. That would damage ... the whole expedition ... considerably more; it is one of the few dark spots which it is best to allow to rest in peace for ever.

In his diary, he was considerably less stoical: 'I shudder at the sudden reminder of the toil up there in the north,' he wrote around this time.

Yet on the other hand there was struggle and there was a goal, something definite at least.

And he added, reiterating the crux of his philosophy:

When all is said and done, happiness is the struggle towards a summit, and when that is attained, it is happiness to glimpse new summits on the other side.

Nansen had earned by his American lectures the sum of $14,000 (£140,000 or $225,000 in present terms). 'When you return home, you will be absolutely independent financially,' wrote his brother Alexander, who was still managing his affairs.

But this money had been painfully earned. Nansen's American impresario, Richard Heard, an ingratiating and persuasive character, had fixed a contract which committed him to fifty lectures, with an option (at Heard's discretion) for fifty more. Nansen now discovered, too late, that he was obliged to deliver this second series for virtually nothing because he had not made up the original guarantee. After a flurry of litigation he managed to cut short the new tour, and on 29 January, to his inexpressible relief, boarded the Cunard liner *Campania* in New York to sail home, at least a month earlier than would otherwise have been possible, having reached no further west than Davenport, Iowa.

What with Eva's emotional letters, the strain of concentrated lecturing, and finally the trouble with Heard, it had not been a happy tour. Nor had he felt at home with the Americans, as his diary copiously makes clear. 'Look at [their] import duties,' ran a typically critical entry during the Atlantic crossing. 'This unhealthy protection of their own industry for the benefit of a few at the cost of the many.... A blinkered and short-sighted breed.' Unmoved by the raw energy of a new country in the process of gestation, he scorned what he saw as American materialism, commercialism and absence of culture. He tellingly disdained American society as 'plebeian'.

On 6 February, he reached London, and felt once more at ease.

58

A Record Lost

To Eva's distress, Nansen did not go straight home. He had arranged a small lecture tour in England on the way to squeeze more money out of the *Fram* expedition while he could – and also to enjoy, as he hoped, a return to hero-worship after three months in America as a curiosity.

He achieved both, but also in England came another, sadder echo of *Fram*. Paid for by Nansen, Blessing was in an institution in Copenhagen, seeking a cure for his morphine addiction, but without success. Nansen now received a pathetic letter from Blessing, asking him to help him find treatment elsewhere. 'Which naturally I will do as far as I can,' Nansen wrote to Eva. 'I feel so terribly sorry for him.'

At last, on 1 March, Nansen returned to Eva, having been away for over four months. 'How happy we will be, my lovely little friend,' he had written out in the Atlantic. 'All misery will be forgotten.'

But first there was another hurried round of recognition, while there was still time. Eva had promised on this occasion to accompany him. Kåre meanwhile went down with scarlet fever, which delayed departure. They finally set off in the middle of April, leaving both children behind in the care of a nurse.

Nansen was on his way to St Petersburg, Vienna, and the marches of central and eastern Europe he had so far missed. He began with a detour via London where, on 20 April, at a lunch given by Scott Keltie at the Royal Societies' Club, he was publicly reconciled with Frederick Jackson. For a variety of reasons, they had fallen out. Jackson was huffed at being overshadowed by Nansen whom, not unjustifiably, he felt that he had as good as rescued and who, in his turn, was sensitive on the point. Jackson had more or less accused him of 'stealing' some of his discoveries in Franz Josef Land.

The Royal Geographical Society had not made things easier. For all his faults, Jackson had led the most innovative and successful British polar expedition for a generation. Nonetheless he had been ostentatiously snubbed by the Society. For him, there was no medal and little recognition. In this could be discerned the wily hand of Sir Clements Markham. He grovelled fashionably before Nansen, but abominated a man like Jackson because he had flouted authority, acted on his own, and diverted private funds which otherwise would have fallen to his, Sir Clement's, own

Antarctic schemes. Nansen and Jackson had met only once since their time at Cape Flora, at a private lunch the previous October when Nansen was on his way to America. Now, with the aid of intermediaries, the antagonism between them was at least publicly laid to rest. That done, Nansen finally left on the long train journey to St Petersburg, and the real business of the trip.

The Swedish-Norwegian Legation in St Petersburg had reported with concern that officials were offended because Nansen had delayed his visit and thus 'slighted Russia ... our northern neighbouring Great Power'. By sheer force of personality Nansen smoothed all ruffled feathers. He attended banquets and gave his obligatory lecture (in English) to the Russian Geographical Society, in the process being presented with the now obligatory gold medal. He again demonstrated his singular talent for gaining an entrée to the ruling circles wherever he went. On 27 April he was received in audience by the Tsar, Nicholas II, who had already awarded him the Grand Cross of Stanislaus.

By way of Moscow and Warsaw, Nansen moved on to Vienna, where he arrived on 5 May for another round of ceremonial, medal and award. Here the royal audience was with the venerable old Austro-Hungarian Emperor Franz-Josef. He questioned Nansen closely about Franz Josef Land; understandably since, after all, it had been named after himself.

The reception in Vienna differed in certain respects from any that Nansen had experienced so far. At the Franz Josef railway station to meet him (and with flowers for Eva) waited a deputation from the Austrian Ski Federation. To them he was not so much the man with the record for the Furthest North as the prophet of skiing, and his visit provided uncovenanted propaganda for their sport. Among them was a great admirer, Toni Schruf, who, since the first crossing of Greenland, had been one of the skiing pioneers in Austria. Schruf now persuaded Nansen to visit Mürzzuschlag, his home town in the foothills of the Alps, and approve the ski terrain. For Nansen, all this was a new experience.

Also in Vienna, around this time, Sigmund Freud was reading *In Nacht und Eis*, the German edition of *Farthest North*. His womenfolk, Freud wrote to a friend, were 'mad about Nansen', while he himself could 'make good use of Nansen's dreams', of which several were recorded in the book. 'They are absolutely transparent,' Freud declared. He was then starting his work on the interpretation of dreams, and Nansen provided some of the raw material:

> That his psychological condition is quite simply typical of those who try something new with confidence and, in a roundabout way, probably discover something new, and not so much as he had imagined, I know from my own experience.

After Vienna, Nansen travelled to Budapest for another reception,

377

another lecture – and a meeting with Adolf Ónodi, still vividly remembering what he always called 'the wonderful days in Naples'. They had not met since then. Ónodi, in his picturesque phraseology, was 'stricken with the most intense Nansen fever', and overcome with what he called an 'unforgettable reunion'.

As a Hungarian Ónodi, in his own words, was 'happy and very gratified' that Nansen had visited Budapest and thus 'honoured Hungary with your distinguished presence'. Under the Habsburgs the Hungarians, reigned over by an Austrian emperor, were as nationalistic and discontented in their dual monarchy as the Norwegians in theirs.

Returning to Christiania from Budapest after a short holiday in Venice (which Eva had never seen before), Nansen was faced with another experience. Shortly after *Fram* had returned from her famous voyage in September 1896, his old benefactor, Axel Heiberg, together with the brothers Ellef and Amund Ringnes, both Christiania brewers, had formed a syndicate to send the vessel north again and pay all the costs. Otto Sverdrup stood on the bridge of *Fram* now, both as expedition leader and captain of the ship, and Nansen was there to see him off. It was 24 June, five years almost to the day since he himself had sailed on her down the fjord.

For Nansen, this was a melancholy experience. He had quarrelled with Sverdrup over some trifling affair. 'In better hands,' he said, Sverdrup 'could have been a fine fellow. In one way he is like wax, one could make anything you like out of him. As long as he was in my hands, he was completely different.' And now Sverdrup was sailing out again; not on another transpolar drift but to explore the Canadian Arctic and Northern Greenland.

Two days later, an American journalist turned explorer called Walter Wellman left Tromsø for Franz Josef Land with the very definite intention of reaching the North Pole. He was followed after another few days by Peary, who sailed out from New York on the selfsame quest by another route. And at the end of July another polar vessel sailed down the fjord from Christiania, this time Antarctic bound. She was a Norwegian sealer, originally *Pollux*, renamed *Southern Cross*, built and refitted by Colin Archer; the expedition ship of Carsten Egeberg Borchgrevink.

Borchgrevink was a Norwegian consumed by the ambition of becoming the first man to winter on the Antarctic continent. He had asked for Nansen's help, but Nansen, who unfairly disparaged him as a fraud, for some reason declined to give it. Finally Borchgrevink persuaded the English newspaper magnate Sir George Newnes to pay for him to go south, albeit with the stipulation that he sail under the English flag.

One after the other, Antarctic expeditions began to follow in the wake of Borchgrevink and de Gerlache. In April 1899, from nationalistic considerations, the German government gave a grant for Erich von Drygalski, a Professor of Geography at the University of Berlin, to go south. Three months later Nansen received a letter from Sir Clements Markham to say that the British government would be following suit with a subsidy for a national Antarctic expedition. Antarctic plans were also afoot in Sweden and Scotland.

'As to my own Antarctic expedition,' Nansen wrote around this time to Sir John Murray, a Scottish oceanographer and Antarctic enthusiast,

> the plan ... was worked out in its outline, to a great extent even in detail, partly on board the Fram, partly also in the winter hut of Franz Josef Land, where Johansen and I had plenty of time at our disposal. At that time I did not know, however, that any other expedition was starting.... Finding upon my return that several expeditions were probably going, I saw [that] I should consequently have to alter my plans [depending on] the discoveries which might be made in the Antarctic.

However, he continued, 'I have compelled myself not to think of my plans for new enterprises, as I wished first to see that the scientific results of the last one were properly worked out.'

Early in April 1899, a few weeks before he wrote to Sir John Murray, news arrived that de Gerlache, in *Belgica*, had arrived back in Punta Arenas, in the Straits of Magellan. His expedition had been shot with dark episodes. *Belgica* had been beset in the pack ice of the Bellingshausen Sea, and only with difficulty escaped, but de Gerlache had achieved his aim of being the first to spend a winter above the Antarctic circle.

In September the same year Nansen, together with Eva, went to Berlin for the Seventh International Geographical Congress. 'We are ... horribly tired, we have constantly been to receptions, some ... so boring you could weep tears of blood,' Eva wrote to a friend.

> I know in advance what people are going to ask ... Weren't those 3 years horrible? Is Nansen going to the South Pole? You, who knew how to wait, are a far greater hero than your husband, etc. etc. It makes you sick.

Nansen was respectfully treated as the polar oracle, thus prolonging yet further the season of acclaim. At the same time, he was brought face to face with those intimately concerned with the future British and German Antarctic expeditions; Sir Clements Markham from the one and Erich von Drygalski from the other. Nansen argued with them about sledge dogs.

Both opposed their use in the Antarctic. Sir Clements, an urbane though wily relic of the mid-Victorian era, pontificated from theory and sentiment. In his youth he had once briefly been to the Arctic but had never actually driven dogs. He despised or feared them because they interfered with his devotion to the national ethos of heroic endeavour. Drygalski, by contrast, although deeply professorial in the classical German mode, had done considerable exploration in Greenland and driven dogs himself. He reasoned that they could only be used near open water, where seals were available for fodder. Inland, they would have to haul their own food, which reduced the useful load. Moreover, in the broken terrain at the edge of the ice cap they would be a hindrance.

'I agree ... that ... on rough ice, dogs are not much use. Johansen and I learned that,' Nansen replied in the debate.

> Nonetheless, I do not regret having taken them, because without dogs we would never have come back alive. [And] if it is a matter of penetrating the Antarctic ice cap, then I am certain that dogs are best.

Prophetic words, politely discounted, especially by Sir Clements Markham. Nonetheless, despite their disagreement, Sir Clements, in the course of his Antarctic preparations, wrote to Nansen in November, asking for a list of the firms that had supplied him with food for his own expedition on *Fram*.

This acted like a goad. In December Nansen asked Colin Archer to design two ships for an Antarctic expedition. That suggested the plan that he had evolved on *Fram*: both ships to sail to the Antarctic, one to stay for the winter and, as a precaution, the other to return to Australia or New Zealand.

For one reason or another, those ships never left the drawing-board. Events were now following hard upon one another. In April 1900, Borchgrevink returned to civilisation, having spent a year at Cape Adare, at the entrance to the Ross Sea, thus realising his ambition to be the first man to winter on the Antarctic continent. He had also made the first landing on the Ross Ice Shelf where, on a short ski tour, he set a record for the Furthest South of 78°50′ and opened the race for the South Pole. Once more, Nansen had been forestalled.

But the tolling of the bell came from another quarter.

On 16 January 1899, Nansen received in his home Luigi Amadeo of Savoy, the Duke of the Abruzzi. He had fleetingly approached Nansen the year before, in London, while Nansen was on his way back from America, but silence had supervened. The Duke had now turned up in Christiania unannounced to consult the oracle and begin preparations. He had designs on the North Pole.

Even among the motley crowd that were polar explorers, Luigi Amadeo stood out. Solitary and reserved, he was, in that order, a fervent patriot, a naval officer and a scion of the Italian reigning House of Savoy. He was one more explorer self-confessedly to have been inspired by reading *Farthest North*. Behind a formal, precise and mildly effete appearance, Luigi Amadeo hid all the traits of a man of action. He was an accomplished mountaineer, with first ascents to his credit, among them Mount St Elias, in Alaska. With Peary and Wellman also aiming for the Pole, he was now a man in a hurry. At the age of barely twenty-six, twelve years younger than Nansen, he was a disturbing symbol of youth knocking at the door. He was paying for the whole expedition out of his own pocket. Three days after meeting Nansen he bought *Jason* – the selfsame vessel which had taken Nansen to Greenland – and which, renamed *Stella Polare* ('The Polar Star') became his expedition ship. His plan was to winter on Franz Josef Land and then with sledge dogs (but not skis), head over the pack ice. In less than six months Luigi Amadeo was ready. On 12 June 1899 he became the next to sail down the Christiania fjord heading for high latitudes.

About two months later Nansen was vaguely comforted by the return of Walter Wellman to Tromsø, his expedition a fiasco. Nansen still held the record. But there was yet another melancholy echo of *Fram*. Bernt Bentsen, who made the pierhead jump at Tromsø, had joined Wellman and mysteriously died on Franz Josef Land at the beginning of the year. It was a strange and restless time.

On 2 November 1899, in Christiania, Eva Nansen gave her farewell concert. The programme included the first complete performance of Grieg's song cycle *Haugtussa*, 'The Earth Spirit', a setting of verses published four years earlier by the same Arne Garborg who had been at the farewell dinner on the eve of *Fram*'s departure. It was poetry of the national awakening, rooted in the world of Norwegian folk tales with their pagan overtones in which Nansen, for one, was steeped. The eerie central character is Veslemøy, literally 'Little Maiden', a girl possessed by super-natural powers. She was a seer in whom the forces of good and evil clashed, an uncomfortable creature of light and shadow. 'You have caught ... the unearthly music I tried to sing in verse,' Garborg wrote to Grieg after the concert. Eva Nansen 'sang wonderfully ... she *was* Veslemøy'. Nansen had long since observed the same thing. Even the yacht he had bought two years earlier in England he had chosen to call *Veslemøy*.

The months drifted by in suspense. In March 1900, with Luigi Amadeo hidden in the ice, Nansen hurried off to Germany to squeeze in another lecture tour while he was still the man who had been farthest north. Around the middle of July he was off again; now on an oceanographical cruise to Iceland and Jan Mayen Island in a newly-built Norwegian research vessel, *Michael Sars*, named after Eva's celebrated father. This was her maiden voyage. In his irregularly kept diary Nansen gave vent to the moody nihilistic restlessness by which he was now plagued: 'The ideal I had as a boy, independence, has it been realised? I came closest in the hut up there in the North.' 'The great emptiness envelops me again.' 'The struggle for nothing, in nothing, about nothing.' 'You are basically a perverse creature, in rain and bad weather your depression always lifts.' And: 'It is my lot to desert what means most to me in order to seek that which is cold and hard.'

The year before, Nansen had bought a remote mountain *sæter*, or alpage, called Sørkje, two days' journey by train, horse and carriage west of Christiania, on the border of Telemark. 'Here on this patch of God's green earth,' he proclaimed,

> I have chosen my kingdom, by the side of a mountain lake, ringed by the dark, grave conifer forest, interspersed with birch woods and topped by naked mountains above the timber line.

In other words, he had found himself a summer retreat. It comprised some wooden buildings, a small, disused hotel, and all the land, fishing and hunting within sight. During the winter, for Eva's benefit, he had a piano hauled up on a horse-drawn sledge over the snow – in that terrain the usual way of transporting heavy loads. Thereafter a piano tuner regularly came up from the valley.

That summer of 1900, while Nansen was on *Michael Sars*, Eva went to Sørkje alone. She was eight months pregnant, and could not ride up the bridle path which was the final approach. So, in notably high spirits, she was carried by two men from the valley in a kind of sedan chair improvised from a wicker seat. The family doctor, a midwife and a nurse followed in due course, and on 9 August, in a wild, romantic setting, Eva was delivered of Irmelin, her third child and second daughter. It was a scene that might have been acted out by the eerie Veslemøy whom Eva had so memorably portrayed in song.

Nansen, meanwhile, had been in the sombre waters off Jan Mayen, a gloomy island of volcanic origin of which, in his own words, 'I thought I had seen enough.' Now homeward bound he continued pouring out his emotions into his diary: 'I am tired of everlastingly trying to penetrate the unknown.' And: 'Man, why are you writing? Have you nothing better to do? Is it in order to preserve your great thoughts and sickly moods for posterity?' On 19 August, having disembarked from the *Michael Sars* and travelled hard for four days, he reached Sørkje around midnight. After recovering from the journey he wrote, in very different mood:

> Eva is singing at the piano downstairs, wonderful sounds ... A new little creature in the cradle ... Ah, life is wonderful.

About ten days later a buoy with a message from Andrée, more than three years old, was washed up on the North Norwegian coast. It brought no new latitude, and was the last heard of Andrée. It was not until 1930 that his remains were found, on White Island in the Spitzbergen archipelago. His flight had ended disastrously after only three days, on 14 July 1897, at around 83°N. He and his companions probably died from trichinosis, contracted from eating contaminated polar bear.

Meanwhile at Tromsø on 6 September, soon after the message from the doomed balloonist had been found, there was dispatched to Nansen the half-dreaded telegram from Luigi Amadeo:

58. A Record Lost

STELLA POLARE ARRIVED ... EXPEDITION REACHED EIGHTY SIX THIRTY THREE.

After five years Nansen had lost his record for the Furthest North, if only by twenty miles. He had known it was inevitable, but the expected is usually hard to bear. 'Our goals are what we ourselves decide,' ran a bitter and confused outpouring in his diary during the aftermath:

Is it the struggle towards the goals which makes mankind happy?... Is the Eskimo's goal, his hunting, his struggle against Nature, not as great [as that of] a Newton discovering gravity?... What is the value of having goals for their own sake?... they all vanish.... It is merely a question of time.

This was all too reminiscent of Faust's despairing words:

Verflucht, was uns in Träumen heuchelt,
Des Ruhms, der Namensdauer Trug!

'Cursed be that within our dreams,
Which cheats with thought of lasting fame!'

Such, for Nansen, was the beginning of the new century, and the divide within his life.

Part IV

Diplomat

The Oracle Speaks

Nansen had lost a rôle. Henceforth, consciously or not, he began the long search for another one, in wider fields perhaps. It was a gradual process. For the moment, he remained the supreme polar oracle.

Luigi Amadeo turned out surprisingly to pose no threat. For one thing, his personality was no match for Nansen's and his book about his expedition, when it eventually appeared, was surprisingly flat. For another, having snatched the record, he vanished from the Arctic, returned to mountaineering and, in Africa, eventually made the first ascent of Ruwenzori, 'The Mountains of the Moon'.

It was not only that the romantic aura of his great journeys still clung to Nansen and his ceremonial benison was sought by hopeful explorers. He was an authority on the technique of polar travel. He had, after all, founded a school. He had amassed a fund of practical knowledge. Above all, he had turned Christiania into a prime source of the equipment he had pioneered, notably the Nansen sledge, unobtainable elsewhere. A visit to Nansen had therefore become an indispensable preliminary to a polar expedition. And in the course of 1900 a variety of pilgrims turned up.

The first, in October, were some members of Drygalski's German Antarctic expedition. Hard on their heels came Sir Clements Markham, accompanied by a Royal Naval officer, Commander Robert Falcon Scott, newly appointed leader of the forthcoming British Antarctic Expedition.

Scott was very different from Luigi Amadeo. For one thing, he was no aristocrat, but indelibly middle class. For another, he had not conceived the enterprise, but been appointed to it. He was an unmistakable adventurer. Above all, as Nansen observed, Scott

> had no training which made him specially fit for the task ... no experience in snow and ice ... and had never tried skiing or sledge travelling.

Scott remained in Christiania for about a week, during which time, as was now becoming a habit, Nansen arranged for the supply of equipment, in particular the insulated cooker that now bore his name. He also crammed Scott with as much theoretical instruction as he could on the rudiments of snow travel.

Dr Reginald Koettlitz who, since the never-to-be-forgotten encounter at

Cape Flora, had struck up a correspondence with Nansen, was now one of the doctors on the British Antarctic Expedition. He was soon writing to Nansen: 'How much better it would have been if someone had been placed in command who had had former experience!' As for the expedition's organisers:

> After all the experience of others, notably yourself, [our] preparations are largely governed by the precedents of British expeditions, so ignorantly and blindly followed by men of the official class ... who join ... committees ... The ... final result will, I fear be much blundering [and] it will be muddled through *à l'Anglais*.

The next supplicant to appear before Nansen, in the winter of 1900, was a man diametrically different from Scott. In Nansen's words, Scott was 'handsome ... with [a] genial expression'. Of the newcomer, neither could be said. Tall and angular, he had intense, hooded eyes and a massive hawk-like nose. He was an officer, not in the navy but in the Norwegian mercantile marine. He was well versed in snow and ice and skiing. He had been *Belgica*'s second mate, one of the polyglot company under de Gerlache and, in the summer of 1899, had diffidently offered to tell Nansen the story in person. He had been on the first sledging journey known to have been made on Antarctic *terra firma*. Now he wanted to organise his own expedition. He wanted to be the first man to navigate the North-West Passage, the legendary seaway between the Atlantic and the Pacific through the Canadian Arctic which had haunted the Western mind for three centuries past, and which nobody had sailed through on one and the same keel. His name was Roald Amundsen.

Unlike his predecessors at Nansen's door, Amundsen was not interested in technical advice on snow travel. He had his own ideas on the subject. There his mentor had been Astrup. What he wanted was Nansen's patronage. Only thus, Amundsen felt, could he acquire the standing that he needed to launch his enterprise. Fortunately for him, he made 'a very good impression', Nansen wrote to a friend, 'and, after the little I have seen of him, I believe that it would be rewarding to help him as much as we can'.

Meanwhile, between 1901 and 1902, Scott, the Germans, and the various other Antarctic expeditions sailed off. 'If a man's good wishes can bring success you will have it,' Nansen wrote in farewell to Scott. 'No one will look forward more keenly than I to see you back safe and sound ... I hope I shall not have sailed on a new expedition before then.' By the summer of 1904 all the expeditions had returned. Koettlitz, ever the faithful correspondent, wrote to Nansen asking, as he had often asked before:

> Are you still of the same mind as you were with regard to doing work in the Antarctic ... if you go there, I am sure you will be able to eclipse anything which all these other expeditions have done.

To Nansen, however, the Antarctic had descended into the half-world between imagination and reality. Since the *Fram* expedition he had been possessed by oceanography, as he had once been possessed by the central nervous system. It had begun with his discovery of the deep polar basin while still on *Fram*, before starting on the sledge journey. He had also been intrigued by the 'dead water' phenomenon which, off the Siberian coast, like an unseen hand, had clutched at *Fram*. It had first been recorded in Roman times by Pliny the Elder. All this and much else was going into the scientific results of the expedition, which were to be in English. Nansen was editing them, all six massive tomes, besides writing some of the papers.

Nansen initiated the explanation of dead water, which turned out to be due to standing waves where fresh water lies on top of sea water, as, for example, outside the estuary of a river. More significant was the reversible bottle for taking deep sea water samples that he had designed, and Anton Amundsen had constructed on *Fram*. Modified by a Swedish oceanographer, Otto Petterson, it has come down to us as the Nansen-Petterson water bottle, and to this day remains the standard device for taking such samples.

But Nansen's main accomplishment lay on another plane, with ironical consequences for himself. It all began when *Fram* was frozen into the ice in September 1893, and he observed that the drift did not follow the wind, as accepted theory had it, but consistently diverged by a certain angle to the right. He quickly discerned that this was due to the effect of the earth's rotation. He further concluded that, as the depth increased, each successive layer of water, moving over the next like a wind, would produce increasing deviation until, at a certain depth, the movement would be *against* the current on the surface.

Deficient in mathematics, Nansen now looked for someone to give his reasoning mathematical proof. By a chain of circumstances the choice fell on a Swedish physicist in Stockholm called Walfrid Ekman. In a letter to Nansen of 14 November 1901 Ekman effortlessly sketched out the formulae. The conclusion was that the effect of wind on the surface of the sea produced currents which, in Ekman's own words, 'formed something like a spiral staircase ... down towards the depths'.

This was a seminal formulation. It appeared at the time when oceanography was turning from an empirical to a mathematical science; it ended as a fundamental principle of the behaviour of all fluids and gases and is one of the foundations of modern meteorology. It has come down to us as the 'Ekman spiral'.

By rights, of course, it ought to be called the 'Nansen-Ekman spiral'. It was another object lesson in how priorities of discovery are perceived. Nansen had made the observation, and known what question to ask – which is often the real creative work. But Ekman had provided the mathematical formulation. To be fair to him, he gave Nansen his due from the first. And the historic fact remains that Nansen, having already become one of the founders of neurology, had now made himself the same in oceanography and fluid dynamics.

Nansen still hankered for the South Pole, although not just yet. For the present he was involved in the establishment of the first international oceanographical organisation – the International Council for the Exploration of the Sea. This began with a conference in Stockholm during the summer of 1899. The countries round the North Sea were represented but the then Great Powers concerned, notably England and Germany, would not allow the Council to have its seat on any of the others' soil. Oceanography was still a young science and many of the pioneering oceanographers happened to come from Scandinavia. Three years later, after much negotiation, the Council established its secretariat in Copenhagen and Nansen managed to have the Central Laboratory, as it was called, located in Christiania under his leadership.

Other more private matters also preoccupied him. The marriage of his old love, Dagmar Nicolaysen, 'The Treasure', had broken up, and she was in a parlous state. Nansen helped her by giving her translation and editing work in the preparation of the *Fram* scientific results. Then, on 6 December 1901, Eva gave birth to their fourth child, a son, christened Odd. Meanwhile Nansen really was planning a new house. The old one was no longer substantial or grandiose enough to match his standing. He wanted 'a fortress with broad moats and drawbridges ... where we can shut [out] the whole world', he told Eva. Like Ibsen's Master Builder he wanted a tower – literally.

Having bought a plot near his old home at Lysaker, outside Christiania on the fjord, he arranged an architects' competition, complained that the designs were too 'domestic', and took a hand himself. What he had in mind was something like the house outside Manchester of his old supporter in England from the *Fram* days, Henry Simon – a typical baronial structure expressing the aspirations of the successful Victorian manufacturer. In the end that is what he got. There was a hall, a grand staircase, a gallery, and a tower, all based on Simon's plans. Onto this Nansen had grafted an exterior with Italian Renaissance touches and, inside, what were deemed to be Nordic features, notably heavy carved woodwork and lintels, and, in time, neo-Romantic murals drawn from the sagas. The design ended up substantially Nansen's own; so, too, the supervision of the building work, to the dismay of everyone concerned. The outcome, a sombre mass that appeared to rise out of the bedrock, was indisputably an extension of his own personality. 'Good heavens, it has taken a long time to materialise,' wrote Johansen. 'Don't you remember, this is what you thought about in happy moments on the sledge journey!'

The housewarming was held on 4 April 1902. It took the form of a masked ball with about 200 guests, each of whom was announced by a fanfare from a trumpeter, a head taller than the crowd, decked out as a herald. 'My consort is wild on such occasions,' Eva ironically wrote to a friend.

> The latest is that he folds his socks down and his trousers up and dances with bare legs.

Nansen explained in his speech of welcome that the party should actually have been held on 7 April because that was the anniversary of a turning point in his life: the attainment seven years earlier of his furthest north. However, at this time, the winter's snow still lay on the ground, and to have delayed even a day or two would have risked the final depressing thaw and slush. Now, said Nansen in delphic terms, he was faced with another turning point. Therefore he wanted to commemorate his furthest north or highest latitude which, in his own idiosyncratic words, he called his greatest 'polar elevation' – *Polhøiden* in Norwegian – and so *Polhøiden* was to be the name of the house. In a curious wordplay, *Polhøiden* also meant 'The Polar heights', which implied something glacial and inaccessible.

It was here, on 2 October 1902, that Otto Sverdrup was admitted to a dinner with his men. He had returned to Norway on 19 September in *Fram* after four years in the Canadian Arctic. He had discovered 300,000 square kilometres of new land – more than all the expeditions of the past half century together. He had perfected the art of travelling with dogs and skis initiated by Nansen on the first voyage of the *Fram*. The one blemish had been the suicide of the doctor, Johan Svendsen. Although not setting a new record for the Furthest North, Sverdrup was widely admired for a successful and economical expedition. He and Nansen had, however, not yet made up their quarrel, but in public maintained a polite truce.

Up in his tower, Nansen arranged his study, with a view down over the trees to a distant view of the fjord. Eva was somewhat lost among the grandeur – the elaborate and cluttered furnishing, the dark decor, the atmosphere laden with a sense of something awry. On 20 March 1903, in these forbidding surroundings, she gave birth to her fifth and last child, a son called Åsmund.

While Eva was pregnant, Amundsen visited Nansen one day with a tale of woe. He had indeed managed to organise his expedition. He had put all his money into it, but he was being hounded by his creditors and needed to pay them off before he could depart. Nansen gave him 5,000 kroner of his own (£12,000 or $20,000 in present terms), and then hastened personally to drum up support. He approached Alfred Harmsworth who, having financed the Jackson-Harmsworth expedition might, he thought, be disposed to help.

> I have had to give £5,000 to the [British] Antarctic Expedition [Harmsworth

replied], and I do not feel disposed to spend any more on that kind of research at present.

Just now I am going in for chemical inquiries. They interest me very much, and I can supervise them myself

In the end Nansen managed to raise most of the money required – King Oscar II himself being among the donors. At midnight on 16 June 1903 Amundsen's ship, *Gjøa*, a sloop of only 47 tons, slipped her moorings a mile or so from Nansen's home and, in gloomy drizzle, became the next in the line of ships that sailed down the fjord bound for the polar ice.

60

Writing to *The Times*

Born in 1872, Amundsen was eleven years younger than Nansen and therefore was one more disturbing personification of youth knocking at the door. However, in the complex, dichotomous relations between the two men, extraneous motives had a hand in persuading Nansen to help. The Swedish-Norwegian Union was approaching another of its recurring crises, and he discerned that, if successful, Amundsen could be used for political purposes.

Ever since returning from the first crossing of Greenland, Nansen had taken it upon himself to exploit his reputation abroad in order to advance the drive to Norwegian independence. In February 1897, for example, when he arrived in London in the aftermath of the *Fram* expedition to begin his lecture tour, he was entertained to dinner at the House of Commons by Sir George Baden-Powell, meeting there both George Nathaniel Curzon, shortly to be ennobled and Viceroy of India, and Arthur Balfour, the future Prime Minister. Nor did Nansen forget his self-appointed rôle of private envoy when he went on to Paris. There he was received by Félix Faure, the President of the Republic, who made him a commander of the *Légion d'honneur*.

Early in 1893, Nansen had written a letter to *The Times*, rounding off almost a whole fiery column by excoriating the Norwegian-Swedish Union as 'a constant source of hatred and separation ... which irritates and humiliates every Norwegian who has a sense of honour in his breast'. This deeply hurt King Oscar, who felt he had always shown every consideration for his Norwegian subjects. This was the time when *Fram* was preparing to sail, and on being shown round the ship the King told Nansen that now he regretted having given a donation to the expedition. 'I [only] acted on my conviction, and what I considered my duty,' Nansen naïvely wrote to Colonel Theodor Frölich, the Court Chamberlain, and offered to return the money. In the event he kept it, but the incident encapsulated the tensions building up. It marked Nansen's first formal incursion into foreign affairs.

Then in April 1898, when he visited St Petersburg to receive his Russian accolade for the *Fram* expedition, he was entrusted by the Norwegian government with a confidential mission. He was to moot the possibility of a separate trade agreement between Norway and Russia. He was received by the Tsar, of course, but – even more important for the task he had been sent to perform – by the earthy and mighty figure of Count Witte, Minister of Finance and architect of Russian industrialisation: in short, the real ruler of Russia. The outcome of his mission, which he telegraphed from Vienna – not from St Petersburg 'on account of Russian spying', as he put it – was that Russia did not wish to be implicated in the domestic strife between Norway and Sweden.

In fact Russia, like the other Powers, was deeply concerned with Norwegian strivings for independence. They were likely to have repercussions far beyond the borders of the country. They potentially threatened the whole delicate balance of Europe. Norwegian separatism could have a dangerously unsettling effect on burgeoning nationalist agitation elsewhere, notably in Finland within the Russian Empire itself, but also in the patchwork edifice of Austro-Hungary where Czechs, Hungarians and Croats were particularly restive. In short, a rupture in the Swedish-Norwegian Union would exacerbate instability in an already psychologically disturbed climate.

'Purely sentimental', was how *The Times*, in a leader, once characterised Norwegian grievances.

> Norway ... hardly pretends that she suffers any material wrong. Her dissatisfaction springs from incompatibility of temper.

The Times had a point. Sweden, once the scourge of Russia and the terror of Europe, was a great Power in the final stages of decline. Norway was a subject province in the process of revival. They were perverse rôles for senior and subordinate, of which both were uncomfortably aware.

In fact, Norway possessed greater sovereignty than the states of the European Union today. Although the King appointed the government and could veto legislation, parliament and judiciary were sovereign, and subject to no outside interference; taxation likewise. There was no Union parliament. The writ of the Swedish bureaucracy stopped at the border. In Stockholm there was a permanent Norwegian ministerial delegation under a Minister of State to keep contact with the King and conduct matters affecting Norway. The only formal Union body was the combined ministerial council, composed of Swedish and Norwegian cabinet ministers, which advised the King on strictly Union matters. Otherwise, each country was independent, even having its own army and navy. Foreign affairs remained the Union link, and the only sphere in which Norway was subject to Sweden. Nonetheless, even under such liberal auspices, Norwegians became more irked with each passing year.

Nationalism in Norway, as almost everywhere else in Europe, and indeed in the shape of the pan-Slav movement in Russia, had its origins in the fertile brain of Johann Gottfried Herder, one of the German Romantics, Goethe's teacher and reputedly a model for his Faust. Broadly speaking Herder equated nationhood with folklore, language and what by a far-reaching antithesis he called 'folk-poetry' as against 'art-poetry'. His distant heirs were now fulfilling his work.

Nansen was one of the motley figures thrown up across Europe by the nationalist movements coming to fruition. In some ways, he resembled Thomas Masaryk, the founder of the Czech republic. Both were university professors; both passionate hunters and nature worshippers; both fanatically devoted to the truth and absolutely incorruptible. As Nansen was a skier, so was Masaryk a Sokol member. The Sokol was a society for mass gymnastics, purposely contrived by a Bohemian nationalist to generate patriotic feeling. It is a moot point whether skiing or the Sokol was the first case of sport being consciously used as an agent of national self-assertion.

Nansen and Masaryk were children of the zeitgeist. They differed in one important respect. Masaryk fervently believed in popular democracy; Nansen's instincts were all in the direction of an enlightened oligarchy – if such a thing were possible. At home he continued to despise politicians, as he had done all along. 'One acquires more distaste for the breed the more one has to do with them,' he said around this time.

The drive to Norwegian independence, in the latter stages of which Nansen had become embroiled, was a bitter and confused process in which, by historical accident, events such as constitutional reform, which elsewhere had taken centuries, were here squeezed into decades. One issue on which emotions ran high was the flag question. Both Sweden and Norway each had a separate national flag which, when used as a naval or merchant ensign, was quartered by a so-called 'union mark'. The Norwegians wanted it officially removed. This was achieved by the end of 1898 and they got their 'clean' ensign, as it was called. It was, however, the consular question that the Norwegians chose as their final battleground.

Although there were Norwegian ambassadors, Swedes dominated the foreign service. Norway was a nation of seafarers and, for a maritime country, the consul in the port was a vital figure. He had to understand the mentality of the seamen with whom he had to deal. The Norwegians demanded a separate consular service. The Swedes refused. The conflict festered, reaching a crisis in 1892 and, with increasing virulence, 1895. In both cases, the Norwegians, having overreached themselves, were forced to retreat.

The crisis of 1892 produced Nansen's letter to *The Times* that so distressed King Oscar. In November 1898 Nansen once more wrote to *The Times* about the Swedish-Norwegian Union, spreading himself over more than two columns. He was replying to an article inspired by King Oscar, putting the official Swedish point of view. In neither case was Nansen acting on his own.

His first letter to *The Times* bore the stamp of his brother-in-law, Professor Ernst Sars, an historian and one of the more rampant Norwegian separatists, whose view of history was that it ought to be used to re-create the past in order to encourage national consciousness. The next one betrayed a different, cannier influence. Either way, Nansen had lent himself to propagating views abroad that would not otherwise have commanded attention.

This did not go down too well at home. 'The great sportsman [who] crossed Greenland on skis one summer, and our sports-mad age ... gives him authority both as a scientist and statesman,' was the sarcastic comment of one diehard newspaper. Not only politicians and journalists thought thus. After the return of the *Fram*, a wit wrote from Paris that 'Nansen has exceeded Ibsen. He has entered the *Musée Grévin*. [Ibsen] has still to enter the celebrated waxworks.' What rankled was that by his handful of letters to *The Times* Nansen – 'the great sportsman' – had commanded more attention than the tireless efforts in the foreign press of all the approved polemicists put together.

In January 1899, Nansen once more wrote to *The Times* about the Union conflict. Thereafter he faded from the political scene. And when he lost his record for the Furthest North to Luigi Amadeo he lost something of his glory, among his fellow-countrymen at least. Until one of the Poles was conquered, however, he would not actually face eclipse.

His family suffered as his Faustian wails rang out. 'A goal! Great or small, just one on which all one's powers could be concentrated,' Nansen wrote in his diary around this time.

> I have arrived precisely where I did not want to go, broken and torn by the heavy burden of unrelieved trivialities.

Eva was faced by an ever more introspective and tyrannical husband who was prey to shifting, unpredictable moods. He would shut himself away in his study in the tower to work, and their eldest child, Liv, recalled how if he was heard humming a certain melody 'we knew that all was well ... and the barometer was rising'. From the start, Nansen had imposed a Spartan regime on his children. Food was simple, with everlasting gruel twice a day. He thrashed his sons when he thought it necessary. He forbade Eva to praise or show affection because he believed that weakened character. She of course knew how to circumvent this, but in the gloomy house among the trees the tensions mounted.

Money played its part. Eva could not manage the household accounts and had to bear her husband's thunderous reproaches on that score. Unfairly, he did not personally concern himself with finance but left it all to his brother Alexander. Eva did not exactly have an allowance but when she needed housekeeping money would have to brave Alexander in his office – where he knew all too well how to play the parsimonious, admonitory family lawyer.

In fact, however, from early in 1902 Alexander himself was in financial trouble, which left Nansen himself exposed. During the 1890s, Christiania had been in the grip of a building boom and Alexander, shrewdly as he thought, had invested some of Nansen's literary earnings in property. The boom then collapsed. Alexander's investments slumped, and he was being harried by the banks. To complicate matters, it was proving difficult to sell Nansen's old house, *Godthåb*.

Nonetheless each summer Nansen and his family moved to their country retreat at Sørkje, which swept away depression. Here, in the wild and mountainous landscape, they were really in tune with their surroundings. Nansen could hunt to his heart's content and there was music to lighten his mood. Eva was often at the piano singing Schubert *lieder*, which appealed to his sentimental streak.

Although at *Polhøiden*, Nansen tolerated no intrusion while at work, he was no hermit. When he descended from his tower he wanted company. He indulged in a habitual round of entertainment. In characteristic Dionysian swings of mood, he would overturn his demands for domestic economy and tell Eva to spare no expense to ensure a grand reception. The children did not fail to observe the contrast between these outbursts of profligacy and their own spartan fare.

Among those he most frequently entertained were a colony of artists who had sprung up round his home. Called the 'Lysaker Circle', after the place in which they lived, they were mostly in the national romantic tradition. In the decorative arts, inspired by William Morris and the Arts and Crafts movement, they reinvented a medieval high Norse style. The discovery and excavation of three Viking long ships in Norway between 1867 and 1903 – now national showpieces – spurred the trend. So did a movement to save and restore stave churches – strange quasi-pagan medieval wooden structures in the countryside which themselves seemed to echo the design of a Viking ship.

None of the the Lysaker Circle became world famous – unlike their fellow-countryman, the Expressionist painter Edvard Munch, the herald of the neurotic in art and their aesthetic opposite in every way. They themselves, in the spirit of the age, were consciously promoting symbols of national consciousness. Nansen's own High Norse appearance was unashamedly exploited. Around the turn of the century there was a state-subsidised, popular illustrated edition of the Norse sagas. One of the illustrators was Nansen's particular friend among the Lysaker Circle, an accomplished draughtsman called Erik Werenskiold. He very recognisably used Nansen as a model for some of the medieval Norwegian heroes. That neatly symbolised Nansen's elevation to a national totem. It also explained part of his frustration. He yearned for at least the similitude of action.

From time to time he did emerge onto the public stage. In February 1903, for instance, he made the closing speech at the Nordic Winter Sports Week in Christiania, an early forerunner of the Winter Olympics. However ambiguously he might otherwise be regarded, there was no doubt of his services to skiing – 'the most national of all Norwegian sports', as he himself had memorably written. He was a figure with whom every Norwegian skier could identify and a timely image of the Norwegians to themselves. With his didactic cast of mind, Nansen was no orator. But when he spoke from the heart he could carry his audience. On this occasion he had a singular theme: 'Winter sports ... are something that bind the nordic peoples together.' Swedes had participated by invitation, so he added for their benefit: 'I hope you will go home with memories of ... the spontaneous and genuine cheering ... that greeted the Swedish ski jumpers.' They had been trounced by the Norwegians, which prompted a further homily: 'Take that as a sign,' Nansen went on,

> that we are a people who admittedly wish to defend our honour and independence with the tenacity and stamina of a sportsman, but who also, like a sportsman ... will welcome our friends and companions.

The event took place against a background of rising tension. The Swedish and Norwegian governments were once more negotiating over the consular question, and hence the future of the Union. Meanwhile campaigning was already under way for the Norwegian general election in the autumn. For decades the Union with Sweden had bedevilled politics; now it was the only issue. The party of the Left – Liberals of a kind – was in power, and wanted immediate secession, even at the risk of war. That frightened off one faction which, on this question, had more in common with their opponents, the party of the Right – equivalent roughly to Conservatives elsewhere – who advocated caution. The upshot was an electoral pact, dubbed the 'Coalition Party', uniting those who wanted peaceful negotiation, leaving the Radical Left as the 'war party'. As usual the politicians were depressingly humdrum. Once more leadership came from the outside.

'I believe that it must be possible for ... a solution satisfactory to both [Sweden and Norway] to be found,' Nansen wrote to King Oscar.

> In any case I am determined to do what little I can in that direction ... What I consider more important, and what will perhaps surprise Your Majesty even more, is that in this matter I have Bjørnstjerne Bjørnson on my side.

Bjørnstjerne Bjørnson – 'the poetical politician' as *The Times* once irritably called him – was an exuberantly radical and romantic literary figure. Playwright, novelist, publicist, Ibsen's rival, and the national poet, he wrote the words of the Norwegian National Anthem. He was an implacable opponent of the Union – 'That treaty by which we are befouled', he once called it in an enraged couplet – and had long agitated for instant independence, whatever the cost. Larger than life, with florid posturing, he was regarded as a chieftain in the land, and had enormous public influence.

And now in April 1903 Bjørnson – 'the bellows of the nation' as someone called him – in a sensational *volte face*, published a newspaper article forswearing his old fiery radicalism and endorsing the Coalition Party. That gave it legitimacy. The Coalition duly won the election and, in October, a well-meaning Professor of Law called Francis Hagerup became Prime Minister.

Talks on the consular question ambled along. In November 1904, they took an unexpected turn. The Swedes abruptly became intransigent and imposed new conditions. Meanwhile, international tension was rising. In February that year, the Russo-Japanese war broke out, entailing for Russia from the outset a string of disasters. In January 1905, the first Russian revolution began.

Such was the backdrop to the new crisis in the Swedish-Norwegian Union. The Great Powers were even more concerned than before with events in Scandinavia. On 7 February the negotiations between the Swedes and Norwegians broke down. 'A new feature of the situation,' Sir Rennell Rodd, the British Ambassador in Stockholm, reported towards the end of the month,

> is the appearance on the scene in the character of a political agitator of the popular arctic explorer Frithiof [*sic*] Nansen.

61

A Gentlemanly Revolution

As the negotiations with Sweden were breaking down, the Norwegian government seemed prey to drift and indecision. What leadership there was shifted to the Press. One of Nansen's old friends, Ola Thomessen, editor of a Christiania newspaper of the moderate Left faction called *Verdens Gang* ('The Way of the World'), felt that Nansen was the only figure who could rally the country.

The upshot was a succession of articles by Nansen, published between 12 February and 2 March 1905 and challengingly titled 'The Way Ahead', 'Courage', 'Recklessness' and 'Willpower'. This was Nansen's first incursion into domestic politics and constituted a highly personal manifesto on the Union crisis. 'Have we ... forgotten that once in a while, even in this country, we need something more than even the bravest words, and that is *action*,' ran an operative passage.

Nansen was denouncing the appeasers, who wanted to continue negotiating, for years if need be. He seized on the consular question as the question of national sovereignty. He advocated the immediate establishment of a separate Norwegian consular service, with or without Swedish consent, letting the consequences take care of themselves. It was, as he might have said, no time for wobbling. He brought down upon himself an assortment of reproach. Bjørnson, in his new rôle of moderate, declared that there was 'too much polar bear in him'. Sigurd Ibsen, the dramatist's son and now Norwegian Minister of State in Stockholm, summoned him to a meeting (in a Christiania hotel), and gave him a dressing down. This was no Nansen plan, but 'an Andrée plan', he told him in a cutting allusion to the vanished balloonist, who had become a byword for foolhardiness. Hagerup, the Prime Minister, received a letter from a Swedish politician saying that 'Nansen's ... pronouncements ... make the same impression here as a village actor playing Shakespeare – declamation and nothing more'.

But Nansen had caught something in the public mood. He was not to be so easily by-passed. The breakdown of the consular negotiations precipitated a cabinet crisis. The Norwegian constitution rigidly fixed the parliamentary term at three years, with dissolution precluded. The next general election was more than a year hence. The unfortunate Hagerup was removed and, on 11 March, a bare nine days after the last of Nansen's articles appeared, a new government took office. It was an altogether more decisive constellation, its brief unequivocally to bring the whole Union crisis to a head.

The new Prime Minister was a shipowner of substance called Christian Michelsen. It was the Norwegian shipowners, with their resource, ingenuity, and consummate ruthlessness who created the wealth that eventually modernised Norway. They had displaced the officials at the top of society. Michelsen came from Bergen, and Nansen had known him slightly during his own years there two decades before. He had not then entered politics but looked on life with a rough, jeering wit. In the summer of 1904 Nansen once more visited Bergen. Michelsen, now a Cabinet Minister, sobered by the years and uncertain in health, received him, and thenceforth they met sporadically.

Nansen was thirsting for personal action. Michelsen was altogether foxier. Of the moderate faction of the Left Party, stiff-suited, dark-haired, bearded, pouchy-eyed, vaguely Mephistophelean, he was by taste a gambler with a gift for bringing off a coup with small resources. They found a happy symbiosis. It was Nansen's newspaper articles that generated the climate of opinion needed to push Michelsen to power. Once there he wanted Nansen in his cabinet, if only for prestige.

It was not the first time that office for Nansen had been mooted. There were even calls for him to lead the country. Edvard Grieg who, besides being a composer, was something of a wit, was driven despairingly to write to one newspaper editor:

> I am a great admirer of Nansen, but I would rather have [you as] Prime Minister ... than ... Nansen. It would be 1,000 times preferable! And if dilettantism is to rule ... why not Prime Minister Grieg? He's not as bad as you think.

Nansen happened to agree. He declined all blandishments of political office. In his own words: 'I feel unsuited to the work of a minister ... I can do better work outside the cabinet.'

On the evening of 16 March he left hurriedly on an unorthodox mission. Norway was generally considered a holiday destination and little more. The urgent need was to have the country taken seriously abroad. A committee had been formed to finance propaganda. Norway having no independent official representation, private agents were despatched to fill the void. Nansen was sent to London. He had a reasonable cover since he was to lecture to the RGS.

First he made a detour via Berlin, where Michelsen had asked him to try to see the Kaiser. He failed for once, and was left kicking his heels. His diary reads:

> My journey wasted, blocked by a wall of formalism. My time and trouble thrown away. Alien people, who speak a language I do not understand.

401

Feelings of justice, patriotism [which] are not expedient, ridiculous. Enthusiasm for ideals naïve silliness.... This well organised society, where each ant has its place and its lead round its neck, is repulsive.

To pass the time, he saw Wagner's *Das Rheingold* which, he wrote to Eva in another outburst,

> seemed pure nonsense. God help me, I didn't understand a word, and it did not make me feel more kindly towards [the Germans] ... the whole thing was so ... far removed from what was natural [and] human that I felt nauseous.

In fact, Nansen's arrival in Berlin was thoroughly inopportune. Among other things, after his previous indifference, the Kaiser now wanted the Union preserved at almost any cost. This was connected with his desire for stability in the north. He wanted no irritating diversion from his grand designs elsewhere. He wanted Sweden within the German ambit. In his own pregnant words: 'A customs union must be established and [Sweden] converted to a federal state.' Wilhelm had no intention of encouraging separatism by receiving a Norwegian 'revolutionary'.

On 21 March Nansen left Berlin – 'this desert' – for London, not having seen the Kaiser or any significant officials. However, as he wrote to Eva, his stay had been more useful than at first he supposed: 'I have now obtained a fairly reliable insight into conditions and the atmosphere as they really are.' Nevertheless he was 'pleased at the prospect of being in surroundings where they speak an intellectual language that I understand a little.... It is a great relief to leave dreary Germany and come here to England, where one can breathe freely, and there are individuals one can talk to [and] feel welcome.' The easygoing flamboyance of Edwardian London was a contrast to the brash nationalistic vulgarianism of Berlin under Kaiser Wilhelm II. For one thing, there was not the throng of uniforms in the streets that had irritated Nansen in the German capital.

Nansen's true purpose in visiting London was to be on hand when a certain letter was published in *The Times* – 'the tribal notice board of the Establishment', as someone once called it, and as such internationally revered. The letter appeared on 25 March over his signature. It presented a legal case for separate Norwegian consuls and whatever else might follow. Spread over more than two closely argued columns, it was clearly not all his own work. In fact it had been drafted by the foreign department of the Norwegian Ministry of the Interior. Nansen had only lent his name.

It was enough. He was 'a representative figure in no merely party sense', *The Times* declared in a leading article commenting on his letter and published in the same issue.

> His fame as an explorer, his prowess in the Furthest North, have given him a unique place in the affections of Norway, just as they have made his name known and honoured throughout the length and breadth of Europe.

Nansen was in fact rather more popular in England than the native polar hero, the newly promoted Captain Robert Falcon Scott, despite Scott's having returned from the Antarctic with a new record for the Furthest South of 82°17′. As Koettlitz, the ever-faithful correspondent, wrote to Nansen, reflecting some public criticism, it 'might have been much further had the Captain [Scott] been a man of more experience'. Scott was also under a slight cloud in that he allowed his expedition ship *Discovery* to be beset in the Antarctic for two years. She was rescued by a relief ship, the Dundee whaler *Terra Nova*, whose captain, Harry Mackay, skilfully blasted a passage through the ice – an uncomfortable fact which Scott tried to cover up.

Nansen's polar reputation, however, remained unblemished. Socially, too, he was more desirable than Scott. Thus a prolix and hair-splitting legalistic screed, which otherwise might have sunk into oblivion, turned into a vehicle for highly effective Norwegian propaganda. For two days on end Nansen was interviewed, with the result that, as he wrote to Eva, there was 'a deluge in approximately all the papers here about the Union and the future position of Norway, etc. etc.'

This attention to his views was all the more remarkable because on the day that his letter was published, *The Times* ran a whole page on the Battle of Mukden, the final rout of the Russian army by the Japanese in Manchuria. It was 'destined to take rank with Austerlitz, Waterloo ... and to be reckoned among the most decisive of modern times', the paper wrote of it. And indeed it was. It was the first battle in history involving a million men, the first defeat of a European power by non-Europeans for centuries. Already there was talk of the 'yellow peril'.

In the face of all this counter-publicity Nansen had prevailed by the force of what *The Times* called his 'vivid personality'. In order to maximise the impact he had avoided all journalists until his letter appeared. Now, in his own words, he was playing

> the diplomat and servant of the gentlemen of the press. I unconstrainedly admire myself, I don't believe I have ever been so pleasant and cooperative, haven't thrown a single reporter out ... I think that has made a deep impression on them.... They were used to other treatment before.

More to the point, when the letter was published and Nansen had appeared in his true colours, as it were, he was officially noticed. He was soon courteously received by the Foreign Secretary, Lord Lansdowne. It was all very different from his comprehensive snub in Berlin.

The message, however, was essentially the same. In its leader *The Times* made the point. While broadly sympathetic to Norwegian aspirations, it regarded with its old misgivings 'the possible complications of a northern question, which, if the Union were severed, might be added to those tangled problems that already vex the mind of Europe'. That, more

403

or less, was what Nansen heard from Lord Lansdowne and most of the other politicians whom he met in the next few hectic days, including the Prime Minister, Arthur Balfour.

In between, Nansen delivered his lecture to the RGS. 'It says in [the newspapers] that you are going to organise an expedition to the South Pole,' Eva wrote to him. 'Are you going to mention it?' For Nansen, the South Pole was becoming an albatross. He did not touch on it at all. His lecture was on the rise and fall of shore lines due to deformation of the earth's crust during ice ages. This was a new topic of current scientific concern. It was another echo of the *Fram* expedition – Nansen's interest in geology that was formed during his stay at Cape Flora in Franz Josef Land. His main scientific interest remained oceanography, and he had begun the work that was to lead to a classic study of the Norwegian Sea – work from which he had torn himself away to come to London earlier than he had intended.

Nonetheless, as he justifiably wrote to Eva, he had a 'comforting sense of being of some use'. This was an age in which personality still counted in policy. By sheer force of character, Nansen had sailed into the centres of power as if he had been some national leader and not an itinerant spokesman for a suspect cause. He had been plainly told that because of international complications which Britain, beset by troubles elsewhere, wished to avoid, differences ought to be settled without breaking the Union, so in substance he had been rebuffed in London, as in Berlin, though much more gently. All the same, he had brought the Norwegian view to the fore. He had generated goodwill for later exploitation. In short, he was showing himself an early master of the nascent craft of public relations.

He had certainly taken the Swedes aback with his propaganda coup. His privateering had overcome their official diplomacy. In Stockholm Count Gyldenstolpe, the Foreign Minister, complained to Sir Rennell Rodd. As the British Ambassador Sir Rennell, in his own words, was compelled to 'maintain an attitude of strict impartiality. But I ventured to suggest that they had also a famous explorer whose name was as well known to my countrymen as that of Nansen. Why should they not get Sven Hedin to enter the lists.' Hedin was the celebrated explorer of Central Asia, who had even been to Tibet. The Swedes took the hint. On 1 April, as Nansen was leaving London to return home, he found a long riposte in *The Times* to his own letter. It put the Swedish case and was signed 'Sven Hedin'.

Nansen and Hedin had been friends since they had first met in Stockholm, almost twenty years before, when Nansen had gone there to prepare for the crossing of Greenland. They now had a fierce exchange in the columns of *The Times*. That is to say, they allowed their names to be used by their respective governments to present official views in an unofficial guise. It did not impair their friendship, but politics did obtrude. For instance, Hedin had invited Nansen to Stockholm for the presentation of the Vega medal in April (awarded that year to Captain Scott). It was the twenty-fifth anniversary of the return of Adolf Erik Nordenskiöld in *Vega* from an expedition as a result of which, in Hedin's words to Nansen, 'both you and I ... received powerful stimuli ... which were decisive in our lives'. Hedin particularly wanted to use the occasion to commemorate Nordenskiöld, who had died four years earlier. Nansen, for his part, would have been nothing loath. Nonetheless he refused the invitation because, as he put it, the Union crisis had become

> a matter of emotion ... We Norwegians all feel that our national sense of honour has been hurt [and] so you will understand [that] I do not feel like coming even if it hurts me to stay away. Not least because I will be prevented from honouring the memory of my wonderful friend Nordenskiöld ... to whom I owe so much.

Hedin replied understandingly. 'I am fairly indifferent towards the Union as such,' he wrote. But he feared Russian aggression if it was dissolved. And: 'To count on England's help in case of war is dangerous. England grovels before Russia.'

On 8 February, after the consular negotiations broke down, King Oscar, old and sick, withdrew from government for a rest. He appointed his eldest son, Gustaf, the Crown Prince and future King Gustaf V, Regent in his stead. At the age of 47, Gustaf had long been waiting in the wings. Tall, slim, foppish, unappealing, lacking his father's charm and slightly depraved in appearance, he cut an unfortunate figure. Nonetheless he concealed surprising political acumen. So far he had been a staunch upholder of the Union. A single conversation with Christian Michelsen, whom he himself had appointed Norwegian Prime Minister in March, made him turn a mental somersault. 'The consular question,' he observed in some jottings on his return to Stockholm, was

> merely [a] pretext ... for Norway to withdraw from the present Union, which *not a single soul* in Norway wants to continue [and] it might be politically more sensible ... if Sweden herself were to propose a separation ... instead of being kicked out of the Union, as it were.

Far-seeing, he wanted to act 'in the *least* possible brutal way so that a dissolution of the Union does not leave too much bitterness behind'.

This was his message when, on 23 March, he addressed the ominous-sounding Secret Committee. This was a body appointed by the Riksdag – the Swedish parliament – in a national emergency, and rarely resorted to. On this occasion it had been invoked two days before Gustaf's address for the purpose of hinting at a threat. It was a moment of crisis, and Nansen was drawn into the propaganda war once more.

His original article in *The Times* had also appeared in both a French and a German newspaper – *Le Temps* and the *Kölnische Zeitung* respectively – and seemed to be serving as the Norwegian manifesto. Now he put his name to a small book – *Norway and the Union with Sweden* – a pamphlet prepared once more by officials, elaborating the legalities of the Norwegian case for separate consuls. It appeared in English, French and German, early in June. Like so much else, it was overtaken by events.

On 4 May, Eva Nansen gave one of her Thursday musical 'at homes'. Because of the crisis it turned into a political and intellectual mobilisation. There were 150 guests out at the Nansens' towered home. 'I do not think that I was alone in thinking of a royal palace,' as Arne Garborg, who was among them, put it.

> If by chance the Swedish Union is dissolved, there is no doubt that Nansen will be one of the most important figures [because] he is now ... the Norwegian ... with the greatest European reputation, and he is not only 'educated'. They say he is of royal descent ... When the dancing began ... he was constantly on the dance floor; and he was the best dancer as well as the greatest name – as a royal pretender should be.

Following a carefully constructed plan, events began following their preordained course. On 18 May, a bill for a separate consular service was laid before the Storting, and on 23 May completed its passage. Next day, following the usual procedure, it was sent to Stockholm for the Royal Assent. On 26 May King Oscar resumed power. He wished to take upon himself all responsibility for what was about to happen.

The next day the Norwegian Ministerial Delegation in Stockholm presented the law in formal council. The King refused assent. Thereupon the Minister of State – no longer Sigurd Ibsen, but a former journalist called Jørgen Løvland – announced that the government had resigned. He had their letters of resignation, which he now produced. They were dated the previous day. The King refused to accept the resignations on the grounds that no other government could then be formed.

All this took place in an atmosphere of high drama. In Christiania, meanwhile, the politicians were petrified of a conciliatory royal gesture, for that would have wrecked their gambit. It was announced that the Storting would meet on the morning of 7 June. When the session opened, nothing luckily had yet been heard from the King. The proceedings barely took an hour. After the preliminaries the President of the Storting, Carl Berner, a stolid, bearded, commonplace yet somehow dignified figure, read out a carefully drafted statement, the crux of which was that since the Cabinet had resigned and, by his own admission, the King was in no position to appoint a government, the constitutional monarchy had 'lost its function'. Therefore:

> The Storting authorises the members of the cabinet which has resigned this day to exercise, until further notice, as the Norwegian government, the

authority delegated by the King in conformity with the Constitution and current laws of the Kingdon of Norway – with those modifications necessitated by the fact that the union with Sweden under one King has been dissolved as a consequence of the King's having ceased to function as the King of Norway.

'Quite a gentlemanly revolution,' Hugh Blakistone of *The Times* remarked to another journalist. And revolution it was, albeit couched in legal terms and hidden in a subordinate clause of a syllogistic argument. An illegal secession had been declared and a king deposed.

Nansen had been responsible for Blakistone's presence in Christiania. He had complained to Moberley Bell, the manager of *The Times*, about his paper's biased reporting from Stockholm, and proposed a local newspaper editor instead to act as 'stringer' in Christiania. Bell, however, an old foreign correspondent, smelt a story and despatched Blakistone instead.

In most respects Nansen had been on the sidelines while these crucial events were unfolding. In consolation, as it were, he received from his old Hungarian friend Adolf Ónodi yet another letter, reminiscing about the 'splendid days in Naples' when they were hopeful young neurobiologists together but giving a wistful view of events from that other dual monarchy of the Habsburgs on the Danube:

> I must congratulate you [Ónodi wrote] with all my heart on the unique action of your great admirable nation ... Where we in Hungary are concerned the struggle is still hopeless, and we do not have the slightest idea of what is going to happen.

62

To Fill a Throne

The Norwegians had acted in the aftermath of the Battle of Tsushima, the naval engagement off Korea on 27-28 May in which the Japanese, under Admiral Togo, annihilated a Russian fleet. Like most naval battles, this one produced a moral effect out of all proportion to its military significance. It was the ultimate Russian disaster in the war against Japan. In St Petersburg a British diplomat reported 'a widespread feeling of consternation and despair.... The cup of humiliation has been filled to overflowing.' For the time being Russia could be discounted. This reduced foreign complications. Had the Norwegian politicians deliberately planned it their action could scarcely have been better timed.

The Kaiser also helped. At the end of March, he had created a flashy diversion by landing in Tangier to stake a German claim in North Africa, thus clashing with French colonial interests and precipitating the so-called First Moroccan Crisis. It had brought Europe to the brink of war. The Powers, in a high state of nervousness, wanted no new Balkans in the north. They tacitly agreed to remain neutral in the Scandinavian imbroglio.

In Scandinavia itself meanwhile, the crisis was pursuing its course. Nansen, however, was still waiting in the wings. Early in July Eva moved to Sørkje for the summer with the children as usual, leaving him alone for once at *Polhøiden*. There was good reason for this. Beneath a surface calm matters were becoming thoroughly tangled. Perhaps there was a rôle for him in the offing. At any rate he was soon involving himself. He fired off a telegram to a political acquaintance and kindred spirit in London, the polymath James Bryce, MP (later Lord Bryce), a former Cabinet Minister, a historian still remembered for his classic study *The Holy Roman Empire*, and a mountaineer to boot. Nansen's wire to Bryce ran as follows:

WAR AGITATION IN SWEDEN APPROACHING SERIOUS DANGER STRONG WARNING FROM YOUR GOVERNMENT WOULD CERTAINLY HAVE GREAT EFFECT PREVENT THIS TERRIBLE CALAMITY FATAL TO SCANDINAVIA AND DANGEROUS TO EUROPEAN PEACE USE YOUR INFLUENCE.

An Ulster Protestant, Bryce understood all too well the complexities of another Union. He conveyed Nansen's telegram to the Foreign Office and promised to help where he could.

Nansen also wrote directly to Lord Lansdowne, alleging that Sweden would mobilise and asking Britain and the other Powers to intercede. As Foreign Secretary, Lord Lansdowne could not 'correspond officially with ... Dr Nansen upon these subjects', he telegraphed to Viscount Melville, the British Consul-General in Christiania.

> Please explain privately [Lord Lansdowne continued,] that so far as my information goes there is no reason for supposing that Swedish Gov't have the intentions he attributes to them. He may rest assured that our influence will be exerted in the interests of a peaceful settlement.

The situation, however, had been bedevilled by misjudgement. The Swedes, accepting a cliché that the Norwegians were all talk and no action, had been taken by surprise. For their part, the Norwegians had expected quick recognition of their independence. The Powers swiftly disabused them of that notion. It would be a pernicious example for restless nationalities elsewhere, from Catholic Ireland to the Carpathians. It was widely made clear that abrogating the Union, being the work of one party, was invalid. Recognition depended on legalising the rupture, which in turn meant the agreement of the Swedes. Until then the consequence was diplomatic isolation. The Norwegians frantically set about finding a way out of the impasse. They sent out private emissaries, Nansen being one, who were received by the back door.

Despite considerable republican feeling, the Norwegians had decided to preserve the monarchy because, except for Switzerland and France, Europe was still wholly monarchical and they wished to allay suspicions of revolution in their secession. In fact, on declaring their independence, the Norwegians had simultaneously asked King Oscar to nominate a Prince of his own House of Bernadotte as their King. The Bernadotte Proposal, as it was known, had also been intended as a conciliatory gesture. It turned out to be a trump card handed to the Swedes.

Until he formally abdicated, Oscar was still King of Norway. Until he explicitly rejected the Bernadotte Proposal Norway was deprived of a head of state. Meanwhile Norway was trapped in an interregnum.

Into this limbo, armed with a plan of action, stepped Nansen's cousin Frederik Hartvig Herman – 'Fritz' – Wedel Jarlsberg, a relation of the landowner of the same name who had once memorably threatened to prosecute Nansen for poaching. A curious blend of child and *grand seigneur*, Wedel had been the Swedish-Norwegian Ambassador in Madrid. Like other Norwegians in the joint diplomatic service, he resigned immediately on the declaration of independence in order to serve his own country. He wanted Prince Charles of Denmark on the Norwegian throne.

There were legitimist arguments in favour of this choice, since the Danish Royal Family traced its origins back to the medieval Norwegian kings. More importantly, Charles was the second son of Frederik, the Danish Crown Prince, one of whose sisters, Dagmar, was, as Maria Feodorovna, the Dowager Empress of Russia and the mother of the Tsar. Still better, another of his aunts, Alexandra, Dagmar's sister, was the consort of King Edward VII and hence Queen of England. To clinch matters, he also happened to be Edward's son-in-law, having married his third daughter, Princess Maud. With the might of the British Empire thus behind him, and reinsurance in his Russian connections, Charles, in Wedel's view, would make an ideal Pretender.

Before approaching Charles, however, Wedel wanted King Edward's permission – for this, as people nowadays forget, was still an age of royal foreign policy and the King clearly held the key. With Michelsen's approval Wedel made a flying visit to London.

He arrived early on 19 June. It was Ascot week and the King, of course, was at the races. Wedel hurried round to visit Sir Rennell Rodd, whom he knew from the diplomatic corps and who, as Ambassador in Stockholm, was in England for the Royal wedding of Prince Gustaf Adolf, eldest son of Prince Gustaf, and King Edward's niece, Princess Margaret of Connaught. Sir Rennell had a ticket for the Royal Enclosure at Ascot but, as an intellectual, an aesthete and a sometime friend of Oscar Wilde, was uninterested in the Turf and had had no intention of using it. Now, however, in his own words, he

> caught the first available train. I managed to have a message conveyed to the King, who left his party and gave me a brief interview on the lawn ... Resisting tempting offers to lunch from friends ... I returned to London immediately, having stayed barely an hour on the course, [and] explained the situation [to] Lord Lansdowne.

Lansdowne then discreetly received Wedel, who left again next morning for Christiania, Lansdowne having told him that, under the right conditions, King Edward would have no objections.

The King was, in fact, a step ahead of Wedel. Very sensibly not quite trusting the Foreign Office, he had personal agents among diplomats in strategic embassies who wrote directly to himself or his Private Secretary, Lord Knollys. Even less did 'The Uncle of Europe' trust his two nephews, the Tsar and the Kaiser. He too wanted Charles, a friendly presence, on the throne of Norway – for power politics quite as much as dynastic preferences were here involved – and had already put the wheels in motion. At least a week before Wedel reached London the British Chargé d'Affaires in Copenhagen was talking to the Prince.

Charles was a reluctant Pretender if ever there was one. An amiable family man and a naval officer, he had a nice house in the centre of

Copenhagen. He liked being a prince in an easygoing society that allowed him to live incognito. He was not sure that he wanted to move to a palace and be a king. However, after much prodding by British diplomats and, telegraphically, by King Edward, swayed by his knowledge of the wishes of Queen Alexandra and spurred by a belated cloak-and-dagger introduction to Wedel at the British Ambassador's residence, Charles tentatively accepted the offer of the throne.

Despite sabre-rattling by both sides, it was at any rate clear by now that the Union was going to be dissolved by negotiation. It was at this point, and partly for this reason, that Michelsen sent Nansen to Copenhagen to ensure that Charles would indeed act.

Again Nansen needed a cover for his mission, and again there was one conveniently to hand. He was a participant in the fourth conference of the Permanent International Council for the Exploration of the Sea, which happened to be about to take place in Copenhagen between 18 and 21 July.

'Just one big rush,' Nansen wrote to Eva,

> idiotic nonsense, which I think it is crazy that grown-up men should be compelled to sit through.

Obviously Nansen had not lost his old distaste for scientific congresses, even though counterbalanced by his new-found but secret rôle of confidential agent. The years and the weight of responsibility had taken their toll however.

'How much has this man not changed since he was here many years ago and was honoured ... for his celebrated [Greenland] expedition,' wrote one Danish journalist after an interview with Nansen.

> Then he was an agile young sportsman ... with a bright look in his eye and a ready smile.... The look is different now.... The light of the snowy wastes in [his] eyes is not yet extinguished, but their expression has become more serious ... and his mouth, which is now obscured by a large, grave moustache, does not smile as easily as before. [He is] still slim and active.... Only the forthright behaviour of a sportsman has been replaced by the elegance of a man of the world.

Because the negotiations with Charles were secret, Nansen had to be painfully circumspect, but soon after arrival he was introduced to Prince Charles and Princess Maud. 'The Royal couple,' said Wedel, keeping himself to the fore in this complex affair, 'were naturally overwhelmed by Nansen's celebrated charm.' They were 'extremely pleased to hear that I very much wanted to have them in Norway', Nansen himself told Eva in a letter.

> They had been afraid of me, believing that I wanted a republic so that I could

become President.... That's what they generally believe abroad. Good Heavens, people can't imagine that everyone doesn't want to be a president.

Nansen was only one of many republicans in principle who, in practice, had now turned monarchist. Foreign policy aside, their feelings had been expressed by Anton Amundsen in the now distant days on *Fram* who, when faced with Nansen's departure on the sledge journey, had said that 'it is better to be ruled by one king than by many petty kings'.

'Prince Charles ... seems to be a good chap,' Nansen wrote to Eva, 'and the most intelligent of the Oldenburgs [the Danish ruling House] although admittedly that is not saying much.'

He had a reason for his mockery. There was talk, and more than talk, in the Nansen family of illegitimate descent from Frederik VI, King of Denmark from 1808 to 1839 and hence, until 1814, King of Norway too. He was said to have been the natural father of Nansen's paternal grandmother, Vendelia Christiane Louise. Even allowing for a break in the succession, that made Nansen a distant blood relation of the Danish, British and Russian reigning houses, and hence a kind of cousin of Prince Charles. His father's nickname as a child was 'the Oldenburger', and the Danish royal family was said to have acknowledged the connection. Perhaps this made Nansen a noticeably acceptable emissary. He believed the story anyway.

Radiating trustworthiness and force of character, still with the patina of the great explorer of the age, Nansen brought authority in his wake. He convinced Charles that this was no frivolous palace intrigue. He relieved the Prince of a feeling of being used by others, and gave him a sense of purpose of his own. It was Nansen who crucially persuaded Charles that the Norwegian crown was a concrete possibility.

His position was anomalous. Wedel had credentials of a sort; Nansen was supposedly a private individual. Nonetheless he was treated as the real agent of the Norwegian government. He repeatedly dined with British diplomats. This was understandable because the British Embassy was now in reality directing the affair. His arrival, moreover, was a relief to Alan Johnstone, newly appointed British Minister in Copenhagen, who, in his own words, was

> forced, owing to our lack of direct and controlling intelligence ... to place a certain faith in Baron Wedel ... but I thoroughly distrust the man himself. He came here hoping to carry through matters with a high hand and [return to] his own country ... saying.... 'See! I have brought you a king.'

Johnstone who, through his wife, had connections at court, was able to go behind the Foreign Secretary's back and deal directly with King Edward. To Eva, Nansen reported a 'flaming telegram from King Edward, who considered the matter settled. [He] thinks that Queen of Norway is a splendid title for his daughter'. Needing always a woman in whom to confide, Nansen was sharing secrets with Eva; more so sometimes than with his official masters.

Between them, Nansen, Johnstone and King Edward were nagging Charles to act. Charles resisted all these blandishments. Until the Bernadotte Proposal was formally rejected, the throne of Norway was not his to take. At the outset, King Oscar had privately explained that he would eventually reject the Bernadotte Proposal, but only when the Union had been formally dissolved. This was unknown outside the Danish court and government. It was enough to explain Charles's obduracy.

All this was happening in a vacuum, because the Swedes had not yet officially responded to the Norwegian declaration of independence. It was only early in August that the Riksdag finally made up its mind. The Union would be dissolved, but only by mutual consent. To regularise matters, Norway was to ask Sweden to end the Union. Certain conditions were stipulated. The Swedes insisted on successful negotiation first, then abrogation of the Union, and finally a declaration that the Norwegian throne was vacant. The Norwegians jibbed at this. They wanted a king first and negotiations after, as a recognised State. Deadlock ensued.

However, the Norwegians felt that they could comply with one of the Swedish demands. This was that in order to prove that the rupture of the Union was not a mere parliamentary whim, without a mandate, the Norwegian approach was to be contingent on a test of public opinion, either by an election or a referendum. The Norwegians quickly chose a referendum, to be held on 13 August. The electorate duly approved the end of the Union by 368,208 votes to 184 with a turnout of 85.4%. Added to this were a quarter of a million 'Yes' votes in a private poll of women, Norwegian female suffrage still being eight years away. The virtual unanimity made a deep impression abroad, but not as deep as Nansen for one had hoped.

Two rebuffs in Stockholm, besides the urging of Alan Johnstone in Copenhagen, finally convinced the Norwegians that, having won the principle, they would do best to submit to the rest of the Swedish demands. So they requested Sweden to dissolve the Union and open talks on the conditions laid down. The question of the crown was left in abeyance.

With relief, the Swedish government agreed. After a little discussion Karlstad was accepted as the venue for the talks. This was a sleepy lakeside Swedish town on the railway line between Stockholm and Christiania. Most importantly, by the communications of the day, it was isolated from the febrile atmosphere of both capitals. Negotiations finally began on 31 August.

For Nansen, however, there was no part to play, and he fled back to Sørkje. As usual, he ran down the last slope behind the buildings, shouting to let Eva and the children know that he was arriving. The exuberance hid a tortured state of mind. As he had told Eva,

If the Norwegians settle things [without Prince Charles] they might say why the devil do we need a prince, seeing that we have managed everything by ourselves, and we can make do with a republic. I am afraid of that.

Nansen's fear went deeper than politics. 'We can never kill the vanity in ourselves,' ran a telling passage in his diary.

If you yourself have played a part in [what is now happening] you must be content with the knowledge that you have done something useful, but not demand recognition.... If you rejected the presidency, or did not seek it, everyone would praise you as honourable and unselfish, but they would not understand the true reason; that I would abhor the consequent trouble and the constrained life, and am enough of an egoist to prefer ... being my own master.

In other words, a republic would be a mortal temptation.

Nansen's eldest child, Liv, regularly went back late to school because of the hunting season. Now, not even the old pleasure of shooting grouse over his own preserves could lighten Nansen's mood. 'We are living in difficult times, the old values have been destroyed, the new ones have not yet been created,' he lamented.

The solid earth on which we have built has crumbled beneath our feet ... Our ideals have become shadows in the mist.... Everything seems an empty and miserable ... chaos, where only one thing is certain: *everlasting change*. But whither? whence? Like the wind.

'The whole antheap seems so far off up here, and I cannot understand why I think it is all so important,' Nansen was soon writing up in his corner of the heath,

and in the dusk I sit before the fireplace and stare into the flickering flames from birch logs.

Only a few weeks after these questing passages were penned a certain clerk in the Swiss patent office in Berne called Albert Einstein published an innocent sounding paper of exactly thirty pages which launched the theory of relativity. Whatever his faults and bleakly pessimistic moods, Nansen had given tongue to the zeitgeist.

63

Unofficial Envoy

On 7 September, a man arrived from the valley with a telephone message recalling Nansen to Christiania. He had a suitcase already packed in expectation of this summons, for which he had been half hoping. He left the same afternoon. But to get away from Sørkje and reach the capital was a complicated undertaking. First he had to row across 'his' lake. Then came what he called 'a romantic ride in darkness and moonlight on muddy roads'. Only on the last lap was he able to travel by train. He reached Christiania late the next morning. Still in his shooting clothes, he cycled off without delay to see Michelsen who, as Prime Minister, was leading the Norwegian delegation to the conference at Karlstad and had hastily returned.

The cause of Nansen's summons was a crisis in the talks. Michelsen wanted him to go to London yet again and secure British diplomatic support. He hurried off by the night train that same evening, 8 September.

The agenda of the Karlstad Conference was short and clear-cut. Its purpose was to regulate the consequences of separation. They were few, and mostly uncontentious. The stumbling block was the Swedish demand for demilitarisation of the southern border zone, and in particular demolition of the Norwegian frontier forts. This touched national pride and aroused high, irrational emotion. On the afternoon that Nansen had left Sørkje for Christiania the Swedes suddenly issued an ultimatum on the forts, demanding a reply within forty-eight hours, with the veiled threat of war.

This was such an abrupt change of mood that the Norwegians suspected hidden influences at work. They were not all that hidden. The conference had clashed with a Swedish General Election. Because of the emotional atmosphere both sides had been warned against this, notably by *The Times*. It was another manifestation of the turbulent spirit of the age. The year 1905 was an echo of 1848. Everywhere, political systems were in turmoil. The Right was losing its grip, grappling with a confused lurch to the Left. The Swedish delegates at Karlstad, whatever their private inclinations, had to consider their domestic constituents. It was enough to explain the change of tack. Eventually, the Swedes extended their ultimatum. They finally agreed to an adjournment of six days so that the delegates could consult their governments. It was this respite that Nansen was being sent to exploit.

Yet again he was a private envoy with no official credentials. He travelled via Copenhagen where, on the evening of 9 September, he asked Count Raben, the Danish foreign minister, for diplomatic help against the Swedes as well. Raben, wishing to avoid foreign entanglements, was greatly perturbed. Eventually he found a way round by promising that Denmark would ask England, France, Germany and Russia to put pressure on Sweden. This was a neat device to involve the Powers without the impression of gratuitous interference.

At midnight, Nansen continued on his way, arriving in London early in the morning of Monday, 11 September. He booked in at the Royal Societies' Club, of which he was a member, and where he could discreetly hide. His mission depended on working behind the scenes, and much now rested on his shoulders.

He began with the Press. He quietly visited *The Times* and the *Morning Post*, as a result of which both published almost embarrassingly pro-Norwegian leaders over the next few days.

The day after his arrival Nansen saw Sir Thomas Sanderson, Permanent Under Secretary of State at the Foreign Office. Here his reception was considerably less warm than at the newspaper offices. Sir Thomas had just received the Danish request for British intervention which Nansen had manifestly come to support, and he practically accused Nansen, together with Wedel, of having put the Danes up to making the approach by exaggerating the danger of war.

Nansen was deeply concerned, for the following day, 13 September, the Karlstad Conference was to reassemble. He had hoped to see the King, but quickly understood that this was now unlikely. He suggested going to meet the Foreign Secretary only to be told that it was 'not judicious'. Lord Lansdowne was away on one of his estates in Ireland, and a visit now would bring undesirable publicity.

The fifth Marquess of Lansdowne was one of the eminent Edwardians. A classical scholar, the product of Eton and Balliol, infinitely courteous, reticent, and polished in appearance, he was held by his equals to be the greatest gentleman of the age. He was in fact a patrician Anglo-Irishman born to rule. He had been Governor-General of Canada and Viceroy of India. As an English landowner in Ireland, he had an all too intimate acquaintance with a union of irreconcilables. He was the architect of two momentous treaties: the Anglo-Japanese Alliance, and the understanding with France.

King Edward, having received a letter from Wedel, was pressing Lansdowne for action in the Norwegian affair. Lansdowne deplored royal interference in foreign policy. He declined to act directly on the Danish request and make a formal representation. Rennell Rodd would be unobtrusively exerting pressure in Stockholm. On 14 September Sir Thomas

Sanderson called Nansen to the Foreign Office to convey this message. Having reported his original conversation with, and impressions of, Nansen and in consequence received new guidance from Lord Lansdowne, Sir Thomas was considerably more amicable than before.

Nansen's presence, however, caused the Foreign Office some unease, by virtue of its novelty alone. Until he arrived, Norway was somehow an amorphous concept, her politicians unimpressive and unknown abroad. Nansen gave his country stature and a face. By sheer personal magnetism and the lingering glory of the snows he had ensured his country a status out of all proportion to its size. He had the kind of presence that suggested he was speaking for one of the Powers instead of a small nation on the periphery. He appeared at the right moment to counteract Wedel's suspect machinations and present authoritative arguments. He gave the British authorities the impulse they needed to shift their neutral stance in order to break the Scandinavian impasse.

He also, in his own words, 'thought it best to ... beard the lion in his den', and called on Baron Bildt, the much respected Swedish (and still technically Norwegian) Minister in London. Bildt, no chauvinist, was relieved to find Nansen dignified and moderate. They had a guarded but friendly conversation, each disparaging his own countrymen for their excesses. Bildt in fact disliked the recent antics at Karlstad. He unwittingly touched a raw nerve when, as Nansen observed, he remarked that 'he had always imagined [Norway] as a republic, with myself as President. I thanked him for the compliment, but said that it would never happen.'

The following day, 14 September, Nansen's presence in London was revealed by the *Daily Mail* and, as usual, he was besieged by reporters. He kept all except the chosen ones at bay by hiding in the library of the RGS. Having been forced out into the open, he now once more exploited his old reputation with the Press.

At this point, Henry Wilkinson, acting Editor of the *Morning Post*, presented Nansen with what was arguably a calculated leak. Wilkinson arranged a meeting with his brother-in-law, who worked in the Foreign Office, and who confidentially disclosed, as Nansen recorded in his diary, that 'the Swedish government had [said] that they had no hostile intentions towards Norway, but they had to keep up the pretence in order to "play to the gallery" '. The contours of Foreign Office tactics were beginning to emerge. The Norwegians were being reassured that the Swedes would keep their share of the original bargain.

A lone, unofficial agent, Nansen had only sporadic contact with Michelsen at Karlstad. Often he had to glean what he could from the Foreign Office. He dared not trust a secretary, and therefore had to do all the routine work of encoding and decoding telegrams and so forth. On 15 September, when he wrote a vital letter to Lord Lansdowne, in longhand, he had no time to make a copy. Prompted by a telegram from Michelsen, Nansen asked Lansdowne if Britain, together with other Powers, would guarantee a neutral frontier zone. Of his own accord he asked whether, in case the negotiations broke down and the Norwegians elected Charles their King, Great Britain would immediately recognise their country.

Lansdowne characteristically replied that 'while the secret negotiations were still in progress, any attempt on our part to put what is usually spoken of as diplomatic pressure upon the Swedish [government] would only have the effect of defeating our objects ... particularly if [it] were to take place in an obtrusive manner'. And about the frontier zone: 'Our experience of ... such joint liabilities is not altogether reassuring.' As far as Prince Charles and immediate recognition went, the answer was another polished 'No'. The letter was dated 19 September. Lansdowne had held it back for 24 hours, he explained,

> in the hope that I might end it by offering you my congratulations ... My latest information ... affords every reason for believing that a settlement will be come to, if it has not already been reached.

On 13 September, the day that the conference reassembled at Karlstad – by coincidence the day when away in Manchuria an armistice brought the Russo-Japanese war to an end – Nansen's work on the way through Copenhagen bore fruit to the extent that the French, Russian and subsequently the German ambassadors made representations to the Foreign Ministry in Stockholm. The Swedes were furious, accusing the Norwegians of 'perfidy' in approaching the Great Powers while in the same breath maintaining that the action had had no effect. Clearly the authorities in Stockholm were shaken by the unexpected foreign pressure. By now, it was clear that if negotiations did break down, the Powers would intervene.

Nansen, however, was again on the sidelines. Now he had nothing to do but wait. His letters to Eva showed another change of mood. 'This is a horribly trivial life,' he wrote. 'I won't say that I can't do anything useful. I think I can, in a way, but not enough considering the time I'm spending.' He consoled himself by going to the theatre – a typical piece of parental inconsistency since he had forbidden his eldest child, Liv, to do so, and she was now nearly thirteen. He laid it down that actors were vacuous and vain, that theatres were unhealthy for children, besides which plays – as Ibsen himself in fact once maintained – could be better understood through reading.

On 23 September an agreement was at last signed at Karlstad. For an accurate report of the terms Nansen had to wait three days until it appeared in *The Times*. After all the fuss, the Norwegians had submitted to the Swedish demands. They had to give up their frontier forts, as required. They were, however, allowed to salvage something to hold up to their critics at home, and avoid charges of capitulation.

In the chancelleries of Europe there were sighs of relief that a powder keg had been defused. In Sweden there was a sense of deliverance from a burden of destructive irritation, August Strindberg, for instance, characteristically writing that he had

> hoisted a pure Swedish flag, without the Union mark. The mark of Cain has disappeared, for now brother has ceased fighting brother – as we hope!

In Norway, however, as Eva wrote to Nansen,

> people are screaming horribly, and no one is happy any more. They say that the glory of [the declaration of independence on] 7 June has disappeared, etc., I don't understand it, but can only wait until you return home, *you are really needed here*, you must try and cure all this sickliness and declamation.

The cause of the discontent was the demolition of the frontier forts and the historical legacy of bitterness. Exactly as Prince Gustaf had foretold, this was the outcome of not immediately conceding Norwegian independence. In Nansen's view,

> the agreement at Karlstad was quite good [so he told Eva], all things considered ... one must not confuse the great with the small, and last winter if anyone had been offered the dissolution of the Union in exchange for demolition of the forts, who would have hesitated ...

Elsewhere, there were undertones of unease articulated notably in London, by Sir Horace Rumbold, the former Ambassador in Stockholm, writing in the *Westminster Gazette*. 'In bursting asunder the Union, the Norwegians have violated ... a European trust,' Sir Horace wrote.

> For Europe, and especially for ourselves, the Union was a guarantee of internal peace in the Scandinavian Peninsula, and it was distinctly as such that it was favoured by those who were answerable for the general European rearrangement of 1814-5 ... one can scarcely help being angered by the thought that ... national vaingloriousness ... threatens the general peace.

Since the formation of Belgium in the previous century Norway was in fact the first of the subject nations of the post-Napoleonic settlement to achieve independence. With hindsight it might appear the prelude to the unravelling of the European settlement that, one way or another, had stood for the best part of a hundred years.

Nansen, at any rate, found himself subtly transformed from confidential agent to ambassador in waiting. King Oscar had given a long interview to *Le Temps* in Paris – one of the first reigning monarchs to agree to be interviewed by the Press – the essence of which was that 'the Norwegians have behaved badly'. *Le Temps* quickly followed up by printing an interview with Nansen in which 'speaking English easily and most correctly,

he defended his fellow-citizens against the bitter reproaches of King Oscar
... but without the least touch of bitterness himself'.

> Very tall, with square shoulders, with his energetic countenance and heavy
> blond moustache, in which his fifth decade is putting a touch of grey, Doctor
> Nansen [the paper continued], makes a certain impression: behind the
> diplomat of today, one sees and one senses the explorer of yesterday, who has
> risked his life a thousand times for the glory of his country as well as the
> benefit of science; he has left the shifting pack ice in order to venture just as
> rashly into the even more shifting terrain of difficult negotiations.

Lord Lansdowne now finally wished to meet Nansen, who therefore had
to wait until the Foreign Secretary's return. Meanwhile, on 1 October, in
an interlude to politics, Sir Clements Markham had Nansen to tea. A few
days earlier, Sir Clements had finally resigned as President of the RGS,
an event which seemed to close an age. Nansen told Sir Clements that he
was worried about Amundsen's financial difficulties when he should return. Nothing had been heard from Amundsen for over two years. In a
disturbing contact with the polar world Nansen also met Dr Jean Charcot,
a French explorer who had just returned from the Antarctic.

Finally, on 3 October, Nansen and Lord Lansdowne met discreetly at a
small dinner given by Sir Thomas Sanderson at his home in Wimpole
Street. Nansen, in authoritative form, turned to the question of Norwegian
security. Divorced from Sweden, Norway, he said, would be cast adrift,
small and alone in an increasingly dangerous world. It was an issue
already exercising the government in Christiania.

Nansen asked about the so-called November Treaty. This was a guarantee given by Great Britain and France in November 1855 of the
territorial integrity of Sweden-Norway. It was part of the diplomacy of the
Crimean War and aimed against Russia. Nansen wanted to know whether
it would be applied to Sweden and Norway after their separation.

Writing to Sir Rennell Rodd, Lord Lansdowne reported that

> Dr Nansen asked me whether ... such a Guarantee would be more difficult
> to obtain in case Norway adopted a republican form of government. I said
> that I could not see why [that] should preclude the possibility of a Guarantee,
> but that the selection of Prince Charles might predispose public opinion here
> in favour of the Guarantee.
>   Dr Nansen told me that he would leave immediately for Norway, with the
> hope that he would be able to bring about a calmer state of public opinion
> than at present existed.

Back in Christiania Nansen found the atmosphere exactly as Eva had
described it. 'What do people want?' he wrote in a newspaper article
ironically headed *Heroism!*

> Naturally rejection of the Karlstad agreement, thereafter war ... republic.

That will secure us 'splendid isolation'. It is so fortifying to stand alone, and now there is a risk of being recognised by other states.

Now that the end of the Union was in sight, Prince Charles's candidature for the Norwegian throne had been reopened. Once more Nansen was conscripted by the government, this time to ditch the republicans, quickly fill the throne, and avoid any further suspense.

On 9 October, the Storting ratified the Karlstad agreement. Opposition was confined to a small embittered faction on the Left. In London, Nansen had frankly explained to Lord Lansdowne that

If the British [government] could take some step ... in connection with a guarantee for the integrity of [Norway] when the time comes it would decidedly make the election of Prince Charles of Denmark much easier.

Writing on the same day as the ratification of the agreement, he now reinforced this, asking Lansdowne whether the Storting could be authoritatively told in secret session that

the election of Prince Charles of Denmark would greatly help us ... in ... that it would strengthen the bonds with Great Britain, and make the British government more willing to ... guarantee the absolute integrity of Norway.

Prodded by telegram, Lord Lansdowne telegraphed his approval on 15 October. Deliberately or not, he had waited until the Riksdag in Stockholm also had ratified the Karlstad agreement, which they did on 13 October. When on 19 October, in Christiania the Storting met to consider the election of Prince Charles as King, Lansdowne's message swung waverers behind him. But the Danes, frightened off by the republican clamour, now wanted the Norwegians to hold a referendum first. Michelsen, fearing the consequences of delay, immediately sent Nansen – still as a private agent – to Copenhagen to persuade them to change their mind.

Nansen left the following day and arrived in Copenhagen on 21 October. That same evening he met Prince Charles at the home of Count Raben. Tall, thin, dark, unassuming, conventionally self-possessed in the fashion of the age, Charles at first sight could give the impression of a pliable nonentity. Nansen was swiftly disabused of that notion. 'During the summer, I had talked to a relatively callow youth,' he records,

but now he had developed into a grown up man, and my respect grew as he warmed to his subject. I had come in the belief that he would be easily persuaded ... but I was confronted with a man who had thought the matter through from different angles.

The Prince shrank from ascending the throne against the popular will. He insisted on a referendum to remove all doubt. 'I argued as well as I could,' Nansen wrote to Eva, 'but he stood his ground and defended his standpoint admirably.'

Nansen, supported by the Norwegian government, objected to a referendum because, although one had been held at the behest of the Swedes, it was not recognised by the Constitution. Interestingly enough, Alan Johnstone, now once again intimately concerned in the negotiations as British Minister in Copenhagen, declared a few days later 'what a bad invention the plebiscite was', as Nansen recorded in his diary.

> It could easily be used against parliament. Napoleon III had invented the personal plebiscite in order to oppose the legal national assembly, and it was no admirable example, etc.

In other words, both men were at heart parliamentary despots. The Prince turned out to be the better democrat. On 29 October Nansen left Copenhagen for Christiania empty-handed. A referendum there was going to be.

Meanwhile, on 26 October, the last act of the separation of the dual kingdom had been played out. In Stockholm the Riksdag repealed the Act of Union and the Karlstad Agreement was signed, while King Oscar recognised Norway and rejected the Bernadotte Proposal. The Union was at an end. Norway had achieved its sovereignty without a drop of blood being spilled. Both sides could take credit for a unique and civilised performance.

Russia was actually the first Power to recognise an independent Norway, on 19 October, followed by Great Britain the next day. The referendum was held on 12-13 November. Nansen campaigned frantically on the royalist side. The republicans fought a bitter rearguard action, but in the end the royalists won with 79% of the vote. In the Storting on 18 November Prince Charles was unanimously elected King – a piece of magnanimity on the part of the republicans by which the new monarch was greatly touched.

As for Nansen, he had at least achieved what he had been asked to do. Yet: 'Everything is empty and hopeless,' he wrote in his first diary entry after the event.

> This tinsel world is unbearable ... the whole town, indeed almost the whole country and all newspapers are full of the forthcoming entry of the King, and everything connected with it: pomp, ceremony, play-acting ... Are we living by externals, just appearance and forms ... Michelsen is furious at what he is seeing and hearing ... he had never thought ... that there was so much snobbery ... In truth European society is bankrupt. Our values have shrivelled and collapsed, and we ourselves are shipwrecked on an islet in the middle of Eternity's stormy sea. The next moment we will be swept away. Slogans no longer have any power; what are we to live on now? ... I am afraid that our culture ... has come to the end of its tether. A new culture must be found, a new attitude to life ... Does the East possess them? No one knows.

This outpouring had perhaps been triggered by a disturbing voice from the wilderness. On 1 November Nansen received a letter from Roald Amundsen. It had been almost a year under way and was dated the previous November, from King William Land, in the Canadian Arctic. It was the first sign of life from Amundsen since he had disappeared from human ken in *Gjøa* off the coast of Greenland two and a half years earlier. The letter had been carried to civilisation by Eskimo courier and the Canadian Mounties at Cape Fullerton in Hudson Bay. Amundsen wrote that so far all had gone well, that he had reached the North Magnetic Pole, and that he hoped to finish sailing through the North-West Passage that summer. 'If we finally succeed in [doing so],' he ended his letter,

> my first telegram will be to you, Herr Professor. Not a day has yet passed, and scarcely one will go by, without my thanking you in my thoughts for what you have done for me. I know that so far I have not failed the trust you have shown me, and I dearly hope that in the future I will be able to say the same thing.

Meanwhile, on 25 November, Prince Charles sailed up the fjord and arrived in Christiania on the Danish Royal yacht *Danebrog*, after a stormy crossing of the Skagerrak. He had assumed the title of King Haakon VII, after one of the old Norwegian kings. His two-year-old son and heir, originally Alexander, he renamed Olav, another historic Norwegian royal name.

In snowfall against dark waters, together with Eva, Nansen was down at the quayside to welcome Haakon. Because he was still a mere private citizen he deliberately kept in the background, in the shadow of the official welcoming dignitaries. In his own words:

> Both the King and Queen made a good but somewhat self-conscious impression as they came ashore in this foreign [country] which was to be their fatherland.

After the ceremonial landing Nansen went to the Palace to renew his acquaintance privately with the King and Queen. Almost from the start, he had become a family friend. At the year's end tributes to his work descended on Nansen from the Prime Minister downwards. This did not prevent his writing gloomily in his diary:

> The fog is as solid as a wall out there. Heavy and dismal and hopeless in this land of fog. It is as if we all go blundering about in this fog seeking the meaning of life. As if it had any meaning.

Nansen faced the New Year with more than his usual burden of ambivalence. Attainment, as usual, brought a hollow sense of anticlimax. And his very success had brought ill will in its train.

In his innocence, Nansen assumed that Sweden and Norway would instantly bury the past. Prince Gustaf had been more realistic in foreseeing a legacy of bitterness. Nansen found himself cut by old Swedish friends. They included Gustav Retzius, his once boundless admirer in neuroscience. Even Prince Eugen, tolerant, no chauvinist, a royal Jacobin, could no longer bring himself to communicate directly with Nansen. Instead, he sent greetings through Erik Werenskiold, their mutual friend among the artists round Nansen's home:

> I find it difficult to swallow much of what [Nansen] did before the break [Prince Eugen wrote]. I understand that he did it for his country, but half truths are not the truth, and that brings its own deserts.

Nansen meanwhile was disturbed by a voice from the past. Hjalmar Johansen wrote 'concerning money matters', as he put it. After the sad hiatus on returning from *Fram* he had finally achieved his old ambition and been given a permanent commission in the army. He was gazetted a full lieutenant, with five years' seniority into the bargain. He had also married his old love Hilda Øvrum, for whom he had been pining in the Arctic. He was now in Tromsø, promoted Captain, but somehow lost. He had discovered that he could not cope with the return to everyday life after his moment of fame. His posting to northern Norway he felt to be a kind of internal exile. He could not stand the boredom of garrison routine in a conscript army. Money matters defeated him. He had a wife and three children to support, and they, for some reason, as he explained in his catalogue of woe,

> have been living back [at home] in Skien and I here in Tromsø [which] has added to my outlays ... more than usual ... I have therefore not been able to pay my tax and some old debts ... I cannot manage because of debt ... I will be sold up within the next few days unless I pay my taxes ... a lawyer is suing me ... I have never been in such a jam before. – For that reason I must ask you for a loan of 1,000 – one thousand kroner [£2,500 or $4,000 in present terms]. I am only begging you for this, because I see no other way out.

It was almost as if there had been a curse on *Fram*. Blessing still could not shake off his morphine addiction. Aside from Sverdrup and Scott Hansen, most of the crew had been in need at one time or another. Down the years Nansen, unshakeably loyal to those who had followed him, helped every one of them, and their families too.

Johansen was the saddest of them all. This latest cry for help was the fifth or sixth in four years, and Nansen had hitherto always come to the rescue. Like a seaman only at home with a coast disappearing astern, Johansen was a misfit in the toils of life ashore; a distorted reflection of something within Nansen himself, a charge upon his conscience for neglect. For some reason, Nansen delayed answering this appeal. It needed a telegram – 'WILL YOU HELP ME AS I WROTE DISTRESS IN SIGHT' – to secure the money.

Nansen was simultaneously confronted by a call with yet more troubling implications for himself. On 9 December he heard once more from Amundsen. Now it was a cable requesting five hundred dollars, but also announcing the completion of the North-West Passage.

Strictly speaking, this was not quite true. Amundsen had been caught by the ice at King Point, on the north coast of Alaska, and forced to winter there. He still had to pass through the Bering Strait and actually enter the Pacific. But since his letters from King William Land he had sailed *Gjøa* through the last unnavigated Arctic channels linking the Atlantic with the Pacific, so that he had actually completed the North-West Passage in all but name. By ski and dog sledge he had travelled eight hundred miles overland from King Point to the cablehead at Eagle, on the Yukon, in the Alaskan hinterland. Before returning to King Point, he told Nansen, he would wait at Eagle for a reply.

By the first crossing of Greenland, Nansen had become the latest to achieve one of the last great geographical goals. Now, after seventeen years, he had finally been deposed. Despite that, he hastened to arrange with Michelsen for official help through the Norwegian consular service, then in the hasty process of being established. He now confirmed the arrangement, and after a slight delay the $500 (£4,800 or $7,600 in present terms), was cabled to Amundsen in Eagle.

Nansen observed to Michelsen that 'an expedition as successful as this one would have a certain significance for our country, perhaps now especially, because it will draw attention to us'.

To Amundsen himself Nansen wrote that he had never doubted that he would carry out his plan,

> but this exceeds all expectations, it has gone so well. What is more, it has come just at the right time, as a shining chapter in the new history of the new Norway.

He then gave Amundsen a résumé of recent events, the burden of which was that he had sailed from a subject country but would be returning to an independent one. King Haakon, in Nansen's own words, 'made his entry ... exactly a fortnight ago today. And now there comes the news of your triumph.' He suggested that, when Amundsen reached port,

> it might not be a bad idea ... to cable ... our ... King Haakon. If for old times' sake you would telegraph a few words to King Oscar, I leave to you; it is not necessary, but perhaps would be considerate to the old gentleman.

The whole affair was clouded by an uneasy aftertaste. Nansen had heard the news not, as Amundsen had wished, directly from himself, but at second hand, in a newspaper. Amundsen's telegram had been intercepted in America, the gist leaked to the Press, and the news first published in Christiania two days before finally being delivered to Nansen.

Almost as unsettling as Amundsen's achievement was gloomy news from Adolf Ónodi, in Budapest, who wrote:

> Everything is miserable where we are concerned, simply a bloodless absolutism. Nobody knows what is going to happen ... taxes and loans for the army are collected with force. We have no idea whether elections will be carried out, or whether we will be governed in an absolutist way for a long time.... It is a hopeless, miserable situation. There is a general depression.

From Marion Ure, now living in Shanghai, came a letter also touched with unease: 'I scarcely know, Fridtjof, whether to congratulate you or not upon this outcome of the revolution in your country,' she began.

> Will you write us, & also say if it is true that you have been offered the post of ambassador [in London] & whether you have accepted. Of course it is a very splendid position & I congratulate you very heartily if this is true & yet ... I wonder – for it seems ... very unlike the old Fridtjof of Viking days, but then do we not all change as the years advance & very likely you can serve your country better in this way than in hunting for more Poles!

Nansen had indeed been appointed to the post. 'So I'm here ... Why am I here? How did it happen?' he wrote in his diary as soon as he had arrived. It was a great moment and a great chance.

64

Riding Mistress

Independence seemed almost to have taken the Norwegians by surprise. Foreign affairs were clouded by improvisation. A.N. Krupensky, the first Russian Minister to an independent Norway, wrote from Christiania to the Foreign Minister in St Petersburg that

> this new capital ... does not know where to lodge its foreign guests. It is difficult to find a suitable apartment.... A representative of the English Foreign Office is tramping the streets to find a house to lease or buy for the British Legation.

It was only on 21 March 1906, five months after formal sovereignty, that the first ministers to the Powers were appointed. There were few trained diplomats and a dearth of men of stature. King Edward VII wanted Nansen in London, and there he was accordingly sent. It was the most important post in the fledgling diplomatic service.

Nansen arrived in London on 15 April 1906 and started, as he wrote to Eva, by 'rushing round like a cockroach looking for rooms where I could settle down, but have temporarily given up'. He lodged instead at the Royal Palace Hotel in Kensington (now the Kensington Palace).

'THE MINISTER FROM THE NORTH POLE' was the headline under which the *Bystander* greeted Nansen's arrival, accompanying its article with a caricature of him on skis.

> Dr Nansen ... may not be experienced in the paths of diplomacy, but as he himself coyly confesses, he has 'seen life' of another kind in another locality, notably up at the North pole, where I believe the carryings-on of the polar bears are really a scandal ... I suppose Dr Nansen was sent to us because King Haakon knew from personal experience the rigours of an English spring, and decided that only an Arctic Explorer could stand it.

The routine business of the Legation was conducted by the erstwhile Chargé d'Affaires, now transformed into First Secretary, Johannes Irgens, a Christiania lawyer, who was installed in a pleasant house in the Boltons, South Kensington. To begin with, Nansen had little to do but settle in.

One of his first public actions was a newspaper interview on the death of Henrik Ibsen on 23 May. He was asked for his estimate of Ibsen's work. 'I am not a critic,' Nansen replied,

> it is not my business to formulate an 'estimate'.... But this at least can be said, that Ibsen's influence in shaping the Norway of to-day, and the Norwegian character, has been incalculable. If I may use myself as an example, it is no exaggeration to say that my character, such as it is, has been largely of Ibsen's making. The suggestive influence of such a poem as 'Brand' upon the men of my generation has been more than you would easily believe.... He stimulated the national self-consciousness and self-respect. He was above everything a bracing influence, and, like most bracing influences, he was sometimes more wholesome than pleasant.

Nansen's interlocutor was William Archer, who had originally translated and introduced Ibsen to England. He was a cousin of Colin Archer, who had built *Fram*. 'Ibsen was a great man,' Nansen wrote to a friend.

> It is terrible how the great men are being thinned out ... and where are the new ones?

The London to which Nansen had returned was different to the one he had known the year before. In January, there had been a general election, the result of which was that the Conservatives, in power for a decade, had been routed, and the Liberals returned to office by a landslide. This was more than the time-honoured change of party at the helm. It was a violent shift of power. It belonged to the political earthquake shaking Europe, other manifestations of which included the breaking of the Swedish-Norwegian Union and revolution in Russia.

In England, the patricians were being deposed. The new Prime Minister was a down-to-earth Scot called Sir Henry Campbell-Bannerman. Lord Lansdowne had been replaced as Foreign Secretary by the altogether different, bird-watching Sir Edward Grey. The real portent was the first parliamentary appearance in force of the Labour Party, and hence, ultimately, 'The Strange Death of Liberal England', to quote the title of a celebrated book. Nansen himself saw the writing on the wall. 'The course is set for Socialism,' he wrote in his diary. 'Before, the individual was the tyrant; now it is much worse, [it is] society.'

On the surface, London remained its Edwardian self. 'Birth is of no account here,' wrote Baron Bildt, the Swedish Ambassador, now about to leave his post, in a memorandum for his successor, 'but wealth is desirable.' The young Norwegian diplomatic service was the victim of political parsimony, and Nansen himself was not 'moneyed' in the full sense. He could not therefore afford premises of the correct diplomatic standing. But Edwardian London, with its frantic pursuit of pleasure laced with a sense of doom, also hungered for celebrities, and Nansen was still counted among them. His old fame, garnered long ago in the days of *Fram* and the

428

crossing of Greenland, mysteriously still clung to him. Having presented his credentials to the King on 10 May he saw the social invitations begin to flow from the Court and Society hostesses. He was soon summoned to Windsor Castle, from where one afternoon he wrote to Eva that he was going for a drive – these were the salad days of early motoring – with the King, Lord Milner (the great Imperial administrator) and the statuesque Lady de Grey, a reigning beauty of the age.

> The King and Queen both say that you must come over soon [Nansen told Eva], everyone is asking after you, and feel sorry for me, having to be here alone, and I heartily agree.

Eva had refused to follow him to London because she could not bring herself to leave her own home and familiar surroundings, or so she said. She had a double pretext in that Nansen had promised that he would only stay in London for as long as it took to arrange the 'territorial guarantee' – the safeguard, that is, of Norwegian territorial integrity. That was his real mission. In his innocence, he expected this to be a matter of months. Eva considered it senseless to uproot herself and the children for so short a time. 'It annoys me,' she wrote, 'that people smile and say "he'll remain there all right".' She could not answer back. Because of its political and diplomatic ramifications, Nansen's mission was a secret although he trusted her and she knew about it.

Soon after his arrival he reported to her (but probably not to his own Foreign Minister) a meeting with the French Ambassador, Paul Cambon:

> Our conversation proceeded in a peculiar way; he spoke French, and I spoke mostly English. But he understands my English considerably less than I his French, which is a model of clarity.

One of the great characters of the diplomatic corps, Cambon was, as Nansen told Eva,

> a devilishly intelligent man.... He told me many interesting things ... also about the treaty that we want to achieve for the protection of Norway. In his view it was very important, but it is a delicate matter, and it was necessary to deal tactfully with Germany, and it will not be quickly settled.

Nansen would therefore probably have to remain in London far longer than he expected. To Eva, this was naturally a disappointment. She also had to cope with other strains.

On 9 June the previous year, two days after the declaration of independence, there had been a ceremony in Christiania at which the old Union flag was lowered for the last time and the new 'clean' Norwegian tricolor raised. Nansen had been among the crowd, *incognito* as he thought. Afterwards, however, he received snapshots of himself, anonymously sent. They showed him together with a woman. The woman was not Eva, but Sigrun Munthe, the wife of a neighbour at Lysaker. All three used to go riding together.

Nansen had become a passionate horseman. Sigrun was tall, stately, and sat well on a horse. Eva did not. She was, moreover, older than he, while Sigrun was younger. Nansen was now forty-four, and growing restless. For some time he had been paying court to Sigrun, and during that spring they had started an affair.

By her own account, Sigrun said to him: 'Be careful. I'm not like the other scalps you have hanging on your belt.' Her husband was a painter called Gerhard Munthe, one of the national romantic 'Lysaker Circle' around Nansen. Munthe was twenty years older than Sigrun. He had married her when she was seventeen. They were childless. They had been man and wife for the best part of two decades.

To begin with, Eva did not appear to suspect her husband's liaison. Her gossipy letters to Nansen while he was abroad during that summer of 1905, and before she moved to the country, had been full of artless references to Sigrun, mostly about riding together. But when Nansen was in Berlin in March, on his first foreign mission, she had blandly written:

> It is sad for you that you don't have me with you – perhaps you are sitting and longing for me in your hotel ... no, no, you and I are not that much in love with each other.

With his habit of resorting to English poetry when trying to express his feelings, Nansen at one point quoted to Sigrun some verses from Tennyson's *Idylls of the King*:

> In Love if love be love if love be ours,
> Faith and unfaith can ne'r be equal powers.
> Unfaith in aught is want of faith in all.
> It is the litle rift within the lute,
> That by and by will make the music mute ...

It was not, in the circumstances, a very good choice of text. Sigrun responded in the classic manner by demanding that he leave his wife and family for her, and threatened suicide when he refused. This was in 1905, and not a helpful background to his missions to London and Copenhagen.

Nansen lived in mortal fear that Eva would find out. He wanted to avoid the consequences by confessing to her but dared not. He needed an intermediary. He found one in her accompanist and closest friend, Ingeborg Motzfeldt. In the autumn of 1905, Ingeborg having returned to Christiania after studying in Italy, Nansen overwhelmed her with an uninhibited recital of the difficulties plaguing him. She thought it best to try to save Eva from the truth. From this point of view Nansen's move to London was timely. But exposure came – and in the worst possible way.

64. Riding Mistress

'It is just as if you and I are no longer married,' Eva sadly remarked in a letter soon after Nansen departed; 'as if I am finished with that part of my life.' A few weeks later she was writing: 'There is much talk about Mrs Munthe, and they say that she is unhappily in love with you and has become another person since you left ... I mention this, particularly after having heard this gossip ... today.'

[The subject] had been plaguing me for a long time, I have often been on the point of talking to you about it, but always stopped myself at the last minute – Have you not begun to be a little fond of Mrs Munthe? You know that you have been visiting her more than you ought to have.

More penetratingly she continued:

I often felt as if you were naturally fond of me in one way, and were sorry for me, but could not withstand the temptation of being together with her. I have borne this unpleasant and destructive [feeling] since she fell off [a horse] last year, and I saw you holding her in your arms, looking down at her with a strange expression.

Nansen replied, in all too well remembered terms, that 'if only you had spoken ... to me about this long ago, it would have saved me much *misery*'.

Mrs M. is not quite normal; if I have often sought her, it has not been for my own pleasure, rather the reverse, because she always made me sad and depressed, but it was because I thought I had to *take a little care of her* and treat her like a patient.

There was a grain of truth in all this. Sigrun was evidently frustrated in her marriage, and in part Nansen acted out of pity. He ought to have known better. Sigrun had turned out to be uncomfortably like Ibsen's neurotic heroine, Hedda Gabler, and now he had to extricate himself from a disastrous entanglement. Once again, he needed an outsider's help, and once again he chose Ingeborg Motzfeldt. He rushed off a letter to her asking her to intercede.

It is not for my sake ... that I am asking you for this [he wrote]. I have acted badly, been weak and cowardly ... Had I been more of a man from the start it would have been different ... Do what you think is best for Eva.

Nansen wanted Eva to be convinced that it was she he really loved. In this he was successful. 'Had Ingeborg not come ... and told me that she knew you loved me,' Eva wrote,

and that you had unburdened yourself to her before, I think I would have gone mad and taken my life, I was already looking in the medicine cupboard.

Then she rang up and said she wanted to dine with me and I thought she is the only one I can stand and [who might] dampen my misery, and then she came and told me all, and I was as if transformed.

From Nansen's reply, in Eva's words, 'there poured true love for the first time for many a long day'. And later: 'I have become a happy human being again.... Time heals all.' And: 'I discovered ... when I thought that I had lost you for good – that I care more for you than for the children – Heaven help me it is horrible to admit it, but that is how it is.'

But she also reproached him: 'How could you keep the comedy going and look me in the face?' she asked. 'Because I loved you above all else and ... felt that you ought to be shielded,' was his reply. As before, at a distance, with pen and paper, Nansen had patched the rift. His affair – what Eva now called 'The Other's evil' – seemed the key to the revival of their own brand of possessive love. It was as if Sigrun drew off the destructive emotions which Nansen and Eva otherwise spent on torturing each other. But each was still enmeshed in the isolation that had been the root of their unhappiness from the start.

Somehow, through a fraught exchange of letters and telegrams, Nansen managed to break off the affair without disaster. It was all so much easier at a distance. Sigrun was left with a sense of shame at having betrayed her unsuspecting husband. Nansen persuaded her not to enlighten him, for fear of destroying him. Eva was left to cope with a close neighbour and erstwhile companion who had been the other woman. For his part, Nansen, relieved at last of tension and guilt, could face his duties in London with greater peace of mind.

One final twist in the comedy still remained. King Haakon's coronation was to take place on 22 June in the Nidaros cathedral at Trondheim, where the medieval Norwegian kings had been crowned. The King wanted all the Norwegian ambassadors to attend, and in London King Edward VII asked Nansen to accompany the Prince and Princess of Wales (later King George V and Queen Mary), who were to represent him at the ceremony. They were to sail directly in the royal yacht there and back, so Nansen would not be able to go home. In one way this suited him, because he wished to avoid Sigrun. But he did want to see Eva. She too had been invited to the Coronation. For no clear reason, she refused. Perhaps she was afraid to see her husband until she had completely mastered her feelings. Like a hurt child, she was still withdrawing, looking inwards on the self. To Nansen she had written: '*Nevermore* will I make *new* friends.'

Early in July, Nansen returned to London, still without seeing Eva and still without instructions from his government. This meant that he had little to do except continue with the social round. He complained of being

the honoured guest ... a new creature to exhibit for the entertainment of the high life.... What a ridiculous invention are these social conventions.... Exterminate all these banal relics of semi-barbarism.

In reality, he liked being part of the passing scene. He went riding in Rotten Row with political contacts or fashionable ladies, both efficient routes to the seats of power. He regaled Eva with his roll of distinguished visits. One day it was the King at Windsor, another Lady Aline Sassoon, née Rothschild, who had pretensions as an artist, at her studio in Park Lane. He stayed with the Duke of Rutland at Belvoir Castle and visited the dowager Duchess of Manchester,

> a thoroughly amusing person, American, intelligent, ageing ... garrulous, chattering away undeterred, whether there are kings or princes present. [She is] big and fat, with a face like the Emperor Nero.

At last, at the beginning of August, Nansen was free to go home. The dog days had arrived. With parliament in recess there was little to be done, as Sir Edward Grey explained to him. Everybody, as usual, had left town. The Legation could look after itself. Nansen went directly to Sørkje, where Eva had long since moved with the children for the summer. He deliberately avoided his home at Lysaker for fear of meeting Sigrun.

For nearly two whole months he remained among the untenanted mountains, in 'the land that speaks my language', as he put it. There, once more, he found an interlude of peace. Having gone through purgatory during that summer of 1906, he and Eva now experienced an interlude of great contentment. His diary, to which he normally resorted only in moments of dark introspection, was singularly thin. For once his energies were turned outwards from the self. Politics were banished. He worked happily once more on oceanography, writing up the results of his accumulated cruises. An ancient Greek would have recognised in him a man who, temporarily at least, had come within appreciable distance of *aretê*, the virtue of being suited to what one is doing and consequently approaching a state of goodness and inner peace – according to Aristotle, the only prize worth having.

Even his discouraging financial state, revealed when his annual accounts arrived from Alexander, could not breach a sense of wellbeing. His old home, *Godthåb*, had finally been sold, but because of the persistent property slump in Christiana rents were low and his income correspondingly reduced. He was also supporting his step-brothers and sisters, and especially his old confidante Ida. Still with children to care for, she was now separated from her husband, Axel Huitfeldt, who had become an alcoholic.

All too soon Nansen was on the boat back to England. On return, early in October, almost his first duty was to write to someone who had come even closer to *aretê*. During the summer, Amundsen had finally passed the Bering Strait and become the first man to sail from the Atlantic to the Pacific on one and the same keel, thus formally completing the North-West Passage. He had put into Nome, in Alaska, to cable the news.

433

You have carried out to the letter what you intended [Nansen wrote], and what you had signified in advance as your goal.

It was the classic, unfudged definition of success.

From first to last, your journey is one of the most successful and best organised expeditions known to polar history. And its charm is that it has been carried out with such small means ... I believe that it will be the model for many future expeditions, and will introduce a new kind of polar exploration with small, cheap vessels adapted to accomplished scientific work.

But, he warned, revealingly:

It is all very well to travel in the polar regions, but it is much more trying to come home and be feted.... Save yourself as much as you can, and don't wear yourself out by celebrating and chattering with all kinds of people.

This was one of the first letters written from the new Norwegian Legation. Nansen had at last moved out of his hotel into suitable rooms. They were modest enough, in a block of service flats at 36 Victoria Street, convenient for Parliament, Whitehall, the Foreign Office – and Buckingham Palace. The premises had been found by an admirer called Marie Lewis. She was the German-born daughter-in-law of Sir George Lewis, a famous (or infamous) Jewish criminal lawyer, who belonged to King Edward's raffish set, had infiltrated the underworld, had saved His Majesty himself from various scrapes, and was said to know enough to ruin half the Dukes and Duchesses of England. During the summer, Nansen had broken a dinner engagement with Scott Keltie, where he would have been introduced to Captain Scott, in order to go down and see Marie Lewis at the seaside resort of Sheringham instead. 'I cannot blame you,' was Keltie's mild reproach. 'I think Sheringham is an excuse for committing any crime.' For her part, Mrs Lewis had reported to Nansen chattily after his departure:

We have been bathing every day & of course my sister has missed you in the water & also for giving her the finishing touches with powder.

Eva was not exactly kept *au fait* about these gallivantings, but she knew at second hand. 'You are so loved everywhere,' she wrote to her husband with a touch of pride. For making love to a neighbour and little foreign escapades were two quite different things. In any case she had agreed to come over in the autumn, arriving about a fortnight after him. She had left the children behind, but with her came Ingeborg Motzfeldt. Both she and Nansen seemed glad of this third presence.

Now that Eva was with him, Nansen wanted to show her off in society. He wished her to be well dressed and, whatever her own inclinations, sent her to a fashionable dressmaker. In Ingeborg Motzfeldt's slightly ironic words,

> Nansen, who knew so much, was very particular about the material, so Eva had to bring back samples before she ordered the white silk gown for dressy occasions. He wanted to feel for himself whether the silk was soft and thick and genuine enough!

Nansen meanwhile was disturbed by another echo from the past. In Stockholm, in December, Camillo Golgi and Santiago Ramón y Cajal were jointly awarded the Nobel Prize for 1906 for physiology and medicine. It recognised their work in Nansen's old field of neurobiology. Cajal was rewarded for developing, or at least propagating, the now generally accepted neuron theory, in the pioneering of which Nansen had so notably played his part two decades before. Cajal had obliquely recognised this in a paper published fifteen years earlier. It was however not Cajal but Golgi, honoured for the anatomical discoveries that made Cajal's work possible, yet looking backwards and still clinging pathetically to the outmoded network theory, who now, in his address of acceptance, actually mentioned Nansen, albeit quixotically claiming him in support. To Nansen, it was all long ago and far away. The award, however paradoxically, had recognised his work too, and drawn a line under lingering regrets for that part of his vanished self.

In London, at the beginning of the month, as a favour to Marie Lewis, and to repay her father-in-law's hospitality to him, Nansen persuaded Eva to sing at a dinner given by Sir George in his town house at Portland Place. There his German-born wife kept a salon frequented by artists, writers and musicians. With or without *arrière pensée* Eva ended her recital on the Faust motif. She performed her old favourite, Schubert's setting of Goethe's *Gretchen am Spinnrade* – 'Margareta at her Spinning Wheel':

> *Wo ich ihn nicht hab,*
> *Ist mir das Grab,*
> *Die Ganze Welt,*
> *Ist mir vergällt.*

> 'Him gone, my room
> Is like a tomb,
> Him gone, all
> The world to me is gall.'

Ingeborg Motzfeldt, who was accompanying Eva, described how,

> as if through a mist of powerful emotion, I glimpsed how the others were gripped, the hostess with tears streaming down her cheeks and Nansen's face as white as the wall against which he was sitting.

65

A-Hunting He Would Go

Norwegian independence had quickly been followed by a wave of parochialism. One consequence was a disregard in Norway for diplomats and diplomacy, partly because they were seen as an aristocratic relic of the now dissolved Union. It was widely held that representation abroad should be consular rather than diplomatic, and devoted to the encouragement of trade. Above all, ninety-one years of uninterrupted peace had left the Norwegians with the illusion that it could be taken for granted. On the whole, even their leaders considered that the best foreign policy was not to have one. They believed in the efficacy of good intentions. The Norwegian General Election of 1906 had brought a further swing to the left. Only with difficulty – helped by Nansen – had Michelsen been kept in office, on the grounds that a change of government so soon after independence would make a bad impression abroad. The new mood did not make the diplomatic corps more popular, and added to the obstacles with which the Norwegian Foreign Minister, Jørgen Løvland, had to contend.

Of farming stock Løvland, the last Norwegian Minister of State in Stockholm, was a novice in foreign affairs. Nonetheless he displayed an acute judgement of underlying forces. In the face of compact disbelief, he was convinced that war between England and Germany was inevitable. He expected it soon. He wanted his country kept out of it. His aim was an international guarantee by the Great Powers of Norwegian territorial integrity and neutrality. Because of political opposition at home he had to work in secret before starting the process. What with one thing and another it had all taken time.

In the small hours of 9 November Nansen finally received a telegram from Løvland instructing him officially to raise the question of the territorial guarantee. At last, after nearly seven months, he could begin the work he had been sent to do.

On the face of it, Nansen had the easiest task of the Norwegian envoys to the Powers, all of whom had simultaneously been sent identical instructions. By design or not, the telegrams went out as King Haakon and Queen Maud were setting off for England on the first State visit of their reign. Haakon considered that he had been promised the guarantee as a condition for accepting the throne. He saw in his visit an opportunity to redeem the pledge. He quickly told King Edward so. To begin with Edward, both as statesman and father-in-law, unreservedly agreed.

The Foreign Office, however, was a very different place from the one that Nansen had known the year before. This was not only due to the recent change of government. It was also due to the strange personality of Sir Edward Grey. Although his policies were the same as those of his predecessor Lord Lansdowne, he was a Foreign Secretary of a very different stamp. Count Benckendorff, the Russian Amdassador in London, summed it up:

> Grey, something of a novice ... caught between three or four different fires, does not really know how to act. It is the King, with his common sense and politicial instincts and royal dignity, who has maintained the equilibrium.

Besides all that, Grey was weak, indolent, evasive and ambiguous. A man of peace, he was the prisoner of events leading inexorably to war. Above all, he was burdened by the liberal conscience, parading a high moral stance which clouded policy and confused his utterances, so that interpreting him was perilous. He was the antithesis of Nansen in character, but the two men had one thing in common. Grey, who came from a minor branch of the old Whig aristocracy, shared Nansen's dislike of stiff etiquette and preferred informality.

The real change at the Foreign Office, however, lay in the character of the Permanent Under-Secretary, the chief official. Sir Thomas Sanderson had been replaced by Sir Charles Hardinge. Sanderson, who had rarely been abroad, was a kind of superior clerk, at the beck and call of his political masters. Hardinge was a bird of another feather. Lofty, self-certain, overbearing when need be, he enjoyed being the power behind the throne. He had a formidable intellect. A product of Harrow and Trinity College, Cambridge, he succeeded adequately in the mathematical Tripos. Grey, by contrast, just scraped through in Jurisprudence at Oxford. Stronger and more intelligent than Grey, Hardinge was in many ways the real Foreign Secretary. He also had the ear of the King who called him 'Charli' (thus spelt). It was with Hardinge that Nansen, as often as not, had to deal, and they did not get on. Nansen wanted a swift settlement of what came to be known as the integrity treaty.

Until recently Ambassador in St Petersburg, Hardinge understood the slippery convolutions of the Russian mind and the hidden complexities of the Scandinavian question. He was opposed to the treaty in the first place, a fact which he scarcely troubled to conceal. The negotiations had developed into a duel between him and Nansen.

Nansen was vouchsafed glimpses of the fascinating, hidden twists of policy. King Edward, apparently contradicting himself, once told him that Norway, with a thousand years of history as a recognised kingdom, was demeaned by asking for foreign guarantees. Admiral Sir John Fisher, the great, free-spoken naval reformer and First Sea Lord, told Nansen, when the two men accidentally met in the street,

> that he had told Sir Edward Grey ... that England ought not to commit herself to respect Norwegian neutrality alone without the other [Scandinavian] countries ... since if, in a war with England, Germany occupied Denmark and closed the Straits, it would be an absolute necessity for England to occupy a Norwegian harbour to secure a base for her operations in those waters.

Nansen secretly agreed with the Admiral in part. He too spurned neutrality, but in his case because he wanted the freedom of action to conclude a defensive alliance with Sweden.

This was going to be a long haul. In between excursions to the Foreign Office, Nansen was repeatedly summoned with Eva to court ceremonies attended by King Haakon and Queen Maud, both at Windsor and Buckingham Palace. After a family visit to Sandringham in December, Nansen took Eva and Ingeborg Motzfeldt back to Norway for Christmas, returning to London alone at the end of January.

Eva devoutly hoped that 1907 would see an integrity treaty finally signed and her husband home again for good. 'It will surely be all over by Christmas?' she wrote. 'If I didn't believe that, I couldn't hold out.' Nansen felt the same, or so he wrote in his reply.

> How happy I was at what you said about me when I was home, that I 'have never been so nice before' ... You will see that being away so much will make me appreciate the time spent at home. Perhaps eventually I won't be so difficult to live with after all. I really think that I have become a little less unreasonable than I used to be; but perhaps it is just imagination.

In the meantime, the everlasting calls at the Foreign Office ground on; drafts and memoranda continued drifting from one country to the other. 'This life has become a wilderness,' Nansen complained in his diary a few weeks after his return.

> I, whose pride was independence ... where am I now, everybody else's servant but my own. How has it happened, is it all just to serve my country's cause? Don't waste your time on what others can do just as well, was once my principle. But is not everyone else better suited to this kind of life? Unquestionably! And still I continue.... Why is this life so dismal? Is it perhaps mainly because I am doing nothing that makes a mark, no milestones.

This particular outburst of depressive interior monologue seemed divorced from an outward appearance of almost manic pleasure. Nansen had become part of the Edwardian scene. He was the stuff of gossip, moving where other ambassadors did not. An exotic, half-tamed figure, he was unceasingly lionised. At one extreme, he met the wealthy Fabian couple Sydney and Beatrice Webb – 'distinguished and entertaining', he told Eva in a gossipy letter. 'On principle they never serve wine in their home, only whisky and soda.' In a very different milieu, under the heading 'FAVOUR-ITES AT COURT', the *Tatler* could reveal that

> Four of the most popular men are the Marquis de Soverol, Sir John Fisher, Dr Nansen, the Norwegian Minister, and Lord Esher. These are to be seen at country houses where the King is a guest probably more than any others.... Since the marquis's advent as Portuguese ambassador his popularity has scarcely been exceeded by anyone. Dr Nansen is now running him close.

Nansen had in fact for some time been a Court favourite. De Soverol, ribald and uninhibited, appealed to one side of the King's nature, but Nansen was a breath of fresh air. Edward, heavy-bellied, with protruding eyes and a deep, guttural voice, rolling his r's, speaking French, German, Italian and Spanish, seemed not quite English, but a cosmopolitan king. He could appreciate Nansen for what he was. He treated him like a friend – or even one of the family. As the *Tatler* explained, Nansen was

> very adaptable. He dances with great enthusiasm, [He] is a keen sportsman, one of the best bridge players at Court ... and a good story-teller.... It is, however, hinted that the great Norwegian explorer is not quite immune from the temptations of 'Furthest North' and may one day fit out another expedition.

Temptations perhaps, but real events had now moved on. Amundsen returned home in November from America after his attainment of the North-West Passage and in the new year visited London for his accolade. On 10 February, Nansen took him to see the Prince of Wales and the next day Amundsen lectured to the RGS. 'As always it was nice to see him,' Nansen wrote to Eva.

> He was much appreciated here ... His lecture was very good, although his pronunciation of English was often a little incomprehensible to Englishmen because he put the accent on the wrong syllable.

But Nansen was listening to a man who, in every respect, had done exactly what he had set out to do. 'What has not been accomplished with large vessels and main force, I will attempt with a small vessel and patience,' Amundsen had declared in advance. How he had achieved that was the burden of what he had to say. Nansen was the first among the audience to speak after Amundsen's lecture. He made the point that the two great historic quests of the English navigators, the North-East and North-West Passages, had finally been attained by Scandinavians, 'the North-East by a Nordenskiöld, and the North-West by an Amundsen'.

439

But the fine thing is the way you are able to appreciate what little we have done ... when we want to send out a man to an unknown region...Amundsen ... is the sort of man we should send.... And we may see him start again on a new exploration. And I feel certain, next to his own country, he will have many well-wishers in this country.

Nansen compounded this delphic utterance by quoting from Tennyson's *Ulysses*:

> One equal temper of heroic hearts
> Made weak by time and fate, but strong in will
> To strive, to seek, to find, and not to yield

The poem is about the last voyage of the ageing Greek hero. This incident does not appear in Homer; it comes from Dante. In the *Divine Comedy*, Dante puts Ulysses, archetype of the explorer, in hell, and makes him tell the story of his end. Driven by uncontrollable restlessness, Ulysses, after all his adventuring, sails on just one more voyage out into the Atlantic and reaches the southern hemisphere where, overtaken by a storm, his ship founders, and the waters close over his head.

In Nansen's mouth, Tennyson's lines rang like the valediction of the old king finally surrendering to the new.

But if anything, his physical energies now increased. The very day after his gloomy outpouring in his diary, Nansen had asked his old lecture agent, Gerald Christy, to introduce him to fox hunting. 'Now I'm crazy about hunting,' he was writing to Eva soon after Amundsen had left. And, he added after a day out with the Belvoir hunt:

> It's a heavenly pleasure ... I only wish you could be with me.... The strange thing is that I feel as if I had never done anything else in my life, as Lord Robert Manners, who was with me ... said. He found it a little hard to believe that I had never hunted before. For my part I believe that I really could become a first class fox hunter, and have a feeling that many are not better ... at the start there were 300 riders ... what a beautiful sight it is when they all race off over fields and ditches and hedges ... I saw many of them fall [but] I haven't come off once ... I look after myself, you know I have that gift.

Unhindered by the complexities of the integrity treaty, Nansen now hunted as often as he could.

In the middle of December the year before he had unofficially presented to the Foreign Office the first Norwegian drafts for a treaty. They revealed a naïveté that irritated and amused professional diplomats in all four Powers. There was much minuting and criticism and counter-drafting between the capitals. As a result, on 11 March 1907, Nansen presented to the Foreign Office the second Norwegian draft. This went some way to meet the criticisms provoked by the first.

But while Nansen continued shuttling back and forth to the Foreign

Office, in the manner of the age his hunting and the social round were left untouched. He went avidly to the theatre and the opera, seeing everything from Wagner and Shakespeare to Puccini, Oscar Wilde and, as he wrote to Eva, 'a lovely children's comedy called *Peter Pan*'. He thought it would suit their eldest son, Kåre, now nine years old,

> with its fairy floating in mid-air, mermaids and pirates ... not forgetting Indians and crocodiles ... I was ... moved [and] became like a child again. When all is said and done, I am so unpredictably sentimental.

He found time to write occasional letters to his eldest child, Liv, but, as he explained to Eva, 'taking care not to treat her as a grown-up, thinking human being'. Liv was now fourteen years old and of her own accord had started reading Ibsen. When *Ghosts* was kept away from her (because it dealt with venereal disease and other un-childlike themes) she promptly got hold of a copy and could not understand the fuss.

> I honestly agree with you that she is quite impressive [Nansen commented to Eva], but we must take care not to let her see that we think so, in case it makes her overestimate herself somewhat ... I do believe she is something of a personality, and too good to become an ordinary boring person.

Eva wrote, half-teasingly, that she was hearing that Nansen was being pursued by ladies in Society. He brushed this off, but it would have been out of character if he had been left unaffected by the customs of Edwardian – and King Edward's own – sexuality.

Nansen found himself involved, in particular, with Leonie Leslie, Winston Churchill's aunt – at least to the point of unburdening himself to her and going out with her on various occasions. One Tuesday, at a matinée, they saw Ibsen's *Hedda Gabler* – 'quite well acted', Nansen reported to Eva (although not the fact that he had seen it with Mrs Leslie), 'but what a horrible play it fundamentally is'. (The final scene in which Hedda, thwarted in love and ambition, commits suicide, and her husband can think of nothing better to say than 'that's simply *not done*', still has power to shock.)

In the same muddied waters between mistress, mother-figure and female confidante, Nansen was also drawn to Millicent Fanny Erskine St Clair, fourth Duchess of Sutherland. One of the most beautiful women of her day, Millicent was also highly intelligent, romantic and married to a prosaic, uninteresting husband whose only distinction was his title. Behind the façade of an aristocratic society hostess, Millicent was a scholar, a poet, and an occasional playwright good enough to have had her work produced in the West End, and she had the common touch. She was also an imperious reformer, among her soubriquets being the Democratic Duchess and – less flatteringly – Meddlesome Millie. She was always

441

looking for her ideal man. When Nansen met her, she had already taken a lover, which ended in humiliation.

Meanwhile, Nansen was pouring out a stream of truly fond letters to Eva, and at his entreaty she came over in April for six weeks or so. Ingeborg Motzfeldt once more accompanied her. Later in the month, they all went to a reception given by Millicent at Stafford House, her London home, where she held a salon for celebrities in the arts. Next day Nansen sent her a copy of *Farthest North* to take with her to Sicily, which she was about to visit. *Fram* was somehow never far from his thoughts. 'It is the contrasts that make life,' he wrote to Millicent.

> I remember well that when I was up there hibernating in the darkness, I often thought with longing of the Mediterranean, but when I come under that sky I long for the ice-fields of the North.

While Nansen and Eva were frequenting the grand houses of the West End, barely two miles away in the somewhat less fashionable precincts of Islington a group of Russians was plotting the end of that kind of world. One of them, with a fixed stare, and the face of a Mongol tribesman, was born Ulyanov. Another was a seedy looking Georgian, about whom little was known except that he was a bank robber, and whose travel documents were made out in the name of Ivanovitch. They also called themselves Lenin and Stalin. They were in London for the fifth congress of the Russian Social Democratic and Labour Party which, being banned in Russia, had to work in exile. It was the occasion when Lenin, after years of subversion, seized control of the party, founding what came to be known as the Bolsheviks. The congress, held in the Brotherhood Church, a dingy non-denominational tabernacle, and ironically financed by a well-meaning capitalist, a soap manufacturer called Joseph Fels, continued verbosely for the whole month of May. It complicated Nansen's work, because the Russian Government was not best pleased with Britain for harbouring this nest of revolutionaries ('What a set of self-righteous crooks!', a Russian exile of another sort called them), and that led to diplomatic cross-currents.

Eva and Ingeborg Motzfeldt went home on 18 May. At about the same time Nansen received a letter from Marion Ure to say that she and her husband were coming to England from Shanghai on a visit, and could they please meet? With reluctance, Nansen agreed. They had not seen each other since the days in Naples, now twenty years in the past. He shrank from another reminder of the passage of time. 'You must look out for an old lady with gray curls & spectacles that's *me!*' wrote Marion. To Eva, Nansen judiciously wrote that Marion's husband was 'a kind and pleasant Englishman. She had become very old.'

Nansen was also troubled by another appeal for help from Johansen. He had now resigned, or been discharged from the army. He was still in

Tromsø, separated from his wife, destitute, sold up, and by now an alcoholic. He wanted money to pay his debts. On this occasion, Nansen declined. Instead, he wrote to the local police chief for information.

> I feel no obligation to pay the debts he has incurred by his actions [Nansen explained]. That is the concern of those who have given him credit, and thus enabled him to run up debts.

For once, help appeared of itself. Out of charity or not, various expeditions to Spitsbergen that summer signed Johansen on, and so, for a while, Nansen was spared a charge on his conscience.

Meanwhile, negotiations for the integrity treaty dragged on. By the middle of the summer France, Germany and Russia, each for their own reasons, wished to sign immediately. England, which earlier had agreed, now suddenly refused. Everything now seemed to depend on Nansen. On 28 June he personally delivered to Edward VII a message from Haakon to the effect that unless the treaty was concluded before the Norwegian parliamentary recess in a week's time Haakon's position would be weakened, and the old spectre of a republic revived. Edward turned the matter over to Hardinge, who, the same evening, at a Foreign Office dinner, plainly told Nansen that the government would not submit to having a pistol held to its head.

'Concepts such as perfidy do not much trouble English foreign policy,' Nansen wrote in his report of this conversation. 'Where Sir Charles Hardinge is concerned, I think that he regards [such considerations] as ridiculous weakness.' Hardinge made it abundantly clear, as he himself noted in a letter the following day to Lord Knollys, the King's private secretary, that British policy

> must not depend upon the national political situation in Norway, but upon what we considered to be our own particular interests.... It was not a question in which sentiment could be allowed to predominate.

The Russians, he added, had just shown their hand. They had produced another counter-draft of a treaty, but now for the first time unpleasantly coupled with a demand to fortify the Åland Islands, demilitarised by treaty since the Crimean War. The Ålands, part of Finland, are a rocky archipelago, pointed like a dagger at the heart of Stockholm, to which they command the approaches. Hardinge reminded Nansen of this and more besides.

> If, I said, we ... conclude the Treaty guaranteeing the integrity and neutrality of Norway and ... permit the fortification of the Åland Islands it would place Sweden in a position of complete isolation and entirely at the mercy of Russia.... It was unnecessary of me to ask him what the position of Norway would be under such circumstances.

This news was evidently a great surprise to Nansen & he appeared much perturbed by it.

Hardinge, from his position of virtual control, reined in both Sir Edward Grey and the King. He refused to be rushed into signing the integrity treaty. He saw now that by neutralising Norway and fortifying the Ålands Russia was trying to divide and rule in Scandinavia and, incidentally, was unintentionally driving the Swedes into the arms of Germany. From another point of view, the German Ambassador in St Petersburg reported home that

the new English attitude ... was nothing other than an attempt ... with the pretext of special consideration for Sweden ... to have a say ... in the Baltic.

Through Grey and the King, Hardinge now told Nansen that Britain insisted on dropping the neutrality clause. 'On receipt of that information,' Count Wrangel, the Swedish Ambassador in London, sarcastically reported home,

Dr Nansen was much distressed. [He] bewailed the fact to his personal patron, Norway's chief foreign Minister, King Edward, and also ran round crying to the relevant ambassadors here, and asked them to do something, so that the whole of this question of Norway's integrity and neutrality ... would not be a complete fiasco.

Finding that matters were now out of his hands, and brushing aside the humiliation, Nansen turned his mind to other things. He helped organise the annual congress of the Permanent International Council for the Exploration of the Sea, held in London that year, and became involved in an esoteric dispute over the origin of ocean currents. He had also been appointed President of a well-meaning body called the Social and Political Education League and on 26 June, at University College, London, with Sir Oliver Lodge in the chair, gave an address called 'Science and the Purpose of Life'.

'Life is becoming too complicated,' ran the operative passage.

We have not been able to follow the material development, which has gone so fast that our brain has not accommodated itself to the new arrangement of things.

He also included this apologia:

Melancholy and pessimism, though possibly attractive, are sins if they lead to inactivity.... Let the desire be to do everything as well as possible.... But let it also be impressed upon the young ... never, when there is a choice, to do anything which can be done equally well or better by someone else. How many wasted lives would then be spared ... if each individual tried to find

444

his own line!... To consider yourself fit for something is not the same thing as to consider yourself important.

About this time the Duchess of Sutherland returned to London from Sicily and she and Nansen began to see rather a lot of each other – the *Bystander* commenting, among other thing: 'Grass-Widowers it is proverbial, do see rather a lot of the game.' The true state of affairs was suggested by a quotation from John Greenleaf Whittier that Nansen wrote in Millicent's 'Treasure Book':

> To seek is better than to gain.
> The fond hope dies as we attain;
> Life's fairest things are those which seem.
> The best is that of which we dream.

Millicent had probably followed the other women who withdrew before Nansen's approaches passed a certain point.

Meanwhile the machinations over the Integrity Treaty were untidily proceeding. At the end of July Sir Edward Grey told Count Benckendorff that Britain would drop her objections and sign the Russian draft if the question of neutrality were removed and only the territorial integrity of Norway was included. The question of fortifying the Åland Islands was postponed. The Powers had finally agreed that they wanted no confrontation in the north. That meant that the signing of the treaty was now only a matter of time, or so it seemed.

Hardinge had tried to kill it off by procrastination and might well have succeeded, but for one thing. As Benckendorff put it:

> There is someone, a man of stature who in all this has played a rather curious, vital, and I believe entirely personal rôle. I mean Nansen.... Extremely independent in his views, extremely radical in principle, and at the same time thoroughly opportunist.

66

Integrity Secured

Nansen, meanwhile, had left politicians and diplomats to their own devices and once more fled homewards to join Eva and the children in their mountain retreat. First, however, by Royal Command, he had to accompany King Haakon and Queen Maud – 'or perhaps the other way about, the Queen and King', as he commented to Eva – on their first visit to Northern Norway. From Hammerfest, with *Fram* ever on his mind, he wrote to her:

> I could not think of anything else ... than when we met there, and you arrived on the steamer in the evening, and I stormed up the gangway. Ah can't you remember it all, it was as if it happened yesterday. And then, the telegram about *Fram* in the morning. I seem to be living through it all again.

Early in August Nansen was at Sørkje again, between the upland lakes, under the low rolling mountains amongst which he felt at ease. Once more he and Eva seemed content with each other's company. Given their finances, she had asked if she could bring a piano tuner up from the valley that summer. 'Of course,' was Nansen's reply. 'That piano is an inexpressible pleasure ... and I don't know how we should manage without it.'

His diary was blank, indicating at least superficial contentment, until, on 15 September, at sunset, the first hint of autumn precipitated a melancholy outpouring. At one level it featured an extensive outburst of Nature-worship:

> The mountains have got their yellow-red colours of gold, the lakes are blue, like cold eyes, the air is clear ... the outlines of the hills are sharp and firm. One feels strong and free ...

But this was counterpoint to an interior monologue running underneath. Coaxed by Scott Keltie acting on behalf of Heinemann, Nansen had started writing a history of polar exploration and now, as he recorded in his diary, 'I have been immersing myself in the voyages of the old Norsemen.'

> They were not dreamers, they were men of action ... not weakened by

self-analysis like ourselves.... In their small open boats, they found their way over the ocean [and] attained their goal or went to the bottom ...

What pitiful navigation we have made of life, between sunken reefs in shoal waters, far from the driving spume of the open sea. But why am I writing this now? I can never keep a steady course, always drifting with the changing current ...

Soon this existence will once more finish, and I will have to go down to the valley and the cities where 'people' live. What a fool Lohengrin was to leave his airy realms to descend to earth and interfere in the petty quarrels of mankind.... He felt it himself when he took his melancholy farewell from the swan.

All this and much more Nansen reproduced, almost word for word, in a letter to the Duchess of Sutherland, written that same evening. 'I think of you often,' he interpolated. 'When last I heard from you, you were in the garden dreaming – are you there still I wonder? I cannot say why but just that moon made me wish to write.'

Beneath all this there was an undertow driven by the shadow of Roald Amundsen. In February, when Amundsen visited London, he had, in Nansen's own words,

told me of a plan ... of going through the Bering Strait with a small ship ... and drifting across the North Polar Sea living on the ice, as he could not expect the small ship to stand the pressures. I told him ... that I could not approve of that plan ... the only thing was to go on the *Fram*, which was built for it; but ... I wanted the *Fram* for [an] expedition to the South Pole. He asked then whether I would not let him join me ... and then he could get the *Fram* for his North Polar drift afterwards. I objected that that would be too much for him.... Though he was a comparatively young man he would be a great deal older before he started on his drift, and life is after all short even without wasting so many years in the ice.

For the past five years, since the end of Sverdrup's expedition, *Fram* had been laid up at a harbour down the fjord. Belonging to the State, she was not actually Nansen's to lend, but in practice he had first call. The whole question was left hanging in the air. In May, Amundsen had politely written for an answer; again Nansen had temporised. He was tortured by indecision. Worse, despite all his protestations, he dared not tell Eva what was on his mind. When he wrote to Millicent, it was obliquely to find relief.

A few days later, Nansen was recalled to his diplomatic duties by a telegram carried up from the valley. He had left London believing that the signing of the Integrity Treaty was now no more than a formality, and that therefore he would not have to go back. This proved not to be the case. The Russians produced yet another draft. English intentions were still unclear. Nansen, after all, had to return to London. 'If ... you have not quite forgotten a wandering friend,' he now added in a postscript to Millicent, 'send a line to 36 Victoria Street & mark it *Private*.'

He and Eva packed up for the season. The first of the autumn storms, earlier than usual, made them less reluctant to descend into the valley and go home to Christiania. But now a decision about Amundsen could no longer be delayed. Nansen finally plucked up the courage to do what he had so long dreaded, and broach the subject with Eva. In his own words:

> I ought to have done so long ago ... I cannot forget how sweet and touching you were ... You are a wonderful human being, and I love you more than you know ... What a fool I have been to go and brood on my own instead of talking to you, who ought to know all my thoughts. I imagined that I would be saving you from unnecessary worry ... but, as you say, it was silly and misplaced consideration. Now I am so relieved since talking to you, and see things in quite another way. I believe, as I said to you, that that [Antarctic] journey will not materialise. When all is said and done I have so much other work which I want just as much to finish.

Her own feelings aside, Eva had gently burst the bubble of Nansen's old Ibsenesque 'life-lie', the strange force between hope and delusion that had been buoying him up. There was a time for everything, and Nansen's moment for the South Pole had passed. Indeed it might soon have passed for everyone. An Anglo-Irishman called Ernest Shackleton was leaving that year to attempt its attainment. In London he had already approached Nansen for advice.

One day late in September Amundsen arrived at *Polhøiden* to hear his fate – for in spite of all Nansen had still not quite made up his mind. Slowly, racked by indecision, Nansen descended the stairs to the hall where the tense figure of the younger man was waiting amid the heavy furniture. Self-sacrificingly, Eva had told her husband that he had to fulfil himself, and thus left him free to decide. Hidden in their bedroom, she awaited the result of the encounter.

As Nansen looked into Amundsen's long-nosed, hawk-like face, with its deep-set, burning, bright blue mesmeric eyes, he sensed, for once, the power of an equal personality. He told Amundsen that he could have *Fram*.

*

Writing to Eva on the boat back to England, Nansen exclaimed:

> It was so horrible to leave you ... But I console myself with the thought that this is the last time I will go to London, and so it will not be so long until we meet, and time will pass quickly.

So it did, socially at least. As a good shot, Nansen was welcome at any Edwardian house party. Now, in the second week of October, he was invited to Balmoral. He bagged two stags and two does.

In London he contined his playgoing. 'How little there is often in

Shakespeare's lovers,' he wrote gloomily in the sporadic book of woe he called his diary after seeing *As You Like It* one evening.

> Here he is only a splendid example of the species. She ... loves him simply because he has muscular strength.... Perhaps when all is said and done, love is only this primitive emotion, and we try in vain to ... raise it to a higher level.

Once more, he wrote the same thing in almost the same words to the Duchess of Sutherland. He had just seen her again. Both letter and diary entry were written on her birthday, 20 October. 'All my thoughts are with you today,' he wrote to her. 'And ... if good wishes have any power your life will be ... bright and remote from petty worries.'

> I saw the light in your window last night when I came home from the theatre ... It is indeed funny how you are always thrown across my path. My birthday, which I actually had forgotten till I received your telegram, was on the *tenth*, yours is *ten* days later ... I scribble down my flickering thoughts ... to amuse myself, forgetting that they are less amusing to others.

Once more he quoted Tennyson:

> 'Nothing was born;
> Nothing will die;
> All things will change'

and added:

> You see, the same incurable dreamer, but please do not think me impossible. There is also another side you have not seen, with an unquenched craving for action. It has been starving for a long time now.

As if on cue, about a week later Ernest Shackleton wrote asking Nansen to come and see him off at Victoria Station on the last day of the month when he left on his expedition to reach the South Pole. 'You promised to do so if you were able,' Shackleton reminded him. Though Victoria was just down the road from where he lived, diplomacy kept him away. He was in the process of forcing the negotiations for the Integrity Treaty to the point of culmination.

In a characteristic volte face the Russians suddenly told the Norwegians that they were prepared to sign. Nansen in turn forcefully conveyed the news to Hardinge. With his usual slippery guile, Alexander Isvolsky, the Russian Foreign Minister, had not informed the British, so Hardinge was taken by surprise. Sir Arthur Nicholson, the British Ambassador in St Petersburg, was asked to investigate. He reported that Isvolsky had indeed changed his mind. The die was cast when the King, who had long since lost patience, arranged for this dispatch to be discreetly leaked to

Nansen. That gave him his trump card. In Hardinge's own wry words to Nicholson,

> I did not [at first] believe Nansen ... However when we received the confirmation from you of [his] statement, it was of no use to be 'plus royaliste que le Roi'.

On 2 November, at long last, the Integrity Treaty was finally signed in Christiania. It obliged the Powers to respect the territorial integrity, but not the neutrality, of Norway and, if she were threatened from any quarter to come to her aid if she so desired. At the same time, England, France and Norway abrogated the November Treaty of 1855. Although it took another five months for Sweden to follow suit, that was the end of the matter.

It was also the end of Nansen's mission in London, and time for him to go. The prospect of his departure did not at all please the King. Nansen wrote to Eva that His Majesty had told Princess Victoria: 'That man is forbidden to leave England.' He tried to talk him into remaining as Ambassador.

Nansen was respectfully adamant. On 15 November, he submitted his letter of resignation to King Haakon and told Løvland, now Prime Minister, he wished to be home before Christmas, and home for good. 'I am afraid of the new men,' he told Eva. What he meant, in particular, was that he was afraid of what he called 'socialists and defence nihilists' who, he believed, were living in a fool's paradise and would use the treaty as an excuse to drag the country into disarmament.

These things were not Eva's concerns. 'We two must nevermore be parted in this way,' she now wrote to him in London impatiently. 'I can respect and submit to expeditions – but this!'

67

Too Late, Too Late

'Unfortunately your wife has been in bed again during the last few days on account of a feverish catarrh of the bronchial passages.' Thus began a letter written to Nansen about a fortnight later by Dr Jenssen, their family's old doctor.

> She is particularly troubled by a strong and persistent cough and a bad pain in her right side, presumably because of the cough ... She has had one or two morphine injections, with excellent relief of the pain ... There are absolutely no disturbing symptoms, but your wife asked me to write to you, as she is not able to do so.

This reached Nansen at Sandringham, the Royal country retreat in Norfolk. King Edward by now took Nansen's presence during his peripatetic social round as a matter of course; at his birthday, for example, on 9 November. 'I did not feel at ease,' Nansen wrote to Eva, 'since I was the only one [at Sandringham] who did not have a present for [the King].' He noted that, besides Queen Alexandra, 'King Edward's ... lady friend Mrs Keppel is also a guest at Sandringham ... it is the most peculiar arrangement one can imagine.'

Nansen regaled Eva with this and other piquant Court details in a succession of letters remarkably different in tone from almost any before. They were lighter, chatty, almost content. Innocently he mentioned that Queen Maud, who had come over from Norway for her father's birthday, flirted with him. And one evening after dinner:

> The Queen of Spain ... Queen Maud, the Duke of Alva and I played bridge, which went on with many delays, because at the same time [an] orchestra was playing *The Merry Widow*, and that naturally ended with Queen Alexandra, who was playing bridge at the next table, getting me and Queen Maud to dance on the carpet between the bridge tables, and she had a train of many metres.

'Now don't you go and fall in love with Queen Maud!', Eva replied. 'Or let yourself be tempted by her flirting – just you remember! That is to say, I am not in the least jealous, but am fully aware of the dangers of such circumstances. Flirt as much as you like, but don't go too far. Amen!'

451

Part IV. Diplomat

The first inkling that Nansen had that anything was seriously awry reached him in a letter from Eva dated 21 November. She was in bed with fever and coughing. 'We must make sure we enjoy ourselves in future,' she wrote, 'not go our separate ways too much ... Won't you try?' A few days later she wrote that she was better, but still in bed.

> I have become so thin, and am glad that I have time to put on weight before you arrive. I so want you to be in love with me again as in the old, long vanished days. You will see I will be pretty for your sake ... You write ... we will rack our brains over our finances ... we must help each other ... Expenses and yet more expenses, it is terrible what such a house costs to run ... Now and then, if you are dissatisfied with me, say so straight out and not put on your stiff, cold immovable face and silence, because then we will be back in the old misery again, and I will become old and irritable. Am I wrong to say all this? ... I don't think we have always been sensible and shown confidence in each other; not I in any case. I have often been afraid of you, and on that account failed to say many things.... And then that repulsive woman came between us, which made me more and more bitter and less fond of you with each passing day. Ugh, one can't go through such things without being marked. But everything will be better when we both show good intentions and much love.

When this arrived, Nansen was still at Sandringham, commandeered now as company for King Haakon who, earlier delayed by a political crisis at home, had now come to join Maud on her family visit. But still he failed to take alarm until Dr Jenssen's letter arrived on 6 December, inexplicably delayed. Now only did he telegraph back. The next day, Eva's birthday, Nansen telegraphed to her too:

> ALL GOOD THOUGHTS WITH YOU TODAY MANY HAPPY DAYS IN PROSPECT HOPE YOU ARE WELL TELEGRAPH A FEW WORDS TO SANDRINGHAM.

This crossed a telegram from the doctor reporting a sudden deterioration. A succession of worsening bulletins followed, and only then, on 8 December, did Nansen leave. He hurried by the fastest route via Flushing, but at Hamburg the next day found a telegram that Eva had died. Somehow he continued the journey home. She had been carried off by pneumonia. It had found the old weakness in her lungs. She was forty-nine years old.

Her death took everyone who knew her by surprise. 'It seems to me like a horrible misunderstanding ... I thought she was sure to survive us all,' wrote one of her acquaintances, adding:

> Poor Nansen, he did not arrive in time ... I can see his melancholy equine head in helpless dissolution; there are strong elemental emotions in that man.

452

67. Too Late, Too Late

Prostrated by grief, Nansen collapsed into bed, then sat motionless in one of the rooms, staying silent for days. His children were afraid to approach him. It was many weeks before he could express his feelings, and then only in his diary – a long, sad outpouring which ended with these words:

> So kindly from her heights, where nothing more can reach her, she smiles down on my misunderstood striving, which separated me from her for a time. Now all is shattered ...
>
> One of the last things she said was: 'Poor him, he will come too late.'
>
> Ah yes, he came too late, and now all is lost. The only great thing that life gave has gone.
>
> Ah what have I possessed – now I am poor and alone.
>
> Here everything is so cold and inconsolably forlorn.
>
> Out there in the night the moon is shining down on the frozen, snow-covered ground.
>
> Life? Confused sleep-walking.
>
> What a nightmare, and I wanted only to wake. Now I want to sleep.

It was like the nightmare on *Fram*, when he feared he would return to find Eva dead. Out of the past had come the recollection of one of the farewell letters she had written to him at that time:

> I want to have many happy years before I give up. And then I want to be burned together with my beloved boy, and the pyre will be down on our strand ... and Liv can hide our ashes where she wants.

At intervals, she had reiterated the wish. Cremation, however, was impossible in Norway then, but allowed in Sweden. So Nansen had to take her remains to Gothenburg, have the body cremated and bring the ashes back home, where, as she had wished, they were scattered no one knows where.

*

Duty now rescued him from his grieving by the fjord. His government had declined to accept his resignation immediately, for fear that it might be misconstrued as disapproval of the Integrity Treaty, and he was persuaded to delay. At the end of February he accordingly returned to London to wind up his mission and say goodbye to King Edward VII. 'It makes me sad to think that I am now actually going to leave England for good as minister,' he wrote to Lord Knollys.

> The King has always been so very kind to me, and made my position such an easy and pleasant one.... It seems so strange that my life there will soon belong to the past, as I felt as if I belonged there.

453

Part IV. Diplomat

It was the ending of an age. The day before Eva, King Oscar, the last of the Swedish-Norwegian Union kings, had died at seventy-eight. 'How strange, and not without melancholy,' remarked the same acquaintance who had grieved for Eva and Nansen.

> He suffered much on our account – partly, if not entirely, through no fault of his own.... By and large one has to say ... that he behaved well in 1905, and his kind-heartedness saved us many difficulties. The flag outside my window is flying at half mast.

That spoke for the country. In a touching gesture, everywhere from public buildings and private homes flags were spontaneously flown in Norway at half mast.

On 1 March 1908 Nansen was received in audience and that same evening commanded to accompany the King and Queen to dinner with the Prince and Princess of Wales. A few days later he was asked to dinner with the King at Buckingham Palace and on 5 March, again at the King's request, was at the station to see him off on his annual departure for Biarritz. With the kindliest of intentions Edward was trying to persuade him to remain after all, now that circumstances had changed. It was in vain. But he suggested that, since he was going to make a State visit to Norway in the spring, Nansen might just as well then hand in his letter of recall.

This was a request that could hardly be refused, and Nansen agreed formally to remain as Ambassador until then. He stipulated, however, that his permanent return home should take place by the beginning of April.

Before he left London on 28 March, he received a letter from Leonie Leslie, whom he had continued to meet. She was about to leave for Malta and asked for his photograph,

> just for me to keep *en souvenir* of the good talks we have had – will you?
> I trust that life has still work & happiness in store for you –
> Our paths lie in different directions – but perhaps we will meet again some day. And I shall always think of you as a friend.

On 1 May 1908 Nansen formally resigned from the diplomatic service. The following day in Christiania, as arranged, he presented his letter of recall to King Edward VII, who was parrying the Kaiser on a round of State visits to the Scandinavian countries. Also on 1 May Nansen's chair at the University of Christiania was appositely converted from zoology to oceanography, still titular and still *ad hominem*.

One final task remained. At Sørkje, Eva had decorated some of the furniture, and signed her name. Nansen went back there, taking with him brush and paint, and obliterated everything she had done. He was accompanied by one of his old peasant friends from the valley. They left by different routes, and that was the last time they met. Nansen quickly sold up and never returned to the place where, as he had once said, 'I have chosen my kingdom.'

68

Kathleen Scott

Professor as he was, Nansen now, at the age of forty-seven, relapsed into semi-private life. He was pursued by shadows from the past. His old flame Dagmar, 'The Treasure', now working as a journalist, revived desultory contact. Ingeborg Motzfeldt, imp-faced, kind and all-knowing, filled once more the indispensable rôle of female confidante. 'I have become mummified,' he wrote to her that summer of 1908.

> It is as if something has shrivelled in heart and mind, and I no longer belong to the land of the living, and as if life was over for me ... Basically I like it, and do not long for life ... Suddenly one evening I woke up and felt that I had become very old ... a pleasant feeling (I do not long to be young, and full of vague longings and stupidities, it is so troublesome). But I had to [saddle a horse and] ride out and get some fresh air and see other people living. I rode out ... to see loving couples whispering to each other on the paths.... Can you imagine, it was really pleasant to [be] a spectator and watch life from a long distance.

He kept two nightingales in the house.

> It was so strange [he wrote] when I came down to go to bed last night and I went to look at the two [birds] in the cage on the gallery outside my door as I often do, but they were not there; the door of the cage was open, as it often is at night. I looked round and glimpsed them up on Eva's picture, where they were perched close together and slept ... At night they often go [there]. Do you remember how much she liked animals? I can see her when she came home with those birds, she sat in her room and watched them and busied herself with them all day.

This was a rare glimpse of Nansen's inner thoughts. His diary had almost dried up, and was curiously bereft of emotion. Outwardly, however, he buried himself in his work. Together with a rising younger oceanographer called Bjørn Helland-Hansen he was finishing a monograph on investigations during the first years of the century into the Norwegian Sea – the waters between Norway, Spitsbergen, Greenland, Iceland and the British Isles. Finally published in 1909 as *The Norwegian Sea* it was the first comprehensive treatment of any sea. Long outmoded, it nonetheless remains an historical milestone from the beginnings of oceanography and a classic of its kind.

Simultaneously he was working on the history of Arctic exploration that he had undertaken at the behest of Scott Keltie. He applied now to historical research the same minute thoroughness that he showed in oceanography. (For example, he investigated changes in the earth's magnetic field the more accurately to plot the compass courses of the early voyagers.)

Politically, he was disillusioned. He felt that his compatriots, having achieved independence, did not know what to do with it; that they were sinking into parochialism; that the country was enveloped in an atmosphere of anticlimax. In the early autumn of 1907 came the death of Edvard Grieg and with it the passing of another of the country's giants. Nansen began to feel somehow out of place. Symptomatically, his best friends in public life were the King and Queen.

In his now sparsely kept diary, barely two months after Eva's death, he entered an attack on the rising tide of socialism. It was, he wrote,

a 'feminine' movement, which has already outlived itself.... It is extremely reactionary, grotesquely taking to extremes the desire to protect the weak at the expense of the strong.... It is an inconceivable contravention of the fundamental principles of the living world. It is the religion of all incompetence. Nature and society require that incompetence *must* sink to the bottom.... Nature has only given the strong the right to live.

That hid irony, given the circumstances of his private life. He had been left with five children, the youngest of whom, Åsmund, was mentally retarded and partially crippled. Nansen treated him kindly, but continued to bring the others up as harshly as before.

It is naturally a good thing to bring up nice, well-behaved children [he had once publicly declared]. But it is not enough, it is just as important to form character and willpower [which] are often developed by harsh treatment. I myself am of a weak nature. What character I have is due to a strict upbringing in childhood.

Without a mother, and with servants acquiescing in the regime, the home overlooking the fjord was steeped in a spartan and oppressive atmosphere. The three younger children were at an age which provided its own armour. Liv, now a girl of sixteen, and Kåre, an eleven-year-old boy, were not so fortunate. The best moments for them both were when Nansen took them out skiing. Then, Liv could recall 'we were [both] friends with father.'

We were more at ease than at home. Even if it was only a little Sunday ski tour ... we thought that father was different. Yes, it could be difficult to keep up with him when he swung along, but we were only too pleased to let him be first when we saw how it put him in such a wonderfully good mood.

The polar world continued ambiguously to intrude. On 10 November 1908, at a grand meeting in the Masonic Hall in Christiania, Amundsen formally announced his new expedition. Sailing in *Fram* he was going to repeat Nansen's drift, but try to succeed where Nansen had failed and reach the North Pole itself. Endorsing his own eclipse as it were, Nansen was there and spoke generously in support. He also allowed his name to be used in a public appeal for funds. Amundsen, in whom gratitude was highly developed, wrote after Christmas to express 'heartfelt thanks for all your kindness to me during the old year'.

About this time Nansen also heard from Captain Scott. Undeterred by his shortcomings on the *Discovery* expedition, Scott proposed returning to the Antarctic. He was experimenting with motor sledges and wanted Nansen's advice on where in Norway to conduct trials. Nansen suggested a frozen lake called Mjøsen, north of Christiania where, in his own words, 'that humbug Wellman had some motor-sledges tried ... in the spring of 1906 ... He was going to take them with him in his airship.' (Abortive though it was, that expedition of Wellman's was in fact the first attempt to fly in the polar regions with a proper dirigible aircraft.)

Nansen meanwhile was haunted by the shadow of his own *Fram* expedition. Johansen's wife Hilda had asked for help in obtaining a post in a bank for which she had applied. Thanks to him, she succeeded. Still separated, and now feeling nothing but pity for her husband, she asked if Nansen could get him some work too. For a second season, Johansen was out of charity employed by Arctic explorers on Spitsbergen, and had by now come back, only to face his old insoluble dilemma. Away from civilisation, he was a model of application and sobriety, but once returned he relapsed helplessly into drinking. In his travail he wrote to Nansen:

> I still feel suited to life in the ice for a while yet, and if you could only help me in that direction, I would be devoutly grateful to you, and it is my hope that much that has now gone wrong can be rectified.

Amundsen's expedition seemed the opportunity he had been craving. 'I am writing to ... Amundsen asking if he will take me,' he wrote to Nansen. 'I hope that ... you will put in a good word for me.' Nansen, still hounded by his conscience, did so, and Amundsen, against his better judgment, was persuaded to accept him.

The polar regions continued to obtrude. Shackleton returned from the Antarctic on 23 March 1909, having reached 88°23′S, a mere 97 miles from the Pole, and the closest anyone had yet been to either the South Pole or the North.

Later that summer Nansen sailed out in his yacht *Veslemøy* on another oceanographical cruise. On 1 September, he had to take refuge from a storm at Molde, on the Norwegian coast. In his own words:

A message was delivered ... that I had to go ashore for a telephone call from Christiania ... It must be the children, my God ... I ran ashore [only to learn] that it was a request ... to ring up [a Christiania newspaper about] a man who had come from the North Pole ... Thank God ... it had nothing to do with the children ... But then I lost my temper. What the devil did it concern me if a man had come from the North Pole.

The man whose supposed exploit had disturbed Nansen on his yacht was Dr F.A. Cook. By his own account he had reached his goal on 21 April 1908. After a week his fellow-American, Robert E. Peary, returned to civilisation, he too claiming to have reached the North Pole, but a year later. Nansen took no public part in the controversy that soon erupted – and still simmers to this day – as to whether either had told the truth. He did, however, rapidly concur in private with the general view that Cook was a fraud – if only, as he wrote to Scott Keltie, because of Cook's 'description of how his Eskimos dance continually [for] two hours on the morning before they reached the Pole ... I don't believe it'. He did not doubt, however, 'that Peary has been near the Pole'.

In October Shackleton arrived in Christiania on a whirlwind tour to harvest glory while there was yet time and gave a lecture to the Norwegian Geographical Society. Afterwards, as required, Nansen delivered a short encomium, the text of which he sent to Emily, Shackleton's wife. 'It will give me great courage if I need it in the future, as I fear I may!' she replied, like the stoical explorer's wife that she was.

At the beginning of March 1910, Captain Scott arrived in Norway to test the final version of his motor sledge and to buy equipment for his new Antarctic expedition. With a complicated blend of conceit and uncertainty, he approached Nansen as his mentor. Nansen's feelings were also complicated. He was always flattered to be treated as the oracle. Scott, however, stood athwart the illusion, to which he still clung, of perhaps conquering the South Pole after all. He was, however, alarmed at Scott's hasty and ill-conceived preparations. He urged him to put his trust in dogs for transport. Bungling on the *Discovery* had left Scott with a mistrust of dogs, but he had compromised to the extent of ordering a few as auxiliaries to the motor sledges. Whimsically, copying Shackleton, he had put his faith in ponies. On the other hand, by the time that Scott returned to England in the middle of March, Nansen had somehow managed to overcome his irrational aversion to skis, also derived from ineptitude on the *Discovery* expedition. Less fortunately, Scott took Nansen's word in another matter.

In 1907 Professor Holst, of Christiania University, together with Theodor Frølich, a Christiania physician, had published a paper on their research into scurvy in guinea pigs. They proved the cause to be the lack of a dietary substance as yet unknown, but found in fresh food, and destroyed by prolonged cooking. It was a seminal work that launched the modern concept of deficiency disease and led to the discovery of vitamins.

At the end of 1909, Holst published a popular article on the subject. Nansen responded with a venomous newspaper attack. Scientific verities aside, it was perhaps a settling of old scores. Professor Holst was in fact the same Axel Holst who had excoriated Nansen at his doctoral disputation all those years ago. At any rate Nansen derided Holst for daring to suggest the idea of deficiency disease, rejected the very concept of an as yet unidentified accessory food factor and, ignoring the experimental evidence, vehemently maintained his old opinion that scurvy was due to tainted food. This was still the received wisdom and when, a few months later, Nansen gave Scott an exposition on the subject, Scott fatefully accepted all that he was told.

Nansen meanwhile continued to give Amundsen unstinting aid. Amundsen was in financial difficulty, which seemed to be his fate, and, among other things, Nansen helped him to obtain a grant from a fund which bore his name and which had been established after his own return on *Fram*. In the small hours of 7 June he was sitting up in the tower of his home to watch as *Fram*, in perfect northern summer twilight, emerged from the inner arm of the fjord where she had been anchored outside Amundsen's home down by the water's edge and, with bare masts over windless waters, moved for the third time down the channel to the sea, like a Viking ship slipping out on a raid. Deflecting hubris, Amundsen had avoided the ostentatious farewells of his predecessors. He had raised anchor at midnight, and one of the few to witness his departure was the lonely figure in the tower across the waters of the fjord.

Outside events accentuated in Nansen a forlorn sense of desolation. A month earlier King Edward VII had died. Nansen felt that he had lost a friend. He wrote movingly to Queen Alexandra, who with touching gratitude telegraphed in reply. About the same time he had to speak at the funeral of Bjørnstjerne Bjørnson. 'All those who were Norway for me will soon have gone,' he sadly wrote afterwards. 'He filled the biggest space. I think I am becoming so old, and time will soon run out.' He was barely forty-nine.

His old girlfriend Emmy, still living in Heidelberg, had seen a report of his oration and was prompted by it to write: 'The first and only time I heard you make a speech, you won't remember it any more, it was in '84, 7 August,' her letter ran – referring, in fact, to an occasion in the mountain resort, and the last time that they had met.

> You were a carefree boy then, and spoke with the enthusiasm of youth about 'the mountains'. Next day, you left ... I remember it well. Besides, the date was engraved by you on my little silver watch which you took on your mountain journey.

Soon afterwards Nansen embarked on another oceanographical cruise in the Atlantic, this time on a Norwegian naval vessel, appropriately called *Fridtjof*. His younger children, as usual, he left at home in the care of a nursemaid. Liv, now a rebellious young woman of eighteen, had been sent – banished she would have said – to a finishing school in French-speaking Switzerland for the year.

Profoundly concerned with the puzzling course of the Gulf Stream, Nansen spent much of that summer of 1910 meticulously sinking and raising thermometers, current meters and water samplers to plumb the behaviour of the familiar yet unknown sea. Back home, he received a letter from Johansen, written on *Fram*, while she was held up in the Channel by contrary winds. 'The dogs surprise me,' Johansen wrote.

> I have always thought that the Eskimo dogs were the wildest ... of all sledge dogs, but these are downright saintly ... I have the impression that the Eskimos treat their dogs better than the Siberian tribes. They are splendid big animals, better than those we had.

Those dogs had also surprised Nansen, but for a different reason. There were nearly a hundred on board, all shipped from Greenland. Amundsen was supposed to be heading for the Bering Strait round Cape Horn. That meant the apparently unnecessary strain of bringing the dogs twice through the Tropics. It would have been more sensible to pick up sledge dogs in Alaska.

On the morning of 1 October, Helland-Hansen appeared at Nansen's door. He had with him a letter from Amundsen. It was dated 22 August, at sea, and had been brought by Amundsen's brother Leon from Madeira, *Fram*'s last port of call. Amundsen wrote that he had changed his plans. He was not going north. He was going to race Scott for the South Pole instead. Amundsen candidly explained that Cook and Peary had been 'the death blow to my enterprise'. That was what had made him go about. There was no point in trying for the North Pole now.

It was a bombshell of the very finest vintage. Nansen vigorously de-fended Amundsen, trying to mitigate the criticism with which his tactics were received – writing to Scott Keltie:

> He never told us, as he was afraid (as he now informs us) that we would have stopped him, and ... he thought he would place us in an awkward position [if we knew]. I think this is a mistake, as I see no reason why he should have been stopped ... Amundsen was certainly not afraid of talking the matter frankly over with Scott, but it was, as you will understand, his countrymen he was afraid of.

'It was evidently me he was most afraid of,' Nansen percipiently observed, 'probably because I had told him that I considered his North Polar drift ... more important than my South Polar expedition, and therefore gave up the latter.'

Nansen said that he was relieved that Amundsen had not told him in advance under pledge of secrecy, because it would have put him in an untenable position. If true of him, it would have been true of Amundsen also. Nansen repeatedly declared that he could have helped Amundsen with his preparations, which had probably been one of Amundsen's worst fears. He respected Nansen from afar; he did not want to be disturbed by dogmatic meddling. But fear was not his burden; conscience was. 'Do not treat me too harshly,' he had written to Nansen. 'I am no humbug; necessity forced me ... I beg your forgiveness for what I have done.'

Behind the mask, Nansen was equally troubled; exactly why was hidden in a dark, confused passage in his diary. 'Epitaph?' was the heading, followed by these lines from the old Norse poem *Hávamál* ('The Sayings of the High One'):

> I know a thing that never dies
> Judgment over the dead.

– or, even more to the point in this case, over the living. For what trust still remained between him and Amundsen had now irretrievably broken down. There eventually came to Nansen a letter from Scott himself in New Zealand, sent about ten days before he sailed. Scott had received a cable from Amundsen throwing down the gage – 'Beg leave to inform you *Fram* proceeding Antarctic' – and now asked Nansen if he knew his destination. Although Amundsen had written to Nansen that he was heading for South Victoria Land, 'Unknown' was Nansen's reply to Scott.

There, for some months, the matter rested. Although marine radio was now established, neither Amundsen nor Scott was equipped with it. Both had vanished into the mists. The silence was broken towards the end of March, 1911, when *Terra Nova*, Scott's expedition ship, reached the cablehead off New Zealand, having put him ashore at McMurdo Sound. She brought the sensational news of a meeting with *Fram* at the Bay of Whales on the Ross Ice Shelf. This was the first hint to Nansen of exactly where Amundsen had proposed to land. It was confirmed by the arrival a few weeks later of *Fram* at Buenos Aires.

In England Amundsen was now accused of stealing a march on Captain Scott, and poaching on his preserves. In fact, Amundsen had made his switch before he knew that Scott was going south although this crucial fact was somehow never made plain. Feelings ran so high that the Norwegian Ambassador in London asked Nansen to publish something in his defence. Nansen obliged with a letter to *The Times*, which appeared on 26 April. It had the desired effect – at least where the leader writers were concerned. It would be almost another year before the next news was received from the rivals hidden in the snows, both of whom Nansen had helped.

He had finally finished his book on the history of Arctic exploration with some of the illustrations done by himself. Its form had changed from the original idea of a popular recension into a scholarly albeit vividly written work, beginning with the ancient Greeks, and getting no further than the obscure Portuguese voyages in the direction of Greenland and Labrador in the early fifteenth century. For long, the definitive treatise on the subject – and still required reading today – it concluded with a highly personal apologia by Nansen, redolent of nineteenth-century optimism, fortified by a reference to Alexander the Great:

> The legend about him is an image of the human spirit itself, incessantly seeking, never obstructed by any limits, in an everlasting quest for height after height, depth after depth – always onwards, onwards, onwards.... The world of the intellect does not recognise space, nor does it recognise time.

Its English translation (in two volumes), under the title *In Northern Mists*, was published at the end of the year. Meanwhile, Nansen had embarked on his now annual oceanographic cruise, this season on his yacht *Veslemøy* again. 'Another summer gone,' he gloomily wrote in his diary.

His fiftieth birthday was approaching, which largely explained his mood. Among the greetings came one from yet another figure out of the past: Fritz Zschokke, a Swiss zoologist, whom he had met in Italy a quarter of a century earlier and to whom he wistfully replied: 'Ah yes, I often think about the good old days in Naples.'

In late autumn, he again went to England on a lecture tour. The subject was the Norse discovery of America, one of the topics covered by *In Northern Mists*. But of course it was his fame as an explorer that was the attraction. On the way he wrote two articles: 'The Equipment of Polar Expeditions' for the *Field*, and 'The Race for the South Pole' for *Scribner's Magazine*. In both he quietly extolled Amundsen's chances of winning the race because of his superiority in handling skis and dogs. Of Scott's motor sledges he said in the *Field* article that 'it is naturally unfortunate to have to gain your chief experience with a new invention on the expedition'. The great polar exploits, he pregnantly reminded his *Scribner's Magazine* readers,

> were chiefly attained ... with Eskimo methods [and] Eskimo dogs ... These are the methods ... used by those earliest of polar travellers, thousands of years ago. It is still ... chiefly the man on whom the results of an expedition depend!

On this lecture tour he renewed a brief earlier acquaintance with Scott's wife, Kathleen. He sent her a copy of *In Northern Mists*, dedicated to her husband. They had first met the year before in Norway, where Kathleen accompanied her husband, and where Nansen had arranged for her to be received by Queen Maud. But it was now, for the first time, that he properly took notice of her. She came to his first lecture, on 6 November, to the RGS. Various encounters followed, all culminating, on the day of Nansen's departure, with a lunch, tête-à-tête, given by Kathleen at her home, 174 Buckingham Palace Road (and convenient for Victoria station). Nansen stayed all afternoon.

When he left, he kissed her hand. Thereafter, he bombarded her with passionate letters: 'I lived away from the world for so long now, that I fall in love so easily.' 'The only star I see now is you, whom my longings seek.'

Kathleen was not to know that he had another affair in progress. He had now resumed relations with Sigrun Munthe, a tortured business, since they had to meet in secret. Nansen liked to call himself her 'boy', as if he were looking for another Eva.

Kathleen was quite different, both to Sigrun and to his previous encounters. In his passages with English grand ladies, they had usually withdrawn before things went too far. Kathleen was not a grand lady. Part Greek, and the daughter of a parson, she was tall, dark, quite comely, extravagantly histrionic, and with a self-consciously Bohemian past. She was a trained sculptress, knew the writers and artists of the day, and had an inquiring mind. Wilful and imperious, she was no mother figure. Her marriage to Scott seemed a mésalliance. Self-confessedly a hero-worshipper, she found herself dominating her anything but heroic husband. Most men, in fact, tended to run away from her. In Nansen she had met her match.

He now asked her to join him in Berlin, where a German edition of *In Northern Mists* was about to appear. Jules Sachs, a Berlin impresario, was busy arranging a promotional lecture tour in Germany and Austria. Again the subject was ostensibly the Norsemen in America; again the drawing power really Nansen's name. Sachs wished to make all he could before the first news from Scott – or Amundsen – arrived to kill off interest. Nansen needed the money. He was financing his own oceanographical work and earlier that year was £1,000 (£47,000 or $75,000 in present terms) out of pocket.

Nansen had first asked Sigrun to accompany him to Berlin. She had however declined for fear of scandal. Kathleen was the next best thing. She agreed. They spent a week together at the Hotel Westminster in Berlin. Afterwards, Nansen wrote to her:

I feel like a Faust, who has got a draught of the fountain of life , and has become young again, suddenly and unexpectedly. I feel as if I am just awakening from a beautiful, very beautiful dream.

'Life was grey, lonely, finished, like an empty beaten country road,' another letter ran. 'What kind of bewitching power do you ... have?

464

Strangely enough, when I think of you, in spite of your strange burning soft eyes, it is as if I see blue anemones in the springtime ... and smell the scent of violets.'

There was one thing wrong with this second letter. It was not addressed to Kathleen. The recipient was a lady called Grete, the aristocratic Hungarian wife of Olaf Gulbransson, a Norwegian caricaturist living in Munich and a prominent contributor to the German satirical magazine *Simplicissimus*. Nansen had met her there a few days after leaving Kathleen in Berlin. After he had finished lecturing, Grete and her husband persuaded him to come skiing with them at St Anton am Arlberg in the Austrian Alps. There this slightly bizarre *ménage à trois* shared a mountain hut for a week or so.

It was largely thanks to Nansen and his crossing of Greenland that skiing was now established in the Alps. He promised to send Grete a copy of *The First Crossing of Greenland* – 'Not that it is a book to be proud of,' he deprecatingly remarked. 'In every respect it is an immature work.' Meanwhile, like an exuberant schoolboy, he led the way up the Valuga and other now famous slopes before hurtling down, for ski lifts as yet there were none. By his own account, it was his first true holiday for years.

All too soon he was on a train speeding north from Munich, on his way home. He wrote to Grete, who had been injured while skiing and was now laid up at home:

> I see you before me sitting there alone ... while you wait for Olaf ... who is working at the editorial offices ... Perhaps you think the hours are lonely until he comes. But still how well off you are! Think if you had sat thus for three years, and never knew whether he would ever come back to you – and nonetheless life had to be lived, a difficult life, while one listened anxiously for the quiet whisper of the changing, temperamental aeolian harp of hope.

This was one of Nansen's very rare, and always oblique, references to Eva. Rapidly he continued:

> Why such melancholy images now? I am sitting here in the dark, rattling compartment, where I can hardly write, in a strange mood of gratitude for the rich, happy time I have had together with you two good, kind, wonderful friends.

Home again, Nansen could now only wait for news from the Antarctic. It soon came, on 7 March, in the form of a laconic telegram in code from Amundsen in Hobart, Tasmania, arranged so that he should know before the public: 'THANKS FOR EVERYTHING OBJECTIVE REACHED ALL WELL.' Amundsen had attained the Pole, and beaten Scott to the cablehead.

'He has evidently sailed very fast, and my old ship has done well,' Nansen was instantly writing to Kathleen; 'But still I wish that Scott had come first. Yes, life is very complicated indeed!' To Grete, he wrote in a very different vein: 'Isn't Amundsen wonderful, and has he not done it well?'

By then, Amundsen's reports had swept round the world. He had reached the Pole on 14 December 1911, after what seemed an effortless ski tour, and seen no sign of anyone else. Confirmation came ironically through Scott himself, with the arrival on 1 April of *Terra Nova* at the cablehead in New Zealand, without Scott, but with the news, brought back by a support party from the south, that on 4 January, he had still been struggling 150 miles from the Pole. He had lost the race, and in one sense Nansen too had lost. In public he praised Amundsen in every way he knew. In private he was sick at heart.

'Happiness! Mocking, demanding word,' he wrote in his first diary entry after Amundsen's primacy was settled.

> I stare round about in the endless desert. Not a single place to rest on the endless flight, not a single person in the whole wide world who can give joy of life, the fire that will take one over the abyss. Goethe's Faust never reached a place where he wanted to 'remain!' I cannot even glimpse anywhere worth the attempt.

Response to a Suicide

In the wake of Amundsen's achievement, Nansen underwent some kind of collapse. 'I ... have had a strange gloom or spiritual depression,' he wrote to Grete Gulbransson, 'that has paralysed all my initiative.' It delayed a long planned oceanographical cruise in *Veslemøy* to Arctic waters round Spitsbergen to the late summer of 1912. He was hounded by many a storm, and finally returned in September to face the man who had finally robbed him of his 'life-lie'. Amundsen, who had been back in Norway for several months, came out to visit him at home and make his peace.

Amundsen arrived tense, uncertain and embarrassed. Nansen shook hands, congratulated him warmly, and showed no trace of resentment. Amundsen departed in palpable relief.

There was strain between them nonetheless. Each regarded the other with respect. But they were too different to share any warmer feelings. Amundsen was a ship's captain, who belonged to the freemasonry of the sea, untrammelled by nationality; Nansen, bound to his native soil, was ever the great man trying to escape from a small country. Amundsen was the single-minded man of action with the gift of leadership, Nansen a tortured, isolated polymath always searching for a rôle. Nansen was the explorer as hero; Amundsen an artist in action for whom the deed was all.

However stark their differences, Nansen had unbridled admiration for the younger man's consummate ability; for the planning, technique, elegance and deceptive ease with which he had won the race for the South Pole, bringing all his men back safe and sound into the bargain. It brought to fruition the classic system of travel using dogs and skis. Nansen had written an encomiastic foreword to *The South Pole*, Amundsen's book about his expedition. He wrote in the Press about 'Amundsen's matchless journey' when the news first came through; about 'this man of iron will who goes on his own way quietly ... without a single mishap. Let no one ... speak of luck ... He has the good fortune that accompanies the strong.'

A little later, Nansen received from Johansen a long letter, written on *Fram* during the voyage from the Antarctic back to Hobart, Tasmania, revealing some of the inner history of the expedition. 'After several false starts,' began one passage,

We set off [for the Pole] on 8 September [1911].... But it was too early a start and if Scott had not been at McMurdo Sound it would not have taken place so early. We did not get further than 80°. Temp. was between 50 and 60 degrees of frost and the dogs could not manage, their legs failed, and several were killed by the cold. We had to turn back. All went reasonably well with the exception of the last day's march.

Several men had frostbitten feet. There was a rush, pell mell, for home. At a certain point Johansen decided to wait for the last straggler, who was far behind, in trouble and alone.

> I had to wait ... for several hours [Johansen went on]. We had started at 7 in the morning and [we] arrived [at our base] after many difficulties at 1 a.m. (The others had arrived during the afternoon at different intervals. We two had no Primus stove, only a few dry biscuits.) Darkness fell early, and it was a wonder that we found our way ... the sledgemeter showed 43 nautical miles for the day.

Johansen then revealed that when the polar party, led by Amundsen, finally started on 20 October on the last great terrestrial journey left to man, they left without him. He gave no reason. Amundsen, in a letter received by Nansen at about the same time, did so. Johansen had been excluded from the party because of being violently insubordinate to Amundsen in public. On arriving at Hobart he started drinking again. Amundsen then paid him off and sent him home ahead of the rest.

On 4 January 1913 Nansen was rung up by a Christiania journalist to break the news that during the night Johansen had shot himself. Taken by surprise, all that Nansen could say of his old companion, so the journalist reported, was that in the Arctic 'he was the right man in the right place'.

Meanwhile Nansen was oppressed by the troubled interlude of waiting for the news from Scott. The Norwegian victory, or rather her husband's defeat, had come between Kathleen and himself, while Sigrun's bouts of waywardness and the furtiveness of their affair were telling on his nerves. Nansen was still writing emotionally to Grete, but it was of Kathleen that he was thinking. Queen Maud, he wrote to her, 'always talks to me about you. I believe she has found out that I like you very much.'

Little more than a month after Johansen's suicide the suspense came to an end. On 10 February 1913 *Terra Nova* returned to the cablehead in New Zealand with the news of the disaster that Scott had brought upon himself. It now turned out that while Nansen and Kathleen were together in Berlin, Scott was discovering that he had lost the game. He had reached the Pole, only to find that Amundsen had been there five weeks earlier. The drama was made more poignant by the fact that Nansen had long since expounded to Kathleen the technical incompetence on the part of her husband which now turned out to have caused his death and that of all his companions on their way back. He was nevertheless shocked at what had happened, perhaps more so than Kathleen, who had always considered her husband unlucky. To compound this public tragedy Nansen's youngest child, Åsmund, died, not ten years old. Nansen was grief-stricken. Yet his duty, he felt, was to try to console Kathleen. She had travelled out to meet her husband and wrote to Nansen on board ship two days after a radio message had brought the news.

'You write ... about the haunting thought of his pain and suffering,' Nansen replied.

> You should not think so much of that ... I have some experience and the fact is that the brain becomes soon so numbed, as you say, that one does not feel so very much. One gets so tired and weak and worn out that one becomes more or less indifferent to physical as well as mental pain. And then at last one falls asleep and does not wake again ...

Soon he was making one of his rare references to Eva. 'A loving, kind woman with a warm soul, how often have I not dreamt of one,' he wrote in his diary:

> She who, when the dark, heavy clouds begin to gather round the brow of the man she loves, rushes to him, soft and warm ... while he rests his weary head on her breast, and cries away his worries and his pain next to her heart. I have only met a single one, and she is lost, for ever. Let him console himself who can with [Ibsen's proverbial saying] 'Only what is lost is kept forever.' I cannot.

And afterwards he wrote, in another tirade of lament:

> I want to go into my secret chamber and lock the door and read ... about great women who could forget themselves and their vanity for the man they loved. And what ... do I have to put in the balance? A woman who will not even risk a little blot on her reputation as a good hostess for your sake, however much it meant for you.

It is unclear whether this was aimed at Sigrun or Kathleen, but probably it was the latter. Nansen had invited Kathleen to sail with him on *Veslemøy* to Spitsbergen on his oceanographic cruise during the summer of 1912. She had declined.

Meanwhile, Nansen's complex feelings towards Amundsen were undergoing an upheaval. It had been precipitated by Johansen's suicide.

The insubordination which had kept Johansen out of the polar party was this. At breakfast at the Norwegian base of Framheim, on the morning after the return from the false start, he had lost control, flared up and tongue-lashed Amundsen over the flight the day before, attacking his leadership in front of everyone else. Implacable towards those he felt had betrayed him, Amundsen sent Johansen home in disgrace. The quarrel between them was kept private, but Johansen was now a broken man.

Having arrived home almost unremarked, he was briefly included in the festivities when the other expedition members followed him to Christiania early in July 1912. He then drifted down into a squalid part of Christiania destitute, brooding, hopeless, with his long, bitter memories, shunning friends and family, still hounded by the mysterious shadow he had felt on the first drift of the *Fram* all those years ago. His suicide might have been a reproach to Amundsen. But in Nansen it violently touched an uneasy conscience.

Ever since returning from *Fram* in 1896 Johansen had felt slighted, abandoned, living in the shadow of his old leader. Nansen had done all he reasonably could to help Johansen financially, but little to save him as a human being. Although knowing what had happened in the Antarctic, he still did not seek out his old companion. The two men did not even meet. All this now came back to haunt Nansen, and inflame the lingering resentment caused by Amundsen's secret switch from north to south, and his attainment of the Pole.

'He suited the life up north in the ice, the cold and loneliness,' Nansen said in tribute to Johansen. 'But it was as if he could not readjust to trivial everyday town life.' Nansen seemed to be hinting that Johansen had found a happy release. But it was a tragic end to a tragic life.

When Amundsen announced that he was going south, he presented it as an extension to his original plan. Thereafter, he would continue on his northern drift. He now discovered the perils of a promise lightly given. His attainment of the South Pole had closed the era of terrestrial exploration. Of the great symbolical goals, only the highest point on Earth, Mount Everest, remained unconquered. To continue with a northern drift would be to repeat what others had already done. For Amundsen only anticlimax lay in wait. More profoundly, by the attainment of the North-West Passage, and now the South Pole, he had twice done exactly what he intended. Another polar journey would be tempting Fate. None of this had he foreseen. From America, where he was on a lecture tour during part of 1913, he wrote to Nansen, obliquely hinting that he wanted to quit exploration while the going was good.

That released in Nansen all the emotion aroused by the burden of Johansen on his conscience. 'I ... have broken lances for you – and, I might even say, your honour,' he wrote in a long, harsh letter of reproach. In private and in public, he had rallied to Amundsen's defence. Scott's disaster, he had written in the Press, was due to scurvy and nothing else. In private, where necessary, he showed that Scott had been the author of his own downfall. 'He would not listen to my advice,' he wrote to Sir Clements Markham, in answer to an emotional missive. '[His] equipment ... was not adequate to the task ... had he done what I would have him do, we should still have had him amongst us.'

There, indeed, was the rub. Had Scott survived, Amundsen could decently have abandoned his now futile Arctic drift. What he really wanted to do was to return to the Canadian Eskimos he had met on the North-West Passage. There he had discovered an inborn talent for anthropology, and that he now wanted to pursue.

But Nansen harped on his old self-deluding refrain of how with bleeding heart he had renounced his own Antarctic plans so that Amundsen could go north. 'If ... the upshot now turns out to be that you ... did the journey I gave up so that you could do the other,' he bitterly put it, 'and that journey does not now materialise, then I think that life can be strange sometimes.' That alone was enough to exploit Amundsen's sense of obligation. Beyond that Nansen, for Kathleen's sake, or more accurately his standing in her eyes, obliquely played on Scott's death to put another charge on Amundsen's conscience by invoking the spectre of dishonouring the dead. Amundsen was thereby trapped between contending evils. It was the classic dilemma of Greek tragedy. If he continued with his drift, he would be guilty of hubris; if he did not, he would be breaking his word. As if in revenge for having been deprived of the 'life-lie', Nansen drove him back to the first alternative, and he found himself embarked with foreboding on a course from which the fire had gone.

'I am standing at one of the great crossroads of my life,' Nansen wrote in his diary about this time. Shortly after Johansen's suicide, a Norwegian businessman called Jonas Lied – who, incidentally, had been one of the last people to see Johansen alive, and said that he had been sober and given no sign of his intentions – had approached Nansen with a proposal. For some years, he had been trying to open the northern sea route along the River Yenisei to the Siberian hinterland (an obsession he shared with Alfred Derry, of the London department store Derry and Toms, from whom he originally got the idea) and lately he had floated a company to that end. His plan was to send a trial batch of Siberian goods by lighter down the Yenisei to the estuary, where it would be loaded onto a ship that had sailed from Norway with a foreign cargo to discharge. The first attempt, in 1912, had failed because the Norwegian ship was stopped by ice. Lied was determined to try again the following year. His shareholders agreed. They chartered a modern tramp steamer called *Correct* and on 5 August 1913, when she sailed from Tromsø for the Yenisei with a cargo of cement, Nansen was on board. 'How and why,' he subsequently wrote, perhaps with a touch of naïveté, 'is still a riddle to me.'

Lied could have enlightened him. As he himself bluntly put it:

I had the inspiration ... to hitch our wagon to Nansen's lucky star ... I wanted [him] on board ... because nothing that [he] lent his name to failed.

Securing that name, however, had been a delicate operation. Nansen, as Lied perceptively remarked, was 'sensitive to the point of being touchy. He must be dealt with as a very famous man or he might find a hundred excuses for not accepting.'

When I first called on Nansen [so Lied later recalled], he came down the stairs two or three steps at a time, like a boy, with a final jump into the hall, though he was [over] fifty.... Perhaps he wished to give the impression of youthful energy.... He spoke in his habitual melancholy tone, sad even when enthusiastic, mirthless even when eager.

But, Lied's account continued,

He took everything seriously from the start.... [The] new Russian charts were all more up to date than those the explorer himself had had on the *Fram*. There was no doubt that the proposal I had brought ... awakened memories and acted favourably on his imagination ... I sensed that he would join us, if the expedition could be given the flavour of an exploit.

Nansen considered the voyage as a holiday – and after the sadness and confusion that had crowded in on him, he deserved one. This was also the twentieth anniversary of his departure on *Fram*. For the first part of the voyage, until rounding the Yamal peninsula at the mouth of the Kara Sea, he was, with one or two variations, retracing her course. His feeling of nostalgia was accentuated by the presence as ice pilot on board *Correct* of the same Captain H.C. Johannesen whom he had consulted about Arctic navigation before sailing on *Fram* and who, other things being equal, would then have liked to join him. It was observed that when Johannesen was not in the crow's nest, Nansen spent a disproportionate amount of time there, staring out over the waters.

After about three weeks *Correct* arrived at her rendezvous at Nosonovski Ostrov ('Nose Island'), a little way upstream from the mouth of the Yenesei where, to Lied's relief, the barges had already arrived from the hinterland with his return cargo. Also to his relief, after six uncertain days, a motor cutter arrived, having been sent by the Russian authorities to take Nansen off for the rest of his journey. Lied, a calculating and enigmatic character, had engineered an invitation for Nansen to visit Siberia as the guest of the Russian government. Having got what he could out of Nansen's presence, he wanted to proceed with his own business. On 3 September Nansen left on the cutter to be taken up the Yenisei.

This was his introduction to the hinterland of Russia. On either bank of the broad reaches of one of the longest rivers in the world the empty Siberian tundra swept on to the horizon. Here and there, Samoyeds and other native tribesmen appeared, interspersed with strange Russians who might have stepped out of a novel by Dostoievsky. There was of course a sprinkling of political exiles. And even in this remote corner there was a plentiful supply of uniformed officials.

After a journey of more than three weeks and over 2,200 kilometres Nansen and his companions reached Krasnoyarsk on the upper reaches of the Yenisei. To save time and cut off a bend in the river they covered the last two hundred miles or so by a hair-raising ride overland in a horse-drawn vehicle called a *tarantass* through wild terrain reputedly infested by brigands.

Krasnoyarsk was a station on the Trans-Siberian Railway, opened about a decade earlier, and the real reason for the journey up the river. Nansen had been offered a free trip on the Trans-Siberian Express. On 29 September he joined the train, travelling in the private carriage of Wourtzel, the chief engineer of the Russian state-owned railways, who had asked him to join him on a tour of inspection. His other companions travelled as far as Irkutsk. Nansen went on to Vladivostok, the terminus on the Pacific. He returned by an unfinished railway, the Amur line, which the Russians were building to avoid the existing branch through Chinese territory. He had to cover a large stretch by motor car over a primitive carriageway through the virgin taiga, before rejoining the railway some way east of Chita, the junction of the two lines. One of the new stations was named after him, in his presence. Finally, by way of St Petersburg, he returned home on 4 November. He had spent a month almost continually on trains.

Travel, as usual, had acted as a stimulant. His mood lifted. Only when the prospect of home loomed up did oppressive melancholy return. 'It is strange that it is always a little sad to say farewell,' he wrote in his diary when the train passed a station called Viatka, past the line of the Urals, leaving Siberia behind.

For Lied, the venture had been a promising success, backed by the lustre of Nansen's name. For his part, Nansen wrote a book about his experiences, published in English as *Through Siberia the Land of the Future*. Much of the book was devoted to a description of the native tribes that he had met along the way. It had some familiar touches. 'What a country for a sportsman!' Nansen wrote at one point about the route of the Amur railway.

> Bears and elks and wild boars ... And now and then tigers.... But we must go forward, ever forward, to inspect the laying of this line which ... is to open the way for that so-called civilisation which will gradually clear away forests and natives and game.

He extolled the astonishing modernisation that Russia was then undergoing, at a feverish pace, as if there was not much time left. His two main themes were, in that order, the unbounded possibilities of Siberia for developing Russia and settling millions of superfluous Russians, and the threat of Japanese, Chinese, Koreans pressing in, diligent, industrious, aggressive, land-hungry, threatening the empty spaces. He presented Russia as the bulwark of Europe against the 'yellow peril', as it was then called, and which he personally so much feared.

About this time, Nansen changed the name of his house from the original elided *Polhøiden* to the more forceful and expressive *Polhøgda* –

both meaning the same ambivalent 'Polar Heights'. This was an outcome of the Norwegianisation of the language, which in fact was furthering Nansen's disillusionment with his fellow-countrymen. The centuries under Denmark had left Danish as the literary and educated language. The drive to independence involved linguistic nationalism, and a long factional campaign to eradicate Danish influence by imposing a new artificial Norwegian national language, which led to bitter strife, unresolved to this day.

Nansen abhorred the militants of the language movement, fundamentally on the grounds that language is not the plaything of political fashion but naturally evolves with changing circumstances. He was particularly incensed by radical spelling reforms imposed by government decree. He belonged to the school that held to the language inherited from the Danes. Nonetheless, like many others, he adopted Norwegian forms when they seemed appropriate. *Fram*, instead of the Danish *Frem*, was one example; *Polhøgda* now to replace *Polhøiden* was another.

Nansen spent the summer of 1914, the last summer of peace, on another oceanographical cruise ranging from Madeira to the Azores. He returned home a few weeks before the outbreak of war in August.

'These sad days make me think of my friends far away and of sunnier times,' began a letter that arrived not long afterwards. It was from Mrs E.M. Sharpe, Marion Ure's mother, whom he had last met in Italy and Switzerland in the now distant 1880s, when he was still a hopeful young neurobiologist. She had now returned home from Japan.

> I know your country is not at war. Long may it be so. I should like to have a letter ... I do not want to lose you – and there may not be much time. I am nearly 86 ... What can you say of ... Italy? That lovely land is a Camp. Shall it be a battlefield? God forbid.... Do let me hear of you. I like to remember Italy and Brunnen.

Nansen had now acquired an even deeper distaste for politicians than he felt before. The Norwegians had declared themselves neutral in the war. As Nansen reiterated, that was not by itself a guarantee of safety. Neutrality entrenched by treaty had not saved Belgium from invasion. He believed rather in the policies of Switzerland and Sweden, which backed their desire for neutrality by arming themselves to defend it. For the moment, the Norwegians seemed safe, because none of the belligerents wished to take on more commitments. That situation could not be guaranteed to last.

His country's real enemies Nansen considered to be its own rulers: weak, indecisive and complacent. He reserved his deepest scorn for the Norwegian Prime Minister, a moustachio'd shipowner called Gunnar Knudsen, a member of the Left Party who, shortly before the outbreak of war, had famously said that internationally 'there was a cloudless sky'.

Nansen canvassed politicians in an attempt to change the government. He wrote to English acquaintances, explaining that although Norway was neutral, public sympathy lay not with Germany but with England and the Allies. But he was merely a private citizen. He was not taken seriously.

These were the dead years, which had begun when he had left the Embassy in London. Frustrated, unsettled, occasionally sneered at by the Press, he retreated to his *Polhøgda*, shut himself up in his tower, kept the world at bay, and buried himself in writing and working out his observations from his last oceanographical cruises before the war.

Periodically he consoled himself with mountain trips for skiing or hunting – an unimaginable privilege, as he admitted, while on the battlefields the slaughter continued without end. He was becoming gloomier and more introspective than ever. In his diary, at Easter 1915, he entered a long lament for his dead son Åsmund: 'With a big heart, you always thought of others, to the end.'

> But you and Eva had to go and I, who am least made for life, have been left. How long will it last?

About a year later, in March 1916, Nansen dived into the past in a different way. He repeated the downhill run he had last done a generation earlier on the return half of his now almost legendary crossing on skis between Bergen and Christiania. By now there was a railway over the mountains, and the idea struck him on a visit to Finse, the station at the summit of the line. A chance acquaintance egged him on and decided to accompany him. In Nansen's own words:

> Before sunrise [he wrote], we speeded in the train over the plateau to Hallinskeid station, precisely where I had searched for a snowed-in hut that winter night thirty-two years earlier.

And of the run itself:

> I could not remember having had to overcome so awesome a slope as this on that occasion when I travelled that way alone. But I must have done so, and I almost admired myself for having managed it without its having made a deeper impression.
>
> But memory is strange. It made out the climbs to be worse than they were in reality, but the downhill slopes shorter and easier. Is it the effect of age?.... Youth takes all difficulties downhill in its stride.

After catching the next train back to Finse and 'a gargantuan lunch at half-past two':

> What a change ... Until a few years ago [there was] the same [ancient] isolation in these mountains in winter.... But now! The locomotive whistles

broke the silence ... and so-called civilisation creeps higher and higher up to the mountain fastnesses with its big hotels and unavoidable 'tourists'.

Soon after, in May, there came another, distant echo of the Arctic. Dr Blessing died. He had never been cured of the morphine addiction he had contracted on *Fram*. Since returning, twenty years before, he had only irregularly practised; most recently in the Antarctic on a Norwegian whaler. His drug habit had killed him.

Eventually the outside world intruded on Nansen in a way he might have wished. In November that year he was approached by a Bavarian called Wilhelm Filchner. A good-humoured, sharp-witted, regular army captain, he was seconded to the intelligence department of the German Admiralty, and stationed in Bergen to spy on Norwegian shipping. He had been, among other things, a polar explorer, having visited Spitsbergen and led a German Antarctic expedition before the war. On that account he knew various Norwegians. He made contact with Nansen through Helland-Hansen in Bergen and met him discreetly in a mountain hut on the Bergen-Christiania railway. Nansen thereafter invited him to stay at *Polhøgda*.

Despite her declared neutrality, the Germans considered Norway a hostile country, because her mercantile marine was largely sailing in Allied service. In consequence German submarines began sinking Norwegian ships. But it was not these matters with which Filchner was concerned. What he was really interested in was peace feelers with England, and he thought Nansen could help him through his influence in high places.

By Filchner's own account, Nansen offered to mediate if he could, and they agreed to sound out the possibilities, Filchner in Berlin and Nansen through his British contacts. But in London the Foreign Office rejected Nansen's overtures. Meanwhile Filchner, having been unmasked as a spy, had to leave Norway hurriedly. In any case the moment had passed. On 16 December Lloyd George succeeded Asquith as Prime Minister in England, with a brief to fight the war to the death. There were similar changes of men and policies in Germany. Peace was now out of the question.

It was not the first Scandinavian attempt at mediation between the belligerents. In 1915 King Gustaf V of Sweden, the former Prince Gustaf, wrote to the Tsar, Nicholas II, offering his help in making peace between Germany and Russia. 'Never has Russia been so united and so resolute as now upon the question of ... carrying out this war to a *lasting end*,' Nicholas replied in declining the offer.

A few months afterwards in St Petersburg – or rather Petrograd, as the name had been russified in the wake of war to eradicate the German influence – there was a poignant sequel to Nansen's Siberian journey. Jonas Lied, now settled in Russia, presented the Tsar with a copy of the

69. Response to a Suicide

English edition of *Through Siberia the Land of the Future*, 'bound in white pigskin and gold braided'. He was, he wrote in his diary,

> received in private audience, a great honour ... I was astonished to see how small he was and asked myself whether it is possible that this could be the mighty Russian ruler. He was very charming.... His movements were nervous, and he was constantly changing his position ... I handed him the book and he asked me whether it was a present from me or Nansen. I said the latter and he asked me to thank him.

Around the same time, or a little later, in Zürich, Lenin who, like all good revolutionaries, was spending some time in exile in Switzerland, took the same book out of a public library.

Nansen meanwhile, in politics, relapsed once more into the frustrating rôle of spectator at great events. At home, he was in the doldrums. His affair with Sigrun had settled down, her husband was complaisant and she justified her behaviour on the grounds of wanting to give Nansen's children a home. Liv resented her intrusion on her mother's memory. Odd, the youngest surviving son, escaped the gloomy house to live with family friends. Only Irmelin (called 'Immi') really warmed to Sigrun and stayed with her in her home. For all that Nansen could not openly parade Sigrun as his mistress. Their affair had to remain clandestine. Discontented, melancholy and lost as before, he tried his hand at a novel.

It was never finished, much less published. The plot, such as it is, involves the rape and murder of a country girl by an itinerant gipsy, who buries her in a remote upland peat bog. The unnamed, talented hero bears a distinct resemblance to Fridtjof Nansen. He appears out of nowhere in the Norwegian mountains and, having being wounded by a bear, is nursed by an unnamed woman, an idealised version of Eva. The substance of the novel is a dialogue between them, which soon turns into an interior monologue in which the author argues with himself, coming out with such passages as:

> He was everlastingly on the road to somewhere else. In the capricious game of life he had tried everything, found little, and lost much.

A prominent theme was Nansen's old favourite of the conflict between the primitive and the civilised, encapsulated within himself. 'I am truly even less coherent than you think,' the hero is made to say, which just about sums the book up too.

Although through his hero Nansen proclaimed that life had no purpose, he personally was seeking some new satisfaction to give it meaning. At one point in 1917 he was considering an expedition to Mongolia, and actually obtained permission to travel through Russian territory. However, he was at best half-hearted. A new idea, elaborated in his abortive novel, had entered his mind. He was on the brink of seeing himself as the conscience of the world. He had shown early signs of abandoning social Darwinism and turning humanitarian at the beginning of 1916, when he published an article in which he maintained that 'it will be the duty of the neutral countries to maintain the continuity of world morality, and save it from shipwreck'.

In October 1918 he was elected Rector of the University in Christiania, but refused the honour and never took it up. It would have enmeshed him in academic pettifogging and given him no outlet for his new crusading fever. That providentially appeared around the same time with the foundation of a League of Nations. Its purpose was to secure peace and settle conflicts by negotiation. It was an old idea, appropriated by President Woodrow Wilson as one of America's aims on entering the war. It was a cause espoused by idealists who, in various countries, established a League of Nations Union to promote their views. At the end of October a Norwegian branch was formed, with Nansen as chairman. In that capacity, when the moment came, he headed for the Peace Conference in Paris. This began on 18 January 1919, following the defeat of Germany and the Armistice on 11 November 1918.

Sailing from Norway on 22 February 1919, Nansen travelled to Paris via London, staying there for about a week. As soon as he arrived, he met Kathleen Scott once more. It was an odd time for them both. Neither had yet found another spouse. Neither had yet reconstituted their lives. Nansen was still unsatisfactorily entangled with Sigrun, who had finally divorced her husband, so that he could marry her, as she hoped. Kathleen was trying, like others of her kind, to revive the social amenities of the world that had vanished when the guns began to fire. Then, through the agency of Kathleen, several things happened to give form to Nansen's well-meaning but nebulous intentions.

First, she introduced Nansen to J.M. Barrie at one of her carefully arranged little lunches. The creator of Peter Pan was entranced. Here, he sensed, was a real, live hero to set against the dead and martyred Scott. Then, on Sunday 2 March, she took Nansen to a country house at Lamer, the home of someone called Apsley Cherry-Garrard. For related reasons, Arctic and Antarctic were haunting the inner life of both men.

Nansen had exacted retribution from the man who, by the now well-embedded, self-comforting English myth, was held to have caused the death of Kathleen's husband. Amundsen, much delayed, at last had left on his Arctic drift. After three expeditions, and the depredations of the tropics, *Fram* was no longer the ship she had been. Amundsen had had to have another vessel built. He called her *Maud* after the Norwegian queen. Hounded by the shadow of Nansen to the end, he had finally sailed in June the year before. Nansen could rest content. Amundsen *was* continuing his drift, as he had always maintained.

Cherry-Garrard, a novice in the snows, had been with Scott on that second, ill-fated expedition; indeed he had been on the last relief party that

478

might, realistically, have saved Scott and his surviving companions. He had been cruelly driven to the edge of sanity by a mounting obsession that his own shortcomings as a snow traveller were the cause of failure, and consequently that the blood of his friends lay upon his head. Now, at Lamer, under Kathleen's eye, he and Nansen met, and had a long and intricate discussion on the speed of sledges and the different kind of runners. Evidently Cherry-Garrard was still hoping for a technical reason to explain why he had been too late on that distant, sad Antarctic foray now seven years in the past, and thus a chance to lift his burden of guilt. Nansen, tragically, was unable to provide one.

Bernard Shaw, a neighbour, was also present on that occasion. So too was Lady Gregory, friend and ally of W.B. Yeats. She treated Nansen with old-fashioned veneration; he responded with touching, child-like pleasure. Fired perhaps by this charming scene, Kathleen dashed off – on Cherry-Garrard's notepaper – a letter of introduction for Nansen to Colonel E.M. House, Woodrow Wilson's closest and most influential adviser at the Peace Conference, and another celebrity she had ensnared with her imperious charms.

Exactly three days later, in Paris, Nansen presented this letter to Colonel House. 'Lady Scott [having] been kind enough to give me an introduction,' he explained in his accompanying note, 'I would be very grateful for a talk with you ... whenever it would suit your convenience.' All unknowing, he had entered as if on cue.

Part V

The League

70

An Ideal Front Man

The peace conference was a vast cosmopolitan caravanserai of fanatics, supplicants, charlatans and semi-comic characters all seeking to shape a new world order. The old one had collapsed in the aftermath of war. Kings and princes had been swept away. The Habsburgs and the Kaiser had gone. The map of Europe was being comprehensively redrawn. Presiding over the rearrangement were the delegations in Paris of France, Great Britain, Italy and the United States, the Big Four, so called; the most powerful of the victorious Allies.

They had assembled to dictate the terms of peace. Vanquished Germany was not there. The other great absentee was Russia. Having begun the war as one of the Allies, she ended squalidly, neither friend nor foe. In 1917 Lenin had seized power by a coup d'état, dignified by the name of the October Revolution, after the month (Old Style) in which it was carried through.

One outcome was a separate, early peace with Germany. Worse still, Lenin and his coterie – Marxists, broadly speaking, and labelled variously Bolshevik, Communist, Soviet or Red – were preaching world revolution, having incidentally murdered the Tsar and his family, thus ending the rule of the Romanoffs. Understandably, the Allies refused to recognise the Bolsheviks. They pinned their hopes instead on the Whites, adherents of the old regime, whose armies were fighting the Bolsheviks in a vicious civil war and still controlled large tracts of Russia. Here and there, the Allies even intervened themselves.

This, then, was the position when the Peace Conference began. Ostensibly about Germany, in reality it concerned Russia and the threat of Communism. Under any circumstances Russia would have been a problem for the Allies. As a price for her offensives on the Eastern Front she had been promised Constantinople and the Straits, realising the old nightmare of Russia bursting out of the Black Sea into the Mediterranean. The Bolshevik Revolution was a heaven-sent pretext for evading this particular bargain. Russia, past and present, was the spectre haunting the Conference.

The statesmen grappling with these complexities were an inauspicious constellation. Orlando, Clemenceau and Lloyd George, the leaders of Italy, France and Great Britain respectively, were ordinary venal politicians.

The man who stood apart was Wilson, tall, prim, remote, bespectacled, mediocre, an arid moralist but alarmingly high-minded. He had a mystic vision of a new world order. It was founded on his celebrated Fourteen Points – 'Mais le bon Dieu n'avait que dix' ('The good Lord only had ten'), Clemenceau reputedly said in a scurrilous aside – which had formed the conditions on which the Germans had sued for peace and were now the basis of the Conference proceedings.

The founding of the League of Nations was high on the confused agenda of the conference. Since the League was supposed to abolish war and be all-embracing, the neutrals wanted a say in its formation. Woodrow Wilson refused. The establishment of the League was to be an integral part of the peace treaty, and as such remained the prerogative of the victorious Allies. However, mainly as a concession to the French, the neutrals were invited to send observers to an unofficial meeting with a sub-committee. The scene was described by a Danish representative:

> On Thursday 20 March 1919 at 3 o'clock in the afternoon, the repre-
> sentatives of the 13 neutral states [were received] at the Hotel Crillon, where
> the Americans were staying. The whole thing was very confused. The par-
> ticipants, ... approaching fifty in total, were crammed into a room with
> reasonable place for half that number.... The meeting [was chaired] by
> [Lord] Robert Cecil.... He said that ... it was not his intention to enter into
> a discussion of the basic principles; these were to be considered settled.

Nansen's unpopularity with the politicians at home precluded his being named as a Norwegian delegate. So far, he was merely one of the crowd of hangers-on. His opening came through a member of the American delegation in Paris called Vance McCormick. By all accounts, Russia under its new Communist regime was going hungry. McCormick had the idea of offering to feed the population on condition that the Communists ceased fighting and, more importantly, stopped the export of subversion. In other words, he proposed using food as a weapon. Thus was born one of the great innovations of the century.

McCormick put his idea to Herbert Hoover, a conspicuously realistic and supremely able member of Wilson's entourage, a future President himself, holder of many offices, and head of the American Relief Administration, which brought unstinted aid to the victims of the war. They agreed that if they were to have any success with Lenin, the ARA could not openly be involved. They needed a front man, in the shape of some respected figure from a neutral country. They discussed it over dinner on 4 March, the very day before Nansen approached Colonel House with his letter from Kathleen Scott.

Strictly speaking, Nansen needed no introduction. When America came into the war on the side of the Allies on 6 April 1917 she also joined the blockade against Germany and the Central Powers – among other things blocking all supplies to the neutral countries pending agreements aimed at stopping trade with the enemy. The Norwegians were particularly affected, because they were not self-sufficient in food and depended on America for grain. Once more Norwegian politicians were guilty of mismanagement. Once more Nansen was conscripted to save the situation by virtue of his personality and his fame as an explorer which, after a generation, mysteriously still clung to him. On 22 June 1917 he was appointed a plenipotentiary with diplomatic status and, at the head of a small delegation, shortly afterwards went to Washington to negotiate an agreement. It took far longer than expected. Nansen remained in Washington for the best part of a year. He met Hoover, then head of the US Food Administration, and was regularly in touch with others who later appeared at the Peace Conference. On 30 April 1918, when Nansen finally signed an agreement on behalf of Norway, it was Vance McCormick, then head of the US War Trade Board, who did so for the United States. Thus when Nansen appeared in Paris he was already a familiar figure to influential members of the American delegation. He had even met the President himself.

At a certain point, Nansen was approached by the Russian Political Conference in Paris, a kind of goverment in exile. Several members had held office, notably S.D. Sazonov, who had been Foreign Minister under the Tsar. The Conference asked Nansen to head an international movement to buy arms for Russia and raise one hundred million dollars to destroy Bolshevism. Nansen took this seriously enough to visit McCormick at his office in the Hotel Crillon and discuss the matter.

That was on 18 March. By another neat coincidence, that was the very day on which the American delegation received a telegram from one of their number called William Bullitt – 'a young man with ideas', to quote Harold Nicolson, a member of the British delegation – who had been discreetly sent to Russia to report on conditions, there being no official United States representatives on Red territory.

> The Soviet Government is firmly established and the Communist Party is strong politically and morally [his telegram ran]. The Soviet Army is growing [but] the economic conditions of Soviet Russia are tragic ... Everyone ... is pitifully under-nourished ... There are no medicines; men, women and children die by hundreds who might otherwise be saved.

In other words, the moment for the food weapon had arrived. The Allies were blockading Communist-held Russia, so the weapon was real enough. Nansen was wined and dined by McCormick – a bon viveur with a taste for titled ladies but a sharp eye for character ('manners very brusque ... don't see how he holds his popularity', he had, for instance, reported of Hoover) and an understanding of politics – nobody's fool, in fact, whether at the Ritz or elsewhere. In Washington, McCormick had become familiar with Nansen's personality: his forthrightness and his naïveté. It was generally accepted that by sheer force of character, in the face of the pusillanimity of his own government, he had secured an agreement before any of the other neutrals. On 29 March McCormick was writing in his diary: 'I believe he is the man to start a satisfactory neutral relief to aid Russia without recognizing Bolshevist Government.'

By now Hoover had accepted McCormick's general plan and Woodrow Wilson asked Hoover for a memorandum, which he delivered on 28 March. It was a spirited amd closely argued document, with considerable pre-science. 'The Bolshevik,' Hoover wrote, 'has to a greater degree relied upon criminal instinct to support his doctrines than even autocracy did.' The question was,

> whether the Bolshevik ... stirred by great emotional hopes will not under-take large military crusades ... to impose their doctrines on other defenceless people. This is a point on which my mind is divided.

As for Nansen's putative mission:

> Some Neutral of international reputation for probity and ability should be allowed to create a ... Relief Commission for Russia.... He should be told that we will ... help in his humanitarian task if he gets assurances that the Bolsheviki will cease all militant action across certain defined boundaries and cease their subsidising of disturbances abroad.... This plan does not involve any recognition ... of the Bolshevik murderers now in control. [It] would at least test out whether this is a militant force engrossed upon world domination. If such an arrangement could be accomplished it might at least give a period of rest along the frontiers of Europe and would give some hope of stabilization. Time can thus be taken to determine whether or not this whole system is a world danger, and whether the Russian people will not themselves swing back to moderation and themselves bankrupt these ideas. This plan, if successful, would save an immensity of human life and would save your country from further entanglements which today threaten to pull us from our National ideals.

In other words, the food weapon appealed to the American mentality as an alternative to military action and a vehicle of high-minded influence in other people's domestic affairs.

Nansen's intended rôle in all this was still unclear. At first McCormick supposed he would be sent to Russia on a preliminary survey. Hoover took a different view, and he it was who was now directing the affair. Able, unlike both Wilson and Lloyd George, to keep cool and not take fright, he now swung into action. He wished to seize the moment and decided on an immediate, firm proposal addressed to Lenin directly. Hoover was work-ing with Colonel House and an associate on the American delegation called George Auchincloss, a convert to the use of famine relief for political ends. House and Auchinclosss suggested that Nansen be associated with a Swede called Hjalmar Branting, a much respected figure, shortly to become his country's first Social Democratic Prime Minister. Hoover thereupon drafted a letter for both to sign.

Branting and Nansen had earlier had some desultory correspondence, chiefly about a common interest in a genuine plan for Scandinavian military defence to deter aggressors. They both happened to be in Paris now. Nansen, however, possibly urged on by Bullitt, struck Branting's name from the draft.

Bullitt, who had returned to Paris from Moscow on 25 March, had been thoroughly hoodwinked by Lenin. 'The Red Terror is over,' he confidently reported after a week or so in Moscow – which was now the capital – and Petrograd.

> Theatres, opera and ballet ... are now run under the ... Department of Education which ... sees to it that working men and women and children are [able] to attend the performances and that they are instructed beforehand in the significance and beauties of the production ... Lenin ... is ready to make compromises ... he has already [abandoned] his plan to nationalise the land.

In short, Bullitt had started out well disposed to the Russian revolution; he returned a classic Soviet sympathiser. But he was probably the only man in the American delegation with an inkling of how the minds of the Russian leaders worked. Although it was against his own convictions, he found himself intimately concerned in moulding the presentation of Hoover's plan. He could explain, for example, that Branting, being a parliamentary Socialist, would be anathema to Lenin, who believed only in proletarian revolution. In addition, only Nansen had the personality calculated to impress a Russian, imbued as he was with respect for the strong man. Besides which, the rulers in the Kremlin would see through the crude, instant approach. So Nansen was left as the single pawn, and a subtler gambit was devised instead.

Hoover first of all drafted, and Nansen signed, a letter to the Big Four. It made Nansen pose as a disinterested neutral advocating 'a purely humanitarian commission for the provisioning of Russia'. House immediately ordered Auchincloss and a member of the American delegation called David Hunter Miller – who, incidentally, played a leading rôle in establishing the League of Nations – to draft a reply. The Big Four having had their say, Bullitt was asked to revise the document. The object was to make it acceptable to the Russians. Bullitt's final version was the text eventually signed by the Big Four. Nansen's original letter was dated 3 April; it was a fortnight before the agreed reply was ready. In essence it was Hoover's plan of 'food for peace'.

In Nansen's name his letter to the Big Four, beginning 'The present food situation in Russia, where hundreds of thousands ... are dying monthly from sheer starvation and disease, is one of the problems now uppermost in all men's minds,' together with the reply, and a short elaboration, were then embodied in a telegram to Lenin.

Nansen had no inkling of how he was being manipulated. Nor could he see through the tactic of using food as a weapon. To Sigrun he naïvely wrote that 'the only ... sensible policy ... is to show ... the Bolsheviks that there is charity which cares for suffering humanity in spite of all politics'.

When need be, he could still be down to earth – writing home, for example, to make sure that his clothes were protected from moths. He joined modestly in the social round of the Conference, continuing to be entertained by McCormick. While waiting for Lenin's reply he recorded a wild evening that began in the Bois de Boulogne and ended in the studio of a Norwegian artist, where one of the guests injured his knee trying to lift a fat Pole and a girl fell and broke her leg. It was the only action Nansen had experienced at the Conference so far.

Meanwhile there had been delays in the actual sending of the telegram. Neither the French nor the British would transmit it because of a refusal to have direct dealings of any kind with the Communist regime. Hoover finally got it sent via the ARA office in Holland. Nansen also sent a copy via the Norwegian Foreign Ministry in Christiania. One way or another the telegram finally reached Moscow on 4 May.

Lenin told G.V. Chicherine, Soviet Foreign Minister, and his deputy, Maxim Litvinov, each to draft a reply. 'My advice is: use it *for propaganda*,' wrote Lenin in an exhaustive string of comments, 'for clearly it can serve *no other* useful purpose.... Be extremely polite to Nansen, *extremely insolent* to Wilson, Lloyd George and Clemenceau. This is ... the *only* way to speak to them.'

Both Chicherine and Litvinov suggested thanking Nansen and proposing a meeting. Lenin agreed, with this qualification:

> I would ... advise ... elaborating ... the separation of (a) the humanitarian and (b) the *political* aspect ... You mention the humanitarian ... nature of the proposal? For this all thanks and compliments to Nansen *personally*. If it's humanitarian aims, then do not *bring* politics *into it*, dear sir, but *just start shipping* (stress this.)

But if the proposal concerned what Lenin called a '*truce*',

> then this is *politics*! You are an educated man, Mr Nansen, you know perfectly well that *every* war and *every* truce is *politics*. This means YOU have linked the 'humanitarian' with the 'political'. *You* have lumped them together! Explain to him, as you would to a 16-year-old schoolgirl, why a truce is *politics*.

'Is it a good thing – to mix the "humanitarian" with "politics?" ' Lenin went on.

No, it is a bad thing, because it is hypocrisy, for which *you* are not to blame, and it is *not you* we are blaming. For one must talk *frankly* about politics without taking cover behind 'humanitarianism'.

'Wind up with a *résumé*,' Lenin concluded.

If it is politics, then we propose a *truce* for peace ... we are always ready for talks with those *who are really to blame* for the [civil] war. If it is *not* politics *but* humanitarianism, we say thank you ... we must not miss the opportunity of replying to Nansen in a way that would make *good* propaganda.

And that fundamentally was the reply which, over the name of Chicherine, was sent to Nansen on 7 May by radio.

Via Stockholm and Copenhagen it eventually reached Paris on 15 May. By then Nansen, exhausted, confused and in despair, like most others at the Conference, and shrinking from more exorbitant hotel bills, had left Paris and returned to Christiania. Unable to see through Russian motives, any more than through those of the Americans, he took comfort from Chicherine's reply and, through the American Embassy in Copenhagen, telegraphed Hoover that he proposed to meet Soviet delegates, probably in Stockholm. In polite terms, Hoover ordered him to do nothing of the sort.

The Big Four understood that they had failed again. They had no Russian policy, and the Nansen plan had only been one more expedient. In any case, interest was waning. The Conference was dominated by a belief in the transience of the Communist regime, and Admiral Kolchak, the main White Russian commander, with his capital at Omsk in Siberia, was making notable progress. 'I am beginning to believe Nansen's relief expedition a mistake,' McCormick himself wrote in his diary. In one of the mercurial changes of mood that characterised the Peace Conference the Big Four and others now took the sanguine view that Kolchak, after all, would overthrow Lenin, removing the need for the food weapon or other diplomatic stratagems.

Nansen himself clung to a belief that he would still, somehow, be going to help Russia. He made desultory moves on his own behalf. He spent months waiting at home for the call that never came, before grasping that he and the plan attached to his name had been quietly dropped. To fill the vacuum, he returned to his novel, which took the place of the diary he had now ceased to keep. 'One sits here quite powerless,' he made his hero say.

Just think of the poor ill-treated Russian people – the victorious civilised world sits there playing with those dying people like pieces in a game of chess – and meanwhile allows them to continue being tortured.

As was his wont, he repeated the gist in current letters, notably to his old friend Pastor Vilhelm Holdt from the now distant Bergen days. 'In my loneliness, I often think of you and the many happy years we were together,' he concluded.

In gloomy *Polhøgda* overlooking the fjord he was faced with his insoluble dilemma of being unable to make contact with his children when they were present and missing them when they were not. The two girls, Liv and Immi, were at university in America. Nansen himself had sent his sons away. Kåre, the elder, was now working in Northern Norway as a lumberjack; Odd, his younger brother, had been placed with family friends while preparing for matriculation.

In November Nansen briefly visited London to speak once more on behalf of the League of Nations, but in a state of disillusion. The League, he had told Sigrun, was 'an outward form with very little substance'.

For some time, Nansen had been begging Kathleen Scott to marry him. Knowing about Sigrun, however – besides being seventeen years younger – she had hesitated all along, and now with finality said No. On 17 December, upon this rejection, and soon after returning home, Nansen married Sigrun at last. It was a very quiet civil wedding with only one or two friends present. At least after twelve years Nansen was no longer on his own, and the house had a mistress again. This did not altogether remove his everlasting melancholy. The auguries of his marriage aside, twice in one year a mission had slipped from his grasp. As he tried fictionally to convey in his abortive novel, he felt the classic superfluous man.

71

Getting Them Home

'The Council of the League of Nations,' began a telegram that reached Nansen unexpectedly one day in April 1920,

> proposes to pass the following resolution ... that Prof. Fridtjof Nansen be appointed ... to investigate ... measures ... to relieve the sufferings of the ... large numbers of Prisoners of War still ... in captivity in foreign lands.... The Council is anxious to know ... whether you would accept this invitation if it were made.

The telegram was signed by Sir Eric Drummond, first Secretary-General of the League of Nations, but it was to someone else that Nansen owed this call to action.

This was an Englishman called Philip Baker, better known under his later name of Philip Noel-Baker, a member of the British Delegation to the Peace Conference. He had been closely concerned in the drafting of the Covenant of the League, as its constitution was called, and then joined the permanent Secretariat. After a fleeting encounter during the Conference Baker (as he was still known), like many another, was overwhelmed by Nansen's personality and saw that it might be turned to the League's account.

Brought into being by the signature at Versailles on 28 June 1919 of the peace treaty with Germany, the League was unable to become operative until the treaty itself came into force on 10 January 1920. It was then an obscure body mainly concerned with administering certain provisions of the Treaty of Versailles. Further to diminish its standing, the United States Senate had refused to ratify the Treaty of Versailles and the Covenant of the League, so that the Americans had withdrawn. As quickly as possible, Baker wanted to give the League a proper title to existence. The repatriation of prisoners of war was his chance.

Except for a handful in Russia, their erstwhile co-belligerent, the victorious Allies had repatriated their own prisoners of war. The problem concerned Germany and the Central Powers, the defeated enemies. More than a year after the Armistice something like a quarter of a million of their prisoners of war were still held in Russia and perhaps 200,000 Russians in Germany. There had been various suggestions that the

491

League might somehow help, though the International Committee of the Red Cross would actually do the work.

Baker adroitly manipulated these circumstances to appropriate from the Red Cross the whole question of the prisoners of war to the League. The two bodies were preposterously different. For half a century the ICRC had protected wounded soldiers and prisoners of war. Its founding father was Henri Dunant, a citizen (like Rousseau) of Geneva, which had become its seat. Wholly Swiss, the ICRC was the product of self-interest tempered by public service; practical, businesslike, free of cant, and universally respected.

By contrast, the League of Nations was generally derided for high-mindedness, compounded by a vein of frivolity. Few wanted to work for it, because it was held to be a transitory freak. Baker, on that account, saw in the League a stepping stone in his as yet undefined career. It was he who first suggested to Drummond the appointment of a 'special Commissioner' for the prisoners of war, proposed Nansen, and quickly ensured that his proposal was adopted by the League's ruling bodies.

When Drummond's telegram arrived Nansen was once more in the grip of restlessness. Sigrun had turned out a good housewife, restoring warmth to the empty shell that he had called his home, but it was not enough. The first reports had just arrived from Amundsen, saying that he had doubled Cape Chelyuskin, but was beset in *Maud* just to the east. It was enough to rouse his wanderlust, and he dredged up his old idea of an expedition to Mongolia. He also acted as an intermediary in Soviet peace overtures to England.

'The proposition is so entirely new to me that I do not know what to answer,' Nansen replied to Drummond.

> As I understand it ... the whole task would mean years of work ... in that case I cannot accept this important appointment as it would mean that I had to give up my scientific work. But if I am mistaken, and it would mean less work than I expect, I might of course reconsider it.

'The work ... will not be as great as you suppose,' Sir Eric mellifluously telegraphed back.

> Actual execution of measures decided on might be placed in other hands if you personally found it impossible to continue. It is true that for next few months any other work would no doubt be difficult.... Nevertheless ... the League would urge you very strongly to accept their invitation as they could find no one with such great experience and authority to carry out the negotiations required.

Three days later, on 17 April, Nansen telegraphed that he 'might be able to accept' provided that the preliminary work could be done at home, 'as I could then finish my scientific work here now [on] hand'. As it happened, he and Bjørn Helland-Hansen, pioneers in their still esoteric field, had just finished an article on the effects of sunspots on climatic change. Now Nansen was writing a paper on the formation of coastlines and the continental shelf. Of all this Sir Eric was naturally ignorant, but his appeal had been nicely pitched. By the time Nansen replied he had already started preparations. 'I am offered good assistance here,' he telegraphed.

> It would however be desirable to get a suitable man for assistance from you as your representative ... and bring all information.... We could then start work at once as there is certainly no time to lose if prisoners shall be back before winter.

Sir Eric immediately sent Philip Baker post haste to Norway. It was not merely to bring information. It was to make absolutely sure that Nansen would cease to wobble.

Baker arrived in Christiania on 23 April. Being on an official mission he stayed at the British Legation, from which he telephoned to Nansen, expecting to be summoned to the presence. Instead, it was the celebrated figure of awe that speedily descended on *him*, at the wheel of a Model 'T' Ford and clearly a menace on the roads. While in America on his wartime food mission, Nansen had become utterly captivated by the motor car, and the Ford had been among his baggage when he returned. Henceforth it replaced horses in his affection. He allowed no one else to drive.

Baker found little difficulty in persuading Nansen finally to confirm his acceptance of the post. For hours they talked, sizing each other up. Though concealed from themselves, they had at least one thing in common: each had developed a visible taste for good works, while concealing within himself a morose streak of harshness or even cruelty. Even now Nansen's eldest daughter Liv, twenty-eight years old and out in the world, living in America, was haunted by 'the everlasting thundercloud at home' and hoped that 'with the passage of time I shall get over the painful memories'. Nansen's other children all felt more or less the same. In Baker's case, it was his wife, Irene, who bore the brunt. Such displays of outward charity and arid inner harshness are an old contradiction, of which modern 'humanitarians' are only the latest example.

Born in 1889, and thus nearly thirty years younger than Nansen, Philip Baker was a product of King's College, Cambridge. He was up before the war, at a time when the university was distinguished by a certain foetid atmosphere of bachelor dons swooning over attractive undergraduates. He was a contemporary of Maynard Keynes, the economist, and Rupert Brooke. More to the point where Nansen was concerned, Baker had been climbing and skiing in the Alps. He was an Olympic athlete. At the Stockholm Olympic Games in 1912 he had run in the 800 metres and 1,500 metres, coming sixth in the latter. To Nansen Baker represented the spirit of youth, for which he was beginning to pine.

Baker happened to be a Quaker. On that account, and being a conscientious objector, he chose non-combatant service in the war. Together with some Cambridge friends he served creditably in a volunteer ambulance unit. He was decorated for bravery. In 1918, through family connections, he was appointed by the Foreign Office to the section dealing with the League of Nations.

At the Peace Conference, and later in the embryonic League, Baker exerted considerable influence, out of all proportion to his junior position. He displayed a formidable combination of determination, plausibility and guile. Small, neat and dapper, what he lacked was presence and trustworthiness. Both Nansen possessed aplenty. They complemented each other. Nansen, looking for a sense of purpose, was given a mission and a new lease of life. In return Baker had found someone through whom, as he thought, he could attain his own ends. This was the compact into which they tacitly entered at the British Legation in Christiania on that day in April 1920.

After their talk, Baker telegraphed to Drummond confirming Nansen's final acceptance, but chiefly about squaring the ICRC 'because am privately informed [they] consider themselves discarded and are resentful'. This was hardly surprising. The care of prisoners of war properly belonged to the ICRC.

For all his naïveté and Baker's supercilious talk, Nansen grasped that the ICRC held the key to success. He proposed a meeting. The ICRC quickly organised one in Berlin, on 18 May, at the Hotel Esplanade. Besides the ICRC, German organisations were represented and, in the person of a former Russian prisoner of war, Viktor Kopp, the Soviet authorities too. Of Nansen a German delegate, Gustav Hilger, noted that

> his humane attitude and integrity raised him far above the surroundings into which the chaos of post-war Europe had plunged him. Everything that Nansen said and did was directed exclusively and without compromise to the welfare of suffering humanity. He was quite simply incapable of understanding that ... anyone could make political capital out of ... problems like the repatriation of prisoners of war ...

Hilger was a member of the *Reichzentralstelle für Kriegs- und Zivilgefangene*, the central German organisation for repatriating prisoners. Moritz Schlesinger, head of the organisation, was also at the meeting. From both men Nansen learned at first hand one essential fact: without any dabbling by the League – to which Germany did not in any case belong – but with the help of the ICRC, the *Reichzentralstelle* had negotiated an agreement with the Soviets for the exchange of their own prisoners. Likewise a representative of the ICRC, Edouard August Frick, had made a similar arrangement for the prisoners of the Central Powers.

This latter group came chiefly from the successor states of the now defunct Habsburg Empire: Austria, Hungary, Czechoslovakia, and the various Balkan satrapies congealing into what eventually became Yugoslavia. Still chaotic and penurious, they were in no condition to help their nationals, to whom revolution and anarchy in Russia had caused horrible suffering. The breakdown of society meant that the organisations responsible for them had collapsed. Moreover, by a cruel paradox, the Bolsheviks had released all prisoners of war. This meant that they were technically free to go where they pleased but had nobody to take responsibility for them. Many tried making their way home independently. Probably worst off were a hundred thousand or so in Siberia. Under agreements already made, the Soviets had undertaken to collect and transport the prisoners to the border. The difficulty was to get them home from there. Transport in eastern Europe had largely broken down. Nansen now understood that this was his essential problem.

At the Berlin meeting he explained that 'at first, he had been inclined to reject the mission of the League of Nations, because it appeared insoluble', to quote the minutes of the proceedings.

> But after he had heard and seen here how much had already been efficiently done, the mission no longer appeared so difficult. If the representatives of ... the Red Cross were prepared to continue ... the work already begun, then his duty was mainly to solve financial difficulties.

That basically was the bargain struck. As Gustave Ador, its President, had indicated, the ICRC had long since laid its plans. Its delegates had gone out into the field, often at great risk to themselves. So the ICRC would continue to do the work but the League of Nations would collar the prestige. Ador was prepared to accept this arrangement as the price for being able to complete what he had begun. To their eternal credit, the ICRC never publicly complained.

The main repatriation route was via the Baltic, from the Estonian port of Narva to Schweinemünde in Germany. The bottleneck was shipping. As Nansen had foreseen, his task would be to speed the process to save the prisoners from another disastrous winter in captivity, ravaged by cold, malnutrition and disease.

To that end he had to find funds. Neither the League nor the ICRC had money of their own, but had to beg it for any project. To complicate matters, there was antagonism between the ICRC and its offshoots, the national Red Cross societies, which Nansen would have to smooth out. As for the League, Nansen agreed with Baker that it needed £670,000 (£11,000,000 or $18,000,000 in present terms) for the work of repatriation, and hurried off to London to get it, arriving on 4 June. He became involved in a succession of inconclusive meetings. For all his fame and personality he was helpless when faced with the intricacies of government finance. He was rescued from this predicament by Thomas Lodge, an English businessman and former civil servant who had represented the ministry of shipping at the Peace Conference. Lodge was still in Paris and, in his own words,

> I received a pressing invitation from the League of Nations to help Nansen in the administration of the finances of ... repatriation ... I was convened to a meeting with Nansen in London and I went there with the outline of the general basis.... To me at that moment Nansen was just a name, distinguished in ... exploration but an unknown quantity in that strange world of post-Versailles politics.
>
> Had I found in that room the ordinary European politician, even the most reputable of that class, I think I would have found some excuse for wriggling out of the venture. But when I met Nansen I found a man living on a plane where wriggling just was not done. I don't mean that Nansen gave expression to any very impressive lofty sentiments.... What I found was a man completely single-minded, influenced only by the consideration as to where his immediate duty lay ... and, with some misgivings but with no hesitation, I began the most satisfying episode in my life, a personal collaboration with Nansen.

Meanwhile, Nansen was confronted with another hurdle. Speeding the repatriation depended on the goodwill of the Soviet authorities within Russia, but relations between her and the West were fluid and ill-defined. By now the civil war had all but ended and the Soviets had won. In London Nansen was introduced to a Russian called Leonid Krassin, sent over by the Soviets to pave the way for the opening of diplomatic relations. Once they met, curiously enough, at No. 10 Downing Street, in the presence of Lloyd George, suggesting that Nansen was being used in the tortuous byways of Anglo-Soviet relations. Then in Copenhagen on 26 June, by way of Geneva for a meeting with the ICRC, Nansen met Maxim Litvinov, the deputy Soviet Foreign Minister, who was staying in the Danish capital similarly to open relations with the West. As a result he decided that he would have to go to Moscow.

After an arduous journey by sea and rail via Tallinn in Estonia, Nansen reached Moscow in the second week of July. There he met Georgiy Chicherine and, for the first time, could put a face to the signature of the Soviet Foreign Minister on the verbose reply to his telegram from Paris the year before. Chicherine turned out to be small, nervous, eccentric, fluttering and effeminate. With his high-pitched voice, hypochondria, formidable intellect and aristocratic background, he was one of the weirder characters thrown up by the revolution.

Since the Soviets did not recognise the League of Nations – to them it was a capitalist conspiracy – Chicherine began by rejecting Nansen's credentials. Nansen, by way of riposte, demanded a special train to take him back to the frontier. Upon which Chicherine backed down. The Soviets were hungry for recognition and international respectability. Chicherine, like Baker, saw in Nansen a means to his own ends. He agreed that

Nansen could be considered as representing the member states individually.

Having settled that matter, Nansen was introduced to the man in charge of evacuating all prisoners of war. This was the proletarian, gangster-like, revolver-toting Comrade Alexander Vladimirowitch Eiduk. Like so many of the nastier Communist officials he was a Latvian, and a sometime member of the Cheka, as the Soviet Secret Police was then called. Eiduk gave assurances that prisoners would be gathered, looked after, and regularly transported to borders and ports. There seemed no need to question that this would be done: enforcing orders was clearly Eiduk's métier.

However, the question of money for repatriation was still unresolved. The League had chosen to raise funds through the International Committee on Relief Credits in Paris. This had been formed in April that year as a mechanism for financing post-war European reconstruction. While Nansen was in Moscow the League's application was blocked by Britain and France. However, Sir Eric Drummond, nineteen years in the Foreign Office, was the quintessential Whitehall mandarin, and therefore understood the ways of government. He sent Baker to see A.J. Balfour, a member of Lloyd George's Cabinet. Balfour remembered Nansen vividly from his previous contacts before the war, and now interceded on his behalf. As a result, when Nansen went to Paris for a meeting about Relief Credits on 28 July he got what he wanted. That disposed of his immediate financial difficulties.

Meanwhile, he received from Philip Baker a letter saying:

> I shall be leaving for Antwerp on the 9th or 10th August ... If necessary I will, of course, stay later than that, although that would, I am afraid, prejudice still further my very slender chances of doing any good in the Olympic Games!

These were the seventh modern Olympics, the first since the war. Baker had been selected to run for Great Britain in the 800 and 1,500 metres, as he had done in Stockholm, eight years previously. Somehow, among all his scurrying around, Baker had found time to train. He was in fact a pioneer in systematic athletic training. In any case, he had enormous natural talent. Although now thirty-one years old, he came back with the silver medal in the 1,500 metres. If nothing else, it made Nansen admire him all the more and, conversely, strengthened the hold he had on Nansen.

In the meantime Balfour who, behind a foppish pose, concealed great humanity, was helping Nansen with ships. Under the Treaty of Versailles the German mercantile marine had been sequestrated as part of war reparations. Since the vessels were interned in German ports and would be manned by local German crews, they could rapidly be put into service. Balfour quickly arranged for as many ships as necessary to be released.

Somehow, men of infuence were attracted by Nansen's personality. Charter rates were lowered, so he was able to husband his finances. Eventually, fifteen ships were put on the Baltic run.

Eiduk at any rate was as good as his word. The trains kept rolling; the prisoners arrived at the transit camps on time, often in larger numbers than promised. More Baltic ports were used; other routes were opened. There was one through the Black Sea from Novorossisk to Trieste. Some prisoners in eastern Siberia were evacuated through Vladivostok; one of Nansen's assistants (not of the League) cut down costs by letting ships take cargo as well as passengers.

Nansen was however balked in his hope of getting all prisoners out by the winter. In the middle of September 1920 he presided over a conference on the subject at Kovno, the capital of Lithuania, on neutral ground.

One reason for the delays in repatriation had been the closure of most land routes by the war between Poland and Russia. In the spring of 1920 the Russians invaded Poland. It was the first campaign in what Lenin himself called 'the creation of a world soviet republic'. The Red Army reached the gates of Warsaw. There, in the middle of August, in one of the decisive battles of the century, sometimes called 'the miracle of the Vistula', the Polish Army, under Marshal Pilsudski, routed the Russians and drove them out. When Nansen arrived at the conference in Kovno, however, the Russian delegates were not noticeably chastened by defeat.

To care for the prisoners still stranded in Russia for another winter, relief had to be organised. The Russians still declined to deal with any existing international body, least of all the League. They were content, however, to treat with Nansen as an individual. So at Kovno an organisation was established under his personal responsibility. Called *Nansenhilfe* ('Nansen Aid'), with headquarters in Berlin, it collected funds and distributed food, clothing and medical aid. The Russians refused entry to most of the foreign supervisors, including those from the ICRC. They were meticulous, however, in distributing the supplies themselves.

Nansen had changed much since the days on *Fram*, when he intruded on other people's work. He had learned to delegate, too much, perhaps. Indeed, as time went on he became more or less a figurehead. Yet on 18 November 1920 he could stand up during the first Assembly of the League of Nations – after a nomadic existence at last installed in its permanent home in Geneva – and announce that nearly 200,000 prisoners of war had been repatriated in both directions. It was the only concrete accomplishment on the part of the whole organisation. He had saved the League – temporarily at least – from being an otiose talking shop. There were those who felt that he might have saved it altogether.

By the summer of 1922 repatriation had been completed. In his final report to the League, Nansen announced that nearly 430,000 prisoners of war had been repatriated, of whom 200,000 had been Russians from

Germany and Central Europe. The total cost was around £400,000 (£7,000,000 or $11,000,000 in present terms).

When a member of the League Secretariat tried to belittle the work of the ICRC and, in his own words, 'make a splash about this event' in order to appropriate all prestige for the League, Baker had the grace to object. Nansen also knew full well to whom praise was really due. 'It is through the agency of the International Committee of the Red Cross,' he told the Assembly of the League, 'that practically the whole of the work in which I have been able to take a part has been accomplished.'

72

Seduced by Lenin

'I have just come from a country with the least freedom I have yet known,' wrote Nansen on the long way home from his mission to Moscow in 1920. The addressee was a young Swedish woman called Estrid Linder, whom he had met on the Atlantic crossing in 1917, when going on his food mission to America – she was on her way to Japan – and with whom he had kept up a sporadic correspondence. 'My dear sweet friend,' his letter actually began, 'if only you had been here ... I would have taken you in my arms and hugged you ... so that you would nearly have suffocated.' One of his latest female confidantes, Miss Linder was light-hearted, adventurous, intelligent, well-bred, with aristocratic good looks. The letter proceeded:

I felt as if I was in a prison or under surveillance the whole time ... I think of Hamlet's words:

'The time is out of joint; oh cursed spite
That ever I was born to set it right!'

Don't think that I ... attach any significance to my own little self ... but nonetheless there is this corrosive feeling of not being able to detach oneself, and which gives one no peace unless one does all one can to help, even if little comes of it. But there is no point in being melancholy, it doesn't help, one has to be cheerful and believe in the future, otherwise it's no use. But Heavens above it is sometimes difficult, one becomes so tired; people are often so difficult to deal with, and cause so much unnecessary trouble.... In Russia there was a complete drought both in the wheatfields and among the population, a country deserted by its good genius, everything was muted, even emotions.... The present kind of communism is hardly sustainable in the long run.

Nansen heard of a food shortage in Petrograd, and made a half-hearted, abortive attempt to organise relief. As his outpouring hinted, he was disenchanted with Russia. Sometimes he now appeared disenchanted with life itself. When Colin Archer died, in February, at the age of eighty-nine, not even memories of *Fram* could send Nansen down the fjord to Larvik for his funeral. 'A huge pile of telegrams ... had to be answered immediately,' he wrote to a friend, so I had to give up the idea, and was represented by the ... mayor.... But I should like to have been there.... Alas, there are not many like him.

Like many another, Nansen felt that the giants were passing away and pygmies were taking over. 'It is the individual and not the masses who can save the world from the misery of our times,' he declared. '[We ought] to establish the Fourth International for individualism against Communism.' That was a dig at the Third International, formed in Moscow two years earlier to propagate Communist revolution. It was Lenin's answer to the League of Nations.

To console himself, Nansen returned to his scientific work. He had three projects under way. He was finishing off his paper on the formation of coastlines, and also considering two further monographs on climatic change. 'This is after all my real work,' he told Frick,

and in the long run it is no good to split oneself up in doing soon one thing, soon another; so now I have to concentrate ... on my real work, because I have found that all this splitting takes very much out of one.

Nansen was unusually content to be at home. Immi, his younger daughter, had returned from America and, in her merry, inconsequential way, brought a touch of happiness to *Polhøgda*. What is more, when he had to travel, Sigrun had been prepared to go with him, which Eva had rarely done.

Besides his post as High Commissioner for the repatriation of prisoners of war, Nansen had been appointed a Norwegian delegate to the Assembly of the League of Nations. Despite his protests he enjoyed, and psychologically needed, the public persona that this offered. After all, it merely involved a few weeks in Geneva during the autumn. As in the past, he was the only man of stature his country could provide. But he was suffering the strains of a fragmented personality. Approaching sixty, with heavy features, a massive, drooping moustache, and a slightly puzzled cast to his habitual melancholy gaze, he looked like a Viking who had lost his ship.

Early in October 1920, Nansen called on the British Minister in Christiania, Sir M. Findlay, to urge the admission of Germany to the League of Nations – a highly contentious proposal. Nansen's interest could be traced, on the one hand, to his German contacts, on the other to his experience with the Russians. He thought Britain might welcome a proposal from a neutral power, but the Foreign Office refused to discuss the matter.

For their part, the Americans were cheerfully using Nansen to try and free citizens of theirs taken hostage by Russia in a bid to break out of diplomatic isolation by forcing the United States to recognise the Communist regime. Then, on 13 July 1921, he received, along with other people, a surprising telegram from Russia. It was signed by Maxim Gorky, the celebrated novelist who four years earlier had sent him a letter urging him to write a biography of Columbus. Marked 'Collect, 103.10 Norwegian kroner' (about £100 or $160 in present terms), the telegram ran:

TO ALL HONEST PEOPLE
SOUTHEAST RUSSIAN CORNGROWING STEPPES SMITTEN BY CROPFAILURE CAUSED BY DROUGHT STOP THIS CALAMITY MENACES HUNGER DEATH TO MILLIONS OF RUSSIAN POPULATION STOP THINK OF RUSSIAN PEOPLES EXHAUSTION BY WAR AND REVOLUTION WHICH REDUCED CONSIDERABLY ITS RESISTANCE TO DISEASE AND ITS PHYSICAL ENDURANCE STOP GLOOMY DAYS HAVE COME FOR COUNTRY OF TOLSTOY DOSTOYEVSKY MENDELEYEV PAVLOV MUSSORGSKY GLINKA AND OTHER WORLD-PRIZED MEN AND I VENTURE TO TRUST THAT CULTURED EUROPEAN AND AMERICAN PEOPLE CONCEIVING TRAGEDY OF RUSSIAN PEOPLE WILL IMMEDIATELY SUCCOUR WITH BREAD AND MEDICINES STOP ... RUSSIAS MISFORTUNE OFFERS HUMANITARIANS SPLENDID OPPORTUNITY TO DEMONSTRATE VITALITY OF HUMANITARIANISM STOP I THINK PARTICULARLY WARM SYMPATHY IN SUCCOURING RUSSIAN PEOPLE MUST BE SHOWN BY THOSE WHO DURING IGNOMINIOUS WAR SO PASSIONATELY PREACHED FRATRICIDAL HATRED ... I ASK ALL HONEST EUROPEAN AND AMERICAN PEOPLE FOR PROMPT AID TO RUSSIAN PEOPLE STOP GIVE BREAD AND MEDICINES STOP

On several counts, this is an interesting document. To begin with, it was the first Soviet admission of disaster to be released abroad. Iron censorship and carefully guided tours for foreign sympathisers had so far veiled reality from the outside world. More to the point, this opened the first charity chantage of the century. The words were ascribed to Gorky, but the formula was Lenin's. He had invented the exploitation of famine as moral blackmail on the West. We are living with the echoes still.

Gorky had been ordered, or persuaded, to issue his appeal as a result of dire need. Lenin, the new autocrat of all the Russias, with his lust for power, was now uncertain in the saddle. Early in March, there had been a mutiny at Kronstadt, the naval base outside Petrograd. It was the second of its kind. The first Kronstadt mutiny had been a prelude to the Bolshevik revolution in 1917. This one was provoked by a feeling that the revolution had been betrayed. To quote one of their own slogans, the Kronstadt sailors were now rebelling against the 'yoke of the Communists'. They had merely exchanged one autocracy for another. In a military onslaught on 17 March, amid scenes of horrifying butchery, the uprising was ruthlessly crushed. Before that happened, the unrest had spread to Petrograd itself. The régime was shaken to the core.

Lenin was beset by other troubles. 'War communism' – that is, regimentation of labour, absolute state control, abolition of private property – had left the economy in ruins. The political dangers were worse, to which the Kronstadt mutiny bore witness. The supreme exponent of the tactical retreat, Lenin sanctioned the New Economic Policy – NEP for short. This was a kind of half-caste capitalism. It allowed private enterprise up to a certain level, with the state holding the commanding heights of heavy industry and transport. The first of the decrees establishing the NEP was promulgated a week after the Kronstadt uprising was suppressed.

Worst of all was agricultural disaffection. As Nansen had observed, there had been a drought the year before. This was followed by a hard winter and a second successive drought. By the early summer of 1921, in certain parts of the country, a crop failure was looming. This was nothing new. A cycle of good years and lean ones was part of Russian history. On this occasion, political dogma gave an abominable twist to events. Collectivisation was still in the future. Instead the new Communist régime ordered the peasants to deliver their surplus to the state. They refused to comply. As a result, they were subject to requisition by armed patrols. That kindled even deeper resentment.

The NEP abolished requisition, and substituted a tax in kind. But by then it was too late. The peasants had responded to the old dispensation by hiding food from the requisition patrols, and only tilling enough for their own needs. That meant they had no reserves. Now in a country like Russia, straddling a variety of climatic zones, famine is a contradiction in terms, because a poor harvest in one region will be balanced by a bumper crop in another. What was happening now was that the transport system was on the verge of collapse, so that grain could not be moved where it was needed. The upshot was incipient famine in the so-called 'Black Earth' provinces. This was the densely populated fertile region round the Volga, in which about one third the inhabitants of European Russia then lived. The impending disaster was an artificial product of the system.

It was another miscalculation of Lenin's warped mind. He wanted to crush the peasants because, in their devotion to the land, he saw the citadel of capitalism and the heart of resistance to Communism. He had been prepared to starve them into submission. He had not counted on a famine. It threatened the foundations of his régime. Lenin was left with the only alternative of appealing to the capitalist world. He could not, however, publicly admit a mistake. So he resorted to a characteristic stratagem.

It began with a loosening of press censorship. On 26 June 1921 *Pravda* admitted famine among a population of around 25,000,000. About a month later an ostensibly non-governmental body, dubbed the All-Russia Famine Relief Committee, was called into being. To produce a sheen of independence for the benefit of what Lenin liked to call 'useful idiots' in the West, a majority of non-Communist public figures from the suppressed and officially forgotten past, some just released from prison, were appointed to the Committee. To keep an eye on them, Lenin planted what he called a 'Communist cell' among them. In fact, on the committee were early members of the *nomenklatura*, the Communist ruling class. The chairman happened to be Lev Borisovitch Kamenev, Chairman of the Moscow Soviet. Thus was born one of the embryonic 'front' organisations of the Soviet era.

The most famous, and therefore most useful, member of the committee was Maxim Gorky. It was in that capacity that he had issued his appeal. To enhance the pathos, the Patriarch Tikhon, head of the Russian Orthodox Church, had been allowed to attach a call of his own to the telegram from Gorky.

Nansen quickly telegraphed back to Gorky:

ONLY PEOPLE WHO CAN HELP MATERIALLY NOW ARE AMERICANS BUT SERIOUS OBSTACLE WILL BE THAT AMERICAN CITIZENS ARE RETAINED IN RUSSIA ... MUST THEREFORE MOST URGENTLY ADVISE THAT THEY ARE RELEASED AT ONCE OTHERWISE I FEAR YOU CANNOT EXPECT MUCH HELP FROM AMERICA.

The American Minister in Christiania, A.G. Schmedeman, who may or may not have drafted the reply, thanked Nansen for sending it.

In the meanwhile Nansen had become modestly involved in relief on his own. This followed an earlier request by Gorky for aid for Petrograd. Nansen was presented with a stock of salted fish in Finland to help feed the population of the city. He offered the fish to the Russians provided that a Norwegian representative, nominated by himself, be admitted to supervise distribution. Lenin agreed to the demand, 'as an exception, with the exception strictly specified', he told the Politbureau. They in their turn rubber-stamped acceptance on 11 July, two days before Gorky made his emotional appeal.

Gorky's sentimental bombast had left Nansen unmoved, but a letter from Paris, in Nansen's own words, 'has thrown a new match into my soul'. The writer was John Gorvin, Secretary of the International Committee on Relief Credits, and closely connected with Nansen in the repatriation work. Prompted by reports filtering through to the Press, he now, for unclear reasons, wanted Nansen to persuade the American and European governments to start international relief for Russia. 'If I can be of any real use for the organisation,' Nansen declared, 'I ... cannot take the responsibility of refusing.' Put another way Gorvin, unlike Gorky, promised action, and the continuation of the public persona which Nansen desperately needed. As a first step, he immediately telegraphed Chicherine for Soviet views.

Gorvin's letter arrived on 27 July, just as Nansen was about to drive off in his old Ford to go fishing in the mountains. 'I fear the nerves are giving way, and I must try to escape for a little while', Nansen wrote to another of his female confidantes. On this occasion it was Lili Sulzer, the beautiful and elegant wife of the Swiss Ambassador in Washington when Nansen was there on his food mission during the war. He had written to her 'in my tower looking out on the fjord at the many white sails glittering in the setting sun', soon after returning home in 1918, reminiscing about week-end excursions together en famille into the country outside Washington. The Sulzers were probably his closest friends during that phase of his life. 'Is it not cruel, how we must meet to part,' he then continued. 'Now the whole Atlantic Ocean is between us, and we can only meet in our thoughts.' The Sulzers had since returned to Switzerland but still it had seemed hard to meet.

Nansen came home from his fishing holiday to find himself overtaken by events. Herbert Hoover had replied to Gorky upon his appeal being printed in the Press and offered aid through the American Relief Admini-stration. The Russians had been taken by surprise. Hoover demanded as part of his price the release of the American hostages. The Russians capitulated, and were already negotiating with the ARA in Riga, which left Nansen without a rôle in that particular affair.

However, waiting for him at home he found an invitation from Gustave Ador to a conference in Geneva on the Russian famine organised by the ICRC and the League of Red Cross Societies. He also received a telegram from Berlin, signed by Frick, Gorvin and Lodge, old cronies from the repatriation of prisoners-of-war, proposing that they all meet at Riga to discuss aid to Russia. The latter promising more, Nansen accepted it instead.

What he did not know was that Philip Baker lay behind this. Frick and his companions had originally planned a trip at this time to inspect prisoner-of-war transit camps which Nansen, incidentally, had refused to join. The journey had been diverted to the famine instead. Frick was on his way to Moscow on behalf of the joint Red Cross Conference in Geneva. Baker persuaded him to call for Nansen. Behind the scenes, Baker was also canvassing the conference. This was an extensive gathering, mainly of private charities. It took place on 15-16 August. It invited Nansen and Herbert Hoover to be its joint High Commissioners. Hoover, now Secretary of Commerce in President Harding's Republican administration, besides being head of the ARA, declined. Because of Baker's assiduous lobbying, the conference then appointed Nansen on his own. He was apprised by telegram on 17 August, just as he was leaving for Riga. He immediately telegraphed his acceptance, and so departed with credentials of a kind.

He arrived at Riga on 20 August. In the same place, on the same day, the ARA and the Russians concluded their agreement. Maxim Litvinov, Deputy Commmissar for Foreign Affairs, signed for the Soviet Union; Walter Lyman Brown, its European Director, signed for the ARA.

On the face of it, as at the start of the Peace Conference in Paris, Nansen had come all the way merely to join the hangers-on. Since the newly-won independence of the Baltic States and the borderlands, Riga, the capital of Latvia, an austerely beautiful seaport, had become the main crossing point into Russia from the West, and hence a listening post too. An assorted flock of journalists, diplomats, spies and agents of one kind or another had turned the city into a shady mart of news, rumour and intrigue.

Barely half an hour after the signing of the ARA agreement Litvinov received Nansen and his party. They claimed that they could raise £10,000,000 in credits for relief. This was transparently an attempt to outbid Hoover. Nansen wanted to enter Russia to see things for himself. Litvinov objected on the grounds that the information was available in Riga. However, he did ask the Kremlin. The upshot was rapid permission to proceed. On the evening of 22 August Nansen and all his party left by train for Moscow. Before departing, Nansen had hastily to answer a lengthy document from Philip Baker, who was now trying to appropriate famine relief for the League of Nations in order once more to raise its status and, incidentally, help himself in his career.

To the Kremlin, Nansen was a possible counterpoise to Hoover. Chicherine himself negotiated with Nansen, representing the Geneva conference. In two days they raced through their discussions, and on 27 August signed an agreement on famine relief. In part, it was explicitly modelled on that with the ARA. They differed however in certain vital respects. The ARA had secured complete financial and operational independence, recognising none but its own authority, with its own staff brought in from abroad. To help work in the field it was even allowed to form local committees, without official interference. It was a bitter pill for the Soviet authorities to swallow. Nansen, by contrast, was authorised to raise credits on behalf of the Russian government. Besides, he had submitted to Russian authority. His organisation was under the control of a committee of two in Moscow, one member to be nominated by the Kremlin and the other by himself.

In his innocence, Nansen suggested to Chicherine that, instead of an official government nominee, someone from the Famine Relief Committee be appointed as the Russian member of his own committee of two – the International Russian Relief Executive, as it was officially known. What Lenin called 'Nansen's most brazen proposal' in a characteristic note to Stalin, proved that

> we are going to blunder badly unless we keep our eyes peeled ... the ... Committee [is] a screen [for holding] forth against the government.... What are we waiting for?... I propose: this very day, Friday 26 August [the Committee] should be dissolved ... motive: their refusal to work. *Appoint one man from the ... Cheka* to supervise the liquidation.... The whole thing will be done before Nansen leaves. Nansen will be faced with a clear 'ultimatum'.

In other words, the Famine Relief Committee had served its purpose. Western aid had been secured. The Committee was accordingly dissolved. Obviously, Nansen was unaware of this clandestine by-play. He only knew that Chicherine had refused his request. Despite this rebuff, on the day he

signed his agreement Nansen left Moscow (in a special train) with unabated zeal to pursue his mission. He was heading first for London.

There he found scant sympathy. Raising government credits turned out
to be a chimera nurtured by Frick, Gorvin and others of his entourage. 'I
was greatly struck by Dr Nansen's sanguine views,' observed the official
who received him at the Foreign Office. 'I received the impression that the
Bolsheviks had thrown dust in [his] eyes.' Oddly enough, in Moscow, Lenin
was thinking along similar lines. Hoover, he regarded as an inflexible
opponent against whom, in a letter to Chicherine, he called for 'relentless,
persistent warfare'. By contrast, learning that Nansen was being derided
in the British Press for his efforts, Lenin told Chicherine that

> we ... shall ... gain by winning over the 'pro-Nansen' elements and *put an
> end* to the game of the anti-Nansenites.

From London, Nansen hurried on to Geneva where, as he wrote to
Sigrun, 'I am naturally together with [Philip] Baker every day, and he is
just as charming and indefatigably helpful as always.' To put it another
way, Baker once more personally could use Nansen for his own ends,
which still circled round appropriating Russian famine relief for the
League. In fact, Baker induced Nansen to persuade the Norwegian government to raise the matter in the Council, even drafting the necessary
memorandum, with the telling rider that 'it would be fatal if it were known
to *any one* that I was mixed up in it at all!'

For the best part of a month, Nansen remained in Geneva trying, under
Baker's guidance, to cajole the League into approving his agreement with
Chicherine, to adopt the cause of famine relief, and to persuade governments to give credits. The Second Assembly was in session, so it was a time
for oratory. When Nansen stood up to make a speech, he dominated the
gathering. By his presence, he stirred the public galleries as no other
delegate could. But when he sat down, it was with a turgid sense of
anticlimax.

For one thing, he had to contend with the locale. Geneva was only
beginning its rôle of international centre and all it could offer the League
as a debating chamber was the dim and uninspiring *Salle de la Réforma-
tion*. Even in his mother tongue Nansen was no orator. Besides, Baker
wrote his speeches and, tainted by officialese or bathos, or for some other
reason, somehow they did not ring true. In any case, the atmosphere of
Geneva eviscerated the passionate appeal. 'They only use ... words to
conceal their thoughts,' as the jeering Voltaire, once exiled just over the
border at Ferney, had put it, might have been a motto for the League in
the Calvinist city on the lake.

Nansen seemed suddenly a baffled hero. He had naïvely trusted in a
pathetic personal appeal. That illusion was neatly dispelled by Giuseppe
Motta, the Swiss delegate. They were not there as individuals, said Motta,

but as the delegates of States ... Dr Nansen, whose personality was such that
he might be said to be representing himself was, nevertheless, the Delegate
of Norway ... approval of [his] arrangement ... would raise political questions. [I do not] desire the interference of the League ... in the domestic
affairs of a Government.... Only ... charitable organisations ... could usefully
direct this kind of undertaking.

Motta articulated the feelings of the Assembly – and, in particular,
attitudes to Nansen. The underlying dilemma had been posed by Aristide
Briand, the French Prime Minister. Any action 'must be limited to saving
the victims of the famine without the Soviets' being able to exploit the
opportunity to consolidate their position'.

In Moscow not merely had the Famine Relief Committee been dissolved,
but the non-Communist members had been arrested and some of their
leading figures condemned to death by the Cheka. Lenin candidly admitted that they were innocent of any crime, 'but it was necessary for us – for
political reasons – to destroy ... the Committee'. This of course was then
hidden from the world. In the end, chiefly because Hoover protested, Lenin
reprieved the condemned prisoners and deported them to the West. But at
the time the news made an impression in Geneva and elsewhere. 'I knew
that the world was wicked,' Nansen wrote to Sigrun, 'but so much heart-
less villainy is too much.' He did not in fact mean the death sentences, but
the indifference of the League to his appeals.

On the last day of September Nansen made his final remonstrance
before the Assembly. 'I do not think that we shall strengthen the Soviet
government by showing the Russian people that there are hearts in
Europe,' he solemnly declared. 'I appeal to the peoples of Europe ... to the
whole world for their help.... Hasten to act before it is too late to repent.'
The upshot was rejection, clothed in a string of anodyne resolutions. On
the lines of Motta's reasoning, the League declined to engage in Russian
famine relief. Having been widely lauded for his success with the prisoners
of war, Nansen was perplexed by this rebuff. It was the first public failure
of his life.

Early in October, Nansen returned to London once more to appeal to
the authorities. There he again met Kathleen Scott, together with Philip
Baker and Leonid Krassin, now head of the Soviet trade delegation in
London, and Soviet ambassador in all but name. Kathleen was both
irritated and amused at Nansen's obvious naïveté and Krassin's equally
obvious exploitation of it. She was also irritated by Baker's obsequiousness
towards Krassin.

Kathleen berated Krassin for stealing much of her income. Before the
war, the trustees of the Scott Memorial Fund, collected by public subscrip-
tion after her late husband's Antarctic disaster, had invested some of it in
Russian shares because of the astronomical returns. The Bolshevik revolution had put paid to that. Given her own financial loss, Kathleen was

infuriated by Krassin's dapper, imperturbable, opulent, highly capitalistic figure, adorned by white waistcoat, with a Rolls Royce waiting to take him home.

By now, an international conference in Brussels, outside the ambit of the League, had confirmed the refusal of government credits. Nansen would have to call for private charity. So far he had been insulated from the famine. He hurried back to Russia now to see for himself. For his convenience in Moscow, he arranged for a motor car to be shipped from Warsaw. Unfortunately, under the aegis of the luckless Polish chauffeur-cum-mechanic, the vehicle caught fire an hour after first starting in the Russian capital.

On 28 November Nansen reached Saratov on the Volga, in one of the worst afflicted areas. 'So much unhappiness and misery in this world!' he recorded in his diary. 'In ... two days I have seen more than in a whole lifetime.' About ten days later he was back in Moscow, thereafter wiring his colleagues in that spirit.

Have returned from land of shadows [he telegraphed]. All ... people must unite ... to make the governments of Europe grant sufficient credits immediately before it is too late.... Hundreds and thousands are dying daily. People are lying helpless in their houses without food.... We can still save millions of lives if only time left be used to utmost advantage.

Home for Christmas at *Polhøgda*, he continued to issue a stream of heart-rending appeals. To his old friend Vilhelm Holdt in Bergen, he wrote tellingly about 'feeling that one is bearing on one's shoulders all the sorrows of the world'.

The year 1922 opened with little encouragement for Nansen. Towards the end of January he returned to England, once more to try and get money out of the government but also to tour the country and raise private funds. His first appearance was at the Queens Hall in London where Kathleen Scott was in the audience. To Nansen's puzzlement, she was unmoved, believing that since the famine was caused by evil rulers, it was therefore not a worthwhile object of sympathy.

This was an unusually dispassionate reaction among Nansen's audiences. The majority belonged to the well-intentioned, with deep reserves of sentiment. For analogous reasons, the tour was ill organised. Along the way Nansen expressed a passionate desire for a day's fox hunting. The last time had been as Ambassador in London, fourteen years before. He was taken out with the Heythrop Hounds, near Oxford, his host recalling

a very bad day in pouring rain and I ... retain a vivid picture of Nansen galloping about at top speed on every possible occasion, regardless of what the hounds were doing.

After about a fortnight Nansen was back in London, having acquired some personal goodwill and raised perhaps £15,000 (£340,000 or $550,000 in present terms). Despite having met Lloyd George, however, he had still been unable to coax a grant out of the British government. He realised that henceforth he would have to depend on private charity.

To the Soviets this was deplorable. Their foreign propaganda deprecated 'bourgeois philanthropy' and was agitating for foreign credits instead. It was a way of exploiting the famine to promote trade and break out of economic isolation. It was food as a weapon in reverse, as it were. Hoover was out of the question but the Soviet authorities had some hopes of Nansen and now he had failed them – at least in their economic objective. All the same, they felt that politically he might still be of use.

Returning to *Polhøgda* late in February, Nansen received a letter from Vilhelm Holdt saying that his wife, Maria, was mortally ill. 'You two faithful friends,' Nansen wrote, 'gave me a ... home ... associated with some of the best ... of a frequently nomadic and hard-working life.'

> How I would have liked to go to Bergen to see her once more ... but I cannot get away now, I have to remain at my post to do my work for the many starving people in the East.

It was only some hours away by train, and Nansen was not wholly indispensable. As in the case of the prisoners of war, he could not bear to move permanently abroad, and insisted on working from his home, but the real headquarters lay in Geneva. It was a small office called the 'High Commissariat of Dr Nansen'. This belonged to the International Committee for Russian Relief, the body that had emerged from the joint Red Cross Conference that appointed Nansen in the first place. Frick was Nansen's deputy, and there was a Moscow office led by Gorvin. Since mid-February, Nansen had also been represented in the Ukraine.

In the new year he had received from the Norwegian minister in Helsinki, Dr Andreas Urbye, a letter recommending his military attaché, a Captain Vidkun Quisling, who was about to return to the General Staff in Christiania. Quisling, wrote Urbye, 'has a great interest in your work'.

> In every respect – particularly in character, intelligence and knowledge – he is a first-class man, and since he writes and speaks Russian well I imagine he would be of great use to you.

This arrived opportunely. The Kremlin had belatedly admitted to famine in the Ukraine as well. Nansen appointed Quisling his delegate there, and sent him post haste to Kharkov, the Ukrainian capital, at a monthly salary of £60 (£1,400 or $2,200 in present terms). 'He is a very nice and quiet man, whom I am sure you will like,' Nansen wrote to Gorvin in a letter introducing the man whose name, as the arch-collaborator under the Nazi occupation of Norway during the Second World War, eventually became a synonym for traitor.

Nansen's organisation had a dual function. Besides collecting money for its own work it was, through his agreement with Chicherine, a legal umbrella for other charities. One of them happened to be the Swedish Red Cross. They were working at Samara, on the left bank of the Volga. 'The Nansen organisation in Moscow is an unfortunate fiasco,' wrote their head of mission, Eric Einar Ekstrand, a Swedish diplomat seconded to the post, in a confidential report on 23 January.

> There is no order, they had no idea of the whereabouts in Russia of the trains carrying their food supplies, and Gorvin ... was absolutely incapable of dealing with the Russian authorities.

This view was confirmed when British charities sent out their own inspector, Sir Benjamin Robertson, a civil servant from India with experience of famine. 'He felt rather strongly on the subject of Dr Nansen's organisation,' Colonel Haskell, Director of the ARA Russian operation, reported.

> He stated that ... the office in Moscow was in chaos ... There was no distributing organisation in the field, and to his great surprise [a Soviet official] had informed him that the distribution of the Nansen relief was to be made through the Government cooperatives.... Of our own work, he had only the kindest things to say.

At the outset, when the ARA had protested that they merely wanted to feed the starving, Litvinov reiterated that 'food is a weapon'. Hoover, having anticipated the idea, could hardly disagree. He had well-defined objectives. Besides the release of the American hostages, he wanted to absorb an American grain surplus and, to that end, secured a Congressional appropriation of $20,000,000 (£450,000,000 or $600,000,000 in present terms). He wished to deplete Soviet resources to conduct foreign propaganda, and so compelled Russia to hand over gold reserves worth $12,000,000 (£240,000,000 or $360,000,000 in present terms), also spent, incidentally, on American grain. On the assumption that the Communist régime was now permanent, the ARA itself was used both for spying and also to gain a foothold in Russia for future American industrial concessions. Hoover achieved his aims with notable efficiency.

At the height of the famine in the spring and summer of 1922 the ARA was feeding about 8,500,000 people against 400,000 by all other charities combined. It was also distributing grain and seed corn for the harvest. With a staff of about 300 Americans in Russia, and 80,000 local employees, the ARA was practically an autonomous body working with military efficiency. It had its own distribution network, down to soup kitchens in the remote villages of the Volga, and the economic power to bring recalcitrant authorities to heel. It even bent the inefficient Russian railways to its will.

By political calculation Hoover had accomplished rather more than Nansen, who proclaimed unsullied, albeit self-indulgent humanitarian motives. Yet Hoover was reviled by the Soviets and their supporters in the West. To them, he was a capitalist ogre who had exposed their system. In an early ideological campaign, they exploited Nansen's naïveté to promote his reputation and obscure Hoover's services.

At any rate, the ARA kept its distance from Nansen's organisation, and most charities nominally affiliated to it dissociated themselves as far as they could. The British Red Cross and Save the Children Fund were notable examples. In Samara, for instance, the Swedish Red Cross, with proven efficiency, found themselves distributing supplies from an assortment of bodies, including Nansen's own office. Only Quisling, working independently in the Ukraine, seemed exempt from charges of incompetence.

'As self-certain and convincing as [Nansen] seemed in Geneva, so fumbling and indecisive did he appear in the Russian environment, with which he was not familiar,' wrote Ekstrand who had known him from both places.

> He meant well ... A better messenger of the *idea* of aid ... was not to be found in the whole world.... But where putting it into practice was concerned [he] was on uncertain ground.

Other impressions of Nansen around this time paint a confused picture. In a very different context a Norwegian called Tryggve Gran, who had been with Scott in the Antarctic as a ski instructor, told a story of meeting Nansen hunting reindeer in Norway and described how

> he got quite wild ... By nature Nansen was ... brutal ... But he knew it was wrong ... and he fought against it ... when he went in for [humanitarianism] and that sort of thing it was because his brain said that was right. It was not his heart.

At home, in similar vein, Sigrun observed that her husband 'has become an idiotic Good Samaritan'. He started cutting down expenses. He had worked out that £1 saved a Russian from starvation and so, as Sigrun bitingly recorded of one trip to Berlin, he 'travelled 2nd class ... thus saving [£5] = 5 human lives!'

From a different point of view Karl Radek, of the Bolshevik old guard, asserted that Nansen 'deeply sympathised with the revolution ... here we have something more than a mere philanthropist, namely *an intrepid Arctic traveller, whose heart was intimately bound in sympathy with the travellers to the New Land of Socialism*'. Then Mrs Tweedie, with her memories of the Nansen preparing to leave on *Fram* thirty years before, met him in Geneva and saw an

512

old man with grey hair and a stoop.... What a sad contrast to the wonderful
young Viking of those ... days.... He had become very Bolshevistic ... while
feeding the destitute, they had fed him with revolutionary ideas. Geneva did
not trust him – it was sad to see.

Along the same lines, a Soviet official called Rakovsky told Nansen to his
face: 'You ... are [a] Bolshevik without knowing it.'

Nansen was now suspect among Western governments. 'I am against
any further association with Dr Nansen or any organisation connected
with him,' the British trade representative in Moscow typically reported
to the Foreign Office. 'I distrust the motives which underlie, if not of Dr
Nansen himself, at all events of his close associates.' Nansen was now
blatantly a cover for the Soviets, their sympathisers, and various shady
operators in exploiting the famine for political or financial purposes. For
example, Philip Baker had discreetly seized the moment to use him as an
intermediary with the British government to urge full recognition of the
Soviet regime.

The Danish Embassy in Berne reported that the ICRC felt 'a certain
dissatisfaction with the policy of ... Dr Nansen ... in combining his
function as High Commissioner for [famine relief] with that of a kind of
agent for the Soviet government'. This referred to a deal by which the
London office of ARCOS, the All-Russian Co-Operative Society, a Soviet
organ, had opened a revolving credit of $1,000,000 (£23,000,000 or
$36,000,000 in present terms) for Nansen to buy grain. Nansen appeared
as the purchaser, and the Soviet connection was masked. He had naively
lent his name to an ambiguous transaction, designed to break an embargo
and acquire foreign credits. The ICRC, which had originally spawned
Nansen's organisation, now quietly disowned it, and wanted it shut down.

Nansen was further compromised by attacks on his deputy, who was
said to combine his own business with famine relief. He was supposed to
be negotiating for concessions in Russia using Nansen's name as a cover.
The allegations happened to be true. Frick spent most of his time in Berlin,
in touch with Soviet agents and their intermediaries. The ICRC thought
fit to remind Nansen that Frick was no longer a delegate of theirs.

In any case, by the early autumn of 1922, the famine had largely been
overcome. Nobody knows how many had died; one million is a widely
accepted figure. Lenin had the last laugh. Western charity, and Nansen in
particular, had saved him when, in his own words, he was 'barely hanging
on', and death by starvation had weakened the hated peasants into the
bargain.

His work efficiently done, Quisling went home in August to resume his
interrupted military career. Nansen, like so many charitable workers,
wishing to prolong his own organisation, continued with alarmist predic-
tions of more dire starvation to come. Unfortunately the Russians
announced that they were about to start exporting grain once more.

Nansen plaintively cabled to Kamenev, his liaison with the Soviet authorities, and now one of three regents appointed by the ailing Lenin:

UNLESS A CATEGORICAL DENIAL IS ISSUED PROPAGANDA FOR HELP WITH THE RUSSIAN FAMINE ... IS QUITE USELESS AND WE MUST GIVE UP ALL WORK ... PLEASE REPLY URGENTLY TO SAVE OUR WORK.

Nansen received an indirect, emollient reply, that he was very welcome to redirect his energies from relief to reconstruction.

Without his knowing it, Nansen had become a mouthpiece of the Soviet regime. In his propaganda in the West he proclaimed the necessity of Soviet rebuilding for the revival of Europe. Only trade with Russia, he now declared, could save Europe's economic troubles. 'The reconstruction of Russia,' he told the Assembly of the League of Nations, 'is vital ... for the prosperity of the whole world.' Indeed he went further. Out of Russia, he liked to say, would come the regeneration of a decadent West. He was only echoing the historic Russian messianic delusion.

In a word, he had become what the historian Ronald Hingley calls a 'Russia-Fancier'. This is someone who,

indoctrinated by Russians with the patter characteristic of the subject, [returns] home to regurgitate it, acting in effect as [an] unpaid public relations officer ... exposure to Russia tends to provoke Russian-like behaviour in even the most stolid of aliens.

It is an old syndrome, known before the Revolution. It has its roots in the romantic mis-translations into English of the great Russian novelists at the turn of the century, with their wholly deceptive idealisation of the Russian character. The Soviets were merely latter-day beneficiaries of this literary illusion.

To those who thought that way, Nansen had become entrenched as a high-minded world-improver. Partly on that account, he was awarded the Nobel Peace Prize for 1922. It was in recognition of his famine relief in Russia. But there were other, more compelling reasons too.

73

'The Nansen Passport'

At the beginning of 1921 some 800,000 Russians, having fled the Communist regime, were refugees in Europe; some wealthy, most penurious. In February, the International Committee of the Red Cross called a select conference of organisations directly concerned in helping them. This action had been precipitated by the arrival in Constantinople the previous November of the defeated army of the White Russian General Wrangel. He had been driven out of the Crimea by the onslaught of the Red Army that virtually ended the Russian Civil War. In a decrepit armada of rusting hulks, he brought with him across the Black Sea 100,000 souls, of whom half were civilians. Edouard Frick was temporarily detached from his prisoner-of-war work and sent by the ICRC to investigate. He grasped the historical significance of what he saw. This, he wrote in his report to the ICRC, was

> beyond the limits of private charity and even of the large Red Cross organisations. The League of Nations would appear ... morally obliged to assume responsibility.

The ICRC agreed and, that being the outcome of their conference, on 20 February they approached the Council of the League. This was a momentous step. It began the institutionalisation of the political refugee. Among other things the ICRC suggested that

> a [High] Commissioner for the Russian refugees should be appointed by the League, who would do for the Russian refugees the kind of work which Dr Nansen had so successfully undertaken on behalf of prisoners of war.

It was against this background that Nansen received, in the middle of June 1921, a letter from Frick asking him to go to Moscow on behalf of these unfortunates. This was followed, on 6 August, by a telegram from Sir Eric Drummond, asking if he would agree to be nominated League High Commissioner for Russian Refugees. Behind both approaches lay the scheming of Philip Baker, whose relations with Nansen are worth more than a passing glance.

Baker, an obsessive manipulator, wanted to continue using Nansen for his own purposes. He had by now a good grasp of his psychology. That is

515

why, in the first instance, he had chosen to act through Frick because, in any language, Frick could, when he chose, be inexpressibly persuasive. Both he and Baker were prepared when Nansen, as expected, went through the now familiar gavotte of initially declining but hoping, indeed expecting to be persuaded otherwise.

Nansen was now a much more desirable candidate than ever before. As High Commissioner for the Repatriation of Prisoners of War he had created one of the rôles of the century. This is the highly publicised, not to say media-conscious, international civil servant. When he started, nobody wanted such a job; now it had turned into a desirable object of intrigue. The Americans suggested someone who turned out to be one of the early embezzlers of charitable funds. The Italians put forward a 'working class' candidate of their own called Turatti. The British had their nominee in Sir Samuel Hoare, later Lord Templewood. In other words, one of the first supra-national carousels of its kind was in progress. It was a dress rehearsal for the United Nations, of which the League was the inglorious precursor.

At one point, while Nansen's attitude was still uncertain, Baker had fleetingly supported the candidature of Sir Samuel Hoare. He turned against him on account of his uncompromising anti-Bolshevik opinions, which would complicate dealings with Russia, but also because he was a practised politician who, under the public face of sweet reason, hid private cunning difficult to counter. Nansen was the reverse: behind an uncompromising persona lay a malleable human being. Baker, however, did not only see Nansen as a grand puppet – although Nansen himself once said that 'It is he [Baker] who writes all my speeches, and I only deliver them.' His attitude was more complex. He admired Nansen the explorer to the point of hero worship. One of his treasured memories was sitting enthralled in the buffet of the Gare du Nord in Paris, while Nansen dipped into the past to talk about his adventures on *Fram*. He did not often do so, but it was only then – as Baker, like others, memorably found out – that Nansen somehow came alive, and another being momentarily escaped before being returned to its shell.

On another level Nansen was a considerably more entertaining companion than most of the earnest functionaries now flocking to the League. It was whispered with a sneer that, like the view of Mont Blanc across the lake, he had become one of the sights of Geneva. Long gone was the exhibitionist Jaeger outfit of his younger days. He dressed conventionally in lounge suit, collar and tie, his distinguishing eccentricity now a wide-brimmed hat. All the same, there was much laughter in the office during his visits to Geneva. Even now he was a cut above the mediocrities putting their stamp on the organisation; even now he was the one personality to bring prestige in his wake and dominate them all.

He and the shorter, neat, dapper Philip Baker made an incongruous, but in some ways complementary and inseparable, duo. Both liked dancing, at which Baker was the more skilled performer. At decent intervals

516

they would slip away from the office to hotel lounges and slightly louche bars in the steep, narrow streets of the old town up on the hill in the shadow of Calvin's cathedral of St Pierre, or further out on the south side of the lake at Chêne-Bourg, near the French border. (Geneva is really two cities in one. On the north side of the lake, it is sober and very Swiss; on the south, more provincial French.) Baker, incidentally, had an extramarital liaison, platonic or not, with Dame Rachel Crowdy, an Englishwoman who was head of the social section of the League, and the first female senior international civil servant. Nansen, still attractive to a certain kind of woman, picked up partners as required and, 'well oiled', to use Dame Rachel's phrase, cut loose on the dance floor, so that the years dropped away and once more he became *il gran' giovane*, 'the overgrown boy', of the vanished days in Naples in another century. Dame Rachel, incidentally, had a yacht on Lake Léman and asked Nansen to sail with her. It was, she recalled, a terrifying experience. Nansen, of course, took command and, in her own words, 'wanted to do all the things I had learned not to do'.

Other considerations aside, Baker had no wish to lose a colleague so human. He exploited the new psychological climate that followed the Russian famine to make Nansen agree after his ritual refusal to take the post. Within the Secretariat, he made the point that Nansen, alone among the candidates, was untainted by lobbying. He was clean. He was still the dominant personality of the League. In the words of Rachel Crowdy, Nansen was distinguished by 'supreme honesty, supreme courage and extraordinary innocence'. Or, as others might see it, he was the ideal compromise candidate.

Frick, a good psychologist, was preparing the ground. 'What I hope,' he had written to Nansen, was that the work for refugees

> would be entrusted to an energetic man *who knows and loves the question*, who possesses the initiative, the courage, and a little of that utopian idealism without which ideas, like those of the League of Nations, are not even partially realised.

So when Sir Eric Drummond telegraphed his request to Nansen at home in Christiania, Nansen immediately agreed. He could, Sir Eric went on to explain, combine this with famine relief: 'BELIEVE THE TWO QUESTIONS MAY BECOME ... INTERWOVEN AND SOLE CHIEF FOR BOTH WOULD GREATLY FACILITATE MATTERS.' In this he was echoing a memorandum from Baker, and a letter from him to Nansen, in the course of which he had said: 'Your acceptance of the post of High Commissioner for Russian Refugees would improve the prospects of the League taking action on the famine question as well.'

Four or five days after acceding to Drummond's request, Nansen was chosen as High Commissioner for Russian famine relief, not by the League, but by the Red Cross conference in Geneva. On 23 August, he was finally appointed High Commissioner for Refugees by the League. By then, he was on his first mission to Moscow to sign his famine relief agreement with Chicherine. His formal acceptance to the League was dated 1 September. He was now in London, on his way to Geneva.

As High Commissioner for Refugees Nansen was an early victim of the casuistry that distinguished the League and descended to its heirs. The League disclaimed responsibility but undertook to pay the administrative expenses of an exiguous office and lend the services of the Secretariat. Nansen, however, would have to raise his own funds. He was supposed to co-ordinate the relief work of private charities, rather like his function as High Commissioner for famine relief. His was in fact an autonomous appointment, kept at arm's length. This meant that the League would share any kudos, but avoid blame if things went wrong.

By the same token, Nansen was spared pettifogging interference. In particular, he had a free hand in choosing his staff. That turned out to be providential. The League was growing up. It had obviously come to stay. No longer was it disdained as employment. It was developing a bureaucracy, laced with political intrigue. Already member states were demanding national quotas, so that the Secretariat would reflect the composition of the League. This would not have suited Nansen at all. He had a stubborn faith in Anglo-Saxon administration. He had long surrounded himself with Englishmen and Scots, leavened by a Swiss or two. In another contradiction, he matched pride in being Norwegian with rising scorn for the governance of the country, and certainly wanted no Norwegians in his office – although, as in the case of Quisling, he was prepared to make an exception in the field.

So the old familiars from the work on prisoners of war and the newly started famine relief joined Nansen in his refugee mission too. Thomas Lodge was once more co-opted as financial adviser. So too, as business agent, was an ambiguous figure called John Hamilton. A shrewd City operator, he was a director of Guéret, Gait & Co., a trading company registered in London which, amongst other things, chartered ships and dealt in grain. He knew how to bargain with Russians. As deputy in the refugee work, Nansen appointed Frick. Multilingual, well-read, speaking Russian like a native, Frick was Nansen's indispensable assistant. Frick's enemies in the League, of whom he had many, called him Nansen's evil genius. In the background remained the ubiquitous, ill-defined figure of Philip Baker. They were all adept at juggling responsibilities. This was the help that Nansen needed now. Repatriation of prisoners of war, Russian famine relief, and now Russian refugees: he had amassed three concurrent rôles.

Finally, as personal secretary, Nansen installed a Major T.F. Johnson, a former British Army officer, who had served on the Eastern Front during the war, and was probably connected with Intelligence. It was Johnson who stayed in Geneva – in Room 98 at the Palais des Nations (once the old

Hotel National) – exclusively devoted to the refugee work, and gathered the threads into his hands. A keen observer of character, Johnson also, in his own words, saw Nansen as 'a bundle of paradoxes'.

> In many ways he was simplicity itself ... he professed to scorn ceremony ... he refused to travel first class on League affairs, although even modest officials were entitled to [it]. He would turn up at a banquet with his numerous high decorations in his pocket as if they were so many halfpennies – but heaven help the person who presumed on that display of simplicity. I witnessed once a rebuke he administered to the Ambassador of a Great Power, who had given the place to which Nansen was entitled to a Minister he was canvassing, which that exalted person will remember to his dying day.
>
> The paradox which was Nansen showed itself in another striking way. No one who travelled with [him] could reconcile the intrepid North Pole explorer, whose Arctic exploits fired the imagination of middle-aged men ... when they were boys, with the 'windy traveller' who was never happy unless he was at the station long before the due departure of the train and who, at the last minute, sent out SOS in all directions for forgotten articles varying from passport to pyjamas.

Setting up the refugee office in September 1921 coincided with the start of famine relief. Nansen concentrated on the latter, leaving the refugee work to take care of itself. As usual, the ICRC did the first work in the field. As usual too, it was Frick who took the first practical step.

The ICRC saw the crux of the Russian refugee question as legal status. The Russian refugees were in judicial limbo. They could scarcely claim the protection of the Soviet regime. As foreigners, they could not legally travel, marry, be born, work, or even simply stay where they were. They raised unheard-of complications; by most legal codes they simply did not exist.

According to an apocryphal Russian saying, 'A man consists of a body, a soul and a passport,' and that went to the heart of the matter. It was Frick who, in between his work on the Russian famine and the prisoners of war, at one of the interminable discussions at the Palais des Nations, hit upon the solution. He suggested an identity document, serving as a passport, to be recognised by international agreement. With or without Nansen's permission, he called it a 'Nansen passport' and the name stuck. Hugh McKinnon Wood, deputy head of the Legal Department of the League, worked out the details.

By the end of the year, the matter was coming to a head. On 15 December 1921, Lenin signed a decree which deprived those Russians of their nationality who were living abroad without permission. That meant something over a million refugees. At the stroke of a pen, the Soviet leader had created a stateless horde.

Nansen seemed untouched. He was curiously lukewarm towards the Russian refugees as a whole. With his flawed insight into natures other than his own, he could not understand the psychology of exile. Down the ages émigrés have been abnormally sensitive and suspicious. As a result they have not easily been turned into objects of facile sympathy. In any case, starving Tolstoyan peasants more easily tapped the powerful emotion of self-indulgent pity.

At home for Christmas that year, Nansen published an article entitled 'Brotherly Love' in a Norwegian magazine:

> I see no other salvation for mankind than the rebirth of brotherly love [this article ran]. Perhaps it sounds childish ... I can see politicians shrugging their shoulders ... what we need is practical politics ... I am also a practical politician ... I am only interested in reality. But no practical politics are conceivable in a civilised society except based on brotherly love, reciprocity, helpfulness, confidence.... Brotherly love is practical politics.

Nansen was writing exclusively about the Russian famine. That monopolised his sympathy, and for some time he all but ignored the refugees. He made an oblique comment in a passage from his Christmas letter to Vilhelm Holdt:

> For my part, life has been somewhat changeable, and somewhat different from what I imagined – less coherent, less concentrated on one goal than I believed a human life should be; more fragmented, more chasing from goal to goal than was perhaps good for me.

Meanwhile Nansen's assistants continued working on the refugee question without him. For most of February 1922 he was immersed in his English tour for the Russian famine. 'I think Nansen has had a violent attack of nostalgia & has taken to the woods with a firm determination to chase hares instead of chasing politicians,' Philip Baker thereafter complained to Eric Drummond. In fact, Nansen had gone home for some spring skiing. From time to time he exasperated his assistants with telegrams unexpectedly announcing that he was retreating to his native mountains for a much-needed rest. On this occasion his disappearance was even less opportune than usual.

> If we make him come [to the Council meeting] he will be in a great temper [Baker continued]. But I think if he doesn't they will try & turn him out.... And [Sir Samuel] Hoare as Commissioner wd. really be intolerable!

There was, in fact, a plot to remove Nansen. It began with an invitation by Nansen, through Frick, to Sir Samuel Hoare, in November 1921, to report on the plight of Russian refugees in Constantinople. The choice was understandable. Sir Samuel was a conspicuously able Conservative backbench MP. He had been a British Military Intelligence officer in Russia during the war, rising to the rank of Lieutenant-Colonel. He and Nansen had met during the Peace Conference in 1919. In any case, Sir Samuel agreed to Nansen's request. In December 1921 he visited Constantinople and toured the Balkans to investigate resettlement. On returning to London he reported to a political colleague that

> things are drifting, money is being wasted, the refugees are being demoralised and in a few months time there will be a calamity when there is no more relief ... After talks with Nansen ... and other Geneva officials I do not believe that they realise in the least the serious position in which the League has been placed.

To Nansen himself Sir Samuel wrote: 'I cannot be associated in any way with a policy of drift.' Nor had he confined himself to words. In Constantinople he had established an office of the League and formed a local committee to care for the 23,000 Russian refugees stranded there. He put the office under the direction of Captain Burnier, delegate of the ICRC, and a Lieutenant-Colonel Procter, an Englishman stationed in Constantinople to represent British bondholders of the Ottoman debt. Oddly enough, Sir Samuel was merely acting on a proposal of the ICRC, hitherto ignored by the League. He returned to London with a fairly common reaction. He was disillusioned both with the League in action and with the ineptitude of the work done in Nansen's name compared with his formidable personality and good intentions. In his own words, he discovered that the Foreign Office was 'determined to get Nansen removed from the post of High Commissioner for Russian Refugees. He was obviously so incompetent.'

Sir Samuel decided to help. On 24 March 1922 there was a League Council meeting in Paris, at which he spoke, and canvassed appropriately in the corridors.

It was this meeting that Baker was so anxious for Nansen to attend. Nansen obstinately insisted on staying at home. Chiefly, it seemed, this was to concentrate on the famine, but also perhaps it stemmed from an instinct that tactically it was the right thing to do. Baker, however, did go to the meeting. Sir Samuel, in his own words, was sure of

> Nansen's deposition ... Baker, however, became very active and eventually bluffed most of the members of the Council into a promise to support Nansen.

For the moment, Nansen was safe. Baker, incidentally, was now Noel-Baker. After six years of marriage, he had added the maiden name of his wife, Irene Noel, who came from a family of means.

The following July, in Geneva, a League conference quickly adopted Frick's and McKinnon Wood's proposal for the 'Nansen Passport'. Again, Nansen himself was not actually present; he was once more at home in *Polhøgda*. The conference was run by Kuno de Watteville of the ICRC, who was acting for Nansen among the refugees. It became known as 'de Watteville's Conference'. In essence, it was agreed that the 'Nansen

521

Passport' would be issued by the country of residence as a certificate of identity and a travel document. It did not confer nationality; it merely gave the holder a title to existence. For the first time, the concept of stateless-ness was enshrined in law. By ensuring re-entry the document removed the main barrier to crossing borders. The refugee himself would generally be under the protection of the High Commissioner, who thereby became a kind of international consul. That too was an innovation.

Fifty-four countries ultimately recognised the arrangement. Even the term 'Nansen Passport' eventually became the official title of the document. Thus Nansen was not only – half-heartedly perhaps – the first High Commissioner for Refugees but, under his aegis, for the first time, the position of the refugee was regularised. The principles still hold. It was an object lesson in what could be achieved by the magic of a name. The Nansen Passport became almost a badge of honour. It enabled many a Russian émigré to move as freely as other citizens of the age, and start a new life elsewhere. Stravinsky, Chagall, Pavlova and Rachmaninoff were some illustrious holders.

Aside from incompetence, one of the accusations against Nansen that persuaded Sir Samuel Hoare to join the plot against him was concentration on the famine to the detriment of the refugees. Another, more serious, was conflict of interest. By now at least the repatriation of prisoners of war had been finished. Still, famine relief and the resultant comfort to the Kremlin were held to be irreconcilable with helping refugees from the Soviet regime. Nansen thought only that he was displaying brotherly love in different ways. His naïveté blinded him to the suspicions that his dual rôle aroused. Noel-Baker explained to a fellow-Quaker that Nansen

> considers his work for the famine and his work for the refugees to be two parts of one whole ... the reconstruction of Russia. He is profoundly convinced that Russia can never be built up again ... until the famine has been stopped ... On the other hand, his experience in Russia ... is that ... reorganisation ... will be greatly impeded ... by the fact that the whole country has been denuded of its educated classes ... It is vital, therefore, to build up ... a new educated class ... among the émigrés ... in Europe.

Whether this point of view emanated from Nansen or Noel-Baker was a moot point. In any case, the upshot was that Nansen advocated repatriation as the preferred solution, not so much for the comfort of the refugees, as their country's good. He really believed that by obtaining an amnesty from the Soviet authorities he would ensure a mass idealistic return to the motherland. This proved to be the great miscalculation of Nansen's life. Only a few thousand refugees ever chose repatriation. They knew their fellow-countrymen all too well. Nansen was left with a long-lasting problem on his hands. An undertone of coolness towards the Russian refugees confided to his care was probably due to a prejudice of Noel-Baker's. He found them 'disagreeable' and trenchantly said so.

73. 'The Nansen Passport'

The conflict of interest was partly resolved on 20 September. On that date, at the second conference in Geneva of Nansen's International Committee for Russian Relief, 'paying ... tribute ... to Prof. Nansen ... for his great energy ... the nobility of his convictions and the authority of his pronouncements', to quote one of the resolutions, the ICRC finally had the Committee dissolved. Nansen nonetheless decided to persevere with his aid to Russia in a personal capacity.

The day before, the Assembly of the League had given Nansen the solace of another mission. He was asked to take care of a new outflow of refugees. He found himself playing a part in a Greek tragedy.

74

Fair Exchange

When Nansen was at the Peace Conference in Paris in 1919, caught up in Hoover's first, abortive essay in aid to Russia, another sub-plot was being played out round Greece. The leading rôle was filled by the Greek Prime Minister, a politician from Crete called Eleftherios Venizelos. A mixture of charm, cunning, brigandage and high policy, given to reciting Homer, bespectacled, and wearing a square skull-cap of black silk, Venizelos was one of the most extraordinary characters at the Conference. 'He and Lenin,' said Harold Nicolson of the British Delegation, 'are the only two really great men in Europe.'

One of the issues confronting the Peace Conference was Turkey. The Great War had led to the defeat of the long decaying Ottoman Empire, which was finally dismembered and reduced to Turkey proper. The peace-makers, all-powerful, and all-ignorant, were not sure what they wanted. Venizelos was. A legacy of the Ottoman Empire was a large Greek minority in Asia Minor and Thrace. Within Greece itself there flourished a movement for a 'Greater Greece'. That aimed at redeeming the Greeks of Asia Minor into one motherland, which in turn meant annexing the relevant parts of Turkey. Venizelos was the apostle in Paris of these aspirations.

The Allies, notably England, France and America, were prepared to use Greece as a proxy to attain their unclear ends. Lloyd George thought it would be nice to have a state friendly to England in possession of a strategic swathe of Turkey. He and Venizelos connived at a military occupation.

Venizelos was hankering for Smyrna. It was a prosperous city with a large Greek colony, and an ancient centre of Christianity in Moslem Turkey. It also happened to be a strategic Eastern Mediterranean port. On 14 May 1919, with the Peace Conference still in session, Allied forces landed at Smyrna. The next day a Greek army followed, and in due course occupied the surrounding territory. There was another conference, another treaty, this time at Sèvres. It was signed on 10 August 1920. It broadly ratified the status quo. Smyrna and a surrounding zone were ceded to Greece. As elsewhere, the peacemakers had merely begotten another piece of paper.

While Nansen repatriated his prisoners of war, took on famine-stricken Russia and was landed with Russian refugees, the Greek army marched into Anatolia. In two victorious offensives during 1920 and 1921 they advanced far beyond the Smyrna zone to occupy vastly more territory and almost bite off the western part of Turkey. Nemesis was not far behind.

The Greeks threatened Constantinople, the Sublime Porte, the Ottoman capital. The Allies objected. Their arrangement, embodied in the Treaty of Sèvres, was to internationalise Constantinople and the zone around the Straits – that is to say the exit from the Black Sea into the Mediterranean. The Greeks had to desist.

The Allies, meanwhile, had been dealing with the rump of the old Ottoman Empire under the last Sultan in Constantinople. They were confronted with the rise of Mustapha Kemal, later surnamed Attatürk, the founder of modern Turkey. In the Anatolian hinterland Kemal was leading a nationalist insurrection, and building up an army. He controlled a rival government whose seat was at Ankara. He repudiated the Treaty of Sèvres. In late August 1922 he attacked the Greek army. Within a month, it had been routed and driven out of Turkey. In the wake of the disaster stumbled a forlorn exodus of the Greek population. That was what led to the call on Nansen.

*

The Kemalist government had announced that the country was to be purged of non-Muslims. Greeks would no longer be tolerated on Turkish soil. According to circumstance, they were to be eliminated by massacre or expulsion. Of the former, there was plenty, including a notorious one at Smyrna.

The Greeks of Asia Minor were defined, not by race, which through historical miscegenation was meaningless anyway, but by religion. They were Ottoman subjects of the Greek Orthodox faith. These were the melancholy victims fleeing to Constantinople, among other places. On 16 September 1922, in Geneva, Nansen received from Colonel Procter, still his delegate in Constantinople, a telegram appealing for help. Armed with this, Nansen demanded that the League extend his mandate as High Commissioner for Russian refugees to the Greeks, and allow him to use his existing organisation to care for them as well. Somehow he forced the Assembly to act quickly. On 19 September it voted him the powers he wanted, with the now all too characteristically pusillanimous rider that 'the League undertakes no responsibility for these refugees'. By the first week of October, Nansen was installed in the Pera Palace Hotel in Constantinople. Sigrun, who had been with him in Geneva, he left in Athens. He was accompanied, however, by Noel-Baker.

In pursuit of his career, or driven out by irritated enemies, Noel-Baker had left the League Secretariat and was now working for the League of Nations Union in London. Nansen, increasingly afraid of acting on his own, called for his old assistant. There were reasons of his own for

Noel-Baker to go to Greece. His wife's family had Greek connections going back nearly a century. They had a large property on the island of Euboea, near Athens, which Irene had now inherited. Noel-Baker wanted to help her with some business. Because of the property they lived apart, meeting periodically.

More than a million refugees were flooding into Greece. Most were destitute, having fled to the coast with what they could carry before the advancing Turks, and then evacuated by sea with the help of British and American ships. The country could not immediately house and feed them all. They were distributed over Greece billeted on the inhabitants, or squalidly living in the streets or ramshackle camps. They were left to survive on charity, most of it international. It was obviously a temporary expedient.

As in the case of the Russian famine, Nansen was criticised for the way he carried out relief. 'The Americans and other charitable organisations all consider him unpractical and anxious to obtain credit for work for which they supply money,' the British Embassy in Athens reported. 'Colonel Corfe, his representative here, is so dissatisfied that he is going to refuse to represent him any longer.' It was becoming a familiar pattern. When it came to practical details, Nansen was found wanting. High policy was different.

'The fundamental problem,' Nansen wrote to Venizelos, 'is the ultimate fate of these refugees.'

> They must ... be settled elsewhere and I presume that it will be the purpose of the Greek government ... for the exchange of populations with the Turkish government ... to settle [the refugees] in the vacant lands.

In other words, to make space for the Greek refugees from Asia Minor, Nansen was proposing a reciprocal expulsion of the Moslem minority in Greece.

'I believe this policy,' as Nansen put it to Venizelos, 'falls properly within the scope of the mission with which the League of Nations has charged me.' That was debatable. Nansen, however, had a taste for elastic interpretation. He had already discussed informally the exchange of populations with Hamid Bey, the Kemalist representative in Constantinople. He found a receptive listener. The Turks faced a complementary problem: the expulsion or slaughter of the Greeks had left vacant land and houses waiting for new occupants.

With his capacity for holding contradictory opinions, Nansen could jettison his lofty ideals of brotherly love when circumstances required. Greek and Turk evidently did not get on, so it was pointless forcing them to live together. He – or Noel-Baker? – saw in the Greek disaster an opportunity to unmix the population and, in his own words, achieve 'true pacification of the Near East'.

526

74. Fair Exchange

Venizelos was no longer Greek Prime Minister. After losing an election in 1920 he had been living abroad in self-imposed exile. Since a revolution in Athens late in September 1922, following the military disaster, he had however been acting as the diplomatic emissary of the new rulers. When Nansen wrote to him he was in Paris. On 14 October a telegram arrived from Venizelos asking Nansen officially to negotiate with the Turks for an immediate, compulsory exchange of populations.

The following day, Nansen received a similar request from the Allied High Commissioners in Constantinople. These were the representatives of Great Britain, France, Italy and Japan administering what was still the International Zone of the Straits. Nansen and Noel-Baker had come expecting to deal with a simple refugee crisis. Instead, they found themselves involved in something for which the most recent historical precedents were the expulsion of the Jews from Spain in 1492 and the revocation of the Edict of Nantes in 1685 which led to the flight of the Huguenots from France.

In short, Nansen was being used both as a mediator and the originator of a proposal for which moralistic politicians would be shy of accepting responsibility. Both Venizelos and the High Commissioners were anxious that the exchange be settled quickly and therefore independently of the forthcoming peace negotiations between the Allies and the Ankara government of Kemal, the new rulers of Turkey.

So Nansen suddenly became a diplomatic shuttlecock. 'I am afraid ... that it is going to be absolutely impossible for me to leave him,' Noel-Baker wrote to Lord Robert Cecil, an erstwhile colleague in the League, asking him to pacify his employers at the League of Nations Union in London, and extend his leave.

[Nansen] is extremely tired and if I left him the burden of work ... on him would be considerably greater ... As I happen to know a great many people in this part of the world, and particularly in Athens, I can be of rather special help.

Nansen now tried to complete the circle by officially starting to negotiate with the Kemalist authorities. He was prepared to go to Ankara. He found himself the victim of delay, intentional or otherwise. 'I am not fit for waiting,' he wrote to Lili Sulzer, whom he still used as confidante.

I do not mind difficulties, I do not mind fighting, you know, I do not mind sufferings and hardships of any kind – but waiting!... that one can drive one mad...But what shall I do, I know that ... the future of a whole people is involved [and] very much may depend on my behaviour – I have to be patient, nay even try to be polite.

Nansen used the delay for a quick tour of Bulgaria and Greece, spending a day in Athens, where the government reiterated its desire for a quick

527

population exchange. In fact, they returned him forthwith to Constantinople in a Greek naval vessel. Nansen arrived on 23 October to find a telegram from Mustapha Kemal himself, somewhere in Anatolia, saying that the exchange of populations was 'acceptable in principle'. Haggling over details dragged on.

Meanwhile, on 11 October Greece and Turkey had signed the Armistice of Mudania. One provision was that the Turks would retain Eastern Thrace, awarded to Greece under the now defunct Treaty of Sèvres. Before the Turkish forces arrived, the whole Greek population, as if driven by ancestral memory, spontaneously fled into Greece. That meant another 300,000 souls. Nansen drove out with Philip Noel-Baker to see what was happening. 'I long so much for you,' Nansen wrote to Lili Sulzer afterwards.

> Life seems so very very sad.... The roads were simply one continuous series of wagons, people and cattle. I have never known what it meant to see a whole people on foot before, it was a real 'Volkswanderung' as in old times, I imagine. When at night we came on top of a hill I thought I saw a whole city before me with its thousands of lights – it was their camps spread out over the plain, camp-fire by camp-fire, and there they were sleeping on the ground without shelter of any kind.... They do not know where they are going and will find no shelter where they come – oh, misery.... How difficult life seems sometimes, and men are certainly not making it better. What a Hell they can make of it – and fancy how beautiful it could be.

And quoting from Edward FitzGerald's translation of Omar Khayyám, which had momentarily replaced Shakespeare as his favourite source of English quotations:

> Ah, Love! could thou and I with Fate conspire
> To grasp this sorry scheme of things entire,
> Would not we shatter it to bits – and then
> Remould it nearer to the Heart's Desire!

Meanwhile, the Powers, Turkey and Greece had agreed to hold a peace conference in Lausanne. Early in November, Nansen started off from Constantinople on the long route first by ship to Athens, and then by train through the Balkans. Lausanne had been chosen for the conference because it was in Switzerland, and on neutral ground but, unlike Geneva, unburdened by the League of Nations, which was already becoming tainted as the home of lost causes.

In the grand but jaded Hotel du Château at Ouchy on the shore of Lake Léman the diplomats and politicians, like creatures out of an epilogue by Gibbon, crowded to settle the fate of Greece and Turkey. The meetings took place in the congested dining room with its low, shabby ceiling, heavy chandeliers and *table d'hôte* atmosphere. The proceedings were dominated by Lord Curzon, once Viceroy of India, the last British Foreign Secretary in the old aristocratic tradition, inner complexities hidden by a superior, overwhelming and idiosyncratic manner.

An American diplomat at the conference, meeting Nansen, recorded having seen him once

> more than twenty-five years ago, when he strode through the Touraine Hotel in Boston after returning from his world-famous Arctic expedition. He was a proud and forbidding figure then without much sympathy in his face. Now he is a powerful, forceful old man, but gentle and with blue eyes filled with a kind of patient sadness ... He talks of the refugee thousands, of the transfers and exchange of [populations] as if sympathy had outgrown all individuals and had attached itself now only to masses of misery.... There is something comforting about Nansen's size, his great hands, his deep northern voice booming out English.

The Conference of Lausanne opened on 20 November. On 1 December Nansen, accompanied by Philip Noel-Baker, appeared before the Territorial and Military Commission to hear his report on his negotiations on the exchange of populations read out. He was an unofficial guest, debarred from speaking himself by the Turks' old objection that his mandate was from the League, with which they had no official relations.

The operative passage in Nansen's report was on his old theme that 'to unmix the populations of the Near East will ... secure the true pacification of the Near East'. He added the rider that 'from the political and psychological point of view' the exchange would best be carried out immediately, while a sense of crisis still persisted.

A sub-commission on the exchange of populations was then appointed. It first met the following day, 2 December when, by diplomatic manipulation, in a rather more relaxed atmosphere, Nansen expounded in person on his proposal. 'In dispassionate tones he described the condition of the million refugees,' wrote Harold Nicolson of the British delegation. 'Dr Nansen's lecture proved a salutary counter-irritant.' Feeling that his usefulness was then at an end, Nansen left the next day for Norway. 'It is fair to say,' reported Noel-Baker to Sir Eric Drummond, still League of Nations Secretary-General,

> that unless [Nansen] had been here the matter would never have been discussed at all and that he is entirely responsible for the lines on which the discussion has begun.

The upshot was the signing on 30 January 1923 of the Convention of Lausanne. It was a long document, of nineteen articles, of which the first said all:

> As from 1 May 1923, there shall take place a compulsory exchange of Turkish nationals of the Greek Orthodox religion established in Turkish

territory, and of Greek nationals of the Moslem religion established in Greek territory.

These persons shall not return to live in Turkey or Greece respectively without the authorisation of the Turkish government or of the Greek government respectively.

The only exceptions were certain Greeks established in Constantinople, and the Moslems of Western Thrace.

In short, the Convention ratified the Greek exodus from Turkey, and regulated the forthcoming expulsion of Moslems from Greece. It closely followed Nansen's proposals, especially the creation of a Mixed Commission of Greeks, Turks and neutrals to regulate the exchange. In particular this meant valuing property left behind so as to arrange for rough and ready compensation. Because the Peace Treaty was only signed on 24 July 1923 the exchange of populations was delayed by agreement for a year, and actually commenced on 1 May 1924.

With a population of 5,500,000, Greece was expected to absorb well over 1,000,000 refugees. Far-seeing, Nansen had proposed to the League in November 1922 the flotation of an international loan to finance the process. It was two years before the loan was finally raised: £12,300,000 (£290,000,000 or $464,000,000 in present terms), through banks in London, New York and Athens. It was actually over-subscribed.

By the end of 1924 the migrations were substantially complete. Over 350,000 Moslems had been moved to Turkey; nearly 190,000 more Greeks returned from Asia Minor. However well conducted, it was a melancholy process. There were heart-rending scenes as Greek and Moslem were uprooted from land which had been theirs for generations. Historically, it was the final destruction of Hellenism in Asia Minor, and the end of a long chapter going back for millennia. On the other hand, the face of Greece was changed for good with the influx of an enterprising breed of farmers, merchants and shipowners. Above all, despite the hardship, a festering minority problem had been excised. We are still enjoying the benefits today. Nansen could take most of the credit. It was arguably his greatest achievement as an international statesman.

75

A Nobel Accolade

It was during the Conference of Lausanne that Nansen learned that he had been awarded the Nobel Peace Prize for 1922. 'I felt ashamed in many ways,' he wrote to Philip Noel-Baker, 'but if our work is worth it, it is first of all you who should have had it much more.' This was not empty self-deprecation. Nansen was indicating that to Noel-Baker he owed his persona as international statesman. To put it differently, Noel-Baker, an unlikely Mephistopheles, had been the ambiguous agent of his Faustian compact.

Among the five legendary eponymous prizes founded by Alfred Nobel, the Swedish chemist who, among other things, invented dynamite, that for peace stands apart. Those for physics, chemistry, physiology and medicine, and literature are awarded by Swedish learned institutions. The peace prize, however, is bizarrely the business of a committee of five elected by the Norwegian Storting. It is presented in the Norwegian capital, and not in Stockholm, like the others. The recipients have been largely a gallimaufry of the opportunist, the virtuous and the well-intentioned. Nansen was among the very few worthy winners.

He had to hurry home from Lausanne for the presentation ceremony on 10 December. This was the anniversary of Nobel's death in 1896, and has traditionally been the date on which the prizes are awarded. 'The Peace Prize has been awarded to ... Nansen for [his] international work ... during the past few years,' ran the citation.

> Especially his work for the repatriation of the prisoners of war, his work for the Russian refugees, his work to bring succour to the millions of Russians afflicted by famine, and finally his present work for the refugees in Asia Minor and Thrace. Even although this work has only been accomplished during the last few years, it covers such a range, and is of such importance, that the Nobel Committee wish to recognise it.

There seems to be a blight on the obligatory acceptance speech for the Nobel Peace Prize, and Nansen's, alas, was no exception. It teetered on the brink of bathos. 'Christmas ... is on the way, when the message to mankind is: Peace on earth,' ran the peroration.

> Never before has erring, suffering mankind waited with greater longing for the Prince of Peace, for ... the prince of brotherly love bearing aloft the white

banner with a single word gleaming in golden letters: Work. Each one of us
can be a worker in his [cause] to bring the wish to work and pleasure in work
back to mankind – to bring faith in the dawn.

Nansen was however true to himself in answering the faithful Vilhelm
Holdt's rhymed telegram of congratulations:

> To me ... the Peace Prize is strange and incomprehensible; since I was forced
> by chance into this work, which was not mine at all ... My scientific work has
> convinced me ... that everything goes in cycles, in waves, it is my consolation,
> even if the periods of decay can be long, and the wave troughs deep; a crest
> comes again, if only one can wait ... even after the Twilight of the Gods there
> is another world.

Between the presentation of the prize and the New Year, Nansen now
finished the work on coastlines he had had to abandon for the repatriation
of the prisoners of war. Entitled *The Strandflat and Isostasy*, it concerned
the rise and balance of the earth's crust after the weight of the ice cap
disappeared with the end of the last ice age. It was long, abstruse, closely
argued, a major contribution to the subject – and written in English. 'The
author much regrets the late appearance of this treatise,' he began the
foreword.

> It has been written and printed with many interruptions due to various
> circumstances over which he had no control. The greater part of the manu-
> script was ready for the press more than eighteen months ago.

The previous November, while Nansen was travelling to the Conference
of Lausanne, the ship on which he sailed from Constantinople was Italian
and, as he wrote to Frick,

> does a regular trade with Novorossisk. The officers ... assured me that in the
> last few voyages their Company have brought away at least 25,000 tons of
> grain destined for foreign countries.

At the same time grain was being supplied by foreign charity via Odessa.
In other words, while there was supposedly a famine in Russia and
pathetic appeals were being broadcast on behalf of the starving masses,
the Soviet authorities were secretly exporting grain to earn foreign exchange. Nansen was disconcerted, not so much because the stratagem had
been hidden under the cover of his name but because, as he phrased it, 'if
such exports were known to have taken place they would completely ruin
our work'.

Even Noel-Baker had by now turned against the Soviets. As he wrote
to Nansen, they seemed 'determined to make the reconstruction of Russia
impossible ... you will have to have a complete break with them and tell
them that it is quite impossible to do relief work while they continue their

exports.' Nothing, however, could dent Nansen's emotional obsession with Russia, or his determination to prolong his charitable work. He considered the Nobel Prize to be mainly in recognition of his famine relief. The prize that year was worth about £12,000 (£284,000 or $450,000 in present terms). To that, Christian Erichsen, a Danish publisher, had added a like amount, in the vain and sentimental hope that other rich men would follow his example. Against Noel-Baker's urgent suggestion that the Greek refugees were more deserving, Nansen decided to spend almost the whole combined sum on Russia.

He first wanted to see things for himself, however, and in the middle of January went off to Moscow. Sigrun was left behind. The journey moreover meant two or three days by train and, as she wrote to a friend:

> I am so afraid for him in that horrible typhus-ridden land – he forgets that he is over 60 and *terribly* worn out.

In Moscow Nansen was fêted – less as a saviour of famine victims than as a defender of the Soviet régime against its detractors in the West. He was received by various dignitaries, notably Felix Dzerzhinsky, the bland, soft-spoken, sometime head of the secret police – now, incidentally, no longer the Cheka, but reorganised as the GPU – and the architect of the 'Red Terror'. Dzerzhinsky was now Commissar of Transport, transferred to use modified terror to impose some kind of efficiency on the railways. He coolly admitted to Nansen what ought to have been obvious from the start, that the famine had been caused 'more by an unequal distribution of cereals than by a true shortage'. Consequently 'reorganisation of the transport system [is] essential ... for the struggle against the consequences of the famine'.

Nansen had brought Frick with him and, at the end of January, to gauge conditions in the Ukraine, they visited Kharkov. A Gogol-like event there, and a sidelight on the workings of the system, was the summary imprisonment of managers of the opera house for (1) failing to produce cocktails, (2) using a dirty tablecloth and (3) not providing enough chairs for a grand reception in Nansen's honour.

The head of Nansen's mission in Kharkov was a Danish Red Cross nurse called Lena Tideman, a handsome capable woman who could deal, single-handedly, with armed Ukrainian brigands. After Nansen departed she wrote to him that she had gone for an evening walk,

> and looking up at the sky – which I do day and night – I immediately saw the shining star Jupiter, and lo! my thoughts said: Fridtjof Nansen is like Jupiter; big, calm and chieftain-like, it shines above the others – Now for ever after, I will always associate Jupiter with Fridtjof Nansen.

This was an uncanny harkback to the days on *Fram* when Nansen saw Jupiter, shining above Cape Chelyuskin, as Eva's star.

Back in Moscow, the Soviet authorities made it clear to Nansen that the famine was over, and hence relief was no longer required. The ARA was to cease operations on 15 June. Nansen reluctantly agreed to close down his organisation on 15 August. Frick for one was greatly relieved. He had long complained of the cost, and evidently suspected incompetence or dishonesty in the Moscow office. In fact, it was waste of money, or worse, that had partly persuaded the Red Cross to disband Nansen's International Committee for Russian Relief. Chicherine had spoken for many when he once told Nansen of his 'unbounded confidence in you personally.... Unfortunately [your] choice [of] agents ... is not always a happy one.'

Nansen decided to spend nearly all his Nobel prize money and Erichsen's matching contribution in establishing two model farms, one in the Volga region and one in the Ukraine. This being reconstruction, the Soviets were pleased to accept, and the decision was reported by *Izvestia* on 4 February as Nansen was leaving Russia. Part of the new scheme meant importing tractors. Frick had a hand in that, on commission no doubt. It was the start of his trade with Soviet Russia. It was also one of the earliest introductions of the tractor to Russian farming.

On the way back from Moscow, Nansen made a detour to stay with his old Swiss friends, Hans and Lili Sulzer at St Moritz. He was much affected by the surroundings of the upland valley of the Engadine, with its touch of Shangri-La. 'Dear friend,' he wrote to Lili from the train on the way home,

> Those days in the heights must have changed my sight, life seems healthy and strong again, and the plains not so horribly dull after all ... That bath of heavenly light in that pure atmosphere, that feeling of space, of freedom high above the plains and the towns, does change the colour of life from grey to blue and rosa [*sic*] and a depressed soul is lifted up into another existence. How can I thank you for having made me come up there? Thank you for those wonderful days. To say that they have done me a world of good, at a time when it was especially needed, would sound rather banal and tame, wouldn't it? But I think you know and you will have noticed how the wings grew for every day up there.

In Moscow Nansen had announced that, as part of his change from pure famine relief to economic reconstruction, he would turn his office there into a centre for the distribution abroad of reliable information from Russia. He himself, on returning home, wrote a series of internationally syndicated articles, eventually collected in a book published in various languages. The English edition appeared during the course of 1923 as *Russia and Peace*.

It was a muddle-headed work. Nansen naïvely repeated the party line, notably that under the Tsars there had been no industrial development, when he himself with his own eyes had seen the opposite on his visit to Siberia in 1913. He justified both the 'Red Terror' and the secret police, the one as the revenge of the 'formerly oppressed classes', the other, on the grounds that the 'legal right of personal security has never been strongly safeguarded in Russia'. His message was his old one – namely, that the spiritual renewal of the West would come out of Russia, and that Russian trade was needed for Western economic recovery.

Probably the book owed something to Quisling, who at that time had pronounced Soviet leanings, and for whom Nansen had formed a high regard. In fact, he sent Quisling back to the Ukraine to oversee the last months of his famine relief, and also used him on another errand. While in Moscow, Nansen had confirmed an agreement which, as he thought, ensured the safety of returning refugees. This included inspection by his own appointed agents. Gustave Ador of the Red Cross denounced the guarantees as worthless – and inded, in the end, most of the repatriated refugees were imprisoned, deported or shot. Nonetheless, in November 1923, Nansen sent Quisling to the Balkans for a short while to supervise the repatriation of some few thousand Russian refugees who wished to return home.

Russia and Peace, although not widely read, branded Nansen yet again as a Soviet sympathiser and 'Russia-fancier'. He was further stigmatised by being elected, admittedly without his knowledge and against his will, an honorary member of the Moscow Soviet, which increased antagonism to him among Russian émigrés and their supporters. At one point the League, by now a warren of spite and intrigue, tried to close his office down, but Nansen put paid to this by one of his outbursts of cold public fury. In Geneva he was beginning to be regarded, in amusement or irritation, as the conscience of the League.

Towards the end of 1923, he made a short lecture tour of the eastern United States to promote the cause of peace and the League. He sent Herbert Hoover, still Secretary of Commerce in Washington, an autographed copy of *Russia and Peace*. Hoover did not approve of it. More practically, he talked about the Greek refugees from Asia Minor and tried, unsuccessfully, to have the new American national quota system of immigration relaxed in favour of Russians. Sigrun and his younger daughter Immi accompanied him on this trip. They were all back home early in the New Year.

'I have felt so depressed and unfit for every kind of life ... and still no entertaining company,' Nansen was soon writing to Lili Sulzer.

No, there is something wrong in existence, man is really meant to be bright and happy; and it was not the intention of the 'creator' that we should make life such a monotonous drudgery as we often make it.

Nansen had become a stranger in his own home. Once more he found himself unable to live with a woman. Rightly or wrongly, Sigrun had become jealous of his affection or otherwise for Lili's sister. Even the sister's recent marriage had not healed the wound. Sigrun and Nansen were at odds; her feelings for him were turning to frustration and contempt. She drove his old friends away. It was Liv, now returned from America, married and settled down, who enabled her father to escape to her home and entertain his companions. She now also had a daughter, Nansen's first grandchild, with his consent called Eva. Like a character from Ibsen, Sigrun was haunted by the power of the past.

Immi too was giving him 'anxieties'.

> I wish she could have found a good man [he wrote to Lili], but there are so few of them, and I am afraid she is now badly in love with a young man, who is one of our best ski-runners especially jumper. He took the price [*sic*] for jumping in Chamonix; but that is not enough. I am afraid he needs some other qualities too.

This referred to the first Olympic Winter Games in January-February 1924. Immi's 'young man' was Jacob Thullin Thams, the gold medallist. Whatever his brilliance on the jumping hill, the affair and Nansen's anxieties turned out to be transient. Immi began studying art, and eventually married one of her teachers, Professor Axel Revold, a leading Norwegian painter.

With Kåre things were otherwise. After much trouble, he had finally scraped through his examinations as a forestry inspector and Frick found him a job at one of Nansen's own model farms at Arkadak in the Volga region. It was still a time when foreigners could work in Soviet Russia and move about fairly freely. Kåre left for this job in May 1923. 'I am rather anxious for him,' Nansen wrote to Lili Sulzer, in another bout of confession,

> not knowing how he may develop, whether there will ever become a man of him, or whether he will always remain the same extremely weak character.... My only hope now is that the feeling of having some real responsibility may help to make at least somewhat of a man of him.

Kåre had been psychologically maimed by his harsh upbringing at his father's hands. His mother was a dim memory, and the arrival of Sigrun meant kindness and approachability in the home at last. But it was too late. After a year or so Nansen's model farms were on the way to failure, and on that account or not Kåre was out of a job. However, a Norwegian called Frederik Prytz, an enterprising associate of Quisling, gave him work in his forestry concession in Northern Russia. That lasted until 1926. Finally, in 1929, Kåre was sent to work in Canada, and his father never saw him again.

Odd, by contrast, had an unimpeded education, qualifying as an architect. He too had been hurt by his harsh upbringing but, with a stronger character and robust humour, survived with fewer mental scars. Still there remained the barrier between himself and his father which, like others of the family, partially lifted only on the ski track. Odd described how his father still insisted on using only one ski stick, with a heavy iron spike and no basket, although two sticks had long been accepted, and he himself had used them on the crossing of Greenland. Nor would he consider the new frame rucksacks just being introduced. ' "Oh no! Don't imagine you can teach me anything about skis and ski equipment, my boy!" Upon which he forged ahead,' Odd recalled of one particular ski tour in 1925.

> It was as if as long as he lived all his ski tours – even if they were only around his home … were still taking place on the Greenland ice cap … or on the pack ice of the polar sea.

In addition to the strains with his father, Odd had to cope with a dislike of Sigrun he found it difficult to conceal. Probably on that account, he moved to America in 1927, having recently married, and settled in New York. Eventually he returned home, joined the Norwegian resistance during the second world war and, with grotesque irony, given his father's association with Quisling, spent several years in a German concentration camp.

When Odd left, *Polhøgda* turned into an empty shell. Since Nansen had been travelling so much, and immersed for so long in foreign affairs, he had all but turned his back on the domestic politics he so openly scorned. At the end of October 1924, however, he received a letter from Christian Michelsen, the architect of Norwegian independence. Michelsen had long since retired from parliamentary politics to devote himself to shipping, although sporadically he did work behind the scenes. 'A large number of young people in Christiania have asked me to help them to start their new association against communism,' Michelsen now wrote to Nansen,

> and they have urgently asked me to use what influence I might have on you to ask you to do the same…. The name [of the] movement [will be] 'fædre-landslaget' [The Fatherland League] … I need scarcely say what great importance … I *also* attach to *your* participation at the beginning.

The upshot was that Nansen went to Bergen, stayed with Michelsen for three days, and agreed to join. On the face of it, this could hardly have been more contradictory. The author of *Russia and Peace*, branded as a Soviet sympathiser, was preparing to act against Communism. But Nansen believed that Communism, a Western import anyway, was suited only to Russia, and even there it was dying away. He certainly wanted no Communism in his own country, if only because of the menace of the collective and the threat to individualism.

This was not the first time that Nansen had helped to start a political movement. In 1906, he had been involved in founding *Frisinnede Venstre* – 'Liberal Left' – whose aim was roughly to abolish faction and install a government of national unity. *Fædrelandslaget* had analogous aims, but the situation was more critical, for in 1924 Norway seemed on the verge of revolution.

On the one hand the Norwegian Labour Party was radical, Marxist, allied to Moscow, and subscribed to the Communist aims of revolution, class warfare and dictatorship of the proletariat. There had actually been clashes with police and army, and the party, still in opposition, was prepared to seize power by force. On the other hand, the non-socialist parties, then in power, had piled error upon ineptitude as if bent on suicide. Speculation in shipping and the high cost of living experienced during the war, followed by unemployment and economic collapse, opened the door to revolutionary forces. To complicate matters, the parties of the centre and right were quarrelling among themselves. *Fædrelandslaget* was one of the movements that were emerging across Europe as a reaction to the threat of Communism. Most were Fascist which, by definition, were produced by that reaction. *Fædrelandslaget* was not.

The year 1924 was one of turmoil. There was a widespread mood of apprehension. It partly explains why Michelsen approached Nansen just then. Lenin died, and Stalin was replacing Trotsky as his heir. Hitler was writing *Mein Kampf* in a German prison after an abortive *putsch*. In Italy, Mussolini finally divested himself of his liberal allies, and consolidated his pure Fascist government.

On 29 January 1925 *Fædrelandslaget* was launched in meetings across the country. Nansen spoke in what was now Oslo. From the beginning of the year Christiania had reverted to its medieval name and another relic of the Danish centuries was removed. The core of Nansen's somewhat academic oration was this. 'If revolution can ever be justified,' he said,

> it can only be in a society where there is no civil liberty ... and because of lack of political liberty people have to live under conditions lacking human dignity. On that account, revolution in a country like Russia seems unavoidable because of all that has happened there. But to talk of the right to revolution in a society with full civil liberty, universal suffrage, equal treatment for everyone, where anyone can work his way up to the highest position, sounds really like idiotic nonsense.

On several occasions, *Fædrelandslaget* tried to instigate a national government under Nansen as Prime Minister. Each time the idea in general and Nansen in particular were rejected by the professional politicians. This had its parallel in Geneva, where Nansen was consistently defeated in elections for Vice-President of the Assembly of the League of Nations. In fact it was the lustre of Nansen's name, not his political participation, that *Fædrelandslaget* wanted. This it obtained: the two were associated until his dying day. *Fædrelandslaget* never made much of a parliamentary impact but its association with Nansen offered an indefinable reserve of stability. It held the fort, while the extremists withered away, and the Norwegian Labour Party began to tread the path of democratic socialism, eventually coming to power through the proper parliamentary process. As he had done in 1905, when Norway broke away from Sweden, for the second time he saved his country from a clouded fate.

When all was said and done, however, Nansen could not raise himself to the right pitch where domestic politics were concerned. The years only accentuated the inherent conflict between a great man and a small country. His passion seemed only to flow freely abroad. At the Assembly of the League of Nations, year after year, in his capacity as Norwegian delegate, he discoursed on a variety of wrongs. He was steered not so much by the Norwegian authorities to whom, by rights, he was subordinate, as by Philip Noel-Baker and other Englishmen, notably Lord Robert Cecil. Nansen even had English secretaries. In many ways he was a diplomatic privateer in the service of an English faction, and he pursued a selection of freebooting crusades. One was for the admission of Germany to the League. To the confusion of his own foreign ministry he negotiated in Berlin with the authorities on his own responsibility, and without or against instructions. Finally, in September 1926, Germany was admitted, and for this Nansen could probably take some of the credit.

But the cause which really touched him, and with which he persevered with dogged quixotry, was on behalf of the Armenians. His brush with Turkey over the Greeks in Asia Minor brought him into contact with the tragic fate of these people. Harried and massacred by Turks, forgotten by the Allies, ignored in the Treaty of Lausanne, they opened up in Nansen a hitherto untapped well of sympathy. He conducted a highly personal crusade to establish a national home for Armenian refugees in Soviet Armenia. His willing assistant was Quisling, who now replaced Noel-Baker as his travelling aide. Stolid, enigmatic and taciturn, Quisling was a thoroughgoing contrast to Noel-Baker, but he served as the youthful character that Nansen now always seemed to need by his side. Noel-Baker was now changing direction. He eventually became a Labour politician.

In the summer of 1925, Nansen carried out a tour of inspection in Soviet Armenia, with Quisling in his party. He later thanked Quisling for his

> untiring kindness as a travelling companion, and for the ... help he has given [me] through his knowledge of Russian and his many-sided attainments.

It was Quisling who, in fact, worked in Russia for Nansen's Armenian plan. In June 1929 he finally had to tell Nansen that the Russians had rejected it. Russia was now in the grip of Stalin, yet Nansen still clung to the illusion of liberalisation. Years of effort had been wasted. Even a short lecture tour to the United States in 1928 seemed to serve no useful purpose. Nansen had given too much of himself to a lost cause. It may have shortened his life.

In Great Britain, however, the old 'Nansen fever' lived on. Here he was still the hero who had made the first crossing of Greenland and reappeared after the *Fram* expedition like someone returning from the dead. Early in November 1925 he received a letter informing him that he had been elected Lord Rector of St Andrews University in Scotland. A year later, after a postponement due to the General Strike in Britain, he arrived for his installation.

He came to St Andrews on the afternoon of 2 November. The stuffed head of a polar bear, clad in academic gown and mortar board, adorned the locomotive of his train, held by a student riding on the footplate. From the station more students hauled Nansen in an open carriage. Next day he was installed as Rector.

'I have been wondering how on earth you ever came to think of making me your rector?' he said in his address after the installation ceremony.

Was it because long ago, before you were born, I expect, a young fellow with the same name as mine made some journeys through the Frozen North? ... Or could it be because, during more recent years my name has happened to be connected with several undertakings intended to alleviate the sufferings of unfortunate fellow-creatures?

I could not find out; and that was disheartening, as it might have given me my cue for this address, the delivery of which, I understand, will be my chief duty as your rector.

This was one of Nansen's more felicitous speeches. The thoughts were his own, but the text had actually been written by Noel-Baker, with the help of Leonard Woolf. They had beecome acquainted through Irene Noel-Baker's friendship with Virginia Woolf.

In a grim drill hall Nansen faced a sea of scarlet undergraduate gowns. He was speaking to his constituency, for at St Andrews the Rector is chosen by the students. Nansen was the first foreigner to be elected. His immediate predecessor had been Rudyard Kipling, who in turn succeeded J.M. Barrie.

'Here I stand,' said Nansen, 'your rector, rather an old man, I am sorry to say, and I have to deliver an improving address.'

Barrie proposed that a good subject for his successor's rectorial address [Nansen went on], would be: "the mess the rector himself has made of life." Little did he know how much to the point that subject would be for your present rector. Barrie warned you against M'Connachie, his imaginary other half, who is always flying around on one wing, dragging him with him. And what shall we other poor mortals say, whose M'Connachies do not write charming plays for us, like Barrie's, but merely lead us astray?

Adventure was the title Nansen had chosen for his address. M'Connachie, however, was not to be mistaken for the spirit of adventure.

75. A Nobel Accolade

Far from it, he is just Master Irresponsible – an emotional, impulsive and quarrelsome person who is very easily bored, and thinks it extremely dull when you go on with the same thing for long.

Nansen, in the words of the local newspaper, 'had a tall, commanding figure, and a magnetic personality. The earnest spirit which inspired his whole address held the close attention of the gathering for an hour and a quarter. He is gifted with a strong, clear voice and is a very effective orator. He has a wonderful command of English and speaks it remarkably well, his native accent obtruding itself very little.' Afterwards, until long past 1 a.m., 'Dr Nansen attended the Rectorial dance, into which he threw himself with wonderful vigour, taking part in fox-trots, waltzes, eightsome reels, etc. For an hour he was "up" at every dance.'

'I was an undergraduate once,' Nansen explained in his oration.

I went in, body and soul, for Zoology, and especially for microscopical Anatomy. For six years I lived in a microscope. It was an entirely new world, and Master Irresponsible kept fairly quiet during those years, and we were well on the way to become a promising young zoologist.

But, he said,

Master Irresponsible took advantage of a weak moment, and played me one of his most fatal tricks. We had just finished a treatise on the nervous system, with the result that the author's own nervous system was over-strained and needed a little rest. Then he brought back the Arctic dreams and told me that the time had come to carry out our old plan of crossing Greenland. It would not take long, and we could soon return to the nervous system again with renewed vigour.

He had launched into a review of his life, using this opportunity, as he used all others, to strike a blow for the League of Nations. But it was talking about the Arctic that made him come alive in a way that nothing else could.

Of course, having once really set foot on the Arctic trail and heard the 'call of the wild' ... we could not return to the ... histology of the nervous system again, much as I longed to do so.

Nansen then told the story of the *Fram* expedition. And then in what might have been a profession of faith:

You may notice that in the case of these plans, as also on many occasions in life, I had the misfortune to have most of the competent authorities ... against me.... However, I had the advantage of living a great deal alone ... and had thus acquired the habit of making up my mind without asking the opinion of others. Ibsen said that that man is strongest who stands most alone.

541

But that did not imply, he warned,

> that every man who stands alone is strong.... Beware of obstinacy and
> foolhardiness! For a strong man there is a great danger in resistance and
> contradiction ... I think it was Montaigne who wondered whether the fanati-
> cism which is created by unflinching defiance of the judge's violence ... has
> not more than once made a man persist, even to the stake, in an opinion for
> which – among friends and in freedom – he would not have singed his little
> finger. There is certainly a profound truth there. It is the spirit of adventure,
> but the reverse side of the medal.

And in a telling conclusion:

> My friend Amundsen observed the other day that he was glad he was not
> born later, as then there would have been nothing left for him to explore
> except the moon [but] there will be more than enough for you too, my friends.

Here was unconscious irony. Since 1924 Nansen had been involved in
German plans to cross the Arctic by airship. That is to say, his name and
reputation were being used. Philip Noel-Baker wanted to go with him, to
which Nansen replied that 'there is no man I would like to take with me
on any expedition [more] than yourself'. Money, however, was hard to
raise. Nansen was hoping against hope that he would reach the North Pole
at last. But on 17 May 1926 he received a cable from Roald Amundsen, in
Teller, Alaska:

MY TASK COMPLETED MY WARMEST THANKS FOR EVERYTHING
YOU HAVE DONE FOR ME ALL THESE YEARS.

Once more, Amundsen had beaten him to his goal. He had just crossed
the Arctic by airship, passing over the North Pole, and become the first
man indisputably to have reached both Poles of the earth. It was the end
of a tortured saga. The drift of the *Maud* had been a failure, although he
did navigate the North-East Passage – the second man known to have
done so – and finally reached Nome. Thereafter, he tried unsuccessfully to
fly to the North Pole by aeroplane. By now, he was a driven man, widely
thought to be unbalanced. Like the Flying Dutchman, he had been forced
by Nansen to continue with exploration against his will, with no escape in
sight. At least he had raised money for his enterprises where Nansen now
could not. The two men made a rare appearance together in public at a
meeting in Oslo in the middle of July, organised by *Fædrelandslaget*. But
when Nansen asked Amundsen to join him in his German airship enterprise, Amundsen declined. His own achievement had been his revenge.

Two years later, in October 1928, Nansen had to broadcast a memorial
oration for Amundsen on the Norwegian radio. Amundsen had disappeared over the Arctic during the summer while trying to relieve the
Italian airship commander, Umberto Nobile, who had crashed in an

attempt to reach the North Pole. Nansen likened Amundsen to the old Norse sea-kings, typically as expounded by Carlyle.

> Carlyle says: 'The first duty of a man is to conquer fear.' I wonder if Amundsen ever had any fear that required conquering.... The deed itself ... was perhaps what he considered most important.... And so, when his work was finished, he returned to the Arctic wastes, where his life's work lay. He found an unknown grave under the clear sky of the icy world with the whirring of the wings of eternity through space.

It was the end that Nansen had wished for himself. What he did not know was that Amundsen had been a sick man. He had had radium treatment in America. It was perhaps an exit half-deliberately chosen.

Nansen had outlived almost all the great figures of the classic age of polar exploration. Shackleton and Peary had died some years before. Even Scott Keltie, his faithful old friend at the Royal Geographical Society in London, was dead.

For the first few months of 1929 he was in the United States, alone, on a lecture tour, still trying to raise money for his Arctic airship flight. He received little encouragement, and returned home in disappointment.

On the outward voyage he had written to another of his female confidantes, Nini Roll Anker, a Norwegian authoress. 'Why could you and [your husband] not be on this ship also?' he sadly asked. 'What a nice crossing we would have. But that's how it is with our short lives, everything is so perversely organised.'

It was to Nini that Nansen confided his new political and philosophical ideas. He now combined humanitarianism fervour abroad with an interest in eugenics at home. 'We are threatened,' he wrote to her, 'with "the survival of the unfittest." ' All round, he was gloomy and pessimistic.

Nansen was now patently a sick, unhappy man, suffering from cataract and trapped in a miserable marriage. Nini, meeting him at dinner, recorded in her diary that it was

> sad to see Fridtjof and Sigrun. He seemed unbearably miserable; she hard, on her guard, almost hateful when she looked at him.... My God, that people can harden themselves to such an extent, steep themselves in hate ... I would give much to help Sigrun and Fridtjof, but how? It is hopeless ... and perhaps he will soon be blind – how will he manage then?

Still the Arctic would not relax its grip. At the end of 1929 Nansen received a telegram from Russians wintering on Franz Josef Land 'TO WISH THE CELEBRATED TRAVELLER A HAPPY NEW YEAR AND THE BEST POSSIBLE ARCTIC WORK'. It was another reminder of *Fram*; yet he was strangely ambiguous about the preservation of the ship. It was, he had written to a government department, extremely difficult for me to express an opinion in this matter, as it is a question of feeling ... It is obvious that if *Fram* remains in the water it will decay sooner or later ... so perhaps it would be best to scrap it immediately, especially if one could prepare a good large model of the ship.

It was Scott Hansen, now retired from the navy, and Otto Sverdrup, who made the preservation of *Fram* their own impassioned cause. Sverdrup, dying in 1930 at the age of 76, never saw the work come to fruition. Scott Hansen lived long enough (dying in 1937) to see the ship brought up on dry land, and housed in the museum, on the fjord in Oslo, where she can be seen to this day.

In February 1930, Nansen went up to a mountain hut at Geilo, on the Oslo-Bergen railway, for a reunion in the snow with two old skiing friends. One was Wilhelm Morgenstierne, a diplomat whom he had first met on his food mission to Washington in 1917-18. The other was Professor Jac. S. Worm-Müller, whose acquaintance he had first made in a sleeping car on a railway journey in Norway in 1914. They noticed that Nansen was not his usual self, so they kept to the easy runs. Morgenstierne had 'flu. But after a few days Worm-Müller and Nansen returned to Oslo, blithe as usual. The evening of their arrival, Nansen talked to a military society on the different gliding properties of wood on snow. It turned out to be his last public lecture.

Soon after, Nansen went down with 'flu himself, caught no doubt from Morgenstierne. He had had a heart attack while out hunting in 1928, and there had been other incidents since. But he had continued to press on with his work. He was now found to have phlebitis, a blood clot in one lung, and his heart was beginning to fail. He was ordered to bed. Odd and his wife were called home from America. King Haakon, who had kept his friendship with Nansen down the years, visited his sickbed.

Nansen refused to rest, continuing to write letters and plan new books. On 7 May he wrote to Fritz Zschokke, his old Swiss friend from the long vanished days in Naples, and now a Professor in Basel. Zschokke had invited him to his seventieth birthday party on 27th May. Nansen had to reply:

> I have been bed-ridden for 9 weeks ... but am now much better. It will however take some time before I can undertake a journey. I send you my very best wishes.... Yes, my dear friend, we are now growing old, and a long time has passed since we were together in Naples, and much has happened in that time ...

It was one of the last letters he wrote. On 13 May 1930 he died suddenly, at home, from a heart attack.

On 17 May, the Norwegian national day, he was given a State funeral. Otto Sverdrup, all quarrels forgotten, was one of the pall bearers at the lying in state at the University of Oslo; so too were Philip Noel-Baker, and

544

Oluf Dietrichson from the Greenland expedition. There was a two minutes' silence, and flags were flown at half mast. Nansen's coffin, drawn by four black horses, almost like royalty, went in procession through the streets of the city, lined with crowds. He was cremated, and his ashes laid to rest under a tree at *Polhøgda*.

Epilogue

On his last visit to America Nansen had met Dr Harvey Cushing, 'the founder of neurosurgery', whose work so depended on Nansen's contribution to the neuron theory. The wheel had come full circle. Nansen sent him his papers on neuroscience, now forty years in the past. 'It has always interested me that a man of your type, who was interested in things on a large scale,' Cushing wrote in a letter of appreciation,

> should as a young man have spent so long a time in microscopic work. It is almost like turning from a study of the microcosm to that of the macrocosm.

This was as good an epitaph as any. Another tribute came to Nansen, also on that last visit to America, from Admiral Byrd, the American explorer of the new generation, on his Antarctic expedition at Amundsen's old base at the Bay of Whales. Byrd cabled to Nansen through an intermediary:

> SORRY I CANT BE [THERE] TO GREET THE DEAN OF ARCTIC EXPLORERS IN PERSON I WILL HAVE TO DO IT THROUGH MY GOOD FRIEND KENT COOPER. I HAVE STUDIED DR NANSEN'S STUFF USED IT IN THE ARCTIC AND EXPECT TO USE IT DOWN HERE TOO ... AGAIN DR NANSEN WE SALUTE YOU BUT THIS TIME FROM ANTARCTICA

In Greenland Nansen lives on in a poem that has become part of Eskimo folklore. Translated this runs:

> From Norway
> Six men came out.
> Four Norwegians Two were Lapps
> Together with the Norwegians.
> They landed on our East Coast
> And with them they had all their belongings.
>
> They wandered over the Inland Ice,
> Suffering great need.
> Scarcely did they have enough food or change of clothes
> They had too little coffee, and it gave out.

Epilogue

And the same with their tobacco.
At last they came over the ice.

Nansen was not exactly a leader of men, but he could inspire them. He opened the era of modern polar exploration, the last chapter of terrestrial discovery, and inspired his successors, and his life encompassed its extent. He was one of the great explorers of the Age of Discovery, which began with the Italian, Spanish and Portuguese navigators of the fifteenth century and ended only with the attainment of the South Pole. With his wide attainments, he approached the Renaissance ideal of the universal man.

Also on that last visit to America, a journalist called Brenda Ueland had made his acquaintance. She recorded in her diary:

When he says good-bye to me and kisses my hand, I shall never forget his face and I know that he loves me, for there is the terrible look of the sense-of-eternity or the sense-of-death in it. In the cab on the way to the train, he spoke one sentence of great sadness, 'I wonder if I will ever again …' Earlier in the evening … he speaks of 'Faust' (I cannot remember what he said).

Perhaps he had quoted to her the last lines of Goethe's tragedy:

Das Ewig-Weibliche
Ziet uns hinan

'Eternal womanhood
Raises us on high.'

That expresses the yearnings of a driven and tormented man who, in spite of his triumphs, felt himself strangely unfulfilled.

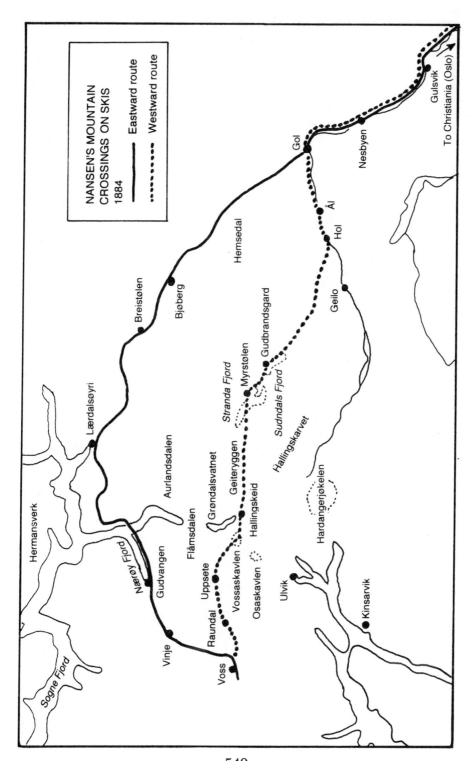

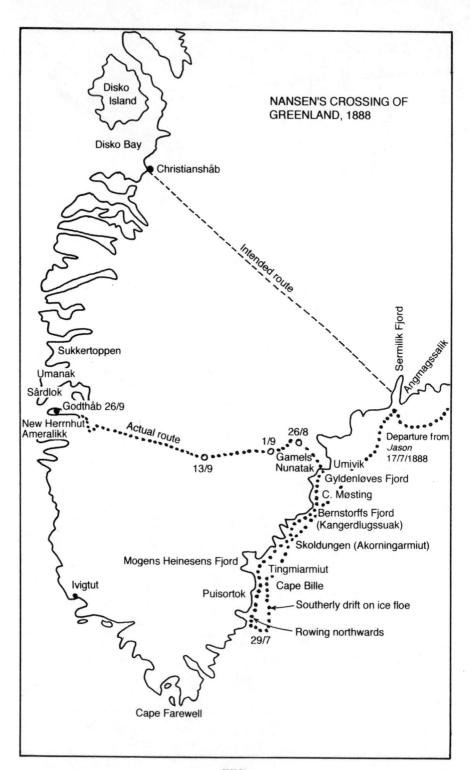

Disko
Island

Disko Bay

Christianshåb

NANSEN'S CROSSING OF
GREENLAND, 1888

Intended route

Sermilik Fjord

Angmagssalik

Sukkertoppen

Umanak

Sårdlok

Godthåb 26/9

New Herrnhut
Ameralikk

Actual route

26/8

1/9

13/9

Gamels
Nunatak

Umivik

Departure from
Jason
17/7/1888

Gyldenløves Fjord

C. Møsting

Bernstorffs Fjord
(Kangerdlugssuak)

Skoldungen (Akorningarmiut)

Mogens Heinesens Fjord

Tingmiarmiut

Cape Bille

Puisortok

Southerly drift on ice floe

Ivigtut

Rowing northwards

29/7

Cape Farewell

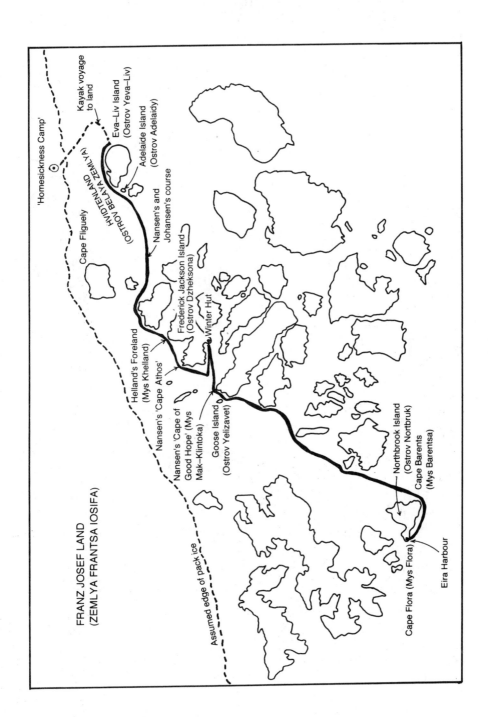

FRANZ JOSEF LAND
(ZEMLYA FRANTSA IOSIFA)

Assumed edge of pack ice

"Homesickness Camp"

Kayak voyage
to land

Cape Fliguely

Eva–Liv Island
(Ostrov Yeva–Liv)

Adelaide Island
(Ostrov Adelaidy)

HVIDTENLAND
(OSTROV BELAYA ZEMLYA)

Nansen's and
Johansen's course

Frederick Jackson Island
(Ostrov Dzheksona)

Winter Hut

Helland's Foreland
(Mys Khelland)

Nansen's 'Cape Athos'

Nansen's 'Cape of
Good Hope' (Mys
Mak–Klintoka)

Goose Island
(Ostrov Yelizavet)

Northbrook Island
(Ostrov Nortbruk)

Cape Barents
(Mys Barentsa)

Cape Flora (Mys Flora)

Eira Harbour

551

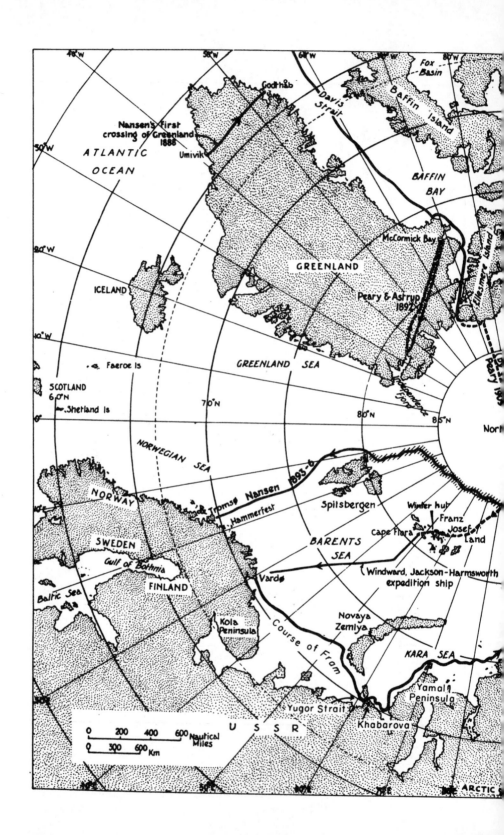

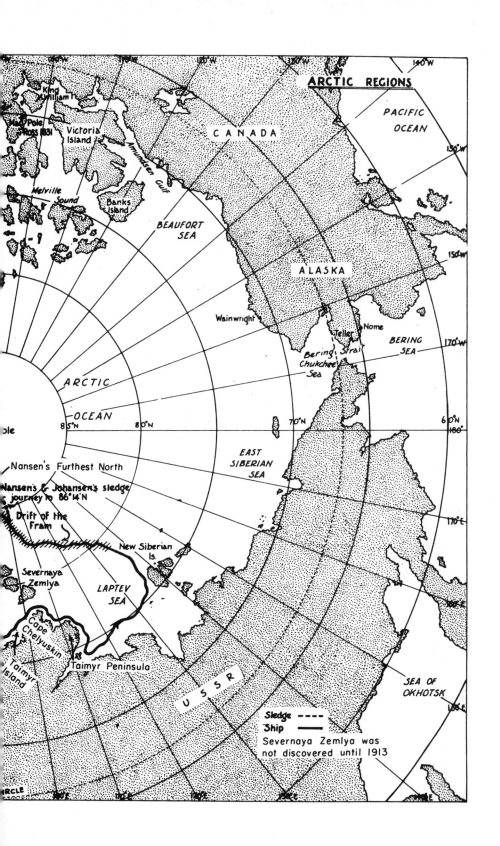

ARCTIC REGIONS

PACIFIC OCEAN

King William I.

Mag Pole Ross 1831

Victoria Island

C A N A D A

Amundsen Gulf

Melville Sound

Banks Island

BEAUFORT SEA

A L A S K A

Wainwright

Teller

Nome

Bering Strait

Chukchee Sea

BERING SEA

ARCTIC

OCEAN

85°N

80°N

70°N

60°N

180°

Nansen's Furthest North

EAST SIBERIAN SEA

Nansen's & Johansen's sledge journey to 86°14'N

Drift of the Fram

New Siberian Is.

Severnaya Zemlya

LAPTEV SEA

Cape Chelyuskin

Taimyr I'sland

Taimyr Peninsula

U S S R

SEA OF OKHOTSK

Sledge ----
Ship ——

Severnaya Zemlya was not discovered until 1913

RCLE

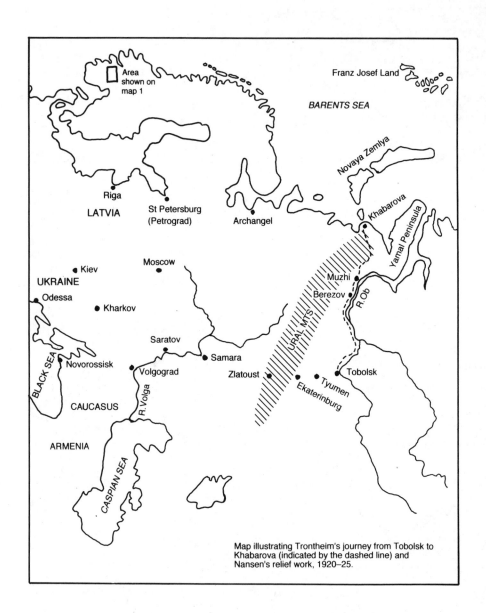

Map illustrating Trontheim's journey from Tobolsk to Khabarova (indicated by the dashed line) and Nansen's relief work, 1920–25.

Notes

References are given when not clear from the context, manuscript sources or bibliography; also when required by significance.

Manuscript sources are identified by archive and class mark within square brackets.

Printed works are identified either by date – in parentheses for articles – or shortened title from the bibliography.

Numbers in **bold** refer to the pages of this book.

Abbreviations:
BD: *Documents on British Foreign Policy 1919-1939*.
NB: *Fridtjof Nansen Brev*
US Papers: *Papers Relating to the Foreign Relations of the United States*.

Prologue
1 'I'm the': Mill 1951, p. 8.

Chapter 1
5 'deep, sombre': Nansen, diary, 27 March 1894 [UB Ms.8°2201].
6 'dismal and': Nansen, 'Fra barneaarene', p.7.
7 'It was': A.O. Vinje, 'Fra Thelemarken', *Skrifter i Samling*, i, p. 155.
8 'I did not': *Quoted* Worm-Müller, *Historiske Optegneleser*, Vol. IX p. 66 [UB Ms.fol. 2656].

Chapter 2
10 'that strange': Knut Hamsun, *Sult*, p. 7.
12 'of all the states': Forester 1850, p. v.
12 'the great European': Moe 1915, p. 267
15 'a means of travel': 'Om Hurtigløb på Ski' [UB Ms.fol. 2269].

Chapter 3
Quotations from Nansen, *Viking*

diaries [UB Ms.fol.2262:1], 'Langs Grønlands Østkyst', 'Om Isbjørn og isbjørnjagter'.

Chapter 4
22 'It is': Fridtjof Nansen, letter to Baldur Nansen, 30 March 1885 [UB Brevs. 48].
23 'and nobody': Nansen, draft of a novel, p. 59 [UB Ms.8°2229:2].
25 'I admire': Koht 1968, p. 288.

Chapters 5 & 6
Nansen's narrative: 'En Skitur fra Voss til Kristiania'. Press coverage of Huseby ski races: 'Skirendet ved Huseby'.

Chapter 7
44 'divide ... without': G. Armauer Hansen (1881), p. 741.

Chapter 8
46 'never in': Fridtjof Nansen, letter to Armauer Hansen, 21 March 1886 [BUB Ms.1571.14e].
47 'Look and learn': Nansen,

Naturforskerliv under opholdet i Neapel [UB Ms.fol.2269].
50 'not to crow': Nansen, *I Sacretia nuova* [UB Ms.fol.2269].

Chapter 9
52 'He had loved': Fridtjof Nansen, *På jagd ved løvfald* [UB Ms.fol.2269].
53 'Anastomoses': Nansen, 'Preliminary Communication', p. 220.
56 'Freud covered his tracks': Changeux 1986, p. 28. Freud (1882), (1884). Sulloway 1979, pp. 7, 422.

Chapter 10
63 'In polar': A.E. Nordenskiöld, letter to Fridtjof Nansen, 2 January 1888 [UB Ms.fol.1924:1a(2)].

Chapter 11
The source of quotations from Balto in this and subsequent chapters is his *Med Nansen over Grønlandsisen i 1888*.

Chapter 12
Quotations from Nansen in this and subsequent chapters come from his Greenland diaries and *Paa Ski over Grønland*

Chapter 14
Quotations from Dietrichson in this and subsequent chapters come from his 'Fra Dr. Nansens Grønlandsexpedition'.

Chapter 18
119 'I first addressed': Gustav Baumann, letter to KGH 4 October 1888 [DRA KGH Div. Korr.- Sager 29b].

Chapter 19
123 'had no wish': Nansen, *Eskimoliv*, p. 176
125 'He found our': Signe Rink, 'Nachhall der ersten Nansen-Expedition', p. 680.

Chapter 20
128 'During the morning': Per Rygh, diary, 30 May 1889 [UB Ms.8° 2278].
131 'a new method': Schmelck (12 December 1888).

Chapter 21
138 'When I': Eva Nansen (3 March 1893).

Chapter 24
155 'acquired a': Beyer 1923, p. 118.

Chapter 25
157 'Nine hours': Clements Markham, diary, 19 July 1892 [RGS].

Chapter 26
164 'What a strange': Tweedie 1894, p. 190.

Chapter 30
183 'dressed in': Trontheim, *Nansen imøde*, p. 1 [UB Ms.fol. 1924:2hII].

Chapter 31
Except where otherwise indicated, quotations in this and the succeeding chapters come from the *Fram* diaries of Nansen, Anton Amundsen, Theodor Jacobsen, Hjalmar Johansen, Bernhard Nordahl, Scott Hansen and Otto Sverdrup. Also: Nansen 1897, Johansen 1898, Nordahl 1898.

Chapter 33
204 'a certain': D'Arcy Thompson (Avril 1930), p. 147.
205 'difficult to deal': Fossheim, diary kept on the second *Fram* expedition, 10 October 1899 [NSM Ark.998.09].
208 'that irredeemable': Nansen, draft of novel [UB Ms.8°2209].

Chapter 34
218 'knew how': Waldeyer, *Deutsche Medisinische Wochenschrift* (1891), p. 1287.
218 'I propose': Waldeyer, *Berliner*

Klinische Wochenschrift (1891), p. 691.

Chapter 52

Quotations from and about Jackson: diaries [SPRI Ms. 287/1/2]. Also Jackson 1899 and 1935; Peel 1894

341 'I ... walked': Stanley 1872, p. 411.

Chapter 54

352 'our companions': Armitage 1924, p. 109

358 'You here?': Brandes 1968, p. 237.

Chapter 56

366 'belonged to': *Le Figaro*, 27 March 1897.

Chapter 57

370 'simply finished': Guttridge 1986, p. 330

373 'Thou art the siren': Waldesgespräch, von Eichendorff 1987, p. 86

Chapter 58

377 'mad about': Freud 1950, p. 277.

379 We are': Eva Nansen, letter to Anna Schjøtt, 22 September 1899 [UB Brevs.48].

Chapter 60

396 'Nansen has': Gunnar Heiberg 1900, p. 37.

396 'we knew': Høyer 1954, p. 193.

Chapter 61

401 'I am a great': Edvard Grieg, letter to Ola Thomassen, 1 March 1905 [UB Brevs. 100].

405 'The consular': 'Några tankar ... 18:de mars 1905' [BFA Gustav V:s arkiv vol.76].

406 'I do not': Arne Garborg 1924, p. 20.

Chapter 62

408 'a widespread': Charles Hardinge, letter to Lord Knollys, 6 June 1905 [RAW Geo. V. W.46].

408 'WAR AGITATION': Fridtjof Nansen, telegram to James Bryce,

26 June 1905 [BOD Bryce papers, uncatalogued].

409 'correspond officially': Lord Lansdowne, telegram to Viscount Melville, 7 July 1905 [PRO FO 73 654].

412 'forced, owing': Alan Johnstone, letter to Lord Knollys, 9 August 1905 [RAW W.46 198].

Chapter 63

419 'hoisted a': August Strindberg (1920).

Chapter 64

427 'the new capital': A.N. Krupensky, letter to Count Lamsdorff, 25 December 1905 [UDO Deponert Arkiv No. 31].

435 'Cajal had obliquely': De Felipe 1988, p. 24.

435 'Nansen, who': Løchen 1962, p. 69.

Chapter 65

437 'Grey, something': Iswolsky 1939, p. 323.

443 'Concepts such': Fridtjof Nansen, letter to Løvland, 5 July 1907 [UD Oslo].

443 'must not': Charles Hardinge, letter to Lord Knollys, 29 June 1907 [RAW W.52].

444 'On receipt': Count Wrangel, letter to Count Trolle, 23 July 1907 [RAS 1 0 10 Vol. 50].

445 'There is someone': Iswolsky 1939 p. 76.

Chapter 66

447 'told me': Fridtjof Nansen, letter to Sir Clements Markham, 4 April 1913 [UB Brevs. 48].

Chapter 67

452 'It seems': Gerhard Gran, letter to Bjørnstjerne Bjørnson, 8 December 1907 [UB Brevs. BB].

453 'It makes': Fridtjof Nansen, letter to Lord Knollys, 18 February 1908 [RAW Geo V W.53].

Chapter 68
457 'It is naturally': *Om Opdragelse og Undervisning*, p. 63.
457 'we were': Høyer 1955, p. 38.

Chapter 69
471 'I had': Lied 1943, p. 109.
475 'Before sunrise': Nansen, *Frilufts-Liv*, p. 51.
476 'Never has Russia': Tsar Nicholas II to King Gustaf V of Sweden, 27 February 1915 [RAS UD 1902 HP 1944b].
479 'Lady Scott': Fridtjof Nansen, letter to Col. E.M. House, 5 March 1919 [YALE].

Chapter 70
484 'On Thursday': Munch 1963, p. 71.
485 'The Soviet': US Papers 1919, Russia, pp. 81-83.
486 'The Bolshevik': Herbert Hoover, letter to Woodrow Wilson, 28 March 1919 [YALE].
487 'The Red Terror': US Papers op. cit., pp. 85-95 *passim*.
487 'purely humanitarian': Fridtjof Nansen, letter to V.L. Orlando, Lloyd George, Woodrow Wilson and Georges Clemenceau, 3 April 1919 [HI].
488 'My advice': Lenin 1960- xliv pp. 224-6 *passim*.

Chapter 71
494 'because am': Philip Baker, telegram to Sir Eric Drummond, 24 April 1920 [LN 40/4026/2792 Box R 1574].
494 'his humane': Hilger 1964, p. 42.
496 'A chance': Lodge (1943) i p. 31
497 'I shall': Philip Baker, letter to Fridtjof Nansen, 30 July 1920 [UB Ms.fol. 1988: K10A- K10X].

Chapter 72
500 'A huge': Fridtjof Nansen, letter to Peter M. Anker, 20 February 1921 NB iv p. 49.
506 'Nansen's most': Lenin 1960- xlv p. 268.
507 'I was greatly': BD 1976 p. 734.

507 'we ... shall': Lenin 1960- xlv p. 290.
507 'it would be': Philip Baker, letter to Fridtjof Nansen, 7 March 1922 [UB Ms.fol. 1988: R1].
509 'Have returned': Fridtjof Nansen, telegram to Comité International de Secours à la Russie, 18 December 1921 [UB Ms.fol.1988.R 1].
509 'a very bad': Schuster 1979, p. 37.
510 'has a': Andreas Urbye, letter to Fridtjof Nansen, 31 December 1921 [UB Ms.fol.1988 RU01].
511 'The Nansen': Eric Einar Ekstrand, letter to Prince Carl, 23 January 1922 [RAS UD 1920 HP 72 V].
511 'He felt': Wm. L. Haskell, letter to American Relief Administration London, 30 January 1922 [HI ARA records].
511 'As self-certain': Ekstrand 1944, i p. 277.
512 'he got': Tryggve Gran, personal communication to the author, 1973.
512 'has become': Sigrun Nansen, letter to Toralv Øksnevad, 20 January 1923 [UB Brevs. 611]
512 'something more': Radek 1935, p. 250.
513 'old man': Tweedie 1933, p. 92.
513 'I am against': BD 1976, p. 911.
513 'a certain': Danish Legation, Berne to Danish Foreign Ministry 11 September 1922 [DRA UM. Kontor 1 6 U 275]
514 'UNLESS A': Fridtjof Nansen, telegram to L.B. Kamenev, 28 July 1922 [CHL NBKR 4/613].
514 'indoctrinated': Hingley 1977, p. 164.

Chapter 73
519 'a bundle': T.F. Johnson 1938, pp. 156-7.
520 'I think': Philip Baker, note to Sir Eric Drummond, 18 March 1922 [CHL NBKR Addnl. Acc. 878].
521 'things are': Sir Samuel Hoare, letter to H.A.L. Fisher, 8 March 1922 [CUL Templewood Mss. II.8].

522 'considers his': Philip Noel-Baker, letter to Manley O. Hudson, 4 March 1922 [LN 45/16957x/12930 Box R 1719].

Chapter 74

524 'He and': Nicolson 1944, p. 271.

526 'The Americans': Mr. Lindley (Athens) to Foreign Office, 5 November 1922 [PRO FO 371/7957].

526 'The fundamental': Fridtjof Nansen, letter to Venizelos, 10 October 1922 [CHL NBKR].

527 'I am': Philip Noel-Baker, letter to Lord Robert Cecil, 19 October 1922 [CHL NBKR 4/471].

529 'more than': Child 1925, p. 83.

529 'to unmix': *Lausanne Conference* 1923, p. 114.

Chapter 75

537 'Oh No!' Odd Nansen 1970, p. 40.

537 'A large': Christian Michelsen, letter to Fridtjof Nansen, 27 October 1924 [UB Brevs. 48].

539 'untiring kindness': Nansen 1931, p. 7.

540 'I have': Nansen 1927, *passim*.

543 'Carlyle says': *Nansens Røst*, p. 692.

543 'Why could': Fridtjof Nansen, letter to Nini Roll Anker, 12 January 1929 [UB Ms.8° 2668:7].

544 'extremely difficult': Fridtjof Nansen, letter to Kirke og Undervisningsdepartementet, 24 October 1924 [UB Ms.fol.1924:2hI].

Epilogue

546 'It has always': Dr Harvey Cushing, letter to Fridtjof Nansen, 27 November 1929 [UB Brevs. 48].

546 'SORRY I CANT': R.E. Byrd, radiogram to Fridtjof Nansen, 25 January 1929 [UB Brevs. 48].

546 'From Norway': Balto 1980, p. 28

547 'when he says': Ueland 1939, p. 244.

Sources

Unpublished sources

Archives consulted, with abbreviations

Arbetarrörelsens Arkiv och Bibliotek (Archive and Library of the Labour Movement), Stockholm. (AAB)
Archives of the Marquess of Salisbury, Hatfield House.
Astrup Family Papers, Oslo. (AST)
Beauvais Industri A/S, Tåstrup, Company Archives. (BEA)
Bergens Offentlige Bibliotek (Bergen Public Library). (BOB)
Bernadottske Familiearkiv (Bernadotte Family Archives), Stockholm. (BFA)
Bodleian Library, Oxford, Department of Western Manuscripts. (BOD)
British Library, London. (BM)
Bundesarchiv, Bern, Switzerland. (BE)
Cambridge University Library, Manuscripts Department. (CUL)
Churchill College, Cambridge, Churchill Archives Centre. (CHL)
Comité Internatonal de la Croix-Rouge, Geneva, Archives. (CICR)
Dartmouth College Library, Hanover, NH, USA. (DART)
Det Kongelige Bibliotek (The Royal Library), Copenhagen. (KBK)
Gilchrist, John H., Family Papers, CT, USA. (GIL)
Harvard Law School Library, Cambridge, Mass., USA. (HAR)
Herbert Hoover Library, West Branch, Iowa, USA. (HH)
Hoover Institution on War, Revolution and Peace, Stanford, Cal., USA. (HI)
Houghton Library, Harvard University, Cambridge, Mass., USA. (HL)
Jaeger Company Archives, City of Westminster Archives Department, Victoria Library, London. (JAG)
Kungliga Biblioteket (The Royal Library), Stockholm. (KBS)
Kungliga Vetenskapsakademien (Royal Swedish Academy of Sciences), Stockholm. (KVA)
La Trobe Library, State Library of Victoria, Melbourne, Australia. (TRO)
League of Nations Archives, Palais des Nations, Geneva. (LN)
Library of Congress, Washington, DC, USA. (LCW)
Museo della Storia della Università, Pavia (PAV)
National Archives and Records Administration, Washington DC, USA. (NAR)
National Library of Scotland. (NLS)
National Maritime Museum, Greenwich. (NMG)
Norsk Polarinstitutt (Norwegian Polar Institute), Oslo. (NPI)
Norsk Privatarkivinstitutt (Norwegian Institute of Private Archives), Oslo. (NP)
Norsk Sjøfartsmuseum (Norwegian Maritime Museum), Oslo. (NSM)
Prince Eugens Waldemarsudde, Stockholm. (WAL)

Sources

Public Record Office, London. (PRO)
Rigsarkivet (Danish State Archives), Copenhagen. (RAK)
Riksarkivet (Norwegian State Archives), Oslo. (RAO)
Riksarkivet (Swedish State Archives), Stockholm. (RAS)
Royal Archives, Windsor Castle. (RAW)
Royal Geographical Society, London, Archives. (RGS)
St Antony's College, Oxford. (SAO)
Sandefjordmuseene (Museums in Sandefjord). (SM)
Save the Children Fund, London, Archives. (SCF)
Scott Polar Research Institute, Cambridge. (SPRI)
Simon Engineering Group, Head Office, London. (HS)
Staatsarchivs Basel (Basle State Archives), Switzerland, Zschokke Archives. (BSL)
State Library of Victoria, Melbourne, Australia.
Sulzer Brothers, Winterthur, Switzerland. (SUL)
Sutherland Family Papers, Dunrobin, Scotland, (SUTH)
Universitetet i Oslo, Universitetsarkivet (Archives of Oslo University), Oslo. (UO)
Universitetsbiblioteket i Bergen (University Library), Bergen. (BUB)
Universitetsbiblioteket i Oslo, Håndskriftsamlingen (University Library, Department of Manuscripts), Oslo. (UB)
University Library, The University of St Andrews, Scotland. (STA)
University Library, University of Reading, Publishers' Archives. (REA)
Utenriksdepartementet (The Royal Ministry of Foreign Affairs) Records Division, Oslo. (UDO)
Wintersport- und Heimatmuseum (Winter Sports and Local History Museum) Mürzzuschlag, Austria. (MUR)
Yale University Library, New Haven, Conn., USA. (YALE)
Carl Zeiss Oberkochen, Germany. (CZ)

Diaries and journals

Amundsen, Anton, *Fram* diaries, 1893-96 UB Ms.8° 638b.
Amundsen, Roald, diary, 1925. UB Ms.8° 3108.
Anker, Nini Roll, diaries, 1925-30. UB Ms.8° 2669:7.
Auchincloss, Gordon, diaries, 1918-19. HHA
Dietrichson, Oluf, Greenland diary, 1888. UB Ms.4° 4057:2.
Edward VII, appointment diary, 1906-07. RAW.
Fossheim, Ivar, diaries kept on second *Fram* expedition, 1899. NSM Arkivalier 998.09.
Fram, ship's log, 1893-96. NSM.
Garborg, Hulda, diaries. UB Ms.8° 2022:1-9.
Duke of York (George V) diaries, 1896-1922. RAW.
Hansen, Sigurd Scott (from 1909 Scott-Hansen), *Fram* diaries, 1893-96. UB Ms.8° 3423.
    Navigation rough books, 1893-96. UB Ms.fol. 1924: 2dII.
    Aurora notebooks. UB Ms.fol. 1924: 2dIII.
Jackson, F.G., Franz Josef Land diaries, 1896. SPRI Ms. 287/1/2.
Jacobsen, Theodor, *Fram* diaries, 1895-96. NSM A540.
Jakhelln, Fritz, Norwegian representative in Moscow, diaries, 1921-24. In private ownership.
Johansen, Hjalmar, *Fram* diaries, 1893-96. UB Ms.8° 2775.
Lied, Jonas, diaries, 1913-26. NSM.
Hudson, Manley O., Peace Conference diaries, 1919. HAR Ms. Box no. 166.

Sources

McCormick, Vance, Peace Conference diaries, 1919. HI
Markham, Sir Clements, diaries, 1885-1908 RGS.
Miller, David Hunter, Peace Conference diaries, 1919, HI.
Nansen, Fridtjof, leaves of diary, 1903. UB Brevs. 149.
    Diaries, 1886-90. UB Ms.8° 2204.
    Diaries, 1900-15. UB Ms.8° 1802.
    Diary extract, Svartisen myth, 1893. UB Ms.fol. 1924:2dIII.
    Diary, 1907. UB Ms.8° 2227.
    Fram diaries, 1893-96. UB Ms.8° 2201; Ms.fol. 1924: 2e.
    Greenland diaries, 1888-89. UB Ms.8° 2224.
    Greenland diary, 1888. (In private ownership)
    Diaries, 1886-1900. UB Ms.8° 2204.
    Diaries, 1906-1929. UB Ms.8° 2227.
    Diary, Germany 1886. UB Ms.8° 2205.
    Diary, laboratory notes, 1884. UB Ms.8° 2227.
    Diary and notebook, 1929. UB Ms.8° 2855.
    Diary, Russia 1921. UB Ms.8° 2227.
    Diary, Siberia 1913. UB Ms.8° 2203.
    Veslemøy diary, 1912. UB Ms.8° 2202.
    Viking diaries, 1882. UB Ms.fol.2262:1.
Nordahl, Bernhard, *Fram* diaries, 1893-96. UB Ms.8° 638c. *Fram* electrical log 1893-95. UB Ms.fol.1924: 2d II.
Rygh, Per, diary, 1889. UB Ms.8° 2278.
Sverdrup, Otto, *Fram* diaries, 1893-96. UB Ms.fol. 4171.
Windward, ship's log, 1896. DART

Select list of correspondence and other manuscript sources consulted

Auswärtiges Amt, selected archives on microfilm. SAO.
Armenia, attempts at resettling. UB Ms.fol. 1942, Ms. fol. 1988. CHL NBKR 4/30, 4/609, Addnl. NBKR Acc.878. LN boxes R696, R697.
Cajal, Santiago Ramón y, letters to Gustav Retzius. KVA.
Christensen, Thv., notes on Nansen family. UB Ms.fol. 2820:2.
Crowdy, Rachel, interview with Lise Lindbæk for the Norwegian Academy of Sciences, November 1935. UB Ms.fol. 1942: D1(2).
King Edward VII, correspondence with King Oscar II of Sweden-Norway. BFA O II Ark. Vol. 109. RAW W.46.
Exchange of minorities between Greece and Turkey. UB Ms. fol. 1942; Ms.fol.1988; CHL NBKR 4/471, 4/473, 4/619, 4/620, 4/628; Addnl. NBKR Acc. 878. LN boxes R1322, R1749, R1759, R1760. PRO FO 371 7955, 7956.
Famine Relief in Russia, abortive attempt 1919. UB Ms.fol. 1942; Ms.fol. 1988. AAB Branting Archives Vol. 13. CHL NBKR 4X/34. HH. HI Herbert Hoover Archives. RAS UD Handarkiv Serie 3 Herman Wrangel. UDO J.Nr.15864/1919, 16319/1919, 16595/1919, 30298/1919. YALE Col. E.M. House Papers.
Famine Relief in Russia, 1921-23. UB Ms.fol. 1942; Ms.fol. 1988. CHL BULL 5/8; NBKR 4/438, 4/444, 4/445, 4/450. 4/450a, 4/450b, 4/459, 4/470, 4/471, 4/472, 4/608, 4/609, 4/610, 4/610b, 4/611, 4/613, 4/615, 4/616, 4/617, 4/628; Addnl. NBKR Acc. 878. CICR H.Com.sec.Rus. NANSEN Cr. HC5 boxes 47, 49, 50. HI American Relief Administration (ARA) Archives boxes 80, 90, 271, 288. LN boxes R822, R823, R1725, R1727, R1746, R1752, R1753, R2452. PRO FO 371 6851, 6913, 6920, 6921, 6922, 6924, 8148, 8149, 8163, 8218. RAK Danish Red Cross Archives DRK Ark.10.001 pk.14; UM 17C1 Hj.R.Fl.Int.N.Kt Pakk 1. RAS

Sources

UD 1920 HP vols. 1471, 1472, 1473; Swedish Red Cross Archives UD 1920 HP 1472 V.

Fram expedition. UB Ms.fol. 1924:2. BFA NKKJ 1892-1904 35e-f. RAO Priv. Ark. 61. RAS 1902 [45 A 7] Vol. 2780.

Greenland expedition, 1888-89. UB: Ms.fol. 1924:1. RAK: Fam. Gamél Pr. Ark. Nr. 5444 Pk. Nr. 5, KGH Div. Korr Sager 29b FN Rejse.

Hardinge, Sir Charles (Lord Hardinge of Penshurst), correspondence and papers. RAW.

Hoare, Sir Samuel (Lord Templewood), correspondence and papers. CUL.

Hoover, Herbert. Papers, HI ARA; Hoover Archives. HH.

House, Col. E.M. Papers. YALE.

Integrity Treaty for Norway. UDO documents published in Omang, *Norge og stormaktene 1906-14.* PRO FO 371 295; FO 657; RAS Inkommande från beskickningar, Novembertraktaten vols. 50, 51, 52. RAW Geo V: W.47; W.52; W.53.

Jones, A.G.E., 'Captain Scott's Service Record', unpublished manuscript

Mission to Washington, 1917-18. UB Ms.fol. 1988: Am. I, II, III; Ms.fol. 2274:E10; Ms.fol. 2821:2. HI Herbert Hoover Archives. KBS Fridtjof Nansen, letters to Estrid Linder, 1917.

Nansen, Baldur. Correspondence. UB Ms.8° 2329.

Nansen, Eva (née Sars). Correspondence. UB Brevs. 48, Brevs. 201, Brevs. 755. Music. Ms.fol. 2204.

Nansen, Fridtjof. About 1,200 of his letters, a fraction of the total, have been printed in *Fridtjof Nansen Brev*, the main published source. The bulk of Nansen's papers is in the Department of Manuscripts, University Library in Oslo. Most are in catalogue numbers Brevs. 48, Ms.8° 2201-30, Ms.fol.1924, Ms.fol. 1942, Ms.fol. 1988, Ms.fol. 2260-70, 2273-5, Ms.fol. 2381, 3920. A significant proportion is also held in CHL, LN and RGS. In particular:

Correspondence

Anton Amundsen. UB Ms.fol. 1924:2c(1).

Roald Amundsen, UB, especially Ms.fol. 1924:5 and Leon Amundsens arkiv vedrørende Roald Amundsen.

S.A. Andrée. UB Brevs. 48.

Colin Archer. UB Ms.fol. 1924:2hI; Ms.fol. 3875:3.

Samuel Balto. UB Ms.fol.1924: 1a, 1b.

'The Big Four', letter to, 3 April 1919, reply from, 9 April 1919. HI Hoover archives Box no. 318.

Bjørnstjerne Bjørnson. UB Brevs. 48; Bjørnsonarkivet.

Dr Henrik Blessing. Ms.fol. 1924: 2c, 2i; Ms.fol. 2282.

Ida Bølling (Huitfeldt). UB Brevs. 48; Ms.fol. 1924: 1c; Ms.fol. 2273.

Waldemar Brøgger. UB Brevs. 298; Ms.4° 2593; Ms.fol. 1924: 2hII.

Emmy Caspersen (Endemann). UB Brevs. 48; Ms.fol. 2273.

Georgiy Chicherine. Ms.fol. 1924: 5(4), 7(III,IV); Ms.fol. 1988: R(1), R(6)A, RUO (1).

Gerald Christy. UB Ms.fol. 2381.

Dr Daniel C. Danielssen. BUB Ms. 700/14-18. UB Brevs. 48; Ms.fol. 1924.

Oluf Dietrichson. UB Ms.fol. 1924: 1b(2), 2hII.

Sir Eric Drummond. UB Ms.fol. 1988:F,K. LN boxes R1574, R1575, R1702, R1705, R1707, R1749.

Walfrid Ekman. KVA. UB Brevs. 48.

Dagmar Engelhart (Nicolaysen) UB Brevs. 48; Ms.fol. 1924:13d.

Sources

Edouard August Frick. LN boxes R1721, R1727, R1741. UB Brevs. 48; Ms.fol. 1988.

Augustin Gamél. UB Ms.fol. 1924: 1b(1), 1c, 2hII. RAK Fam. Gamél Pr. Ark. Nr. 5444.

Emma Gamél. UB Brevs. 48.

Vilhelm Garde. UB Brevs. 48.

Camillo Golgi. PAV.

Maxim Gorky. UB Brevs. 48; Ms.fol. 1988: R(1)

John Gorvin. CHL NBKR 4/449, 4/450b, 4/610b, 4/611, 4/617, 4/627, 4/628, 4x/43. UB Ms.fol. 1988: R(1), R(6), RU(6), RUO(1), RUP(4).

Grete Gulbransson. UB Brevs. 610.

Olof Gulbransson. UB Brevs. 610.

Dr G. Armauer Hansen. UB Ms.fol. 1924:1c, 2iI. BUB Ms.1571.14e.

Sigurd Scott Hansen. UB Brevs. 48; Ms.fol. 1924: 2a(6), 2a(12), 2c(1).

Sven Hedin. RAS SH Ark.Brevs.EI:427. UB Brevs. 48.

Marie Holdt. UB Ms.1924: 1c.

Vilhelm Holdt. BOB. UB Brevs. 48; Ms. fol. 1924:1c.

Gustav Holm. UB Brevs. 48; Ms.fol. 1924:1a(2).

Herbert Hoover. HI Hoover Archives.

Dr Jens Jenssen. UB Brevs. 48.

Hjalmar Johansen. UB Ms.fol. 1924: 2C(1), 2i III.

John Scott Keltie. UB Brevs. 48. RGS Nansen Corr.

Dr Reginald Koettlitz. UB Brevs. 48, RGS Library Ms.

Lord Lansdowne. RAW Geo. V W.47. UB Ms.fol. 1924: 10a(4-5).

Lenin, telegram to, 17 April 1919. HI Hoover archives Box no. 318.

Leonie Leslie. UB Ms.fol. 1924: 10a(6).

Marie Lewis. UB Brevs. 48; Ms.fol. 1024: 10a(7).

Estrid Linder. KB i:Ep.L 32.

Luigi Amadeo of Savoy. UB Brevs. 48.

Ingeborg Motzfeldt (Løchen). UB Brevs. 149.

Louis Alphonse Mourier. UB Brevs.48; Ms.fol. 2269.e.

Sir Clements Markham. UB Brevs. 48.

Christian Michelsen. *Fridtjof Nansen Brev*, ii-iv. UB Brevs. 48.

Sigrun Munthe (Nansen). *Fridtjof Nansen Brev*, iii-v.

Sir John Murray. UB Brevs. 48

Alexander Nansen. UB Brevs. 48; Brevs. 199.

Baldur Nansen. UB Brevs. 48; Ms.8° 2319.

Eva Nansen. UB Brevs. 48.

Philip Noel-Baker. UB Brevs.48; Ms.fol. 1988. CHL NBKR; Addnl. NBKR Acc. 878.

A.E. Nordenskiöld. KVA Ms. Nordenskiöld Brev. UB Ms. 1924: 1a, 1c, 2a, 2c.

Dr. Adolf D. Ónodi, UB Brevs. 48; Ms.fol. 1924: 2hII, 2iI.

R.E. Peary. UB Ms.fol.1924: 2a(3). NAR Record Group No. 401-1 Peary letters sent and received.

Vidkun Quisling. UB Ms.fol. 1988; Ms.fol. 3920 V:1.

Gustav Retzius. KVA. UB Brevs. 48.

Capt. R.F. Scott, SPRI. UB Brevs. 48; Ms.fol. 1924: 14(a).

Mrs E.M. Sharp. UB Brevs. 48.

Marion Sharp (Ure). UB Brevs. 48.

Johanne Sylow. UB Brevs. 48.

Lili Sulzer. UB Brevs. 48.

The fourth Duchess of Sutherland. SUTH. UB Ms.fol. 1924: 10a(7).

Sources

Otto Sverdrup. UB Ms.fol. 1924: 1a, 1b, 2c, 2h.

Lena Tidemand. UB Brevs. 48.

Edouard von Toll. UB Brevs. 48.

Alexander Invanovitch Trontheim. UB Ms.fol. 1924: 6a.

Fritz Zschokke. BSL P.A. 767. UB Ms.fol. 1924: 2iI, 14d(1).

Draft of novel. UB Ms.8° 2229: 1-2.

'I Sacretia Nuova', unpublished ms. UB Ms.fol. 2269.

Naturforskerliv under opholdet i Neapel, mai 1886, unpublished ms. [UB Ms.fol. 2269].

Notebooks. UB Ms.8° 2227; Ms.8° 2855; Ms.fol. 3920 V:4.

'Om Hurtigløb på Ski', unpublished ms. UB Ms.fol. 2269.

'Paa jagd ved løfald', unpublished ms. UB Ms.fol. 2269.

'White Face Mountain', unpublished essay. UB Ms.fol. 2274: E2.

Tsar Nicholas II of Russia, correspondence with King Gustaf V of Sweden, February 1915. RAS UD 1902 HP 1944b.

Noel-Baker, Philip. The main collection of Noel-Baker's political papers is held by CHL, under the general classification NBKR. LN and UB are other substantial sources.

Quisling, Vidkun, political papers. LN boxes R696, R697, R1727, R1745, R1746. UB Brevs. 48; Brevs. 428; Ms.fol. 1942: C, GG; Ms fol. 1988: A, F, R(6), RU(2), RU(3), RU(6), RUL(6), RUO(1), RUP(5), RUT(3); Ms.fol. 3920:V.

Rae, John, manuscript of autobiography. SPRI Ms. 787/1-2.

Repatriation of Prisoners of War. UB Ms.fol. 1942; Ms.fol. 1988. CHL NBKR 4/449, 4/480, 4/450b, 4X/43, 4/613, 4/621. CICR. LN boxes R1574, R1575, R1576, R1582, R1702, R1703, R1704, R1705, R1706, R1707, R1709. PRO FO 371 4672, 5390, 5450. RAK UM 1 Kont. 6U263; Danish Red Cross Archives DRK Ark. 10.001 pk. 13

Reuterskiöld, Lennart, corrspondence with Foreign Ministry in Stockholm about *Fram* expedition. RAS UD 1902 [45 A 7] vol. 2780.

Russian Refugees, High Commissioner for. UB Ms.fol. 1942; Ms.fol. 1988. CHL NBKR 4/436, 4/449, 4/450, 4/450a, 4/450b, 4/470, 4/471, 4/472, 4/473, 4/606, 4/610b, 4/611, 4/613, 4.617, 4/618, 4/619, 4/620, 4/621, 4/622, 4/623, 4/624, 4/625, 4/627, 4/628, 4/629, 4x/43, 4x/78, 7/62. CHL Templewood II.8. LN boxes R1719, R1720, R1721, R1722, R1723, R1724, R1725, R1726, R1726, R1727, R1728, R1729, R1739, R1740, R1741, R1742, R1743, R1744, R1745, R1746, R1747, R1748, R1749, C1321, C1322. CICR. PRO FO 371 7955.

Scott, Kathleen (Lady Scott), correspondence with Col. E.M. House, YALE. Correspondence with Nansen and other papers, copies in the possession of the author. UB Ms.fol. 1924:14a.

Separation of Norway and Sweden and election of Prince Charles to the throne of Norway, 1905. UB Ms.fol.1924:10. BFA Gustav V Ark. Vol. 76; Oscar II Ark. Vols 41, 65, 109. PRO FO 22 584; FO 63 1424; FO 73 649, 650, 654; FO 188 252. RAK Ny. kgl. Saml. 4465 4°. RAS UD 1902 Vols. 232b, 234. RAW Geo.V W.46. UDO Deponert Arkiv Nr. 31.

Torup, Sophus, letter to Nansen 18 February 1890 about diet on Greenland expedition. UB Ms.fol. 1924: 1f.

Trontheim, Alexander Ivanovitch, *Nansen imøde* ('To meet Nansen'). UB Ms.fol. 1924: 2hII.

Worm-Müller, Prof. Jacob S., Historiske Optegneler. UB Ms.fol. 2656.

Sources

Published Sources

Newspapers and periodicals consulted

Norwegian newspapers:

Aftenposten
Arbeiderbladet
Bergens Aftenblad
Bergensposten
Dagbladet
Norges handels og Sjøfartstidende
Morgenbladet
Morgenposten

Tidens Tegn
Tromsø Stiftstidende
Trondhjems Adresseavis
Vardø-Posten
Verdens Gang
Ørebladet
Various local newspapers

Other newspapers:

Aftonbladet
Berlingske Tidende
Dagens Nyheter
Daily Chronicle
Daily Mail
Frankfurter Zeitung
Göteborgs Handels-och
   Sjöfarts-Tidning
Kölnische Zeitung
L'Express
Le Figaro
Le Matin
Le Petit Parisien
Le Temps
Manchester Guardian

Nationaltidende
Neue Freie Presse
New York Times
Observer
Pall Mall Gazette
Paris Daily Mail
Politiken
Svenska Dagbladet
Sketch
Standard
The Times
Washington Post
Westminster Budget
Westminster Gazette

Norwegian journals:

Årbok, Forening til Ski-idrettens
   Fremme
Bergen Museum Skrifter
Bergens Museums Aarsberetning
Budstikken, (Anden raekke)
Byminner
Det Norske Geografiske Selskabs
   Aarbog
Det Norske Turistforeningens Aarbog
Det Norske Videnskabs-Akademi,
   Avhandlinger & Aarbok
Edda
Geofysiske Publikasjoner
Historisk Tidsskrift
Illustreret Tidende for Børn

Illustreret Maanedskrift
Kirke og Kultur
Kristiania Turistforeningens Aarbok
Naturen
Norsk Geografisk Tidskrift
Norsk Idrætsblad
Norsk Kirkeblad
Norsk Polarinstitutt, Aarbok
Personalhistorisk Tidsskrift
Ringeren
Sameliv
Samtiden
Syn og Segn
Teknisk Ukeblad
Urd

Sources

Other journals:

Abhandlungen für die kunde des
    Morgenlandes
Academy
Alpine Journal
American Geographical Society,
    Bulletin
American Geologist
American Historical Review
American Scandinavian Review
Anatomischer Anzeiger
Annals and Magazine of Natural
    History
Annual Register
Arch. Math. Naturv.
Arch. f. Anat. u.
    Entwickelungsgeschichte
Archiv für Psychiatrie und
    Nervenkrankheiten
Archives de Physiologie, Deuxieme Serie
Arctic
Arktis
Athenaeum
Bankers' Magazine
Berliner Klinische Wochenschrift
Biological Bulletin
Biologische Untersuchungen, Neue
    Folge
Blackwood's Magazine
British Ski Year Book
British and Foreign
    Medico-Chirurgical Review
Bystander
Century Illustrated Monthly Magazine
Century Magazine
Contemporary Review
Current History, New York
Dansk Tidskrift
Das Ausland
Det Grønlandske Selskabs Skrifter
Deutsche Medisinische Wochenschrift
Die Alpen
Die Umschau
Echo de Paris
Falk
Field
Forschungen und Fortschritte, Berlin
Forum
Gads danske Magasin
Geografisk Tidskrift

Geographical Journal
Good Words
Grønland
Hibbert Journal
Historische Zeitschrift
Historisk Tidskrift [Swedish]
Historisk Tidsskrift [Danish]
Household Words
Ideas
Illustrated London News
Inter-Nord
Internat. Monatsschrift für Anatomie u.
    Physiologie
Internat. Rev. der gesamten
    Hydrobiologie und Hydrografie,
    Leipzig
International Journal of Ethics
Internationale Monatschrift f.
    Anatomie u. Histologie
Jahrbuch des Schweiz. Ski-Verbandes
Jahrbuch des Schweizer Alpenclub
Jenaische Zeitschrift für
    Naturwissenschaft
Journal du Conseil
Kungl. Svenska Vetenskapsakademiens
    Årsbok
Lady
Lancet
League Publications, Social Questions
Leprosy Review
Les Prix Nobel
London Medical Gazette
Longmans Magazine
Mariner's Mirror
McClure's Magazine
Meddelelser om Grønland
Mittheilungen der Geographischen
    Gesellschaft in Hamburg
Monthly Review
Musk-Ox
Nation and Athenaeum
Nature
Nautical Magazine
Neue Denkschriften der Schweiz.
    Naturforsch. Ges.
Neue Freie Presse
Nineteenth Century
Nordisk Tidskrift för Vetenskap, Konst
    och Industri

Sources

Nordisk Medicinhistorisk Aarsbok
Nordisk Medicinsk Arkiv
Nordisk Musik-Tidende
Nordisk Tidskrift
Norseman
North American Review
Ny Illustreret Tidende
Ny Jord
Ottar
Outing [NY 1905-11]
Outlook
Paa Skidor
Petermann's Geographische
  Mittheilungen
Polar Record
Polarboken
Popular Science Monthly
Proceedings of the Royal Geographical
  Society
Publications de Circonstance,
  Copenhagen
Punch
Review of Reviews
Revista Trimestral de Histologia
  Normal y Patologica
Revue Internationale de la Croix-Rouge
Russian Affairs

Russian Review
Scandia, Stockholm
Science
Scottish Geographical Magazine
Scribner's Magazine, New York
Self Culture
Sitzungsber. d. kais. Akad. Wiss. Wien
Skandinaven
Snø og Ski
Spectator
St. Antony's Papers
Svensk geografisk Årsbok
Symons Meteorological Magazine
Tidsskrift for Dansk Røde Kors
Tidsskrift-for-Sygepleje
U.S. Congressional Hearings (Senate
  Library) 41st-73rd Congress
Verhandlungen der Anatomischen
  Gesellschaft, Jena
Verhandlungen der Gesellschaft für
  Erdkunde zu Berlin
Washington Academy of Sciences,
  Journal / Proceedings
Wide World Magazine
Ymer
Zeitschrift der Gesellschaft fuer
  Erdkunde zu Berlin

Books

Aasheim, Stein P., *Gjennom Sibir i Nordmenns Fotspor*, Oslo, Ernst G. Morten-
  sens Forlag, 1991.
—— *Vestkysten eller døden*, Oslo, Scanbok Forlag, 1989.
Abrikossow, Dmitrii I., *Revelations of a Russian Diplomat*, Seattle, University of
  Washington Press, 1964.
Amundsen, Leiv, and Seip, Didrik Arup (eds), *Henrik Wergelands Skrifter*, Oslo,
  J.W. Cappelens Forlag, 1962.
Amundsen, Roald, *Mitt Liv som Polarforsker*, Oslo, Gyldendal norsk Forlag, 1927.
—— *Nordostpassagen*, Kristiania, Gyldendalske Boghandel, 1921.
—— *Nordvestpassagen*, Kristiania, Aschehoug, 1907
—— *Sydpolen*, Kristiania, Jacob Dybwads Forlag, 1912.
Amundsen, Roald, og Ellsworth, Lincoln, *Den første flukt over Polhavet*, Oslo,
  Gyldendal norsk Forlag, 1926.
Andersen, Magnus, *Vikingefærden*, Kristiania, Eget Forlag, 1895.
Andrée, S.A., Strindberg, Nils, och Frænkel, Knut, *Med Örnen mot Polen*, Stock-
  holm, Albert Bonniers Förlag, 1930.
Archer, Lt.Col. C., *William Archer*, London, George Allen & Unwin, 1931.
Archer, James, *Colin Archer, A Memoir*, Gloucester, privately printed, 1949.
The Arctic Pilot, The Hydrographer of the Navy, 1975.
Armitage, Albert B., *Cadet to Commodore*, London, Cassell, 1924.
—— *Two Years in the Antarctic*, London, Edward Arnold, 1905.

Sources

Arnesen, Odd, *'Fram' Hele Norges Skute*, Oslo, Jacob Dybwads Forlag, 1942.

Asbjørnsen, P. Chr., *Norske huldre-Eventyr og Folkesagn*, Christiania, P.F. Steensballe, 1870.

Asbjørnsen, P. Chr., og Moe, Jørgen, *Norske folke-Eventyr*, Christiania, Jacob Dybwad, 1868.

Astrup, Eivind, *With Peary Near the Pole*, London, C. Arthur Pearson, 1898.

Auswärtiges Amt, *Die Diplomatischen Akten des Auswärtigen Amtes 1871-1914, Kommentar*, Berlin, Deutsche Verlagsgesellschaft für Politik und Geschichte, 1926.

────── *Die Große Politik der Europäischen Kabinette*, Berlin, Deutsche Verlagsgesellschaft für Politik und Geschichte, 54 vols., 1922-27.

Avrich, Paul, *Kronstadt 1921*, Princeton, New Jersey, Princeton University Press, 1970.

Baddeley, John F., *Russia in the 'Eighties'*, London, Longmans, Green and Co., 1921.

Baedeker, K., *Norway and Sweden*, Leipzig, Karl Baedeker, 1889.

Baker, Ray Stannard, *Woodrow Wilson and World Settlement*, London, William Heinemann, 1923.

────── *Woodrow Wilson, Life and Letters*, Vol. 8, London, William Heinemann, undated.

Balabanoff, Angelica, *Impressions of Lenin*, translated by Isotta Cessari, Ann Arbor, University of Michigan Press, 1964.

────── *My Life as a Rebel*, London, Hamish Hamilton, 1938.

Balto, Samuel J., *Med Nansen over Grønlandsisen i 1888*, Oslo, Universitetsforlaget, 1980.

Barry, Richard Ritter von, *Zwei Fahrten in das nördliche-Eismeer*, Pola, Druck und Verlag von Carl Gerold's Sohn in Wien, 1894.

Bauer, Walter, *Fridtjof Nansen: Humanität als Abenteuer*, München, Kindler, 1979.

Beauvais i Hundrede Aar, Copenhagen, Beauvais, 1950.

Benestad, Finn, and Schjelderup-Ebbe, *Edvard Grieg mennesket og kunstneren*, Oslo, Aschehoug, 1980.

Berg, Karin, *Ski i Norge*, Oslo, Aventura, 1993.

Beyer, Marie (ed.), *Breve fra Edvard Grieg til Frants Beyer 1872-1907*, Kristiania, Steenske Forlag, 1923.

Bilton, William, *Two Summers in Norway*, London, Saunders and Otley, 1840.

Bjørnson, Bjørnstjerne, *Artikler og Taler*, Kristiania, Gyldendalske Boghandel Nordisk Forlag, 1913.

────── *Samlede Værker*, Oslo, Gyldendal norsk Forlag, 1940.

Bjørnsrud, Halvor H., *Fridtjof Nansens Kongerike*, Oslo, Noregs Boklag, 1961.

Bjørnstjerne Bjørnsons og Christen Collins Brevveksling 1889-1909, Oslo, Gyldendal norsk Forlag, 1937.

Bjørnstjerne Bjørnsons Breve til Alexander L. Kielland, Oslo, Gyldendal norsk Forlag, 1930.

Bjørnstjerne Bjørnsons Brevveksling med Svenske 1858-1909, Vol. III, 1889-1909, Oslo, Gyldendal norsk Forlag, 1961.

Blehr, Sigurd, *Mot Frigjørelsen*, Vol. 1, Oslo, Cammermeyers Boghandel, 1946.

Bomann-larsen, Tor, *Den Evige Sne*, Oslo, J.W. Cappelens Forlag, 1993.

Bompard, Maurice, *Mon Ambassade en Russie*, Paris, Librairie Plon, 1937.

Bonsal, Stephen, *Suitors and Supplicants*, Bonsal, Stephen, Port Washington, N.Y., 1969.

Brandes, Georg, *Literære Tendenser*, København, Gyldendals Uglebøger, 1968.

Sources

Brändström, Elsa, *Amongst Prisoners in Russia and Siberia*, London, Hutchinson, undated.

Breve fra Alexander L. Kielland, Udgivne af hans sønner, København, Gyldendalske Boghandel Nordisk Forlag, 1907.

British Documents on the Origins of the War 1898-1914, Vol. VIII, London, His Majesty's Stationery Office, 1932.

Brøgger, W.C., and Rolfsen, Nordahl, *Fridtiof Nansen 1861-1893*, Kristiania, Det Nordiske Forlag, 1896.

Brunchorst, Dr. J., *Bergens Museum 1825-1900*, Bergen, John Griegs Forlagsexpedition, 1900.

Bull, Edvard, et al., *Det norske Folks Liv og Historie*, Oslo, Aschehoug, 1929.

Bull, H.J., *The Cruise of the 'Antarctic'*, London, Edward Arnold, 1896.

Bullock, Theodore Holmes, and Horridge, G. Adrian, *Structure and Function in the Nervous System of Invertebrates*, London, W.H. Freeman, 1965.

Caraman, Father Philip, S.J., *Norway*, London, Longmans, 1969.

Carlsson, Sten, and Rosén, Jerker, *Svensk Historia*, Stockholm, Svenska Bokförlaget/Bonniers, 1964.

Carr, Edward Hallett, *A History of Soviet Russia: The Bolshevik Revolution, 1917-1923*, (3 vols.), London, Macmillan, 1950-53.

Carroll, E. Malcolm, *Soviet Communism and Western Opinion 1919-1921*, Chapel Hill, University of South Carolina Press, 1965.

Castberg, Frede, *Minner*, Oslo, Universitetsforlaget, 1971.

Castberg, Johan, *Dagbøker 1900-1917*, Oslo, J.W. Cappelens Forlag, 1953.

Cecil, Robert, *Life in Edwardian England*, London, Batsford, 1969.

Cecil of Chelwood, Viscount, *A Great Experiment*, London, Jonathan Cape, 1941.

——— *All the Way*, London, Hodder and Stoughton, 1949.

Chamberlin, William Henry, *The Russian Revolution 1917-1921*, London, Macmillan, 1935.

Changeux, Jean-Pierre, *Neuronal Man*, Oxford, Oxford University Press, 1986.

Child, Richard Washburn, *A Diplomat Looks at Europe*, New York, Duffield, 1925.

Christensen, Olav, *Skiidrett før Sondre*, Oslo, Ad Notam Gyldendal, 1993.

Churchill, Winston, *The World Crisis, Part IV, The Aftermath*, London, Thornton Butterworth, 1929.

Coates, Vary T., and Finn, Bernard, *The Transatlantic Cable of 1866*, San Francisco, San Francisco Press, 1979.

Coe, Brian, *The Birth of Photography*, London, Ask & Grant, 1976.

Cole, Margaret I. (ed.), *Beatrice Webb's Diaries, 1912-1924*, London, Longmans, Green and Co., 1952.

Collett, Camilla, *Amtmandens Døtre*, Kristiania, Alb. Cammermeyers Forlag, 1897.

Collin, Chr., *Studier og Portræter*, Kristiania, Det norske Aktieforlag, 1901.

Conquest, Robert, *The Harvest of Sorrow*, London, Hutchinson, 1986.

Conway, Sir Martin, *The First Crossing of Spitsbergen*, London, J.M. Dent, 1897.

Cooper, Diana, *The Rainbow Comes and Goes*, London, Rupert Hart-Davis, 1958.

Corder, Percy, *The Life of Robert Spence Watson*, London, Headley Brothers, 1914.

Cowles, Virginia, *Edward VII and his Circle*, London, Hamish Hamilton, 1956.

Craig, Gordon A., and Gilbert, Felix (eds), *The Diplomats 1919-1939*, Princeton, New Jersey, Princeton University Press, 1953.

D'Abernon, Viscount, *The Eighteenth Decisive Battle of the World*, London, Hodder & Stoughton, 1931.

Dahl, Hans Fredrik, *Vidkun Quisling, en Fører blir til*, Oslo, Aschehoug, 1991.

Dass, Petter, *Nordlands Trompet*, Oslo, Aschehoug, 1958.

Sources

Davis, Kathryn W., *The Soviets at Geneva*, Geneva, Librairie Kundig, 1934.

De Capell Brooke, A., *Travels in Sweden, Norway and Finmark*, London, Rodwell and Martin, 1823.

—— *A Winter in Lapland and Sweden*, London, John Murray, 1827.

De Coussange, Jacques, *La Scandinavie, Le Nationalisme Scandinave*, Paris, Librairie Plon, 1914.

De Felipe, Javier De, and Jones, Edward G., *Cajal on the Cerebral Cortex*, New York, Oxford University Press, 1988.

De Long, Emma (ed), *The Voyage of the Jeannette. The ship and ice journals of George W. De Long*, New York, Houghton Mifflin, 1883.

De Taube, Baron M., *La Politique Russe d'Avant-Guerre et la Fin de L'Empire des Tsars*, Paris, Librarie Ernest Leroux, 1928.

Degras, Jane, (ed.) *The Communist International 1919-1943, Documents*, Vol. I, 1919-22, London, Oxford University Press, 1956.

—— *Soviet Documents on Foreign Policy*, Vol. I, London, Oxford University Press, 1951.

Derry, T.K., *A History of Modern Norway 1814-1972*, Oxford, Clarendon Press, 1973.

Didring, Ernst, *Sveriges Hjälp till Krigsfångarna*, Stockholm, P.A. Nordstedt & Söners Förlag, 1920.

Diebitsch-Peary, Josephine, *My Arctic Journal*, New York, Contemporary Publishing Company, 1894.

Dietrichson, L., *Svundne Tider*, 4 vols., Kristiania, J.W. Cappelens Forlag, 1896-1901.

Dietrichson, Vera, *Knut, du lyver!*, Oslo, Aschehoug, 1991.

Dillon, The Hon. Arthur, *A Winter in Iceland and Lapland*, London, Henry Colburn, 1840.

Dillon, E.J., *The Eclipse of Russia*, London, J.M. Dent, 1918.

—— *The Peace Conference*, London, Hutchinson, undated.

Documents Diplomatiques Français (1871-1914) 2ᵉ Série (1910-11), Paris, Imprimerie Nationale, 1938.

Documents on British Foreign Policy 1919-1939, First Series, Vol. III 1919, London, H.M.S.O., 1949; Vol. XX, London, H.M.S.O., 1976.

Dostoyevsky, Fyodor, *The Devils*, translated by David Magarshack, London, Penguin, 1971.

Durand, André, *From Sarajevo to Hiroshima*, Geneva, Henry Dunant Institute, 1984.

Eagar, M., *Six Years at the Russian Court*, London, Hurst and Blackett, 1906.

Eckhoff, Professor Lorentz, (ed.), *De var fra Norge*, Oslo, Alb. Cammermeyers Forlag, 1956.

Edberg, Rolf, *Nansen – Europén*, Stockholm, Tidens Förlag, 1961.

Egeland, John O., *Kongeveien*, Oslo, Aschehoug, 1973.

Eichendorff, Joseph von, *Werke*, Vol. I, Frankfurt am Main, Deutscher Klassiker Verlag, 1987.

Ekstrand, Eric Einar, *Jorden Runt på trettio år*, Stockholm, P.A. Nordstedt & Söners Förlag, 1944.

Ellsworth, Lincoln, *Beyond Horizons*, New York, Doubleday, Doran, 1938.

Eudin, Xenia Joukoff, and Fisher, Harold H., *Soviet Russia and the West 1920-1927*, Stanford, Cal., Stanford University Press.

Falnes, Oscar J., *National Romanticism in Norway*, New York, Columbia University Press, 1933.

Sources

Farnsworth, Beatrice, *William C. Bullitt and the Soviet Union*, Bloomington, Indiania University Press, 1967.

Fasting, Kåre, *Nils Claus Ihlen*, Oslo, Gyldendal norsk Forlag, 1955.

Filchner, Wilhelm, *Ein Forscherleben*, Wiesbaden, Eberhard Brockhaus, 1951.

Fischer, Louis, *Men and Politics*, New York, Duell, Sloan and Pearce, 1941.

Fisher, H.H., *The Famine in Soviet Russia*, New York, MacMillan, 1927.

Fitzmaurice, Lord Edmond, *The Life of Granville George Leveson Gower Second Earl Granville*, London, Longmans Green and Co., 1905.

Fønhus, Mikkjel, *Der Villmarka Susar*, Oslo, Aschehoug, 1987.

────── *Jerv*, Oslo, Aschehoug, 1906.

────── *Varg*, Oslo, Aschehoug, 1987.

Footman, David, *Civil War in Russia*, London, Faber & Faber, 1961.

Forel, August, *Out of My Life and Work*, translated by Bernard Miall, London, George Allen & Unwin, 1937.

Forester, Thomas, *Norway in 1848 and 1849*, London, Longman, Brown, Green, and Longmans, 1850.

Fredborg, Arvid, *Storbritannien och den ryska frågan 1918-20*, Stockholm, P.A. Norstedt & Söners Förlag, 1951.

Freud, Sigmund, *Aus den Anfängen der Psychoanalyse*, Briefe an Wilhelm Fliess, Abhandlungen und Notizen aus den Jahren 1887-1902, London, Imago Publishing, 1950.

────── *Gesammelte Werke*, ii and iii, *Die Traumdeutung, Über den Traum*. London, Imago Publishing Co., 1948.

Friedman, Robert Marc, *Appropriating the Weather: Vilhelm Bjerknes and the Construction of a Modern Meteorology*, London, Cornell University Press, 1989.

Frings, Paul, *Das internationale Flüchtlingsproblem*, Frankfurt am Main, Verlag der Frankfurter Hefte, 1951.

Fristrup, Børge, *Inlandsisen*, København, Rhodos, 1963.

Fueloep-Miller, René, *The Mind and Face of Bolshevism*, New York, Harper Torchbooks, Harper & Row, 1965.

Futrell, Michael, *Northern Underground*, London, Faber & Faber, 1963.

Gad, Finn, *Grønlands Historie*, København, Ejnar Munksgaards Forlag, 1946.

Garborg, Arne, *Bondestundentar, Skriftir i Samling*, Band I, Kristiania, Aschehoug, 1921.

────── *Dagbok 1905-1923*, Kristiania, Aschehoug, 1924.

────── *Trette Menn*, Oslo, Aschehoug, 1991.

Garborg, Hulda, *Dagbok 1903-1914*, Oslo, Aschehoug, 1962.

Garnett, David, *The Golden Echo*, London, Chatto & Windus, 1953.

Gehr, Margarete, and Permi, Jaakko, *Fridtjof Nansens zoologische und neuroanatomische Arbeiten, seine Beziehung zu Camillo Golgi und seine Bedeutung als Neuroanatom*, Ostermundingen, Hirnanatomisches Institut, Psychiatrische Universitätsklinik, 1979.

Geikie, Sir Archibald, *A Long Life's Work*, London, Macmillan, 1924.

Gilbert, Martin, *Winston S. Churchill*, Vol. IV, Companion Parts I and II, London, Heinemann, 1977.

Gillies, A., *Herder*, Oxford, Basil Blackwell, 1945.

Goethe, Johan Wolfgang, *Faust*, Stuttgart, Philipp Reclam Jun., 1991.

Gorky, Maxim, *Days with Lenin*, London, Martin Lawrence, undated.

Gosse, Edmund, *Ibsen*, London, Hodder and Stoughton, 1907.

Graham, Stephen, *The Way of Martha and the Way of Mary*, London, Macmillan, 1915.

Gran, Gerhard, *Norsk Aandsliv i Hundrede Aar*, Kristiania, Aschehoug, 1915.

Sources

Gran, Tryggve, *Fra tjuagutt til sydpolfarer*, Oslo, Ernst G. Mortensens Forlag, 1974.

Grant, N.F. (ed.), *The Kaiser's Letters to the Tsar*, London, Hodder & Stoughton [1920].

Greely, Adolphus W., *Three Years of Arctic Service*, London, Richard Bentley, 1886.

Greve, Tim, *Fridtjof Nansen 1861-1904*, Oslo, Gyldendal norsk Forlag, 1973.

—— *Fridtjof Nansen 1905-1930*, Oslo, Gyldendal norsk Forlag, 1974.

Grew, Joseph G., *Turbulent Era*, London, Hammond, Hammond & Co., 1953.

Grey of Falloddon, Viscount, *Twenty-five Years*, London, Hodder & Stoughton, 1925.

Grønvold, Marcus, *Fra Ulrikken til Alperne*, Oslo, Gyldendal norsk Forlag, 1925.

Gulbransson, Dagny Björnson, *Das Olof Gulbransson Buch*, München, Langen Müller, 1977.

Gunther, A.E., *The Life of William Carmichael M'Intosh, M.D., F.R.S., of St. Andrews, 1838-1931*, St. Andrews University Publications No. LXI, 1977.

Günther, Ernst, *Minnen från Ministertiden i Kristiania Åren 1905-1908*, Stockholm, P.A. Norstedt & Söners Förlag, 1923.

Guttridge, Leonard F., *Icebound*, Annapolis, Maryland, Naval Institute Press, 1986.

Haakonsen, Daniel, *Henrik Ibsen, mennesket og kunstneren*, Oslo, Aschehoug, 1981.

Hakluyt, Richard, *The Principall Navigations Voyages and Discoveries of the English Nation*, London, 1589, Facsimile Edition, Cambridge, at the University Press, 1965.

Hall, Charles Francis, *Arctic Researches and Life among the Esquimaux*, New York, Harper & Brothers, 1865.

Hammer, S.C., *Det Merkelige Aar*, Oslo, Aschehoug, 1930.

—— *Kristianias Historie*, Kristiania, J.W. Cappelen, 1923.

Hamsun, Knut, *Det Vilde Kor*, in *Samlede verker*, Fjerde bind, Oslo, Gyldendal norsk Forlag, 1934.

—— *I Æventyrland*, in *Samlede verker*, Fjerde bind, Oslo, Gyldendal norsk Forlag, 1934.

—— *Pan*, Kristiania, Gyldendalske Boghandel, 1920.

—— *Sult*, Oslo, Gyldendal norsk Forlag, 1971.

—— *Victoria*, in *Samlede Verker*, Første bind, Oslo, Gyldendal norsk Forlag, 1934.

Hansard, Third Series, ccciv; Fourth Series, x.

Hansen, G. Armauer, *Livserindringer og betragtninger*, Kristiania, Aschehoug, 1910.

Hardinge of Penshurst, Lord, *Old Diplomacy*, London, John Murray, 1947.

Harrison, Marguerite, *Born for Trouble*, London, Victor Gollancz, 1936.

Hartmann, Sverre, *Fører uten folk*, Oslo, Tiden norsk Forlag, 1970.

—— (ed.), *Det norske Studentersamfundets Skrift til minne om 1905*, Oslo, det norske Studentersamfundet, 1955.

Hayes, Dr.I.I., *The Open Polar Sea*, London, Sampson Low, Son & Marston, 1867.

Hayes, Paul M., *Quisling*, Newton Abbott, David & Charles, 1971.

Haymaker, Webb, and Schiller, Francis, (eds), *The Founders of Neurology*, Springfield, Illinois, Charles C. Thomas, Publisher, 1970.

Hedin, Alma, *Min Bror Sven*, Stockholm, Wahlström & Wickstrand, 1926.

Hedin, Sven, *Stormän och Kungar*, Vol. i, Helsingfors, Söderström & Co., 1950.

Heiberg, Gunnar, *Pariserbreve*, Kristiania, Aschehoug, 1900.

Sources

Heiberg, J.V., *Unions Opløsning 1905*, Kristiania, J.M. Stenersen & Co.s Forlag, 1906.

Heilbrun, Carolyn G., *The Garnett Family*, London, George Allen & Unwin, 1961.

Helland-Hansen, Bjørn, and Nansen, Fridtjof, *Temperature Variations in the North Atlantic Ocean and in the Atmosphere*, Smithsonian Miscellaneous Collections, Vol. 70 No. 4, Washington, Smithsonian Institution, 1920, pp. 408.

Helle, Karen B., et al., *The Nansen Symposium on New Concepts in Neuroscience*, Bergen, Sigma Forlag, 1987.

Henriksen, Bredo, *Polarfareren Hjalmar Johansen og Skien*, Skien, Eget Forlag, 1961.

Herbert, Wally, *The Noose of Laurels*, New York, Atheneum, 1989.

Herder, Johann Gottfried, *Werke*, Band 2, *Schriften zur ästhetic und Literatur 1767-1781*, Frankfurt am Main, Deutscher Klassiker Verlag, 1993.

Hertling, Knud, et al. (ed.), *Greenland Past and Present*, Copenhagen, Edvard Henriksen, undated.

Hertz, Johanna (ed.), *Heinrich Hertz Memoirs, Letters, Diaries*, San Francisco, San Francisco Press, Inc., 1977.

Hewins, Ralph, *Quisling, Prophet without Honour*, London, W.H. Allen, 1965.

Hildebrand, Fil. Dr. Karl, *Gustav V som Människa och Regent*, Stockholm, Aktiebolaget svensk Litterature, 1945.

Hilger, Gustav, *Wir und der Kreml*, Frankfurt am Main, Athenäum Verlag, 1964.

Hingley, Ronald, *The Russian Mind*, New York, Charles Scribner's Sons, 1977.

Hjälp Ryssland, Stockholm, Centrala Hjälpkommittén för det hungrande Ryssland til förmån för Rysslandshjälpen, 1922.

A History of Technology, Vol. V, *The Late Nineteenth Century*, Oxford, Clarendon Press, 1958.

Hoare, Sir Samuel, *The Fourth Seal*, London, William Heinemann, 1930.

Hodin, J.P., *Edvard Munch*, London, Thames & Hudson, 1972.

Holberg, Ludvig, *Dannemarks og Norges Beskrivelse*, Kjøbenhavn, Johan Jørgen Høpffner, Universitets Bogtrykker, 1729.

——— 'Første Brev til en højvelbaaren Herre', *Ludvig Holberg Værker*, vol. xii, Rosenkilde og Bagger, 1971.

Holland, Clive *Arctic Exloration and Development c. 500 B.C. to 1915*, New York and London, Garland, 1994.

——— (ed.), *Antarctic Obsession*, Alburgh, Bluntisham Books/Erskine Press, 1986.

Holm, G. og Garde, V., *Den Danske Konebaads-Expedition til Grønlands Østkyst*, Copenhagen, Forlagsbureauet i Kjøbenhavn, 1887.

Hoover, Herbert, *Memoirs, Years of Adventure 1874-1920*, London, Hollis & Carter, 1952.

——— *Memoirs, The Cabinet and the Presidency 1920-1933*, London, Hollis and Carter, 1952.

——— *The Ordeal of Woodrow Wilson*, London, Museum Press Ltd., 1958.

Hovdenak, Gunnar, *Roald Amundsens siste Ferd*, Oslo, Gyldendal norsk Forlag, 1934.

Høyer, Liv Nansen, *Eva og Fridtjof Nansen*, Oslo, J.W. Cappelens Forlag, 1954.

——— *Nansen og Verden*, Oslo, J.W. Cappelens Forlag, 1955

Høygaard, Arne, og Mehren, Martin, *'Ajungilak' eller Grønland på Tvers*, Oslo, Gyldendal norsk Forlag, 1931.

Huitfeldt, Fritz, *Lærebog i Skiløbning*, Kristiania, Haffner & Hille, 1896.

Huntford, Roland, *Scott and Amundsen*, London, Hodder & Stoughton, 1979.

——— *Shackleton*, London, Hodder & Stoughton, 1985.

Sources

Hydén, Nils, *Den siste Vikingen*, Stockholm, Lindquists Forlag, 1934.

Henrik Ibsen, *Samlede Verker*, Oslo, Gyldendal norsk Forlag, 1940.

Ibsen, Sigurd, *Udsyn og Indblik*, Kristiania, Gyldendalske Boghandel Nordisk Forlag, 1912.

Idrætsforeningen Odd, *Beretning ved 25 års Jubileet*, Kristiania, W.C. Fabritius & Sønner [1930].

Imbrie, John, and Imbrie, Katherine Palmer, *Ice Ages*, London, Macmillan, 1979.

Ingstad, Helge, *Landet under Leidarstjernen*, Oslo, Gyldendal norsk Forlag, 1960.

Irgens, Francis, *En Norsk Diplomats Liv*, Oslo, Dreyer, 1952.

Iswolsky, Alexandre, *Au Service de la Russie, Correspondence Diplomatique, 1906-1911*, Paris, Les Éditions Internationales, 1939.

Jackson, Frederick, *The Great Frozen Land*, London, Macmillan, 1895.

—— *The Lure of Unknown Lands*, London, G. Bell & Sons, 1935.

—— *A Thousand Days in the Arctic*, London, Harper Brothers, 1899.

Jackson, Holbrook, *The Eighteen-Nineties*, London, Grant Richards, 1913.

Jackson, Stanley, *The Sassoons*, London, Heinemann, 1968.

Jacobson, Marcus, *Developmental Neurobiology*, Third Edition, New York, Plenum Press, 1991.

Jaeger, Dr Gustav, *Selection from Essays on Health-Culture*, London, Dr Jaeger's Sanitary Woollen System Co. Ltd, 1884.

Jaeger, Hans, *Fra Kristiania Bohêmen*, Kristiania, Eget Forlag, 1885.

Jæger, Henrik, *Bergen og Bergensere*, Bergen, F. Beyer, 1889.

—— *Kristiania og Kristianienserne*, Kristiania, F. Beyers Forlag, undated.

James, Patricia (ed.), *The Travel Diaries of Thomas Robert Malthus*, Cambridge, Cambridge University Press, 1966.

Jensen, J.A.D., *Om Inlandsisen i Grønland*, Copenhagen, Forlagsbureauet i København, 1888.

Jensen, Jens Marinus, *I Folkeforbundets Tjeneste*, København, C.A. Reitzels Forlag, 1931.

—— *Fridtjof Nansen*, København, Woels Forlag, 1926.

Jensen, Magnus, *Norges Historie, Unionstiden 1814-1905*, Oslo, Universitetsforlaget, 1971.

Jessen, Franz v., *Begivenheder Jeg Oplevede*, in *Egne, Begivenheder, Mennesker*, København, Gyldendalske Boghandel nordisk Forlag, 1909.

—— *Mennesker Jeg Mødte*, in *Egne, Begivenheder, Mennesker*, København, Gyldendalske Boghandel nordisk Forlag, 1909.

Johansen, Hjalmar, *Selv-anden paa 86°14'*, Kristiania, Aschehoug, 1898.

Johnson, Henry, *The Life and Voyages of Joseph Wiggins, F.R.G.S.*, London, John Murray, 1907.

Johnson, Robert A., *Transformation*, San Francisco, Harper, 1991.

Johnson, T.F., *International Tramps*, London, Hutchinson, 1938.

Jones, A.G.E., *Polar Portraits*, Whitby, Caedmon of Whitby, 1992.

Jungar, Sune, *Ryssland och den Svensk-Norska Unions Upplösning*, Acta academiae Aboensis, Humaniora, Vol. 37 nr. 3, Åbo, Åbo Akademi, 1969.

Juritzen, Arve, *Privatmennesket Quisling og hans to kvinner*, Oslo, Aventura Forlag, 1988.

Just, Karl, *Carl Johans Gate*, Oslo, Ernst G. Mortensens Forlag, 1950.

Kane, Elisha Kent, *Arctic Explorations*, London, Nelson, 1892.

Katkov, George, et al. (eds), *Russia Enters the Twentieth Century*, London, Temple Smith, 1971.

Kazemzadeh, Firuz, *The Struggle for Transcaucasia*, New York, Philosophical Library, 1951.

Sources

Keilhau, Wilhelm, *Norge og Verdenskrigen*, Oslo, Aschehoug, 1927.

Kennan, George, *Siberia and the Exile System*, London, James R. Osgood, McIlvaine & Co., 1891.

Kennan, George F., *Soviet-American Relations, 1917-1920, The Decision to Intervene*, London, Faber & Faber, 1958.

—— *Russia and the West under Lenin and Stalin*, London, Hutchinson, 1961.

Kennedy, Capt. Alex. W.M., *To the Arctic Regions and Back in Six Weeks*, London, Sampson Low, Marston, Searle, & Rivington, 1878.

Kennet, Lady, Kathleen, Lady Scott, *Self-Portrait of an Artist*, London, John Murray, 1949.

Kerguelen Trémarec, *Relation d'un Voyage dans la Mer du Nord*, Paris, De l'Imprimerie de Prault, 1771.

Kern, Stephen, *The Culture of Time and Space 1880-1918*, London, Weidenfeld & Nicolson, 1983.

Kielland, Eugenia, *Nini Roll Anker i Liv og Arbeid*, Oslo, Aschehoug, 1948.

Kinck, Hans E., *Rormanden overbord*, Kristiania, Aschehoug, 1920.

Kirwan, L.P., *The White Road*, London, Hollis & Carter, 1959.

Kish, George, *North-East Passage*, Amsterdam, Nico Israel, 1973.

Kjær, Nils, *Epistler*, Samlede skrifter iv, Kristiania, Gyldendalske Bokhandel, 1922.

Kjærheim, Steinar (ed.), *Fridtjof Nansen Brev*, vols. i-v, Oslo, Universitetsforlaget, 1961-78.

Kjetsaa, Geir, *Maksim Gor'kij i Norge*, Universitetet i Oslo Slavisk-Baltisk Institutt, *Meddelelser*, Nr. 6 1975.

Kloster, Knut Ulstein, *Krigsår og Gullflom*, Oslo, Gyldendal norsk Forlag, 1935.

Knaplund, Paul (ed.), *British Views on Norwegian-Swedish Problems 1880-1895*, Oslo, Norsk Historisk Kjeldeskrift-Institutt, 1952.

Knudsen, Chr., *Spredte Minder fra 1905*, Kristiania, J. Aass Forlag, undated.

Koelliker, A., *Erinnerungen aus meinem Leben*, Leipzig, Verlag von Wilhelm Engelmann, 1899.

Kohn, Hans, *The Mind of Modern Russia*, New Brunswick, New Jersey, Rutgers University Press, 1955.

Koht, Halvdan, *Henrik Ibsen*, Oslo, Aschehoug, 1954.

—— (ed.), *J.E. Sars Brev 1850-1915*, Oslo, Gyldendal norsk Forlag, 1957.

—— *Johan Sverdrup*, Oslo, Aschehoug, 1925.

—— *Minne frå unge år*, Oslo, Aschehoug, 1968.

—— (ed.), *Norske brev – særlig fra 1905 – til Ann Margret Holmgren*, Oslo, Gyldendal norsk Forlag, 1955.

Kokk, D., *Otto Sverdrups Liv*, Oslo, Jacob Dybwads Forlag, 1934.

Det Kongelige Fredriks Universitetet 1811-1911, Festskrift, (2 vols.) Vol. I, Kristiania, Aschehoug, 1911.

Kristensen, Kaptein L., *Antarctic's Reise til Sydishavet*, Tønsberg, Forfatterens Forlag, 1895.

Krogvig, Anders (ed.), *Fra det Nationale Gjennembruds Tid*, Breve fra Jørgen Moe, Kristiania, Aschehoug, 1915.

Kuhlenbeck, Hartwig, *The Central Nervous System of Vertebrates*, Vol. 3, Part 1, Basel, S. Karger, 1970.

Ladas, Stephen P., *The Exchange of Minorities: Bulgaria, Greece and Turkey*, New York, Macmillan, 1932.

Laing, Samuel, *Journal of a Residence in Norway, during the Years 1834, 1835, and 1836*, London, Longman, Rees, Orme, Brown, Green, & Longman, 1836.

Sources

Landquist, John, *Knut Hamsun*, Kjøbenhavn og Kristiania, Gyldendalske Boghandel, 1917.

Lansing, Robert, *The Big Four*, London, Hutchinson, 1922.

Lasson, Bokken, *Slik var det Dengang*, Oslo, Gyldendal norsk Forlag, 1938.

Lausanne Conference on Near Eastern Affairs 1922-1923 Records of Proceedings and Draft Terms of Peace, Cmd. 1814, London, His Majesty's Stationery Office, 1923.

League of Nations, *Records of the First Assembly, Plenary Meetings*, Geneva, 1920.

—— *Records of the First Assembly, Meetings of the Committees*, Geneva 1920.

—— *Records of the Second Assembly, Plenary Meetings*, Geneva, 1921.

—— *Records of the Second Assembly, Meetings of the Committees*, Geneva 1921.

—— *Records of the Third Assembly, Plenary Meetings*, Geneva, 1922.

—— *Records of the Third Assembly, Meetings of the Committees*, Geneva 1922.

League of Nations Council, *Procès-Verbal*, Session 1-5, 1920; Session 6-9, 1920; Session 10-11, 1920.

Leather, John, *Colin Archer and the Seaworthy Double-Ender*, London, Stanford Maritime, 1979.

Lee, Sir Sidney, *King Edward VII*, London, Macmillan, 1927.

Lenin, V.I., *Collected Works*, 45 vols., Moscow, Progress Publishers, 1960-.

Leslie, Anita, *Edwardians in Love*, London, Hutchinson, 1972.

Levine, George, and Knoepflmacher, U.C. (eds), *The Endurance of Frankenstein*, Essays on Mary Shelley's Novel, London, University of California Press, 1974.

Liddell Hart, B.H., *History of the First World War*, London, Pan Books, 1979.

Lie, Michael, *Fra Mit Liv som Diplomat*, Oslo, Gyldendal norsk Forlag, 1929.

Lied, Jonas, *Siberian Arctic*, London, Methuen, 1960.

—— *Return to Happiness*, London, Macmillan, 1943.

Liljequist, Gösta H., *High Latitudes*, Stockholm, Swedish Polar Research Secretariat, 1993.

Lindberg, Folke, *Scandinavia in Great Power Politics 1905-1908*, Acta Universitatis Stockholmiensis, Stockholm Studies in History, No. 1., Stockholm, Almquist & Wiksell, 1958.

—— *Den Svenska Utrikes Politikens Historia*, III:4, 1872-1914, Stockholm, P.A. Norstedt & Söners Förlag, 1958.

Linder, Estrid, *Tretton Kapitel om en lycklig Resa*, Stockholm, Albert Bonniers Förlag, 1919.

Linder, Gurli, *Sällskapsliv i Stockholm under 1880- och 1890-talen*, Stockholm, P.A. Norstedt & Söners Förlag, 1918.

Lindgren, Raymond E., *Norway-Sweden*, Princeton, NJ, Princeton University Press, 1959.

Løchen, Ingeborg Motzfeldt, *Minner fra et Vennskap*, Oslo, Aschehoug, 1962.

Lockhart, R.H. Bruce, *Memoirs of a British Agent*, London, Putnam, 1932.

Løvland, Jørgen, *Menn og Minner fra 1905*, Oslo, Gyldendal norsk Forlag, 1929.

Lowenthal, David, and Bowden, Martyn J. (eds), *Geographies of the Mind*, New York, Oxford University Press, 1976.

Loyrette, Henri, *Gustave Eiffel*, New York, Rizzoli, 1985.

Ludwig, Emil, *Leaders of Europe*, London, J. Nicholson and Watson, 1934.

Luigi Amadeo of Savoy, Duke of the Abruzzi, *On the 'Polar Star' in the Arctic Sea*, London, Hutchinson & Co., 1903.

Lunn, Arnold, *Ski-ing*, London, Eveleigh Nash, 1913.

McCance and Widdowson's The Composition of Foods, London, Royal Society of Chemistry and Ministry of Agriculture, Fisheries and Food, 1991.

Sources

M'Clintock, Admiral Sir F. Leopold, *The Voyage of the 'Fox' in Arctic Seas*, London, John Murray, 1908.

McCollum, E.V., *A History of Nutrition*, Boston, Houghton Mifflin Company, 1957.

McCullagh, Francis, *A Prisoner of the Reds*, London, John Murray, 1921.

McFarlane, James Walter, *Ibsen and the Temper of Norwegian Literature*, London, Oxford University Press, 1960.

McKinlay, William Laird, *Karluk*, London, Weidenfeld & Nicolson, 1976.

McLynn, Frank, *Stanley*, 2 vols, London, Constable, 1989-91.

Mach, Ernst, *The Science of Mechanics*, translated by Thomas J. McCormack, Chicago, Open Court Publishing Co., 1893.

Madariaga, Salvador De, *Christopher Columbus*, London, Hodder & Stoughton, 1939.

Magnus, Olaus, *De Gentium Septentrionalium*, Basilieæ, Ex Officina Henric Petrina, 1567.

Mantoux, Paul, *Les Délibérations du Conseil des Quatre*, Paris, Editions du Centre National de la Recherche Scientifique, 1955.

Markham, Admiral Sir Albert H., *The Life of Sir Clements R. Markham*, London, John Murray, 1917.

Maxwell, Gavin, *Seals of the World*, London, Constable, 1967.

Mayer, Arno J., *Politics and Diplomacy of Peacemaking*, London, Weidenfeld & Nicolson, 1968.

Mehl, Prof. Dr Erwin, *Grundriss der Weltgeschichte des Schifahrens*, Schorndorf bei Stuttgart, Verlag Karl Hoffmann, 1964.

Mennesker jeg Møtte, Tolv Radioforedrag, Oslo, J.M. Stenersens Forlag, 1936.

Meyer, Michael, *Henrik Ibsen*, 3 vols., London, Rupert Hart-Davis, 1967-71.

Militärt kring 1905, Stockholm, Hörsta Förlag, 1958.

Mill, Hugh Robert, *An Autobiography*, London, Longmans Green and Co., 1951.

—— *The Record of the Royal Geographical Society 1830-1930*, London, The Royal Geographical Society, 1930.

—— *The Siege of the South Pole*, London, Alston Rivers, 1905.

Miller, David Hunter, *The Drafting of the Covenant*, New York, G.P. Putnam's Sons, 2 vols., 1928.

Moe, Jørgen, *Fra det Nationale Gjennembruds Tid*, Kristiania, Aschehoug, 1915.

Mohr, Adrian, *Allermanns Gast in Norwegen*, Leipzig, Grethlein & Co, 1931.

Møller, Arvid, *Jo Gjende*, Oslo, J.W. Cappelens Forlag, 1979.

Monflier, Georges, *Le Docteur Fridtjof Nansen a Rouen*, Rouen, Imprimerie Cagniard, 1897.

Moorehead, Alan, *The Russian Revolution*, London, Collins with Hamish Hamilton, 1958.

Munch, Anna E., *Et Nordisk Digterhjem*, København, Fischers Forlag, 1954.

Munch, P., *Die Völkerbundpolitik der drei nordischen Staaten*, Berlin, Verlag von Georg Stilke, 1929.

—— *Erindringer 1870-1909, Fra Skole til Folketing*, København, Nyt Nordisk Forlag Arnold Busk, 1959.

—— *Erindringer 1918-1924, Freden, og Genforeningen og de første efterkrigsaar*, København, Nyt Nordisk Forlag Arnold Busk, 1963.

Munthe, Gerhard, *Karlstad 1905*, Bergen, J.W. Eides Forlag, 1954.

Murav'eva, L.L., and Sivolap-Kaftanova, I.I., *Lenin V Londone*, Moskva, Iédatel'stvo Politicheskoì Literatur'i, 1981.

Næss, Harald, *Knut Hamsun*, Boston, Twayne Publishers, 1984.

Nag, Martin, *Hamsun i russisk åndsliv*, Oslo, Gyldendal norsk Forlag, 1969.

Sources

Nansen, Fridtjof, *Adventure and other Papers*, London, Leonard and Virginia Woolf, 1927.
—— *Blant Sel og Bjørn*, Oslo, Aschehoug, 1961.
—— *Dagbok fra 1905*, Oslo, Aschehoug, 1955.
—— *Eskimoliv*, Kristiania, Aschehoug, 1891.
—— *Fram over Polhavet*, Kristiania, Aschehoug, 1897.
—— *Frilufts-Liv*, Kristiania, Jacob Dybwads Forlag, 1916.
—— *Gjennom Armenia*, Oslo, Aschehoug, 1962.
—— *Gjennem Sibirien*, Kristiania, Jacob Dybwads Forlag, 1914.
—— *Nord i Tåkeheimen*, Kristiania, Jacob Dybwads Forlag, 1911.
—— *Norway and the Union with Sweden*, London, MacMillan, 1905.
—— (ed.) *The Norwegian North Polar Expedition 1893-1896 Scientific Results*, 6 vols, London, Longmans, 1900-06.
—— *Paa Ski over Grønland*, Kristiania, Aschehoug, 1890.
—— *Russia & Peace*, London, George Allen & Unwin, 1923.
—— *Through the Caucasus to the Volga*, London, George Allen & Unwin, 1931.
—— *Through Siberia the Land of the Future*, London, William Heinemann, 1914.
Nansen, Odd, *Langs Veien*, Oslo, Gyldendal norsk Forlag, 1970.
Nansens Røst, Oslo, Jacob Dybwads Forlag, 1945.
Nares, Capt. Sir George, *Narrative of a Voyage to the Polar Sea*, London, Sampson, Low, Marston, Searle & Rivington, 1878.
Negri, Francesco, da Ravenna, *Viaggio settentrionale*, Padova, Nella Stamperia del Seminario, 1700.
Nerbrøvik, Jostein, *Antiparlamentariske straumdrag i Noreg 1905-14*, Oslo, Universitetsforlaget, 1969.
Nicolson, Harold, *Peacemaking 1919*, London, Constable, 1944.
—— *Curzon: The Last Phase*, London, Constable & Co., 1934.
Nielsen, Yngvar, *Da Unionen skulde Briste*, Kristiania, Gyldendalske Boghandel Nordisk Forlag, 1915.
—— *En Christianiensers Erindringer*, Kristiania, Gyldendalske Boghandel Nordisk Forlag, 1910.
—— *Norge i 1905*, Horten, C. Andersens Forlag, 1906.
Nietzsche, Friedrich, *Thus Spoke Zarathustra*, translated by R.J. Hollingdale, London, Penguin, 1969.
Nissen, Bernt A., *Gunnar Knudsen*, Oslo, Aschehoug, 1957.
Nobel Lectures, Physiology or Medicine 1901-1921, Amsterdam, Elsevier, 1967.
Nockher, Dr Ludwig, *Fridtjof Nansen*, Stuttgart, Wissenschaftliche Verlagsgesellschaft, 1955.
Nordahl, Bernhard, *Framgutterne*, Kristiania, Edv. Magnussens Forlag, 1898.
Nordenskiöld, A.E., *Den Andra Dicksonska Expeditionen till Grönland*, Stockholm, F. & G. Beijers Förlag, 1885.
—— *Vegas färd kring Asien och Europa*, Stockholm, F. & G. Beijer, 1880-81.
Norland, Andreas, *Hårde Tider*, Oslo, Dreyers Forlag, 1973.
Norge 1814-1914, Kristiania, Albert Cammermeyer's Forlag, 1914.
Norsk Biografisk Leksikon, Oslo, Aschehoug, 1923-86.
Norske Skiløpere, Oslo, Skiforlaget Erling Ranheim, 1955.
O'Brien, Francis William, *Two Peacemakers in Paris*, College Station, Texas A & M University Press, 1978.
Olrik, Axel, *Folkelige Afhandlinger*, Kjøbenhavn, Gyldendalske Boghandel, 1919.
Om Opdragelse og Undervisning, Fra Mødet i det Pædagogiske Samfund den 23de April 1900, Kristiania, Aschehoug, 1900.

Sources

Omang, Reidar, *Norge og Stormaktene 1906-14* (Skrifter utgitt av Det. Kgl. Utenriksdepartments Arkiv 3), Oslo, Gyldendal norsk Forlag, 1957.

───── *Norsk Utenrikstjeneste, Grunnleggende år*, Oslo, Gyldendal norsk Forlag, 1955.

Ore, Oystein, *Nils Henrik Abel*, Minneapolis, University of Minnesota Press, 1957.

Oscar II, *Mina Memoarer*, Stockholm, P.A. Norstedt & Söners Förlag, 1960.

Østvedt, Einar, *Hjalmar Johansen*, Skien, Selskapet for Skien Bys Vel, 1967, 1978.

Papers Relating to the Foreign Relations of the United States, 1919, Vol. XI, Washington, United States Government Printing Office, 1945.

Papers Relating to the Foreign Relations of the United States, 1919, Russia, Washington, U.S.G.P.O., 1937.

Papers Relating to the Foreign Relations of the United States, The Paris Peace Conference, 1919, Vol. V, Washington, U.S.G.P.O., 1946.

Papers Relating to the Foreign Relations of the United States, 1921, Vol. II, Washington, U.S.G.P.O., 1936.

Papers Relating to the Foreign Relations of the United States, 1922, Vol. II, Washington, U.S.G.P.O., 1938.

Papers Relating to the Foreign Relations of the United States, 1923, Vol. II, Washington, U.S.G.P.O., 1938.

Pares, Bernard, *A History of Russia*, London, Jonathan Cape, 1955.

Parkinson, Claire L., *Breakthroughs*, London, Mansell, 1985.

Parry, Captain William Edward, *Narrative of an Attempt to Reach the North Pole*, London, John Murray, 1828.

Paulsen, John, *Mine Erindringer*, Kjøbenhavn, Gyldendalske boghandels Forlag, 1900.

───── *Samliv med Ibsen*, København, Gyldendalske Boghandel, Nordisk Forlag, 1906.

Payer, Julius, *Die österreichisch-ungarische Nordpol-Expedition*, Wien, Alfred Hölder, 1876.

Payne, Robert, *Lenin*, London, W.H. Allen, 1964.

Peary, Robert E., *Northward over the 'Great Ice'*, London, Methuen, 1898.

───── *The North Pole*, London, Hodder & Stoughton, 1910?

Peel, Helen, *Polar Gleams*, London, Edward Arnold, 1894.

Perry, Bliss, *And Gladly Teach*, Boston, Houghton Mifflin, 1935.

Petersen, H.C., *Skinboats of Greenland*, Roskilde, National Museum of Denmark, 1986.

Pound, Reginald, and Harmsworth, Geoffrey, *Northcliffe*, London, Cassell, 1959.

Prins Eugen, *Brevene forteller*, Oslo, Gyldendal norsk Forlag, 1946.

Quigstad, J.K., *Lappiske Eventyr og Sagn*, Oslo, Aschehoug, 1927.

Quisling, Vidkun, *Russland og vi*, Oslo, Jacob Dybwads Forlag, 1930.

Radek, Karl, *Portraits and Pamphlets*, London, Wishart Books, 1935.

Ramm, Agatha, *Sir Robert Morier*, Oxford, Clarendon Press, 1973.

Ramón y Cajal, Santiago, *Histologie du Système Nerveux de l'Homme et des Vertébrés*, Paris, Maloine, 1909.

───── *Les Nouvelles Idées sur la Structure du Système nerveux*, translated by Dr L. Ayoulay, Paris, C. Reinwald, 1894.

───── *Neuron Theory or Reticular Theory?*, Madrid, Instituto 'Ramon y Cajal', 1954.

───── *Recollections of my Life*, Cambridge, Mass. M.I.T. Press, 1937.

Ransome, Arthur, *Six Weeks in Russia in 1919*, London, Independent Labour Party, 1919.

Sources

The Record of the Save the Children Fund, London, Vol. 2, 1921-22.

Recueil de lettres, Proclamations et Discours de Charles Jean, Stockholm, de'limprimerie de C. Deleen, 1825. Seconde partie 1838.

Reed, John, *Ten Days that Shook the World*, London, Lawrence & Wishart, 1961.

Report of the Sixth International Geographical Congress, Held in London, 1895, London, John Murray, 1896.

Retzius, Gustaf, *Biografiska Anteckningar och Minnen*, Vol. II, Uppsala, Almquist & Wiksells Boktryckeri AB, 1948.

Reynolds, E.E., *Nansen*, London, Geoffrey Bles, 1932.

Rich, E.E. (ed.), *John Rae's correspondence with the Hudson's Bay Company on Arctic Exploration 1844-1855*, London, Publications of the Hudson's Bay Record Society, no. 16, 1953.

Richardson, Sir John, *Arctic Searching Expeditions*, London, Longman, Brown, Green and Longmans, 1851.

Lord Riddell's Intimate Diary of the Peace Conference and After, London, Victor Gollancz, 1933.

Riffenburgh, Bruce A., *The Anglo-American Press and the Sensationalization of the Arctic 1855-1910*, Unpublished thesis submitted to the University of Cambridge for the degree of Doctor of Philosophy, 1991.

Rink, H., *Om Grønlands Indland*, Kjøbenhavn, G.E.C. Gad, 1875.

Riste, Olav, *The Neutral Ally*, London, Allen & Unwin, 1965.

Risthelhueber, Réné. *La Double Aventure de Fridtjof Nansen*, Montreal, Les Éditions variétés, 1944.

Risting, Sigurd, *Kaptein C.A. Larsen*, Oslo, J.W. Cappelens Forlag, 1929.

Robbins, Keith, *Sir Edward Grey*, London, Cassell, 1971.

Robbins, Richard J., Jr., *Famine in Russia 1891-1892*, New York and London, Columbia University Press, 1975.

Rodd, Sir James Rennell, *Social and Diplomatic Memories 1902-1919*, London, Edward Arnold, 1925.

Rumbold, Sir Horace, .*Further Recollections of a Diplomatist*, London, Edward Arnold, 1903.

—— *Recollections of a Diplomatist*, London, Edward Arnold, 1902.

Sanness, Tor Borch, *Fram*, Oslo, Norsk Maritimt Forlag, 1989.

—— *Colin Archer skipene*, Oslo, Bokhandlerforlaget, 1978.

—— *Colin Archer skøytene og lystbåtene*, Oslo, Norsk Maritimt Forlag, 1979.

Schapiro, Leonard, *The Communist Party of the Soviet Union*, London, Eyre & Spottiswoode, 1970.

Scheme for the Settlement of Armenian Refugees, Geneva, League of Nations, 1927.

Schley, Commander W.C., and Soley, Professor J.R., *The Rescue of Greely*, London, Sampson, Low, Marston, n.d.

Jakob Schønings Dagbøker, Oslo, Johan Grundt Tanum Forlag, 1950.

Schück, H., et al., *Nobel, The Man and his Prizes*, Stockholm, Sohlmans Forlag, 1950.

Schulte, Gabriéle, *Hamsun im Spiegel der deutschen Literaturkritik 1890 bis 1975*, Frankfurt am Main, P. Lang, 1986.

Schuster, Sir George, *Private Work and Public Causes*, Cowbridge, D. Brown and Sons, 1979.

Scott Russell, *The Modern System of Naval Architecture*, London, Day and Son, 1864.

Scott, George, *The Rise and Fall of the League of Nations*, London, Hutchinson, 1973.

Scott, Captain Robert F., *The Voyage of the 'Discovery'*, London, Macmillan, 1905.

Scott's Last Expedition, London, Smith, Elder, 1913.

Seeger, Charles Louis (ed.), *The Memoirs of Alexander Iswolsky*, London, Hutchinson, 1920.

Seton-Watson, Hugh, *The Russian Empire 1801-1917*, Oxford, Clarendon Press, 1967.

Seymour, Charles, (ed.), *The Intimate Papers of Colonel House*, Vol. IV, London, Ernest Benn, 1928.

———*Letters from the Paris Peace Conference*, New Haven, Yale University Press, 1965.

Shepherd, Gordon M., *Foundations of the Neuron Doctrine*, Oxford, Oxford University Press, 1991.

Sherrington, C.S., *A Text Book of Physiology*, Part III, *The Central Nervous System*, London, Macmillan, 1897.

Simson, Gerhard, *Fünf Kämpfer für Gerechtigkeit*, München, C.H. Beck'sche Verlagsbuchhandlung, 1951.

Slingsby, W. Cecil, *Norway: The Northern Playground*, Oxford, Basil Blackwell, 1941.

Smith, Michael Llewellyn, *Ionian Vision*, London, Allen Lane, 1973.

Smythe, F.S., *Edward Whymper*, London, Hodder & Stoughton, 1940.

Snorre Sturlason, *Kongesagaer*, Nationaludgave, Kristiania, J.M. Stenersen & Co's Forlag, 1900.

Sørensen, Jon, *Fridtjof Nansens Saga*, Oslo, Jacob Dybwads Forlag, 1940.

Spengler, Oswald, *Der Undergang des Abendlandes*, München, C.H. Beck'sche Verlagsbuchhandlung, 1923.

Stafford, Marie Peary, *Discoverer of the North Pole*, New York, William Morrow & Company, 1959.

Staib, Bjørn O., *Nanok – Over Grønland i Nansens spor*, Oslo, Ernst G. Mortensens Forlag, 1962.

Stalin, J.V., *Works*, Volume 2, Moscow, Foreign Languages Publishing House, 1953.

Stanislavski, Constantin, *My Life in Art*, London, Geoffrey Bles, 1962.

Stanley, H.M., *How I found Livingstone*, London, Sampson, Low, Marston, Low and Searle, 1872.

——— *In Darkest Africa*, 2 vols., London, Sampson Low, Marston, Searle & Rivington, 1890.

Statsråd Edvard Hagerup Bulls dagbøker fra 1905, Oslo, Gyldendal norsk Forlag, 1955.

Steen, T.E., *Négociations pour les Prisonniers de Guerre*, Paris, Librairie Hachette & Co., 1918.

Steffens, Lincoln, *The Autobiography of Lincoln Steffens*, vol. ii, London, Harrap, 1931.

Stenseth, Bodil, *En norsk Elite*, Oslo, Aschehoug, 1993.

Steveni, William Barnes, *The Scandinavian Question*, London, T. Fisher Unwin, 1905

Stokland, Olav, *Av Norges indre Historie*, Oslo, Dreyers Forlag, 1969.

Stone, Norman, *Europe Transformed 1878-1919*, London, Fontana Press, 1990.

Street, C.J.C., *President Masaryk*, London, Geoffrey Bles, 1930.

Stuart, Denis, *Dear Duchess*, London, Victor Gollancz, 1982.

Suarez, Georges, *Briand*, Paris, Librairie Plon, 1952.

Sulloway, Frank J., *Freud, Biologist of the Mind*, London, Burnett Books, 1979.

Sundman, Per Olof, *Ingen fruktan, intet hopp*, Stockholm, Bonniers, 1968.

Sources

———— *Ingenjör Andrées luftfärd*, Stockholm, P.A. Nordstedt & Söners Förlag, 1968.

Szamueli, Helen, *British Attitudes to Russia*, 1880-1918, Unpublished thesis submitted for the degree of D. Phil. at the University of Oxford, July 1982.

Tallents, Sir Stephen, *Man and Boy*, London, Faber & Faber, 1943.

Tegnér, Esaias, *Frithiofs Saga*, in *Samlade Skrifter*, Stockholm, P.A. Norstedt & Söners Förlag, 1921.

Temperley, H.W.V. (ed.), *A History of the Peace Conference of Paris*, London, Henry Frowde and Hodder & Stoughton, 1920-24.

Thesen, Rolv, *Ein diktar og hans strid*, Oslo, Aschehoug, 1991.

Thompson, Ruth D'Arcy, *D'Arcy Wentworth Thompson*, London, Oxford University Press, 1958.

Trotsky, Leon, *On Lenin*, London, Harrap, 1971.

Tuan, Yi-Fu, *Topophilia*, Englewood Cliffs, NJ, Prentice-Hall, Inc., 1974

Turi, Johan, *Turi's Book of Lappland*, edited and translated into Danish by Hatt, Emilie Demant; translated from the Danish by Nash, E. Gee, original title, *Muittalus Samid Birra*, London, Jonathan Cape, 1931.

Turville-Petre, E.O.G., *Myth and Religion of the North*, London, Weidenfeld & Nicolson, 1964.

Tveterås, Harald L., *Et norsk Kulturforlag gjennom Hundre år*, Oslo, Aschehoug, 1972.

Tweedie, Mrs Alec, *A Winter Jaunt to Norway*, London, Bliss Sands & Foster, 1894.

———— *Tight Corners of My Adventurous Life*, London, Hutchinson & Co., 1933.

Ueland, Brenda, *Me*, New York, G.P. Putnam's Sons, 1939.

Ullman, Richard H., Anglo-Soviet Relations, 1917-1921, Vol. II *Britain and the Russian Civil War*, Princeton, NJ, Princeton University Press, 1968.

———— Vol. III *The Anglo-Soviet Accord*, Princeton, NJ, Princeton University Press, 1972.

United States Senate, Committee on Foreign Relations, *US Congressional Hearings (Senate Library)*, 41st-73rd Congress, 1869-1934, Vol. 159, (1919) p. 1161, Friday 12 September 1919.

Urdahl, Laurentius, *Handbog i Skiløbning*, Kristiania, Hjalmar Biglers Forlag, 1893.

———— *Greenland*, Copenhagen, C.A. Reitzel, 1928.

Vaage, Jakob, *Norsk Idrettslitteratur gjennom 200 år*, Horten, Jørgensens Trykkeri, 1970.

———— *Norske Ski Erobre Verden*, Oslo, Gyldendal norsk Forlag, 1952.

———— *Skienes Verden*, Oslo, Hjemmenes Forlag, n.d.

Vahl, M., Amdrup, G.C., Bobé, L., Jensen, Ad. S. (eds), *Greenland*, Copenhagen, C.A. Reitzel, 1928.

Verhandlungen des Siebenten Internationalen Geographen-Kongresses, Berlin, W.H. Kühl, 1901.

Vestgrønlænder Kateket Hansêraks Dagbog, Copenhagen, H. Hagerup's Forlag, 1900.

Victor, Paul-Emile, and Joelle, Robert Lamblin, *La Civilisation du Phoque*, Armand Colin, Raymond Chabaud, 1989 [no place of publication].

Vinje, A.O., *Skrifter i Samling*, Kristiania, J.W. Cappelens Forlag, 1916.

Vogt, Nils Collett, *Fra gutt til mann*, Oslo, Aschehoug, 1968.

Voit, C. von, *Physiologie des Stoffenwechsels*, in Hermann, L., *Handbuch der Physiologie*, Sechster Band, I. Theil, Leipzig, Verlag von F.C.W.Vogel, 1881.

Von Enzberg, Eugen, *Fridtjof Nansen*, Dresden, Verlag von Carl Reitzner, 1898.

583

Sources

Von Franz, Marie-Louise, *Puer aeternus*, Santa Monica, Sigo Press, 1981.

Von Laue, Theodore H., *Sergei Witte and the Industrialization of Russia*, New York and London, Columbia University Press, 1963.

Von Moltke, Generaloberst Helmuth, *Erinnerungen, Briefe Dokumente*, Stuttgart, Der Kommende Tag A.-G. Verlag, 1922.

Walters, F.P., *A History of the League of Nations*, London, Oxford University Press, 2 vols., 1952.

Ward, Sarita, *A Valiant Gentleman*, London, Chapman and Hall, 1927.

Wedel Jarlsberg, F., *Reisen Gjennem Livet*, Oslo, Gyldendal norsk Forlag, 1932.

–––––– *1905 Kongevalget*, Oslo, Gyldendal norsk Forlag, 1946.

Weems, John Edward, *Peary*, London, Eyre & Spottiswoode, 1967.

Wegener, Georg, *Zum Ewigen Eise*, Berlin, Algemeiner Verein für Deutsche Litteratur, 1897.

Weibull, Jörgen, *Bernadotterna på Sveriges tron*, Stockholm, Bonniers, 1971.

Wetterfors, Paul, *Fridtjof Nansen*, Uppsala, J.A. Lindblads Förlag, 1931.

Wheeler, Sara, *An Island Apart, Travels in Evia*, London, Little Brown, 1992.

White, John Albert, *The Diplomacy of the Russo-Japanese War*, Princeton, NJ, Princeton University Press, 1964.

White, Stephen, *Britain and the Bolshevik Revolution*, London, Macmillan, 1977.

Whitehouse, J. Howard (ed.), *Nansen, a book of Homage*, London, Hodder & Stoughton, 1930.

Whittaker, D.J., *Fighter for Peace*, York, William Sessions, 1989.

Widén, Johan, *Dagboksanteckningar 1901-1913*, ed. Arne Wåhlstrand, Stockholm, Kung. Samfundet för utgivande av handskrifter rörande Skandinaviens historia. Handlingar del 10, 1984.

Wille, C., *Den norske Nordhavs-Expedition 1876-1878 Historisk Beretning*, Christiania, Grøndahl & Søns Bogtrykkeri, 1882.

Williams, W. Mattieu, *Through Norway with a Knapsack*, London, Smith, Elder, 1859.

–––––– *Through Norway with Ladies*, London, Edward Stanford, 1877.

Winter, Ella, and Hicks, Granville (eds), *The Letters of Lincoln Steffens*, Vol. I, Westport, Conn., Greenwood Press, 1974.

Wolfe, Bertram D., *The Bridge and the Abyss*, London, Pall Mall Press, 1967.

–––––– *Three Who Made a Revolution*, New York, Dial Press, 1948.

Wood, Charles W., *Round about Norway*, London, Richard Bentley, 1880.

Young, Louisa, *A Great Task of Happiness*, London, Macmillan, 1995.

Zachariassen, *Karl Johanssen*, Oslo, det norske Arbeiderpartis Forlag, 1932.

Zeilau, Th., *Fox-Expeditionen i Aaret 1860*, Kjøbenhavn, Fr. Woldikes Forlagsboghandel, 1861.

Zeman, Z.A.B., and Scharlau, W.B., *The Merchant of Revolution*, London, Oxford University Press, 1965.

Die Zweite Deutsche Nordpolarfahrt, Erste Band, Leipzig, F.A. Brockhaus, 1873.

Articles

'A Traveller', 'The Norway Stare', *The Bystander* (14 August 1907), p. 334.

Agardh, I.G., 'Om den Spetsbergska Drif-vedens ursprung', *Öfversigt af Kongl. Vetenskaps-Akademiens Förhandlingar* (1869), no. 2, pp. 97-119.

Amundsen, Captain Roald, 'To the North Magnetic Pole and through the North-West passage', *Geographical Journal*, xxix (1907), 486-518 [paper read at the RGS 11 February 1907].

Sources

Andrée, S.A., 'A Plan to reach the North Pole by Balloon', *Report of the Sixth International Geographical Congress*, pp. 211-27.

H.A. [H. Angell], 'En Skitur fra Hardanger til Kongsberg', *Morgenbladet* [Christiania] (10 March 1884).

Anker, Øyvind, 'Gerhard Gran og Bjørnstjerne Bjørnson', *Edda*, xxxv (1935).

Archer, Colin, 'On the Wave Principle Applied to the Longitudinal Disposition of Immersed Volume', *Transactions of the Institution of Naval Architects*, xix (1878), pp. 218-31.

———— 'The Fram', *The Norwegian North Polar Expedition 1893-1896, Scientific Results*, Vol. 1, pp. 5-16.

Archer, William, 'Dr Nansen on Ibsen', *Tribune* (26 May 1906).

———— 'Ibsen as I knew him', *Monthly Review*, xxiii (June 1906), pp. 1-19.

'Arctic Exploring Expeditions', *Geographical Journal*, ii, no. 5 (November 1893), p. 463.

Astrup, Eivind, 'Løitnant Peary's Grønlandsekspedition 1891-92', *Det Norske Geografiske Selskabs Årbog*, v (1891-92), pp. 25-44.

Atkinson, Meredith, 'Soviet Russia and the Famine', *The Nineteenth Century*, xci (April 1922), pp. 603-12.

'Av Edvard Griegs Breve til Aimar Grønvold', *Samtiden*, xxxviii (1927), pp. 79-88.

Baldwin, E Briggs, 'The Baldwin-Ziegler Polar Expedition', *Wide World Magazine*, x (1903), pp. 396-402, 432-36, 587-93.

Barr, Professor William, 'The Last Journey of Peter Tessem and Paul Knutsen, 1919', *Arctic*, xxxvi, no. 4 (December 1983), pp. 311-27.

Berelowitch, Wladimir, 'La diplomatie de la famine', *L'Express* (15 August 1985), pp. 40-5.

Bjørlykke, K.O., 'Den norske nordpolsekspedition', *Det Norske Geografiske Selskabs Årbog*, no. IV (1892-93), pp. 86-104

Bjørnson, Bjørnstjerne, 'The Political Crisis in Norway', *Review of Reviews* (June 1892), p. 362.

Bloch-Hoell, Nils E., *Fridtjof Nansen og religionen – Kirken og Fridtjof Nansen*, Nansen Minneforelesning (10 Oktober 1984).

Bobé, Louis, 'Borgmester Hans Nansens Efterslægt', *Personalhistorisk Tidsskrift*, Tredje Række, 1 Bind, (1892), pp. 9-17.

'The Book of the Month, Nansen's "Farthest North"', *Review of Reviews*, xv (1897), pp. 276-85.

Brandes, Georg, 'Friedrich Nietzsche', I 'En Afhandling om aristokratisk Radikalisme', 1889, *Samlede Skrifter*, syvende Bind, Kjøbenhavn, Gyldendalske Boghandels Forlag (1901), pp. 596-644

———— 'Søren Kierkegaard', *Samlede Skrifter*, Kjøbenhavn, Gyldendalske Boghandels Forlag, ii, pp. 251-404

Brassey, Annie, [Lady Brassey], 'Mr. Gladstone in Norway', *Contemporary Review*, xlviii (July-December 1885), pp. 480-502.

Brice, Arthur Montefiore, 'The Jackson-Harmsworth Polar Expedition', *Geographical Journal*, viii (December 1896), 543-65.

Brinkmann jr., August, 'Fridtjof Nansen som Zoolog', *Naturen*, lxxxv (1961), pp. 387-404.

Brøgger, W.C., 'Fridjof Nansen og Videnskapsakademiet', *Morgenbladet* (24 May 1930).

Brown, Dr Robert, 'Das Innere von Grönland', *Petermann's Geographische Mitttheilungen*, 17 Band (1871), pp. 377-89.

Browne, T.L. Murray, 'The Glittertind and Uledalstind in Norway', *Alpine Journal*, v, no. XXXII (February 1871), pp. 154-70.

Sources

Bull, E. Hagerup, 'Fra 1905', *Samtiden*, vol. xxxvii (1926), pp. 197-207, 269-80, 333-45, 385-95, 449-63, 521-42.

Bullitt, W.C., 'United States Senate, Committee on Foreign Relations, Statement of Mr William C. Bullitt, September 12th 1919', *U.S. Congressional Hearings (Senate Library) 41st-73rd Cong.1869-1934*, clix, pp. 1161-297, Washington, D.C., Congressional Information Services (1984).

Busk, Douglas, 'Prehistoric Ski-ing in Russia', *British Ski Year Book* (1960), pp. 30-3.

Campbell, J.R., 'Excursions in Norway', *Alpine Journal*, v, no. XXX (August 1870), pp. 49-62.

'Captain Sverdrup's Expedition to Northern Greenland', *Geographical Journal*, xii, no. 2 (February 1899), pp. 136-47.

Carlgren, W.M., & Lindberg, Folke, 'Ett svenskt förslag till stormaktsintervention i unionskonflikten våren 1899', *Historisk Tidskrift*, lxxiii, pp. 258-69.

Cereghini, Mario, 'Le ski dans la littérature et l'iconographie italiennes du 16ᵉ siècle', *Die Alpen*, xxvi (1950), pp. 114-20.

'Colonel Feilden on Current Polar Exploration', *Geographical Journal*, iv, no. 3, (October 1894), pp. 365-6.

Cyriax, Richard J., 'Arctic Sledge Travelling by Officers of the Royal Navy, 1819-49', *Mariner's Mirror*, xlix, no. 2 (May 1963), pp. 127-42.

Dainelli, Giotto, 'The Geographical Work of H.R.H. The late Duke of the Abruzzi', *Geographical Journal*, lxxxii (1933), pp. 1-15.

Dalager, Lars, 'Grønlandske Relationer indeholdende Grønlændernes Liv og Vedtægter' [1752], *Det Grønlandske Selskabs Skrifter*, II (1915).

De Quervain, A., and Mercanton, P.L., 'Ergebnisse der Schweizerische Grönlandexpedition', *Neue Denkschriften der Schweizerischen Naturforschenden Gesellschaft*, Band LIII (1920).

'Det festlige Møde i Anledning af Dr Fridtjof Nansens Expedition', *Geografisk Tidskrift*, 10de Bind (1889-90), pp. 53-64.

'Die arktische Campagne, 1880', *Petermann's Mittheilungen*, 26. Band (1880), p. 424.

'Die Erschliessung eines Theiles des nördlichen Eismeeres', *Petermann's Mittheilungen*, 17. Band (1871), pp. 97-110.

Die Reisen des 'Jason' und der 'Hertha' in das Antarktische Meer 1893/94, Separatabdruck aus den Mitteilungen der Geographischen Gesellschaft in Hamburg (1891-92).

'Die Südküste von Franz Josef-Land nach B. Leigh Smith', *Petermann's Mittheilungen*, 26. Band (1880), pp. 464-5.

Dietrichson, O.C., 'Fra Dr Nansen's Grønlandsexpedition', *Aftenposten* (23 May 1889).

—— 'Hvad man kan Opleve under en Kajakktur i Polaregnen', *Polar-Årboken* (1935), pp. 15-18

—— 'Otto Neumann Sverdrup', *Norsk Geografisk Tidsskrift* (1931), pp. 285-9.

'Diplomatarium Groenlandicum 1492-1814', *Meddelelser om Grønland*, Bd. 55, Nr. 1 (1936).

Doyle, Sir Arthur Conan, 'A Ski Tour in 1893', *The British Ski Year Book* (1924), pp. 245-9.

'Dr Fridtof Nansens Brev fra Godthaab til Etatsraad Augustin Gamél', *Geografisk Tidskrift*, 10de Bind (1889-90), p. 3.

'Dr Fridtjof Nansens officielle Rapport til Etatsraad Gamél', *Geografisk Tidskrift*, 10de Bind (1889-90), pp. 65-72.

Sources

'Dr Nansen's Advance towards the North Pole', *Scottish Geographical Magazine*, xii (1896), pp. 481-3.

'Dr Nansen's Book', *Daily Chronicle*, 15 February 1897.

'Dr Nansen's Arctic Expedition', *Geographical Journal*, i, no. 6 (December 1893), p. 554.

'Dr Nansen's Expedition', *Geographical Journal*, ii, no. 2, p. 174.

'Dr Nansen's North Polar Expedition', *Geographical Journal*, vii, no. 3 (March 1896), p. 317.

'Dr Nansen's Polar Expedition', *Geographical Journal*, ii, no. 1, p. 69; ii, no. 4, p. 36.

'Dr Nansen's Progress', *Geographical Journal*, ii, no. 3 (September 1893), p. 272.

'Dr Nansen's Return', *Geographical Journal*, viii, no. 3 (September 1896), p. 279.

'Dr Nansen's Scientific Results', *Geographical Journal*, xviii, no. 3 (September 1901), pp. 284-7.

'Dr Nansen's Scientific Researches', *Nautical Magazine*, xlviii, no. 5 (May 1899), pp. 328-9.

'Dr Nansen's Statements', *Nautical Magazine*, lxvix, no. 9 (September 1900), pp. 521-2.

'Dr Nansen's Third Volume of Scientific Results', *Geographical Journal*, xx, no. 4 (October 1902), pp. 332-4.

'Duality in Scandinavia: Dr Nansen', *Review of Reviews*, xxxi (1905), pp. 366-7.

Dudden, Arthur P., and von Laue, Theodore H., 'The RSDLP and Joseph Fels: A Study in Intercultural Contact', *American Historical Review*, LXI, no. 1 (October 1955), pp. 21-54.

Duff, Sir Mountstuart E.Grant, P.R.G.S., 'The annual address on the Progress of Geography, 1892-93', *Geographical Journal*, II, no. 1, p. 1.

Eberlin, Peter, 'Fridtof Nansen's Plan at løbe paa Ski tværs over Grönland', *Ny Jord* (February 1888), pp. 186-90.

——— 'Sundet, der i gamle Dage skal have gaaet tværs over Nordgrønland', *Geografisk Tidskrift*, 9de Bind (1888-89), heft IV, pp. 73-5.

Edwards, John S., 'Nordic Polymath', *The World & I* (April 1991), pp. 324-31.

Ekman, V. Walfrid, 'Om jordrotationens inverkan på vindströmmar i hafvet', *Nyt Magazin for Naturvidenskaberne*, Bind 40 (1902), pp. 37-63.

——— 'On Dead-Water', in Nansen, Fridtjof, *Norwegian North Polar Expedition Scientific Results*, London, Longmans Green and Co. (1906).

——— 'On the Influence of the Earth's Rotation on Ocean-Currents', *Arkiv för matematik, Astronomi och Fysik*, Band 2, no. 11.

——— 'On a New Current-Meter Invented by Prof. Fridtjof Nansen', *Nyt Magazin for Naturvidenskaberne*, Bind 39 (1901), pp. 163-87.

Erslev, Ed., 'Udtog af A.E. Nordenskiölds Rapport om Grønlands-Expeditionen 1883', *Geografisk Tidskrift*.

'Et 60 år gammelt brev om å lage ski', *Foreningen til ski-idrættens Fremme, Årbok 1949*, pp. 135-43. 'Festsitzung zum Empfang von Dr Fridtjof Nansen am 3. April 1897', *Verhandlingen der Gesellschaft für Erdkunde zu Berlin*, xxiv (1897), pp. 223-39, 249-64.

Florey, Ernst, 'The Zoological Station at Naples and the Neuron: Personalities and Encounters in a Unique Institution', *Biological Bulletin*, 168 (supplement) (June 1985), pp. 137-52.

'Food-Supply for the Nansen Expedition', *Lancet*, 29 April 1893, pp. 1027-30.

Forel, August, 'Einige hirnanatomische Betrachtungen und Ergebnisse', *Archiv für Psychiatrie und Nervenkrankheiten*, XVIII Band (1887), pp. 162-97.

'A Forthcoming Recall', *Bystander* (6 March 1907).

Sources

Freud, Sigmund, 'Eine neue Methode zum Studium des Faserverlaufs im Central-nervensystem', *Arch. f. Anat. u. Entwicklungsgesch.* (1884), pp. 453-60.

────── 'Über den Bau der Nervenfasern und Nervenzellen beim Flusskrebs', *Sitzungsber. d. kais. Akad. Wiss. Wien* (1882), LXXXV, Band. III., Abtheilung, pp. 9-46.

────── 'Über den Ursprung der hinteren Nervenwurzeln im Rückenmark von Ammocoetes', *Sitzungsber. d. kais. Akad. Wiss. Wien* (1877), LXXV Band. III, Abtheilung, pp. 15-27.

────── 'Über Spinalganglien und Rückenmark des Petromyzon', *Sitzungber. d. kais. Akad. Wiss. Wien* (1878), LXXVIII, III. Abth., pp. 81-167.

Frick, Edouard-Aug., 'En Souvenir de Fridtjof Nansen', *Revue Internationale de la Croix-Rouge*, Genève, Douzième Année no. 137 (Mai 1930).

Fürst, Carl M., 'Magnus Gustav Retzius', *Kungl. Svenska Vetenskapsakademiens Årsbok för År 1921*, pp. 241-88.

'G.', 'Skisport i Thüringen', *Norsk Idrætsblad* (7 March 1884), p. 44.

Garde, V., 'Nogle Bemærkninger om Øst-Grønlands Beboere', *Geografisk Tidskrift*, 9de. Bind (1887-88), Hefte V-VI, pp. 93-6.

Gladstone, W.E., 'Further Notes and Queries on the Irish Demand', *Contemporary Review*, LIII (March 1888), pp. 321-39.

Gløersen, Kristian, 'Ski-idræt og Huseby-rendet', *Illustreret Tidende for Børn*, 6te Aargang (1890-91), pp. 121-3, 133-5.

Golgi, Camillo, 'The neuron doctrine – theory and facts', *Nobel Lectures, Physiology or Medicine 1901-1921*, pp. 189-217, Amsterdam, Elsevier (1967).

────── 'Sulla Sostanza grigia del cervello', *Gazzetta medica Italiana* (1873).

────── 'Sulla fina Anatomia del Cervelletto Umano', *Archivio Italiano per la Malattie nervose* (1874).

────── *Sulla fina anatomia degli Organi centrali del Systema nervoso*, Rivista sperimentale di Freniatra (1882-83).

Gran, Gerhard, 'Gerhard Armauer Hansen. Hans Personlighed', *Aftenposten* (17 February 1912).

Granville-Barker, 'The Coming of Ibsen', in Walter de la Mare (ed.) *The Eighteen-Eighties*, Cambridge University Press (1930), pp. 159-96.

Greely, A.W., 'Will Dr Nansen Succeed?', *Forum* (August 1891), pp. 710-16.

────── 'Will They Reach the Pole?', *McClure's Magazine*, III, no. 1 (June 1894), pp. 39-44.

Greve, Tim, 'Fridtjof Nansen og kongevalet i 1905', *Nansen minneforelesning 15 october 1974*, Oslo, Universitetsforlaget (1975).

Groeben, Christiane, 'Anton Dohrn – The Statesman of Darwinism', *Biological Bulletin*, 168 (supplement) (June 1985), pp. 4-25.

Grundström, H., 'Den store skidtävlingen Purkijaur-Kvikkjokk', *På Skidor*, 1934, pp. 32-52.

Guberti, Vincenzo, 'Le ski et sa technique au 17ᵉ siècle', *Die Alpen*, XXVI (1950), pp. 129-31.

Hagen, Nils U., 'Fridtjof Nansen's crossing of Greenland in 1888', *Norsk geografisk Tidsskrift*, 43, pp. 175-82.

Hamberg, Axel, 'Til skidans femtioårsjubileum såsom Redskap vid Arktisk Forskning', *På Skidor* (1933), pp. 5-19.

Hambro, Edvard, 'Den internasjonale statsmann', *Naturen*, 85 (1961), pp. 495-503.

Hammerich, Dr F., 'Præsident Hans Nansen den Ældre', *Historisk Tidsskrift*, Tredie Række, Første Bind (1858-59), pp. 131-260.

Hansen, G. Armauer, 'Om Nervenderne i Iglens Volontære Muskler', *Arch. Math. Naturv.*, 6 (1881-82), pp. 460-4.

Sources

—— 'On the Etiology of Leprosy', *British and Foreign Medico-Chirurgical Review*, LV (January-April 1875), pp. 459-89.

—— 'Terminaison des Nerfs dans les Muscles du Corps de la Sangsue', *Archives de Physiologie*, Deuxième Serie – Tome Huitième, Treizième année – (1881), pp. 739-41.

Helland-Hansen, Bjørn, 'Fridtjof Nansen og hans videnskapelige innsats', *Det Norske Videnskaps-Akademi, Årbok*, 1930, pp. 65-84.

—— 'Gerhard Henrik Armauer Hansen', *Bergens Museums Aarbok*, 1911.

Helland-Hansen, Bjørn, and Nansen, Fridtjof, 'The Norwegian Sea', *Report on Norwegian Fishery and Marine Investigations*, Vol. II (1909), no. 2, Kristiania, Det Mallingske Bogtrykkeri.

Herlitz, Nils, 'Unionsupplösningen 1905 sedd med svenska ögon', *Nordisk Tidskrift för Vetenskap, Konst och Industri*, Stockholm, Årg. 44 (1968), pp. 145-70.

'Hertugen av Abruzzerne og hans ekspedisjon mot Nordpolen i 1899', *Årbok Sandefjord Byseum*, 1957-58, pp. 24-34.

Hestmark, Geir, 'Brøgger og Nansen – en vitenskapelig romanse', *Norsk vitenskapshistorisk Selskap Årbok* (1989-91), pp. 7-42

—— 'Fridtjof Nansen og arktisk geologi', *Nansen Minneforelesning 9 oktober 1992, Det norske Videnskaps-Akademi Årbok 1992*, pp. 345-72.

Heuglin, Th.v., 'Kapitän E.H. Johannesen's Umfahrung von Nowaja Semlä im Sommer 1870', *Petermann's Mittheilungen*, 17. Band (1871), pp. 35-7.

His, Wilhelm, 'Zur Geschichte des Menschligen Rückenmarkes und der Nervenwurzeln', *Abhandlungen der mathematisch-physischen Classe der Königl. Sächsichen Gesellschaft der Wissenschaften*, xiii (1886), pp. 479-513.

Holdt, Vilhelm, 'Fridtjof Nansen', *Norsk Kirkeblad* (1930), pp. 324-6.

Holst, Axel, 'Skjørbug og Skibs-beriberi', *Morgenbladet* (22 December 1909).

Holst, Axel, and Frölich, Theodor, 'Experimental Studies Relating to Ship Beriberi and Scurvy', *Journal of Hygiene*, vii, no. 7 (1907), pp. 634-71.

Holtedahl, Hans, 'Fridtjof Nansen som geolog', *Naturen*, 85 (1961), pp. 476-86.

Holtedahl, Olaf, 'Fridtjof Nansen Forskeren', *Samtiden*, Oslo, 70 (1961), pp. 487-95.

'Honours to Dr Nansen', *Geographical Journal*, IX no. 4 (April 1897), pp. 452-53.

Hovgaard, Captain A., 'The Kara Sea and the Route to the North Pole', *Scottish Geographical Magazine*, Vol. VI (1890), pp. 25-39.

Ibsen, Sigurd, 'Da Unionen løsnede', *Samtiden*, xvii (1906), pp. 197-236.

'In Northern Mists', *Spectator* (27 January 1912), pp. 154-5.

Ingstad, Helge, 'Skispor fra Telemark', *Polarboken 1957*, pp. 7-18.

'Interessante Nansen-brev om forberedelsene til 1.Fram-Ferd', *Norges handels og Sjøfartstidende* (14 December 1937).

Irgens, L.M., 'The Discovery of *Mycobacterium Leprae*', *American Journal of Dermatopathology*, 6 no. 4, pp. 337-42.

—— 'Leprosy in Norway', *Leprosy Review*, Vol. 51, Supplement 1 (March 1980).

Irminger, O., 'Ældre Beretninger om Østkysten af Grønland', *Geografisk Tidskrift*, 7de Bind, Hefte VII og VIII (1884), pp. 117-21.

Isachsen, Gunnar, 'Otto Sverdrup', *Norsk Geografisk Tidskrift*, Bind III (1930-31), pp. 290-6.

Itkonen, T.I., 'Finlands Fornskidor', *På Skidor* (1937), pp. 71-89.

Jakhelln, Fr., 'Noen Minner fra 1905', *Samtiden*, LXIV (1955), pp. 61-70.

Jansen, Jan K.S., 'Fridtjof Nansen og Hjerneforskningen ved slutten av forrige århundre', *Det norsk Videnskaps-Akademiets Årbok* (1982).

Johannesen, Edv.H., 'Observationer av Strömsætninger, Iisforholde og Dybde

Sources

under Fangstreisen paa *Novasemlia* i Sommaren 1869', *Öfversigt af Kongl. Vetenskaps-Akademiens Förhandlingar*, 1870, no. 2, pp. 111-15.

—— 'Hydrografiske Iaktagelser under en Fangsttour 1870 rund om Novaja-Semlia', *Öfversigt af Kongl. Vetenskaps-Akademiens Förhandlingar*, 1871, no. 1, pp. 157-63.

Johanssen, Karl, 'Fridthjof Nansen', *Arbeiderbladet* (23 May 1930).

Johnsen, Ragnvald, 'Fridtjof Nansen og norsk ski-idrett', *Naturen*, 85 (1961), pp. 487-94.

Johnson, B. Connor, 'Axel Holst', *Journal of Nutrition*, 53, pp. 3-16.

Jones, A.G.E., 'Benjamin Leigh Smith: Arctic Yachtsman', *Musk-Ox*, no. 16 (1975), pp. 24-31.

—— 'Frederick George Jackson 1860-1938', *Musk-Ox*, no. 20 (1977), pp. 97-103.

—— 'Rear Admiral Sir William Edward Parry: A Different View', *Musk-Ox*, no. 21 (1978), pp. 3-10

—— 'What Nansen Saw in 1882', Unpublished paper.

Just, Gunnar, 'Fridtjof Nansen i Infanteriets Vinterskole Hans siste offentlige foredrag, om tresorters glidning på sne', *Skiforeningens Årbok* (1930), pp. 135-40.

'Kapitän E.H. Johannesen's Umfahrung von Nowaja Semlä in September 1870', *Petermann's Mittheilungen*, 17. Band (1871), p. 230

Karr, Henry Seton, 'The Rupture between Norway and Sweden', *Nineteenth Century*, lviii (October 1905), pp. 539-44.

Katkov, George, 'The Kronstadt Rising', *St Antony's Papers Number 2. Soviet Affairs Number Two*, London, Chatto & Windus (1959).

Keilhau, Baltazar, 'Nogle Efterretninger om et hidtil ubekjendte Stykke af det søndenfjeldske Norge', *Budstikken*, (Anden række) II (1820-21), no. 49-50.

Keltie, J. Scott, 'Thirty Years' Work of the Royal Geographical Society', *Geographical Journal*, xlix, no. 5 (May 1917).

Kiærland, Lars, 'Ski og Skiløpning i Gamle Dager', *Foreningen til Ski-idrættens Fremme Årbok* (1934), pp. 138-49.

Kjærheim, Steinar, 'Nansen i hans Brev', *Nansen Minneforelesning 10 Oktober 1972*, Oslo, Universitetsforlaget (1973).

Kleivan, Helge, 'Fridtjof Nansen som etnograf', *Naturen*, 85 (1961), pp. 447-61.

Klingenberg, K.S., 'Fridtjof Nansen', *Det norske Turistforeningens Årbok* (1931), pp. 1-3.

Koht, Halvdan, 'Da den Norsk-Svenske Unionen vart sprengt', *Historisk Tidskrift*, Oslo, 34te Bind (1946-48), pp. 285-320

—— 'Kongs-vale i 1905', *Syn og Segn*, Oslo, 53 Årg. (1947), pp. 15-29; 64-76.

Kropotkin, P., 'Recent Science', *Nineteenth Century*, xvi (February 1897), pp. 250-69.

'Lappernes Skifærd paa Grønland 1883', *Geografisk Tidskrift*, 7de Bind, Hefte V og VI (1883-84), p. 116.

Larsen, Kapt. C.A., 'Nogle optegnelser af sæl-og hvalfanger "Jasons" reise i Sydishavet 1893 og 94', *Det Norske Geografiske Selskabs Aarbog*, v (1893-94), pp. 115-31.

Lindberg, Folke, 'Englands Nordiska Politik Sommaren 1905', *Historiska Studier tillägnade Nils Ahnlund*, Stockholm, P.A. Nordstedt & Söners Förlag (1949).

Lodge, Thomas, 'Fridtjof Nansen', *The Norseman*, i (1943), pp. 30-4.

Lundeby, Einar, 'Fridtjof Nansen og språket', *Nansen minneforelesning 10 oktober 1989, Det Norske Videnskaps-Akademi Årbok* (1989), pp. 324-33.

Luther, Carl J., 'Hippopodes (Horse-footed men)', *British Ski Year Book for 1952*, pp. 57-68.

590

Lytzen, Carl, 'Levninger fra Jeannette-Expeditionen paa Grønlands Vestkyst', *Geografisk Tidskrift*, 8de Bind (1885-86), Hefte III, pp. 49-51.

Maigaard, Chr., 'Beretning om den af Civilingeniør Robert E. Peary ledede Expedition paa den grønlandske Indlandsis', *Geografisk Tidskrift*, ix (1887-88), pp. 86-93.

Markham, C.R., 'Address to the Royal Geographical Society', *Geographical Journal*, iv (1894), p. 1.

—— 'Address to the Royal Geographical Society', *Geographical Journal*, viii (July 1896), pp. 1-15.

—— 'The Arctic Expedition of 1875-76', *Proceedings of the Royal Geographical Society*, xxi (1877), pp. 546-47.

—— 'Dr Nansen on North Polar Exploration', *Geographical Journal*, xxxix (January 1912), pp. 26-30.

—— 'Second Voyage of the "Eira" to Franz-Josef Land', *Proceedings of the Royal Geographical Society*, v (April 1883), pp. 204-28.

—— 'The Voyage of the "Eira" and Mr. Leigh Smith's Arctic Discoveries', *Proceedings of the Royal Geographical Society*, iii (1881), 129-50.

Meier, Gudrun, 'Aufzeichnungen über Grönland-Expeditionen des späten 19. Jahrhunderts in den Stationsdiarien der Herrnhuter Missionare', *Polarforschung*, vi (1969), pp. 260-3.

Mill, Hugh Robert, 'Adventure and other Papers', *Geographical Journal*, lxxi (January 1928), p. 99.

—— 'The Petterson-Nansen Insulating Water-Bottle', *Geographical Journal*, xvi (November 1900), pp. 469-71.

Millhouse, O. Eugene, 'The Golgi Methods' in Heimer, Lennart and Robards, Martine J. (eds), *Neuroanatomical Tract-Tracing Methods*, New York, Plenum Press (1981), pp. 311-44.

'The Minister from the North Pole', *Bystander* (30 May 1906).

Moe, Moltke, 'Det nationale gjennembrud og dets mænd', in Liestøl, Knut (ed.), Instituttet for sammenlignende Kulturforskning, Serie B: Skrifter IX, *Moltke Moes samlede Skrifter* iii, Oslo, Aschehoug (1927), pp. 3-196.

Morgenstierne, Wilhelm, 'Samvær med Fridtjof Nansen', Unidentified cutting.

Morier, Victor A.L., 'A Reindeer Journey in Arctic Russia', *Murray's Magazine*, vi (1889), pp. 170-84, 364-78.

Mosby, Håkon, 'Fridtjof Nansen som oceanograf', *Naturen*, lxxxv (1961), 462-75.

Murray, John, 'The Renewal of Antarctic Exploration', *Geographical Journal*, iii (January 1894), pp. 1-42.

'N——n', 'Den nordamerikanske Greely-Expedition', *Geografisk Tidskrift*, 7de Bind, Hefte VII og VIII (1884).

Nansen, Eva, 'Skiløbningen', *Verdens Gang* (3 March 1893).

'Nansen, Eva Helene', *Norsk Biografisk Leksikon*.

'Nansen, Fridtjof', *Norsk Biografisk Leksikon*.

Nansen, Fridtjof, 'Akvariet i Neapel', *Illustreret Tidende for Børn*, ii (1886-87), pp. 2-3

—— 'Anatomie und Histologie des Nervensystemes der Myzostomen', *Jenaische Zeitschrift für Naturwissenschaft*, xxi (Neue Folge, Vierzehnte Band, 1887), pp. 267-321.

—— 'Avgjørelsen straks', *Verdens Gang* (16 October 1905).

—— 'Bidrag til Myzostomernes Anatomi og Histologi', *Bergen Museum Skrifter*, Bergen (1885).

—— 'Bjørnejagt ved Ishavet', *Illustreret Tidende for Børn*, i (1885-86), pp. 27-9, 58-61.

Sources

—— 'Changes in Oceanic and Atmospheric Temperatures and their Relation to Changes in the Sun's Activity', *Journal of the Washington Academy of Sciences*, viii (1918), pp. 135-40.

—— 'Closing-Nets for Vertical Hauls and for Horizontal Towing', *Publications de Circonstance*, Copenhagen, no. 67 (July 1915), pp. 3-8.

—— 'Den Norske polarexpedition 1893-96', *Det norske Geografiske Selskabs Aarbog*, viii (1896-97), pp. 53-76.

—— 'Den zoologiske station i Neapel', *Naturen* 1887, pp. 39-46.

—— 'Die Entdeckung Amerikas durch die Nordmänner und die Sagas vom Vinland', *Zeitschrift der Gesellschaft für Erdkunde zu Berlin* (1912), pp. 41-58.

—— 'Die Erforschung der unbekannten inneren Arktis', *Arktis*, ii (1929), pp. 3-10.

—— 'Die magnetische Abweichung in anfang des 16 jahrhunderts', *Petermanns Mitteilungen*, lviii (1912), pp. 8-12.

—— 'Die Ursachen der Meeresströmingen', *Petermanns Mitteilungen*, li (1905), pp. 25-31, 62-3.

—— 'Fra Grønlandsfærden', *Den Norske Geografiske Selskabs Årbog*, no. 1 (1889-90), pp. 1-18.

—— 'Geological Sketch of Cape Flora and its Neighbourhood', in Pompeckj, J.F., 'The Jurassic Fauna of Cape Flora', *Norwegian North Polar Expedition Scientific Results*, i.

—— 'Die Nervenelemente, ihre Struktur und Verbindung im Centralnervensystem', *Anatomischer Anzeiger*, iii (15 February 1888), pp. 157-69.

—— 'En Skitur fra Voss til Kristiania', *Aftenposten* (29 March; 1, 9, 16 April 1884).

—— 'Endnu lidt om Kvindesagen', *Bergensposten* (17 November 1886).

—— 'Foredrag på Akershus 10. Mars 1905', *Nansens Røst*, ii, pp. 323-6.

—— 'Foreløbig Meddelelse om Undersøgelse over Centralnervesystemets histologiske Bygning hos Ascidierne samt hos Myxine glutinosa', *Bergens Museums Aarsberetning* (1885), pp. 55-78.

—— 'Fra barneaarene', *Illustreret Tidende for Børn*, viii (1893), pp. 6-7.

—— 'Gjennem Grønland?', *Illustreret Tidende for Børn*, iii (1887-88), pp. 129-32.

—— 'Grønlands indbyggere', *Naturen* (1888), pp. 109-19.

—— 'Grønlands indlandsis', *Naturen* (1888), pp. 1-12.

—— 'Haren paa Færøerne og dyrenes hvide vinterdragt', *Naturen* (1904), pp. 257-61.

—— 'Heltemot!', *Verdens Gang* (6 October 1905).

—— 'Hjalmar Johansen. Noen spredte Minner', *Det norske geografiske selskapets Årbok*, xxiv (1912-13).

—— 'How can the North Polar Region be Crossed?', *Geographical Journal*, i (January 1893), p. 1.

—— 'How the North Pole will be Reached', *Wide World Magazine*, i (April 1898), pp. 53-62.

—— 'Hvad nu?', *Samtiden*, xvi (1905), p. 68.

—— 'Hvad vi vil', *Verdens Gang* (24 September 1905).

—— 'I dagens Spørsmål (1909)', *Nansens Røst*, ii, pp. 384-406.

—— 'Journey across the Inland Ice of Greenland from East to West', *Proceedings of the Royal Geographical Society*, xi (August 1889), 469-87.

—— 'Journey across the Inland Ice of Greenland from East to West', *Scottish Geographical Magazine*, v (1889), pp. 393-405, 503-4.

—— 'Klima-vekslinger i historisk og postglacial Tid', *Avhandlinger utgit av Det Norske Videnskaps-Akademi i Oslo I. Matem.-Naturvid. Klasse* (1926), no. 3.

Sources

—— 'Klima-vekslinger i nordens Historie', *Avhandlinger utgit av Det Norske Videnskaps-Akademi i Oslo I. Matem.-Naturvid. Klasse* (1925), no. 3.

—— 'Kongedømme eller Republikk? 11. November 1905', *Nansens Røst*, ii, pp. 361-9.

—— 'Langs Grønlands Østkyst', *Geografisk Tidskrift*, vii, Hefte III og IV (1884), pp. 76-9.

—— 'Letsindighet', *Verdens Gang* (24 February 1905).

—— Letter on Scott Keltie, *Geographical Journal*, lxix (March 1927), pp. 286-7.

—— 'Lidt om heluldbeklædningen', *Bergens Aftenblad* (6 and 7 November 1883).

—— 'Mænd', *Verdens Gang* (13 February 1905).

—— 'Methods for Measuring Direction and Velocity of Currents in the Sea', *Publications de Circonstance*, Copenhagen, no. 34 (February 1906).

—— 'Mod Nordpolen', *Illustreret Tidende for Børn*, vi (1890-91), pp. 2-4.

—— 'Mot', *Verdens Gang*, 18 February 1905.

—— 'Nationenes Forbund', *Tidens Tegn* (14 February 1919).

—— 'Nerve-elementerne, deres Struktur og Sammenhäng i Centralnervesystemet', *Nordisk medicinsk arkiv*, xix (1887), pp. 1-24.

—— 'Næstekjærlighet', *Samtiden*, xxxiii (1922), pp. 1-11.

—— 'Nobel-Foredrag', *Les Prix Nobel en 1921-1922*, Stockholm, P.A. Nordstedt & Söner (1923), pp. 1-11.

—— 'Nordens stilling og opgaver under og efter krigen', *Samtiden*, xxviii (1917), pp. 1-9.

—— 'The Norsemen in America', *Geographical Journal*, xxxviii (December 1911), pp. 557-80.

—— 'Northern waters: Captain Roald Amundsen's Oceanographic Observations in the Arctic Seas in 1901', *Videnskabs-selskabets Skrifter*, I Mathematisk-Naturv. Klasse (1906), no. 3.

—— 'Om den kommende norske polarekspedition og dens udrustning', *Det norske Geografiske Selskabs Årbog*, iii (1891-1892), pp. 91-118.

—— 'Om drivisen, dens dannelse og grustransport', *Naturen* (1887), pp. 213-17.

—— 'Om hvirveldyrenes tredje øie, pandøiet', *Naturen* (1887), pp. 65-71.

—— 'Om Isbjørnen og isbjørnjagter under Grønlandskysten 1882', *Norsk Idrætsblad*, nos. 5, 10, 11, 12, 13 (1883).

—— 'Om Kvindens Natur og Evolutionstheorien', *Bergensposten* (27, 28, 29 December 1886).

—— 'On North Polar Problems', *Geographical Journal*, xxx (1907), pp. 469-87, 586-601.

—— 'Oscillations of Shore-Lines', *Geographical Journal*, xxvi (1905), pp. 604-16.

—— 'Plan til en ny Polarexpedition', *Den Norske Geografiske Selskabs Årbog*, no. IV (1892-93), pp. 53-82.

—— 'Plan til en ny polarekspedition', *Naturen* (1890), pp. 65-96.

—— 'Preliminary Communication on some Investigations upon the Histological Structure of the Central Nervous System in the Ascidia and in Myxine glutinosa. *Ann. Mag. Nat. Hist.* xviii, Fifth Series (1886), pp. 209-26.

—— 'A Protandric Hermaphrodite (*Myxine glutinosa*, L) amongst the Vertebrates', *Bergens Museums Aarsberetning for 1887*, pp. 2-34.

—— 'Roald Amundsen', *Arktis*, ii (1929), pp. 1-3.

—— 'Roald Amundsen', *Norsk Geografisk Tidsskrift*, 3.-4. Hefte (1928), pp. 141-6 [broadcast 24 October 1928].

—— 'Roald Amundsens Færd', *Politiken* (11 March 1912).

—— 'Robert Edvin Peary', *Naturen* (1920), pp. 64-8.

Sources

——— 'Science and the Purpose of Life', *Hibbert Journal*, vi (July 1908), pp. 743-57.

——— 'Skiløb i Thelemarken', *Illustreret Tidende for Børn*, ii (1886-87), pp. 87-9.

——— 'Skjørbuk og Skibs-Beriberi', *Morgenbladet* (24 December 1909).

——— 'Some Oceanographical Results of the Expedition with the Michael Sars in the Summer of 1900', *Nyt Magazin for Naturvidenskaberne*, bind 39 (1901) pp. 129-61.

——— 'Some Results of the Norwegian Arctic Expedition, 1893-96', *Geographical Journal*, ix (1897), pp. 473-505.

——— 'Spitsbergen Waters', *Videnskabsselskapets Skrifter I. Mat.-Naturv. Klasse* (1915), no. 2.

——— 'Spitsbergens opdagelse', *Naturen* (1920), pp. 1-12.

——— 'Svartale på Folkefesten for 'Fram'-mennene', *Morgenbladet* (14 September 1896).

——— 'Tale 17 Mai 1905', *Nansens Røst*, ii, pp. 345-53.

——— 'Tale for idrætten', *Forening til ski-idrættens Fremme, Aarbok* (1903), pp. 20-6.

——— 'Tale ved stiftelsen av "Fedrelandslaget"', 29 January 1925, *Nansens Røst*, ii, pp. 636-41.

——— 'The Earth's Crust, its Surface-forms, and Isostatic Adjustment', *Avhandlinger utgit av Det Norske Videnskaps-Akademi i Oslo I. Matem.-Naturvid. Klasse* (1928), no. 12.

——— 'The Equipment of Polar Expeditions', *Field*, cxix, pp. 39 & 95 (6 & 13 January 1912).

——— 'The Proposed Expedition in the *Graf Zeppelin*', *Geographical Journal*, lxxv (January 1930), pp. 67-70.

——— 'The Race for the South Pole', *Scribner's Magazine*, New York, li (1912), pp. 305-10.

——— 'The Relations between Sweden and Norway', *The Times* (2 January 1893).

——— 'The Sea-Route to Siberia', *Geographical Journal*, xliii (1914), pp. 481-500.

——— 'The Strandflat and Isostasy', *Videnskapsselskapets Skrifter. I Mat.-Naturv. Klasse* (1921), no. 11.

——— 'The Structure and Combination of the Histological Elements of the Central Nervous System', *Bergens Museums Aarsberetning for 1886*, pp. 29-195.

——— 'The Swedish-Norwegian Conflict', *The Times* (25 March 1905).

——— 'The Swedish-Norwegian Conflict', *The Times* (12 April 1905).

——— 'The Waters of the North-Eastern North Atlantic', *Internationale Revue der gesamten Hydrobiologie und Hydrographie*, iv Hydrographisches Supplement, Serie II Schlußheft (Juli 1913).

——— 'Til "Maud"s Menn', 3 February 1926, *Nansens Røst*, ii, pp. 646-51.

——— 'Towards the North Pole', *Longmans Magazine*, xvii (1890), pp. 37-48.

——— 'Ved Bjørnsons Gravfærd', *Morgenbladet*, 4 May 1910.

——— 'Veien', *Verdens Gang* (12 February 1905).

——— 'Videnskab og moral', *Samtiden*, xix (1908), pp. 1-14.

——— 'Vilje', *Verdens Gang* (5 March 1905).

——— 'Vorschlag für ein Zelt aus Segeltuch mit Schneepackungung für Polarstationen', *Arktis*, i (1928), p. 37.

——— 'What I Believe', *Forum*, lxxxii (1929) pp. 360-5.

Nansen, Fridtjof, and Brunchorst, Dr J., 'Lavstaaende dyrs og planters naturhistorie', *Naturen* (1887), pp. 12-21, 106-12, 129-39.

Nansen, Fridtjof, and Guldberg, Gustav, 'On the Development and Structure of the Whale', *Bergens Museum Skrifter* (1894), V.

Sources

Nansen, Fridtjof, and Helland-Hansen, Bjørn, 'Om Sammenhængen mellem de aarlige vekslinger i Norskehavets vandmasser og vekslinger i klima, agerbruk og fiskeri i Norge', *Naturen* (1909), pp. 193-219.

―― 'Klimavekslinger og deres aarsaker', *Naturen* (1920), pp. 12-28, 101-16, 347-61.

Nansen, Fridtjof, and Mohn, Professor H., 'Wissenschaftlige Ergebnisse von Dr F. Nansens Durchquerung von Grönland, 1888', *Petermanns Mitteilungen*, Ergänzungsheft no. 105 (1892), pp. 1-111.

'Nansen's Farthest North', *London Quarterly Review*, lxxxviii, New Series xxviii (1897), pp. 132-49.

Nash, Roderick, 'The American Invention of National Parks', *American Quarterly*, xxii, pp. 726-35.

Nathorst, A.G., 'Et Møde med Eskimoer i Nordvestgrønland', *Geografisk Tidskrift*, vii (Hefte V og VI, 1883-84), pp. 115-16.

―― 'Oscar Dickson', *Ymer*, xvii (1897), pp. 159-65.

―― 'Otto Torell', *Ymer*, xx (1900), pp. 455-59.

Neale, W.H., 'Benjamin Leigh Smith', *Geographical Journal*, xli (1913), pp. 396-7.

Needham, Dr.Joseph, 'An Excerpt from "Science and Civilisation in China" ', *British Ski Year Book* (1962), pp. 15-17.

Nicolaysen, Ragnar, 'Arkstisk ernæring', *Nansen minneforelesning* (9 oktober 1970).

Nissen, Kristian, 'Samer i Polarforskningen', *Sameliv* (1961-63), pp. 48-80.

Noel Baker, Philip, 'Nansen and Norway', *Nation and Athenaeum* xlvii (31 May 1930), pp. 279-80.

―― 'Nansen som Internasjonal Politiker', *Samtiden* xlii (1930), pp. 371-6.

―― 'Nansen: The International Statesman', *Nation and Athenaeum* xlvii (7 June 1930), pp. 292-3.

Nordenskiöld, A.E., 'Den blifvande expedition til Grönland, promemoria afgifven til d:r O.Dickson', *Ymer* (1883), pp. 101-12.

―― 'Den svenska expeditionen til Grönland, år 1883, rapporter afgifna til d:r O.Dickson', *Ymer* (1883), pp. 211-60.

Nordgaard, O., 'Nogen minder fra den biologiske station ved Puddefjorden', *Naturen* (1922), pp. 206-20.

Norman, Axel Otto, 'Fridtjof Nansen i Genève', *Urd* (1930), pp. 662-3.

'The North Polar Problem', *Geographical Journal*, ix (1897), pp. 505-29.

Ónodi, Dr A.D., 'Entwickelung der Spinalganglien und der Nervenwurzeln', *Internationale Monatschrift für Anatomie und Histologie*, i (1884), pp. 204-9, 255-84.

'Opdagelsesrejser til Grønland 1473-1806', *Meddelelser om Grønland*, Bd. 55, Nr. 1 (1936).

Orstadius, Axel, 'Skilda drag från den s.k. "Nordenskjöldstäflingen" å skidor i Jockmock den 3 April 1884', *Föreningen för Skidlöpningens Främjandet i Sverige*, Årsskrift (1897-98), pp. 237-48.

Palmstierna, C.F., 'Sweden and the Russian Bogey', *Nineteenth Century*, cxiii (1933), pp. 739-54.

Peary, R.E., 'A Reconnaissance of the Greenland Inland Ice', *Bull. Amer. Geog. Soc.*, xix (1887), pp. 261-89.

Philippi, Felix, 'Mein Vekehr mit Henrik Ibsen', *Neue Freie Presse*, Vienna (27 October 1902).

Plumstead, E., 'Dr Nansen and his Lunar Tables', *Nautical Magazine*, lxvii (1898), pp. 517-31.

―― 'Nansen's Longitude Observations and their Scientific Results', *Nautical Magazine* lxviii (1899), pp. 247-63.

Sources

—— 'The Norwegian Polar Expedition, 1893-96', *Nautical Magazine*, lxx (1901), pp. 233-45.

'Pour la Russie', *Revue Internationale de la Croix-Rouge*, Genève, iii (1921), pp. 887-918.

'Premierlieutenant J.A.D. Jensens Indberetning om den af ham ledede Expedition in 1878', *Meddelelser om Grønland*, Første Hefte (1879).

'Private Collection of Food taken by Dr. Nansen's North Pole Expedition, 1893', *Sixth International Geographical Congress, London, 1895, Catalogue of Exhibits*, pp. 172-3.

Rabot, Charles, 'Fridtjof Nansen som jeg minnes ham', *Samtiden*, xlv (1934), pp. 67-76.

Rae, Dr John, 'Exploration of the Faeroes and Iceland &c.', *Proceedings of the Royal Geographical Society*, v (1861), pp. 80-90.

Ramón y Cajal, S., 'Estructura de los Centros Nerviosos de las Aves', *Revista Trimestral de Histologia Normal y Patológica* (1 May 1888), pp. 305-15.

—— 'Morfología y Conexiones de los Elementos de la Retina de las Aves', *Revista Trimestral de Histologia Normal y Patológica* (1 May 1888), pp. 317-22.

—— 'Sur l'origine et la direction des prolongations nerveuses de la couche moléculaire du cervelet', *Internationale Monatsschrift für Anatomie und Physiologie*, vi (1889), pp. 157-74.

Rasmussen, Knud, 'Fridtjof Nansen', *Geografisk Tidskrift*, xxxiii (1930), pp. 179-88.

—— 'Fridtjof Nansen', *Norsk Geografisk Tidskrift* (1931), pp. 297-305

—— 'Manden uden Retræte-Linier', *Samtiden* xlii (1930), pp. 385-91.

Reeves, E.A., 'Dr Nansen and his Lunar Tables', *Nautical Magazine*, lxvii (1898), 887-8.

Refsum, Helge, 'Some Aspects of Norway's Contributions to Ski History', *British Ski Year Book* (1937), pp. 7-21.

Remack, Dr, 'Ueber die Structur des Nervensystems', *Neue Notizen aus dem Gebiete der Natur- und Heilkunde*, vi (Juni 1838), pp. 342-6.

Retzius, Gustaf, 'Untersuchungen über die Nervenzellen der cerebro-spinalen Ganglien und der übrigen peripherischen Kopfganglien', *Arch. f. Anat. u. Entwickelungsgeschichte* (1880), pp. 369-98.

—— 'Zur Kenntnis des Nervensystems der Crustaceen', *Biologische Untersuchungen*, Neue Folge I (1890), pp. 1-50.

Rink, H., 'Om Dr Nansens Grønlandsrejse og dens Resultater', *Geografisk Tidskrift*, x (1889-90), pp. 3-9.

—— 'Resultaterne af de nyeste danske Undersøgelser i Grønland, med Hensyn til Indlandet og de svømmende Isbjærges Oprindelse', *Geografisk Tidskrift*, ix heft IV, pp. 63-73.

Rink, Signe, 'Nachhall der ersten Nansen-Expedition. Berichte der Eskimos Arkaluk und Wéléme in Goothaab', *Das Ausland*, lxvi (1893), pp. 662-3, 679-82.

—— 'Aus dem Leben der Europäer in Grönland', *Das Ausland*, lxvi (1893), pp. 747-9, 758-64, 777-9.

'N.R.' [Nordahl Rolfsen], 'I skodden', *Julehilsen 1898*, pp. 22-3.

Rudmose Brown, R.N., 'Fridtjof Nansen', *Geographical Journal*, lxxvi (1930), pp. 92-5.

Rumbold, Sir Horace ['H.R.'], 'The Breaking Away of Norway', *Westminster Gazette* (29 September 1905).

St George Saunders, Hilary, 'Nansen as I knew him', *Norseman*, iii (1945), pp. 2-8.

Sabro, G.N., 'Skiløbningen før og nu i isterdalene', *Foreningen til Ski-idrættens Fremme Årbok* (1934), pp. 119-28.

Sources

Sars, E., 'Keilhaus opdagelse af Jotunheimen', *Det norske Turistforeningens Årbog* (1872), pp. 54-65.

Savours, Ann, 'The 1773 Phipps Expedition towards the North Pole', *Arctic*, xxxviii (1984), pp. 402-28.

Schäffer, Edward Albert, 'Observations on the Nervous System of *Aurelia aurita*', *Philos. Trans.*, clxix (1879), pp. 563-75.

Scheibert, Peter, 'Über Lenins Anfänge', *Historische Zeitschrift* clxxxii (1956), pp. 549-66.

Schjøtt, Mathilde, 'Fru Sars', *Ringeren* (1899), pp. 14-15, 31-2, 45-6.

Schmelck, Ludvig, 'Norsk Nordpolsexpedition', *Morgenbladet* (12 December 1888), p. 1.

Scott, E.J., 'The Cheka', in *Soviet Affairs*, St Antony's Papers, Number 1, London, Chatto & Windus, 1956, pp. 1-23.

Seebohm, H., 'The North Polar Basin', *Geographical Journal*, ii (1893), p. 331.

Shetelig, Haakon, and Volgelsang, Th. M., 'Ved Hundreårsjubiléet for Armauer Hansen', *Samtiden*, lii (1942), pp. 573-92.

Skedsmo, Tone, 'Hos kunstnere, polarforskere og mesener', *Kunst og Kultur*, lxvi (1982), pp. 131-51.

'Skiløbermøde', *Morgenbladet* (14 December 1892).

'Skirendet ved Huseby den 4 februar 1884', *Norsk Idrætsblad* (8 February 1884), p. 28.

Slingsby, Wm. Cecil, 'Round the Horungtinder in Winter', *Det norske Turistforeningens Årbog* (1880), pp. 87-107.

Smith, Emil, 'En Prokonsular', *Samtiden*, xli (1930), pp. 392-4.

Solano, E. John, 'Scandinavia in the Scales of the Future', *Monthly Review*, xx (1905), pp. 1-21.

'Some Results of the Norwegian Arctic Expedition, 1893-1896', *Geographical Journal*, ix (1897), pp. 473-505.

Stephen, Leslie, 'Nansen', *International Journal of Ethics*, vol. viii (1897), pp. 1-22.

Story, Alfred T., 'Mr. Andrée's Balloon Voyage to the North Pole', *Strand Magazine*, xii, no. 67 (July 1896), pp. 77-91.

'The Story of Nansen's Achievement', *The Times* (15 February 1897).

Strindberg, August, 'Ett fritt Norge', *Samlade Skrifter*, Stockholm, Albert Bonniers Förlag (1920), liv, pp. 429-42.

Svensen, Åsfrid, 'På Eventyr i Språket og i villmarka. Fridtjof Nansen som Populærvitenskapelig Forfatter', Nansen Minneforelesning (10 October 1991).

Sverdrup, H.U., 'Fridtjof Nansen', *Arktis*, iii (1930), pp. 1-4.

—— 'Fridtjof Nansen som Videnskapsmann', *Norsk Geografisk Tidsskrift* (1931), pp. 306-13.

Sømme, Jacob D., 'Fridtjof Nansen som videnskabsmand', *Morgenbladet* (17 May 1930).

Sørensen, Jon, 'Den Røde Horisont – Fra White Face Mountain', *Kirke og Kultur*, xxxix (1932), pp. 470-6.

—— 'Fridtjof Nansen', *Kirke og Kultur* (1930), pp. 326-40.

'The Nansen Meeting in the Albert Hall', *Geographical Journal*, ix (1897), pp. 249-56.

Thompson, D'Arcy W., 'Fridtjof Nansen', *Journal du Conseil*, v (Avril 1930), pp. 142-7.

Thoresen, Distriktslæge, 'Nogle Bemærkninger i Anledning af Sidste Premieskirend ved Huseby', *Morgenbladet* (17 February 1881).

Tidemand, Lena, 'Fridtjof Nansens Besøg i Kharhof Januar 1923', *Tidsskrift for Dansk Røde Kors* (1923), pp. 48-51.

597

Sources

—— 'Om Hjælperaadet i Ruslands Hungerdistrikter og Smaaskildringer fra Livet derovre', *Tidskrift-for-Sygepleje*, xxv (1925), pp. 47-52, 79-81, 97-100, 210-14.

—— 'Oplevelser i Rusland', *Tidskrift-for-Sygepleje*, xxv (1925), pp. 329-33, 352-7.

Togan, A. Zeki Validi, 'Ibn Fadlan's Reisebericht', *Abhandlungen für die kunde des Morgenlandes*, xxiv, 3 (1939).

Törnebohm, Dr. A.E., 'Mikroskopische Untersuchung von Schlammproben, eingesammelt von Dr. F. Nansen', Anhang I, *Petermanns Mitteilungen*, Ergänzungsband xxiii, Heft 105 (1893), pp. 104-8.

Torup, Sophus, 'Fridtjof Nansens Livssyn', *Samtiden* xlii (1930), pp. 377-84.

Tozer, H.F., 'Norway', *Vacation Tourists and Notes of Travel in 1860* [ed. Francis Galton], Cambridge, Macmillan (1861), pp. 362-421.

Tuan, Yi-Fu, 'Desert and Ice: Ambivalent Aesthetics', in Kemal, Salim, and Gaskell, Ivan (eds), *Landscape, Natural Beauty and the Arts*, Cambridge University Press (1993), pp. 139-57.

Undset, Sigrid, 'Gaterne', *Kristiania* (1918), pp. 79-92.

Vaage, Jakob, 'De limte skis historie', *Foreningen til ski-idrettens Fremme, Årbok for 1962*, pp. 10-20.

—— 'Et 60 års minne', *Foreningen til ski-idrettens Fremme, Årbok for 1948*, pp. 35-43.

—— 'Hvordan skiløperne i hovedstaden skaffet seg ski i det forrige århundre', *Foreningen til ski-idrættens Fremme, Årbok for 1949*, pp. 118-24.

—— 'Premieskirenn i Norge 1767', *Foreningen til ski-idrættens Fremme, Årbok for 1932*, pp. 74-80.

—— 'Skibindingene gjennom 4000 år', *Foreningen til ski-idrettens Fremme, Årbok for 1966*, pp. 42-53; *1968*, pp. 36-47.

—— 'Skismørning gjennom tidene', *Foreningen til ski-idrettens Fremme, Årbok for 1963*, pp. 19-32.

—— 'Sportsforretninger i det forrige århundre', *Byminner*, no. 4 (1971), pp. 31-41.

—— 'Skistavernes Historie', *Snø og Ski* (1975), pp. 84-94; (1977), pp. 16-23.

Vesterlund, Otto, 'En skidlöperveteran', *På Skidor* (1904-05), pp. 45-52.

'Videnskabsselskabet', *Morgenbladet* (30 November 1884).

Vinje, A.O., 'Fjøllstaven min', *Nytaarsgave for Nyhedsbladets Abonneneter* (1862), pp. 26-36.

Von Toll, Baron E., 'Mitteilungen über eine Reise nach den Neusibirischen Inseln', *Petermanns Mitteilungen*, xl (1894), pp. 131-9, 155-9.

Vorren, Ørnulv, 'Med Samer på Ski over Grønland', *Ottar*, Nr. 88 (1976), pp. 36-41.

—— 'På Ski i Nordkalottens Fortid', *Ottar*, Nr. 115 (1979), pp. 11-17.

Waaler, Erik, 'Patologi og mikrobiologi i Bergen', *Nordisk medicinhistorisk Årsbok*, Supplementum XI (1985).

Waldeyer, W., 'Ueber einige neuere Forschungen im Gebiete der Anatomie des Centralnervensystems', *Berliner Klinische Wochenschrift*, xxviii (1891), p. 691.

—— 'Ueber einige neuere Forschungen im Gebiete der Anatomie des Centralnervensystems', *Deutsche Medisinische Wochenschrift*, xvii (1891), pp. 1213-18; 1244-6; 1267-70; 1287-9; 1331-2; 1352-6.

Ward, Herbert, 'The Departure of Dr Nansen's Arctic Expedition', *Illustrated London News* (8 July 1893), p. 39.

—— 'Dr Nansen's Farewell', *Sketch* (12 July 1893), pp. 590-1.

Weibull, Jörgen, 'Kronprins Gustaf inför unionsupplösningen 1905', *Scandia*, Stockholm, xxvi (1960), pp. 167-229.

Sources

Wellman, Walter, 'The Wellman Polar Expedition', *National Geographic Magazine*, x (1899), pp. 481-504.

Wendell, Winifred Lee, 'Some Modern History-Makers of Scandinavia – IV', *Self Culture* (August 1900), pp. 546-51.

Werenskiold, Erik, 'Fridtjof Nansen', *Samtiden* xlii (1930), pp. 364-70.

Whitaker, Ian, 'Late Classical and Early Mediaeval Accounts of the Lapps (Sami)', *Classica et Mediaevalia*, xxxiv (1983), pp. 283-303.

—— 'Tacitus' *Fenni* and Ptolemy's *Phinnoi*', *Classical Journal*, lxxv (1980), pp. 215-24.

Whymper, Edward, 'Explorations in Greenland', *Good Words* (1884), pp. 38-43; 96-103; 184-9.

—— 'Greenland', *Alpine Journal*, v (1870), pp. 1-23.

—— 'Some Notes on Greenland and the Greenlanders', *Alpine Journal*, vi (1873), pp. 161-8; 209-21.

—— 'The First Crossing of Greenland', *Proceedings of the Royal Geographical Society*, xiii (1891), pp. 55-9.

—— 'Nansen's "Farthest North" ', *Leisure Hour*, xlvi (1897), pp. 369-72.

Wiggins, Captain Joseph, 'The State of the Siberian Sea: The Nansen Expedition', *Geographical Journal*, iii (1894), pp. 121-4.

Wiklund, K.B., 'Mera om skidans historia', *På Skidor* (1929), pp. 252-79.

—— 'Några tankar om snöskors och skidors upprinnelse', *På Skidor* (1926), pp. 1-18.

—— 'Ur skidans och snöskons historia', *På Skidor* (1928), pp. 5-56.

Williams, Beryl J., 'The Revolution of 1905 and Russian Foreign Policy', in Abramsky, C., and Williams, Beryl J., *Essays in Honour of E.H. Carr*, London, Macillan (1974), pp. 101-25.

Worm-Müller, Jacob S., 'Fridtjof Nansen', *Foreningen til ski-idrættens Fremme, Årbok 1930*, pp. 65-7.

—— 'Fridtjof Nansen, Patrioten og Verdensborgeren', *Samtiden*, lxx (1961), pp. 496-504.

Wright, G. Hagbert, 'Russia's View of her Mission', *Nineteenth Century*, lvii (1905), pp. 181-97.

Wyke, Barry, 'Fridtjof Nansen', *Annals of the Royal College of Surgeons of England*, xxx (1962), pp. 243-52.

Index

Ador, Gustave, 495, 505, 535

Alert (ship): sets Furthest North on Nares expedition (1876), 221

Amadeo of Savoy, Luigi, Duke of the Abruzzi: plans expedition to North Pole, 380-1; breaks N's record for Furthest North, 383, 396

American Relief Administration (ARA), 505, 506, 511, 534

Amundsen, Anton: Chief Engineer on *Fram*, 180, 210, 259, 347, 389; diary, 192, 200, 225, 321, 323; constructs water sampler and current meter for N, 221

Amundsen, Roald Engebreth Gravning, 1, 388, 420, 423, 439, 458, 542; appearance, 388, 448; N's opinion of, 388, 440, 463, 465, 466, 543; N's patronage of, 388, 391-3, 425, 458, 460; completes North-West Passage, 424, 433, 470; attitude to N, 447, 542; races Scott, 461-3; first to reach South Pole, 465, 467-8, 470-1; British outcry, 462; tries to abandon Arctic drift, 470-1, 478, 542; first to reach both Poles, 542; death, 542-3

Andrée, Salomon August: attempts to reach North Pole by balloon, 349-50, 400; meets N, 357, 367-8; disappears, 382

Antarctic, 364, 365, 379, 388, 448; Borchgrevink first to spend winter on, 380; knowledge of, 365, 379; use of sledge dogs in, 379; Cape Adare, 380; Ross Ice Shelf, 380

Angell, Lt. Henrik, 64-5, 67

Archer, Colin, builder of *Fram*, 150-1, 157-8, 161, 166, 173, 365, 378, 380, 428, 500

Archer, William, translator of Ibsen, 428

Arctic, 362-3, 364, 365, 379; knowledge of, 18, 188, 190-1, 194, 212, 259, 303, 352-3, 364-5; first explorers of, 18; first navigation of North-East Passage, 28, 63, 439; trans-polar current, 148, 149, 162, 193, 194, 212, 355, 370; first crossing of Spitsbergen, 356; first navigation of North-West Passage, 425, 433, 439; first attempt to cross by airship, 458; northern sea route, 471-2; first air travel to North Pole, 542;

Spitsbergen, 62-3, 356, 382, 189-91; Khabarova, 183-4, 186, 305, 321; Novaya Zemlya, 183; Kara Sea, 184, Yugor Strait, 184, 185, 189; Yamal Peninsula, 189, 190, 349; Cape More Sale, 189; Cape Chelyuskin, 190, 191, 192, 193, 305, 493; Yenisei River, 190; Taimyr Peninsula, 191, 192; Olenek River, 188, 193, 194; Laptev Sea, 193-6; Lena River, 194; New Siberian Islands, 194, 322; Kotelnoi, 194; Cape Fliguely, 266, 269, 322; Wilczek Land, 303; Cape Felder, 305; Karl Alexander Land, 305, 306; Brøgger's Headland, 306; Eira Harbour, 307, 310; Helland's Foreland, 308; 'Cape Athos', 309; 'Cape of Good Hope', 331; White Island, 333, 382; Cape Flora, 337, 342, 351, 352, 363, 377, 387; Northbrook Island, 337, 342; Elmwood, 342, 343, 351, 352; Eva-Liv Island, 352, Adelaide Island, 352; Frederick Jackson Island, 352; Hvidtenland (White Land), 353; Cape Fullerton, 423; *see also Fram expedition; Franz Josef Land; Furthest North; Greenland; North Pole*

Armitage, Albert, second-in-command on Jackson's expedition, 341-2, 343, 352; admires N, 352

Astrup, Eivind, Peary's companion on Greenland expedition, 159-60, 320, 388

Austria, 376, 394, 399, 464; Mürzzuschlag, 377; Vienna, 376, 377, 394

Baden-Powell, Sir George, 356, 369, 374, 393

Baker, Philip: *see Noel-Baker, Philip*

Balfour, Arthur, 393, 404, 497

Balto, Samuel Johannesen: on Greenland expedition, 73-4, 78, 79, 80, 82, 86, 88-9, 90, 93, 94, 102, 106, 107, 113, 126, 138, 147; rejected for *Fram* expedition, 165; narrative by, 143-4

Barrie, Sir James, 441, 478, 540

Baumann, Gustav, acting Governor of Godthåb, 119-20

Belgian Royal Geographical Society, 369

Belgica (ship), first to winter above Antarctic Circle, 369, 379, 388

Benckendorf, Count, Russian Ambassador in London, 437, 445